DIRECTIONS IN DEVELOPMENT

Access to Financial Services in Brazil

DIRECTIONS IN DEVELOPMENT

Access to Financial Services in Brazil

A study led by Anjali Kumar

THE WORLD BANK
Washington, D.C.

1818 H Street, NW
Washington DC 20433
Telephone: 202-473-1000
Internet: www.worldbank.org
E-mail: feedback@worldbank.org

1 2 3 4 07 06 05 04

Library of Congress Cataloging-in-Publication Data

Kumar, Anjali.
Access to financial services in Brazil / Anjali Kumar.
p. cm. — (Directions in development)
Includes bibliographical references and index.
ISBN 0-8213-5716-6
1. Finance—Brazil. 2. Financial institutions—Brazil. I. Title. II. Directions in development (Washington, D.C.)

HG185.B7K85 2004
332.1'7'0981—dc22 2004045528

Contents

Figures

Tables

Foreword

The challenge of alleviating poverty and improving living conditions for the poorest populations is a formidable one. It is increasingly apparent that such a betterment of the lot of poor people requires an effort that spans all sectors of the economy and may not be easy to achieve through economic growth alone. Improved access to financial services helps poor people by enabling payment transactions that then bring them into the formal sector. Access to deposit services helps people save safely and thus handle fluctuations in consumption needs. Financial services also enable poor people to use profitable business opportunities and thus raise earnings. And financial services help better manage risk. Beyond the role of financial systems in providing economic stability and contributing to growth, there is an increasing awareness of the importance of financial services as a wider part of the development agenda.

Yet, there is relatively little accumulated knowledge of present levels of financial access in poor countries or of the factors that are important in expanding access. How should access be measured? The establishment of financial institutions or service outlets does not in itself guarantee access for poor people. Should access then be measured in terms of services actually used by them? Or by reductions in the unmet demand for financial services? These are some of the initial questions pondered by this study, which incorporates the results of a major survey conducted in Brazil in several cities concerning present levels of financial access and its impediments. Frequently, access to financial services has been popularly equated with access to credit. Yet credit needs are often described as a secondary financial need by poor people, whose need for a stable store of value for their savings or mechanisms for making and receiving payments is often paramount. One contribution of the present work is its attempt to unbundle the concept of financial access.

The genesis of the present work lies in the recognition, at multiple levels, of the need to develop new analytic and policy tools for directly addressing problems of financial access beyond the establishment of the precondition of more stable and solvent financial systems. Brazil has shown a sustained interest, in recent years and across different government administrations, in addressing issues related to poverty alleviation and reduction in inequality. It was Brazil's Central Bank that first raised the theme of financial access as an area for joint exploration with the World Bank. And in parallel, the World Bank's Financial Sector Network has encouraged the development of an understanding of financial access in response to the World Bank's Board and in support of the Millennium Development Goals. Within the Latin America and Caribbean Region of the World Bank, a series of new initiatives for exploring themes of financial access has been launched in countries such as Mexico and Colombia in addition to Brazil. New dimensions of access are under investigation, following on the present work, examining issues specific to financial access for enterprises, in contrast to the focus on poor individuals adopted in this study. The present study on Brazil may thus be regarded as an early and perhaps pioneering effort in part of a widespread move toward the adoption of issues of financial access as a key theme in World Bank–led work on financial systems.

Eventually the value of such a work lies in its messages for policymakers and financial institutions and in the extent to which it provides them with a functional framework with which to address problems of access. The book shows that, despite a contraction in the number of banks, Brazil has made important strides in financial access in recent years, and thus it is not underbanked in comparative terms. While recognizing that the expansion of financial access presents enormous challenges to a government focused on poverty reduction, the study cautions that traditional approaches toward the expansion of access may be both more expensive and less successful than desirable. Options for policy discussed here draw on the experience of several countries, illustrating that solutions to the difficult dilemma of incentive compatible service expansion lie in not one but in several directions. These include the use of products and institutional interfaces designed specifically for the target group of clients, as well as appropriate lending techniques, incentives, and instruments; the expansion of information; and adoption of new technology.

We hope that this volume fills a gap in our development knowledge and that it will assist policymakers, researchers, and practitioners in the efforts to expand financial access to poor people.

March 2004

Fernando Montes-Negret
Manager
Financial Sector Unit
Latin America and the Caribbean Region
The World Bank

Danny Leipziger
Director
Finance, Private Sector Development and Infrastructure
Latin America and the Caribbean Region
The World Bank

Acknowledgments

This study was conceived and undertaken under the joint leadership of the Brazil Country Unit of the World Bank, led by Gobind T. Nankani and Vinod Thomas, Country Directors, and Joachim von Amsberg, Lead Economist, and of the Financial Sector Unit of the Latin America and the Caribbean Region, led by Fernando Montes-Negret, Sector Manager, and Danny Leipziger, Director. The project has received extensive support from the World Bank's Financial Sector Board, in recognition of the importance of access to financial services for reducing poverty and inequality and raising welfare. This work is the outcome of a collaboration of an extensive team of people from within the World Bank, from Brazil, and external consultants. The team was led by Anjali Kumar, Lead Financial Economist in the Finance Cluster of the Latin America and the Caribbean Region of the World Bank.

Scholars in Brazil who collaborated and participated with this effort include, notably, Professor Rosane Mendonça and students from the Institute of Applied Economic Resarch (IPEA) and the Federal University of Nateroi (Rio de Janeiro), in particular Cristine Campos and Daniel Santos. Professor Mendonça also helped coordinate a field survey, undertaken by the firm Sensus (Belo Horizonte), led by Ricardo Guedes. The team benefited from the guidance of Professor Ricardo Paes de Barros, IPEA. Core background papers were prepared by Armando Castelar Pinheiro (IPEA), the firm of Thomas Felsberg and Associates (São Paulo), and a team headed by Professor Ricardo Leal and students from the COPPEAD Business School (Rio de Janeiro). Contributions were also received from Moysés Kessel, formerly of the Central Bank of Brazil.

The study was also enriched by discussions and contributions from the Comunidade Solidária and Serviço Brasileiro de Apoio às Micro e Pequenas Empresas and with Jaime Mezzera and Henry Jackelen of the Brasília offices of the International Labour Organisation and the United Nations Development Programme. The team met with numerous financial institutions in Brazil, and close discussions were maintained during the process with financial-sector associations, notably FEBRABAN, the association of banks, and also ANFAC and ABEL, which represent the factoring and leasing industries. Particularly valuable collaboration was extended by the team of Beatriz Azeredo da Silva of the Banco Nacional de Desenvolvimento Econômico e Social (BNDES) and Lara Goldmark, consultant to BNDES.

World Bank and International Finance Corporation (IFC) staff and consultants contributing to this report included, notably, Thorsten Beck, McDonald Benjamin, Soumya Chattopadhyay, Thomas Glaessner, Mario Guadamillas, Margaret Miller, Nataliya Mylenko, Susana Sanchez, Sophie Sirtaine, and Jacob Yaron. Contributions were also provided by Alfredo Ebentrich, Lydie Ehouman, Daniela Klingebiel, Peer Stein, and Robert Vogel. Significant background papers were prepared by a team from Shorebank Advisory Services (Chicago and Washington). Ricardo Gonçalves and Adam Parsons contributed technical notes and participated in the initiation, preparation, and finalization of all parts of the study. Micky Ananth provided extensive support with document preparation.

Thoughtful comments from several World Bank colleagues as well as external persons are reflected in this study. Reviewers and advisors in the World Bank have included Mauricio Carrizosa, Robert Christen, Francisco Ferreira, Joselito Gallardo, James Hanson, Aart Kraay, Soledad Martinez, Steven Schonberger, Shahid Yusuf, and Dimitri Vittas. Comments and contributions have also been provided by Marguerite Berger and Rogerio Studart of the Inter-American Development Bank and Ashoka Mody and Kenichi Ueda of the International Monetary Fund. Professor Robert Townsend of Chicago University provided valuable insights on alternative frameworks for analysis. Professor André Urani of Instituto de Estudos do Trabalho e Sociedade was a special advisor to the project, and Professor Marcelo Neri of the Fundação Getulio Vargas provided helpful comments on Brazilian data sources at the outset of the study.

The key counterpart agency for the project has been Brazil's Central Bank. Initial endorsement for the study came from the Central Bank Governor Armínio Fraga, and discussions of the final report continued with Central Bank Governor Henrique Meirelles, Afonso Bevilaqua, and Eduardo Loyo. Director Sérgio Darcy and his office, including Clarence Hillerman Jr. and Marden Soares, provided guidance throughout, especially on microfinance and financial regulation in Brazil. Subsequent discussions on themes of financial access within the Central Bank included especially Eduardo Lundberg and Márcio Nakane. Discussions with the Ministry of Finance were held with Marcus Lisboa and Otaviano Canuto. The report benefited immensely from intensive reviews by technical teams within the administration, including notably Wagner Guerra Jr., Roberto Shoji, and Otávio Damaso at the Ministry of Finance and Amaro Gomes at the Central Bank.

Early versions of this study have been presented and discussed at seminars and workshops in Washington and Brazil. In Washington, early results from Brazil have been compared with ongoing parallel work in Mexico and Colombia, organized by Tova Solo of the Latin America region, FPSI unit. Events organized in Brazil have included an IETS/ World Bank seminar on inequality and social justice at Rio de Janeiro, held in tandem with an IFC workshop on microfinance; a workshop that included themes of urban poverty, by the Cities Alliance at São Paulo, in October 2003; and a Central Bank workshop on microfinance. And recently, results of this study were shared with an audience in Delhi, India, drawing comparisons between India and Brazil on financial access. Valuable messages were received from participants at these events, which also have been reflected. We would like to take this opportunity to thank all the people in government, financial, and academic communities who have provided their time, thoughts, and contributions to the team and to the study.

Executive Summary

This study evaluated present levels of access to financial services in Brazil and government policies that have had an impact on access. Based on these findings, the study explored options for increasing future access to financial services in Brazil. The first section of this summary highlights the core conclusions to emerge from the study and their implications for government policy. The next section describes the findings and recommendations of each chapter, and is followed by an in-depth look at specific areas examined by the study.

Principal Conclusions

Financial markets constitute a significant part of a broad group of factor markets, including land and labor markets, which are the basic institutions underlying the effective functioning of an economy and the production and sale of its goods. Financial exclusion reduces the potential welfare of individuals and the productivity of enterprises in an economy. Effective participation in financial markets and other factor markets, which are different from normal (product) markets, is a precondition for effective participation in the economy.

Access of disadvantaged groups to financial markets is thus of strategic importance for social and economic development and social inclusion. Market failures in these markets have particularly detrimental effects on economic productivity and social benefit. Therefore, these markets are typically closely regulated. But regulation, in turn, generates risk of regulatory failure, and many regulations may hinder access to the poor. These are the reasons for analyzing financial access and for reviewing the role of public policies to promote access.

The overarching message to emerge from this study is that increased financial access would be promoted by sound overall macroeconomic and financial sector policy. Beyond that, the government could and should undertake regulatory reforms to enable financial markets to function more smoothly, and undertake targeted policies to improve access. However, care should be taken to ensure that such targeted policies let the excluded groups participate efficiently in financial markets. This would direct the focus toward a review of incentives rather than public financing of special programs.

Sound macroeconomic policy implies, first, the reduction of the government's borrowing requirement, which will enable more borrowing by individuals and enterprises in the economy, and, second, the reduction and harmonization of taxes on the financial sector that will reduce the burden on overall intermediation and also reduce current opportunities for regulatory arbitrage across different segments of the financial system. Beyond that, efforts should be made to ensure that competition is maintained in financial markets.

Regulatory reforms, which would stimulate outreach and affect disadvantaged groups, require a move away from expensive special public financing that often fails to meet target groups, toward improved regulatory regimes that stimulate access. Present subsidies on some costly special programs, such as those for the rural sector, could be reduced in a phased program. Subsidies, mandatory lending targets, and measures that seek to curb market prices could perversely lead to reduced access over time. Examples of desirable regulatory reforms include a review of Brazil's extensive regulatory and reporting requirements for microfinance, compared to what may be merited by its present non-deposit-taking nature. Reliance on relatively low-cost credit could be gradually weaned, although alternative sources of funds may be needed and deposit-taking could be considered once the industry adopts mature microcredit practices.

In microfinance, a series of new regulatory initiatives have been adopted, many positive. However, many other recent programs that rely on subsidies, lending limits, and mandated lending could limit the development of some credit markets. Care should be taken not to overburden financial institutions with the task of intermediation of special government assistance programs, which could detract from the establishment of orthodox credit practices. In the banking sector, several new regulations have been adopted recently that are moves in the right direction, including the simplification of processes for opening accounts, expanding the scope for correspondents to financial institutions, and establishing basic accounts. Bank branch opening could also be simplified. However, microlending by microfinance institutions (MFIs) such as Civil Society Organizations with a Public Interest (OSCIPs) and Microcredit Companies (SCMs) could find their activities restricted by controls on onlending interest rates. New policies in this area should be monitored in terms of cost and impact.

For nonbanks there is a fragmentation of regulation in some areas such as factoring, which is outside the defined scope of financial sector activities, and which otherwise might help to contribute to the sector's development. Such policies could extend beyond financial institutions themselves to the overall infrastructure for financial intermediation. A first concern in this area relates to creditor rights; regulatory reform can focus on attention to procedural delays in reaching judgments in credit disputes and examining the rationale of tax write-offs on uncollected small claims. To enhance credit reporting, regulations limiting information to five years, restricting the sharing of information, and limiting the use of positive information should be reevaluated.

Targeting and programs of special outreach imply not so much the public financing of programs as their appropriate design, to insure their outreach to and impact on desired groups of the population. For example, geographic targeting should go beyond efforts to place a service outlet in each broadly defined geographic area, such as a municipality, to focus on the identification of deprived neighborhoods, which could include inner city areas within broader urban municipalities. Such targeting would be based on systematic tracking of deprivation. Appropriate designs would include designing community outreach strategies to target customers with limited access, introducing image differentiation, adopting new lending methodologies and technologies, strengthening credit reporting, easing the use of secured credit, and offering incentive-compatible support. Basic accounts and 'lifeline' services, which provide minimal service packages, can be reinforced with government support to employees or banks to open such accounts. Government could also support the use of such accounts to deposit government transfers as well as provide careful monitoring of the costs of basic service packages.

Incentive-compatible support can take forms such as start-up support, initial tax breaks, matching grants, partial risk or credit guarantee support for the development of community finance institutions, and enhancement of regulatory measures to increase disclosure of practices aimed at access. In the context of microcredit institutions, there is now a series of recognized sound practices for microcredit that boost its sustainability, and microfinance entities that can demonstrate the incorporation of such good practice should be the recipients of funding support for institutional development or expansion. Encouragement can also be offered for the establishment of formal or informal partnerships and institutional support programs between banks, nonbanks, or even nonfinancial entities (such as factoring companies) and microfinance. Finally, judicial education as well as programs of financial education and literacy are also key.

Concern about financial exclusion increased over the last decade in Brazil, with the decline in the number of banks since the late 1990s. Only some 60 million of Brazil's population of 176 million have bank accounts, or around a third of its population. Meanwhile, not only is the cost of credit high, but bank spreads are arguably among the highest in the world.

The study points to a series of factors that affect volumes and costs of financial intermediation. It emphasizes that despite the absence of simple remedies, areas exist in which actions can be taken that together would help to expand access and lower the cost of financial intermediation. Twenty key findings and areas for future action follow.

1. *This study finds that there is no evidence of a trend decline in access to bank services in terms of numbers of banking service outlets,* although such services, measured in traditional terms, may have stagnated. Despite concerns regarding diminishing numbers of banks over the last decade, comparing Brazil with other countries at similar levels of development, Brazil is not 'underbanked' in terms of bank branch presence.
2. *The wide regional disparities in bank service provision can be significantly ascribed to differences in population density and income. Also, disparities in financial access can be at least as significant between neighborhoods within a city as between regions of the country.* Locational emphasis, which is based on the importance of providing a basic service outlet in each municipality, may need to be refocused and supplemented by a locational policy that looks more at deprived areas, which may well be identified at a smaller and more disaggregated level than municipalities. Moreover, even if properly identified, the provision of a service outlet in itself is not sufficient to ensure access by lower-income groups, without more explicit design features to reach the excluded.
3. *Initial measures designed to expand access adopted over the last few years, especially for the microfinance and cooperative sectors and later for banking correspondents, have been successful and point toward new modes of access to financial services.* More recently, a number of new initiatives have been made that have relied more on mandated lending and controlled interest rates for target groups. The mainstay of policies to expand access remains traditional, focusing on the allocation of credit, frequently at low interest rates, with considerable reliance on large public banks to support this mandate; some recent measures are also in this tradition.
4. *Traditional policies to expand access that emphasize the quantitative rationing of credit at low interest rates, based on low-cost sources of funding and administered substantially through Brazil's public banks, have a high cost.* Conservative estimates suggest that concessions and support could amount to several billion Reals. The cost of a special program such as the National Program to Strengthen Family Agriculture (PRONAF) is estimated at R$1.1 billion. As illustrated by the analysis of rural finance programs, many such programs fail to reach intended beneficiaries, and tend to be captured by a small number of the better-off, to the detriment of broad-based access. In agriculture, which

is the beneficiary of many special programs, the largest 2 percent of borrowers receive 57 percent of loans, whereas the smallest 75 percent of borrowers receive only 6 percent of credit. Programs that propose ceilings on lending rates for target sectors or clients are costly, as measured by the volume of credit provided and by the interest rate differentials that are eventually borne by society. Additional costs are the crowding out of intermediation at market rates. It is recommended that such programs, including some recently introduced special programs for microcredit, be closely monitored for cost. The regressive incidence of some directed credit interventions may be compounded if they are funded through broad-based and popular programs such as the Worker Assistance Fund (FAT), which imply lower returns to the workers, who are the intended beneficiaries of the FAT fund.

5. *Alternative measures to the traditional programs could include new instruments that offer possibilities for market-based expansion of services.* For example, in agriculture, new forms of index-based yield insurance, or loans combined with put options on crop prices, and the combination of different instruments (for example, credit and insurance) should be explored. The costs of individual programs, and implied subsidies, need to be systematically tracked. Also, there is scope for gradually phasing in reductions in quantitative allocations (such as earmarked funds for housing and rural lending) and for allowing rates to more closely reflect market rates. Successful programs for microcredit, such as the CrediAmigo program, which has achieved outreach to the poorer segments, demonstrate the possibility of onlending at market rates. New forms of technology-based microfinance can also be considered.
6. *Measures to expand the role of the banking system as a whole in the area of access are valuable, but care should be taken that they are established on a sound footing.* Brazil's banks provide the bulk of the country's financial services and remain the mainstay of all intermediation. As the study shows, Brazil's private banks are already servicing small clients and scale of transaction may be less of an issue than costs of basic services. Surprisingly, private banks dominate the provision of current and deposit accounts to small account holders. Survey results suggest that public banks do not demonstrate a clearly dominant role in terms of access, except with regard to certain types of services such as payment services. Recently simplified procedures for opening accounts affecting low-income clients are welcome, especially simplifications in the proof of identity and income. The possibility of alternatives to taxpayer numbers could also be considered. Such measures could gradually be extended to all bank clients. Many obligatory costs

of maintaining bank branches could be examined, such as security aspects, bank hours, and staffing obligations.

7. *Recently introduced measures for the provision of 'lifeline' banking with basic services for lower-income persons are also beneficial and have been successfully introduced in many countries.* However, the costs involved in providing such services should be carefully examined, to ensure that participating institutions' operating costs are covered, and monthly fees for such basic accounts are priced at affordable, nonzero levels. In most countries such accounts do not usually include automatic access to loans or low-interest loan features. The government can encourage the establishment of such accounts, for example, by channeling public payments through such accounts, by offering incentives to employers or their financial institutions for the establishment of such accounts for payroll purposes, and by initial tax breaks to financial institutions for setting up such accounts.
8. *The government could adopt disclosure-based requirements to promote financial services for the underserved.* Tools such as the Community Reinvestment Act and the Home Mortgage Disclosure Act, when appropriately combined with disclosure requirements, have been valuable in limiting discriminatory practices and in expanding access. Especially if combined with systematic tracking of bank records in different categories of lending, possibly in partnership with the private bankers' association, such moral suasion has been found to be very effective in other countries. The government could also consider measures such as partial guarantees or credit insurance for loans provided by banks to excluded groups. In contrast with interest rate subsidies, such measures are incentive-compatible with the increase of private credit to such groups, and would still encourage the prudent use of loanable funds. Finally, the government could also consider a review of banking sector competition, particularly in areas such as access to payment networks, based on recent experience with such investigations in countries such as the United Kingdom.
9. *Private banks could go further toward downscaling or expanding their services to the underserved, through efforts that make use of new lending methodologies and technologies, with appropriate incentives and support from the government.* Such lending methodologies include practices such as image differentiation, or having a different type of bank service outlet for poorer people, and partnerships with local or community-based organizations, including in some cases partnerships with microfinance organizations. The specialized subsidiaries set up by banks such as Unibanco for this purpose are an example, and these features are to be included in the new Banco Popular. Efforts should be made to ensure that such organizations, while user friendly, follow

sound banking principles. The experience of other countries with Community Development Finance Institutions can also be considered in this regard. New technologies such as risk-assessment or credit scoring models may also be useful in evaluating small clients, as would many new technologies that permit easier operation in remote areas or field locations. These technologies have been used successfully elsewhere and are detailed in the study. Although technologically sophisticated, Brazil bank efforts in technology, such as internet banking, are geared largely toward the better-off. Start-up assistance for adopting such technologies could be considered.

10. *Brazil's encouraging progress with the expansion in recent years of its limited microfinance sector, albeit supported by funding from the National Bank for Economic and Social Development (Banco Nacional de Desinvolvimento Economico e Social or BNDES) and from the Northeast Bank (Banco do Nordeste or BNB), has shown in the CrediAmigo program that both outreach and efficiency can be achieved, and that microlending can approach sustainability on a cash flow basis.* The CrediAmigo program is supported by funding from the BNDES and from the BNB. Onlending rates adopted by most of the private MFIs were, until recently, freely determined and approached market rates. Considerable international experience has demonstrated that interest rate caps are unnecessary and may lead to inefficient use of such funds and obstruct spontaneous expansion of microfinance. Rather, the incorporation of good lending practices and methodologies by such MFIs—for example, exploring solidarity group lending, gradual loan size increase, and repayment beginning with immediate effect—is suggested.
11. *On the funding side, many of Brazil's new MFIs have enjoyed privileged access to BNDES funding at the TJLP or long-term interest rate. A phased and gradual increase to market levels would be desirable, at least to the interbank deposit rate, as adopted in CrediAmigo.* However, a sudden significant increase could adversely affect the microfinance sector, given that the majority of MFIs are still deemed to be nonprofit or civil society operations, and could reverse the gains of recent years. The impact of recent escalations in funding costs by loan threshold should be kept under review. Convergence of size thresholds and interest rates combined with gradual transition and guidance on the incorporation of good lending practice would be desirable.
12. *Expansion of microfinance on a significant scale will be difficult—even in the absence of recent measures—unless large-scale partnerships with formal financial institutions can be considered, or, alternatively, a radical change in services could be offered, to include deposit-taking.* This could be contemplated as a future possibility, once there is evidence of maturity in the industry, to expand the funding base. However, new regulations

would need to be introduced for attendant increases in risk, which would include new models of shared, delegated, or independent supervision. The rationale for present multiple regulatory windows for different institutional forms of microfinance should be examined. Harmonizing such regulations in the future would be desirable.

13. *Evidence suggests that cooperatives have a less-restricted funding base than microfinance because of their ability to accept deposits, despite membership restrictions.* The recent easing of membership restrictions on new cooperatives to permit 'open' structures, although admittedly for more sparsely populated areas with meager financial services, requires additional supervision and oversight. Recent regulations include some appropriate safeguards, but it should be noted that membership restrictions are usual even in advanced countries and provide a form of 'reputational collateral' to contain the risks of such institutions, especially in view of constraints in supervisory capacity.
14. *The establishment of a liquidity facility for credit cooperatives is suggested, to reduce opportunity costs relative to commercial banks backed by the Fundo Garantidor de Créditos (FGC) deposit insurance fund.* Until recently, leverage and liquidity restrictions may have been more important for cooperatives than membership restrictions. Recent measures introduced in June 2003 have partially alleviated these. Although there may be indirect access to such liquidity through participation in cooperative banks, more direct support would be desirable. It is noted that some cooperatives are also assuming the role of transferring funds for government-sponsored agricultural programs. If this becomes the practice on a significant scale, it could steer the cooperative sector away from good risk management practices, unless this is clearly a fee-based administrative operation with no credit risk for the cooperatives concerned.
15. *The contribution of nonbanks to access has so far been based to some degree on regulatory arbitrage opportunities with the banking system, and the nonbanks have suffered to varying degrees from lack of legal clarity.* The most promising area for attention in this context is the potential contribution of nonfinancial companies, such as factoring companies, which are already sizeable in terms of the provision of credit to small enterprises, and have made promising contributions in other countries. A first step to take in this regard would be the clarification of the fragmented legal framework for this activity, and passage of a pending law for its consolidation. Wider access to finance through commercial bills and debentures and easing international factoring through permission to set up foreign currency accounts are also recommended.

16. *Credit to small borrowers is impeded by difficulties in loan recovery,* caused in part by 'judicial activism' and also in part by difficulties in the use of collateral. Recommendations in this context are awareness programs for judges, combined with the reinforcement of self-executable instruments used for small borrowers, like, for example, the overdraft facilities offered over the ATMs or the *duplicatas* of small firms. Legal recognition of these debts, which at present is not possible because of their lack of signature and computerized entry, could be explored. An examination of the possibilities of changing the procedural codes to speed up judgments is also advised, as well as the opening of special (small claims) courts for small credits. Finally, current tax write-offs against profits on uncollected small claims can be evaluated in a wider context, because these may be sending perverse signals to both borrowers and financial institutions for debt repayment.
17. *The infrastructure for perfecting security interests use can be strengthened by the adoption of electronic filing, retrieval, and indexation systems at all registration offices in the country and the establishment of networks for the linkage of registries.* The present five-day time period and the cost to conduct a search and certification could be reduced by a self-guided web search. Deadlines for turnover time for registries of deeds and documents could be adopted, and documentation requirements for secured transactions in real estate could be simplified. Additionally, efforts should be made to address the regressive tariff structures of registries and notaries public, and the extent to which notarial and registration services are still operating on a franchise basis could be examined through the offices of judicial oversight.
18. *Further improvements in credit registries and credit reporting will help to ease lending to small borrowers with limited credit history.* Brazil already has effective core systems, but these could be strengthened by more positive information (on utilities payments, for example), and some easing of restrictions on the sharing of such information. There could also be a reconsideration of current time restrictions on information that limit credit data to five years. Brazil is an outlier in this respect. Utility tariffs could also be structured to provide incentives for good payment records.
19. *The ultimate success of policies to expand access is predicated on an appropriate macroeconomic environment, which has a profound influence on overall access.* All the microeconomic interventions discussed above must be viewed against this backdrop. The government's large borrowing needs have a negative impact on private credit, and the high taxation of the financial system, partly to finance such needs, is another deterrent. High reserve requirements add to implicit taxation. Moreover, the impact of taxation is not uniform across the financial

system, which leads to opportunities for regulatory arbitrage across different financial entities. Such regulatory arbitrage also occurs with regard to different forms of financial institutions, where some institutional forms grow popular in response to regulatory constraints in other areas of the financial system.

20. *There is a role for more proactive government policies toward access to financial services at a microlevel through the creation of a better enabling environment in regulation, monitoring, and disclosure and selective support.* Yet the eventual success of these policies will be the greatest if they are backed by fundamental changes in overall approach to access through broad-based financial sector reforms that limit constraints on the price and quantity of credit and reduce the overarching role accorded to a small number of public institutions in their delivery.

Background and Organization of the Study

The remainder of the executive summary provides a more detailed account, by chapter, of the background and the findings of the study, and explores the research areas that were the study's focus and the recommendations for financial access reform that grew out of those findings.

Brazil's financial system is by far the largest in Latin America. Beyond its sheer size, the overall depth of financial intermediation in Brazil, at almost 140 percent of gross domestic product, is greater than that of its large neighbors in the region such as Mexico or Argentina, despite their higher average per capita income. Financial depth and stability are increasingly recognized as contributing to poverty reduction through growth and crisis prevention, but, beyond this, it can be argued that a more broad-based distribution of financial services would raise welfare and productivity.

Individuals with access to financial services can meet unusual or unexpected demands for income, or safeguard against periods of low income or unexpected fluctuations in income. Access to savings and borrowings could also have longer-term welfare implications, permitting people to borrow when young for building human capital, and then save for retirement when they are older. For producers, access to credit for fixed or working capital enables an increase in production possibilities benefiting not only the producer but affecting economywide productivity, employment, and growth. Financing has featured prominently as a constraint for small and medium-size enterprises in some investigations. Some studies indicate that Latin American firms find lack of access to financial markets to be the major obstacle to expansion.

Limits to financial access are pointed out by the Central Bank: around 60 million or a third of Brazilians are estimated to have bank accounts. Nearly 30 percent of all municipalities, or 1,680 out of a total of some 5,600 municipalities, have no bank branch. The 1,400 or so credit cooperatives offer basic financial services to only about 1.5 million Brazilians, mostly in urban areas. But expanding the supply of financial services to underserved segments of society can pose particular difficulties for financial intermediaries such as banks, because of limited information, high risks, and high unit costs. The challenge is to identify ways of expanding access that acknowledge the risks and costs involved but provide measures to mitigate their impact. This is the fundamental objective of the present study, which attempts to assess constraints to access and their determinants, in different segments of financial markets, and then identify alternative public and private choices for improved access.

There are multiple concepts of the underserved: first, the poorer segments of society or, second, those in specific geographic regions that may or may not combine characteristics such as remoteness or sparseness of population with economic backwardness. Third, specific communities such as racial groups, migrants, or minorities may be disadvantaged in terms of financial access. Additionally, the criterion of small size is often applied, particularly to micro- or small-scale entrepreneurs in contrast with individuals. Measures of access and actions to expand access vary depending on which groups of the underserved are being examined. In the present study, poverty is the primary consideration, though small size for producers and location are also factors that are considered. The study pays greater attention to factors that directly affect access. Thus indirect impacts on access, operating via their effect on the overall depth of financial services (for example, the potential crowding out of private credit provision by government borrowing, or the impact of financial sector taxation) are not investigated in detail.

There is also a series of possible indicators of financial access, and the report discusses the tradeoff between the relevance and certainty of conclusions that may be drawn regarding levels of access and the ease of obtaining information. Typically, more disaggregated information is harder to get, and lends itself less easily to international comparison than more aggregated data, which, however, is less conclusive. The study points to simple disaggregations, such as the unbundling of financial services—for example, money transmission, and savings and credit services—and demonstrates their application.

Brazil's government and Central Bank have been concerned about financial exclusion, particularly in the period of the post-Real Plan, when mergers or closures of a number of banks, both private and public, occurred, leading to concerns about contractions in bank services, especially in geographically remote regions. To what extent has there really been a contraction in bank services, and is there, as a consequence, an overall decline in access? To what extent are needs for financial services met? And what explains present levels of access? These are some of the questions addressed in chapter 1 of this study, which sets the stage for the rest of the analysis, by undertaking a broad overview of current patterns of access. It looks first at patterns of supply of financial services, through aggregate data on financial institutions and their branches, and then at the demand for financial services, largely from the perspective of urban consumers and, briefly, from an enterprise perspective. The study is based on the results of a survey undertaken for this report. In particular, policies adopted by the government to expand access are evaluated.

The government has also been increasingly aware of the relatively underdeveloped provision of financial services by smaller players such as cooperatives and microfinance, which have been very successful elsewhere in Latin America. Microfinance has increasingly been hailed in global communities as the new solution to financial exclusion. As a result, several steps have been taken recently in Brazil to expand potential outreach for such institutions, and more such measures are planned. How successful has this been and how much farther can it go? What is the best mix of policies to adopt for the future expansion in the supply of financial services from these sectors? These issues are addressed in chapter 2 of this study, which launches an analysis of the supply of financial services through different institutional segments of the financial market.

In view of the dominant role of banks in Brazil's financial system, chapter 3 of the study examines the role of private banks with regard to financial access. Because of the reduction in bank numbers and some increase in concentration over the latter 1990s, questions may justifiably be raised regarding the impact of these trends on banking outreach. Beyond its analysis of the private banking system's present role in outreach to the underserved, this section also draws extensively on international experience with regard to the provision of private bank services for underserved communities. The study also investigates the potential for expansion of the role of nonbank financial systems such as finance and leasing companies and factoring, which have contributed successfully to access elsewhere (chapter 4).

Traditionally, Brazil's government has attempted to address issues of financial access through its publicly owned financial institutions, which have been accorded a social obligation to attend to the disadvantaged segments of society. The large federal banks, as well as a number of state-owned banks, have been responsible for outreach, not only through the extension of their own resources but also through the administration of earmarked budgetary funds and payroll deductions (such as the FAT fund). Because some of the sectors served by such public financial institutions are known to face a number of market imperfections that may make a case for public intervention, chapter 5 explores one such market segment: rural finance. Even if some intervention is warranted, there are issues of appropriate design. The extent to which these programs may have achieved their own objectives of large-scale outreach to the poor is a first issue for debate. The chapter investigates the efficiency implications of present programs of outreach, as well as other new alternatives.

Following the investigation of service providers, chapter 6 of the study investigates relevant elements of the institutional infrastructure for financial services. Such institutional factors affect particularly the cost of provision of financial services and hence bank spreads. Some of the issues examined here are the implications of current legal processes for creditor rights and contract enforcement, registries for secured credit and their potential impact on the use of collateral, and credit information systems and the application of credit scoring processes.

The study concludes with a discussion of the potential role of policymakers in the expansion of access through different instruments and institutions. The study points out that macroeconomic factors such as large public sector deficits or high taxation significantly affect financial services. Policies that affect other market segments, too, can have significant effects on access—for example, labor market policies and policies relating to competition in the banking sector. However, although it may be difficult for a government to act on these in the context of the financial system, there is a more immediate role for the government to play, through policies that focus on the structure of financial system incentives that affect the distribution of credit and other services. Based largely on experience in third countries, chapter 7 discusses options for a more proactive microeconomic role for the government with regard to financial access.

In-Depth Summary of Specific Research Areas

In this part of the executive summary, the following areas are examined in some depth: assessing access, reviewing the policy implications of findings, expanding microfinance, downscaling private banks, partnering nonbanks, channeling specialized finance, installing institutional infrastructure, and enlisting the government.

Assessing Access

Core analysis in this part of the study rests first on an investigation of aggregate supply side information on banks and other financial institutions, based largely on Central Bank data, followed by a demand side investigation of individual use of financial services, based on the World Bank's survey data.

The analysis of aggregate supply side data suggests, first, that despite contractions in bank numbers, delivery of financial services has not declined over the last decade but has remained largely static. There have been some expansions of new forms of service delivery points, such as ATMs and banking correspondents, and, also, an increased presence of some small financial institutions, including cooperatives and microfinance institutions, although these are also numerically small. Moreover, by international comparison, Brazil may be 'underbanked' compared to developed countries in terms of bank branches, but it has performed at least as well or better than its peers among developing or middle-income countries.

It is true that spatial inequalities in the delivery of financial services are significant among Brazil's regions and have been persistent over time. But much of the spatial difference in the provision of banking services can be explained by regional differentials in population and income. Once these factors are corrected, the differences are significantly eroded.

Next, the supply analysis looked at the differential contributions of public and private banks. Underlying the relatively static overall picture in financial service provision, there has been a significant shift in composition of service providers, with a declining share for public banks. Private banks, although relying extensively on new delivery mechanisms such as ATMs, are also surprisingly more branch-intensive than federal banks.

Econometric analyses of the determinants of bank service provision, using a range of indicators of access, find that, for all banks taken together, per capita income tends to be positively associated with broad measures of access such as the number or density of banking institutions or the value of the loan and deposit services they provide. Banks (public and private) have an urban bias and tend not to provide services in rural areas. Nevertheless, the agricultural community is apparently not underserved.

Finally, analyses that distinguish between public and private banks find some differences in the factors associated with the provision of services of these two groups. By some measures, public banks may provide more services to the poor but private banks appear to offer more services to agriculture and to small enterprises. In many respects the behavior of the two is broadly similar: both tend to have a positive association with richer economic areas and both have some urban bias. Especially in thinly served areas, they tend to be substitutable, with either private or public services dominating.

The second part of the overview of patterns and determinants of access is based on an investigation of the demand side: the extent to which individuals use financial services and the extent to which such services meet their needs. This analysis is based on a survey of 2,000 adult individuals located in nine cities and two metropolitan areas; the survey was undertaken for the purpose of this study. Urban areas were selected because around 80 percent of the population of the country is classified as urban, and because of the ready availability of a sample frame. A series of basic facts regarding the current availability and use of financial services emerged from this survey, and these were then correlated with individuals' socioeconomic characteristics.

In terms of current levels of access, illustrative findings are that 43 percent of individuals surveyed have a bank account. The use of nonbank financial institutions such as cooperatives, credit unions, or microfinance institutions is limited (only 4 percent of responses). However, a considerably larger number of persons, who are not necessarily account holders, make use of financial institutions through payment outlets of banking correspondents, especially through the lottery shop chain of the Caixa Econômica Federal; one of the two large public sector banks. An inquiry about the relative importance of different financial institutions reveals that almost half of the respondents to this question (47 percent) find the lottery shop centers to be their most important institution for financial transactions. Private bank branches are second (27 percent) and public bank branches third (19 percent). Surprisingly, aside from the Lotéricas, the majority of respondents (58 percent) for whom banks are the primary financial institution use private banks. Most accounts are limited; only 61 percent of account holders have access to checking facilities.

Only around two-thirds (64 percent) of those who do not have an account indicate an interest in having one. Among the voluntary reasons for not having an account, high fees clearly dominate. Lack of funds, lack of documentation and references, and difficulties in opening an account also matter. By contrast, factors such as hours of operation or distance, which suggest physical inconvenience, are not important. With regard to deposit and savings behavior, more than half the respondents (54 percent) have their largest deposits in private institutions and 41 percent have their largest deposits in public institutions. Other financial institutions, including cooperatives, account for less than 2 percent of responses. Returns on deposit accounts have low price elasticity; for more than two-thirds of respondents, the most important reason cited for making deposits is 'security.'

Not surprisingly, loan and credit services are much more sparingly used. Only 15 percent of respondents claim to have applied for credit in the past 12 months, and only two-thirds of those respondents had their applications accepted. Apart from formal loans, around a quarter of persons have access to a debit card and a fifth have a credit card. Regarding payment services, cash is overwhelmingly the standard medium of payment for all types of transactions and respondents; 77 percent of respondents use cash for all transactions. There is surprisingly little variation by type of payment. Surprisingly, 92 percent of utility bills are paid in cash. The only expenditure categories where cash use is lower are consumer durables: 77 percent for electrodomestic goods and 80 percent for furniture.

Further analysis was undertaken of associations between observed patterns of access, variously measured, and other parameters. Three broad groups of associations were examined. Given the government's efforts to provide access at all locations, associations between differentials in access and location were first evaluated. Location was considered at two levels: regions of the country as well as location in terms of neighborhoods or areas of a city. Second, because public financial institutions have been given a significant role to play in meeting the needs of financial access of a large cross-section of the population, their role in this regard was examined. Third, the importance of individual characteristics in terms of income, wealth, education, employment, and so on in explaining levels of access was investigated.

With regard to the importance of location, the survey of individual financial behavior supports the supply side finding of the importance of location in determining access, but demonstrates that location in terms of the microcharacteristics of an area or neighborhood can be as important a discriminator for access as regions of the country. Although a first look at the supply of financial institutions points to wide regional differentials in the provision of services, these are considerably reduced when differentials in regional GDP and geographical size are corrected for.

Regarding the roles of public and private financial institutions, the survey of users, as in the case of the aggregate supply analysis, indicates that there is some association between lower-income groups and public banks. However, the user survey also shows that use of public banks varies by type of service. Thus, public banks are popular for payment services (because of the Caixa Econômica Federal outlets) for all socioeconomic groups, and also dominate the provision of housing credit, but largely for the better-off groups. For deposit-taking and for credit, both the privileged and less-privileged socioeconomic groups, broadly measured, have some preference for private banks, and with increases in income, both increased their proportional use of private banks.

Finally, the survey strongly corroborates the findings of the supply side analysis regarding the importance of income, at a per capita level, and points also to the significance of a range of socioeconomic characteristics such as education and (for credit services) wealth in determining financial access. The importance of socioeconomic characteristics in access to financial services suggests that there may be problems of information, or of enforcement, which cause lenders to emphasize such information.

Policy Implications of Findings

What are the implications of these findings from the perspective of broad policy directions to adopt in addressing access-related issues? The analysis suggests a number of thematic directions that could help to guide policy choices.

Policies in Regard to Location

First, there could be implications for policies regarding location. The analysis suggests that although location is important and there do seem to be some underserved regions and locations, much of the difference with regard to location can be attributed to levels of economic activity and sparseness of population. Thus, policies focused on the geographic equalization of services may not, on their own, be adequate or effective in targeting access. This is a significant comment in the context of Brazil, where major efforts to expand access have focused on ensuring that there is at least one financial point of service (branch, service post, or correspondent) in each municipality. Such policies cannot ensure that users of financial services in such locations are indeed the poorer segments of the population; the better-off persons even in these neighborhoods may be more successful in achieving financial access.

Another important inference with regard to locational policies is that regions of the country, or even municipalities, are perhaps not the best points of focus for the expansion of access. Rather, location defined at a microlevel in neighborhoods, with service expansion targeted at areas or parts of a city with specific microeconomic characteristics such as high concentrations of low-income housing, should be considered.

Eventually, factors related to location, though initially significant in the analysis, lose significance once socioeconomic factors such as income and education are included in the analysis. Additionally, other socioeconomic characteristics, such as employment-related variables, gender, and role in household, are also shown to be significant in the determination of many measures of access. One implication of this is that these factors have assumed importance in the absence of sufficient direct information on the financial behavior and creditworthiness of individuals. Wealth and collateral are also important in determining access to credit, because these may help with loan recovery. This finding could also suggest that in the absence of adequate enforcement mechanisms for financial claims, the factors noted above could serve as indicators of financial reliability. The implications are therefore that policies that can directly expand information on clients would expand access, such as the sharing of 'positive' information in some credit registries. Equally, procedures that streamline the use of guarantees, secured credit, bankruptcy, or recovery could also help to expand access.

POLICIES RELATED TO INCOME AND EDUCATION

The importance of income-related factors in determining access emerges as a central and consistent theme. A basic deduction is that access will be increased by overall growth-oriented policies, because improved financial distribution in addition to financial deepening are associated with growth. Perhaps a more significant corollary for policymakers is that if access is so significantly influenced by income, then targeted policies that particularly address lower-income groups are likely to be important in addressing access. What does this imply in practice? That policies such as, for example, 'lifeline' or basic accounts, affordable minimum packages of financial services, possibly special criteria related to documentation requirements for low-income persons, or special financial products designed for low-income persons could be important for raising access.

Next in importance to income in terms of individual characteristics associated with access is education. One suggestion to follow up on this finding is that programs of financial education and awareness may be important for low-income persons, even if overall educational policies, just as overall growth-raising policies, may lie outside the scope of the financial sector policymaker.

POLICIES RELATED TO THE ROLE OF PUBLIC AND PRIVATE FINANCIAL INSTITUTIONS

Finally, the type of financial institution was analyzed. Given the broad range of substitutability, apart from the delivery of some specialized services where either public or private banks seem to dominate (for example, public banks for payments or housing), a suggestion is that greater competition in specialized services would be desirable. For example, more private services in housing or in payments are recommended.

Although the analysis did suggest that persons with lower levels of income tended to use public banks proportionately more, it also showed, as noted above, that along a broad spectrum of services, the roles of these institutions could be largely substitutable. Thus, for both public and private banks, deposit and credit services are available to lower-income individuals, but as persons become better-off, they tend to prefer private services for both types of transactions. This suggests that private banks could do more to refocus their products, image, and services in terms of outreach to the less-well-off. Proactive suggestions for how banks might achieve this, and what the government could do to support such efforts, are discussed in chapters 3 and 7 of this study.

Expanding Microfinance

As the preceding section showed, Brazil's financial system so far has been largely bank dominated, and the development of other forms of financial institutions, especially microfinance institutions or credit cooperatives, has remained emasculated. Yet during the last 10 to 15 years, excitement has grown worldwide regarding the potential of such institutions as vehicles for lending to the poor. Today, MFIs are reaching out to more than 9 million borrowers and 29 million savers in more than 53 countries worldwide. The importance of microcredit for the self-employed and for small entrepreneurs, and thus for jobs, is also increasingly recognized. Microentrepreneurs of Brazil account for the vast majority of all firms and contribute substantially to employment and GDP. According to recent estimates, 98 percent of Brazil's 4.1 million micro- and small enterprises account for 45 percent of formal employment and more than 60 percent of urban jobs. Directly or indirectly, they provide the primary source of income to almost 60 million people and generate nearly 20 percent of GDP.

A second group of financial institutions catering to these needs is the community of credit cooperatives. Credit cooperatives were first formed a century ago in the southern states of Brazil, and are a mature alternative to banks in many countries. Both deposit and loan services are offered. Like microfinance, formal procedures and the use of formal collateral are usually absent because the group's knowledge of its members provides the coinsurance needed in place of guarantees.

Regarding Brazil's microfinance sector, the study finds that there was a remarkable acceleration in Brazil's microfinance sector from the end of the 1990s because of a series of factors. First, there was new political support for the sector, leading to legal and regulatory changes favoring the expansion of microfinance, introduction of new institutional forms such as the OSCIPs and SCMs, and expanded funding flexibility. Prior to 1999, microfinance in Brazil could be extended only by NGOs (nongovernmental organizations), constrained in their funding to donations, and limited technically in lending practices to unrealistic ceilings on interest rates under Brazil's Usury Law.

A second factor was the launching of a major, new, large-scale microcredit experiment, the CrediAmigo program, which incorporates many principles of good microfinance practice. And third, active government financial backing was extended to emerging microfinance institutions through credit offered by the BNDES bank.

Despite this rapid acceleration, microfinance penetration in Brazil today remains low, especially compared to neighboring countries. The portfolio growth rate of individual, small MFIs (in other words, the. microfinance lending other than the CrediAmigo operation of the North-east Bank) has not been remarkably high. Much of the growth spurt was caused by the establishment of new firms rather than rapid expansion of existing firms. Growth indicators for the portfolios of MFIs supported by BNDES suggest nominal annual growth of 22 percent a year; much lower for larger MFIs. The slow growth of Brazil's independent MFIs despite apparent large unmet demand is paradoxical. Some factors responsible could include the difficulties encountered by independent MFIs in expanding client outreach without a branch network or savings products. It may also be noted that the presence of some so-called microfinance institutions in Brazil, run mainly by municipal governments to achieve social objectives such as employment, provide highly subsidized credit that could affect the expansion of market-oriented microfinance.

In terms of performance, indicators of loans overdue for the BNDES-supported MFIs have been average, possibly with some trend increase for BNDES-supported MFIs, and loan provisioning may have been somewhat low. But financial sustainability has been good, perhaps because of low-cost funding. Efficiency indicators in terms of loans per loan officer, though low, have been rising. Impact indicators in terms of loan size suggest that outreach is reaching small client segments.

MFI expansion has been significantly motivated by public sector support, through the substantial presence of the public banks, BNB and BNDES. Microfinance institutions also rely substantially on relatively low-cost government lines of credit extended at below comparable market rates. Conversion to the new institutional forms, such as SCMs, although increasing access to wholesale funding, is rendered less attractive by the implications of new regulatory requirements for the provision of both nonprudential information and information on prudential ratios. There are also tax implications that would subject SCMs to the full range of financial sector taxation. Brazil's MFIs are subject to regulatory and reporting requirements that may be more rigorous than comparator models, in view of their non-deposit-taking scope of activities. However should Brazil contemplate the introduction of savings products or deposit-taking, such regulations would need to be retained and further fine tuned.

In terms of suggestions for the future, it should be noted that if Brazil's microfinance sector is to proceed along a sound expansion path in the future, its institutions should make more extensive use of recognized best practice methods. Although extensively used at CrediAmigo, small MFIs do not appear to have followed these principles.

Since June 2003, the government has introduced new measures to support microfinance. Although the broad direction of support is welcome, measures based on interest rate ceilings for microlending or the directing of bank resources toward microfinance (with the alternative of placement as unremunerated reserves) have a negative impact on financial markets. Interest rate ceilings on microlending squeeze profit margins and discourage private microcredit. International experience on microcredit demonstrates that demand is affected relatively little by lending rates; other features such as personal contact, flexible terms, and phased early repayment are more important ingredients of sustainable microcredit. Directed bank lending is an implicit tax on the financial system. Such measures could have a negative effect on the spontaneous growth of the microfinance sector. The real costs of the new programs, for banks and microfinance institutions as well as the government, need to be carefully monitored.

Next, both to attract more wholesale bank funding and to better incorporate good microfinance practice in its MFIs, Brazil could consider organizational forms that allow partnerships with large banks, which could help with training loan officers, tracking quality indicators, and incorporating good practice. The new microfinance subsidiary at Banco do Brasil (Banco Popular) is a first step. The BNDES bank could also consider a more indirect form of support to MFIs than its present model, through the provision of wholesale credit to private commercial banks, which then could liaise with self-help groups either directly or through NGOs. Another possible way to attract commercial banks to microfinance in an initial phase, as in the National Bank for Agriculture and Rural Development (NABARD) model in India, could be through the use of current direct credit limits for rural and housing lending for appropriate microfinance schemes. Care should be taken to ensure that such partnerships are transparent and cost-effective.

Brazil's microfinance sector could also contemplate deposit-taking in the future, once sufficiently mature, not only to expand its funding base if large-scale rollout is to be contemplated, but also to offer needed savings products and expand client interface. Brazil does not allow any form of deposit-taking for its MFIs, and wholesale funding from the banking system has been limited.

Microfinance in Brazil may need a separate regulatory window, but the reasons for the current multiple regulatory windows of NGOs, OSCIPs, and SCMs may be driven partially by the need to counter other regulations that need overhaul, such as the Usury Law. In the future, a simplification of this framework may be desirable. Harmonizing, and perhaps eventually integrating, the framework for regulated MFIs with the banking system may also be considered.

Within current regulatory norms, SCMs have very low entry capital requirements relative to other countries and also to Brazil's own banking system. This could pose a problem for supervision if the numbers of SCMs expand significantly—although this may be unlikely in the new microfinance environment introduced in 2003. Conversely, leverage ratios appear relatively high, even compared with other countries, which frequently use the same capital adequacy ratios as for banks. If separate regulatory windows are maintained, models of shared, delegated, or independent supervision could be considered.

The Brazilian credit cooperative system has made important advances, particularly since the mid-1990s, especially with the permission to allow central credit cooperatives to participate as owners in cooperative banks. This enabled the rapid expansion of credit cooperatives combined with growing professionalism in cooperative management, information, accounting, staff training and incentives, and internally administered prudential standards. Incentives for individual cooperatives to federate have been high, because leverage ratios for federated cooperatives were set at much higher levels than individual cooperatives. In the past, this may have mitigated the extremely low start-up capital requirements, which are even lower than for microfinance institutions.

Federated or central cooperative members benefit through an expanded range of financial services such as internet banking, credit cards, Bills of Rural Product (CPRs), insurance, and custodial services, in addition to more accessible loan and savings products. In most cases, they have been able to count on more reliable prudential oversight of the resources they have invested in cooperatives.

Despite such advances, it is noted that some cooperatives, especially rural cooperatives, continue to channel directed credit to the rural sector, often at below market rates, sometimes at unattractive spreads. This undermines members' sense of ownership and reduces incentives to repay. To compensate, there have been special dispensations in terms of prudential requirements. Policies such as those that doubled the leverage permitted in the event of financing using public rural credit programs such as PRONAF reinforced incentives that undermine the cooperative spirit and the sustainability of the cooperatives. The removal of this facility with new regulations introduced in June 2003 was a welcome move.

Consideration should be given to reviewing the extent to which the relative market positions of Banco do Brasil versus smaller rural credit cooperatives explain their relative shares of the spread on PRONAF loans, and what measures can be taken to better relate spread to credit risk and administrative expenditures on such public transfers. Care should be taken to ensure that the channeling of government support does not dominate the activities of cooperatives.

One constraint on the expansion of the cooperative sector has been the high liquidity requirement, considerably higher than prudential norms advocated by international standards. Although new regulations introduced in 2003 bring the capital requirements of this sector in line with the banking sector, higher liquidity requirements remain. Other prudential regulations recently introduced could improve the soundness of the sector but will raise supervision resource requirements. Nonprudential disclosure-based advances on the regulatory side comprise the inclusion of cooperative clients with loans above R$5,000 in the Central Bank's credit information system (Central do Risco), and of reviews of cooperatives' boards of directors. As in the case of microfinance, over time the harmonization of financial regulation for the credit cooperative sector with other financial institutions is desirable and recent changes have contributed to this. Such harmonization would promote competition and reduce perceived higher risk associated with the lack to access to a liquidity facility and deposit insurance.

Another constraint on expansion that has frequently been alluded to is membership restriction, both geographic and by occupation. Relaxation of this constraint has been recently introduced, especially for remote areas. It should be noted that constraints on membership exist in most credit union systems in developed countries, and are considered a safeguard based on collective responsibility or 'reputational collateral.' The recent relaxations must be carefully monitored in terms of their impact on the safety and soundness of the cooperative system. In this context, the higher minimum capital requirements for the new open-admission cooperatives are appropriate.

Regarding oversight, there is a need to maintain a prudent balance between direct and delegated oversight of credit cooperatives. The present system of delegation appears to be beneficial, although if the sector grows more, formalized delegation may be needed and choice of an appropriate framework for this will need to be selected. The setting up of a special supervision unit for these institutions, following the regulations of 2003, is a welcome move. Additionally, the collection and maintenance of more information on a regular basis should be encouraged and strengthened. This should include information on the performance of microfinance institutions and credit cooperatives and determinants of such performance: for example, data on administrative cost structures in different geographic contexts, risk profiles of clients by location and type of enterprises, and so forth.

Finally, for both the microfinance and credit cooperative sectors, it is suggested that a number of technological innovations are available that can greatly enhance productivity and delivery capacity, and reduce risk in microfinance transactions. These include, particularly, the use of devices such as personal digital assistants, handheld computers, and smart cards, which help credit officers in the field evaluate applications, register client information, and synchronize field and head office information, all of which can ease microlending. The applications of such new technologies to microfinance are discussed with examples from other countries in an annex to chapter 2, and an exploration of possible adaptations in the Brazilian context is suggested.

Although it is hoped that these measures will help to increase the contribution of microfinance and credit cooperatives, their role—especially that of the microfinance sector—will remain small, at least for some time. A big thrust for expanded access could not easily be shouldered by such entities. Especially in the case of microfinance, large-scale expansion would be difficult without partnerships with banks, public or private. If government access to privileged credit is to be avoided, deposit-taking will need to be seriously considered, with its attendant risks and safeguards. The expansion of client interface is another reason for the consideration of this option. The cooperative sector, by contrast, is already much larger than microfinance, and is already in a position to mobilize deposits. Thus, from the scale perspective, it has more potential.

Downscaling Private Banks

Brazil's 175 private banks represent the vast majority of the country's 191 commercial banking institutions in number, and also in the provision of broad aggregates of financial services. Their role in deposit and lending activity has grown to a dominant position over the last decade, from 42 percent of total deposits in 1994 to 52 percent in 2001, and from 44 percent of total loans to 56 percent over the same period. Four of these private banks are substantially larger than the others: Bradesco with 9 percent of total banking assets in June 2001, Itaú with 7 percent, Santander with 6 percent (via their acquisition of Banespa), and Unibanco with 5 percent. Nevertheless, Brazil's two large public retail banks, Banco do Brasil and Caixa Econômica Federal, still account for close to 40 percent of deposits (20 and 19 percent, respectively, in December 2001) and three federal banks (including the wholesale bank BNDES, Banco do Brasil, and Caixa Econômica Federal) account for around 31 percent of total lending (13, 6, and 11 percent of total bank loans, respectively).

To what extent have these private banks already downscaled their services; that is, contributed to the provision of financial services for the poorer segments of Brazil's society? This issue is investigated in chapter 3 of the study, across several dimensions: the provision of small deposit and small loan services, minimum deposits, costs and fees; and delivery channels. The role of new technologies in the provision of financial services to smaller and less-affluent clients is discussed, the present use of such technologies in Brazil is assessed, and examples from other countries are offered. Finally, the experience of banks in other countries that have successfully achieved outreach to less-affluent clients is described in an annex.

The analysis reveals, first, that private commercial banks in Brazil already play a significant role in the provision of financial services to small clients. Small transaction size per se does not appear to be an absolute barrier for private banks in entering this segment. However, there is a high degree of segmentation in the types of banking services private banks wish to provide. On the deposit side, they are more likely to enter the possibly more lucrative segments of the market such as sight deposits, which are unremunerated, or special savings deposits, where remuneration is much lower than the prevailing interbank rates. This appears to be the case despite the directed credit requirements placed on these categories of deposits. Private banks are not keen to serve the term deposit needs of small clients, which are remunerated at rates close to the interbank rate, presumably because its advantages, compared with safe assets such as government securities, decline. Thus, transactions-based needs and needs for safe stores of value are met, though needs for returns and investments are served less often. There is considerable variation in private banks' individual business plans in terms of outreach, whether they are wholly national or partly foreign owned.

One important corollary is that public banks are not the principal providers of services to small account holders; however, they do provide services in this segment to those account holders who are more interested in investments and in returns through term deposits, compared with those whose needs are based on transactions or on safely maintaining the value of their savings. And evidence suggests that low-income clients do not show a strong preference for public banks.

Findings suggest that fees and costs matter. Looking at the prices of banking transactions, although fees for a basic package of banking services do not appear high, they could nevertheless constitute a significant proportion (1 to 2 percent per month) of the income of a less-well-off individual. In terms of institutional variation of transactions costs, although average fees for private and especially foreign banks may be higher than federal banks, the difference is not significant looking at comparable public and private banks. Some large private banks are as competitive in prices and service range as federal banks, and, in other instances, some federal bank service fees may be high. Transaction fees appear to be a greater obstacle for personal banking services than for the provision of credit to enterprises; high interest rates are the most important factor for enterprises, especially small enterprises. Another finding is that some specific banking services appear to be more uniformly available across different banks, such as ATM use and debit card facilities, whereas others are less likely to appear in basic packages of services without extra charges, and may be more competitively priced across institutions: checking facilities, overdraft facilities, provision of printed statements, and debit orders.

The choice of delivery channels for banking services and also the choice between banks and nonbanks appear to be affected by regulatory requirements that raise the costs of establishing banking services, especially bank branches. The growth of correspondent banking has been partly in response to these regulatory restrictions and costs, but correspondents also help to spread fixed costs. In the future, competition in correspondent franchises and further broad-basing of their services, including, for example, government bond distribution, could help to ensure that their competitive edge is maintained. But, also, prices of other types of services such as bank card networks may be affected by limited competition in their provision. Differentiated solutions are required to address these issues.

New technologies based on phone connectivity, telephone- and internet-based, are widely used in Brazil, but not for services to the lower-income segments. Teleconnectivity in Brazil is relatively low in average terms, although there are many well-to-do who use internet banking. Many countries, including Brazil, are making a conscious effort to encourage more universal access to and use of telecommunication services through nondistortive targeted subsidies, and several examples of good practice are available.

New measures have been introduced recently that require banks to expand microlending from their sight deposit resources, up to an obligatory ceiling of 2 percent—alternatively these funds go to raised reserve requirements. This is an implicit tax on the financial system. Other measures such as disclosure requirements, guarantees, or initial tax breaks are more widely used internationally. Another new measure recently introduced, the basic or minimum account, is, however, widely used in many countries, although it is rarely offered on a free basis as in Brazil.

There are a number of additional good practices that have been identified by banks in other countries to promote the downscaling of their business, which could be considered by banks in Brazil. A first group of such practices depends on the development of appropriate products, which apart from appropriately priced basic accounts include employer-sponsored 'payroll' accounts, and the adoption of technologies such as credit scoring, which may aid outreach to small clients. A second approach rests on the development of partnerships with microfinance institutions, or with other partners such as community organizations, and a third rests on image differentiation. Financial training of the target population would be greatly beneficial and can be delivered in combination with outreach programs.

Finally, there are many measures in the overall environment that could help the banking system in terms of outreach. These are discussed in chapter 6, which deals with institutional infrastructure, and in chapter 7, which discusses how the government could help outreach by easing entry requirements for new bank clients, by reducing current regulatory arbitrage between different segments of the financial sector, and through a number of measures that reduce overhead costs imposed on the banking system and programs of active support for bank outreach.

Partnering Nonbanks

Although statistics on the financial system indicate a heavy concentration of assets in the banking system of between 90 and 95 percent, these data may overemphasize the importance of the system. Banking system assets consolidate data for Brazil's multiple banks, and to the extent that departments of these banks also engage in nonbank activities, these would be included under the category of bank assets. Moreover, some activities that provide finance to consumers and producers in the form of trade finance, commercial credit, or through factoring are considered commercial activities and thus not included in the statistics above on financial intermediation. For example, the discount of invoices, included in credit data, amounted to around R$6 billion in 2001, while the estimated factoring portfolio at the end of 2001 was R$27 billion, and factoring represented an estimated 2.3 percent of Brazil's GDP. Credit card receivables are only included in the statistics above to the extent that these may be refinanced by banks. Finance companies' portfolio was 0.4 percent of GDP, amounting to R$4.4 billion in value, compared with an aggregate consumer credit portfolio of R$70 billion for the entire financial system. And Brazil's outstanding leasing portfolio represented 1 percent of GDP at end-2001, with a portfolio of R$11.6 billion. In many countries, nonbank activities, especially trade finance, factoring, and the leasing of equipment, have been valuable sources of financial access. Chapter 4 of the study evaluates their present and potential contributions to access.

Broad findings indicate that weak bankruptcy and secured transaction laws that complicate the use of collateral in Brazil create incentives for forms of financing (factoring, leasing, trade finance) other than straightforward credit. These forms of financing reduce risk by securing repayments against accounts receivable, or by maintaining title and using self-executable legal instruments. Also, financial institutions offering such services do not face many of the high costs of entry of banks, and some nonbanks such as factoring and finance companies are better equipped to handle the high operating costs for small-scale clients. As such, they could have an important role, although factoring and trade financing provide only working capital and cannot meet investment needs. Leasing could potentially contribute to investment finance but has not been used much for this purpose.

The contributions of these sectors have been below their potential, in part because their own legal underpinnings are fragmented and sometimes challenged as to their legitimacy. Factoring does not have a law governing its services and leasing laws are fragmented. The treatment that factoring and leasing have received in civil litigation has sometimes been perceived as arbitrary. In both factoring and leasing, confusion remains between these activities and normal bank credit. Thus, in the case of leasing, it is sometimes concluded that leases are essentially similar to loans; also, distinctions between financial and operational leases are sometimes unclear. For factoring, the discounting of invoices or postdated checks is considered on a par with the purchase of receivables. Until a mature distinction regarding these novel contracts is established, it will be hard to expand the growth of these services in Brazil.

Looking more specifically at individual segments, the greatest potential appears to lie in the relatively overlooked area of factoring, which makes a sizeable real contribution today in finance and services to small enterprises and could be strengthened and legitimized to extend its outreach. At present, the distinction between genuine factoring and the discounting of invoices or checks is not sufficiently clear in practice. Consolidation of the dispersed legal framework of the factoring industry could contribute toward this. A proposed draft law on factoring has been pending in Congress for years. Its final passage would be beneficial to the industry. The legal framework should also clarify distinctions between recourse financing and nonrecourse financing by factors. Financing with recourse, though not forbidden, has not been recognized in legal jurisprudence. Lack of recourse in cases of fraudulent transactions by clients is costly for factoring companies. Also on the regulatory side, the tax treatment of factoring needs investigation. At present, it is subject to all financial transaction taxes as well as to commercial taxes. A case has been pending in the Federal Supreme Court to resolve this.

Permitting factoring companies wider access to finance would be desirable through, for example, the issue of commercial bills or debentures, currently not possible for those factoring entities not constituted as shareholding companies. This could be eased if the proposed draft law is passed. And international factoring could be eased by the relaxation of certain restrictions against holding foreign currency accounts.

The leasing industry has fluctuated markedly in Brazil in the past decade, Regulatory arbitrage in the tax system has considerably influenced its development and contributed to its boom, especially in consumer vehicle leasing, in the late-1990s. Further changes in the tax system together with the impact of devaluation on dollar-indexed loans, and also judicial activism that tended to shelter the lessee, led to its subsequent contraction and to the move away from individual leasing by lessors.

Leasing is not used often for investment finance at small firms; it is used mainly by large firms, where the obsolescence of equipment or contracting of maintenance for operational leasing makes this an attractive option for investment financing. For individuals, leasing has been used largely by the better-off, primarily to acquire vehicles. Leasing is largely beyond the domain of the less-well-off consumers or small firms, and thus today of limited immediate importance in expansion of access. The relatively slow growth in leasing of machinery and equipment has also been ascribed to the availability of alternative sources of finance, such as the Special Agency of Industrial Financing (FINAME) credit lines of the BNDES bank, which are longer term (three to five years).

The industry may also benefit from clarifications in its legal and tax framework. The legal framework for leasing is scattered, and for many purposes leasing falls under the Civil Code. A dedicated leasing law is under preparation and is due to be submitted to Congress. This will be important in clarifying the framework for leasing operations. The tax advantages of leasing may be difficult for smaller firms to realize because this would require the use of more complex tax forms (*lucro real*) that permit itemized deductions, instead of the simplified tax forms (based on *lucro presumido*). The tax regime for leasing is also complicated by the treatment of 'residual value.' If residual value is low, leases are sometimes not recognized but treated as loans. The industry is seeking legal clarification through a pending suit and its outcome will considerably influence the extent to which the industry regains its attractiveness. There also appears to be a need to clarify and correct accounting practices with regard to leasing. In Brazil, financial leases are booked as operational leases, thus allowing capital goods acquisition without raising the gearing (indebtedness) ratio. However, this accounting treatment is unorthodox.

Partnerships between financial intermediaries and commercial companies could constitute a feasible alternative to promote operational leasing for smaller enterprises. This would be promoted by more competition in the industries that enter into leasing contracts.

Finally, finance companies are an important alternative for consumer credit at low- and medium-income levels. They have the advantage for the consumer of easier access than bank accounts. Independent finance companies are a very small market segment today because most finance companies are part of multiple banks and wider financial conglomerates. For financial institutions such as banks, finance company subsidiaries offer an avenue for product differentiation and lower-cost funds (because there are no reserve requirements). However, the implication is that access to funding is tight for those finance companies that operate independently, because they are not deposit-taking institutions. Most of their services could today be provided by multiple banks.

Channeling Specialized Finance

A large part of the issue of financial access that has occupied the attention of policymakers has been the problem of access to specialized financial services, in sectors where it has been particularly difficult to attract private finance. Two areas of the financial system that stand out in this context are rural financial services and access to housing finance. A substantial part of the system of 'targeted' or 'earmarked' credit in Brazil arose from the need to address these specialized credit needs. Chapter 5 examines the evolution of one of these areas: rural finance. It evaluates the rationale for and cost of the present system, and discusses the extent to which it meets goals of outreach and sustainability.

Many have pointed out that rural finance faces special difficulties and thus merits special solutions. There are, first, geographic issues of access in remote rural areas. These are combined with typically high rates of poverty, lower population densities, isolated markets, highly covariant risks, limited opportunities for risk diversification, sharp seasonal variations in income and in the demand for and supply of financial resources, and lack of traditional collateral. All these factors result in high transaction costs and higher perceived risk in providing financial services in rural areas. It is argued that, as a result, credit to rural markets is 'rationed,' in the sense that lenders tend to limit quantity, even if prices are flexible.

Brazil's response to the challenge of rural finance has been similar to that of a number of countries: direction of credit with a combination of quantitative controls, in the form of mandatory lending to agriculture, and price controls, or lending at below market rates of interest. In Brazil, as in many other countries, selective or directed credit has been channeled largely through public financial entities, either directly or through onlending arrangements with private financial entities. Brazil's largest banks, the Banco do Brasil and the Caixa Econômica Federal, have served as the primary vehicles for channelling credit to the rural and housing sectors, respectively. There are also mandated private sector programs for directed credit: 25 percent of demand deposits (unremunerated by law) must be devoted to rural finance, and 65 percent of passbook savings deposits are earmarked for housing loans. Directed credit shrank after mid-2000, as government-financed restructuring of the federal banks led to removal of a substantial volume of directed credit from their books in exchange for government debt. But despite the decline from about 54 percent of total credit in June 2000 to about 38 percent in March 2002, directed credit remains high.

The study analysis found that the Brazilian rural financial system today is far from good practice: it has limited outreach at high cost instead of mass outreach at low cost. Most rural households still had no access to formal financial services. Credit remained highly concentrated, with three-quarters of all clients receiving less than 6 percent of credit, whereas the top 2 percent of contracts accounted for 57 percent of all credit. Public sector programs and institutions played a predominant role in the national rural credit system, and these have crowded out the private provision of credit at market rates. Freely provided private sector resources had declined to as little as 5 percent of formal rural credit.

To move away from the present situation, Brazil needs to implement a gradual but credible transition program to market-determined interest rates on all rural credit and savings. Although overnight removal may create at least a transitory decline in the allocation of resources to the rural sector and may not be politically acceptable, certain measures could be taken. (1) There could be increases in interest rates on the most heavily subsidized programs (notably PRONAF, whose enormous timely repayment rebates result in highly negative nominal interest rates). (2) Another area where phased rates could be applied is with regard to the 25 percent directed lending requirement. (3) Instead of 'equalization payments,' commercial banks could compete for competitively priced administrative fees for administering subsidized funds. Preference would be given to those who require lower 'equalization' or lower fees.

In parallel, remaining subsidies could be explicitly monitored and budgeted, and refocused away from interest rates to transaction costs. Subsidies have largely been captured by well-to-do farmers and nonfarming corporations, for whom there is no justification for a credit subsidy on either equity or efficiency grounds. The net impact has been to inflate rural land prices because subsidies are capitalized into the value of land, and to promote a more regressive rural income distribution. In view of the fact that ultimately public funds finance programs such as CrediAmigo and PRONAF, there is an urgent need to apply a more uniform approach in applying lending interest rates in such programs.

Brazil could also try to address information and insurance constraints to reduce risks in rural lending. There is good potential for advancing a range of related financial instruments for risk management: price risk management for agricultural commodities, area-based index insurance, and warehouse receipts. These instruments allow farmers to increase their specialization and adopt higher-risk, higher-return production strategies. In a wider context, strengthening rural finance requires attention to the same issues as those affecting overall financial intermediation—addressing issues of high spreads, high administrative costs, and relatively high profits for banks operating in Brazil versus in comparable economies, combined with high financial sector taxation.

Installing Institutional Infrastructure

Substantive laws regarding the legal and judicial protection of creditor rights in Brazil are not very different from those in other French civil law countries, and are generally perceived as adequate by creditors. However legislative procedures are protracted, with recourse to successive appeals or injunctions that diminish the value of legal protection. Moreover, judicial decisions on credit disputes are perceived to be pro-debtor, reflecting judicial social activism, sometimes to the disregard of what is established in the law or the contract. Consequently, jurisprudence and patterns of judicial behavior play a role as important as, or more important than, the law itself in regulating credit disputes.

Especially for small loans, judicial processes are avoided as far as possible because of their uncertainty, expense, and time-consuming nature. Instead, extrajudicial collection through collection agencies is relied on, despite tax advantages in proceeding through the court system. The use of self-executable credit instruments that can help to limit court procedures is also popular. However, these are more common for larger contracts than for small retail loans. Small claims courts cannot be used for this purpose either, because only individuals can initiate causes in these courts. Instead, banks rely on collection agencies and the enforcing power of blacklists, through which access of borrowers to credit or even the use of checks is effectively denied.

However, the most popular consumer loan products are not self-executable instruments (the overdraft facility or *cheque especial*). This is largely because of the formality of requirements for the recognition of a contracted loan, including signatures and witnesses. The ease of extending informal consumer loans through ATMs counterbalances for financial institutions the loss of their self-executable nature. Provisions for loan losses are reflected in higher spreads.

Potential areas for reform that could strengthen creditor rights would include, first, efforts to work with the judges and society at large to show that decisions that benefit a specific borrower in a specific case have broad repercussions that harm borrowers as a whole, at a wider level. As a political process, judicial activism must be dealt with in the political arena, by building a constituency in favor of the strict enforcement of credit contracts. Judicial education is also desirable to promote a better understanding of specific financial instruments, such as self-executable instruments and *cédulas,* and to establish more uniformity in jurisprudence.

In addition, the self-execution of instruments used for small borrowers in the modern context can be introduced, for example, through the overdraft facilities offered over the ATMs or the *duplicatas* of small firms. In keeping with new technology, legal recognition of these debts, which at present is not possible because of their lack of signature and computerized entry, could be explored.

A promising area of reform in the short term is in changing the procedural codes to speed up judgments, an initiative that would likely be supported by the magistracy. Judges largely agree that judicial slowness could be substantially decreased with a reform of procedural codes to reduce the possibilities of postponing a decision in the appeals process. Further, to reduce costs and time for judicial execution of debt, the Special (small claims) Courts could be opened to small credits. These courts, which judge exclusively low-value disputes, operate with much lighter procedures and do not require the parties to be represented by a lawyer; also, their decisions cannot be appealed. To enable courts to take small claims cases, either the law that created the Juizados Especiais would have to be amended, to allow banks and other financial institutions to act as plaintiffs, or a new law would be necessary to create special claims courts able to judge small debt collections. The proposed new courts could be designed to combine pro-debtor services as well as the settlement of small loans, in order to make them socially and politically acceptable.

Finally, current tax write-offs against profits on uncollected small claims can be evaluated in a wider context, because these may be sending perverse signals to both borrowers and financial institutions for debt repayment. International practice in the design of more incentive-compatible tax treatment for small claims can be investigated.

The use of collateral is also rendered difficult by current procedures for the creation and perfection of security rights. There ia a series of different registries, and few locations are linked. Systems of registration are in some cases time consuming when the manual transcription of large deeds and documents is needed, and systems of retrieval are complicated by the lack of electronic filing and indexing. Finally, costs of filing tend to be regressive, affecting small transactions disproportionately. These difficulties impede the development of secured transactions. It is also alleged that despite recent improvements, there are still a large number of registries awarded to persons on a franchise basis, sometimes passed down through generations, without the application of appropriate certification criteria.

Measures that could lead to an improvement in the process include the adoption of electronic filing, retrieval, and indexation systems at all registration offices in the country. The establishment of networks for the linkage of registries would also improve the process, initially if necessary on a pilot basis within cities, regions, or state, and eventually across regions and across the different types of registries required for different types of security interests. An example here is pledges versus mortgages, which are currently under different registries. The possibility exists of legal constraints on such networking, and any modifications that may be required in the legal framework, at both the federal and state levels, which could be necessary to accompany such a process of networking of registries, should be explored. Also, deadlines for turnover time for registration of deeds and documents could be adopted; these would shorten the time taken for these processes and might encourage the adoption of modern technologies. And in parallel, documentation requirements for secured transactions in real estate could be examined, to evaluate the scope for simplification or consolidation. The present five-day time and costs taken to conduct a search and certification could both be reduced by a self-guided Web search.

Efforts should be made to address the regressive tariff structures of registries and notaries public, which at present imply disproportionately high costs for smaller transactions. One solution may be to remove the caps on the upper end of the scale and, if necessary, use the proceeds to lower transaction costs for small-scale transactions. Finally, the extent to which notarial and registration services are still operating on a franchise basis could be examined through the offices of judicial oversight, and the extent to which this is likely to remain a longer-term problem could be assessed. Measures can be investigated that could be adopted within the present legal framework to ameliorate the near-term impact of such arrangements.

Especially in view of the difficulties of executing collateral and establishing creditor rights, improved credit reporting may well be a more immediately important route than judicial reform for Brazil to enhance the security of loans to small borrowers. In many countries, including the United States, experience has shown an association between increased credit to small entrepreneurs and the introduction of credit reporting. Brazil already has effective core systems, both public and private, for credit reporting, and competition in the credit reporting industry is developing. Nevertheless, there are areas that could be improved. A first is the limited extent to which positive information is used in credit histories, partly because of legal restrictions on the sharing of such information, and partly because of practical difficulties in establishing information-sharing arrangements. There are signs that this is now evolving within the context of trade associations (for example, for all finance companies, through a new initiative, Acrefi Positivo), and such initiatives should be strongly supported. Also, provisions in the bank secrecy law that refer to such restrictions as well as guidelines on notification could be reevaluated against international norms to ensure an appropriate balance between protection of private information and the sharing of information that may help all borrowers. There could also be a reconsideration of current time restrictions on information that limit credit data to five years. Brazil is an outlier in this respect.

To enhance available positive information, regulations related to the dissemination and collection of payment data from utilities could also be examined, to seek ways to get data from these sectors into credit reports. Utility tariffs could also be structured so that service providers can take into account credit standing and capacity to pay when providing services. It is important to recognize the value of such positive information for low-income consumers who may lack a formal credit history.

In parallel, efforts could be made to prepare consistent strategic directions for the Central de Risco, at Brazil's Central Bank, including data it would collect. Access to other public databases such as the Cadastro Informativo de Créditos não Quitados do Setor Público Federal or CADIN, which is currently limited, could also be examined.

These measures would need to be combined with judicial education and outreach programs on the benefits of credit reports, and records of case law in this regard could be prepared to promote the consistent application of current and new laws. Outreach programs for consumers should also be launched, especially for low-income consumers, so that they are aware of their rights, understand more fully how credit works, and also understand their obligations. Consumer protection norms could be evaluated against international practice, and some areas where current practice may fall short of such norms could be investigated: for example, regarding notification of access of a credit record and the taking of adverse actions based on such records, limits on the marketing of information, or changing erroneous data.

Enlisting the Government

To what extent will markets eventually solve the problem of financial exclusion without government intervention? As the preceding discussion shows, the role and presence of the government is pervasive. The nature of its regulation of financial entities significantly affects the services they can offer and the appropriateness of these services for the financially excluded. Many observers believe that the government needs to take on a more proactive role, ranging from financial support to the indirect establishment of appropriate incentives to formal financial institutions to expand access. Some observers point out that governments have a particularly significant influence on banks because of the latter's particular status.

The strategic economic position of banks, coupled with their government-granted authorization to operate and provide guaranteed deposit insurance, renders them more socially responsible than ordinary undertakings. But social responsibilities may conflict with private profit. To what extent should the government exercise its influence or authority over the banking system to achieve social objectives? These issues are broadly discussed in the concluding chapter, based largely on the experience of major developed countries.

As a prelude, it is pointed out that financial access cannot be considered independent of the overall depth of financial services, and this depth is influenced by a spectrum of government policies that may lie outside the financial sector. The first section of chapter 7 examines the influence of such policies. These include, first and foremost, overall macroeconomic policy, which has a major influence on financial system deepening. Macroeconomic stability, with sound fiscal management, helps to establish the appropriate environment for inflation-free growth and financial system deepening. The government's taxation and public borrowing requirements are a central part of this environment that affects the financial system. Second, government policies in a range of regulatory areas also affect the financial system. For example, bank branch openings are affected not only by regulations pertaining to banks and other financial intermediaries, but also by prevailing competitive forces and labor laws. These factors affect interest rates and spreads and hence the costs of financial intermediation.

In the context of Brazil today, it is clear that macroeconomic policies with high borrowing requirements, financed through the issue of domestic debt held largely by the financial system, have contributed to the crowding out of lending to the private sector. This has been combined with high taxation of the domestic financial system, both explicit and implicit (through high reserve requirements) and a consequent disincentive toward financial transactions and financial deepening. There has also been a high proportion of directed credit in total credit, which has tended to raise the cost of freely allocated credit.

In evaluating the contribution of different segments of the financial system to access, it became evident that the impact of regulatory policy across different parts of the financial system has been uneven, with consequent regulatory arbitrage between its various segments. This explains at least a part of the relative success of some segments of the system compared with others. For overall success in improving access, greater harmonization of such regulatory impact is desirable.

Regulatory policy in other areas has an indirect impact on the financial system, notably labor market policies, which add a considerable burden to hiring costs in the formal financial sector, thus providing incentives for the development of financial sector segments outside this system. Another example, not detailed here, is competition policy. Increased attention to competition in some formal financial sector segments may broaden the base of support for expanded access.

Given the macroeconomic and regulatory setting, the second part of this chapter suggests that policies favorable to the expansion of access to financial services can be, and have been, adopted in a number of countries. Based largely on the experience of developed countries, especially Canada, the United Kingdom, and the United States, a series of policies favoring access is investigated. Broad lessons to emerge from the cross-country examples conclude this summary.

Government support, through legislation or enabling regulation that takes the form of consumer protection for, for example, the prevention of discrimination or predatory practices, better disclosure of lending practices, and the regular collection of quality data on these practices, is critical to inform good policy and to alter the behavior of institutions. Many developed countries have a series of periodic reporting requirements on parameters related to financial access, which Brazil could examine. In many cases, these have been combined with analytic support from academic research, or from research departments of the central banks or ministerial agencies of the countries concerned. Such policies on disclosure, apart from encompassing measures of access, can also help with the appropriate targeting of access, as in the example of the Index of Multiple Deprivation of the United Kingdom.

Laws on financial disclosure, and the implied moral suasion, are powerful tools in shaping the behavior of financial institutions, especially if there is an alignment of financial and nonfinancial incentives to reinforce legislation. Provisions for enhanced disclosure on loans to specific communities or sectors have been powerful tools in enhancing access, as demonstrated by the Community Reinvestment Act (CRA) of the United States. Many countries have since tried to emulate this, such as South Africa, and the threat of CRA-type legislation has led to enhanced voluntary efforts by private banks to expand both disclosure and access in, for example, Canada and the United Kingdom. U.K. banks began to publish statistics on community lending in 2003.

As recently recognized in Brazil, a case can be made for obligatory provision of some form of basic banking services. This is a widespread practice and many examples exist of such programs, from the 'lifeline' or minimum service provision bank laws in many U.S. states, to the basic account requirements in Canada. U.K. banks have also begun to provide basic accounts, although without formal legal requirements. Such basic accounts emphasize access to money transmission mechanisms and the payment system, and also deposit facilities. Services such as check writing and credit need not form a part of a basic account. Credit facilities offered with Brazil's new basic accounts should remain under review. The pricing and operating costs of such accounts also need to be constantly monitored, and accounts with no fees may become expensive over time. Electronic fund transfers for federal payments and 'First Accounts,' as launched in the United States, could accelerate the reduction of the 'unbanked.' Brazil also proposes to transfer federal payments to such accounts.

Encouraging partnerships of formal financial institutions with community-based credit providers to employ alternative delivery channels can be very productive. There are Community Development Finance Institutions in some of the country cases discussed (the United Kingdom), which have a very different role from traditional public development banks. These agencies are typically small and not-for-profit, and they provide a dedicated link between the recipient of financial services and the government. Sound partnerships between the public and private sectors, built around shared understanding of their different roles and what each brings to any transaction, are also valuable. Such institutional support needs to be involved in financial outreach efforts. These include not only business administration and fund administration agencies but also nonprofit agencies and community investment agencies that work closely with target communities and can assess both their needs and their eligibility.

In terms of financial support, most successful examples of credit support for products that serve disadvantaged populations entail indirect support by government, where private credit providers still share in the risk. The U.S. Community Development Financial Institutions Fund is an example. The Small Business Administration's Microloan Program is another, where the Small Business Administration makes funds available to community-based lenders (intermediaries) who, in turn, onlend to eligible small businesses and individuals. The local provider handles all underwriting and decisionmaking. Such initiatives can be combined with policies to promote access by financial institutions to secondary credit markets. Such activities can be designed to complement rather than compete with private sector activities.

Indirect regulatory policy affecting financial sector competition can also affect access, even if this is not immediately apparent. Brazil's banking structure, dominated by a handful of institutions, bears some resemblance to that of the United Kingdom, where a recent investigation of competition issues, particularly with regard to its big four banks, revealed, for example, the payment of service charges for access to money transmission. The impact of competition on other areas of access to financial services has also been detailed and pointed out in other countries. A full evaluation of the status of competition in the provision of downscaling in this context is suggested. Finally, the role of programs of financial education and literacy are also key possible interventions. In this context, programs that offer incentives for family support for financial planning are noteworthy.

The recommendations that have evolved from this study, if implemented, would enhance access to financial services in Brazil and assist in reducing poverty and improving the quality of life of ordinary Brazilians.

Abbreviations

AAA	Atividades Analíticas e Consultivas	Analytic and Advisory Activities
ABEL		Brazilian Leasing Companies Association
ABN AMRO	Algemene Bank	Nederland–Amsterdam–Rotterdam Bank
ABRACOOP	Brasileira para o Desenvolvimento do Cooperativismo	Brazilian Association for the Development of Cooperatives
ABSA		Amalgamated Banks of South Africa
ACC	Adiantamento do Contrato de Câmbio	Advance on Exchange Contract
ACE	Adiantamento de Contrato de Exportação	Advance on Exportation Contract
ACEP	Agence de Credit pour l'Enterprise Privee (Senegal)	Private Enterprise Credit Agency
ACREFI	Associação Nacional das Instituições de Crédito, Financiamento e Investimento	National Association of Credit, Finance, and Investment Institutions
AGAPE	Asociación General para Asesorar Pequeñas	General Association for Advising Small Business
ANFAC	Associação Nacional das Sociedades de Fomento Mercantil—Factoring	Brazilian Factoring Association
ANOREG	Associação dos Notários e Registradores do Brasil	Brazilian Notary and Registry Association
ART		Aston Reinvestment Trust
ASA	Associação para Progresso Social	Association for Social Advancement
ATM/PAE	Posto de Atendimento Bancário Eletrônico	Automated Teller Machine

BAAC	Banco para a agricultura e cooperativas agriculturais de Tailândia	Bank for Agriculture and Agricultural Cooperatives of Thailand
BANCOOB	Banco Cooperativo do Brasil	Cooperative Bank of Brazil
BANEFE	Banco Santander	Santander Bank
BANSICREDI	Banco Cooperativo SICREDI	Cooperative Bank of the SICREDI
BASA	Banco da Amazônia	Amazonia Bank, Brazil
BB	Banco do Brasil	Bank of Brazil
BBA		British Bankers Association
BCB	Banco Central do Brasil	Central Bank of Brazil
BCIE	Banco Centroamericano de Integración Económica	Central American Bank for Economic Integration
BDC		Business Development Bank of Canada
BIS	Banco Internacional de Compensações	Bank for International Settlements
BKD	Badan Kredit Desas	Badan Kredit Desas
BM&F	Bolsa Mercantil de Futuros	Futures Markets Exchange
BNB	Banco do Nordeste	Bank of the Northeast of Brazil
BNDES	Banco Nacional de Desenvolvimento Econômico e Social	National Bank for Economic and Social Development
BNDESpar	BNDES Participações	National Bank for Economic and Social Development–Equity Branch
BOVESPA	Bolsa de Valores de São Paulo	Stock Exchange of Brazil–São Paulo
BRAC	Comitê Do Avanço Rural De Bangladesh	Bangladesh Rural Advancement Committee
BRDE	Banco Regional de Desenvolvimento do Extremo Sul	Regional Development Bank for the Extreme South

BRI	Banco Rakyat Indonésia	Bank Rakyat Indonesia
BVR	Associação de Bancos Populares Alemões e Raiffeisen	Association of German Popular and Raiffeisen Banks
CADIN	Cadastro Informativo de Créditos não Quitados do Setor Público	Federal Registry of Citizens and Firms in Default with the Federal Government
CAM	Centro de Apoyo a la Microempresa	Microbusiness Support Center
CAMELS	Sistema de Ratings Bancários	Bank Rating System
CAPS		Capital Access Programs
CARD	Centro para a agricultura e o desenvolvimento rural	Center for Agriculture and Rural Development
CAS	Estratégia de Assistência para o País	Country Assistance Strategy
CBTAL	Empréstimo de Assistência Técnica à Modernização do Banco Central	Central Bank Modernization Technical Assistance Loan
CCB	Cédula de Crédito Bancario	Bank Credit Bill
CCJ	Cimissão de Constitução Justica	
CCO		Check Cashing Outlet
CDB	Certificado de Depósito Bancário	Bank Certificate of Deposit
CDFI		Community Development Financial Institution
CDI	Certificado de Depósito Interfinanceiro	Interbank Certificate of Deposit
CDs	Certificado de Depósito	Certificates of Deposit
CEAPE	Centro de Apoio aos Pequenos Empreendimentos	Support Center for Small Business, Brazil
CEF	Caixa Econômica Federal	National Savings Banks, Brazil

CERUDEB	Banco Centenary de Desenvolvimento Rural	Centenary Rural Development Bank
CETIP	Central de Custódia e de Liquidação Financeira de Títulos	Center for Securities, Custodial, and Settlement Services, Brazil
CGAP	Grupo Consultivo de Auxílio aos Pobres	Consultative Group to Assist the Poorest
CMAC	Cajas Municipales de Ahorro y Credito	Municipal Savings and Loans Offices
CMM	Corporacion Mundial de la Mujer	Women's World Corporation
CMN	Conselho Monetário Nacional	National Monetary Council
CNH	CNH Capital	CNH Capital
COCECRER–RS	Cooperativa Central de Crédito Rural do Rio Grande do Sul Ltda	Central Cooperative for Rural Credit, Rio Grande do Sul
COFIDE (DFC)	Corporação Financeira de Desenvolvimento	Development Financial Company
COFINS	Contribuição para Financiamento da Seguridade Social	Contribution for the Financing of Social Security
COMPE	Centralizadora da Compensação de Cheques e Outros Papéis	Central Settlement System of Checks and Other Documents
CPF	Cadastro de Pessoa Fisica	Cadastre of individuals
CPI	Índice de Preços ao Consumidor	Consumer Price Index
CPMF	Contribuição Provisória sobre Movimentação Financeira	Financial Transactions Tax
CPR	Cédula de Produto Rural	Bill for Rural Products; Bills of Exchange
CRA		Community Reinvestment Act
CRAC	Cajas Rurales de Ahorro y Credito	Rural Savings and Loans

CRESOL	Cooperativa de Crédito Solidário	Mutual Credit Cooperative
CRSFN	Conselho de Recursos do Sistema Financeiro Nacional	
CTN	Código Tributário Nacional	Brazil's Tax Code
CVM	Comissão de Valores Mobiliários do Brasil	Brazil Securities & Exchange Commission
DAI	Alternativas de Desenvolvimento Inc.	Development Alternatives Inc.
DGRV	Confederação Alemã de Cooperativas de Crédito	German Confederation of Credit Cooperatives
DI	Depósito Interfinanceiro	Interbank Deposit
DID	Desarrollo Internacional Desjardins	Development International Desjardins
DIEESE	Departamento Intersindical de Estatísticas e Estudos Socioeconómicos	Inter-Trade Unions Department of Statistics and Socioeconomic Studies
DIRUR	Diretoria de Estudos Regionais e Urbanos	Directory for Regional and Urban Studies
EDPYME	Empresa de Desarrollo de la Pequeña y Micro Empresa	Small and Micro Business Development Company
ETA		Electronic Transfer Account
ETENE	O Escritório Técnico de Estudos Econômicos do Nordeste	Technical Office of Economic Studies for the Northeast
FACS	Pesquisa da Análise e da Concorrência de Empresas	Firm Analysis and Competitiveness Survey
FAEJ	Fundo de Apoio ao Empreendedor Joseense	Support Fund for Joseense Entrepreneurs
FAEP	Fundo de Apoio ao Empreendimento Popular	Support Fund for Popular Enterprise
FAMPE	Fundo de Aval ás Microempresas e Empresas de Pequeno Porte	Loan Guarantee Fund for Micro and Small Enterprises

FAO	Organizacao das Nacoes Unidas para a Agricultural e Alimentacao	United Nations Food and Agriculture Organization
FAT	Fundo de Amparo ao Trabalhador	Worker Assistance Fund of the West
FCO	Fundos Constitucionais	Constitutional Fund
FDI	Investimento Direto Estrangeiro	Foreign Direct Investment
FED	Fundación Ecuatoriana de Desarrollo	Ecuadorian Development Foundation
FENASEG	Federação Nacional das Empresas de Surguros Privados e de Capitalização	National Federation of Insurance Companies
FFP	Fondo Financiero Privado	Private Financial Funds
FGC	Fundo Garantidor de Créditos	Deposit Insurance Fund
FGPC	Fundo de Garantia para Promoção da Competitividade	Insurance Fund for Promoting Competitiveness
FGTS	Fundo de Garantia do Tempo de Serviço	Employees Severance and Indemnity Fund
FHA		Federal Housing Authority
FHLB		Federal Home Loan Banks
FIE	Fomento a Iniciativas Economicas (Bolivia)	Economic Initiative Development, Bolivia
FINAME	Agência Especial de Financiamento Industrial	Special Agency for Industrial Financing
FINCA	Fundação de para o Auxílio Comunitário Internacional	Foundation for International Community Assistance
FINEM	Financiamento a Empreendimentos	Enterprise Financing
FINSOL	Financeira Solidaria SA	Financial Security Fund
FMM	Fundación Mundo Mujer	World Women's Foundation

FOLADE	Fondo Latinoamericano de Desarrollo	Latin American Development Fund
FONDESIF	Fondo de Desarrollo del Sistema Financiero y de Apoyo al Sector Productivo–Fundo de Desenvolvimento do Sistema Financeiro e de apoio ao Setor Produtivo	Fund for the Development of the Financial System and Support to the Productive Sector
FONSET	Fórum Nacional dos Secretários de Trabalho	National Forum of Labor Secretaries
FSTAL	Segundo Empréstimo de Assistência Técnica	Financial Sector Technical Assistance Loan
FUNCAFÉ	Fundo de Defesa da Economia Cafeeíra	
FWWB		Friends of Women's World Banking
GCI	Inspeção Global Consolidada	Global Consolidated Inspection
GDP	Produto Interno Bruto	Gross Domestic Product
GNI	Produto Nacional Bruto	Gross National Income
GNP	Produto Nacional Bruto	Gross National Product
GTZ	Sociedade Alemã de Cooperação Técnica	German Technical Co-operation Agency
HMDA		Home Mortgage Disclosure Act
HSBC		Hong Kong and Shanghai Banking Corporation
IAF	Fundação Interamericana	Inter-American Foundation
IBGE	Instituto Brasileira de Geografia e Estatistica	Brazilian Institute of Geography and Statistics
IBRD	Banco Internacional para a Reconstrução e Desenvolvimento	International Bank for Reconstruction and Development
ICMS	Imposto de Circulação de Mercadorias	

ICR	Relatório da Conclusão da Execução	Implementation Completion Report
IDAs		Individual Development Accounts
IDB	Banco Interamericano de Desenvolvimento	Inter-American Development Bank
IFC	Corporação Financeira Internacional	International Finance Corporation
IGP–DI/M		General Price Index–Internal Availability/Average
IIC	Corporação Interamericana de Investimento	InterAmerican Investment Corporation
ILO	Organização Internacional do Trabalho	International Labour Organisation
IMF	Fundo Monetário Internacional	International Monetary Fund
IOF	Imposto sobre Operações Financeiras	Tax on Financial Operations
IPCA	Índice de Preços ao Consumidor Amplo	Consumer Price Index
IPEA	Instituto de Pesquisa Economica Aplicada	Institute of Applied Economic Research
IRB	Instituto do Reseguros do Brasil	Reinsurance Institution of Brazil
ISS	Imposto Sobre Serviços de Qualquer Natureza	Tax on Services
LACIF	Fundo De Investimento ao Desafio America Latina	Latin American Challenge Investment Fund
LIBOR	Taxa de Juros Interbancário de Londres	London Interbank Offered Rate
LTN	Letras do Tesouro Nacional	Federal Treasury Bills
MCR	Manual de Crédito Rural	Rural Credit Manual
MDIC	Ministério do Desenvolvimiento, Industria e Comercio Exterior	Ministry of Development, Industry and Commerce

MFIs	Instituições De Microfinance	Microfinance Institutions
MIS	Sistema De Informação Da Gerência	Management Information System
MODERFROTA	Programa de Modernização da Frota de Tratores Agricolas e Implementos Associados e Colheitadeiras	Program for the Modernization of the Fleet of Agricultural Tractors, Associated Implements, and Harvesters
MPME	Micro, Pequena e Médias Empresas	Micro, Small and Medium-sized Companies
NABARD	Banco Nacional para a Agricultura e o Desenvolvimento Rural	National Bank for Agriculture and Rural Development, India
NAFIBO	Nacional Financiera Boliviana	National Bolivian Finance Company
NCUSIF	Fundo Do Seguro Da Parte Da União De Crédito Nacional	National Credit Union Share Insurance Fund
NGO	Organização Não-Governamental	Nongovernmental Organization
OCB	Organização das Cooperativas Brasileiras	Organization of Cooperatives of Brazil
OECD	Organização para a cooperação e o desenvolvimento econômicos	Organisation for Economic Co-operation and Development
ORGAPE	Organização de Apoio aos Pequenos Empreendimentos	Organization of Support to the Small Enterprises
OSCIP	Organização da Sociedade Civil de Interesse Público	Civil Society Organization with a Public Interest
PAA	Posto Avançado do Atendimento	Advanced Service Outpost
PAB	Posto Avançado Bancário	Advanced Banking Outpost

PAC	Posto de Atendimento Cooperativo	Cooperative Services
PACRE	Posto Avançado de Crédito Rural	Rural Credit Outposts
PAE	Posto de Atendimento Bancário Eletrônico	Automated Electronic Banking Machine
PAP	Posto de Arrecadação e Pagamentos	Payment Posts
PAR	Programa de Apoyo a las Iniciativas Regionales	Support Program for Regional Initiatives
PCO	Posto de Compra de Ouro	
PCPP	Programa de Crédito Produtivo Popular	Program for Popular Productive Credit
PCR	Programa de Capital de Risco	Venture Capital Program
PDI	Programa de Desenvolvimiento Institucional	Institutional Development Program
PESA	Programa Especial de Saneamento Agricola	Special Program for Agricultural Recovery
PFSECAL	Empréstimo Programático para Ajuste ao Setor Financiero	Programmatic Financial Sector Adjustment Loan
PIS/PASEP	Programa de Integração Social/Programa de Formação do Patrimônio do Servidor Público	Program of Social Integration/Program for the Development of Assets for the Public Workers
PLANFOR	Plano Nacional de Qualificaçao do Trabalhador	National Plan for Worker Qualification
POF	Pesquisa de Orçamentos Familiares	Periodic consumer expenditure surveys
PPV	Pesquisa Sobre Padrões de Vida	Household survey
PROAZEM		Incentive Program for the Construction and Modernization of Storage Units on Rural Properties

PROCAJU		Development Program for Cashew Farming
PROCERA–FNE	Programa de Créditos Especiais para Reforma Agrária–Fundo Constitucional de Financiamento do Nordeste	Land Reform Program–Northeast Constitutional and Financial Fund
PROCON	A Fundação de Proteção e Defesa do Consumidor	Brazilian Consumer Protection Agency
PRODAMEL		Development Program for Agriculture
PRODECAP		Development Program for Ovine/Caprine Raising
PRODECER	Programa de Cooperação Nipo—Brasiliero para o Desenvolvimento do Cerrados	Japanese/Brazilian Cooperation Program for the Development of the Savannah
PRODEFLOR		Sustained Development Program for Horticulture
PRODEVINHO		Support Program for the Development of Viticulture
PROES	Programa de Incentivo à Redução do Setor Público Estadual na Atividade Bancária	Reduction of State Level Participation in Banking Activities
PROFUTA		Support Program for Horticulture
PROGER	Programa de Geração de Emprego e Renda	Program to Generate Employment and Income
PROINAP	Programa de Investimentos Agropecuários	Agricultural Investment Program
PROLEITE	Programa de Incentivo à Mecanização, ao Resfriamento e ao Transporte Granelizado da Produção de Leite	

PRONAF	Programa Nacional de Fortalecimento da Agricultura Familiar	National Program to Strengthen Family Agriculture
PROPASTO	Programa Nacional de Recuperação de Pastagens Degradadas	National Program for the Recovery of Degraded Pastures
PROSOLO	Programa de Incentivo ao Uso de Corretivos de Solos	Program of Support for the Use of Soil Amendments
PROTRA-BALHO	Programa de Promoção do Emprego e Melhoria da Qualidade de vida do Trabalhador	Program to Promote Employment and Improve the Quality of Life of Workers
RECOOP		Revitalization Program for Agriculture Producing Cooperatives
RFI	Programa de Revitalização de Cooperativas de Produção Agropecuária	Rural Financial Institution
RITS	Rede de Informações para o Terceiro Setor	Tertiary Sector Information Network
ROA	Retorno em recursos	Return on Assets
RTGS	Sistema de Transferência de Reservas	Real-Time Gross Settlement
SAL	Empréstimo para Ajustamento Estrutural	Structural Adjustment Loan
SBA		Small Business Administration
SBEF	Superintendência de Bancos e Entidades Financeiras	
SBIC		Small Business Investment Company
SBS	Superintendencia de Banca y Seguros	Superintendency of Banking and Insurance
SBS	Serviços para Pequenos Empreendimentos	Small Business Service
SCI	Segurança ao Crédito e Informações	Credit and Information Security

SCMs	Sociedades de Crédito ao Microempreendedor	Microcredit Companies
SDI	Índice de Depedência ao Subsídio	Subsidy Dependence Index
SEBRAE	Serviço Brasileiro de Apoio às Micro e Pequenas Empresas	Brazilian Services to Support Micro- and Small Enterprises
SEDU	Secretaria de Estado do Desenvolvimento Urbano	State Secretariat of Urban Development
SELIC	Sistema Especial de Liquidação e Custodia	Overnight Interest Rate
SERASA	Centralização de Serviços de Bancos	Centralization of Banks' Services
SEWA	Associação de Mulheres Profissionais Liberais	Self-Employed Women's Association
SHG	Grupos de Auto Ajuda	Self-Help Groups
SICOOB	Sistema das Cooperativas de Crédito do Brasil	Brazilian Credit Cooperative System
SICREDI	Sistema de Crédito Cooperativo	Credit Cooperative System
SIP	Sistema Integrado de Pagamento	Integrated Payment System
SME	Empresa pequena e média	Small and Medium Enterprise
SPC	Secretária de Previdência Complementar	Secretariat for Complementary Social Security
SRF	Secretária de Receita Federal	Brazilian Internal Revenue Services
SRO	Organização Auto-regulada	Self-Regulatory Organization
SUSEP	Superintendência de Seguros Privados	Insurance Industry Supervisory Body, Brazil
TA	Assistência Técnica	Technical Assistance
TJLP	Taxa de Juros de Longo Prazo	Long-Term Interest Rate
TR	Taxa Referencial	Reference Rate

UAD	Unidade Administrativa Desmembrada	Separated Administrative Unit
UMBNDES	Unidade Monetária do BNDES	BNDES Monetary Unit
UNICEF	Fundo Internacional de Emergência das Nações Unidos para Crianças	United Nations International Children's Emergency Fund
USAID		U.S. Agency for International Development
VRG		Guaranteed Residual Value
WAP		Wireless Application Protocol
WBES	Pesquisa do Ambiente de Negócio Mundial	World Business Environment Survey
WDI	Indicadores de Desenvolvimento Mundial	World Development Indicators
WOCCU	Conselho Mundial de Cooperativas de Poupança e Crédito	World Council of Credit Unions
WWB		Women's World Banking

CURRENCY EQUIVALENTS

Currency Unit: *Real* (R$)

December 2000 US$1= R$1.95
December 2001 US$1= R$2.31
December 2002 US$1= R$3.55
December 2003 US$1= R$2.90

Fiscal Year of Borrower: January 1–December 31

1
Assessing Access

"Access to financial markets is important for poor people. Like all economic agents, low-income households and microenterprises can benefit from credit, savings, and insurance services. Such services help to manage risk and to smooth consumption ... and allow people to take advantage of profitable business opportunities and increase their earnings potential."

"But financial markets, because of their special features, often serve poor people badly.... Since poor people often have insufficient traditional forms of collateral (such as physical assets) to offer, they are often excluded from traditional financial markets.... [T]ransaction costs are often high relative to the small loans typically demanded by poor people. And in areas where population density is low, physical access to banking services can be very difficult."

WORLD BANK, *WORLD DEVELOPMENT REPORT*, 2000–2001

"The area of financial system regulation and organization will increasingly be focused on the following aspects: ... creation and improvement of financial instruments and activities including those intended to broaden and cheapen credit."

"It is a priority to improve the regulation of mechanisms that broaden the access of the population to the financial system."

HENRIQUE DE CAMPOS MEIRELLES,
GOVERNOR OF THE CENTRAL BANK OF BRAZIL, JANUARY 7, 2003

Growth, Poverty Reduction, and Access to Financial Services

Economic growth, by raising the total income of society, is a primary vehicle for improving human well-being and reducing poverty. The quality of growth can be further enhanced by directly targeting education, health, and poverty outcomes. To achieve these goals, "poor people must be empowered to take steps to improve their lives, and governments must assist them by ensuring that they can obtain the services they need."[1] Targeted poverty intervention is especially important in Brazil, which has one of the most unequal income distributions in the world (table 1.1), significantly more unequal than the Latin American average or other upper-

Table 1.1 Income Distribution: An International Comparison

Region/countries	*GDP per capita in 2000 (constant 1995 US$)*	*Gini coefficient*	*Income share of lowest quintile (%)*
Brazil	**4,624**	**60.5**	**2.5**
Latin America and the Caribbean	3,859	49.5	3.9
of which:			
Chile	5,354	56.5	3.5
Mexico	3,806	50.3	3.6
Peru	2,368	44.9	4.4
Upper-middle-income countries	4,783	42.9	6.4
High-income OECD	29,140	31.4	7.0

Note: Country averages are calculated across the most recent observation per country.
Sources: Data for individual countries are for different years and from different sources (Deininger and Squire 1996 and Lundberg and Squire 2001). GDP per capita data are from the World Bank, *World Development Indicators*. Staff estimates.

middle-income countries. The income share of the lowest quintile of the population in Brazil is significantly below the average for middle-income countries.[2] Brazil's government is keenly aware of these issues and has committed itself to reducing Brazil's rate of extreme poverty by 50 percent by the year 2015.[3]

How can the financial system of Brazil contribute to the reduction of poverty and inequality? It is increasingly accepted that greater financial system depth and soundness contribute to broad-based economic growth with poverty reduction.[4] Deep and efficient financial markets promote investment and total factor productivity growth through their role in selecting and monitoring projects; diversifying risks; reducing asymmetries of information; improving resource allocation; and encouraging the optimization of scale, time frame, and technology. It has been shown that, in the case of Brazil, the possible effect of increased productivity on growth could be large (McKinsey Global Institute 1998).

Strong financial systems help absorb shocks. Conversely, weak financial systems and resulting financial crises entail huge fiscal costs that crowd out social spending and, especially if financed by inflation, disproportionately affect the poor. In neighboring Argentina and Mexico, shallow domestic financial markets have magnified international financial market turbulence, affecting the poor adversely. In Brazil the crisis of 1995 is estimated to have had a fiscal cost of about 13 percent of gross domestic product (GDP).[5] Moreover, badly managed financial crises cause severe disruption to economic processes, erode capital stock, erase confidence in the banking sector, and set back poverty reduction for long periods. Recent crises in Mexico (1995), Ecuador (1998), and Argentina (2002) have significantly increased the incidence of poverty (De Ferranti and Perry 2000).

Apart from the large absolute size of Brazil's financial system, by far the largest in Latin America, the overall depth of financial intermediation in Brazil is greater than that of its large neighbors in the region (table 1.2). The share of financial assets in GDP in Brazil is relatively high, at almost 140 percent of GDP, compared to 81 percent of GDP in Argentina and 68 percent in Mexico.[6] Brazil's achievements in terms of financial depth are modest, however, compared to some large East Asian economies like China, with financial assets/GDP of almost 200 percent despite a per capita income of less than a fifth of Brazil's per capita income. Malaysia, too, has a financial assets/GDP ratio of 370 percent, although its per capita GDP is also below that of Brazil: US$3,390 compared to roughly US$4,350 in Brazil in 2000. Brazil exhibits one of the highest interest spreads in the world, and the maturity of loans is very low, mostly less than one year. The banking system has remained highly profitable, at least since 1999, and well capitalized, with capital ratios between 8.4 and 9.5 percent.

But beyond the association of financial depth and stability with growth and crisis prevention, can the financial system also accelerate the reduction of poverty through targeted interventions designed to broaden the distribution of financial services? The Brazilian financial system, which may have been shaped by the unequal distribution of income and wealth in the country, is the largest in the region and offers a broad variety of services to its clients. However, according to estimates, only around 58 million Brazilians have bank accounts, or a third of the total population, while some 80 million, or half of the total population, are considered 'bankable.'[7] Central Bank statistics show that nearly 30 percent of all municipalities have no bank branch (appendix table A1.2). There are 7 states (out of 27), mostly in the North, where more than 70 percent of municipalities have no bank branch. In the country as a whole, about 1,680 of 5,600 municipalities have no bank branches (appendix table A1.2). The 1,400 or so credit cooperatives offer basic financial services to only about 1.5 million Brazilians, mostly in urban areas. The proportion of Brazilian households with access to more sophisticated financial services, such as mutual funds or insurance products, is low. Brazil's government is aware of these constraints and, since 1999, has accelerated its search for means to expand access to financial services.[8]

The improvement of access to financial services should help both consumers and producers to raise their welfare and productivity.[9] Individuals can insure themselves against periods of low income or unexpected fluctuations in income, and maintain their consumption standards

Table 1.2 Depth of Financial Markets: Brazil and Other Emerging Economies, 1999/2000

Country	*Private credit/GDP*	*Equity market capitalization/GDP*	*Equities—value traded/GDP*	*Domestic public bonds on issue/GDP*	*Domestic private bonds on issue/GDP*	*Total financial assets[a]/GDP*	*GDP per capita 1999[b] (current US$)*	*Total financial assets[a] (US$ millions)*
Brazil	**40.5**	**39.0**	**17.0**	**40.9**	**8.9**	**139.7**	**4,350**	**780,739**
Argentina	23.4	44.0	2.1	11.8	1.0	81.0	7,550	231,166
Mexico	28.5	24.7	7.9	9.2	2.1	68.3	4,440	386,366
India	36.4	34.2	104.7	21.8	0.4	92.8	440	437,293
China	128.9	42.5	66.8	19.5	8.5	199.4	780	2,153,717
Malaysia	103.8	146.5	65.5	29.6	50.0	370.9	3,390	331,302

a. Simplified definition based on aggregate of assets described in this table.
b. Computed using the *World Bank Atlas* method.
Sources: World Bank, *World Development Indicators;* IMF (International Monetary Fund), *International Financial Statistics;* IFC (International Finance Corporation), Emerging Markets Database; BIS (Bank for International Settlements).

through the accumulation of financial savings.[10] For example, for rural farmers, savings constitute insurance to protect themselves against periods of drought or crop failure. Savings also provide a vehicle for future expenditure needs, whether expected (for example, for special family occasions or for the purchase of significant assets such as a home) or unexpected. Access to savings and borrowings could also have longer-term welfare implications, permitting people to borrow when young, for example, for education or for other physical or human capital, and then repay and save for retirement when they are older.[11]

For a producer, access to credit for fixed or working capital makes it possible to increase production, which can have far-reaching implications not only for the producer but also for patterns of employment, occupational choice, and even economywide productivity and growth. Financing constraints have been shown to feature prominently among the constraints of small and medium-size enterprises in some investigations (Hallberg 2001). Other studies have indicated that Latin American firms find the difficulty of access to financial markets to be the major obstacle to the expansion of their business activities, ahead of factors such as macroinstability, taxes, and street crime (Galindo 2001). One study of Latin American countries showed that access to financial services for smaller enterprises had a direct impact on poverty, because of the disproportionately large number of persons employed by such enterprises. Survey evidence on 15 countries in Latin America showed that the microenterprise sector accounted for 56 percent of all earners but 70 percent of the region's poor earners (Westley 2001). In Brazil, an estimated 98 percent of registered firms are enterprises with less than 100 workers and accounted for about 45 percent of registered workers (SEBRAE 2004).

But expanding the supply of financial services to underserved segments of society can pose particular difficulties for financial intermediaries such as banks. Limited provision of financial services cannot be interpreted simply as an unwillingness to provide such services. Lending to some segments, especially the very poor, may be very risky, because households at the margins of financial and cash flow resources may have real difficulty in repaying loans, or be tempted to not repay at all. Persons with informal or irregular employment may face real difficulties servicing loans. The possibility of such problems implies that it is important for financial intermediaries to get information on their prospective clients and to assess their creditworthiness, but such information may be difficult to obtain reliably and costly to collect.[12] Because of such difficulties, even potentially good clients may be underserved, and sometimes entire communities may face limits on credit that cannot be increased in volume even by raising interest rates.[13]

Additionally, there are costs associated with the provision of financial services, and if the value of the services provided is small, or services are to be provided in sparsely populated regions, it may be difficult to cover such costs. Costs of administration may be high because of the need for intensive interaction with and education of clients. Maintaining accounts may be costly because the deposits of the poor, which can provide interest income to banks, may be low, while transaction needs, which are costly to provide, may be high. Such issues arise in all countries and are not unique to Brazil.[14] There may also be country-specific factors: for example, particular regulatory requirements could have an impact on costs associated with the provision of specific financial services.

Issues Examined in This Book: The Structure of the Investigation

The challenge for this study was to identify ways of expanding access that acknowledge the special factors tending to limit the expansion of financial services to underserved segments of the population, and to suggest measures to mitigate the impact of these factors. This is the fundamental objective of the present study. The study first attempts to assess the extent to which constraints to access operate, and to identify the nature of these constraints at the level of different types of financial institutions and in different segments of financial markets. The study then seeks to identify alternative strategies for improved access and their implied tradeoffs. Based on this, the study discusses public and private choices to enhance the availability or reduce the cost of provision of such services, consistent with sound financial practices.

Financial exclusion—the inability to gain access to necessary financial services in an appropriate form—can result from difficulties relating to conditions, prices, or marketing of financial services, or from self-exclusion by marginalized populations, often in response to negative experiences or perceptions (Sinclair 2001). Although often implicit, there are many conceptually distinct and sometimes overlapping definitions of groups that are underserved. First of all, the poorer segments of society are usually identified as having disproportionately low access to financial services, and the poor can be defined not only in terms of income but also in terms of wealth and assets.

Other criteria used are specific geographic regions, which may or may not combine characteristics such as remoteness or sparseness of population with economic backwardness. These criteria have been used extensively in Brazil, for example, as discussed below. Third, specific communities of persons may be identified as disadvantaged in terms of financial access. These could, for example, constitute communities of specific racial groups, migrants, or minorities. Also, the criterion of small size is often applied, particularly to producers, so that micro- or small-scale entrepreneurs are often identified as facing special difficulties in gaining access to financial services, especially credit. Sometimes, more than one such characteristic may apply to a particular underserved segment of the population. Measures of access and actions to expand access vary depending on which groups of the underserved are being examined.

In the present study, poverty is the primary consideration or criterion used, though small size and location are also considered. Given the wide array of factors affecting access, selectivity in the analysis has been essential. The study pays greater attention to factors that affect access directly. Thus, indirect impacts on access, operating via their effect on the overall depth of financial services (for example, the potential crowding out of private credit provision by government borrowing, or the impact of financial sector taxation) are not investigated in detail.

The balance of the present chapter sets the stage for the remainder of the book by undertaking a broad overview of current patterns of access, based on a series of alternative measurements, and investigating possible explanations for observed patterns. The chapter summarizes basic findings regarding present patterns of supply of financial services, in terms of the establishment of financial institutions and their branches. It examines trends in such services over the past 10 years, based on countrywide published data, and undertakes an analysis of the factors that might explain the existence, density, depth, and type of financial services provided in different areas. The underlying question is: What factors can be associated with the provision of services by financial institutions? The next four sections look at the demand for financial services relative to availability, especially from the perspective of individual consumers. This information is based on a survey of urban individuals done specifically for the present study. Particular attention is given to an evaluation of broad government policies with regard to access. Finally, the findings of this chapter are summarized.

The other chapters of the study (chapters 2 to 5) examine in more detail the supply of financial services to the underserved, assessing the actual and potential contributions of different forms of financial institutions to increasing access to financial services. Beginning with a range of microfinance institutions (including credit cooperatives), which have been increasingly regarded internationally as promising instruments for the expansion of access, the study examines why the development of microfinance in Brazil has been relatively limited (chapter 2).[15] Next, given the predominance of the banking sector in Brazil's financial system, the study examines its present and potential contributions (chapter 3), and also investigates the potential for expansion of the role of nonbank financial systems such as finance, factoring, and leasing companies (chapter 4). Chapter 5 explores the structure of special market segments important for issues of access, focusing particularly on rural finance.[16]

Following the investigation of service providers, chapter 6 of the study investigates relevant elements of the institutional infrastructure for financial services. Such factors have a particular impact on the cost of provision of financial services and, thus, on bank spreads. This chapter examines the implications of current legal processes for creditor rights for small borrowers, registries for secured credit, and credit information systems.

The study concludes with a discussion of the potential role of policymakers in the expansion of access through different instruments and institutions (chapter 7). Brazil exemplifies the interplay of macro and institutional determinants in limiting the size of the overall credit market. Pronounced market instability, high real interest rates, the crowding-out effect of large public deficits, high explicit and implicit financial sector taxation including high reserve requirements, all have an impact on the overall shallowness of Brazil's financial markets. While accepting the significant role of these factors, the present study attempts to focus rather on microeconomic issues affecting the distribution of credit and other services, and explores the possibility for a more proactive microeconomic role for the government with regard to financial access.[17]

Metrics of Access: Challenges of Measurement

If access to financial services is to be systematically measured or monitored and if the results of policy initiatives are to be tracked, it is important to define standardized measures and indicators of access. Conceptually, a series of alternative indicators may be envisaged, each with potential advantages and drawbacks, which could be applicable in different circumstances. Simple measures, which can be constructed based on easily available statistics and could be usable for purposes of monitoring over time or for cross-country comparison, have conceptual limitations in their interpretation. More sophisticated indices of access can require the collection of specialized data, which would make them difficult to construct or to use for comparative purposes. Some alternative possible approaches are discussed below.

A first simple group of indicators of access is institutional presence—in other words, the supply of financial institutions or service points for the delivery of financial services. This could refer to a count of the number of different types of financial institutions (such as banks, nonbanks, and microfinance institutions), or the number of branches, service posts, ATMs, and so forth of such institutions. Statistics on such institutions are usually easily available, not only on an aggregated basis for the country as a whole, but also for geographic units—for example, at the level of individual states or municipalities. At least at the aggregate level, cross-country comparisons can be made. For geographic units within the country, such statistics can provide indicators of service availability by region or area. This is the measure of access used most extensively in published data on Brazil today.

One limitation of these measures is that in their simplest form they do not indicate the extent to which services provided meet demand for services, in terms, for example, of numbers of inhabitants of a given area. Simple modifications can be introduced by presenting the indicators as ratios—for example, bank branches per unit of population or per given geographic unit. Other limitations are that not all institutions provide the same levels of service: some may be larger or more comprehensive in service provision. Another extension to the measure, therefore, is the volume of deposits, credits, assets, or net worth of financial institutions in specific areas, also already available in some Brazilian statistics. More difficult to address is the limitation that the presence of a financial institution in a given area gives no indication of the types of clients it serves. Even in a relatively poor area of the country, a bank may choose to focus its services on the richer segments of the population. Another drawback is that, with the change of technology today, institutional presence may become less important for the delivery of financial services, which can be provided remotely through the phone or Web, without the need for physical presence.

More detailed supply-side indicators of access attempt to look at the volume of services provided to particular categories of clients. Different types of financial services can be examined: deposits, credit, and other transactions such as payments and money transmission and the provision of card facilities. If the target groups of underserved persons (low-income or poor clients) could be identified directly, such indicators would be very valuable. However, it may be difficult for banks (and perhaps more so for less-formal financial institutions) to have reasonable information on client income. The size of financial transactions is often used as a proxy: small deposits or small loans stand in for poor clients. But this can clearly misrepresent client income, for obvious reasons. Such indicators could perhaps more easily be applied to identify services provided to disadvantaged communities, or to groups with specific socioeconomic characteristics such as gender, color, or migrant status.

Measures of the extent to which the demand for financial services is met are more difficult to construct than supply-side indicators. Not only is unfulfilled demand implicitly conditional on a specific service price, but it also depends on other conditions of service (such as distance and convenience) and on the risk characteristics of the individual or enterprise. Broad proxies of measures of credit needs for enterprises, especially working capital credit needs, can, however, be constructed based on turnover, raw material needs, and other data. Credit needs for fixed capital, being ad hoc, are more difficult to proxy. Individual credit needs, or the needs of microenterprises that do not separate personal and business needs, are harder to assess. Needs for savings or deposits or other financial services also pose difficulties. In such cases, survey-based indicators of individuals, households, or enterprises are a starting point. Undertaking such surveys in tandem with ongoing periodic statistical surveys such as census or other periodic surveys, or the Bank's household surveys, can help to provide data on socioeconomic characteristics and a reliable sampling frame. The assessment of financial constraints is typically based partly on client perceptions and partly on information such as refusals to provide services like opening an account or providing credit. It should not be forgotten, however, that there may be valid reasons for such failures to obtain financial services, based on risk or cost.

Finally, broad-based measures of access could also be constructed based on the pricing of financial services. Clearly, the critical variable in this context is the interest rate. Although interest rate levels would clearly affect overall volumes of access and hence financial depth, interest rate structures can focus more specifically on access issues. A first broad measure in this regard is the average spread between borrowing and lending rates, an issue of which Brazil is keenly aware.[18] Disaggregations of spreads and examinations of the composition of spreads can also lead to the monitoring of trends in the individual subcomponents of spreads. Concerns about access could also be more specifically tracked by looking at the interest rate structure in greater detail (for example, prices of consumer credit, housing loans, and rural credit), and also by examining the degree to which price discrimination may operate across different segments, and assessing the presence or absence of market segmentation.

In practice, measures must be adapted to the end use for which they are intended. Simpler and more aggregate measures may be all that is feasible for cross-country comparisons, or even countrywide or interregional comparisons, but more detailed measures can be developed when institutional or user data permit. Thus, a series of 'nested' measures can be constructed based on simpler uses (such as broad comparisons) or more sophisticated uses (targeted policy interventions). In the medium term, if access is to be tracked systematically, it would be important for agencies such as the government to require the systematic provision of data on access indicators.[19] For the present study, a series of different measures has been used, based largely on availability, with more aggregate supply-side measures in the present chapter and more disaggregated supply measures at the level of the types of financial institutions in subsequent chapters. Demand-side survey-based data have been used extensively for individual consumers and in a more limited way for enterprises.

Basic Supply-Side Measures of Financial Services Offered in Brazil

This section of the chapter examines trends in bank services and in their ownership and distribution, and compares bank services in Brazil with service provision in the international community.

Trends in and Distribution of Bank Services: Branches and Service Points

A first broad analysis of intertemporal as well as interregional or spatial aspects of the evolution of access to financial services, based largely on data from Brazil's Central Bank on access to financial institutions (mainly banks, their branches, and other points of service), reveals the following key points:[20]

- Despite contractions in bank numbers, aggregate delivery of financial services overall has not declined over the last decade but has remained largely static.
- There have been some expansions of new service delivery points and growth of some institutions, including cooperatives and microfinance firms, but these are quantitatively still in the nascent stage.
- In international comparisons, Brazil may be 'underbanked' compared to developed countries in terms of bank branches, but it has performed at least as well or better than its peers among developing or middle-income countries.
- Spatial inequalities in the delivery of financial services are significant among Brazil's regions and have been persistent over time. But much of this difference arises from regional income differentials.
- A significant shift in composition of service providers, with a declining share for public banks, underlies the relatively static overall picture in financial service provision.
- Private banks, although relying extensively on new delivery mechanisms such as ATMs, are also more branch-intensive than federal banks. Municipalities with a larger share of agriculture and small firms are actually better served by private banks.
- Econometric analyses of the determinants of bank service provision, using a range of indicators of access, find that, for all banks taken together, per capita income tends to be positively associated with broad measures of access such as the numbers or density of banking

institutions or the value of the loan and deposit services they provide. Banks have an urban bias and tend not to provide services in rural areas. Nevertheless, the agricultural community did not appear to be underserved.

- Finally, analyses that distinguished between public and private banks find some differences in the factors associated with the provision of services of these two groups: by some measures public banks may have provided more services to the poor, but private banks appear to offer more services to agriculture and to small enterprises. In many respects the behavior of the two is broadly similar: both tend to have a positive association with richer economic areas and both have some urban bias. They tend to be substitutable, especially in thinly served areas, with either private or public services dominating.

At the broadest level in Brazil's bank-dominated financial system, there has been a contraction in the number of banks over the last decade—from 267 in 1993 to 194 a decade later, in 2002 (figure 1.1). This contraction was accompanied by some decline in the number of bank branches, from 17,400 in 1994 to 16,000 five years later, in 1998. These figures largely reflect the rationalization in the banking industry following inflation stabilization and consequent contraction in bank float income, together with stricter prudential regulations on entry and operation and, later, the privatization of state banks (appendix table A1.2)

Data also suggest continued reliance on the banking system for service provision. There has been little diversification in the overall system of provision of financial services in Brazil over the past decade in terms of asset values, with 92 percent of assets in the banking system in 1993, and 93 percent in 2001. A limited role is played by nonbanks such as finance companies or leasing companies, and this role has not shown any trend increase. Cooperatives have increased in absolute numbers from around 800 in 1993 to more than 1,300 in 2002, and in assets, but this has been too small in absolute terms to affect bank dominance (appendix table A1.1).

The apparent decline in bank services is offset if banking portfolios of multiple banks are counted; banking portfolios declined from 334 to only 296 between 1998 and 2001. And overall numbers of bank branches resumed growth after 1998, to reach 17,050 by 2002, so that, over the period of a decade, branch numbers were relatively stable (appendix table A1.2). Recovery of the numbers of branches may reflect specific conditions governing bank mergers and buyouts, especially for state-owned banks, and increased attention to income from credit operations.[21]

The decline in bank branch numbers, moreover, has been accompanied by an expansion of new types of service points, especially automated teller machines. ATMs increased from 3,500 to 22,500 between 1994 and

Figure 1.1 Growth in Numbers of Financial Institutions, 1993–2002

Banks haves declined in numbers... cooperatives have increased...

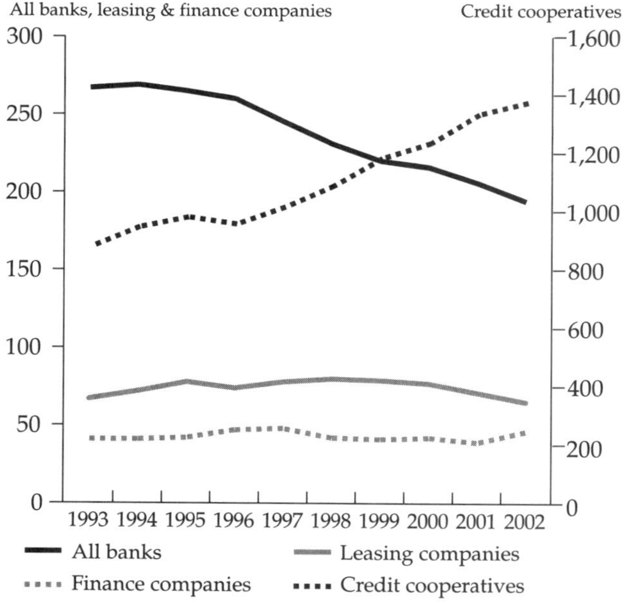

But the share of banks in financial assets remains stable.

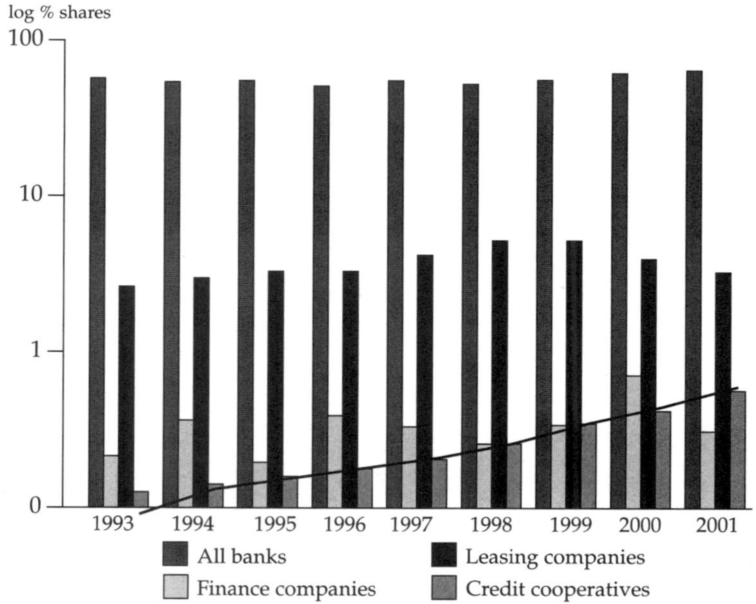

Source: Central Bank of Brazil. (See appendix table A1.1.)

Bank Branch and Service Outposts in Brazil

Brazilian branch regulation distinguishes among different types of branches and branch-like bank offices. At the top of the hierarchy is the *agência*, a bank branch that offers all services, but is also subject to relatively strict security requirements, branch hours, labor laws, and so on. The Posto Avançado Bancário (PAB) and Posto Avançado do Atendimento (PAA) are branch-like offices. PABs are similar to agencies, but provide services only to employees of the private enterprise or public institution in which the PAB is physically located, and can determine their branch hours flexibly. PAAs (established by Resolution 2396/1997) are branch-like offices that can be established only in municipalities where the respective bank does not have an *agência*. The bank can determine branch hours, services offered, and physical location. As of December 2002 there were 7,108 PABs and 654 PAAs in Brazil. However, more than 95 percent of all PABs were located in municipalities already served by bank branches. Finally, the ATMs (Posto de Atendimento Bancário Eletrônico, PAE), which had grown rapidly to 22,428 by end-2002, are largely (nearly 90 percent) on individual rather than associate networks (in other words, they allow access only to accounts with the owner bank).

In 1999 the Central Bank introduced the institution of *correspondente* or correspondent (Resolutions 2640/1999 and 2707/2000). It allows banks to offer limited banking services via nonfinancial companies. Specifically, banks can offer payment and deposit services and limited credit services. The financial responsibility, however, stays with the financial institution. By December 2002 there were more than 16,000 correspondent facilities sponsored by several federal and private banks, notably the lottery shop network of the publicly owned Caixa Econômica Federal, and the postal office network concession won by Banco Bradesco, the largest private bank, in 2001.

2002, principally through the expansion of individual networks (from some 2,800 to more than 20,000) and some smaller expansion of group-operated networks (from around 570 to 2,100 over the same period). More recently there has also been a striking increase in the numbers of correspondent bank arrangements, to some 16,500 by 2002, almost as numerous as bank branches (appendix table A1.2). Apart from credit cooperatives, the number of microfinance companies (SCMs) also grew: 6 were established in 1999, around 26 were in operation at end-2002, and an estimated 36 were close to formal start-up by mid-2003.[22]

Looking within national aggregates at the municipality level, the number of municipalities with no bank branch services increased significantly between 1994 and 1997, from 1,137 to 1,749 municipalities without bank branch service. Thereafter, there has been no further decline in municipalities without bank branches, but some reduction in the number of branches, to 1,665 by end-2002. Meanwhile, the provision of banking service outposts (Advanced Service Outposts or PAAs) grew and municipalities with no branches but with PAAs doubled between 1998 and 2002, from 334 to 654.[23]

The data (figure 1.2) suggest that although there has been no marked decline in access to financial services over the past decade, the overall picture is relatively stagnant, barring some qualitatively significant new institutional segments (cooperatives and microcredit firms) and quantitatively more important development of new delivery channels. These positive signs have accelerated since 1999.

Ownership: Public versus Private Provision of Bank Services

Behind the aggregate numbers, there have been significant changes in ownership composition of bank branches and other service points, with a huge decline in the proportion of public bank branches, which is largely responsible for the faltering overall numbers of branch services. Branches of public banks fell from some 9,000 in 1995 to around 6,700 in 2001 (appendix table A1.3). Meanwhile, branches of private and foreign banks almost doubled from some 5,400 to more than 10,000 over the same period. Public banks rely to a greater extent on branches for delivery; ATMs accounted for only 31 percent of their outlets at the end of 2001, in contrast to almost 50 percent for private domestic banks, including banks with minority foreign ownership.

An analysis of differences in balance sheet structure of banks by ownership category—federal, state, private, and foreign—also revealed that private domestic banks had less assets and fewer loans and deposits per branch than federal banks. In other words, private banks had larger branch networks, relative to their size, compared to public banks. Federal bank branches appeared to be larger, as measured by the number of employees.

Figure 1.3 indicates that private banks have made great strides in client outreach, using delivery systems that are lower cost and use newer technology (chapter 3). Wholly foreign-owned banks, however, have the lowest proportion of ATMs and the highest branch reliance, reflecting possibly their concentration in the high-net-worth segment.[24]

Regional Distribution of Financial Services

A spatial analysis of financial access reveals that there are significant variations in service provision across different regions of the country. Access

Figure 1.2 Evolution of Financial Service Outlets in Brazil, 1994–2002

Bank branch numbers have remained broadly stable while ATMs and correspondents have increased rapidly.

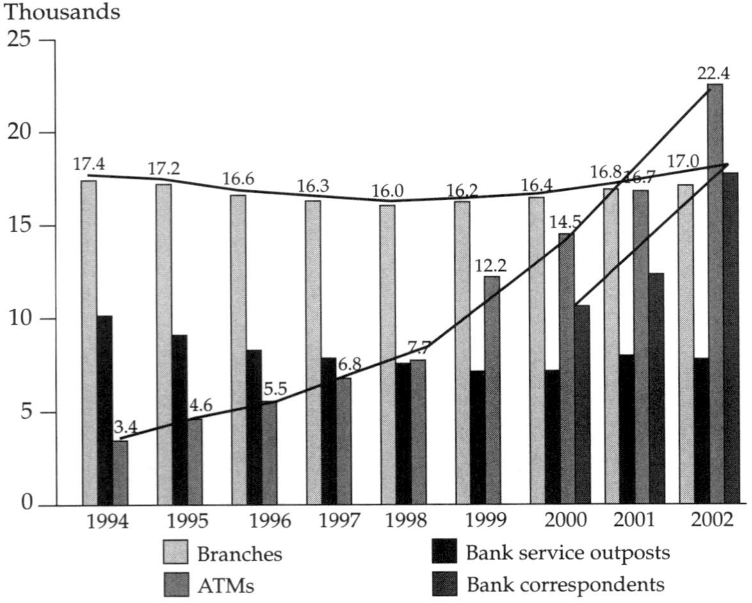

Municipalities without financial services stabilized after 1997 while the number served by PAAs increased.

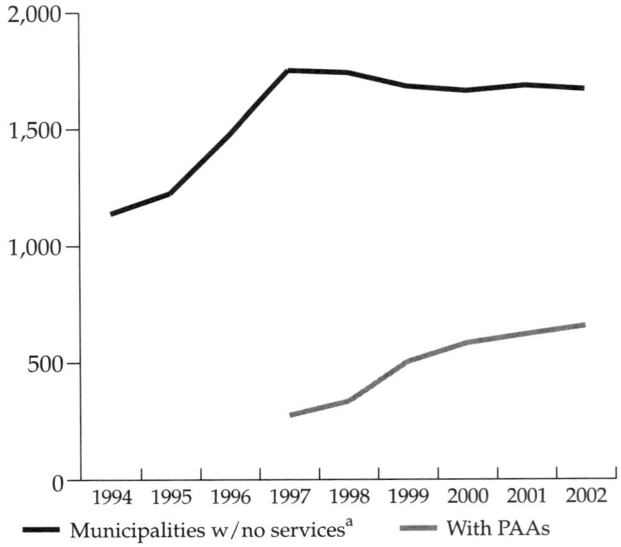

a. Does not include banking correspondents.

Source: Central Bank of Brazil. (See appendix table A1.2.)

Figure 1.3 Ownership of Bank Service Points in Brazil

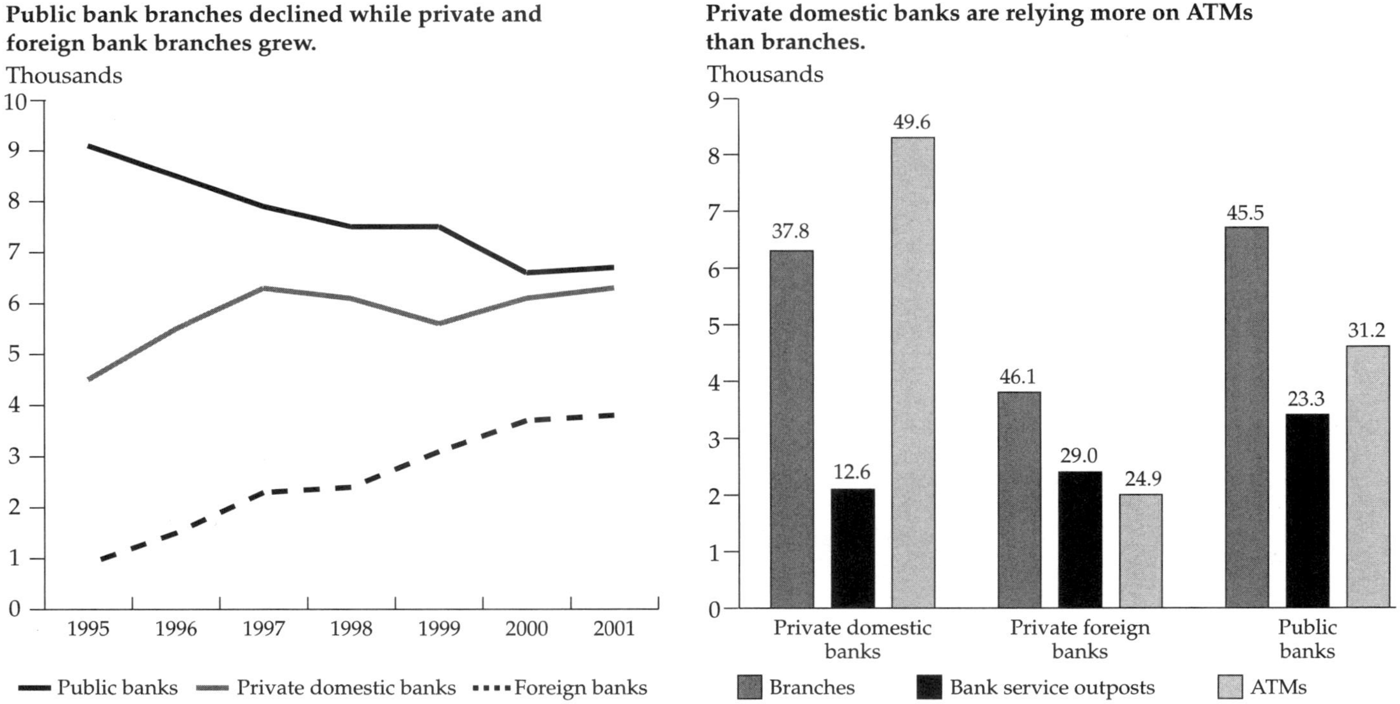

Note: Private domestic banks include those with foreign participation. Numbers correspond to December 2001 data unless stated otherwise.
Source: Central Bank of Brazil.

to financial services is unevenly distributed geographically, with sparse services in the poorer parts of the country. Banking facilities are concentrated in large Southeastern states. Around 57 percent of all municipalities in the Northeast and the North and nearly 20 percent of the population in these states have no access to a bank branch. Nationwide, 30 percent of all municipalities and 6 percent of the population have no access to formal financial services (not including correspondents, as seen in appendix table A1.2). There are 7 states (out of 27), mostly in the North, where more than 70 percent of municipalities have no bank branch. About 1,665 poorer and arguably less-populated municipalities, out of a total of some 5,660 municipalities, have not a single bank branch.

Associating levels of financial services supplied with regional population, area, and GDP or per capita income reveals some interesting findings. Even when bank branches are present, services are more constrained in the North and Northeast. The population per bank branch was nearly three times as high in the North as in the South of Brazil in 1996, and more than three times as high by 2000. Between 1996 and 2000, branch numbers declined in the North and Northeast while they grew in the Southeast. However, branch numbers had also declined in the South and Central–West in the first period, and branch numbers in all regions had improved by 2002. But considering regional GDP differentials, the variation decreases substantially. GDP per bank branch in the North is less than twice as high as in the South, the region with the lowest GDP per bank branch. The smaller number of branches in the North and Northeast, therefore, at least partly reflect lower income levels and hence less potential business (table 1.3).

The relation between average per capita income at the state level and the existence of bank branches is further illustrated in figure 1.4 at the level of individual provinces. As the figure shows, there is a broad positive association between bank services and GDP per capita, whether measured in terms of bank numbers, branch density per capita, or branch density per unit of geographic area.

Some states that appear to be outliers by one measure conform according to other measures. For example, although São Paulo appears to be more intensively branched than predicted by income, if branch density per numbers of persons is the measure of access, this is corrected; thus, the greater population density of São Paulo helps to explain the proportionally higher number of branches than expected on the basis of its average income. If branch density is measured in terms of geographic area, the positive relation overall between per capita GDP and branch density remains. However, in this case the state of Rio de Janeiro is a positive outlier; services are high relative to its small size.

Table 1.3 Branch Density across Brazilian Regions

Region	*GDP/cap 2000 (R$)*	*GDP/ branch (R$m) 2000*	*GDP per branch (R$m) 1996*	*Popn/ branch 1996*	*Popn/ branch 2000*	*Branches 1996*	*Branches 2000*	*Branches 2002*	*Area/ branch 2000 (km²)*
North	3,907	90.5	87.6	17,501	23,161	645	557	580	6,644
Northeast	3,014	61.8	60.3	17,459	20,516	2,546	2,327	2,396	649
Southeast	8,774	71.1	68.4	8,090	8,098	8,281	8,942	9,361	99
South	7,692	57.2	56.0	6,835	7,437	3,440	3,376	3,450	167
Central–West	6,558	63.9	60.8	8,071	9,746	1,301	1,194	1,262	1,273

Source: Branch data: Central Bank of Brazil. GDP data: IPEA (Institute of Applied Economic Research). Population and area data: IBGE (Instituto Brasileiro de Geografia e Estatística).

Figure 1.4 Branch Density by State in Brazil

1. Bank branch (numbers)

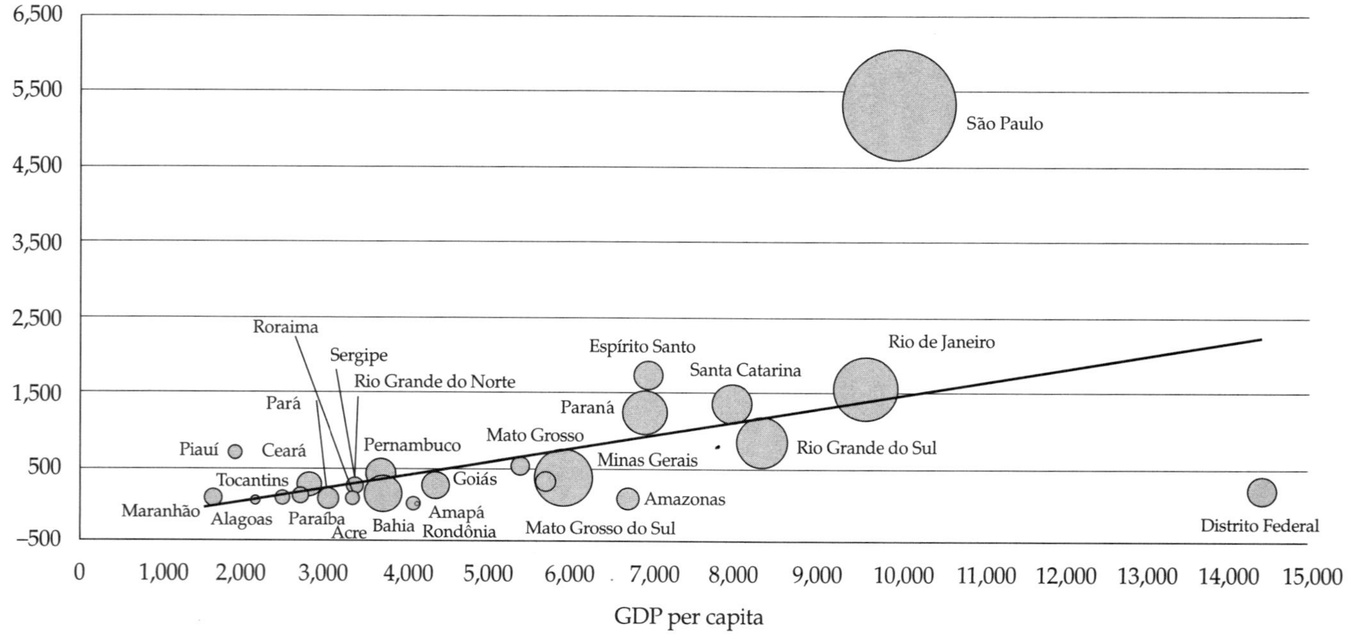

2. Branch density (per 100,000 persons)

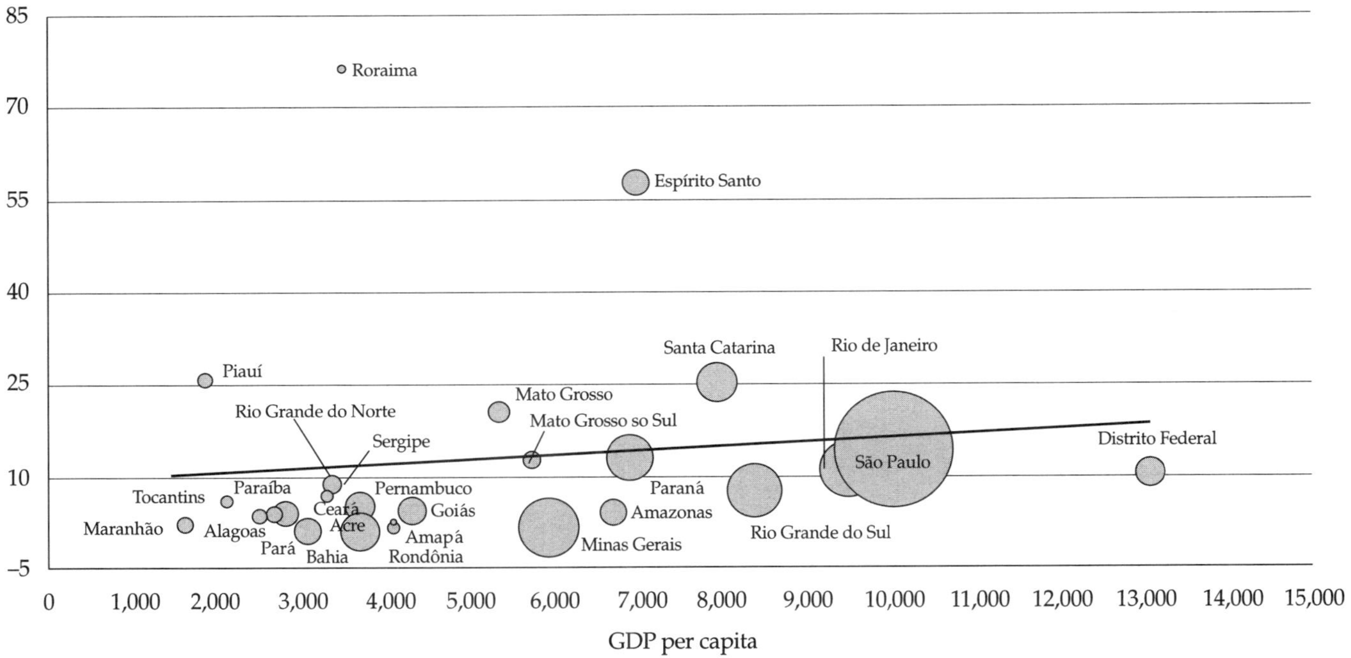

(figure continued next page)

Figure 1.4 *(continued)*

3. Bank density (per 1,000 km^2)

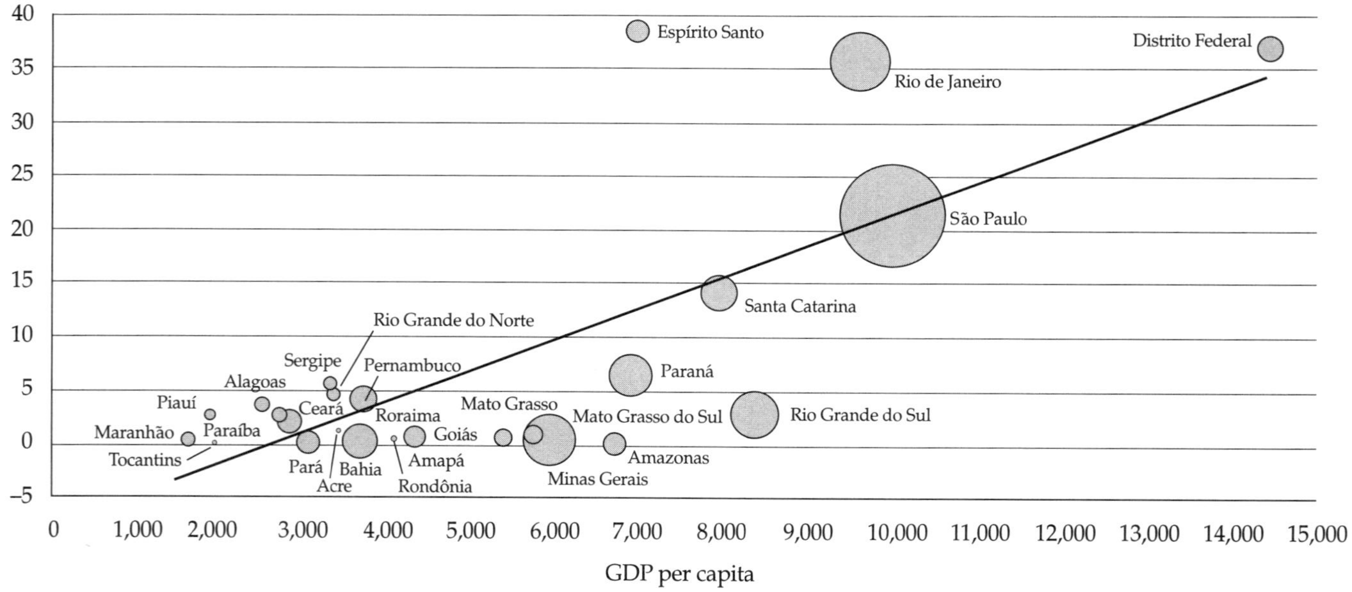

Note: The size of each point represents state GDP.
Source: IBGE.

A few states such as Rio Grande do Norte (NE) or Espírito Santo (SE) remain positive outliers by all of these measures—that is, bank services provided are greater than predicted by per capita incomes by all measures. By contrast, some other states have less than expected services, even after factoring income differentials, by all these measures. They include, for example, Acre, Amazonas, and Rondônia (N), Bahia (NE), Minas Gerais (SE), and Rio Grande do Sul (S). What is interesting here is that some of the better-off provinces are also included among states where services are lower than may be expected on the basis of overall economic size and population. Many states do better than expected on some measures of density and worse on others. Thus, both Mato Grosso and Mato Grosso do Sul (both CW), although apparently underserved according to geographic measures of branch density (per 1,000 square kilometers), are not underserved if their relatively thin populations are taken into account (branch density per 100,000 persons).

However, these diagrams also suggest that for some of the Northern and Northeastern states, which are clustered in the lower left quadrant, a few have lower levels of access than expected on the basis of population density, even once income was factored in. Those states that appear underserved on the basis of population per 100,000 persons include Alagoas, Bahia, Ceará, Maranhão, Paraíba, Pernambuco, and Rondônia. Thus, although regional branch service differentials seem to be significantly related to income levels, access is poorer than the income analysis alone would suggest in these areas.

Finally, the state-level analysis also shows that there is a negative association between per capita GDP and the number of municipalities per state without service (figure 1.5).

If instead of looking at numbers of institutions, the volume of services provided in credits and deposits is examined, and these are adjusted for income differentials, they may provide a more representative measure of financial access. Results of such measures regarding regional variations in the provision of financial services still indicate substantial differences, and the magnitude of variation between regions is especially pronounced again for the North and Northeast, especially compared to the Southeast (table 1.4). However, the variance in per capita credits and deposits is much larger than in credits and deposits relative to GDP. Thus, per capita differentials in regional access to financial services are not only associated with but also greater than per capita income differentials. This could be a reflection of prevailing inequalities in income distribution, so that high mean incomes could nevertheless coexist with large proportions of the regional population at a much lower median income.

Such income differentials are more apparent looking at smaller geographic units, and, not surprisingly, variations in the provision of bank

Figure 1.5 Municipalities with No Services

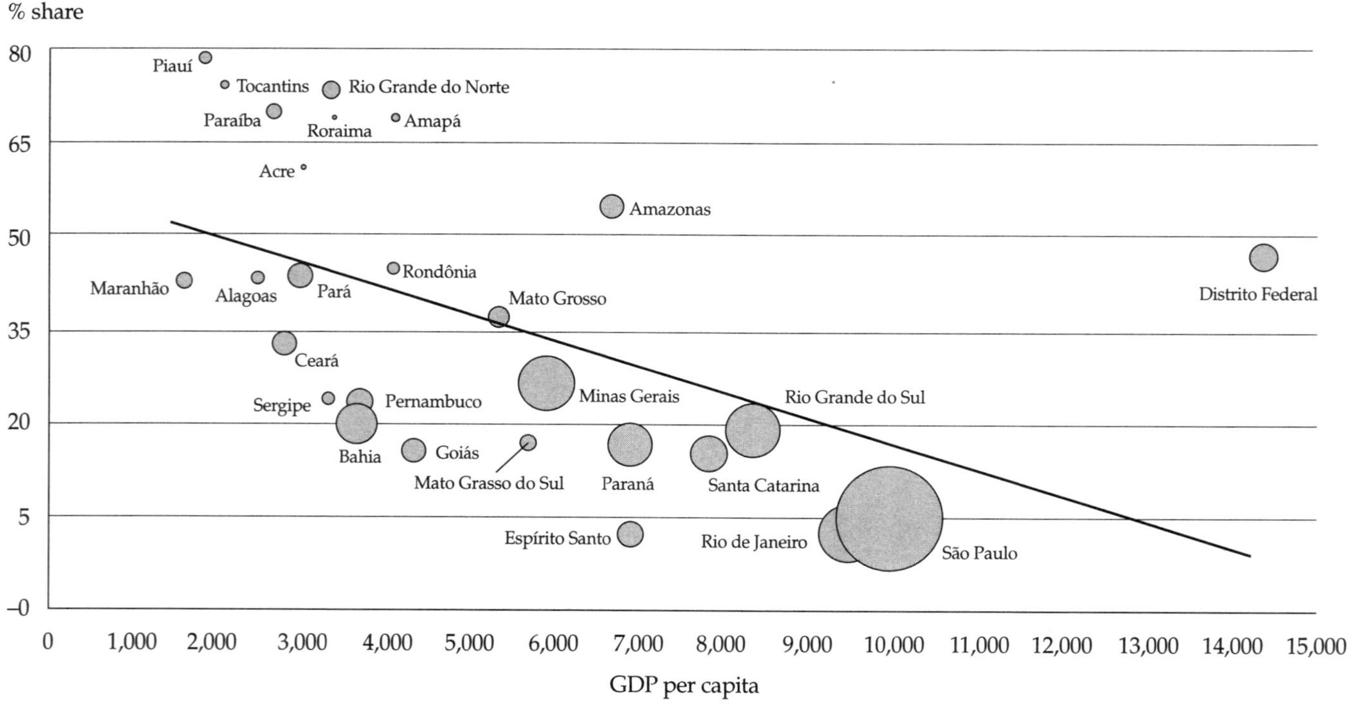

Note: The size of each point represents state GDP.
Source: IBGE.

Table 1.4 Provision of Bank Services across Regions

Region	*GDP per capita (2000)*	*Credit/ GDP*	*Deposits/ GDP*	*Credit per capita*	*Deposits per capita*
North	3,907	21.39	6.19	820	238
Northeast	3,014	19.69	24.14	500	613
Southeast	8,774	31.10	23.25	2,541	1,899
South	7,692	23.65	16.17	1,461	999
Central–West	6,559	33.77	6.18	1,588	291

Note: Brasilia is excluded from the Central–West region.
Source: Central Bank of Brazil, IPEA, and IBGE.

services across municipalities are higher still (table 1.5). Credits and deposits as a share of municipal GDP range from zero to more than 1,000 percent. Similarly, credits and deposits per capita range from zero to R$85,000 (for credits) and R$45,000 for deposits. The large number of municipalities without any bank services explains why the average for the whole sample is so much lower than the aggregate for Brazil.

Finally, combining the examination of the regional provision of services with the nature of bank ownership, it can be seen that the provision of bank services across regions varies significantly between private and public banks (table 1.6). Although public banks dominate in the North and Northeast, private banks dominate in the Southeast. This could reflect the profit orientation of private banks and the 'social' orientation of public banks. Data at the municipal level suggest some complementarity in the branch structure of public and private banks. In 1996, 1,603 municipalities had just one branch, either private or public, while 428 had two, three, or four branches, entirely private or entirely public. In 2000, 1,393 municipalities had just one branch, either private or public, while 397 had two, three, or four branches, entirely private or entirely public. This also suggests that there has been a pattern of segmented delivery of private and public banks, with limited competition between these segments in the more thinly served areas.

International Comparisons of Bank Services

It is clear that, compared to developed economies, Brazilian bank branches serve a much larger number of inhabitants per branch. Whereas an average bank branch in Germany serves a population of 1,479 people and an American branch serves an area with 3,568 people on average, Brazilian branches served an average population of 9,331 people in 1996 and 10,356 in 2000 (figure 1.6).

Table 1.5 Provision of Bank Services across Municipalities, 1996

Item	*Credit/GDP (%)*	*Deposits/GDP (%)*	*Credits per capita (R$)*	*Deposits per capita (R$)*
Average	7.83	4.72	292	179
Median	2.12	2.82	36.71	45.11
Standard deviation	27.78	19.25	1,497	748
Maximum	1,458.24	1,260.09	85,335	44,631
Minimum	0	0	0	0
Observations	4,986	4,986	5,507	5,507
Total Brazil	**30.49**	**22.32**	**1,774**	**1,298**

Source: Estimated from Central Bank of Brazil data.

Table 1.6 Public and Private Provision of Bank Services across Regions

Region	*GDP per capita (2000)*	*Credit by public banks/GDP*	*Credit by private banks/GDP*	*Deposits in public banks/GDP*	*Deposits in private banks/GDP*
North	3,907	19.26	2.09	4.64	1.51
Northeast	3,014	14.73	4.89	19.14	4.97
Southeast	8,774	9.07	21.97	8.55	14.58
South	7,692	14.19	9.45	10.55	5.61
Central–West	6,559	26.78	6.97	3.83	2.33

Note: Brasilia is excluded from the Central–West region.
Source: Central Bank, IPEA, and IBGE.

Figure 1.6 Brazil and Other Countries: Population Served per Bank Branch

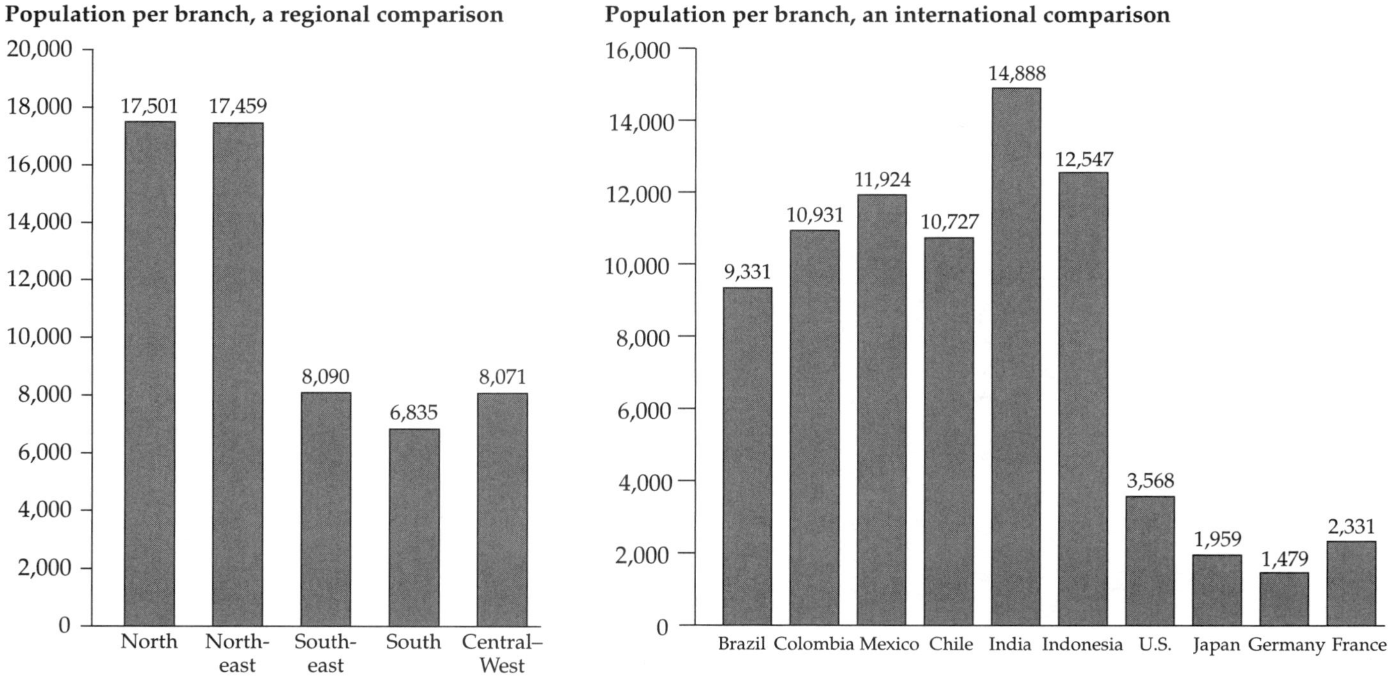

Source: World Bank staff estimates.

But comparisons with other developing countries suggest that Brazil is not obviously 'underbranched' (table 1.7). Brazil has more bank branches relative to population than other Latin American countries, and more than India and Indonesia, two large developing countries. Measured relative to GDP, its bank branch intensity is lower than Colombia, India, and Indonesia, which are all poorer than Brazil, but the two latter countries are much more densely populated. Branch intensity relative to GDP in Brazil is higher than in Chile or Mexico, although both are richer than Brazil. Additionally, as alluded to earlier, the overall proportion of bank account holders to population in Brazil (at least a third of total population, implying a much higher proportion of 'banked' families) is respectable, compared to statistics on other emerging and developed countries: for example, 13 percent of persons in the United States, 15 percent of households in the United Kingdom, and a third of all households in Hungary.

Measured according to average geographic area covered per branch, Brazil appeared at first to be 'underbanked' relative to all other comparator developing countries except Chile. However, this is easily explained by the low population density of Brazil and the vast areas that are not populated. An econometric estimation of predicted branch intensity compared to actual intensity for Brazil and other countries, correcting for differences in branch intensity explained by differences in GDP, total population, and geographic size, found that Brazil is the only developing economy that is not 'underbanked' by this standard, because its actual branch intensity was higher than predicted.

Econometric Analyses of Factors Associated with Bank Service Supply

What explains decisions by banks to locate their services in some municipalities rather than others? Attempts were made to associate three different supply-side measures of access to banking services—including, first, the presence or absence of a bank branch; second, branches per million inhabitants; and third, credits or deposits as a ratio of GDP—with economic characteristics including income per capita; overall economic size of the region in which banks operate in terms of GDP per capita; and locational characteristics such as population density, shares of rural and agricultural population, and the share of small firms to GDP (table 1.8).

For all measures of access used here, except the existence of a bank branch, per capita income is positively associated with access. Thus, banks try to locate in regions where people are better off.[25] Municipalities with higher overall GDP also tend to have better bank access.[26] There is also a clear result, across all measures, that areas with lower rural popu-

Table 1.7 Bank Branch Density: An International Comparison

Country	*GDP per capita*	*Population per branch*	*GDP per branch (current US$ millions)*	*Area per branch (km²)*	*Residual branch intensity*
Brazil	**3,152**	**9,331**	**29.4**	**470**	**0.82**
Colombia	2,085	10,931	22.8	273	–0.53
Mexico	4,969	11,924	59.3	236	–0.42
Chile	4,505	10,727	48.3	535	–0.79
India	448	14,888	6.7	44	–0.00
Indonesia	683	12,547	8.6	110	–0.07
U.S.	33,087	3,568	118.0	117	–0.17
Japan	34,344	1,959	67.3	6	0.22
Germany	25,724	1,479	38.1	6	0.86
France	24,434	2,331	57.0	22	0.14

Note: Residual branch intensity is the deviation of actual from predicted number of branches, derived from a regression of the number of branches on GDP, land area, and population for 28 countries. Positive numbers indicate that actual branch number exceeded predicted values.
Sources: World Bank staff estimates, based on Hawkins and Mihaljek 2001 and *World Development Indicators* data.

Table 1.8 What Explains Bank Branch Services across Municipalities?
(all banks)

Dependent variable	1. *Existence of branch*	2. *Branch density*	3. *Credit/ GDP*	4. *Deposits/ GDP*
Econometric model	*Probit*	*Tobit*	*Tobit*	*Tobit*
Income/capita (R$'000)	–0.05 (0.00)	12.16 (0.00)	0.18 (0.23)	0.16 (0.13)
GDP (R$m)	0.04 (0.00)	–0.00 (0.24)	0.00 (0.03)	0.00 (0.13)
Population density	–0.00 (0.00)	–0.02 (0.00)	–0.00 (0.78)	0.00 (0.00)
Rural population	–0.01 (0.00)	–2.06 (0.00)	–0.42 (0.00)	–0.27 (0.00)
Agricultural share	0.00 (0.93)	0.15 (0.52)	0.08 (0.16)	–0.03 (0.46)
Small firm share	0.02 (0.00)	1.38 (0.00)	–0.01 (0.93)	–0.01 (0.91)
Observations	4,958	4,958	4,958	4,958

Note: Existence of a branch is a dummy variable equal to one if a municipality has a branch and zero otherwise. Branch density is the number of branches per million persons. The regressions control for random state-level error terms. *P*-values in parentheses indicate significance; $0.01>p>0$ indicates significance at the 1% level; $0.05>p>0.01$ indicates results significant at the 5% level. Higher *p*-values indicate weaker association.
Sources: IBGE, IPEA, Central Bank of Brazil.

lations are more likely to have a bank branch. These results, indicating urban bias in the provision of bank services, are very significant. However, high population density is negatively associated with branch existence and branch density, and positively associated only with the provision of deposit services. This could suggest that some more densely populated areas, such as those that are urban and poor, are not particularly likely to attract bank services. The share of small firms in a municipality is positively associated with the establishment and density of bank branches, but there is no clear relation with volumes of credit or deposits.

Finally, the share of work force in agriculture does not show any significant relation with the level of bank services, in contrast to the negative association for rural indicators. This may reflect the series of policy incentive schemes offered for agricultural lending, discussed further in chapters 3 and 5 of this study. These results indicate that although rural areas are indeed underserved, agriculture is not a sector that is obviously neglected by the financial sector.

Next, going beyond the aggregate measures of financial service availability examined above, further analyses were made to examine separately the factors affecting the provision of financial services by private versus public banks to see if bank ownership affects the findings regarding the determinants of access (table 1.9).

Looking at the role of per capita income, all measures of private bank services reflect the aggregate finding of a positive association with per capita income. These results are highly significant except for bank branch existence, where the relation, though also positive, is weaker. However, for public banks, there is no clear-cut relation to per capita income. Three measures (existence of a branch, volumes of credit, and volumes of deposits) indicate a negative relation, but this is significant only for the first of these measures. And for bank branch density, public banks also indicate a positive relation with per capita income, which is significant.

In terms of associations with GDP, the behavior of the two groups, public and private, is similar in many respects: both have the same signs and reflect the generally positive association with GDP of the aggregate group, for all measures except branch density, which are not very significant. The negative association with population density is similar for the first two measures, although, in terms of credit, private banks indicate a greater propensity to lend in more densely populated areas.[27]

The urban bias of both groups is similar on all measures: the share of the population that is rural is negatively associated with bank access measures. The next finding, on the share of the population in agriculture, is surprising. For all measures, public bank services are negatively associated with the agricultural share, while private bank services are positively

Table 1.9 What Explains Public versus Private Bank Branch Services across Municipalities in Brazil?

Dependent variable	*Existence of bank branch*	*Bank branch density*	*Credit/GDP*	*Deposits/GDP*	*Share of public bank branches in total branches*
Econometric model	*Probit*	*Tobit*	*Tobit*	*Tobit*	*Tobit*
Public banks					
Income/cap. (R$ '000)	–0.10 (0.00)	6.81 (0.00)	–0.08 (0.64)	–0.04 (0.72)	–0.03 (0.00)
GDP (R$m)	0.02 (0.00)	–0.00 (0.31)	0.00 (0.98)	0.00 (0.33)	0.00 (0.98)
Population density	–0.00 (0.00)	–0.01 (0.00)	–0.00 (0.07)	0.00 (0.65)	0.00 (0.69)
Rural population	–0.01 (0.00)	–1.28 (0.00)	–0.45 (0.00)	–0.28 (0.00)	0.01 (0.00)
Agricultural share	–0.00 (0.30)	–0.43 (0.04)	–0.03 (0.64)	–0.10 (0.04)	–0.01 (0.00)
Small firm share	0.00 (0.46)	–0.60 (0.02)	–0.32 (0.00)	–0.23 (0.00)	–0.00 (0.00)
Existence of public bank branch	–0.40 (0.00)				
Public branch density		–0.35 (0.00)			
Credit by public banks/GDP			0.57 (0.00)		
Deposits by public banks/GDP				0.00 (0.97)	
Private banks					
Income/cap. (R$ '000)	0.00 (0.32)	11.11 (0.00)	0.16 (0.00)	0.16 (0.00)	
GDP(R$m)	0.02 (0.00)	–0.00 (0.57)	0.00 (0.00)	0.00 (0.05)	
Population density	–0.00 (0.00)	–0.02 (0.00)	0.00 (0.00)	0.00 (0.00)	
Rural population	–0.02 (0.00)	–3.24 (0.00)	–0.14 (0.00)	–0.13 (0.00)	
Agricultural share	0.00 (0.05)	0.72 (0.01)	0.03 (0.01)	0.00 (0.33)	
Small firm share	0.01 (0.00)	1.45 (0.00)	–0.01 (0.66)	–0.01 (0.97)	
Existence of private bank branch	–0.48 (0.00)				
Private branch density		–0.36 (0.00)			
Credit by private banks/GDP			0.02 (0.00)		
Deposits by private banks/GDP				0.01 (0.13)	
Observations	4,958	4,958	4,958	4,958	3,508

Note: Existence of a branch is a dummy variable that takes on the value one if a municipality has a branch and zero otherwise. Branch density is the number of branches per million persons. Brasilia is excluded from the regressions. However, the results do not change when including it. *P*-values are reported in parentheses.
Sources: Central Bank of Brazil, IPEA, and IBGE.

associated with this. Measures are significant for branch density and for the share of credit. As discussed for the aggregate data, this may reflect policies requiring agricultural lending, at least in respect to credit. Results on small firm shares are positive for private banks, unlike public banks, for the first two measures of access, though not significant for measures related to credits and deposits. There are thus indications that municipalities with a larger share of agriculture and small firms are better served by private banks.

The likelihood that a municipality has a public bank branch is negatively correlated with the existence of a private bank branch. Similarly, the likelihood that a municipality has a private bank branch is also negatively correlated with the existence of a public bank branch in that municipality. This suggests some substitutability, and is driven by the fact that nearly half of all municipalities with a bank branch have only public or only private bank branches. Public and private banks may compete for services because they operate broadly as substitutes in many areas.

As a final measure to better capture differences between private and public banks, the analysis defines two categories of municipalities: those served with only private banks and municipalities with only public bank branches. Results reveal that municipalities with only public bank branches are significantly poorer, in per capita income terms, but that they also have a significantly lower share of the agricultural work force and of small firms.[28] Average per capita income for those municipalities with only public branches is R$2,771, compared to R$4,060 for those with only private branches. But the agricultural share of the group with only public branches is 3.8 percent compared to 5.1 percent for those with only private branches.

Summarizing, many characteristics of service provision by public and private banks are not very different, including the urban bias of both groups and also the broadly positive association with GDP. The finding of some degree of substitutability in their service provision is not surprising. But there are also some interesting differences in the factors behind public and private provision of bank services: public banks appear by some measures to be more likely to serve the poor than private banks. However, they do not show the economic structure expected with a poverty focus. They are not more agriculturally oriented and are not associated with greater services to small firms. On some measures, private banks provide better service than public banks to municipalities with a larger share of agricultural firms and small firms.

Demand-Side Measures of Access: An Enterprise Survey

To what extent do Brazil's enterprises perceive the availability of finance to be a constraint? Data from the *World Business Environment Survey* (World Bank 2000f) indicate that Brazilian firms rate high interest rates as the largest financing constraint, affecting operations and working capital needs, followed by collateral requirements and access to long-term loans (table 1.10). Bank access to loanable funds and to lease finance is rated as a relatively minor obstacle. Although Brazilian enterprises perceive the financing of investment and access to long-term loans to be no more constrained than entrepreneurs in other Latin American and upper-middle-income countries, they rate high interest rates and collateral requirements as greater obstacles than enterprises in comparison countries. This might reflect the availability of long-term investment funds from state sources such as the development bank, Banco Nacional de Desenvolvimento Econômico e Social (BNDES), or deficiencies in the legal system and the short maturity of external debt financing in Brazil (Beck 2000).

Brazilian firms of different sizes do not differ significantly in their assessment of financial constraints. Thus, unlike firms in other countries, small firms appear to face relatively fewer financial constraints. There are, however, significant differences in overall financing patterns across firms of different sizes in Brazil. Small firms receive significantly less financing from equity or from development institutions and more from retained earnings and informal sources than medium-size firms. For firms of all sizes, high interest rates are the largest constraint.

Comparing actual financing patterns across countries and firms, the survey found that Brazil, on average, relies to a lesser extent on retained earnings than other Latin American or upper-middle-income countries, and especially relative to other middle-income countries. Brazil relies more on supplier credit and bank finance. External equity financing was also more important in Brazil.

Demand-Side Measures of Access: A Survey of Urban Individuals

Aggregate measures of the supply of financial services do not provide an answer to the question of who has access. Even if a financial institution exists in a given location, it is not clear without more disaggregated data who the clients of such an institution may be. Therefore, to complement the analysis of data on financial institutions and on the financial constraints on enterprises, a survey was launched to examine the financial behavior of individual consumers.[29] The aims of the survey were (1) to

Table 1.10 Financing Constraints in Brazil: An International Comparison

Country/region	*Is financing a constraint?*	*High interest rates*	*Collateral requirements*	*Access to long-term loans*	*Banks lack loanable funds*	*Access to lease finance*
Brazil	**2.69**	**3.71**	**2.91**	**2.90**	**1.81**	**1.71**
Latin America	2.86	3.57	2.79	2.91	2.22	2.08
of which:						
Argentina	2.99	3.57	2.71	3.13	1.98	1.96
Mexico	3.19	3.47	2.82	3.45	3.10	2.50
Chile	2.41	2.35	2.32	2.29	1.75	1.53
Upper-middle-income countries	2.69	3.41	2.37	2.54	1.83	1.71
OECD	2.35	2.65	2.25	1.80	1.59	1.68

Note: The ratings are as follows: 1 = no obstacle, 2 = minor obstacle, 3 = moderate obstacle, 4 = major obstacle. Numbers for individual countries are averages and numbers for country groups are medians, because of the small number of observations.
Source: World Business Environment Survey (World Bank 2000f).

provide information on individual consumers' present patterns of access to financial services and potential additional demand, (2) to explore perceptions of constraints to access, (3) to examine the factors that are correlated with and could explain access, and, in this context, (4) to try to identify policy directions that could be used to expand access. Broadly, the questions addressed are: What financial services do households want, what do they receive, how does this vary by income or poverty levels? What factors can predict the access to and use of financial services by individuals in different socioeconomic groups, and how could this be useful in shaping public policy toward access?

The survey covered 2,000 urban residents in nine metropolitan areas and two cities across 11 states. The unit interviewed was chosen to be any household member of 18 or above.[30] Around 55 percent of the surveyed population are in the two largest cities of Rio de Janeiro and São Paulo; the remainder are distributed across small and medium cities in all geographic regions. In terms of regional distribution, the largest share is in the Southeast: 61 percent in Belo Horizonte, Rio de Janeiro, and São Paulo. There is substantial coverage in the Northeast (17 percent); other regions (Central–West, North, and South) account for 21 percent of the sample.[31] The principal reason why the sample covers urban areas only is that an estimated 80 percent of Brazil's population live in urban areas. Practical reasons were another consideration.

The questionnaire first identified the key socioeconomic characteristics of each interviewee, and then attempted to map the interviewee's access to specific financial services, unbundling access in the following broad categories: (1) general access to a formal financial institution, (2) access to savings and deposit services, (3) access to credit, and (4) access to payment services.[32] Under each category, access is defined in terms of a series of alternative parameters. For example, access to a financial institution can refer to whether a person has an account with such an institution or has made use of it. It can also be described in terms of physical access: in other words, the distance or time taken to reach the financial institution used.

The socioeconomic characteristics of the surveyed population are summarized in the following box. The analysis of findings with regard to financial behavior is discussed below. First, the frequencies of responses to individual questions on financial access under the four broad groups of financial services discussed above are examined. Second, responses are correlated with socioeconomic characteristics of the respondents and the significance of apparent differences is tested. Third, the determinants of access to different forms of financial services are examined and the relative importance of the different factors at work investigated.

Brazil Financial Access Urban Survey: Socioeconomic Characteristics of Respondents

Despite the exclusion of persons below 18, respondents were relatively young; 60 percent of individuals were below 30 years of age. Education levels are low, with 41 percent below secondary school and only 7 percent with higher education. More than half the individuals began to work by age 15. Forty-three percent had left home by age 20, and around half were married by age 25. Forty-three percent are married, and 34 percent are single.

Income is not high. The mean income of R$696.63 and median income of R$358.50 are only 3.5 times and 1.8 times greater, respectively, than the minimum wage. Only 51 percent of the respondents had a job in the last month. Almost two-thirds of these had a full-time job. Around two-thirds of the respondents have wages as their primary source of income; 15.4 percent have pensions or social security as their primary source of income.

Most of the respondents queried about their role at the workplace are employees (597 persons or 60 percent of respondents), and a third are self-employed; 4 percent are employers. Around 400 persons claim to have a work certificate compared to around 600 who do not. Eleven percent of the sample have never worked.

Household size is not large. More than one-third of respondents belong to a household of less than three persons, 41 percent belong to households consisting of three, four, or five persons, and only 21 percent belong to households of five or more persons. Around 40 percent of persons interviewed are heads of households, and another 43 percent are spouses or children. More than 40 percent of individuals interviewed have no dependents, and 25 percent have more than three dependents.

Housing is relatively ample. Only a fifth (19 percent) admitted to living in illegal areas; 83 percent live in a house or apartment. The majority of the respondents live in a house with more than one room per person. More than two-thirds of the individuals (or their households) own their dwelling (70 percent), and less than 20 percent live in rented homes. Yet more than half (56 percent) claimed to have dwellings valued at R$30,000 or less. And more than one-fifth (21.5 percent) have dwellings with values at R$10,000 or less. Less than 5 percent of individuals have dwellings valued at more than R$100,000. Around one-third of the individuals live less than 5 kilometers from basic services such as a bus stop, a post office, or a public or community telephone. Most persons have a TV (96 percent). Few own an automobile (33.4 percent), and fewer still own a computer (14 percent).

Survey Results: Access to Financial Institutions

Forty-three percent of the individuals interviewed have a bank account. This statistic is surprisingly close to estimates made by Unibanco, one of Brazil's prominent banks, which estimated the 'banked' at 42.8 percent.[33] However, a much larger number of persons make use of financial institutions. Perhaps an unusual feature in Brazil, compared to elsewhere, is that for many if not most persons, contact with a financial institution consists of the use of payment outlets, whose establishment may be bank sponsored, but where it is not necessary to be an account holder to use services offered. Such services have been dominated by the Casa Lotérica or the lottery shop chain of the Caixa Econômica Federal (CEF), although other banks are also now beginning to offer such services. For almost half the respondents (47 percent), these correspondent outlets are deemed to be the most important financial institution.

Services provided at the Lotéricas vary; most prominently, the shops offer bill paying services for utilities and deposit services, and such services are offered without the need to open an account. Thus, using this limited form of correspondent financial institution for making payments does not signify that an individual is a bank account holder. Not including these correspondents, 46 percent of the sample claim that banks are the most important financial institution for them.[34] Surprisingly, aside from the Lotéricas, the majority of respondents (58 percent) for whom banks are the primary financial institution use private banks. The use of nonbank financial institutions such as cooperatives, credit unions, or microfinance is very limited (only 4 percent of responses). Combining these, and excluding Caixa's bill payment points, only around half the surveyed persons use any form of financial institution (table 1.11).

An attempt was made to see if physical distance restricts access: are banks far from their clients? But more than half of the individuals are able to reach the financial institution on foot (53 percent); a third use public transport, and only 12 percent use a private vehicle. More than a third of respondents (37 percent) take less than 10 minutes to arrive at their financial institution, and almost three-quarters (73.5 percent) take less than 20 minutes. The relative unimportance of distance may be a reflection of the urban nature of the survey, or a confirmation that branch density, at least in these urban areas, is not an important issue.

To what extent do the figures above indicate unmet demand for financial services? Around two-thirds (64 percent) of those who do not have an account indicate an interest in having one. However, this does not indicate effective demand for bank services because, in many cases, there could be reasons why persons may be ineligible for an account such as

Table 1.11 Indicator of Access: Access to Financial Institutions

Respondents who:	*Frequency (nos.)*	*Frequency (%)*
Have a bank account	854	43
Use banks as their primary financial institution[a]	887	46
Use mainly private banks	515	58
Use mainly public banks	372	42
Use CEF lottery shops as their primary financial institution	909	47
Use mainly nonbank financial institutions[b]	67	4
Are able to reach the financial institution they use on foot	1,014	53

a. This could include family members of account holders who do not hold accounts themselves.

b. Includes credit cooperatives, microfinance institutions, and others.

Source: World Bank survey of access to financial services in urban areas in Brazil done in 2002.

risk characteristics, bureaucratic requirements, bias, or other factors. Possible reasons for not having an account were investigated and grouped in two broad categories: voluntary factors (referred to as 'difficulties due to banks') and involuntary factors ('difficulties due to respondent characteristics'). Among the voluntary factors, high fees clearly dominate: bank services are expensive for many persons. In parallel, individuals cite their own lack of funds as another important consideration. References to factors such as lack of documentation and references and difficulties in opening an account suggest that bureaucratic requirements are also important. By contrast, factors such as hours of operation or distance, which suggest physical inconvenience, are not important.

Difficulties related to the costs of banking services or high threshold levels are also reflected in the responses to a question addressed to those who have had an account and then closed it (629 cases). The main reason for cancellation was the difficulty of maintaining a minimum balance (218 cases) combined with cancellation by the bank, also caused largely by problems in maintaining the minimum balance, and high fees. These three factors combined amount to 54 percent of responses.[35]

Survey Results: Deposits and Savings Behavior

Highlights of deposit behavior to emerge are the following:

- Sight deposits or current accounts and savings accounts made up the bulk of most respondents' recent deposits; 43 percent of persons making a deposit in the past month used a sight deposit, while 41 percent used savings deposits as their primary vehicle. Less than 2 percent of respondents put money in term deposits or certificates of deposit, less than 4 percent used rotating savings schemes (consortia), and less than 1 percent bought or sold shares. Around 10 percent made 'other' investments.
- More than half of the respondents (54 percent) have their largest deposits in private institutions, while 41 percent use public institutions.
- Other financial institutions, including cooperatives, account for less than 2 percent of responses, emphasizing the limited role of financial institutions other than banks for deposit-taking, at least in urban areas.
- There is still client preference for branch bank use. Despite technological change, 60 percent of respondents made their recent deposits at bank branches whereas only 30 percent used ATMs for deposits and 10 percent used bank service posts (figure 1.7)
- The most important reason cited for making deposits is 'security,' especially for current accounts (215 out of 305 valid cases) and special savings accounts (259 out of 354 valid responses), but also, surprisingly, for term deposits. Respondents also acknowledge the lower transactions costs of current accounts (19 out of 305 cases) and special savings accounts (24 out of 354 cases), and, for current accounts, the value of access to other financial services (30 out of 305 cases). Rates of return appear third in order of importance, suggesting, at an aggregate level, a weak association between use of deposit services and the interest rates paid for such services. It also appears that when decisions are made to withdraw funds, the withdrawals are not typically associated with diminishing returns or increased risk but for liquidity needs (92 percent)
- Most account holders have limited accounts; only 61 percent of account holders have access to checking facilities.
- Other forms of savings and investments in nonbank assets are low. Only 147 persons made voluntary contributions to pension funds (7.5 percent of respondents), and most were public (71 percent).

Figure 1.7 Deposit and Savings Behavior: Survey of Urban Individuals

Where do you have the largest amount deposited?

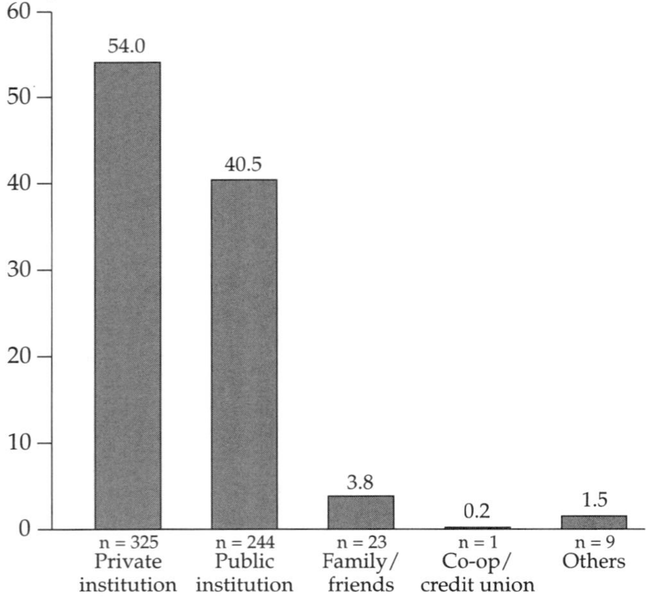

Valid cases = 602

Have you deposited money in one of the following in the last 30 days?

	Frequency (nos.)		
	Yes	No	Valid cases
Bank branch	297	1,482	(1,779)
ATM	150	1,543	(1,693)
Banking service post	48	1,640	(1,688)

	Frequency (%)		
	Yes	No	Valid cases
Bank branch	16.7	83.3	(1,779)
ATM	8.9	91.1	(1,693)
Banking service post	2.8	97.2	(1,688)

Source: World Bank survey of access to financial services in urban areas in Brazil done in 2002.

Survey Results: Loans and Credit Services

Only 15 percent of respondents claim to have applied for credit in the past 12 months, and only two-thirds of those respondents had their applications accepted. The use of guarantees or collateral in successful applications was low—only 12 percent (24 persons out of 194 successful loan applicants).[36] In terms of sources, a third of respondents use private institutions as their primary source of credit, while a quarter (26 percent) use public institutions and a similar proportion (24 percent) use family and friends. Finance companies account for the next big group of creditors with nearly 10 percent; credit unions and shops provide loans to only 1.5 percent of creditors. The reported incidence of pawnbrokers is surprisingly low: only 1 percent accept loans from that source.

In uses of credit, the majority of the respondents apply for a loan for personal purposes (160 persons or 83 percent of respondents). Only 14 borrowers (7.3 percent of respondents) cite business reasons, while the rest cite 'other' reasons. The largest single use of loans (69 cases or 44 percent of respondents) is for family emergencies. Another 15 percent of respondents use the loan to purchase or renovate their homes, and a slightly smaller proportion, 13 percent, use the loan for buying household goods.[37] Unexpectedly, loans for automobile purchase are very low (only 3 percent, perhaps because of the practice of leasing), and loans for education are also low, suggesting a limited borrowing on a 'life cycle'–hypothesis basis.

Borrowing to smooth unexpected consumption needs appears to be common. Among business financing needs, working capital predominates (6 cases out of 12) although payments to creditors (2 cases) and routine maintenance and unforeseen business needs are also cited (1 case each). When not using formal credit, almost half of the respondents (49 percent) use loans from family and friends (35 percent from families and 14 percent from friends). One-fifth (20 percent) use private savings, and around a third (31 percent) use other sources. And 15 percent of respondents have made a loan to their families in the last 12 months.

Average loan amounts are low; 50 percent of respondents applied for R$500 or less; 74 percent applied for loan amounts of R$1,000 or less. Amounts approved closely follow amounts requested, suggesting that in cases of doubtful applicants, credit is rationed by screening out the applicant rather than by reducing the volume of credit extended. On the status of loans received in the last 12 months, a quarter are paid off, suggesting short maturities.[38] More than 62 percent are up-to-date, while around 12 percent of respondents admit to some late payments or to a renegotiation of the loan. Loan processing is surprisingly rapid: more than half receive

Table 1.12 Access to Loans and Credits

Respondents who:	*Frequency (nos.)*	*Frequency (%)*
Applied for a loan and received it	205	10
Applied for a loan but didn't receive it	95	5
Did not apply for loans	1,679	85
Received credit primarily from:		
Private institutions	68	33
Public	52	25
Family/friends	49	24
Finance companies	20	10
Credit cooperatives or credit unions	3	2
Commercial shops	3	2
Others	9	4
Received a business loan	14	8
Received a personal loan	160	92
Did not require collateral to obtain the loan	170	88
Used a financial institution to obtain a loan for real estate	96	37
Have a debit card	503	26
Have a credit card	392	20

Source: World Bank survey of access to financial services in urban areas in Brazil done in 2002.

a response about their loan application on the same day (58 percent); another 26 percent between one and five days.

Finally, apart from formal loans, around a quarter of persons have access to a debit card and a fifth have a credit card (table 1.12). Of these, more than half of respondents (58 percent) have credit card limits of R$600 or less (this is around twice the mean monthly income). Forty-four percent of respondents have credit card debts of R$200 or less outstanding; another 42 percent have credit card debts between R$200 and R$600.

What difficulties do the respondents face in obtaining credit? First, does the low proportion of applicants (only 15 percent) point toward low probabilities of obtaining credit or low credit needs? According to survey responses, most respondents who did not apply for a loan (70 percent) claimed that they did not need the money. However, 17 percent responded that they had assumed the response would be negative. The balance did not know how to apply (4 percent) or had other reasons (13 percent).

Second, what reasons were offered to those who had applied for credit but had been refused? Respondents with loan application rejections cite not having a steady income, not having any guarantees, and not having enough earnings as the primary reasons (table 1.13). However, the

Table 1.13 Access to Loans and Credits: Reasons for Loan Refusals

	Primary reason		*Secondary reason*		*Tertiary reason*	
Respondents	*Frequency (nos.)*	*Frequency (%)*	*Frequency (nos.)*	*Frequency (%)*	*Frequency (nos.)*	*Frequency (%)*
Didn't have a steady income	2	22.2	3	60	—	—
Didn't have any guarantees	2	22.2	1	20	3	42.9
Didn't have enough earnings	2	22.2	1	20	1	14.3
Didn't have a job	1	11.1	—	—	1	14.3
Returns less than expenses	1	11.1	—	—	1	14.3
Others	1	11.1	—	—	1	14.3
Valid cases	(9)	—	(5)	—	(7)	—

Note: — = not available.
Source: World Bank survey of access to financial services in urban areas in Brazil done in 2002.

responses to this question are limited in number, and these results can be considered as only suggestive.

Survey Results: Payments and Money Transmission Services

Cash is overwhelmingly the standard medium of payment for all types of transactions and respondents: 77 percent use cash for all transactions. There is surprisingly little variation by type of payment. Thus, 88 percent of respondents use cash for all daily purchases, but the proportions for education, health, and house rent or mortgage payments are similar; 87 percent, 85 percent, and 88 percent, respectively. And surprisingly, 92 percent of utility bills are paid in cash. The only expenditure categories where cash use is lower are consumer durables: 77 percent for electrodomestic goods and 80 percent for furniture. This could reflect credit offered by consumer finance companies, especially postdated checks. In the two payment categories of utilities and consumer durables, check payment amounts to 12 percent and 13 percent, respectively, of payment method. Credit cards are also used in these two categories, by 9 percent and 6 percent of respondents, respectively. Credit cards or debit cards are used for daily purchases by only 7 percent of the persons surveyed, though debit cards are also used for utility payments by around 5 percent of persons.

For points of payment, a surprisingly high proportion (more than 90 percent) make payments in person at bank branches (54 percent) or other points (38 percent), only 2.5 percent use the mail (44 persons), and just over 1 percent use the internet or telephone. These numbers suggest that retail payments systems are still unsophisticated for the majority of persons. Are the present retail payments systems burdensome? Surprisingly, despite the high proportion of cash payments, between 30 and 40 percent of respondents claim that payments for utilities, education, and health can be made in less than 10 minutes, and, for 50 to 60 percent of respondents, less than 20 minutes. But for 15 to 22 percent of the respondents, these payments take from half an hour to an hour. Payments for furniture and appliances, surprisingly, seem to take the longest time, or more than half an hour for three-fifths of those surveyed.

Payment services were also investigated in terms of income receipt. More than two-thirds of respondents (68 percent) receive their primary income in cash, while 24 percent have direct deposits in their bank accounts. Surprisingly, only 4 percent receive checks. Cash preference is high; the proportion of persons who want to receive cash payments (72 percent) is higher than those who actually receive cash. Checks appear to have the greatest disutility, because the proportion who would like to be paid by check (91.5 percent) is lower than the actual proportion. The proportion of those receiving payment by direct deposit is broadly similar to those who wish to receive their income in this manner, or 24 percent of respondents.

Check cashing is usually done at a public institution (50 percent); the proportion for private institutions is half this level at 26 percent. Eleven percent of respondents use family or friends, and 9 percent use a commercial shop. It is interesting that although there is a preference for private institutions for overall banking services and also for deposit services, preferences are reversed for check cashing. This may indicate that private bank services for check cashing are more onerous or more expensive. Finally, remittances are rare: only 68 persons or 3.5 percent of respondents had sent or received remittances in the last year. Around two-fifths of these were by interbank transfer and another 10 percent through the postal system. Another two-fifths were in cash or through personal transmission.

Analysis of Survey Results: What Factors Are Associated with Access?

The principal aim of this section is to investigate at the broadest level those factors that have been used, in a policy context, to address access issues, and to examine the scope for extending this menu to extend the options for policies favoring access. The associations or correlations between a series of measures of access and selected economic parameters important to policy are analyzed, through the construction of cross-frequencies[39] and, next, through regression analysis. The measures of financial access used are grouped in the same four broad categories as those described above: use of a formal financial institution, access to deposit and savings facilities, access to loans and credits, and access to payment services.

Particular attention is paid to three specific issues. The first of these is location and the association between the location of the respondents and the availability of financial services. Locational measures of access have been the primary means through which the government has tried to track and to address shortcomings in access, as discussed above. A central feature of government policies for the expansion of access has been the attempt to put some financial institution or point of service in each municipality. However, location can be interpreted at two levels: first, the region of the country and, second, the microeconomic characteristics of the neighborhood and dwelling of the respondent. It is proposed here that there may be significant microdifferences in 'location' within a region, state, or even municipality, which could have pockets of poverty within broadly prosperous areas, and, conversely, could have well-to-do persons even in less-affluent municipalities. The association between access and both definitions of location is explored.

Second, the role of different types of financial institutions in the provision of financial services is examined. There has been an assumption that because of market failures in financial markets, there is a need for a public role in the provision of financial services, and that public banks have an important role to play as providers of such services. As already indicated, public banks and private banks often behave in similar ways and are broadly substitutable in services to some segments of the population. Further investigation of the role of public financial institutions is made to see if they better serve the needs of the poorer segments of society.

Third, special attention is paid to the role of information in the provision of financial services. It has been pointed out that one of the key reasons for the limited access to financial services to the poor is the huge difficulty in gathering information on such persons. This is the asymmetric information problem. The extent to which proxies for information on creditworthiness, such as income, wealth, or the possession of collateral, can influence decisions regarding the provision of financial services is investigated. If there are significant asymmetries in the availability of information, these would be illustrated by the importance of such proxy variables for creditworthiness. The policy implication would be to improve overall information on creditworthiness and also to address the specific biases noted.

Impact of Location on Financial Access

Two different aspects of location are analyzed here: location by region in terms of geographic entities as a whole, and location as determined by differing microeconomic characteristics within regions or municipalities.

Location in Terms of Regions of the Country

There is a clear variation in a series of indicators of financial access across regions, which broadly show that the North and sometimes the Northeast of the country are more limited in access than the Central or Southern regions (figure 1.8 and appendix table A1.8).[40] In use of a formal financial institution, for example, 75 percent of the respondents in the North and 71 percent of respondents in the Northeast have no bank account; in contrast, only around half the persons in the South (55 percent) and Southeast (45 percent) have no bank account.

Most persons in the Northeast (70 percent) use banking correspondents as their primary financial institution, while in the Southeast one-half of the persons use banks or their branches as their primary financial institution. Only 6 percent of the respondents who live in the North have deposits in an account, in contrast to more than one-third of individuals who live in the South (37.5 percent). And 97 percent of persons in the North have not applied for loans, compared to 83 percent in the Southeast. Regarding payments, only 18 percent of persons in the Northeast and 16 percent of persons in the North have a debit card, in contrast to 40 percent in the South and 44 percent in the Central–West.[41] Only 2 percent of respondents who live in the Northern region use transfer or direct deposits to make payments, while 15 percent of individuals in the Southeast use that method for payments.

Location in Terms of Microregions: Neighborhoods and Areas within a City

Differences in access can also be strong within a region, at the level of individual neighborhoods (appendix table A1.9). For access to a financial institution, for example, the distinction was made between persons living in legalized areas and those in illegal areas. Forty-five percent are bank account holders in the former areas, in contrast to only 37 percent of persons in the latter or illegal areas. Similarly with regard to type of building, only 34 percent of people who live in informally constructed shacks or in rooms have a bank account, in contrast to almost half (45 percent) the persons who live in regularized houses or apartments. And only 13 percent of individuals with houses of less than 0.5 rooms per person have accounts, compared to more than half the individuals who live in houses of more than 2 rooms per person.

More than half the respondents (59 percent) who live in shacks or rooms use mainly correspondent banks; 47 percent of persons who live in a house or apartment use mainly bank institutions. Again, the same pattern appears when the number of rooms per person in a house is examined. Almost two-thirds (56 percent) of individuals who live in houses that have more than 2 rooms per person use mainly banks, while more than two-thirds of respondents who live in houses with less than 0.5 rooms per person (64 percent) use correspondents.

Results are similar when access to deposit facilities is analyzed: 30 percent of individuals who live in a unique permanent house have deposit balances compared to only 19 percent of individuals who live in collective dwellings.[42] Forty-one percent of the individuals who live in a house with more than 2 rooms per person have deposit balances, in contrast to only 7 percent of persons who live in a house with less than 0.5 rooms per person. Looking at credits, 83 percent of respondents living in homes with more than 2 rooms per person did not apply for loans, compared to 94 percent of people who live in houses with less than 0.5 rooms per person. Thirty-four percent of persons who live in a house with more than 2 rooms per person have a debit card, whereas only 5 percent of persons

Figure 1.8 Role of Location in Financial Access

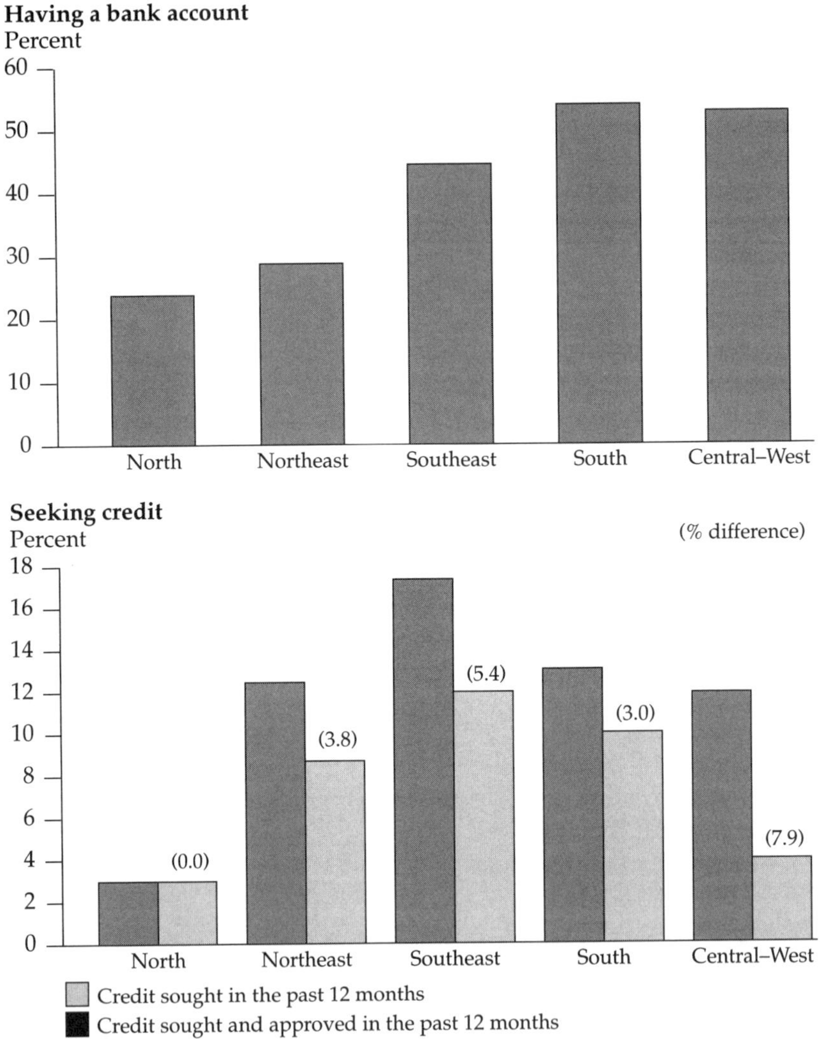

Region	North	Northeast		
City	Pará	Ceará	Pemambuco	Bahia
GDP per capita, 2000 (R$)	3,041	2,794	3,673	3,680

Source: World Bank survey of access to financial services in urban areas in Brazil done in 2002. GDP data provided by IBGE.

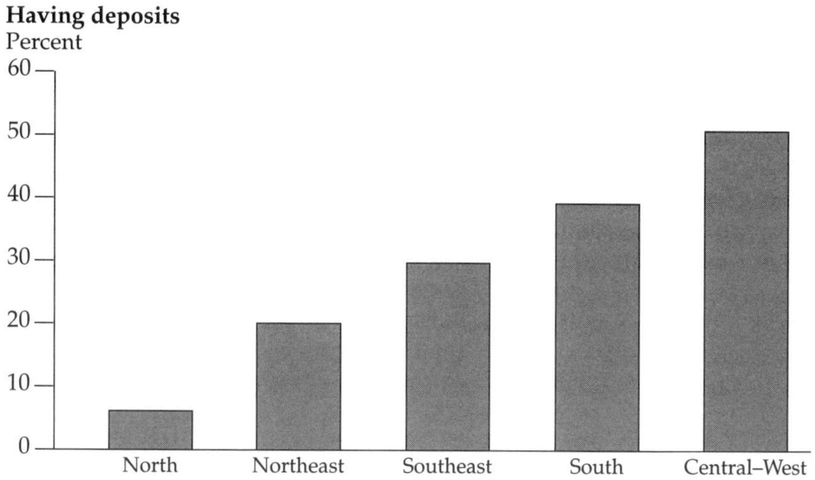

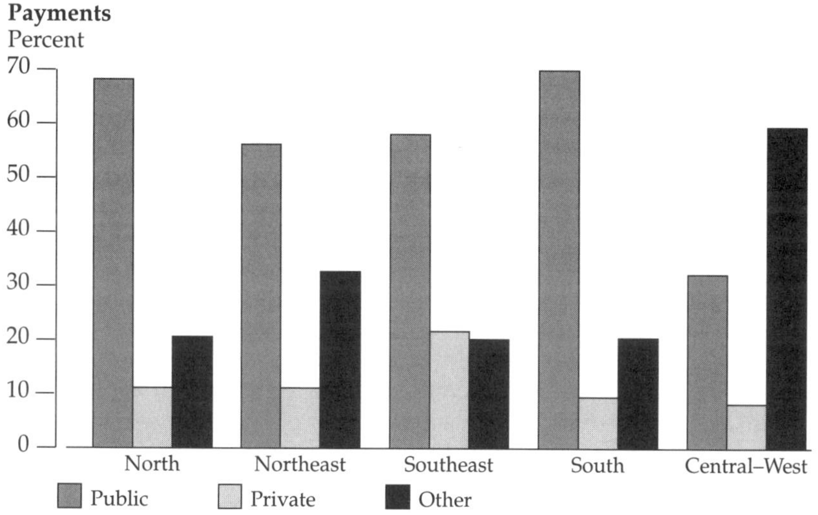

Southeast			South		Central–West	
Minas Gerais	Rio De Janeiro	São Paulo	Paraná	Rio Grande do Sul	Distrito Federal	Goiás
5,925	9,571	9,995	6,882	8,341	14,405	4,316

who live in homes with less than 0.5 rooms per person have a debit card. Differences in proportions for credit cards are also significant. Finally, the percentage of persons who use cash for payments is bigger in illegal areas (84 percent) than in legalized areas (75 percent), whereas the number of persons who use debit or credit card and transfers or direct deposits is bigger in legalized areas. Observations are similar when a comparison is made between respondents who live in houses and apartments with respondents who live in shacks or rooms.

The suggested policy implication of these findings is significant. Although there are indeed differences in the availability of financial services between regions of the country, placing financial institutions in each region or municipality in itself is not a sufficient condition for broadening access. There may well be important differences within neighborhoods and districts of a municipality, region, or state. Even if there is a financial institution present in a given location, its clients may be biased toward the better-off persons. And conversely, areas benefiting from dense networks of financial institutions may still have pockets of the underserved. The implication is that targeted interventions looking at microregions, and at specific groups within regions, may be an important supplement to broad regional policies if access to financial services is to be promoted.

Role of Public and Private Institutions and Financial Access

The next question examined concerns the role of public and private financial institutions as vehicles of access. Brazil's public banks have been considered important vehicles of outreach to underserved communities, and this role has been premised on market failures or imperfections that make it too costly or too risky for private banks to lend to some communities. This section investigates the differences in outcomes for public and private banks in the provision of various forms of financial services, and between groups of persons with different socioeconomic characteristics. The key findings are:

- An individual's use of public and private banks depends on the type of financial service sought. There are significant differences across different types of service.
- Grouping individuals on the basis of those who may be more or less disadvantaged (for example, those in poorer regions versus those in more affluent regions, those in poorer neighborhoods or homes compared to those in more affluent neighborhoods or better homes, or those with higher income or education compared to those with lower income or education) produces some significant results, in which

more-disadvantaged groups make greater use of public bank facilities. However, there are also significant cases of the reverse being true, and many instances where there is no clear association of the less-well-off with public banks.

- Next, looking at different measures of access and first considering overall access to financial institutions, disadvantaged groups do show some tendency to make greater proportional use of public financial institutions. However, the results are significantly influenced by correspondent outlets. Both the disadvantaged and the well-to-do increase their use of public institutions once correspondent outlets are considered.[43]
- For the majority of persons seeking deposit or credit services, there is a general preference for private banks.
- In the case of deposit services, test results find significant differences between public and private bank use and location and personal characteristics, but the results show that the less-well-off groups tend to make less use of both public and private deposit facilities.
- In the case of credit facilities, tests of differences are mostly not significant. An inspection of frequencies again suggests that the association of disadvantaged individuals with public banks is unclear.
- For payment services, in contrast, a clear preference exists for public banks when these are defined to include the correspondent outlets known as lottery shops. In all cases, the proportions of users are higher for public banks than private banks.
- A large part of the preference for public banks may be traced to the services provided by the Lotérica correspondent outlets of the Caixa Econômica Federal. At the time of the survey, the Caixa had a clear advantage in the provision of such services. If the correspondent outlets of private providers, especially the postal outlets of Bradesco, are also able to compete in this market, this advantage may not remain. An implication is that policies adopted toward correspondent outlets will be very important in expanding access and promoting competition in the provision of services to the underserved.
- There is also clearly a greater use of public, compared to private, pension funds, again by both the poorer and the better-off social segments
- Looking at credit for housing, public banks dominate the provision of services, though their services are used more extensively by the better-off segments.

Overall Access to Public and Private Financial Institutions

Examining overall access to a financial institution (our first measure of access), including correspondents and looking across regions, 84 percent of individuals in the North use mainly public banks compared to around two-thirds of individuals in the Southeast. Without correspondents, half the persons in the North continue to use public banks, but in the Southeast the proportion of users of public banks falls to around 38 percent. Both differences are significant, suggesting that many persons use public bank services because of the lottery shops (appendix table A1.10). Similarly, looking at microregions and including correspondents, 81 percent of persons in homes of less than 0.5 rooms per person use mainly public banks compared to 61 percent of individuals in houses of more than 2 rooms per person. But with the narrow definition, only 48 percent of those with less than 0.5 rooms per person use public banks, and only 36 percent of those with more than 2 rooms per person. Both differences are significant (appendix table A1.10).

Looking at individual characteristics, and considering gender, women are less likely to use private banks than men. However, using the narrow definition for public and private banks, the majority of both men and women use mainly private banks. Including correspondent outlets, both women and men use mainly public banks. In terms of income, only 36 percent of persons with income in the highest quintile use public banks as opposed to 49 percent of individuals in the lowest quintile. Again, with the wider definition, use in both groups goes up dramatically, to almost half in the top quintile (51 percent) and 78 percent in the lowest quintile. Looking at wealth, half the persons without collateral use public banks compared to only 40 percent of those with collateral. Including banking correspondents, the majority of individuals with or without collateral use public banks. Similar results are obtained when education and persons with or without jobs are examined.

Access to Deposit, Savings, and Credit Facilities

The next series of measures of access describe access to deposit, payments, and credit services (appendix table A1.11). With regard to deposit and loan services, correspondent outlets, until recently, did not typically offer these services.[44] With regard to payments, public bank outlets and the lottery shops are grouped together. Payment services, as may be expected, are dominated by the public sector (defined to include the lottery shops), and this preference is true across social groups. Some indicators also suggest that public banks may be more oriented toward the underserved. Thus, 62 percent of persons in homes with less than 0.5 rooms per person prefer public banks for payments compared to 55 percent of those with more than 2 rooms per person; similarly, 68 percent of persons in the North use public payment outlets, compared to 34 percent and 58 percent for the Center and Southeast. Perhaps most clearly, 58 percent of persons with less than primary education use public payment outlets while 11 percent use private banks, compared to 41 percent with more than secondary education for public payment outlets and 38 percent for private.

Regarding deposits, the overall pattern in contrast to payment services is some preference for private banks for persons in each geographic or socioeconomic category. Looking at comparisons of the more- and less-disadvantaged groups of persons, according to a range of criteria, a first observation is that the better-off persons have proportionally larger deposits in both public and private institutions than the less-well-off. For example, 18 percent of individuals who live in houses that have more than 2 rooms per person have deposits in public sector institutions and 28 percent have deposits in private sector institutions; in contrast, only 3 percent of persons who live in houses that have less than 0.5 rooms per person have deposits in the public sector and 6 percent have deposits in the private sector.

Similarly, men have more deposits in both public and private sector banks than women. Seventeen percent of the men have deposits in public sector institutions and 22 percent in the private sector, while 11 percent of the women have deposits in the public sector and 15 percent have deposits in the private sector. The differences are pronounced with regard to income and education. Only 7 percent of respondents with low income have deposits in the public sector, and only 6 percent have deposits in the private sector; in contrast, 25 percent of individuals with high income have deposits in the public sector, and 42 percent have deposits in the private sector. Similarly, individuals with high levels of education have more deposits in both public and private sector institutions than individuals with low levels of education.

Do the more disadvantaged persons make proportionally greater use of public facilities for deposits? This hypothesis returns mixed results. Those respondents in the lowest income quintile have marginally more deposits in public banks (7 percent public compared to 6 percent private), while those in the top quintile have 25 percent of their deposits in the public sector compared to 42 percent in the private sector, and persons in the Northeast have proportionally more deposits in public banks (10 percent versus 7 percent, compared to 11 percent public and 22 percent private for the Southeast). However, by contrast, persons living in illegal areas or in shacks or rooms instead of regular houses or apartments have proportionally more deposits in private banks. Similarly, those in the lower educational levels and those without collateral also make greater use of private facilities compared to public facilities. These results, all of which are statistically significant differences, are at first surprising in view of the special savings accounts dominated by the Caixa, but can be explained by the high proportion of current account holders who are offered services at private banks.[45]

Next, looking at credit facilities, the case for public banks remains blurred (appendix table A1.11). In this case, the differences in proportions are usually not significant. They suggest again that the less-privileged have weaker access to both public and private financial services, and there is no general tendency for the disadvantaged to make proportionally greater use of public banks. One significant result obtained is with regard to the microlocation variable on the nature of the dwelling: almost one-third of individuals who live in a house or in a apartment receive credit from private banks and 26 percent receive credit from public banks, while 48 percent of individuals who live in a shack or in a room receive credit from private banks and only 6 percent of those receive credit from public institutions.

The other significant difference is in the proportion of persons who possess collateral, in the form of a car or house, and those who have no collateral. Twenty-six percent of persons who have collateral receive credit from public banks, and 33 percent of those receive credit from private banks. In contrast, only 8 percent of individuals with no collateral receive credit from public banks and 28 percent receive credit from private banks. In both cases, the less-privileged groups have distinctly lower access to both public and private banks, and the frequencies suggest greater use, even by these individuals, of private banks.

A fifth variable used to discriminate between public and private financial services is the voluntary contribution to public versus private pension funds. Results, which are highly significant, show clear differences between contributions in terms of location as well as individual characteristics, and here, as in the case of payment services, both the well-off and more-disadvantaged groups make greater use of public pension funds. Eleven percent of persons with a high level of education have contributed to public funds and 10 percent contributed to private funds, while only 3 percent of individuals with a low level of education contributed to public funds and only 1 percent contributed to private funds.

The same relationship exists between level of income and contribution to public or private funds. In terms of employment, 22 percent of employers have contributed to public funds and 11 percent have contributed to private funds, whereas only 3 percent of employees without a work certificate have contributed to public funds and 2 percent to private funds. This may indicate that incentives to contribute to private pensions funds under a third pillar (*previdência complementar*) need not have matched employer contributions and thus incentives for such savings are limited.

The final variable looked at was the use of credit from public versus private banks for home purchase. With regard to home purchase, the vast majority of the persons in all geographic regions use savings to finance home purchase. But in the North 70 percent of respondents use savings,

10 percent use credit from public banks, and 10 percent use credit from private banks, while in the Southeast 56 percent use savings, 22 percent use credit from public banks, and 11 percent use credit from private banks. Looking at microdefinitions of location, 13 percent of persons with homes of more than 2 rooms per person use public bank credit, while none of the respondents in homes of less than 0.5 rooms per person do so.

Looking at income, almost one-half of respondents with low income (49 percent) finance home purchase by savings, 5 percent use credit from public banks, and 7 percent use private banks, whereas 39 percent of respondents with high incomes finance home purchase by savings and 18 percent use credit from a public institution. Although 12 percent of respondents with a low level of education use credit from public banks to purchase a home, 16 percent of respondents with high levels of education use such institutions. All these results, which are statistically significant, seem to perversely indicate easier access to public bank credit by the more well-to-do social groups, which may partly reflect superior economic capacity to repay.

Role of Information and Respondent Characteristics

As discussed earlier, access can depend on the degree of client information available because of the impact on risks, and hence, costs. Obtaining such information can assume special importance in environments where the capacity to enforce repayment may be difficult because of the limited resources of the client and the nature of prevailing laws and practice with regard to debt recovery or bankruptcy. In the absence of full information, especially on poorer persons with limited credit histories, institutions tend to look for proxies to information on creditworthiness. Such proxy variables could include information on cash flows (income), which could service loans, or assets (wealth), which could aid loan recovery. It appears that banks also desire such information for opening an account, because of the need to service accounts or even to accept a deposit. Other characteristics of this information form could include position in household (heads versus dependents), gender (males versus females), or employment characteristics.

How important are these factors in obtaining financial services in Brazil? The results indicate that information on such characteristics is very important in determining access to financial services. Most important among these characteristics is the income of the respondent, which has a strong positive relation with access to a variety of financial services, including having a bank account and deposit and credit services (figure 1.9). In terms of credit, as income levels increase, the proportion of refusals of credit applications diminishes. Simple trend lines fitted to

Individual Characteristics, Asymmetric Information, and Access to Financial Services

For most measures of financial access, virtually all the socioeconomic characteristics included in the analysis turn out to be highly significant discriminators in determining access to financial services. Foremost among these are characteristics referring to income, wealth (possession of collateral), and education. Many variables related to employment characteristics are also highly significant. Finally, for some measures, gender and the position in the household also matter (appendix table A1.13).

Income: In terms of access to bank accounts, only 15 percent of persons with income in the lowest quintile have a bank account, in contrast to 64 percent of respondents in the highest quintile. Looking at deposits, only 9 percent of the persons with income in the lowest quintile have money in a special savings account, a current account, or a term deposit account, in contrast to 47 percent of persons in the top quintile. Using another measure of deposits, 84 percent of persons in the bottom quintile have no deposits, in contrast to only 32 percent in the top quintile. Income is also important in determining access to credit and loans. Ninety-two percent of respondents in the bottom quintile did not apply for credit, compared to 74 percent in the top quintile. Differences in sources of credit, however, were not very significant among the quintiles of income distribution. Only 5 percent of the persons with a low income have a debit card, in contrast to 40 percent of persons with a high income. Similarly, only 7 percent of the persons with a low income have a credit card, compared to 34 percent of persons with a high income.

Education: Another very important determinant in the access to financial institution is education. Among the significant differences, only 28 percent of persons with education less than primary level have a bank account, while 84 percent of the respondents with more than secondary school have a bank account. When the access to public and private banks is compared, the majority of respondents with a low level of education used mainly public banks (including the correspondents), while 59 percent of persons with high levels of education used mainly private banks (including the correspondents). Only 19 percent of persons with low education levels have money in a special savings account, a current account, or a term deposit account compared to 64 percent of those with higher education. Only 25 percent of respondents with higher education have no deposits, in contrast to 78 percent for those with low education. Ten percent of persons with a low level of education applied for and received loans compared to 23 percent of respondents with high education levels. Only 9 percent of persons with a low level of education have a credit card, whereas almost one-half of respondents with a high level of education (48 percent) have a credit card.

(box continued next page)

(box continued)

Wealth (collateral): Almost one half of respondents who have collateral (45 percent) have a bank account, whereas only 35 percent of the persons without collateral have a bank account. Collateral is also important for the pattern of deposits and savings, but not as important as income or education. However, possessing collateral is the only characteristic that makes a significant difference to credit sources.

Employment—having a job: More than half the people who had a job in the last month (55 percent) have a bank account; in contrast, only 30 percent of people who did not have a job in the last month have a bank account. Thirty-eight percent of individuals who had a job in the last month have money in a special savings account, a current account, or a term deposit account; in contrast, only 19 percent of persons who had no job have money in such accounts. Thirteen percent of respondents who had a job in the last month applied for and received credit, whereas only 8 percent of persons who had no job were in the same situation. Thirty-four percent of respondents who had a job in the last month have a debit card; in contrast, only half (17 percent) of persons who had no job in the last month have a debit card. The difference is very significant. The same pattern occurs with the possession of a credit card.

Employment—having a work certificate: 68 percent of employees with a work certificate have a bank account, in contrast with only 44 percent of employees without a work certificate. Forty-seven percent of employees with a work certificate have money in a special savings account, a current account, or a term deposit account, whereas only 26 percent of employees without a work certificate have money in one of these accounts.

Gender and position in household: Half the men have a bank account compared to a third of the women. One-half of the heads of household have a bank account whereas only 37 percent of the dependents have a bank account. One-half of men use banks as the primary financial institution, while 53 percent of the women use correspondent banks. Thirty-four percent of the men have money in a special savings account, a current account, or a term deposit account compared to 23 percent of the women. But gender is not a good determinant for credit and loan behavior. There are also significant differences between women and men in the possession of credit cards and debit cards.

income and credit applications and acceptances tend to converge as incomes rise. Income levels appear to be particularly positively associated with the use of private banks for deposit and payment services, where their use increases more than proportionately with increases of income, while the use of public banks diminishes.

Figure 1.9 The Role of Income in Different Measures of Financial Access

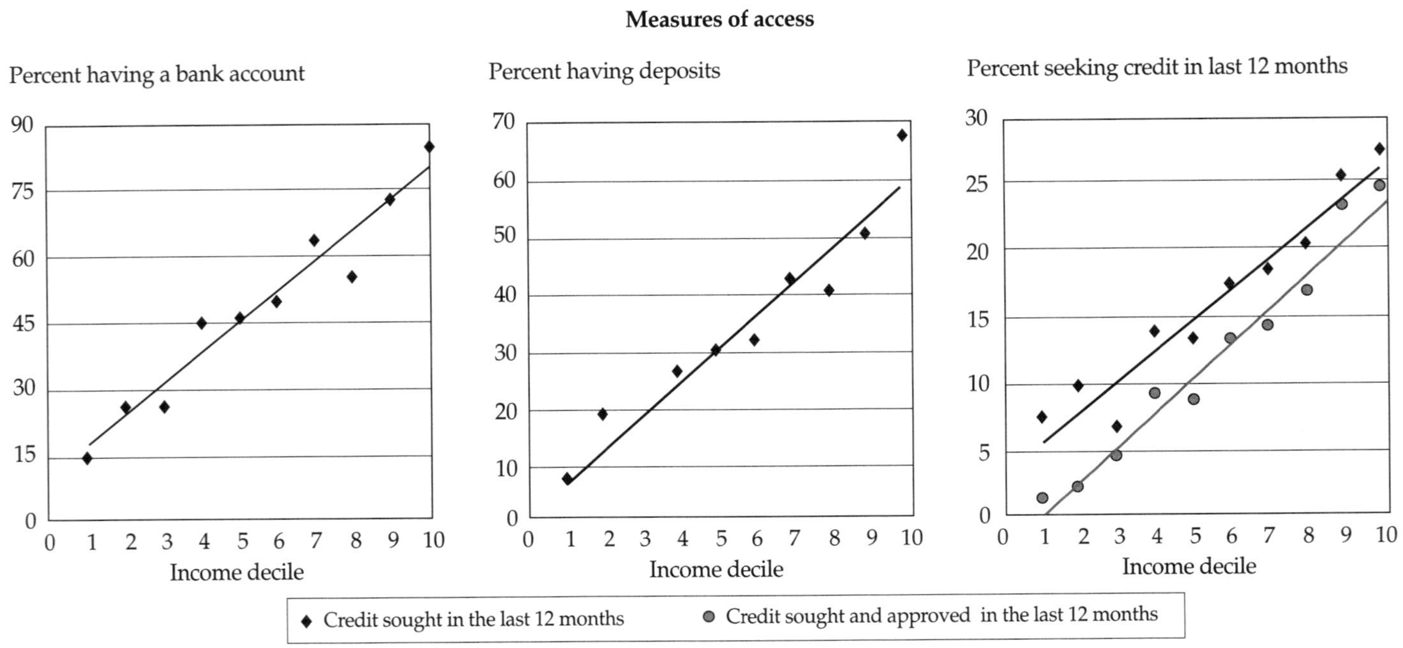

Institutional choice: using public/private institutions (% share)

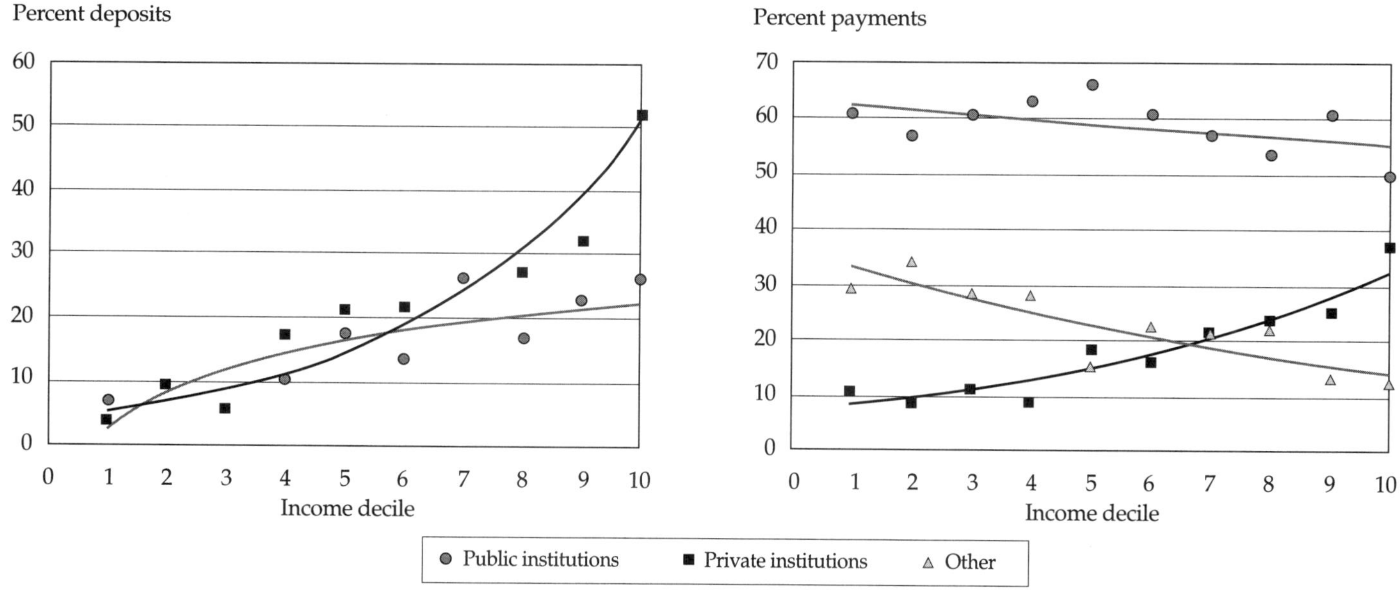

Source: World Bank survey of access to financial services in urban areas in Brazil done in 2002.

An Econometric Investigation of Determinants of Access

The previous section examined the links between financial access and location (both in regions of the country and location in the sense of neighborhoods or areas), institutions (primarily public and private banks), and variables that describe a series of individual characteristics. Following estimations of the cross-frequencies between these variables, the analysis examined the extent to which differences in frequencies are significant. However, tests of difference are not able to evaluate the relative importance of the different factors affecting access. The present section discusses the impact of these factors based on regression analysis.[46] A series of regressions was undertaken, beginning first with locational explanatory variables and then adding variables on individual characteristics.

Determinants of Access to Financial Services

Using a series of different measures of access and using a number of different explanatory variables related to location as well as individual characteristics, the most significant result to emerge is the importance of income, over and above most other parameters, as a determinant of access (table 1.14).[47] Closely parallel to this is the importance of education and of access to credit, wealth, or collateral. Although geographic region, used on its own, is a significant explanatory variable, its importance diminishes considerably after income is added to the equation. Thus, for example, using the probability of having a bank account as a measure of access, geographic region, number of rooms per person, sex, and age are all significant predictors until income, education level, and the possession of collateral are included. Income and education are then very significant and, in the first group of explanatory variables, only geographic location and number of rooms per person continue to be significant. Similar results are obtained if the probability of using banks as the primary financial institution is examined. In this case, once socioeconomic characteristics are included, the importance of geographic location and even dwelling characteristics disappears.

Broadly similar results are obtained when access to specific services are examined. Looking at deposit services, the probability of having money in either a special savings account, a current account, or a term deposit account is significantly linked to income level, education, and two parameters of microlocation. Geographic location is important only before these socioeconomic characteristics are included. In the case of credit services, income is the only independent variable that is related in a significant way to the probability of applying for loans. Income and education are both very important for predicting the probability of having a debit card, and income, education, and the possession of collateral all explain the probability of having a credit card. Geographic region is not an important predictor.

Determinants of the Volume of Credit Requested and Approved

Attempts to evaluate factors determining the volume of credit requested and approved using ordinary linear regression show that income is the only significant explanatory variable. People who have more money request more credit and have received larger loans. This supports the findings in figure 1.9. Variables like age, education, and the number of dependents, which are related to the hypothesis that individuals try to smooth consumption over the course of their lives, are not significant. There is thus no confirmation of the permanent income hypothesis in these results (table 1.15), which also emphasize the importance of income in determining access to financial services.

Determinants of Institutional Choice

The econometric analysis also suggests that income level and education are significant explanators of the probability of using public banks as the primary financial institution, relative to private banks. A high level of education and income decreases the probability of using mainly public banks. These results are true whether a wider or narrower definition of public banks is used (including or excluding correspondent services). However, the probability of having deposits in either the public sector or the private sector (in comparison to not having deposits), while positively and significantly determined by income, is also significantly determined by other socioeconomic and locational variables. When credit is analyzed, only possession of collateral has a significant relationship with the probability of having received credit from public banks, but collateral does not have a significant relationship with the probability of receiving credit from private banks (table 1.16).

Finally, income is the only variable to have a significant (positive) relationship with probability of receiving credit from public banks. Both income and the sector of activity of the respondents are significant explanatory variables for the probability of receiving credit from other government sources for home purchase (table 1.17).

Table 1.14 Determinants of Access to Financial Services: Results

	Institutional access			
	Having a bank account	*Primary financial institution*		
Dependent variable		*Banks*	*Correspon-dents*	*Public banks*
Econometric model	*Probit*	*Multinomial logit*		*Probit*
Geographic region	0.04	0.26	0.16	–0.02
	(0.03)	(0.18)	(0.39)	(0.14)
Sex	–0.05	–0.27	–0.01	0.05
	(0.19)	(0.52)	(0.97)	(0.13)
Age	0.02			
	(0.35)			
Position in the household	–0.07			
	(0.10)			
Illegal vs. legalized area	–0.03			
	(0.57)			
Type of house[a]				
Type of building[b]	–0.11	0.11	0.20	0.07
	(0.04)	(0.86)	(0.74)	(0.09)
No. of rooms per person	–0.05	0.04	0.15	0.02
	(0.00)	(0.85)	(0.45)	(0.11)
Having a job	–0.04	–1.12	–0.86	0.12
	(0.80)	(0.56)	(0.66)	(0.34)
Role in workplace	–0.01	0.43	0.35	–0.02
	(0.62)	(0.18)	(0.27)	(0.46)
Part-time or full-time employment	0.01	–1.06	–1.25	–0.04
	(0.79)	(0.07)	(0.03)	(0.32)
Sector of activity	–0.01	0.31	0.31	–0.01
	(0.62)	(0.31)	(0.30)	(0.56)
Income	0.11	0.48	0.17	–0.06
	(0.00)	(0.00)	(0.27)	(0.00)
Education	0.10	0.35	0.01	–0.05
	(0.00)	(0.02)	(0.94)	(0.00)
Possession of collateral	–0.03	–0.12	0.05	0.01
	(0.50)	(0.82)	(0.92)	(0.71)
Observations	1,069	1,067		1,037

a. Type of house refers to unique, improvised, or collective house.
b. Type of building refers to (i) house or apartment or (ii) shack or room.
Source: World Bank survey of access to financial services in urban areas in Brazil done in 2002.

Deposits				*Loans and credits*		
Having deposit balance	*Having deposits in:* *Public banks*	*Private banks*	*Other institutions*	*Applying for loans*	*Having a debit card*	*Having a credit card*
Probit	*Multinomial Logit*			*Probit*		
0.02	0.3	0.2	–0.6	0.01	0.02	–0.02
(0.11)	(0.00)	(0.08)	(0.00)	(0.20)	(0.25)	(0.15)
–0.08	–0.6	–0.4	–1.3		–0.05	
(0.01)	(0.01)	(0.03)	(0.02)		(0.09)	
0.01				0.02	0.02	0.02
(0.46)				(0.08)	(0.35)	(0.17)
0.03	0.3	0.00	1.8	0.02	0.01	
(0.36)	(0.21)	(0.99)	(0.01)	(0.40)	(0.72)	
–0.11	0.1	0.0	0.7			
(0.38)	(0.75)	(0.94)	(0.49)			
–0.09				–0.01		
(0.01)				(0.67)		
–0.04	–0.1	–0.20	–35.5			0.00
(0.06)	(0.84)	(0.48)	(0.0)			(0.93)
0.18	–0.1	–0.2	–0.5	–0.01	–0.02	0.00
(0.01)	(0.13)	(0.00)	(0.01)	(0.44)	(0.06)	(0.80)
0.18	2.1	0.00	–0.5		–0.06	0.06
(0.18)	(0.02)	(0.99)	(0.72)	(0.20)	(0.54)	
–0.04	–0.3	–0.1	–0.1		0.02	–0.05
(0.05)	(0.04)	(0.32)	(0.71)		(0.38)	(0.39)
–0.01	–0.3	0.00	–0.2			0.01
(0.72)	(0.25)	(0.93)	(0.69)			(0.64)
–0.02	–0.2	0.0	0.2	0.01	–0.03	
(0.29)	(0.10)	(0.94)	(0.27)	(0.14)	(0.01)	
0.08	0.4	0.5	–0.1	0.04	0.09	0.08
(0.00)	(0.00)	(0.00)	(0.44)	(0.00)	(0.00)	(0.00)
0.08	0.4	0.4	0.00		0.05	0.06
(0.00)	(0.00)	(0.00)	(0.86)		(0.00)	(0.00)
0.01	0.1	0.0	–0.2	0.01	–0.04	–0.08
(0.82)	(0.59)	(0.87)	(0.76)	(0.61)	(0.21)	(0.01)
1,077		942		1,200	1,085	1,251

Table 1.15 Econometric Results: Determinants of Volume of Credit Requested and Approved

Dependent variable	*Amount requested for loans*	*Amount approved for loans*
Econometric model	*Linear model*	*Linear model*
Age	–57.43 (0.53)	–21.83 (0.80)
Double age	16.87 (0.35)	5.70 (0.74)
Number of dependents	17.41 (0.73)	63.36 (0.18)
Role in workplace	–4.26 (0.90)	–21.06 (0.51)
Income	45.73 (0.03)	39.50 (0.04)
Education	4.28 (0.88)	24.47 (0.37)
Possession of collateral	–81.41 (0.23)	–42.14 (0.51)
Observations	822	822

Note: P-values are in parentheses.
Source: World Bank survey of access to financial services in urban areas in Brazil done in 2002.

Summary of Findings and Policy Implications

The preceding sections analyzed, first, the factors associated with the supply of financial services, particularly in the form of institutional outlets for such services, and, next, patterns of demand for such services and how these demands have actually been fulfilled at the level of individuals in Brazil's urban areas. Combining and synthesizing the results, the key findings that emerge are:

- Access of Brazil's population to financial services has been dominated by banks. The provision of banking services in the form of bank branches has remained broadly unchanged over the last decade. Brazil is not obviously 'underbanked' in international comparisons.
- Important new trends are emerging in the form of new outlets such as correspondents. As shown by the user survey, these facilities have had a remarkable role and have increased overall use of financial services, both among the better-off and the less-well-to-do sections of society. The effective use of banking services is considerably greater than the number of bank accounts alone would suggest.
- Although a first look at the supply of financial institutions points to wide regional differentials in the provision of services, these

Table 1.16 Econometric Results: The Probability of Using Public Banks for Access, Deposits, and Credit

	Financial institution		*Deposits*			*Credit*	
Dependent variable	*Public banks*	*Private banks*[a]	*Public banks*	*Private banks*	*Other*	*Public banks*	*Private banks*
Econometric model	*Probit*		*Multinomial logit*				
Geographic region	–0.03 (0.33)	–0.02 (0.14)	0.3 (0.00)	0.2 (0.08)	–0.6 (0.00)	–0.26 (0.26)	0.02 (0.90)
Sex	0.05 (0.29)	0.05 (0.13)	–0.6 (0.01)	–0.4 (0.03)	–1.3 (0.02)		
Type of building[b]	0.08 (0.23)	0.07 (0.09)	–0.1 (0.84)	–0.2 (0.48)	–35.5 (0.00)	–1.02 (0.24)	0.73 (0.11)
Number of rooms per person	0.02 (0.39)	0.02 (0.11)	–0.1 (0.13)	–0.2 (0.00)	–0.5 (0.01)		
Having a job	0.06 (0.75)	0.12 (0.34)	2.1 (0.02)	0.0 (0.99)	–0.5 (0.72)		
Role in workplace	–0.03 (0.35)	–0.02 (0.46)	–0.3 (0.04)	–0.1 (0.32)	–0.1 (0.71)		
Part-time or full-time employed	0.00 (0.97)	–0.04 (0.32)	–0.3 (0.25)	0.0 (0.93)	–0.2 (0.69)		
Sector of activity	–0.01 (0.73)	–0.01 (0.56)	–0.2 (0.10)	0.0 (0.94)	0.2 (0.27)		
Income	–0.05 (0.00)	–0.06 (0.00)	0.4 (0.00)	0.5 (0.00)	–0.1 (0.44)		
Education	–0.01 (0.70)	–0.05 (0.00)	0.4 (0.00)	0.4 (0.00)	0.0 (0.86)		
Possession of collateral	0.01 (0.93)	0.01 (0.71)	0.1 (0.59)	0.0 (0.87)	–0.2 (0.76)	–1.28 (0.05)	–0.81 (0.09)
Age						0.54 (0.01)	0.26 (0.10)
Position in the household			0.3 (0.21)	0.0 (0.99)	1.8 (0.01)		
Illegal area vs. legalized			0.1 (0.75)	0.0 (0.94)	0.7 (0.49)		
Type of house[c]							
Observations	450	1,037		942		203	

a. The definition of public banks included lottery shops with banking services and the definition of private banks included post offices with banking services.

b. Type of building refers to (i) house or apartment or (ii) shack or room.

c. Type of house refers to unique, improvised, or collective house.

Source: World Bank survey of access to financial services in urban areas in Brazil done in 2002.

Table 1.17 Econometric Results: The Probability of Using Public Banks for Real Estate Purchase

	Credit for real estate		
Dependent variable	*Public banks*	*Private banks*	*Government finance*
Econometric model		*Multinomial logit*	
Geographic region	0.0 (0.94)	0.3 (0.58)	0.00 (0.97)
Position in the household	0.1 (0.83)	1.2 (0.27)	–0.99 (0.30)
Sector of activity	0.28 (0.03)	0.43 (0.04)	0.42 (0.02)
Income	0.84 (0.01)	0.07 (0.76)	0.98 (0.00)
Observations		130	

Source: World Bank survey of access to financial services in urban areas in Brazil done in 2002.

are considerably reduced when correction is made for differentials in regional GDP and for geographic size.

- The survey of individual financial behavior supports the finding of the importance of location in determining access, but also demonstrates that location in terms of the microcharacteristics of an area or neighborhood can be as important a discriminator for access.
- The survey also strongly corroborates the findings of the supply-side analysis regarding the importance of income, at a per capita level, and points also to the significance of a range of socioeconomic characteristics, such as education and (for credit services) wealth, in determining financial access.
- Gender bias appears to be present in some measures (access to a financial institution and deposit services) but not in all measures (gender bias is not significant for credit).
- The importance of socioeconomic characteristics in access to financial services suggests that there may be problems of information, or of enforcement, which cause lenders to emphasize such information.
- Regarding the roles of public and private financial institutions, both the aggregated supply-side analysis and the survey of users indicate some association between lower-income groups and public banks.
- The user survey also shows, however, that the use of public banks varies by type of service. Thus, public banks are popular for payment services (because of the outlets of the Caixa Econômica Federal) for all socioeconomic groups, and also dominate the provision of housing credit, but largely for the better-off groups. For deposit-taking and for credit, both the privileged and less-privileged socioeconomic groups, broadly measured, have some preference for private banks, and with

increases in income, both increase their proportional use of private banks.

- Thus, in many areas, the user survey corroborates the findings of the supply analysis that, in many respects, public and private banks are broadly substitutable.

What are the implications of these findings, from the perspective of broad policy directions to adopt in addressing access-related issues? The preceding analysis suggests a number of thematic directions that could help to guide policy choices.

A central and consistent theme to emerge from this analysis is the importance of income-related factors in determining access. A basic deduction is that access will be increased by overall growth-oriented policies, because improved financial distribution and financial deepening are associated with growth. Although clearly important, this finding does not suggest immediate measures for policymakers to adopt in addressing issues of access. Of far greater significance as an implication for policymakers is the corollary to this finding: that if access is so significantly influenced by income, then targeted policies that particularly address lower-income groups are likely to be important in addressing access.

What does this imply in practice? That policies that address certain issues—such as (1) 'lifeline' or basic accounts, which provide a minimum package of banking services at very low cost; (2) affordability of minimum packages of financial services; (3) (possibly) special criteria related to documentation requirements for low-income persons; and (4) special financial products designed for low-income persons—could be important for increasing access.

Next in importance to income and individual characteristics associated with access is education. One suggestion to follow up on this finding is that programs of financial education and awareness may be important for low-income persons, even if overall educational policies, just as overall growth-raising policies, may lie outside the scope of the financial sector policymaker.

Equally important are the implications of the analysis with regard to the importance of location. The analysis suggests that although location is important, and there do seem to be some underserved regions and locations, much of the difference with regard to location can be attributed to levels of economic activity and sparseness of population. Thus, policies that rely largely on the geographic equalization of services are not likely to be adequately effective in targeting access. This is a significant comment in the context of Brazil, where major efforts to expand access have focused on ensuring that there is at least one financial point of service (branch, service post, or correspondent) in each municipality. Such policies cannot ensure that users of financial services in such locations are indeed the poorer segments; the better-off persons even in these neighborhoods are likely to have been more successful in achieving access.

Another important inference with regard to locational policies is that regions of the country or even municipalities are perhaps not the best points of focus for the expansion of access. Rather, location defined at a microlevel within neighborhoods, with service expansion targeted at areas or parts of a city with specific microeconomic characteristics (such as high concentrations of low-income housing), should be targeted.

Eventually, factors related to location, though initially significant in the analysis, lose significance once socioeconomic factors such as income and education are included in the analysis. In addition, other socioeconomic characteristics, such as employment-related variables, gender, and role in household are also shown to be significant in the determination of many measures of access. One implication of this is that these factors have assumed importance in the absence of sufficient direct information on the financial behavior and creditworthiness of individuals. Wealth and collateral are also important in determining access to credit, because these may help with loan recovery. This finding could also suggest that in the absence of adequate enforcement mechanisms for financial claims, the factors noted above could serve as indicators of financial reliability. The implications are, therefore, that policies that can directly expand client information would expand access, such as the sharing of 'positive' information in some forms of credit registries. Equally, procedures that streamline the use of guarantees, secured credit, bankruptcy, or recovery could also help to expand access.

When the type of financial institution was analyzed, given that there are some specialized services where either public or private banks seem to dominate (public banks for payments or housing, for example), a suggestion to emerge is that greater competition in these services would appear to be desirable—thus, for example, inviting in private services in housing or in payments, perhaps through an alteration in the present domination of housing finance by one large public institution, or through more competition in the allocation of correspondent franchises.

Finally, although the analysis does suggest that persons with lower levels of income tend to use public banks proportionately more, it also shows that along a broad spectrum of services, the roles of these institutions could be largely substitutable. Thus, for both public and private banks, deposit and credit services are available to lower-income individuals, but as persons become better-off, they tend to prefer private services for both types of transactions. This suggests that private banks could do more to refocus their products, image, and outreach services.

Annex 1.1
Financial Markets and Welfare-Enhancement: Microeconomic Aspects

Access to financial services should improve consumer welfare and producer productivity.[48] The traditional neoclassical approach to demonstrate the advantages of adding financial intermediation to the choices faced by economic agents has been to compare the 'reachable (feasible) utility sets' under two, highly simplified, hypothetical scenarios: one without financial markets and another in which agents can lend (save) and borrow (spend beyond their initial endowment). In the first case, agents are able only to transfer physical goods from one period to the next (for example, trading grain), and are not able to lend or borrow except also in physical goods (for example, seeds).

The addition of financial assets enables agents to reach two objectives: (i) make intertemporal transfers of income and consumption; and (ii) provide an objective reference to the cost of capital ('opportunity cost'), which permits benefits from allowing market-determined interest rates to optimally allocate resources over time. To the extent that these objectives are reached, agents maximize their utility reaching higher utility functions.

In figure A1.1.1 we present a simplified two-period model to illustrate the assertions (i) and (ii) made above. An agent earns income in the two periods, Y_1^a and Y_2^a, and derives utility U_a by consuming C_1^a and C_2^a in the same periods, respectively. In the absence of any form of transfers, the individual must choose $C_1^a = Y_1^a$ and $C_2^a = Y_2^a$ (and hence operate at point "a") to maximize utility. If, however, the person is permitted to save (but not borrow) from income in period 1 for additional budget in period 2, the budget constraint for the individual would become the curve "ae." The concavity of the curve reflects the diminishing marginal utility of greater amounts of income transfer (reflecting the shape of a standard production possibility frontier). The same economic agent now has the option of choosing an optimal point "b" (tangency between the indifference curve and the budget constraint) that allows the person a utility level $U_b > U_a$ by selecting consumption levels of C_1^b and C_2^b in periods 1 and 2, respectively. This new optimal choice between income flows and consumption flows implies a saving of $Y_1^a - C_1^b$ in the first period that results in the financing of an additional consumption of $C_2^b - Y_2^a$ in the second period.

In figure A1.1.2, there is a new scenario where financial instruments that allow savings (though no borrowings) are available. In such a case, the new budget constraint will be governed by the market rate of interest on savings. The new budget constraint, the straight line "aN," allows the individual to optimize cumulative utility at point "c" where $U_c > U_b > U_a$

Figure A1.1.1

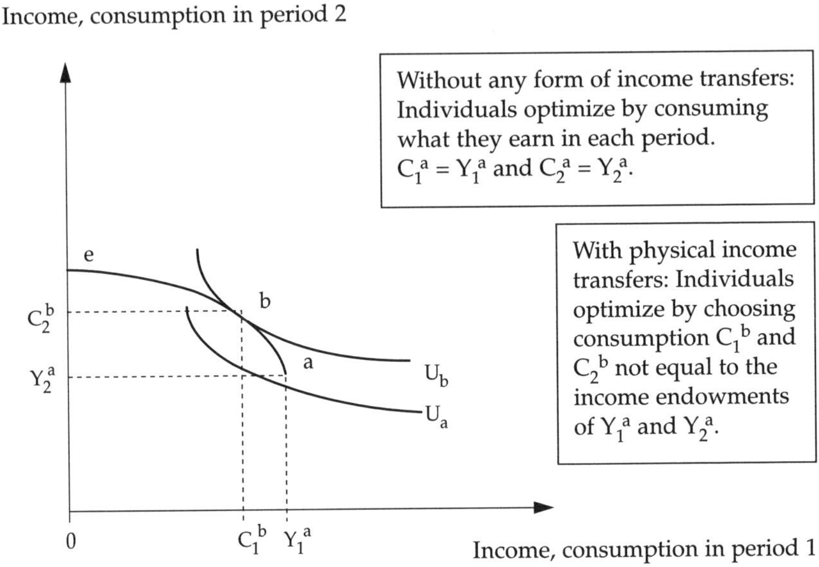

Figure A1.1.2

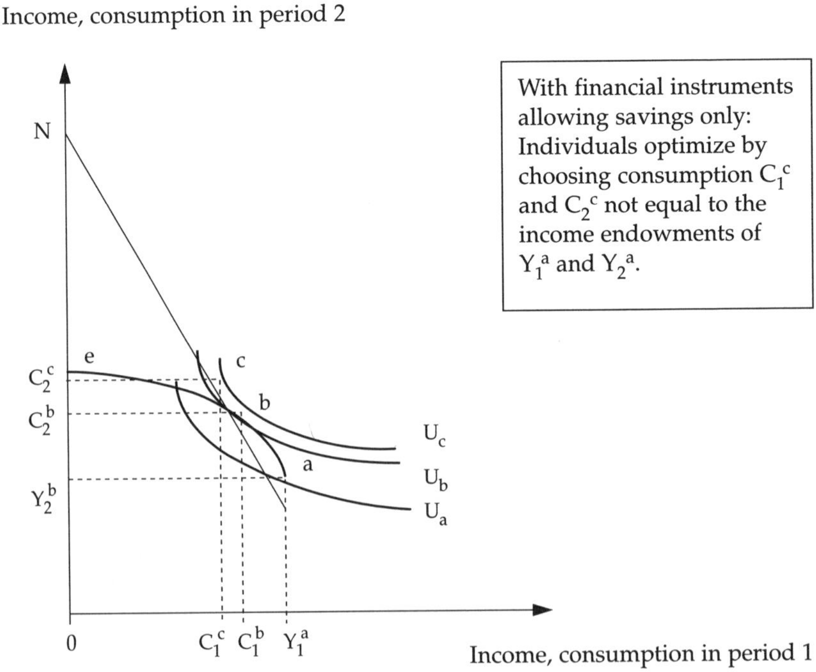

by saving $Y_1^a - C_1^c$ in the first period, resulting in an additional consumption of $C_2^c - Y_2^a$ in the second period.

In addition to the possibility of higher utility to the consumer, the matching of the individual's marginal rate of substitution (the slope of the indifference curve at "c") to the market rate of return (the slope of "aN") provides an objective reference to the cost of capital, the 'opportunity cost.' It is thereby a more efficient outcome than achieving U_a at point "a."

Next, expanding the provisions of financial markets, if financial instruments allow both savings as well as borrowings, the budget constraint in figure A1.1.2 would be extended to "MN" in figure A1.1.3 below.

The implication of being able to borrow as well as save in both periods further expands the range of feasible options. For individuals with marked preference for saving in period 1 (as shown in the shape of indifference curves above) and choosing an optimal point in the range "aN," this additional opportunity may not alter their decisions. But for individuals who prefer an optimal point in the range "aM," the potential to borrow in period 1 offers scope to both maximize utility and achieve optimal allocation between periods based on opportunity cost consideration.

Figure A1.1.3

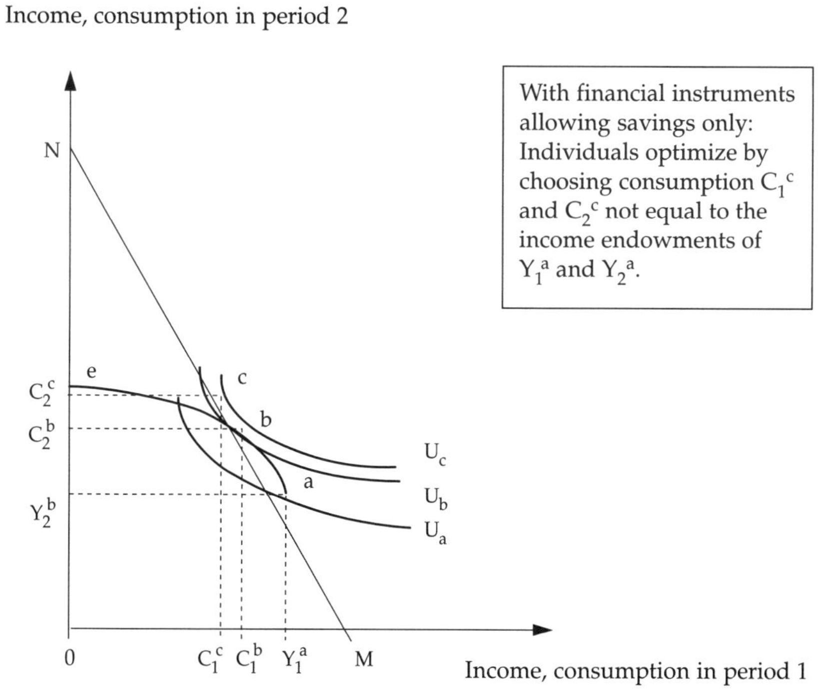

Aggregating this analysis for the entire market, the rate of interest in a competitive financial market can be expected to the equilibrating level that balances the net savers with the net borrowers in period 1, and hence make the mechanism stable and self-sustaining.

The financial instruments thus achieve the multiple objectives of (1) enabling intertemporal asset transfers (2) in a manner that is economically efficient for the individuals and hence the collective society (3) and is robust.

Annex 1.2
Technical Note on Estimation: Urban Financial Survey

This technical note describes the statistical tests used to choose the independent variables of the models and then describes the formulation of the functional forms of models that were subsequently used in the analysis. The econometric models used to determine the measures of access are also described below.

Chi-Square Tests of Independence

The chi-square 'goodness-of-fit' test evaluates the hypothesis that the rows and columns in a two-way table are mutually statistically independent. With dichotomous variables, the chi-square test is similar to the z-test that tests the equality of proportions (or the frequency of incidence) between two variables using large-sample statistics. But unlike the z-test, the chi-square test is not restricted to comparisons of only two sample proportions. For variables with multiple categories, the chi-square test is the most common technique to evaluate the degree of dependence between rows and columns of the categorized data.

Under the null hypothesis that the distribution of observations in the rows and columns is mutually independent (in other words, follows a specified distribution), the chi-square statistic computed indicates the degree to which the distribution variables between the rows and columns differ significantly from the specified norm.

The chi-square statistic for data with (I–1) (J–1) degrees of freedom is computed as:

$$x^2 = \sum_i \sum_j \frac{\left(n_{ij} - m_{ij}\right)^2}{m_{ij}}$$

where n_{ij} = number of observations in i^{th} row and j^{th} column. In our case, n_{ij} is just a count of frequency such that

$$n_{i\bullet} = \sum_{j=1}^{J} n_{ij} \text{ and } n_{\bullet j} = \sum_{i-i}^{I} n_{ij}, \text{ i = 1,..., I and j = 1,...,J}$$

$$n = \sum_{i}\sum_{j} n_{ij} \text{ (overall sum)}$$

$$m_{ij} = \frac{n_{i\bullet}n_{j}}{n}$$

Prior to the regression analysis, chi-square tests were conducted to confirm that the distribution pattern of the dependent variable was different from those that were to be used as the explanatory variables. For example, we checked whether the probability of a woman having a bank account was equal to the probability of a man having a bank account. Only in the cases where the null hypothesis could be rejected were the associated independent variables deemed to be good control or explanatory factors for inclusion in the regression analysis.

Econometric Models

Qualitative response models were estimated using models for binary response and for multinomial choices. Models of binary responses were designed to take the value 0 for persons who did not fulfill the given criterion (such as having access to financial institutions) and a value of 1 for persons who did satisfy the specified criterion. Such variables were associated with additional information that captured personal characteristics, employment information, and location information. Models of multinomial responses associated multivariate variables that followed a logical sequence of progression—such as don't save money, have money in a savings account, have money in a time deposit account—to some independent variables. The second sets of models were thus an expansion of the first set.

In the binary model, we attempted to estimate $E[I/X]$ where X is the vector of independent variables that have some relation with I, and E is the expectation operator. Assuming that vector I follows a Bernoulli distribution, we used the result:

$$E\,[I \mid X] = Pr\,(I = 1 \mid X) = F\,(X : \beta)$$

where *F(.)* denotes the cumulative distribution function of *I* conditional on the values of *X*, and β is an array of parameters that determines this function. In this analysis, we assumed that *X* comprised independent and identically distributed variables and that *F(.)* was linear in its arguments, resulting in the model:

$$F\ (X : \beta) = x'\ \beta + \varepsilon\ .$$

We also assumed that ξ was independent of *X*. This allowed us to use a logit model for regression where the *F(.)* represented a cumulative distribution function of a logistic nature such that:

$$\text{(A1.2.1)} \qquad P\ (I = 1 \mid X) = F\ (X'\ \beta) = \frac{e^{X'\beta}}{1 + e^{X'\beta}}\ .$$

Equation A1.2.1 could be transformed into

$$Log[P(I = 1 \mid X)/(1 - P\ (I = 1 \mid X)] = X'\beta$$

or simply

$$\text{(A1.2.2)} \qquad h(I) = X'\beta\ .$$

Equation A1.2.2 could then be estimated by maximum likelihood estimation techniques. Unlike conventional linear regression models, the coefficients of the regressions cannot be interpreted as the partial derivatives of the dependent variable with respect to the respective explanatory. The partial effects were computed by…

(a) Estimating the probability of access to financial services of an individual with value *J* for a characteristic *k*, which is

$$\hat{P}_i^{\,J}\ (I = 1 \mid X) = \frac{1}{1 + e^{-\sum\limits_{l \neq k} \beta_l X_{il} - \beta_k J}}$$

(b) Estimating the average probability for every J. The difference between the averages calculated for *J* and *J*+1 represented the marginal effect of increasing the value of the explanatory variable *k* of *J* to *J*+1.

Given the limitations of the statistical software used for the analysis, which does not calculate the marginal effects of logit regressions automatically, the marginal effects from probit estimation were used as an approximation of the same results. The probit model is similar to the logit model, with $F(x\beta) = \phi(x\beta)$, where Φ is the standard cumulative normal distribution.

For analysis of multinomial models, multinomial logit estimation is the most widely used technique. In a choice set B = {1,...,m}, where x_B = $(x_1,...x_m)$ denotes the array of observed attributes of the available alternatives, vector $y_B = (y_1,...,y_m)$ has a multivariate probability distribution:

$$f^i(x_B, \theta) = \frac{e^{x\beta^i}}{\sum_{j \notin B} e^{x\beta^j}}$$

with mean $\beta' x_B$ like in the binomial case.

Using maximum likelihood estimation techniques, the sequential series of outcomes in y could be estimated in terms of the explanatory variables X. These results could then be used to estimate the coefficients corresponding to each outcome category such as:

$$\Pr(y = 1) = \frac{e^{x\beta^1}}{e^{x\beta^1} + e^{x\beta^2} + e^{x\beta^3}}$$

$$\Pr(y = 2) = \frac{e^{x\beta^2}}{e^{x\beta^1} + e^{x\beta^2} + e^{x\beta^3}}$$

$$\Pr(y = 3) = \frac{e^{x\beta^3}}{e^{x\beta^1} + e^{x\beta^2} + e^{x\beta^3}}$$

The limitation of this technique is that the estimated solutions for coefficients $(\beta^1, \beta^2, \beta^3)$ need not be unique. Hence by arbitrarily setting one of the β's at the benchmark value of 0, the other coefficients can then be interpreted to measure the change relative to the control group.

In this study, both types of models and estimation—binomial respondents models, logit and probit, and multinomial response models, logit multinomial—were used. Also used were linear models to predict the volume of credit requested by individuals and the volume of credit approved in each request. The logarithm of the amount of money request (or approved) for loans was regressed on identifiable personal characteristics such as age, education level, income, and so forth. The relation estimated was of the type:

$$E[\ln(Y) \mid X] = g(X),$$

where

$$g(X) = \beta_0 + X_1\beta_1 + \ldots + X_k\beta_k + \varepsilon$$

and Y represented the volume of credit requested (approved) and X the characteristics variables.

2
Expanding Microfinance

Microcredit, Access, and Poverty: A New Paradigm?

As discussed in chapter 1, appropriate targeting of policies is needed to strengthen financial access for those groups, especially among the poor, where services are most needed. Largely in the past two decades, excitement has grown worldwide in terms of a new institutional form of delivery of financial services to such communities: the *microfinance revolution*.[1] Loans are made available, in very small amounts, often under a new paradigm: unsubsidized lending at market rates, typically with low levels of formality and limited requirements of collateral, often to particularly vulnerable groups, such as village women. Repayment is undertaken frequently, and rates of repayment in many microfinance ventures are cited to be high. Many microfinance ventures also offer deposit-taking services.

Although many notions of microfinance exist, the small size of transactions involved and delivery through channels other than formal banks are core themes. In addition, *microfinance* has sometimes been defined as the delivery of such services by financial institutions, which are themselves small in size and informal in nature. Today, *microfinance institutions* (MFIs) are reaching out to more than 9 million borrowers and 29 million savers worldwide, in over 53 countries.[2] Microfinance is being considered as a preferred vehicle for extending access to the poorest in many countries.

The importance of microcredit for the self-employed and for small entrepreneurs, and thus for jobs, is also increasingly recognized. Microentrepreneurs of Brazil account for the vast majority of all firms and contribute substantially to employment and gross domestic product (GDP). According to recent estimates, 98 percent of Brazil's 4.1 million micro- and small enterprises account for 45 percent of formal employment and more than 60 percent of urban jobs. Directly or indirectly, they provide the primary source of income to almost 60 million people and generate nearly 20 percent of GDP (www.sebrae.com.br). Firms with up to four employees account for 57 percent of all firms in industry, for 74 percent in services, and for 82 percent in commerce.[3]

In addition, there are an estimated 14 million informal micro- and small-scale enterprises in Brazil.[4] Although the majority of such firms are located in the South and Southeast of Brazil, the impoverished North and Northeast have a higher share of *new* microenterprises. Beyond microenterprises, the need for loans for self-employment by the poorest populations is also widely acknowledged. Such ventures need working capital to survive and investment funds to grow.

Related to the theme of provision of small loans, a second group of financial institutions catering to these needs is the community of *credit cooperatives*. Considerably older than microfinance, the concept of the credit cooperative dates from the 19th century, involving people with a similar trade, employment, or location to pool resources in a democratic economic organization with the objective of serving the common interests of the group. Credit cooperatives were first formed a century ago in the southern states of Brazil. Credit unions, which have grown out from the cooperative system, are a mature alternative to banks in many developing countries worldwide today.[5] As in the case of microfinance, a key characteristic is the small size of transactions handled. Both deposit and loan services are offered, as loans are extended based on the funds accumulated from members, in most cases.

Both microfinance institutions and credit cooperatives have grown in Brazil over the past decade. Although the growth of the microfinance sector has been more rapid, the cooperative sector still dwarfs the microfinance sector in size. The number of credit cooperatives increased from around 950 in 1994 to some 1,400 by end-2002, while their assets grew in parallel from around R$2.5 billion to R$11.5 billion, and loans grew from R$1.4 billion to R$4.6 billion. Members of the credit co-ops could be broadly estimated at around 1.5 million persons.[6]

Many microfinance institutions are largely beyond the purview of formal financial system supervision, but estimates suggest that the total number of clients served increased from around 3,000 in 1995 to around 160,000 by end-2001, while the active loan portfolio grew to some R$140 million. This is small compared to the credit cooperative system and also compared to other countries in the region, once adjusted for country size. Peru and Bolivia had estimated microfinance clienteles of around 185,000 and 380,000 at end-2001, respectively, while small countries such as Nicaragua and El Salvador also had more than 80,000 microfinance clients.[7]

There have been significant recent efforts to detail and analyze Brazil's microfinance sector in the past five years. The contribution of the present chapter lies in identifying and analyzing factors leading to the increase of both the microfinance and the credit cooperative sectors in Brazil and evaluating their future sustainability and potential for contributing to increased access. Alternative models under which there could be an increased potential for expanded access, and preconditions for such models, are evaluated in terms of options for policymakers and for the institutions themselves.[8] The present analysis is based largely on the period ending in 2002. New measures taken by the government in 2003 are briefly described; however, the outcome of such measures has yet to be assessed in detail.

Key observations to emerge from the following sections for Brazil's microfinance sector are as follows:

- There was a remarkable recent acceleration in Brazil's microfinance sector from the end of the 1990s, due to a series of factors: new political paradigms leading to a series of legal and regulatory changes favoring the expansion of microfinance; a major new large-scale microcredit experiment—the CrediAmigo program—which incorporates many principles of good microfinance practice; and active government financial backing to emerging microfinance institutions through credit offered by the Banco Nacional de Desenvolvimento Econômico e Social (National Bank for Economic and Social Development; BNDES).
- Despite this rapid acceleration, microfinance penetration in Brazil today remains low, especially compared to neighboring countries. Yet paradoxically, the portfolio growth of small microfinance institutions is not high.
- Microfinance expansion remains government led, through the substantial presence of the public banks Banco do Nordeste do Brasil (Northeast Bank; BNB) and BNDES. Microfinance institutions have also relied substantially on relatively low-cost government lines of credit extended at below-comparable-market rates. Recent changes introduced by the government include microfinance operations destined for low-income earners and small businesses, to be funded by a minimum 2 percent of the financial institution's sight deposits. The new measures create the possibility of additional reserve requirements for banks that do not participate in certain programs of access. Although such additional reserve requirements would be small, as implemented in tandem with other programs of directed credit, they would add to the already high implicit tax burden of banks and could work against the desired broader development of the microfinance sector.
- Conversion to the new institutional forms, although increasing access to wholesale funding, is rendered less attractive by the implications of new regulatory requirements, both nonprudential reporting as well as prudential requirements. There are also tax implications that would subject the new institutions to the full range of financial sector taxation.
- Growth indicators for the portfolios of microfinance institutions supported by BNDES suggest nominal annual growth of 22 percent a year; much lower for larger microfinance institutions. The slow growth of Brazil's independent microfinance institutions (other than CrediAmigo), despite apparent large unmet demand, is paradoxical. Some

factors responsible could include the difficulties encountered by independent microfinance institutions in expanding client outreach without a branch network or savings product to offer to support their efforts. Partnerships with large banks can help build a client culture; provide a branch network; and also reduce competition from similar products offered by the banks, such as consumer loans.

- In terms of performance, indicators of loans overdue are average (possibly with some trend increase for BNDES-supported microfinance institutions), and loan provisioning may be somewhat low. But financial sustainability has been good, perhaps due to low-cost funding. Efficiency indicators in terms of loans per loan officer, although low, have been rising. Impact indicators in terms of loan size suggest that outreach is reaching small client segments.
- Some so-called microfinance institutions in Brazil, run mainly by municipal governments to achieve social objectives such as employment, provide highly subsidized credit for this purpose. Such price-distorting subsidies could affect the expansion of market-oriented microfinance. Other transfer mechanisms (for example, lump-sum transfers) could be investigated instead, and a clearer distinction could be drawn between these activities and microfinance. Such distinctions between income transfers and the market-based extension of credit may need to be made more extensively in the context of the new microfinance measures of 2003.
- Brazil's formal microfinance institutions, known as its microfinance credit societies (Sociedades de Crédito ao Microempreendedor; SCMs), are subject to regulatory and reporting requirements that may be more rigorous than comparable models, in view of their non-deposit-taking scope of activities. However, should Brazil contemplate the introduction of savings products or deposit-taking facilities, further regulatory fine tuning may be needed.

Suggestions for the future expansion of the microfinance institution sector, based on these findings, follow below:

- An impact evaluation of the new microfinance measures should be undertaken to assess their performance in terms of outreach and sustainability, as well as their impact on participating microfinance institutions and banks.
- Brazil's microfinance institutions could make more extensive use of recognized best practice methods for microfinance; although extensively used at CrediAmigo, small microfinance institutions do not appear to have followed these principles.

- Both to attract more wholesale bank funding and to better incorporate good microfinance practice in its microfinance institutions, Brazil could consider more emphasis on organizational forms that allow partnerships with large banks, which could help with training loan officers, tracking quality indicators, and incorporating good practice. In this context, BNDES could consider a more indirect support to microfinance institutions than its present model, through the provision of wholesale credit to commercial banks, which then form liaisons with self-help groups either directly or through nongovernmental organizations (NGOs). Recent moves to establish microfinance operations in commercial banks, such as Banco Popular, are a step in this direction. In addition to Banco Popular, new programs are also being introduced by public banks such as Caixa and BNB. Care should be taken to ensure that such operations are undertaken on a sound basis.
- In the future, if sufficient maturity and sustainability are achieved, Brazil's microfinance sector could also contemplate deposit-taking, not only to expand its funding base if large-scale rollout is to be contemplated but also to offer needed savings products and expand client interface. Brazil does not allow any form of deposit-taking for its microfinance institutions, and wholesale funding from the banking system has been limited. However, at present, the microfinance institution sector may not be adequately prepared for such a major step, which would also require regulatory reform.
- Microfinance in Brazil may need a separate regulatory window, but the reasons for the current multiple regulatory windows of NGOs, Organização da Sociedade Civil de Interesse Público (Public Interest Civil Societies; OSCIPs), and SCMs may be driven partially by the need to counter other regulations that need overhaul, such as the Usury Law. In the future, a simplification of this framework may be desirable. Harmonizing (and perhaps eventually integrating) the framework for regulated microfinance institutions with the banking system may also be considered.
- Within current regulatory norms, SCMs have very low entry capital requirements, both relative to other countries and to Brazil's own banking system. This could pose a problem for supervision if numbers of SCMs expand significantly. If separate regulatory windows are maintained, models of shared, delegated, or independent supervision could be considered.
- Conversely, leverage ratios, at five times net worth, although not strictly comparable, appear much higher than bank capital adequacy ratios, at 11 percent of risk-weighted assets, and higher than in many other countries, which frequently use the same capital adequacy ratios

as for banks. Especially in view of the present non-deposit-taking nature of Brazil's microfinance institutions, this could be reviewed.

With regard to credit cooperatives, principal findings and suggestions to emerge are as follows:

- The Brazilian credit cooperative system has made important advances, particularly since the mid-1990s, with the permission to establish cooperative banks. These have allowed for rapid expansion of credit cooperatives, combined with growing professionalism in cooperative management, information, accounting, staff training and incentives, and internally administered prudential standards. New measures introduced in 2003 have further favored the expansion of cooperatives, expanding membership in remote areas by allowing 'open-admission' credit cooperatives to be established, and by creating a more level playing field with banks through the harmonization of capital requirements.
- Permission to establish central credit cooperatives has existed since 1971.[9] Incentives to individual cooperatives to federate are high as leverage ratios for federated cooperatives are set at twice the levels of individual cooperatives. This may mitigate the extremely low start-up capital requirements, which are even lower than for microfinance institutions. This may provide a safe way to encourage cooperatives to combine the benefits of local knowledge in mitigating moral hazard and adverse selection problems with the advantages of risk reduction and diversification through networking.
- In turn, federated or central cooperative members benefit through an expanded range of financial services (for example, internet banking, credit cards, Cédula de Produto Rural [bills of rural products; CPRs], insurance, and custodial services) in addition to more accessible loan and savings products, and in most cases, they have been able to count on more reliable prudential oversight of the resources they have invested in cooperatives.
- Nevertheless, the legal and regulatory impediments of earlier decades (notably in the 1960s and 1970s) resulted in a system that still lags behind that in other countries. Penetration ratios remain extremely low by international comparisons. One constraint on expansion has been the high liquidity requirement, required by apex cooperatives, considerably higher than prudential norms advocated by international standards. However, new legislation introduced in July 2003 has harmonized capital requirements for credit cooperatives and banks.
- Other prudential regulations recently introduced could improve the soundness of the sector but will raise supervision resource requirements, notably the expansion to open forms of organization in remote

regions. Nonprudential disclosure-based advances on the regulatory side comprise the inclusion of cooperative clients, with loans above R$5,000 in the Central Bank's credit information system (Central de Risco), and reviews of cooperatives' boards of directors.

- Cooperatives, especially rural cooperatives, have also served to channel directed credit to the rural sector, often at below-market rates, sometimes at unattractive spreads and with regulatory dispensations in terms of leverage ratios. Although the dispensations in terms of higher leverage ended in 2003, there is still the risk that the cooperative sector could be viewed as key to the implementation of government credit programs.

In this light, this study proposes the following recommendations for consideration by Brazilian policymakers and practitioners:

- Provide incentives for the establishment of a liquidity facility for credit cooperatives to reduce opportunity costs relative to commercial banks backed by the Fundo Garantidor de Créditos (Deposit Insurance Fund; FGC). One option to be studied would be to encourage the establishment of a privately managed central liquidity facility for credit cooperatives, run by representatives of cooperatives under Central Bank supervision, and standards for liquidity support, capitalized via a percentage of deposits. In turn, liquidity requirements on sight and time deposits could be eased as the degree of capitalization of the facility increases. After evaluating performance, consideration could be given to public backing for the facility.
- Apply similar financial regulation for credit cooperatives as for other financial institutions. As financial institutions, they should be under the same standards of regulation applied to other financial institutions to promote competition and reduce perceived higher risk associated with the lack of access to a liquidity facility and deposit insurance. However, some special features that would differentiate their regulatory framework need to be taken into consideration.
- Review norms, regulations, and incentives governing public rural credit programs channeled through credit cooperatives. Policies such as those that doubled the leverage permitted in the event of financing using public rural credit programs such as Programa Nacional de Fortalecimento da Agricultura Familiar (National Program to Strengthen Family Agriculture; PRONAF), which undermined the cooperative spirit and the sustainability of cooperatives. These regulations ran counter to what is in general a prudent regulatory framework, and the lifting of this facility with new regulations introduced in June 2003 was a welcome move.

- In addition, consideration should be given to reviewing the extent to which the relative market positions of Banco do Brasil versus smaller rural credit cooperatives explains their relative shares of the spread on PRONAF loans and what measures can be taken to better relate spread to credit risk and administrative expenditures on such public transfers. This undermines members' sense of ownership and reduces incentives to repay.
- Review present capital standards, which are much lower than for microfinance institutions (SCMs) and also compare them to microfinance institutions in other countries. Although these facilitate broad access to cooperative financial services, they also can imply a proliferation of small formal financial institutions, with high costs to the supervisory entity, particularly in a country the size of Brazil.
- Maintain a prudent balance between direct and delegated oversight of credit cooperatives. The present system of delegation appears to be beneficial, although if the sector grows further, formalized delegation may be needed, and a choice of appropriate framework for this will need to be selected.

Finally, for both the microfinance and credit cooperative sectors, it is suggested that

- Several technological innovations are available that can greatly enhance productivity and delivery capacity and reduce risk in microfinance transactions. An exploration of these for adaptations in the Brazilian context is suggested.
- The collection and maintenance of further information on a regular basis should be strengthened. Easing the present shortage of reliable, consolidated data on these sectors would be a first step to strengthening oversight. More detailed information could usefully be obtained for both supervisory and market development purposes on the performance of microfinance institutions and credit cooperatives and determinants of such performance (for example, data on administrative cost structures in different geographic contexts, risk profiles of clients by location and type of enterprises).

Microfinance in Brazil: Evolution and Status[10]

Despite rapid growth in the microfinance sector in neighboring countries such as Bolivia and Peru in the 1980s and 1990s, Brazil's microfinance sector remained dormant through most of this period, for a combination of reasons. First, a strong belief was held that the public sector was key in terms of ensuring financial access by the poor, and a series of specially

Microfinance: New Measures Introduced in 2003

Recent Changes: Microfinance Regulations
Law No. 10735 of September 11, 2003 (formerly Provisional Measure No. 122 of June 25, 2003), and CMN Resolutions 3109 and 3128 of July 24, 2003, and October 30, 2003, respectively, create new vehicles for making microcredit available to low-income earners and small businesses. These have been created in parallel with measures designed to ease conditions for establishing bank accounts and setting up new basic bank accounts, discussed further in chapter 3 of this study.

Under the new regulations, microcredit operations will be funded by a minimum of 2 percent of banks' sight deposits, or alternatively, such deposits will be held as unremunerated reserves. Interest rates of credits based on such funds will be capped at 2 percent per month. Loans will be limited to R$600 for individuals and R$1,000 for small business owners. Loan terms will be no less than 120 days (terms can be smaller as long as rates are adjusted accordingly). Loan originating fees must be less than 2 percent for individuals and 4 percent for small businesses. Individuals and enterprises with simplified accounts (with maximum deposits of R$1,000 for individuals and R$10,000 for enterprises) and low-income individuals will be eligible for such loans, which can be extended directly by the banks or onlent through microfinance institutions.

Recent Changes: Credit Cooperative Regulations
CMN Resolution 3106 of June 25, 2003, eases membership criteria for credit cooperatives, hitherto open only to members of the same activity or profession, by allowing new credit cooperatives to form as 'open-admission' credit cooperatives in municipalities with up to 100,000 inhabitants. Existing credit cooperatives, operating for more than three years, can transform into open-admission credit cooperatives, but only in municipalities (or contiguous municipalities) with up to 750,000 inhabitants. Minimum capital requirements for the transformation are R$6 million for entities located in municipalities in metropolitan regions with more than 100,000 inhabitants and R$3 million for the rest. In the North and Northeast, this requirement is reduced by 50 percent. The aim is clearly to expand the provision of financial services in thinly populated areas, where formal financial institutions may be reluctant to venture.

The same resolution removed the additional leverage permitted to credit cooperatives for extending financing under public rural credit programs such as PRONAF. An additional regulation (Central Bank Circular 3196 of July 17, 2003) harmonized capital requirements for credit cooperatives and banks. It specified new capital adequacy rules for credit cooperatives of 11 percent for cooperatives affiliated to a 'central' cooperative (which is the same ratio as in banks) and 15 percent for cooperatives not affiliated with a central cooperative.

designed programs proliferated, particularly for rural access. The proportion of credit that was 'directed' toward specific sectors was estimated to be as high as 54 percent as recently as mid-2000 and was still as high as 40 percent in March 2003. Second, the regulatory environment for microfinance was limiting. As a result, microfinance was mostly offered through nongovernmental organizations, which relied largely on access to donor funds for onlending; thus, Brazil's microfinance sector was largely driven by philanthropic partnerships with foreign donor organizations. Interest rate caps based on the Usury Law violated the principles of microfinance lending. Third, there was little 'demonstration effect,' in terms of successful large scale in country programs of microfinance. Experience with microfinance was largely anecdotal and limited. The acceleration in microfinance in Brazil in recent years can be attributed to a change in these circumstances, as discussed in the following sections.

Evolution of the Political Debate and the Legal Framework

Parallel to the accelerating international dialogue on the role and contributions of microfinance, as witnessed in the international Microcredit Summit of early 1997, internal debate began in Brazil on the potential contribution of microcredit through the Comunidade Solidária, a public body created in 1995 to strengthen civil society initiatives in Brazil. The Communidade Solidária adopted microcredit as its principal theme of political debate in 1997–98 and resumed this theme in 2001. Largely through the efforts of working groups organized in this context, several legal impediments to the expansion of microcredit were identified. Based on the recommendations of these groups, dramatic improvements in the legal framework for microenterprises have been introduced over the past five years.

New forms of microcredit institutions, excluded from the scope of the Usury Law, were established by regulation.[11] Prior to the changes, microfinance was undertaken largely by nonprofit organizations, and these were constrained by the 1 percent per month ceiling on interest rates imposed by Brazil's Usury Law, which has been meaningless in Brazil's high-inflation periods, and is also limiting in the case of microfinance loans, which traditionally are offered for short periods of weeks or months at higher interest rates than loans in the formal and large-scale sectors. NGOs were also constrained in terms of access to capital—to grants or credit lines from government or foreign donors. Two new legal entities were created in 1999, with considerably more flexibility in terms of both funding and lending and outside the purview of the Usury Law.[12] These were the OSCIPs and the SCMs.[13]

OSCIPs can have a range of objectives, which are not limited to microfinance. OSCIPs exist in many fields such as science, education, and research. Like NGOs, they are deemed to be not-for-profit organizations. Importantly, OSCIPs can sign cooperation agreements with the public sector to implement activities and projects of public interest, which implies that they could have access to public sector funds, in addition to donor funds and owner or sponsor funds. OSCIPs are not able to mobilize deposits from the public. OSCIPs are subject to a low level of nonprudential regulatory requirements, such as some reporting requirements to the Ministry of Justice, but are not required to comply with any prudential regulations.

The second form created, the SCMs, is much closer to a microcredit society, as they exist in many other countries.[14] SCMs are formal for-profit financial entities regulated by the Central Bank of Brazil. SCMs can take loans or lines of credit from foreign or domestic financial institutions, due to regulations issued in July 2001, in which their access to funding was further widened, together with permission to use instruments such as fiduciary alienation for extending credit.[15] However, issuing debt or mobilizing deposits remains restricted. Subsequent regulations issued in July 2001 maintained various prudential norms, including operational limits on capital, leverage, and risk. SCMs are required to comply with minimum start-up capital, ongoing capital adequacy, and limits on risk concentration. The regulations issued in July 2001 also permit SCMs, like banks, to operate through microcredit service points (Posto de Atendimento de Microcrédito) and require them to submit information on their lending operations to the Central Bank's credit risk center—the Central de Risco de Crédito—which in principle could permit them in the future to obtain greatly enhanced credit information on prospective clients (CMN Resolution 2874 of July 26, 2001).

These new institutional forms are clearly a major step forward for microcredit in Brazil. Some existing NGOs, which are microfinance institutions in practice, are considering modifying their legal framework to benefit from the ability to tap external sources of finance, including in some cases splitting up existing organizations into two entities, an NGO rendering nonfinancial services (training and consulting) and an SCM for all financial operations. Ownership of an SCM by an OSCIP is also permitted. SCMs have grown rapidly in numbers, from around 6 in October 2001 to 36 by October 2002 (with 25 functioning and 11 in a start-up phase).

However, this arrangement, with multiple regulatory windows for different forms of microcredit institutions, is complex. Arguably some of these forms have been established to circumvent obstacles elsewhere in the regulatory environment (for example, restraints on interest rates). In

Key Legal Characteristics of OSCIPs and SCMs

OSCIPs

- OSCIPs are nonprofit organizations whose social objectives must fall within a specified list.
- They are exempt from Usury Law restrictions.
- They are subject to reporting requirements (including audited accounts of activities carried out under a cooperation agreement with a public entity) to the Ministry of Justice.
- Sources of financing are limited to donor funding, owners' investments, and government funding (including lines of credits from the Brazilian state-owned development bank, BNDES).
- OSCIPs can own an SCM as a subsidiary.

SCMs

- SCMs are for-profit financial institutions deemed to be a part of the national financial system.
- They are exempt from Usury Law restrictions.
- They are subject to the tax regime for financial institutions, including income tax and Contribuição Provisória sobre Movimentação Financeira (Financial Transactions Tax; CPMF).
- As financial institutions, they are subject to reporting (nonaudited accounts) and regulatory requirements of the Central Bank of Brazil, which supervises them.
- They are subject to minimum capital requirements (R$100,000), liquidity requirements, and restrictions on leverage (five times liquid assets).
- Sources of financing include all those allowed to OSCIPS, plus loan or credit lines from national and foreign financial institutions and from OSCIPs.
- They can extend loans and guarantees to individuals and microenterprises, up to R$10,000 per client, for professional, commercial, or industrial use only; they are prohibited from extending consumer loans.
- They can operate microcredit servicing points, with full flexibility in terms of location, opening hours, and so forth and no additional capital requirement.
- They cannot collect deposits from the public, participate in the interbank deposit market, or issue securities for public offering.

the future, the need for a range of different regulatory windows for microfinance can be investigated, and possibilities for simplifying the present framework can be explored (see below).

SCMs have pointed to their heavy tax burden, in common with other regulated financial institutions. This is a deterrent to NGOs or OSCIPs considering converting to an SCM to expand funding sources. Documentary and reporting requirements have also been considered burdensome, although the reporting of credit operations to the Central de Risco could in future be beneficial to SCMs in terms of enhanced client screening.[16] Third, an extension of the product range of SCMs to include individual or consumer credit is also debated. Most controversial, in terms of further measures to aid SCMs, is the question of whether they should be allowed to mobilize deposits and offer savings products. This issue, and experience in this regard in other countries, is discussed further below.

Establishment of CrediAmigo: A Major Player in Microfinance

In 1997, enthused by its new management and by the new attention to microfinance in political spheres within Brazil, Banco do Nordeste do Brasil, a state-owned development bank with a mandate to promote economic development in the Northeastern states, launched a large-scale microfinance program, which has remained unrivaled in scale in Brazil and constitutes a significant part of its microfinance expansion of the past decade. At end-2001, it served nearly 60 percent of microfinance institution client microentrepreneurs and held about 45 percent of their outstanding loans (figure 2.1).

The program, known as CrediAmigo, benefited from the technical advice of Acción International (a group with strong experience in solidarity group lending) as well as from the CGAP (Consultative Group to Assist the Poorest) and was financially supported by the World Bank (Schonberger and Christen 2001). CrediAmigo was committed to incorporate best practice principles emerging from successful microfinance institutions in the world (see below for further discussion). These included

- Solidarity group lending
- Targeting the informal sector
- Charging interest rates high enough to provide a return on assets sufficient to permit financial sustainability
- Starting with small loan amounts and gradually escalating loan size with repeat loans
- Amortizing loans regularly
- Offering incentives for regular repayment through discounts on the last installment
- Penalizing borrowers if repayment falls behind schedule.

The program also adopted the principles of product differentiation (discussed in greater detail in chapter 3), separating its identity from BNB through a separate entrance or premises for each branch office. Unlike

Figure 2.1 Growth of Loan Portfolio and Client Base of Main Microfinance Providers in Brazil

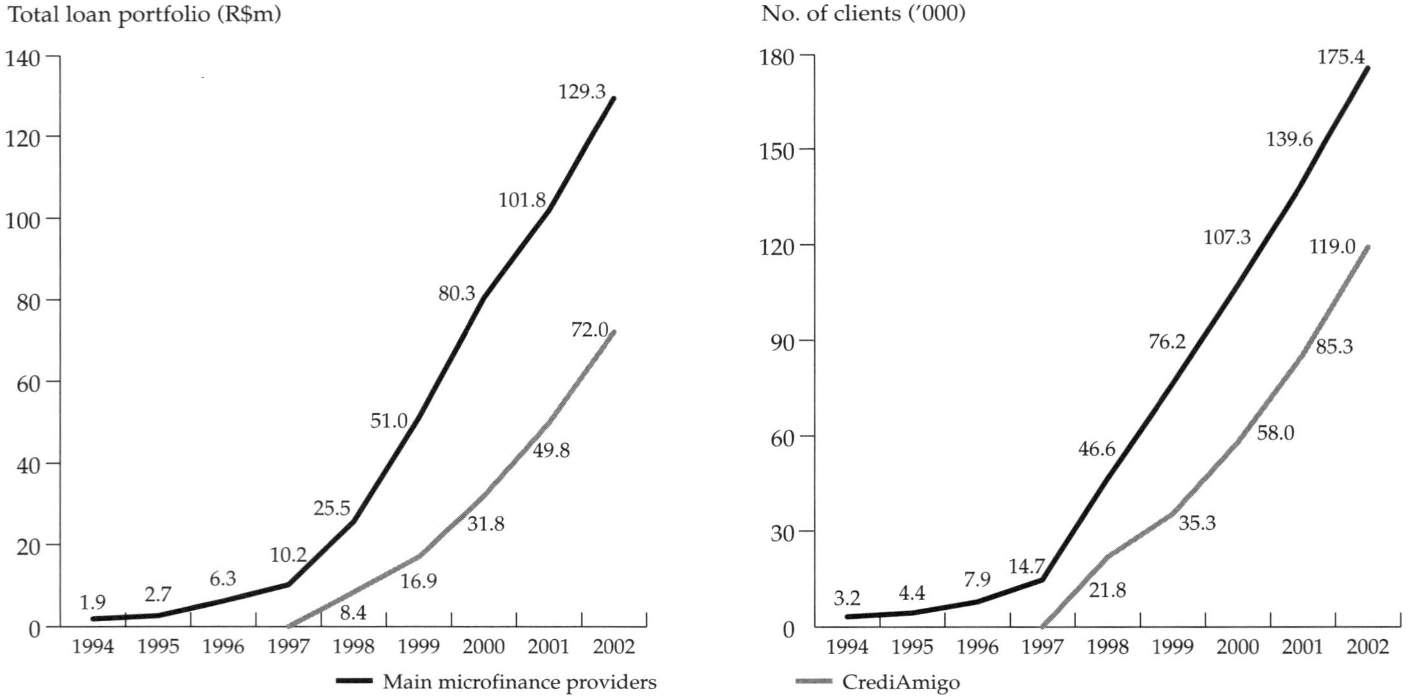

Note: In 2002, June 2001 data were used for three MFIs (Banco do Povo de São Paulo, RioCred, and SindCred), as 2002 data are not available.
Source: Bank staff estimates based on data from BNDES, BNB, and individual institutions' data.

some successful microfinance programs in other countries, there are no obligatory savings requirements (microfinance entities in Brazil cannot accept deposits).

CrediAmigo adopts additional good practices to safeguard its portfolio. A potential client microenterprise must be at least one year old with demonstrated cash flow potential. Its solidarity group members must know each other well, but relatives are excluded. Each group elects a representative and adopts a name. Newly formed solidarity groups undergo training by loan officers on group liability and loan characteristics. Initially, loans were exclusively for working capital purposes. Later, individual loans were introduced based on client records of at least two solidarity group loans. By offering life insurance policies to its borrowers during the term of its loans, CrediAmigo protects itself from eventual death of borrowers.

Products and Growth

CrediAmigo's minimum loan sizes for first-time loans have ranged from R$200 to R$700, and each subsequent loan may be 50 percent larger than the previous loan. Its average loan size in December 2002 was only R$605, confirming a focus on the poor. Female participation, however, corresponds to the population average, at 48 percent. Loan terms range from three to six months for solidarity group loans. Interest rates are higher than popular public bank enterprise loans but lower than consumer credit or even rates charged by some nonbanks such as factoring companies. The program began with a 5 percent flat monthly rate, which has since been reduced to 3.5 percent. Initially, there was a high loan renewal rate, of about 85 percent, and an increasing number of new clients per loan officer.[17] Low transaction costs and quick loan decisions contribute to this. Time between application and disbursement for first-time borrowers is seven days, whereas for repeat borrowers it is 24 hours.

Links to BNB

CrediAmigo represents less than 1 percent of loan assets of BNB and is being managed as an independent profit center with the goal of monitoring progress toward self-sustainability and eventual separation from BNB. As part of BNB, CrediAmigo is supervised by the Central Bank, and the question of how it could in future be separated is not clear. Should CrediAmigo opt for SCM status, it will be required to maintain appropriate capital adequacy. So far, it has received its funds on a 100 percent basis from BNB, which are indexed to the Certificado de Depósito Interfinanceiro (Interbank Certificate of Deposit; CDI) rate, which closely tracks the Sistema Especial de Liquidação e Custodia (overnight interest rate; SELIC) or interbank rate. However, if CrediAmigo had to raise funds from deposits (and comply with reserve requirements) or borrow at market rates from commercial banks or through the issue of its own paper, its funding costs may rise. In terms of operating costs, the program has made every effort to separate its costs from those of BNB and also to prorate the use of BNB resources. Such a separation is, however, partially dependent on the capacity of BNB for monitoring cost centers.

Critically, CrediAmigo has kept costs down and enhanced client focus by separating its labor and staff from BNB. Not only has this permitted the adoption of specialized training and offering of bonuses and incentives, but also it has been relieved of the necessity of paying the wages earned by public sector workers and formal bank employees. However, such arrangements could face increased scrutiny. Its image differentiation in terms of its branches has also relieved it from obligations of complying with costly bank branch-opening requirements.

Portfolio Quality and Financial Performance

CrediAmigo initiated operations in 5 BNB branches in November 1997 and expanded in five months to 50 additional branches, but with ensuing poor portfolio quality. With a renewed commitment to focus on portfolio quality and productivity, CrediAmigo was able to achieve a more stable and sustainable rate of growth. Today, CrediAmigo distributes its products through 164 of Banco do Nordeste do Brasil's 174 branches. By May 2003, CrediAmigo was among the largest microfinance institutions in Latin America, with 123,000 clients and an active portfolio of R$72 million.

Delinquency rates at CrediAmigo were initially uneven. Delinquency rose sharply in the first year following the surge of expansion, but management reacted promptly by writing off bad loans and modifying its performance-based incentive scheme for staff in 1999. It also installed a detailed portfolio-monitoring system for delinquency at the loan officer level. Since its inception, CrediAmigo has been aware of the needs to monitor and control costs and to operate on the basis of profit centers. Today, each branch is a profit center. For example, initially CrediAmigo offered enterprise development services. But when it faced challenges in terms of providing these on a sustainable basis and found also that demand was low, it discontinued such services. CrediAmigo was also aware of its high assets utilization and administrative cost ratios compared to its peers and has launched programs to increase loan officer productivity.

In 2003, its portfolio quality and staff productivity compared favorably with international good practice. Only 4 percent of its loans were overdue, using a strict 30-day portfolio-at-risk measure, in accordance with Central Bank requirements. Its annualized loan loss rate was 2.7 percent, after fully provisioning all loans with payment 360 days or more overdue. As for productivity, loan officers with nine months or more of experience are each handling an average of 313 clients. Salary expenses as percentage of loan portfolio decreased from 139 percent in December 1998 to 27 percent in May 2001.

In terms of profitability, CrediAmigo has progressed positively. About 145 of CrediAmigo's 164 branches are operationally sustainable. Since June 2000, CrediAmigo has presented positive returns on average assets, but in 2002, profits dropped. Learning to maintain good portfolio quality is one of the key challenges that CrediAmigo faces in controlling operating expenses, which remained high at 37 percent of total assets as of December 2002.

Implications for Brazil's Microfinance Sector

The story of CrediAmigo dominates Brazil's microfinance sector. It has clearly demonstrated the existence of a market niche for microfinance and has also demonstrated the means for its achievement. It incorporates many examples of recognized good practice in microfinance lending techniques. It also shows that rapid growth must be tempered with an eye on quality and that learning the microfinance culture takes time.

To what extent does its story provide commercial banks with a model for 'downscaling'? CrediAmigo demonstrates that, under appropriate conditions and following specific practices, a downscaling strategy for commercial banks (that is, targeting lower-income individuals or smaller businesses) could be viable. CrediAmigo also suggests that an existing branch network can greatly help the rollout of microfinance products. Alternatively, partnerships allowing microfinance specialists to distribute their products via bank networks could also be successful strategies to develop large-scale microfinance services.

With the introduction of new measures for microfinance nationwide in 2003, CrediAmigo has also decided to offer microfinance loans under the new terms, accepting the interest rate caps for small-size loans, which other microfinance agencies will now offer. Although CrediAmigo maintains that it will nevertheless be able to sustain its performance, clearly this will be an additional strain and the extent to which it is possible in practice will need to be monitored.

Evolution of the Government's Role: BNDES and SEBRAE

The Communidade Solidária and the government also recognized through their working groups the need for hands-on support to microfinance, both through the provision of wholesale finance and through programs of institution building. Since the late 1990s, a range of new forms of support for microfinance has been provided in particular by BNDES and also by the agency Serviço Brasileiro de Apoio às Micro e Pequenas Empresas (Brazilian Services to Support Micro and Small Enterprises; SEBRAE).[18] The most significant of these was the launching of a new program by BNDES in 1997 for the provision of credit to microfinance entities: the Programa de Crédito Produtivo Popular (Program of Popular Productive Credit; PCPP). This program remained largely unchanged until new microfinance measures were introduced in mid-2003. The analysis below refers to the program from 1997 until mid-2003.

Under this program, BNDES provided revolving wholesale lines of credit to microfinance institutions. Institutions supported by BNDES represented a high proportion of Brazil's microfinance institutions, including most of the larger and more-established institutions.[19] From the time of initiation of the program in 1997 until mid-2001, BNDES had contracted a total value of around R$44 million with 31 microcredit institutions. Of this, around R$25 million represented first-time contracts, and R$18 million represented repeat contracts with around 11 microfinance institutions. Total credits extended by BNDES's client microfinance institutions by end-2000 amounted to R$85.7 million, based on an active portfolio of around R$31.7 million. The active portfolio of these institutions grew to R$41.5 million by end-2002 (table 2.1), representing an estimated 34 percent of total microfinance loans (table 2.2).

Thus, the role of BNDES in Brazil's microfinance industry, albeit indirect, has been large, and its microfinance support program, the PCPP, has contributed significantly to the expansion of microfinance. The role of the BNDES is particularly significant in view of the contribution to microfinance of another public sector bank, the Banco do Nordeste do Brasil, through the CrediAmigo program, discussed further below.

The share of BNDES in the total resources of the microfinance institutions it works with has been constrained by its own regulations; initial leverage ratios have been 1:1 for NGOs and OSCIPs, which could be expanded to 2:1 over time. Leverage ratios of 3:1 (BNDES capital to own capital) were permitted for SCMs. According to BNDES, it provided for 50–80 percent of the funding of these institutions. Loan value averaged R$1,155 in June 2001, which had changed little since 1998, when loans averaged R$1,091 (table A2.1). The average number of clients per institution rose 50 percent from 1998 to 1999, in the early years of the program, from 969 to 1,489, but declined thereafter to around 1,100 by mid-2001. Average portfolio size showed a similar initial increase, from R$0.8 million to R$1.3 million (1998–1999) before diminishing to R$1.1 million in 2000–2001.

This suggests that there was some initial overexpansion, and the early surge then diminished. In terms of loan composition, the majority of loans

Table 2.1 BNDES Program of Support to Microenterprises, 1997–2002

Year	*No. of states*	*No. of municipalities*	*No. of active clients*	*Average nonperforming loans (%)*	*Average loan size (R$)*	*Initial value contracted[a] (R$m)*	*Total value contracted[a] (R$m)*	*Total loan value (R$m)*	*No. of MFIs*	*Active portfolio (R$m)*
1997	n.a.	n.a.	n.a.	n.a.	n.a.	5.9	17.8	n.a.	n.a.	n.a.
1998	14	96	19,382	3.6	1,091	6.0	13.8	46.5	20	16.4
1999	16	199	29,775	4.3	1,120	4.5	4.5	73.2	20	25.0
2000	16	268	36,303	7	1,147	6.9	6.6	85.7	29	31.7
2001	16	n.a.	35,957	4.7	1,169	n.a.	5.0	101.2	33	36.2
2002	16	n.a.	38,027	2.9	1,206	n.a.	2.0	118.7	35	41.5
Total (1998–2002)	—	—	—	23.2	49.7	425.3	—	—		

Note: — = not available; n.a. = not applicable.

a. This may include some contracts other than the 31 MFIs referred to in the other columns.

Source: BNDES Área Social (appendix table A2.1).

Table 2.2 Credit Cooperatives and MFIs in Brazil, 1997–2002

Credit cooperatives	*1997*	*1998*	*1999*	*2000*	*2001*	*2002*
Cooperatives (nos.)	1,015	1,088	1,183	1,235	1,333	1,374
Equity (R$m)	800	1,062	1,357	1,621	2,029	2,584
Loans (R$m)	1,366	1,728	2,203	2,816	3,736	4,562
Deposits (R$m)	1,172	1,730	2,440	3,332	4,840	6,881
Assets (R$m)	2,496	3,339	4,739	6,216	8,451	11,483
Microfinance						
SCMs (nos.)	—	—	3	6	14	26
Equity (R$m)	—	—	—	2.4	5.2	9.7
Loans (R$m)	—	—	—	1.1	4.4	9.3
Assets (R$m)	—	—	—	2.6	8.0	17.2
CrediAmigo						
Clients (nos. '000)	—	21.8	35.3	58.0	85.3	119.0
No. of operations ('000)	—	61.3	114.5	165.9	245.9	359.2
Active portfolio (R$m)	—	8.4	16.9	31.8	49.8	72.0
Amount disbursed (R$m)	—	31.6	81.8	125.8	194.6	287.3
BNDES's portfolio[a]						
MFIs (nos.)	—	20	20	29	31	31
Clients (nos. '000)	—	19.4	24	29.8	36.0 (35.3)	38.0 (37.0)
Active portfolio (R$m)	—	16.4	25	31.7	36.2 (34.4)	41.5 (38.5)
Total clients (these items) (nos. '000)	—	41.2	59.3	87.8	121.3 (120.6)	157.0 (156.0)
Total active portfolio (these items)	—	24.8	41.9	64.6	90.4 (88.6)	122.8 (119.8)

Note: — = not available.

a. Data refer to MFIs supported by BNDES. Numbers in parentheses show numbers net of SCMs (Microcred, Socialcred, and Rótula).

Source: World Bank staff estimates based on data provided by the Central Bank of Brazil, Banco do Nordeste do Brasil, and BNDES.

A Summary of BNDES Lines of Credit to 31 MFIs, 1997 to June 2001

Total active portfolio (June 2001): R$33.9 million
Active clients (June 2001): 34,356
Average nonperforming loans (% > 30 days): 6.1% (4% excluding two lowest institutions)
Average loan value: R$1,155
Average term: 5 years

Loan Distribution by Sector and Client

Informal sector: 76%	Working capital: 90.8%	Industry: 15.4%
Formal sector: 24%	Commerce: 65.9%	Male: 46.5%
Fixed capital: 7.1%	Service: 18.7%	Female: 53.5%

BNDES Loan Terms to MFIs

Maximum amount per loan: R$3 million
Interest rate charged to MFI: BNDES financial costs, Taxa de Juros de Longo Prazo
Term: 8 years, 9 months' grace period, quarterly amortization

Leverage Permitted

(Ratio of BNDES funds to the capital provided by the MFI)
NGOs and OSCIPs: 1:1 in a first operation and 2:1 in a second operation
SCMs: 2:1 in a first operation and 3:1 in a second operation

Other Conditions

- Total leverage should remain below 5:1; in case of excess, funds must be returned to BNDES.
- If nonperforming loans are between 6% and 8% in two consecutive quarters or above 8% in a single quarter, then an amount equivalent to their value must be returned to BNDES.
- If nonperforming loans exceed 15% of total loans in a quarter, total BNDES funds must be returned.
- 15% of funds from BNDES should be put aside for loan-provisioning fund.
- The public sector is allowed to represent only up to one-third of the board of directors of an NGO or OSCIP.

Onlending Terms to Final Client

- Interest rates: Variable by client MFI; maximum spread allowed by BNDES is 6 percent.
- Average loan term: 4.4 months.

Source: World Bank, based on data provided by BNDES Área Social.

went to the informal sector (76 percent), mainly for working capital needs (91 percent), with some preference for women (53 percent of all borrowers). These characteristics conformed to those observed in most international microfinance industries, although the proportion of women is often much higher elsewhere.

The program was very popular. Seven out of 10 applicants were rejected at the first visit, and BNDES worked with one or two of the remaining for a year or two before a loan approval. It maintained that finding quality microfinance institutions was its biggest constraint. BNDES had an institutional development program for its clients, under which it prepared manuals for managers, educational materials on financial management, regulation, information system, accounting, markets, and so forth.[20]

Although the client microfinance institutions' onlending rates, limited to 6 percent per month under these programs, were usually close to market rates, interest rates charged by BNDES to its clients, as with other programs of BNDES lending, were linked to the official long-term interest rate (Taxa de Juros de Longo Prazo; TJLP), which has generally been well below the SELIC (interbank) rate and considerably below commercial lending rates. BNDES was able to sustain this due to its own funding being substantially at below-market rates, based on the Fundo de Amparo ao Trabalhador employment tax. In the case of microfinance institutions, BNDES did not charge a spread over the TJLP, as these loans were deemed to be socially strategic.[21]

In terms of regional distribution, although initially concentrated in the Northeast, which had 68 percent of client borrowers and 56 percent of total loans in 1998, these shares diminished to 51 and 43 percent, respectively, by 2001 (appendix table A2.4). Over time, the more affluent South and Southeast regions taken together have increased their participation, from roughly 26 percent of clients in 1998 to 42 percent in 2001 and from 38 percent in 1998 to 51 percent in 2001 in terms of value. The North, Northeast, and Central–West regions decreased their clients' participation from around 74 percent to 58 percent and from 62 percent to 49 percent in terms of value in the same period. In September 2001, the two regional groups each had around half the total value of loans, although the North and Northeast had a much higher share of clients (58 percent versus 42 percent), implying a much smaller average loan size.

Implications of the PCPP for Microfinance Development

Clearly, the PCPP pushed forward significantly the frontiers of microfinance in Brazil and in scale was surpassed only by the efforts of BNB and the CrediAmigo program. Many sound practices were incorporated, such as onlending at market rates and working with client microfinance

BNDES Client MFIs' Performance, 1998–2001

How well have the client MFIs of BNDES performed over this period? Has performance improved since the association with BNDES began? Based on quarterly data from BNDES, analyses were undertaken to (1) assess the underlying trend growth in client MFI portfolios over this period; (2) examine the extent to which there is any significant difference between the performance of those institutions that received repeated lines of support from BNDES and those that were first-time clients; (3) investigate the correlations between default rates and variables, such as number of clients, number of active credits, and loan size; and finally, (4) examine trends in default rates to see if there had been any improvement over time in performance since BNDES support began. Details on estimations are available in the annex to this chapter.

To summarize results, (1) annual nominal rate of growth averaged around 22 percent for any given institution. Discounting for inflation, annual real rates of growth would be in the range of 16–18 percent. These rates are sedate rather than striking. Variation across individual MFIs is significant, with some, such as PortoSol, doubling their active portfolio, and BluSol tripling its portfolio. (2) Separating the sample between first-timers and repeat performers does not suggest a significant difference in behavior between these groups. Repeat clients do not appear to have better performance than first-time clients. (3) There is some positive correlation between percentages in arrears and number of clients, as well as number of active credits, suggesting that, as institutions grow, control over portfolio quality may suffer. There is also some negative correlation with loan size, suggesting that those microcredit institutions that concentrate on larger borrowers have a better portfolio quality. Finally, (4) average rates of loans in arrears more than 30 days have fluctuated sharply; however, an attempt to see if there had been a trend decline suggested the opposite; weighted average institutional default rates increased over time, by around 11 percent per year. This does not suggest any improvement or learning over time of member institutions in BNDES's portfolio.

institutions to impart good business practices, portfolio monitoring, and evaluation systems. Yet other features associated with sound principles of microfinance were not incorporated. Notable among these was the 'solidarity group' principle of group lending and coinsurance, which is not a requirement of BNDES for its client microfinance institutions. Although some, such as the Centro de Apoio aos Pequenos Empreendimentos (Support Center for Small Business; CEAPE) group of microfinance institutions, follow this practice, it is relatively rare in Brazil.

Moreover, an analysis of the BNDES portfolio and its evolution over this period suggests that its client enterprises did not grow particularly

BNDES and New Microfinance Measures Introduced in 2003

Many microfinance entities faced a huge increase in funding costs after new BNDES programs were established, from September 2003. Under the new programs, the rate at which funds are offered to the onlending microfinance entity are scaled according to loan size. There are three size categories: up to R$1,000, up to R$5,000, and R$5,000 to R$10,000. The cost of funding for the microfinance entities who are recipients of BNDES lines of credit will continue at the TJLP for loans up to R$1,000 and at TJLP + 2 percent and TJLP + 5 percent, respectively, for the larger loan sizes. A minimum of 30 percent of onlending must be used in the smallest size category. In addition, there is a stipulation that onlending rates must be limited to 2 percent or 5 percent per month, depending on loan size.

Although the new measures are designed to expand lending in the smallest size categories and could succeed in achieving this, they could also considerably diminish the incentives for efficient microfinance as a whole. Although some phased increase in funding costs, beyond TJLP, at least toward the interbank rate, would be desirable over time, the one-shot increase undertaken here could impose a severe burden on the borrowing microfinance entities, compounded by the parallel caps on onlending rates. Practical experience of microfinance shows that final borrowers are relatively insensitive to interest rates, and the reasons for the rate caps on onlending will squeeze the microfinance intermediaries. Discontinuities in rates by loan size will provide incentives for evasion, for example, by the taking of numerous small loans instead of a single large loan. Instead of adding emphasis to efficient techniques of microlending, the program shifts attention away from this objective and toward the multiplication of loans that are small by size and increases dependence on unrealistically subsidized funding sources.

rapidly, despite the rapid growth in the BNDES portfolio. Rapid growth episodes, in terms of increases in clients and portfolios, may have been correlated with higher default rates when they occurred. There was no trend decline in bad loans; if anything, there may even have been some increase.

Other good practices as discussed in the context of CrediAmigo and below could also have been followed more consistently.[22] The below-market funding of the client microfinance institutions of BNDES, even if justifiable in a start-up phase, lacked an articulated 'exit' strategy. Ideally, BNDES should have been able to gradually disengage itself from its client microfinance institutions and possibly transfer its role in credit provision for such microfinance institutions to entities such as commercial banks.

Other BNDES Programs: Downscaling through Affiliated Financial Institutions

BNDES also extends credit to small and medium enterprises (SMEs) directly, through its subsidiary Agência Especial de Financiamento Industrial (Special Agency of Industrial Financing; FINAME), and indirectly, through special lines of credit to private financial institutions. Disbursements to micro- and small-scale enterprises amounted to more than R$3 billion in 2000.[23] Adding medium enterprises raises these totals to R$4.4 and R$3.9 billion, respectively. These figures dwarf the R$43 million of BNDES's contracted lines of credit to microfinance institutions under the PCPP and demonstrate that the overall importance of BNDES in programs of financial access for microenterprises and SMEs is huge.

BNDES has a series of products for funding microenterprises' and SMEs' permitted activities (appendix tables A2.6 and A2.7). Prominent among these are the FINAME lines of credit for loans to final borrowers up to R$7 million. Although not restricted to SMEs alone, the criteria for awarding these lines of credit provide incentives for loans to SMEs.[24] Funds are made available at the TJLP rate, plus a markup, which is still somewhat below market sources of funding. The markup has two elements: one based on assessed risk of the agent, which varies by institution, and the other is the spread of the agent, which varies by activity. Spreads for loans to SMEs are 1 percent only, whereas spreads for other activities have been 2.5 percent. Institutions that are able to demonstrate higher proportions of loans to the SME sector obtain more funds. Banks' eligibility limits are re-evaluated every six months. The top 25 financial agents used by BNDES are indicated in appendix table A2.6.

BNDES also participates, together with other federal financial institutions, in other special programs targeted at support to microenterprise for purposes of employment generation: the Programa Brasil Empeendedor (PBE), specially designed to stimulate the development of micro-, small, and medium-size companies. BNDES also participates in a guarantee fund, the Fundo de Garantia para a Promoção da Competitividade, created with resources from the National Treasury, managed by BNDES, which gives collateral to guarantee credits from financial institutions to micro- and SME exporters.[25] Start-up microentrepreneurs in Brazil can also apply for funding from a dedicated fund of R$200 million created to finance 5,000 new microcompanies (Credit Directed to New Entrepreneurs). BNDES received 60,000 applications and approved 4,000.

SEBRAE, a special agency for the support of SMEs, runs programs of technical and financial support to microenterprises through a loan guarantee fund for long-term investments, Fundo de Aval ás Microempresas e Empresas de Pequeno Porte (Loan Guarantee Fund for Micro and Small Enterprises; FAMPE), only available for loans issued by a handful of public banks.[26] In 2000, SEBRAE began a venture capital program, Programa de Capital de Risco, for participation in funds investing in emerging micro- and small companies. And in October 2001, SEBRAE launched a new scheme to provide both technical assistance and credit to microfinance institutions too small to qualify for BNDES assistance, across 300 municipalities with low human development indicator indices. Loans will be available for up to R$300,000 for eight years, with a three-year grace period. Interest rates on SEBRAE lines of credit to microfinance institutions are based on the TJLP, with no spread.

Thus, the government, and especially BNDES, has partnered a wide segment of the nation's financial institutions to improve access through financial incentives and preferential credit rates. But as shown in appendix table A2.6, despite its efforts, it is not clear that BNDES is meeting its objectives. Overall ratios of SMEs in the BNDES lines of credit through its micro-, small, and medium-size programs have been around only half, suggesting that more appropriate targeting mechanisms could be explored (see below). In its PCPP, BNDES has shown a tendency to go toward some of the best-performing institutions in microfinance and also to the more well-to-do regions over time.

Microfinance in Brazil: Present Status[27]

Size and Growth

Given that the incentives to expand microfinance began in the late 1990s, it is not unexpected to find first that, although a handful of the older microfinance institutions date from the 1980s, most (more than 80 percent) have been in existence only from 1998–99 onward. Apart from the state-owned bank initiative, CrediAmigo, microfinance institutions in Brazil are mostly small, private, and independent of formal financial institutions. Private banks in Brazil have not been active players in microfinance.[28] Numbers vary, but estimates suggest that by mid-2002, there were around 120 microfinance players, of which only a dozen catered to more than 2,000 clients.[29]

Among the 40 to 50 larger private institutions, the CEAPE network of NGOs constitutes the second largest microfinance provider in Brazil, with more than 26,000 clients in 220 municipalities across the country served via a network of 13 CEAPE entities. Banco da Mulher, a group of NGOs, some affiliated with Women's World Banking, had more than 2,300 clients and a loan portfolio close to R$2.4 million (US$1.0 million) in June 2001. Several small institutions are also active in the Rio area. They include VivaCred and RioCred, with a loan portfolio of R$2.0 and R$1.2 million and about 2,000 and 1,000 clients, respectively, in June 2001.[30] In terms of nature of services provided, commerce and services in the informal sector dominate (appendix table A2.5). And in terms of regional distribution, most microfinance is urban in character (especially in the Northeast) and thus well equipped to target the urban poor, who account for the bulk of the poor in Brazil (World Bank 2001a).

There are also at least 20 municipal or state-supported microfinance NGOs in Brazil, many of which are expanded versions of public work and employment subsidies. Banco do Povo de São Paulo in São Paulo is now the largest, with a loan portfolio of R$13.8 million and an estimated 16,000 clients. Although these, too, are dubbed microfinance institutions, as they make small loans, they do not attempt to follow the sound financial principles adhered to in microfinance, and their onlending practices are heavily subsidized on the grounds of adhesion to the Usury Law.

As discussed earlier (figure 2.1), microfinance in Brazil began to grow significantly only at the end of the 1990s. There was a rapid burst of growth for the next three to four years, with total clients tripling between 1998 and 2001 (from about 46,000 clients in December 1998 to more than 140,000 in June 2001, an average annual growth rate of 49 percent). Total loan portfolio nearly quadrupled (from R$25 million in December 1998 to R$95 million in June 2001, an average annual growth of 61 percent). But a part of this success is the result of low initial levels. Growth has been unequal across institutions. CrediAmigo has managed to maintain rapid growth since its inception, but some other large microfinance institutions such as the CEAPE network have been largely stagnant. PortoSol, the fourth largest microfinance provider, has also grown slowly.[31]

Supply and Demand Compared; Penetration Ratios

Available estimates suggest that demand for microfinance in Brazil far outstrips supply. The total loan portfolio for microfinance was some R$101 million by end-2001 (table 2.2), for a total clientele of some 140,000 persons (table 2.3). The International Labour Organisation estimates contrast this supply to an estimated 6.4 million potential microfinance clients in Brazil and a potential loan demand of R$11 billion (Mezzera 2002). This implies an average loan size of around R$1,700 per borrower. Even if this is adjusted for our present estimated average loan balance of only R$1,100 per borrower, potential loan demand is around R$7 billion. Thus, according to these estimates, only 2.2 percent of potential microfinance clients, and 1.4 percent of their potential credit needs, are served by microfinance institutions today. Other estimates are similar; 8.2 million potential client enterprises and a penetration rate of 2 percent (Goldmark, Nichter, and Fiori 2002). If this is compared with other countries in the region, using comparable techniques of estimation, Brazil is revealed to have a penetration ratio much lower than that of neighboring countries (table 2.4).

Table 2.3 Main Microfinance Providers in Brazil, end-2001

Institution/group	*Inception*	*Institutions in group*	*Ownership control*	*Active loan portfolio (R$'000)*	*Active clients*
CrediAmigo	1997	1	Public	42,544[a]	80,100[a]
CEAPE	1987	13	Private	17,628	26,368
Banco do Povo de São Paulo	1997	1	Public	13,830[b]	16,266[b]
PortoSol	1996	1	Public	3,881	2,135
BluSol	1997	1	Public	2,467	950
Banco da Mulher	1984	10	Private	2,400[c]	2,334[c]
VivaCred	1996	1	Private	2,043	1,905
Visao Mundial	1996	5	Private	1,592	2,583
Casa do Empreendedor	1997	1		1,435	722
Banco do Povo de Juiz de Fora (FAEP)	1997	1	Public	1,274	853
RioCred	1998	1	Mixed	1,241	1,030[d]
Vitoria Credisol	1998	1	Public	978	693
Rótula	1999	1	Private	823	387
SindCred/Crédito Cidadao	1999	1	Public	746	1,092
ORGAPE	1993	1	Public	684	882
Banco do Povo de Santo Andre	1998	1		463	264
FAEJ	1998	1		412	204
Credimais	1998	1		400	208
Banco do Povo de Minas Gerais	1999	1	Private	391	442
Conquista Solidária	1999	1		306	537
Microcred	1999	1	Private	154	61
Total	—	46	—	95,691	140,016

Note: — = not available.

a. End-2002 figures suggest considerably higher figures.

b. Averages between December 2000 and 2001 data; number of active clients proxied by number of active contracts.

c. Includes three affiliates only (Paraná, Santa Catarina, and Bahia).

d. Estimate.

Source: BNDES; institutions' brochures and websites; data are for June 2001.

Table 2.4 Microfinance Penetration in Brazil and Other Latin American Countries, 2001

Country	*Estimated size of market ('000)*	*Current clients ('000)*	*Market penetration rate (%)*
Bolivia	232.3	379.1	163
Nicaragua	116.4	84.3	72
El Salvador	136.3	93.8	69
Paraguay	83.0	30.2	36
Peru	618.3	185.4	30
Chile	307.8	82.8	27
Brazil[a]	7,875.6	158.7	2

a. Brazil microfinance penetration calculations use 2001 potential demand data, as current market data are also from 2001.
Source: BNDES 2002.

However, these estimates follow a standardized assumption of a 50 percent eligibility rate for all microenterprises. It can be argued that effective eligibility rates may very likely be lower, due to such factors as the availability of special government support, especially in the rural sector, or due to the use of consumer or installment credit in lieu of microenterprise demand, and also because all microenterprises may not wish to borrow. However, the 50 percent ratio was maintained for purposes of comparability with other countries' data. As shown in table 2.4, microfinance penetration in Brazil is much lower than in other Latin American countries, even if the 2 percent estimate is low in absolute terms.

Microfinance Growth: International Comparisons

The apparently high demand estimates for microfinance seem paradoxical compared to microfinance growth rates in Brazil, which outside of CrediAmigo have not been high. As the analysis of the BNDES clients showed, growth rates of the overall microfinance clientele have been high, but this is more due to new microfinance institutions than to the growth in the portfolio of existing microfinance institutions.

True, international experience suggests that developing an extensive microfinance market is generally a long process. After three years of operations, the Grameen Bank of Bangladesh had 377 client solidarity groups, reaching a total of 2,200 poor people. These numbers are close to those reached by recently created Brazilian institutions. Growth at the Grameen Bank started to pick up after about 10 years of operations. The experience of India and Bolivia also confirm that, independent of the structure of the microfinance market, building significant outreach is a lengthy process. India's main microfinance model, the Self-Help Group (SHG) program, was initiated at the beginning of the 1990s. Yet it was only after eight years that it began to witness accelerated growth.

The SHG model was launched by the National Bank for Agriculture and Rural Development (NABARD) in 1991 as a pilot project to link small solidarity groups of poor women, the self-help groups, with financial institutions for funding. The success of the pilot-led NABARD to formalize the Self-Help Group Bank Linkage Program in 1996 as a mainstream activity for commercial banks under their priority sector lending obligations. Under strong impetus from NABARD, the model seems to have taken off, with almost 265,000 self-help groups linked to 318 banks by March 2001 through the participation of more than 750 NGOs. Total loans outstanding amounted to Rs$1,930 million (US$39 million) in March 2000. The government of India is now focusing on making the model sustainable without subsidies and on eliminating barriers to the development of private microfinance institutions. Bolivia, where private microfinance institutions dominate, has also seen its industry grow slowly. Growth started to pick up in 1993 after Prodem, a microfinance NGO transformed into a licensed bank (PortoSol), which prompted similar changes by other NGOs and the creation of a fund to promote private, regulated microfinance institutions (figure 2.2).

These comparisons also suggest that the models of large-scale expansion of microfinance institution portfolios, in tandem with a sponsoring institution such as a bank, may lead to more rapid growth than through small individual microfinance institutions. This is discussed further below.

Institutional Capacity of Brazil's Microfinance: Performance and Impact

Operational and Financial Performance

A large proportion of Brazilian microfinance institutions claim that financial sustainability is a core objective. This section looks at indicators of operational and financial performance, which contribute to the overall assessment of sustainability and performance. First, indicators of the quality of the loan portfolio suggest that Brazil is an average performer relative to comparators, and by some estimates, possibly below average. Analysis of the client institutions of BNDES showed that average rates of loans in arrears fluctuated considerably from 1998 to 2001, from around 3.5 percent to 8.4 percent. In June 2000, loans in arrears averaged 6.12 percent for all 31 clients.[32] Looking at the largest institutions only, the average appears lower, at 4.7 percent, with a range from 1.0 to 10.5 percent (table 2.5).

Figure 2.2 Growth of the Grameen Bank in Bangladesh, Self-Help Groups in India, and Top 10 MFIs in Bolivia

Growth in annual disbursements and outreach

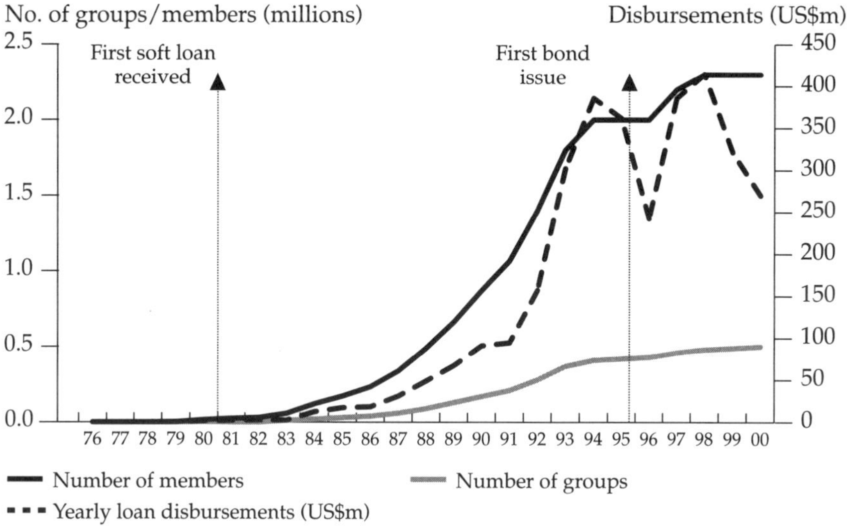

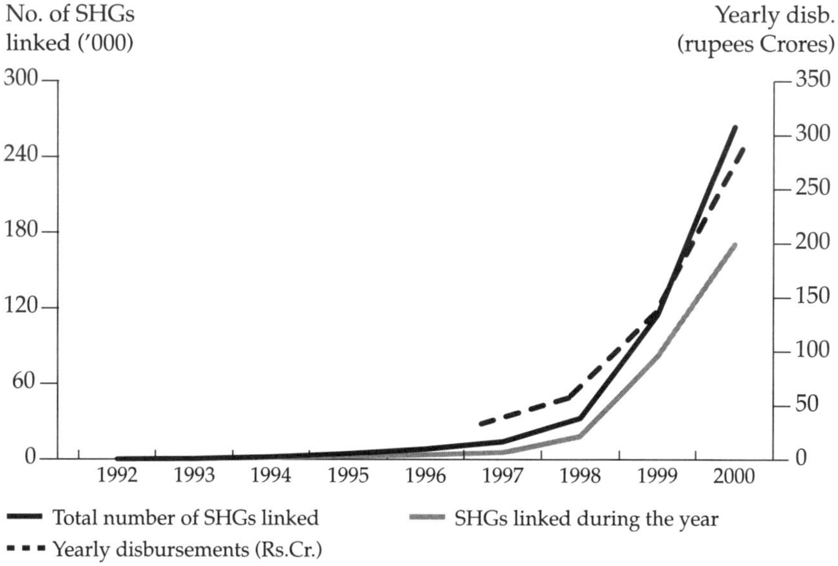

(continued next page)

Figure 2.2 *(continued)*

The growth of Bolivia's 10 largest MFIs

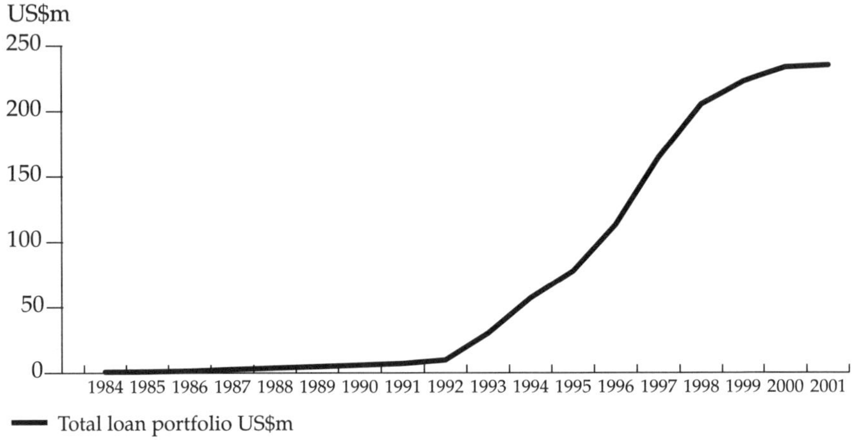

Source: Grameen Bank website; NABARD, India; and individual institutions' data, Bolivia.

Table 2.5 Selected Performance Indicators of Main Microfinance Institutions in Brazil

Institution	*% average annual growth of loan portfolio, 1998–2000*	*% nonperforming loans (overdue > 30 days) 2000*	*Provisions in % total loans 2000*	*% resulting provisioning level of bad loans 2000*
CrediAmigo	94.4	3.8[a]	n.a.	n.a.
CEAPE	0.2	8.6[b]	n.a.	n.a.
PortoSol	20.0	4.6		
Banco do Povo de São Paulo	—	1.6	n.a.	n.a.
BluSol	56.0	1.0	0.7	70.0
Banco da Mulher	83.7	5.2	1.0	19.2
VivaCred	42.0	4.1	n.a.	n.a.
Banco do Povo de Juiz de Fora	—	0.5	2.1	420.0
RioCred	—	10.5	n.a.	n.a.
SindCred	—	3.6	n.a.	n.a.
Average	49.4	4.7	1.3	169.7

Note: — = not available; n.a. = not applicable.
a. August 2001
b. June 2001.
Source: Individual institutions, BNDES.

Variations between institutions are large. Among the BNDES group, eliminating the two worst performers reduced loans in arrears from 6.1 percent to 4 percent. Variations over time are also sharp, even within the same institution; at some points, bad loans have risen to one-quarter or one-third of total portfolio, only to apparently recover six months to one year later. This may reflect the short maturity of loans and periodic write-offs.[33]

A benchmarking table, prepared from a sample of 30 leading microfinance institutions in Latin America, shows that these institutions had an average portfolio at risk (overdue by more than 30 days) of 6.5 percent in June 2001 (table 2.6).[34] This suggests that Brazil is around the reference rate used for similar institutions. Moreover, default rates are dependent on macroeconomic conditions. For instance, BancoSol (Bolivia), which is

Table 2.6 Loan Quality Indicators, Selected Sample of MFIs in Latin America

Country	*Institution*	*% portfolio at risk (> 30 days)*	*% provisions on portfolio at risk*
Brazil	Table 2.3 sample	4.6	169.7
	BNDES 31 sample (June 2000)	6.1	
	DAI estimates (1999)	6.5	
Bolivia	BancoSol, Andes, FIE	8.4	84.9
Colombia	Finamerica, WWB Cali, WWB Popayán, WWB Bucaramanga, WWB Medellín, WWB Bogotá	2.7	84.5
Dominican Rep.	Adopem	2.4	76.5
El Salvador	Calpia, Enlace	8.2	81.3
Mexico	Compartamos	0.4	988.2
Nicaragua	Confia, Finde	7.5	69.1
Paraguay	Visión	7.1	22.7
Peru	CMAC Arequipa, CMAC Trujillo, CMAC Sullana, CMAC Cusco, Edyficar, CMAC Ica, CMAC Tacna, Proempresa, Crear Tacna, Crear Arequipa, Confianza	8.4	100.4
Uruguay	Fucac	6.5	76.3
Average, excluding Brazil		**6.5**	**118.9**

Source: MicroRate website. Ratios are for June 2001.

often cited among best practice examples in microfinance, had a percentage of overdue loans (by one day and more) of 4.5 percent in 1998, but it increased to 16.9 percent in June 2001 as macroeconomic conditions deteriorated.

Next, provisioning for past-due loans may also be low. Most Brazilian microfinance institutions do not disclose their levels of provisioning. Those that do show a wide variety of provisioning levels, from 19 percent for Banco da Mulher's three largest affiliates to 420 percent for Banco do Povo de Juiz de Fora. In their sample of 12 microfinance institutions in 1999, Development Alternatives, Inc. (DAI) estimates an average provisioning level of loans overdue more than 30 days to be 37.5 percent. This compares with 79 percent for BancoSol in 2000 and 68 percent in June 2001. MicroRate's sample of microfinance institutions had a median provisioning rate of 81 percent in June 2001. Applying recommended rates of provisioning for various degrees of past-due loans, DAI estimated that the average provisioning level of Brazilian microfinance institutions should be 64 percent.[35] It has been suggested that the current low level of provisioning may be influenced by loan classification and provisioning norms of the Central Bank, which require full provisioning for a loan with payments overdue by 180 days or more, although these are not applicable to microfinance institutions other than SCMs. Given the short maturity of most microloans, microfinance institutions should be encouraged to provision bad loans earlier.

By contrast, capitalization appears generally strong. DAI calculated the average ratio of capital to gross loans of its sample of institutions at 119 percent. This high average level may be due in part to the young age of most microfinance institutions in the sample, where the loan portfolio is expected to grow substantially from its current level.

Some evidence also suggests that the operating efficiency of Brazilian microfinance institutions appears lower than international best practices. DAI's data suggest that the average number of clients per loan officer was only 191 compared to an average of 326 for a sample of 30 Latin American microfinance institutions used by MicroRate (table 2.7). Similarly, operating costs amounted on average to 49 percent of the loan portfolio for Brazilian institutions compared to 23 percent for MicroRate's sample of Latin American institutions. However, these indicators may be biased upward for Brazilian institutions by the fact that they have not yet reached a size sufficient to benefit from any significant economies of scale.

Yet many microfinance institutions in Brazil seem close to being operationally and financially self-sufficient. Operational self-sufficiency was estimated at 91 percent in the DAI sample of microfinance institutions, adjusted for subsidies but excluding loan loss provisions. Adjusted financial self-sufficiency was estimated at 92 percent.[36] These results compare

Table 2.7 Operational Efficiency Indicators, Selected Sample of MFIs in Latin America

Country	*Institution*	*Clients per credit agent (productivity)*	*% operating costs/average gross portfolio*	*% net income/ average assets (ROA)*
Brazil	DAI sample	191	49.4	6.6
Bolivia	BancoSol, Andes, FIE	287	14.5	–0.7
Colombia	Finamerica, WWB Cali, WWB Popayán, WWB Bucaramanga, WWB Medellín, WWB Bogotá	438	19.9	7.8
Dominican Rep.	Adopem	328	23.2	10.3
El Salvador	Calpia, Enlace	321	42.7	–7.4
Mexico	Compartamos	321	59.4	12.1
Nicaragua	Confia, Finde	195	23.2	5.3
Paraguay	Visión	361	21.1	–3.2
Peru	CMAC Arequipa, CMAC Trujillo, CMAC Sullana, CMAC Cusco, Edyficar, CMAC Ica, CMAC Tacna, Proempresa, Crear Tacna, Crear Arequipa, Confianza	298	21.5	3.2
Uruguay	Fucac	n.a.	11.9	0.3
Average, excluding Brazil		**326**	**23.1**	**3.4**

Note: n.a. = not applicable; ROA = return on assets.
Source: MicroRate website. Ratios are for June 2001.

very favorably with international standards. However, differences across institutions seem to be large, and only 4 of the 12 institutions analyzed reached financial sustainability. Another study of four microfinance institutions conducted by BNDES in May 2000 reached similar conclusions.

These favorable results may be explained in part by high spreads combined with subsidized funding, which compensate for their high operating expenses. Most of Brazil's microfinance providers charge market-based interest rates (refer to table 2.9). Rates are in line with those charged by microfinance institutions elsewhere in Latin America.[37] A comparison conducted by BNDES between four Brazilian microfinance institutions and comparable samples of peers shows that the rates charged by the Brazilian institutions in 1999 were in line with their peers, whose average interest rate reached 53 percent per annum for medium-size institutions and 63 percent for smaller institutions (figure 2.3).

However, some institutions in Brazil charge heavily subsidized interest rates, violating a generally accepted basic principle of sustainable microfinance. This is, for instance, the case for municipal programs such as Banco do Povo de São Paulo or de Juiz de Fora. These programs are essentially social services, financing the creation of work for employment or other welfare purposes, which justify their low interest rates on social grounds. Other microfinance providers cite this unfair competition as a key obstacle to their growth. There is an ongoing debate in Brazil between advocates that microfinance should be sustainable and therefore market driven and advocates that microfinance is a social policy instrument to distribute interest rate subsidies to the poorest. New measures introduced in mid-2003 clearly attempt to support the expansion of credit to the poorest through measures that include lending quotas and interest rate ceilings. It remains to be seen whether these will be effective in increasing sustainable long-term microfinance, as desired.

Low operational efficiency despite high interest rates could be attributed to low-quality loan portfolios, due to problems in loan approval and monitoring. Most institutions have a social objective, with limited experience in business and finance, and little attention devoted to profitability and growth. Some institutions are subject to political influence that affects their ability to make strategically sound decisions regarding branch openings, interest rates, and partnerships. Other challenges mentioned are the capacity of staff, the lack of result-based incentives, too little marketing, and inefficient information flows (Goldmark 2002).

Impact Evaluation

Brazil's microfinance institutions appear to have been successful in terms of outreach to smaller clients. Average loan sizes in Brazil are smaller than for most microfinance institutions in Latin America, in absolute terms and

Figure 2.3 Comparison of Interest Rates Charged on Loans with Other Institutions in Latin America

Interest rate policy, Brazilian microfinance institutions versus peer groups

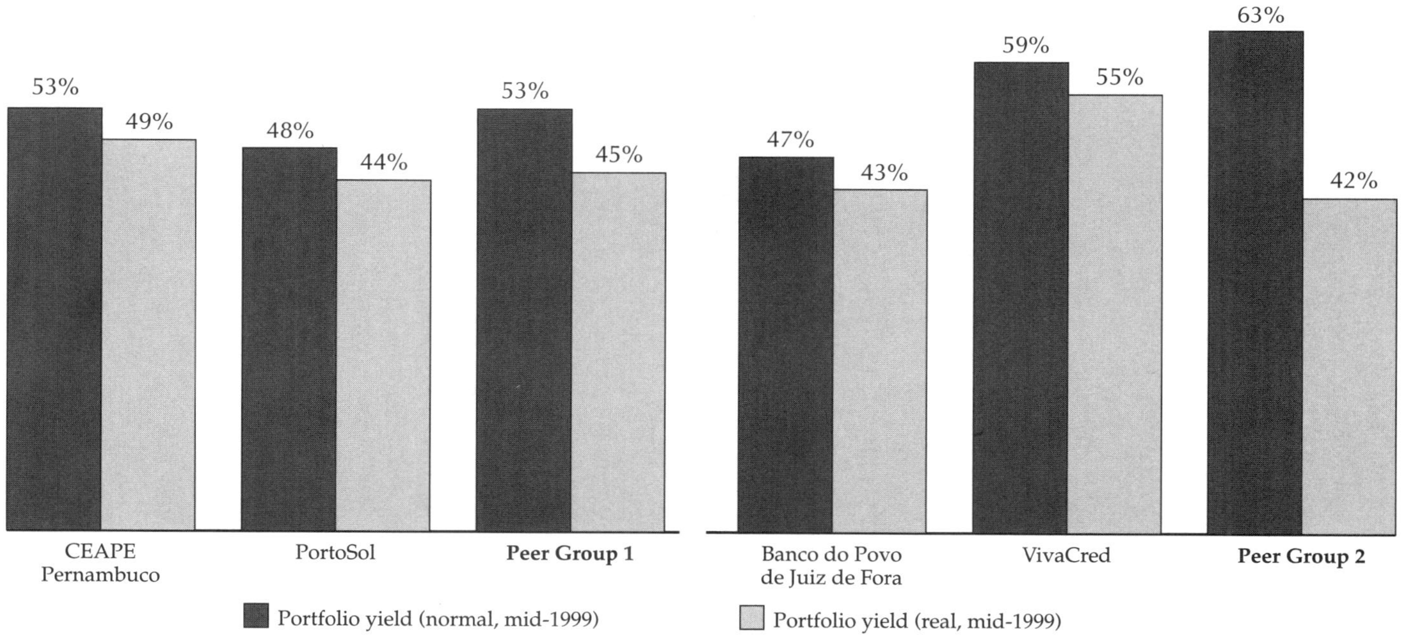

Source: BNDES 2000b.

as a percentage of GDP per capita. As table 2.8 shows, microfinance institutions in Latin America have an average loan size of US$717, varying from US$130 (Enlace en El Salvador) to US$1,225 (Andes in Bolivia), compared to US$460 for Brazil.

To summarize, performance indicators in terms of portfolio quality and loan loss provisioning for Brazil are, at best, average, but overall financial sustainability appears high, largely due to high spreads and low-cost funding. Limited available information on impact suggests that Brazil's microfinance institutions do succeed in reaching out to small clients.

Before concluding, it may be asked how successful microfinance institutions are worldwide. International experience shows that many public and private microfinance institutions have moved toward financial sustainability while offering continued access to financial services to a large number of clients. Among these institutions are the Unit Desas of

Table 2.8 Comparison of Average Loan Size across Latin America

Country	*Institutions included*	*Average loan balance per client (US$)*	*Country GNI per capita (US$)*	*% average loan/GNI per capita*
Brazil	Table 2.3 sample	460	3,570	13
Nicaragua	Confia, Finde	1,178	420	280
Uruguay	Fucac	1,152	6,090	120
Bolivia	BancoSol, Andes, FIE	1,158	1,000	116
Dominican Rep.	Adopem	362	2,100	40
Peru	CMACs in Arequipa, Trujillo, Sullana, Cusco, Ica, and Tacna; Edyficar, Proempresa, Crear Tacna, Crear Arequipa, Confianza	771	2100	37
Paraguay	Visión	613	1,450	35
El Salvador	Calpia, Enlace	466	1,990	23
Colombia	Finamerica, WWB Cali, Popayán, Bucaramanga, Medellín, and Bogota	411	2,080	20
Mexico	Compartamos	231	5,080	5
Average, excluding Brazil		**717**	**n.a.**	**56**

Note: n.a. = not applicable. *World Bank Atlas* methodology (2001) for gross national income per capita, US$2,000.

Source: MicroRate website for average loans data.

the government-owned Bank Rakyat Indonesia. The Unit Desas achieved sustainability in 1989, when their subsidy dependence index turned negative, indicating that they could have lowered their interest rate on loans even if all subsidies were eliminated.[38] Examples of private microfinance institutions include India's Self-Employed Women's Association, which several analyses found to be financially sustainable, and the Association for Social Advancement in Bangladesh, whose Sustainable Financial Services Model focuses on ensuring that the institution remains fully financially self-sufficient (Chen and Snodgrass 1999; Mahajan and Gupta Ramola 1996).

However, only a small proportion of microfinance institutions are totally financially sustainable. Most of these benefited from subsidies at the start of their operations (Mahajan and Gupta Ramola 1996; Morduch 1999, 2000). According to information from 147 participating institutions from 53 countries, tracked by the *Microbanking Bulletin* (Mezzera 2002), two-thirds of their microfinance institutions were able to cover operational costs, and around two-fifths were financially self-sufficient. The adjusted rate of return of this group was 5.5 percent on assets, or 14.1 percent on equity. Financial self-sufficiency is actually higher in microfinance institutions catering to lower-end clients, more than 90 percent. Thus, even under favorable circumstances, microfinance is not a highly profitable activity, although in the right circumstances, returns, although modest, can be positive.

Microfinance in Brazil: Constraints and Challenges

Microfinance Products and Funding Sources

If microfinance in Brazil is to evolve on a large scale, a key future challenge will be the growth of the portfolio of its small-client microfinance institutions, or a change in the form of microfinance activity to allow it to access funding, for example, through deposit-taking. Even before June 2003, a considerable proportion of microfinance in Brazil relied heavily on privileged sources of funding through government banks or donors (table 2.9). Onlending by the BNDES was at the TJLP rate, and onlending at CrediAmigo was at the interbank deposit rate (close to SELIC) interest rate.[39] Some projections indicated that microfinance demand would very rapidly exceed supply as a result.[40] These rates have been much lower than the cost of capital in Brazil for small enterprises. Better-established microfinance groups such as CEAPE, which have NGO status, maintain that funding is a major constraint. Disincentives to a change in status are that, although SCMs can mobilize resources, they are subject to regulatory

Table 2.9 Sources of Funding and Interest Rates Charged by Main Brazilian MFIs

Institution	*Main sources of funding*	*Nominal interest rate on loans*	*Equivalent compounded annual rate*
CrediAmigo	Transfers from the BNB; donor grants and loans (IBRD)	3.5% per month	51% p.a.
CEAPE	Donor grants and loans (IDB, UNICEF); BNDES long-term loans	5.0% per month	80% p.a.
PortoSol	Contributions from city of Pôrto Alegre and state government of Rio Grande do Sul; donor grants (GTZ, IAF); BNDES long-term loans	4.0% per month	60% p.a.
Banco do Povo de São Paulo	State donation; BNDES long-term loans	1.0% per month	13% p.a.
BluSol	Contributions from various associations in the area of Blumenau (craftsmen association, SME association, microentrepreneur association, shopkeepers association) and from the municipality	4.0% per month	60% p.a.
Banco da Mulher	Donor grants (IDB); BNDES long-term loans for some of the NGOs; credit line from HSBC bank	n.a.	n.a.
VivaCred	Donor grants and loans (IDB mostly); BNDES long-term loans; Fininvest start-up funding (consumer company)	3.9% per month	58% p.a.
RioCred	Fininvest investment		
Fundo Carioca	4.2% per month for first loans	3.9% for repeat loans	64% p.a. 58% p.a.
SindCred	Fundo Carioca; contribution from state of Rio's budget	2.4 to 3.6% per month depending on loan size	33% to 53% p.a.

Note: n.a. = not applicable.
Source: Individual institutions.

norms for financial institutions, lose their nonprofit tax-exempt status, and become subject to the stiff taxes imposed on financial institutions. In addition, reporting and supervision requirements are also obligatory. Many microfinance institutions in Brazil receive grant funding, as indicated in table 2.9.

New measures recently introduced have expanded funding offered through banks but are subject to conditions that include constraints on loan size and interest rate caps. For microfinance loans above the small threshold sizes, there has been a significant one-shot increase in funding costs, which may be difficult to sustain for some microfinance firms. The loan size threshold distinctions will provide incentives for loan fragmentation and repeat loans. The challenge for microfinance in Brazil is the expansion of funding without the imposition of such quantitative limits.

One possible area to explore, which is related also to the question of the range of products offered, is the current restriction against the mobilization of deposits for any form of microfinance organization in Brazil today. In many countries, deposit mobilization is permitted not only to offer the client savings products, which are a basic and popular need for many microfinance institutions, but also to permit the expansion of the funding base for microfinance institutions, with the added benefit of increasing contact with a potential client base. Thus, the 147 institutions tracked by the *Microbanking Bulletin* reached 9 million borrowers, but 29 million savers. Indeed, this is most likely the one assured means for substantial expansion of Brazil's microfinance industry.

Clearly, permitting the mobilization of deposits also has risks, first and foremost for the small and likely vulnerable clients of the microfinance institutions concerned. If Brazil decides to move in this direction, appropriate adjustment of supervision methods would be necessary, with concomitant safeguards. A fuller discussion of these issues follows later in this chapter. At this point, it may be noted that, in many countries, regulation of microfinance for deposit-taking institutions is considered necessary; however, for non-deposit-taking, credit-only microfinance institutions, such oversight is not considered important (Christen and Rosenberg 2000; Van Greuning, Gallardo, and Randhawa 1999).

In Brazil, mobilizing of any form of resources other than donor funds for microfinance was constrained for a long time, until the legal changes of 1999 and 2001 discussed above. Although wholesale funding from financial institutions is now available for SCMs, they remain non-deposit-taking institutions; however, they are subject to Central Bank regulatory requirements and, in principle, to its supervision, as discussed earlier. Such an approach is more restrictive than in other countries, as the institutions are subject to prudential regulations despite their non-deposit-taking nature.

Microfinance Organizations' Links to Banks

EXPANDING THE ROLE OF FORMAL FINANCIAL INSTITUTIONS

Especially in view of constraints on deposit-taking, as well as institutional capacity constraints, Brazil's microfinance sector should more closely consider models that progressively increase the market-based financing of microfinance institutions, with a larger role played by formal banking institutions in wholesale financing.[40]

Depending on the institutional capacity of the microfinance institutions involved, various arrangements are possible. In one form, the microfinance institution could be only a point of contact with final clients; in another, it could be entrusted with the carrying out of preliminary credit risk analyses; in yet another variant, it could be a full financial intermediary that carries out its own risk analysis, extends loans, and carries the related credit risks. Such models allow banks to participate in microfinance while reducing the costs involved in providing microfinance services.

But wholesale funding from banks to SCMs has been slow. Only one microfinance institution received such funds in 2001; RioCred, a microfinance institution established in Rio, received funds from Fininvest, a consumer finance subsidiary of the private bank Unibanco. Now transformed into an SCM with the name MicroInvest, its equity is shared with the International Finance Corporation (IFC) in a 75:25 ratio. ABN AMRO Bank has also launched an experimental microfinance NGO, Real MicroCredito, with support from Acción International. Finally, the Caixa Econômica Federal (CEF) piloted a link with a microfinance institution (SindCred) in Rio. However, SindCred's role has been limited to identifying the client and carrying out a preliminary credit risk analysis. If SindCred proves to have sufficient institutional capacity, CEF could consider an arrangement in which SindCred bears full responsibility and risks for onlending.

In some countries, such as India, government-sponsored apex development banks play a large, indirect role in providing wholesale financing to second-tier banks, which then directly provide microfinance through their own microfinance programs or in partnership with NGOs. In 1996, NABARD, an apex development finance institution, launched its Self-Help Group–Bank Linkage Program as a lending activity for banks under their priority sector lending obligations to the rural sector. NABARD's SHGs program takes various forms:

- NABARD–Bank–SHG (without the involvement of an NGO)
- NABARD–Bank–NGO–SHG (with an NGO playing a facilitating role in group formation and development)
- NABARD–Bank–NGO–SHG (with the NGO as financial intermediary).

Examples of Bringing Banks into Microfinance

An interesting example for attracting banks to microfinance is the 'Chilean auction': A fixed subsidy is auctioned off twice a year to those commercial banks that provide the largest number of microloans for the smallest subsidy. Since its inception in 1993, the amount of subsidy has reduced from US$240 to about US$80 on loans that average US$1,200 (roughly 25 percent of GNP per capita). Although these banks are not, and probably will never be, specialized in microcredit, they are the largest microfinance providers in Chile. Because of their size and diversified loan portfolio, the institutional risk associated with microfinance has been reduced. A problem with this case is that it is a subsidy, and it is not certain that those banks that are receiving the subsidy would remain in this market once the subsidy disappears, questioning the sustainability of this effort to formalize microfinance.

Another alternative to a special regulatory window for MFIs is an 'alliance' between unregulated microfinance providers and existing banks or other types of financial institutions, which can also increase the access to financial service by the clientele of the microfinance program.

If the main motivation for licensing an MFI is to offer clients savings products instead of expanding their funding base (and therefore their loan portfolio), yet another alternative is to *allow MFIs to take deposits* as long as they are deposited in a licensed bank, reducing their risk. However, if these funds could be used as a warranty to obtain financing from the bank where they are stored, they could still be at risk.

In March 2000, the second model accounted for 70 percent of SHG linkages. NABARD's main role in the program is the refinancing it provides to participating financial institutions. NABARD also provides technical assistance to participating institutions in the form of grants to NGOs and training of bank staff. The role of the facilitating NGOs is also crucial in the model, allowing banks to decrease the cost of identifying and assessing potential borrowing SHGs. With the help of the NGO, SHGs prepare audited financial accounts for the banks. By March 2001, 263,825 SHGs had been linked to 318 banks through the participation of more than 750 NGOs. The repayment rate of loans has been above 95 percent both at the bank and SHG levels.

NABARD funds are provided to participating financial institutions at below-market interest rates, which has been an incentive for financial institutions to participate in the program. In Brazil, the equivalent would be that a bank such as BNDES, which also onlends at regulated rates, provides indirect funding to commercial banks for onlending to microfinance client groups. It can be argued that BNDES already provides wholesale

Microfinance and Public Banks: Recent Measures

Apart from BNDES, new schemes for the expansion of microfinance have also been set up at Banco do Brasil (BB), CEF, and BNB.

BB: The Banco Popular has been established as an independent subsidiary that will work specifically with microcredit loans. The Banco Popular will focus primarily on Brazil's large informal market with simplified accounts. The Banco Popular will use only correspondent banks to provide its services, which will be contracted on a fee-per-transaction basis. All correspondent banks will need to have an account with BB. A pilot program was to be launched at the end of 2003 and early 2004, with 350 correspondent banks in five cities. The plan is to have 4,500 correspondent banks and 1 million clients by the end of December 2004. The initial business plan will involve US$22 million in total investments and will utilize US$100 million of zero-cost funds onlent by BB (as part of the bank's 2 percent of demand deposits). The Banco Popular expects to break even in its third year.

CEF: The Caixa, with its own brand-name simplified account (Caixa Aqui), claims to have accumulated 750,000 new clients in 2003 after the new measures were launched and expects to reach 1 million by early 2004. Caixa Aqui account holders will have access to pre-approved rotating credit lines of R$200, with interest rates capped at 2 percent per month. Account holders can also receive social benefits, make payments, receive government programs such as the FGTS, and make deposits and withdrawals. Caixa Aqui claims to have expanded to more than 2,000 small municipalities, thus making Caixa present in all 5,561 municipalities in Brazil. As of September 2003, Caixa's network was composed of 2,108 correspondent banks. Caixa plans to contract another 2,250 this year and another 2,000 in 2004. This will expand Caixa's network, including branches, bank service outposts, and correspondents in lottery houses, to more than 20,000 service points.

BNB: Finally, the BNB has modified many features of its CrediAmigo program in accordance with measures taken by other banks, including limits on onlending interest rates.

funds to banks for microentrepreneurs, under the various FINAME products, or through the Brasil Empreendedor programs. But these programs are more for the medium and small sectors than for microcredit. Also, in such cases, the banks lend directly to SMEs, and the principles of microfinance lending are not adopted. There is no role for the NGOs or the solidarity groups that provide the client interface.

Another facet of the NABARD model is that the banks concerned are permitted to use their microfinance lending toward the fulfillment of their quotas for rural credit. In Brazil, to the extent that the earmarking of com-

Bank Rakyat Indonesia (Indonesia), Grameen Bank (Bangladesh), and Bank for Agriculture and Agricultural Cooperatives (Thailand)

Bank Rakyat Indonesia (BRI), one of three state banks, houses the world's largest microfinance network, the BRI Unit Desa. The Unit Desa (village units) were established in the early 1970s to provide agricultural inputs for the cultivation of rice. By the mid-1980s, the system was going to be discontinued, but the Ministry of Finance and the BRI restructured the whole Unit Desa and turned it into a financially viable institution. With the launching of two simple products, the KUPEDES loan and the SIMPEDES savings account, the right mixture of staff incentives and the profit orientation, the Unit Desa soon became very profitable. Clients targeted are not the poorest, however; solidarity groups are not used; and collateral is required.

The origin of the Grameen Bank can be traced to 1976, when Professor Muhammad Yunus launched an action research project to examine the possibility of designing a credit delivery system to provide banking services targeted at the rural poor. The pilot, based largely on principles of solidarity group lending to the poorest, taking advantage of coinsurance and social collateral, was successful, and the project was extended to several districts in the country. In 1983, the project was transformed into an independent bank, which is owned by the rural poor whom it serves (90 percent), and the remaining 10 percent is owned by the government. The Grameen Bank has more than 2.4 million borrowers, over 90 percent women, with 1,170 branches providing services in 40,000 villages. In 1995, the Grameen Bank decided not to receive any more donor funds, as it believes that the growing amount of deposits will be more than enough to repay its existing loans and expand its credit program.

The Bank for Agriculture and Agricultural Cooperatives of Thailand (BAAC) was established in 1966 as a government-owned agricultural development bank. The mandate of the bank has been to provide agricultural credit to farm households. Its success is founded on maximizing outreach to 3.5 million farm households and maintaining financial viability and sustainability of its operations and services. Since 1998, BAAC, with the assistance of the German Technical Cooperation Agency (GTZ), has been pilot testing microcredit programs for extremely poor clients. As of December 2001, BAAC has more than 10 million clients in savings, with more than US$3 billions in deposits.

Source: Bank Indonesia, GTZ, www.grameen-info.org, www.baac.org.th.

mercial banks' lending continues (at present to the rural and housing sectors), it could be more appropriately targeted to the smallest clients, through the establishment of links with microfinance lending.

BNDES (and on an experimental basis, CEF) point out that they are prepared to directly finance small microfinance institutions and also point to the difficulty of finding microfinance institutions with adequate institutional capacity to partner them.[42] Small microfinance institutions do not complain about a financing constraint, and the DAI study highlights the high percentage of microfinance institution funds in liquid investments such as government bonds. However, working directly with microfinance institutions may be more difficult for a wholesale bank, compared to working through the channels of commercial banks, NGOs, and solidarity groups, as the latter provide the client interface and knowledge. Working directly with modestly sized client microfinance institutions may be difficult to expand. Also, as discussed further below, this model requires a separate regulatory window for microfinance institutions. Moreover, in the BNDES model, it would be difficult to apply good principles of microfinance lending to the client microfinance institutions of BNDES.

The CrediAmigo model provides an alternative example of much closer bank support (from the BNB) to a single large-scale microfinance institution, which remains on its books and operates within the regulatory framework of the formal financial institution and concentrates training, expertise, and methodology; deals with large numbers of clients; and allows the use of an existing extensive branch network. The CrediAmigo model at its inception had been closer to the models of the Grameen Bank of Bangladesh or the Unit Desa Banks of Indonesia. Note, however, that the new interest rate policy (including the 2 percent limit) of the CrediAmigo will make this institution a formidable competitor against other microfinance institutions in the Northeast. CrediAmigo risks losing its multiplier effect (as a best practice microfinance institution) and could be perceived as one more government-subsidized credit program.

How extensive is BNDES-style direct support to microfinance institutions in other countries? In Peru, COFIDE, a second-tier, government-owned development finance company, has provided loans to regulated microfinance institutions. But the two most important components of the microfinance institution liabilities are deposits and financing from other financial institutions in Peru, and in some cases, from other countries. In no case do loans from COFIDE constitute more than one-third of liabilities (table 2.10).

In Bolivia, there are two government-owned funds devoted to granting loans and offering technical assistance to financial institutions in the field of microfinance. Of these, the Fund for the Development of the Financial System and Support to the Productive Sector, following its restructuring in 1999, began to finance regulated and unregulated microfinance institutions. However, its role was later limited to the provision of finance for the

Table 2.10 COFIDE Financing to MFIs, by December 2001

MFI	*COFIDE financing (US$m)*	*% share of external financing*	*% share of liabilities*
Mibanco	15.1	68.6	27.2
Cajas Municipales de Ahorro y Credito (CMACs)	33.4	52.2	9.2
Cajas Rurales de Ahorro y Credito (CRACs)	27.6	78.2	32.4
Empresa de Desarrollo de la Pequeña y Micro Empresa (EDPYMEs)	11.8	34.8	31.5

Source: Banking Superintendency, Peru.

unregulated microfinance institutions alone, in addition to the provision of technical assistance to all microfinance institutions.

Public Banks and Competition Issues

The presence of institutions (mostly those established by municipalities), that charge highly subsidized interest rates creates a distortion in the market likely to be a barrier to entry for new private players. Banco do Povo de São Paulo is an example of such an institution that, although apparently successful, is extremely costly to the government, and in which financial self-reliance is clearly a subsidiary objective. In the long run, such a program could perversely choke off total credit to the system, as private providers are not able to compete in its market. The problem of such crowding out, even in microfinance, is accentuated by the existence of numerous 'low-cost' programs and credit lines, implemented mostly by Brazil's development, federal-, or state-owned banks. The danger of such crowding out has increased with the recently introduced measures of 2003, which include large-scale subsidies to small borrowers.

Microfinance Methodology: Principles of Good Practice

As alluded to earlier in the present chapter, economic theory, as well as supporting evidence from several countries, points to several principles that can mitigate the risks and reduce the costs associated with microfinance lending. Many of these principles have been adopted by Credi-Amigo but could be extended especially to newer start-up microfinance initiatives. These principles point particularly to the value of group con-

Banco do Povo, an Example of an Institution with Subsidized Interest Rates

Banco do Povo is a microfinance investment fund created in 1998 by the state of São Paulo. Banco do Povo receives an annual donation from the government of São Paulo's budget. The funds are administered by the state bank Nossa Caixa, which makes disbursements and collects payments on loans made by Banco do Povo.

Banco do Povo's trained credit agents distribute loans aimed mostly at financing fixed capital investments by small businesses and, more recently, start-up companies. The bank's prime objective is to stimulate employment in the state, and it is therefore located in the offices of the City Hall and the Labor Secretary.

Banco do Povo has been quite successful at increasing its loan portfolio while maintaining apparently good quality of loans. Loans disbursed have increased from R$3 million in the first year of operation (September 1998 to September 1999) to R$13 million last fiscal year (September 2000 to September 2001). Nonperforming loans (overdue by 30 days or more) reach only 2 to 3 percent. However, Banco do Povo's loans carry a subsidized interest rate of 1 percent per month in accordance with the limits set by the Usury Law for nonregulated entities.

Source: Banco do Povo.

tracts and dynamic incentives for loan repayment. The Grameen group lending model, in which the default of one member implies that all group members are subsequently denied loans, has been successfully replicated in several countries. Credit cooperatives and rotating savings schemes also use the principle of social insurance, which makes these approaches successful. Such models reduce the risks of 'asymmetric information,' or limited knowledge of the client by the lender. Selection by peers of group members also mitigates 'adverse selection,' in which potential borrowers may include an unusually high proportion of high-risk people who know that their default is too small to be followed up by the lender (Besley 1994; Besley and Coate 1991; Morduch 1999; Udry 1990).

Not all successful microfinance institutions strictly follow the group approach alone, however; BancoSol in Bolivia also required some form of guarantee on around one-quarter of its portfolio, and BRI Indonesia does not use a group-lending mechanism and does require some form of collateral (see below). However, as a consequence, the poorest borrowers are excluded from the BRI model, which targets the group of the 'better-off' poor. Interestingly, some evidence suggests that overall repayment rates are higher in models with greater focus on the poor. Such models tend to rely more on solidarity mechanisms.[43]

Other good practices identified include 'dynamic incentives,' in which loan amounts have progressive or 'step-lending' features, increasing over time; regular repayment schedules that begin immediately after the loan (and help capture a cash flow before it is dissipated); and lending to women or particularly disadvantaged groups with few other options. Finally, although few programs require formal collateral, a collateral substitute is not uncommon; for example, the Grameen Bank requires borrowers to contribute to an emergency fund, in the amount of 0.5 percent of every unit borrowed. An additional 5 percent of the loan is taken out as a 'group tax,' which goes into a group fund account, thus constituting a form of forced savings.

Other Constraints on Expansion

Other factors at play include insufficient information to small entrepreneurs on microfinance availability.[44] This emphasizes the importance of financial education and training efforts for government entities such as BNDES and SEBRAE. The creation of the Portal do Microcrédito (www.portaldomicrocredito.org.br), sponsored by Comunidade Solidária, is a step in the right direction, although the low level of internet connectivity among small entrepreneurs will limit its short-term use.

Parallel to this is the strengthening of information disclosure at the microfinance institutions themselves. Only some of the largest programs publicly disclose financial information on their performance. This contributes to the perception that microfinance providers do not devote sufficient attention to profitability and sustainability. Adopting standard charts of accounts and the publication of results are potential solutions. The microfinance internet portal could also be used for disclosure purposes. An alternative is to encourage the rating of microfinance providers and publish these ratings. Increased communication on the benefits of microfinance compared to other, more-traditional finance sources would also help increase the demand for microfinance.

Second, venture capital funds in Brazil have had a limited interest in microfinance. Although several venture capital funds are active in Brazil, most of them invest in middle-market firms. HSBC, with the InterAmerican Investment Corporation, has recently established a US$105 million private equity fund to invest in SMEs in Latin America, with a special focus on Brazil. It remains very limited, however, compared to the potential demand. The International Finance Corporation of the World Bank Group is also a small actor, and the other player is the government-owned SEBRAE, as described above.

Third, the scarcity of trained loan officers willing to work for small microfinance institutions is also mentioned as a constraint to growth. The difficulties of prevailing labor laws also make it financially difficult to hire good loan officers on a permanent basis, as returns to these activities would not support the maintenance of costly staff with high overheads. Providing additional training to candidate or existing credit officers as proposed by the Comunidade Solidária is therefore certainly needed, at least as a prelude to the investigation of means to make labor laws flexible.

Microfinance Regulation and Supervision: Future Policy Options

The present section does not evaluate in any detail the recent changes introduced in microfinance regulation in 2003. These measures and their potential impact are alluded to elsewhere in this chapter.

Should Microfinance Be Regulated or Supervised?

A discussion of this issue is facilitated if a basic conceptual distinction is pointed out between *prudential* (protective) and *nonprudential* (enabling or preventive) regulation. *Prudential regulation* is concerned with the safety of the financial system and of deposits in institutions that intermediate funds. Such regulation, which comprises, for example, capital adequacy, reserve, or liquidity norms, is usually complex and would typically require a financial regulator's supervision for implementation. *Nonprudential regulation* (for example, disclosure of ownership and control, fees and rates, consumer protection, or financial performance), on the other hand, could largely be self-executing. Until 1999, Brazil's microfinance institutions, as NGOs or nonprofit entities, were not subject to financial regulations and were entitled to special tax treatment. But they were constrained by the Usury Law and limited in their capacity to mobilize funds. Today, the majority of Brazil's microfinance institutions operate under special regulatory windows, as civil society organizations (OSCIPs) or microcredit societies (SCMs). However, one major microfinance institution, CrediAmigo, operates as a department of a bank and is therefore regulated under this umbrella.

Conceivably, other banks, public or private, could also have microfinance operations among their activities. SCMs, as financial institutions, are subject to regulatory requirements that encompass both enabling regulations (reporting requirements) and prudential regulations (minimum capital, leverage, and liquidity). OSCIPs have reporting (nonprudential) obligations to the Ministry of Justice but are not subject to prudential regulation or supervision as a financial entity.

To what extent is the present framework in line with international practice, and what modifications may be needed to support the future evolution of this sector? There is an increasing international consensus on a large range of issues concerning the regulation and supervision of microfinance institutions, and the present section discusses broad guidelines that may be helpful going forward.[45]

Structure of Liabilities and Need for Prudential Regulation

A first consensus area in the microfinance regulation and supervision debate is that it is the structure of the liabilities side of a microfinance institution that determines whether it should or should not be regulated and the extent to which supervision and oversight are required. The emerging consensus points out that credit-only microfinance institutions need not in general be subject to prudential regulation, because the limited resources of a bank authority would be distracted regulating and supervising an institution in which public interest is not at stake. However, this does not preclude nonprudential or enabling regulations, which are aimed at preventing abuses in the industry and also at promotion through greater transparency. Indeed, protection against abusive lending and collection practices, or truth-in-lending, can be particularly relevant for institutions such as microfinance institutions. Ownership and governance criteria (for example, limitations against public sector participation on boards of SCMs) belong to the same category.

Brazil's microfinance institutions today are subject to both nonprudential and, in the case of SCMs, prudential regulations, although its SCMs are not deposit-taking. Prima facie, the present level of prudential regulation of the SCMs appears to be greater than warranted by their funding or scope of activities; it is possible, however, that regulations were imposed with a view to the possible future expansion of the scope of activities of SCMs. Waiting until the microfinance institution sector reveals itself to be sufficiently mature to take deposits can be a prudent strategy. If Brazil believes that the microfinance institution sector is today sufficiently mature for it to contemplate this major step, the structure of the prudential regulation of this sector going forward requires planning.

Are Special Regulatory Windows Needed?

Regarding regulation, the debate focuses on whether there should be a special regulatory window for microfinance activities, or for microfinance institutions, or whether this should come under the code applied to other financial institutions. As discussed above, their risk profile is unique, and regulations may do well to require distinct treatment for microloans or institutions specialized in microfinance. Such regulatory windows may, for example, lower entry requirements or establish a higher capital ratio.

But against this, the proliferation of different, specialized, regulatory windows can rapidly increase the number of regulated microfinance institutions, because the entry requirements can be so low that many microfinance institutions can apply for it. This situation reduces the effectiveness of the prudential supervision, due to both resource constraints and need for appropriate supervisory experience.

Today, Brazil has a specialized framework for SCMs, and their numbers have increased from 0 to 36 in three years. This could swiftly become a supervisory burden. There is also a separate framework for credit OSCIPs; the need for this third window, in addition to the NGO and the SCM, could be reevaluated over time. At present, its major purpose may be as an instrument to avoid the interest rate restrictions on the NGO.

Opinion today is increasingly that integrating microfinance institutions into formal financial systems is key to expanding their outreach and could also facilitate the commercialization or downscaling of banks into microfinance activities. Banks, with their large networks of offices and information systems, have some advantages with respect to smaller microfinance institutions, but in general, they still lack the lending methodologies to enter aggressively into the new field of microfinance. The higher minimum capital requirement of a bank is often cited as a barrier for microfinance institutions, but in some countries, this capital can be so low that sustainable microfinance institutions can afford to comply with it.[46] In Brazil, the new regulatory framework for microfinance institutions has much lower minimum capital requirements than banks, but the largest and arguably most successful of Brazil's microfinance institutions is so far constituted as an arm of a bank, with no special regulatory window.

Specific Prudential Norms: Minimum Capital, Capital Ratios, and Credit Risk

If a special regulatory window is to be established for microfinance institutions, it is argued that the smaller balance sheets of microfinance institutions and, in many cases, the lower capacity of their shareholders to make additional contributions to the equity capital, imply a lower minimum capital, both for entry to the market and for ongoing business operations. Establishing such different capital requirement for microfinance institutions can be very difficult, and appropriate levels can vary from country to country, depending on the size of the existing microfinance providers, the competition in the field of microfinance, and required investments to start the licensed microfinance company, which depends on other requirements made by the bank authority.

The size of existing microfinance providers matters, because if too high, applicants will be few, but too low a level will invite an excessive

Table 2.11 Capital Requirements for Regulated MFIs

Country	*MFI*	*Minimum capital (US$'000)*
Bolivia	Private financial funds (FFPs)	820
El Salvador	Savings and loan societies (SACs)	2,900
Panama	Microfinance banks (BMFs)	3,000
Peru	Municipal offices, rural offices, and EDPYMEs	233
Ghana	Savings and loan companies/rural banks	50/20
Philippines	Rural and cooperative banks, thrift banks[a]	50–260/1,000–6,500
Brazil	Microenterprise credit societies (SCMs)	60

a. For rural and cooperative banks, the paid-up capital varies from US$50,000 to US$260,000, depending on the class of municipality or metropolitan area in which the bank is located. In the case of thrift banks, those operating outside metropolitan Manila are required to have US$1 million of paid-up capital, and those inside, US$6.5 million.
Source: Gallardo 2001; Rosales 2002.

number of applicants, regardless of their sustainability, also posing supervision problems. The degree of competition matters, because the higher the competition, the lower the spread and thus the larger the loan portfolio must be to cover administrative expenses. A larger loan portfolio can be financed either by larger equity or by higher financial leverage, but the latter (as discussed below) is not desirable. Finally, higher regulatory requirements require better information systems, which also argue for higher equity capital. These factors vary considerably by country, and there is no golden rule for establishing a minimum capital requirement, but many factors need to guide the decision. As table 2.11 indicates, Brazil's minimum capital for SCMs is low at present. Whether this is justified in view of the factors discussed above should be debated.

Differences in the minimum capital requirements in countries that have opened regulatory windows for microfinance institutions can also be viewed in terms of the ratio of minimum capital for banks compared to the minimum capital for the licensed microfinance institution. This ratio is 3.3 in Panama, 3.9 in El Salvador, 9.1 in Bolivia, and 19.3 in Peru, to mention some countries. In Brazil, by contrast, the difference in minimum requirements (and thus this ratio) is very high: 175 times for commercial banks and 125 times for development or investment banks.[47]

Capital Ratios and Leverage

Capital ratios establish limits to financial intermediation, reducing the risk from opportunistic behavior from the shareholders, who want to maximize their profits but, at the same time, reduce their risk. Capital ratios also induce asset diversification through risk weighting. Currently, the capital ratio does not discriminate among types of loans in terms of risk weighting. However, microloans are relatively risky for the reasons discussed before: lack of physical collateral and higher volatility and nature of clients, as well as more costly to administer. Especially in countries with low financial intermediation and a large informal sector, these pressures can be compounded by excess demand for microloans, which raises liquidity risk as well as leverage. A higher capital ratio would be required to limit the exposure of microfinance institutions to these risks.

However, conversely, there are two arguments against setting higher capital ratios for microfinance institutions: It results in a less-efficient use of capital, and therefore lower profits, and it restricts microfinance institutions' access to borrowing at market rates, limiting their growth. But cross-country data suggest that sustainable microfinance institutions have achieved operating self-sufficiency with fairly high capital ratios. One option to reconcile these issues is to have a phased approach to capital ratios, with higher initial requirements for some period of time or until some conditions have been achieved, usually financial sustainability, a large equity capital, and better internal and external controls.

As an alternative to reducing capital ratios, institutions may be allowed a wider range of products as their maturity increases. Peruvian regulation adopts such a scheme; more equity capital and better audit systems allow microfinance institutions to perform a wider variety of operations. However, the capital ratio remains at the 9.1 percent minimum. And in many countries, the same capital ratios are required for licensed microfinance institutions as for banks, as is the case in Peru, Bolivia, El Salvador, and Philippines. Panama and Mexico are still determining the capital ratio for these institutions. In Brazil, a credit-only SCM is constrained to lower financial leverage (that is, a capital ratio of five times liquid assets, almost twice as high as the capital ratio of 11 percent of tier 1 and tier 2 capital for the banking system).

Credit Risk Regulation

As discussed, the characteristics of microfinance clients increase their credit risk. This may suggest that more conservative limits on credit risk are needed in terms of provisioning practices. But it is difficult to determine a cutoff limit for microcredit, microenterprises, or microfinance, and any limits set are to some degree arbitrary. Looking at regulatory experiences elsewhere, it is common for the risk of microcredit to be categorized in terms of past-due days, and for each category, a rate of provisioning is determined. Credit risk regulations should also specify how to categorize refinanced or rolled-over loans, loans to related parties, and loan concentration ratios.

Supervision Issues: Who Should Supervise?

Related to this is the issue of who can provide oversight to microfinance institutions: the banking or financial sector supervisor, a separate or delegated supervisor, or self-regulation? These choices are based partially on the changes that regulation imposes on microfinance institutions in the form of more reporting requirements and the corresponding need for more oversight and also on the numbers of such institutions as compared to banks and other entities under formal supervision. It can be argued that the supervision of deposit-taking microfinance institutions should ideally be carried out by a bank supervisor. However, the large number of regulated financial institutions has induced supervisors in many countries to adopt other types of supervision, such as auxiliary, delegated, or hybrid supervision. In the case of *auxiliary supervision,* the bank supervisor is supported in its task by a third party; in the case of *delegated supervision,* the supervision of microfinance institutions is transferred to a new supervisor; and in the case of *hybrid supervision,* some criteria are established to separate those institutions that are supervised by the bank regulator, and the remainder, who are supervised by a delegated supervisor. Usual criteria used in this type of supervision are size of assets, degree of financial intermediation (deposit base), and integration with the payment system.[48]

In Indonesia, indirect supervision is used to supervise credit-only microfinance institutions, the Badan Kredit Desas (BKDs). According to law, all BKDs, a special type of Bank Perkreditan Rakyat, or People's Credit Bank, are to be supervised by Bank Indonesia. However, considering their large number (5,345) and the fact that the BKDs are not mobilizing deposits from the public, Bank Indonesia decided to entrust Bank Rakyat Indonesia with the supervision of BKDs, performing the duty of a delegated supervisor.

Some countries, such as South Africa, have a special supervisor for microfinance. Apart from numbers, there is a case for a specialized supervision approach for microfinance operations, on account of special characteristics: small size and multiple small transactions, inherently greater risk and volatility due to the short maturity of their assets, a market concentrated in low segments of the population with a lack of physical collateral, a lending methodology based on information rather than guarantees, a loan portfolio composed of a large number of microloans with a short-term maturity, high volatility, and an institutional structure in which shareholders have no 'deep pockets.' These features change the risk profile of these institutions, which must be adapted for appropriate supervision methods.[49] These argue for some differences in the approach to supervision, compared to a formal financial institution, as formal supervision could rapidly become very costly.

There is thus a tradeoff between the introduction of prudential regulation and the costs of supervising compliance with this regulation. This will be a key issue for Brazil in going forward if SCMs increase in numbers. Brazil will have to consider the feasibility of maintaining high levels of supervision by the banking superintendent of these entities.

Finally, self-regulation could be appropriate for an infant industry providing limited services and for institutions that do not take deposits from the public. However, self-regulation is rare and, to be effective, should be combined with public ratings of such entities. But few rating agencies in developing countries are able to rate microfinance institutions. Moreover, rating systems lack sanction mechanisms. There is a general consensus today that, although desirable in some circumstances, successful self-regulation is hard to achieve.

The Credit Cooperative Movement and Its Contributions to Access

An Overview of the Credit Cooperative Sector in Brazil

Credit cooperatives were established in Brazil just after the turn of the century in the state of Rio Grande do Sul, and more than 60 were established in the same region until the mid-1960s. At that time, the 'open' form of cooperative, known as the Luzzatti cooperative, prevailed, with no membership restrictions and thus no restrictions against who could obtain credits. Financial scandals coinciding with reforms in the banking laws in the mid-1960s revealed their risks to regulators and made them uncompetitive with banks. In 1967, there was an outright ban on the establishment of new credit cooperatives. A new cooperative law in 1971 sharply restricted the activities of existing cooperatives and set tight membership criteria. Over the following 20 years, more than 50 cooperatives closed down, with losses for their members.

The credit cooperative movement began to witness a renaissance in the early 1980s, when central credit cooperatives were permitted that began to provide apex services to member single credit cooperatives. Thus, the central cooperative, Cooperativa Central de Crédito Rural do Rio Grande do Sul (Rural Cooperative of Rio Grande do Sul), was formed for nine-member cooperatives in Rio Grande do Sul, and similar central credit cooperatives were established in most Brazilian states over the next two decades. These central cooperatives provided a way for liquidity surpluses and needs to be addressed within a network. In 1995, the National Monetary Council authorized the establishment of cooperative banks, which are regular commercial banks that are owned and controlled by cooperatives. This has enabled cooperatives to begin to gain access to sev-

What Is a Credit Cooperative or Credit Union?

Credit unions are legally constituted not-for-profit cooperative financial institutions chartered and supervised, for the most part, under national cooperative law and created to meet the basic financial service needs of primarily low- and middle-income citizens. Credit unions provide a means to learn the value of regular savings and wise use of credit. They are a form of economic empowerment, based on an individual's ability to control and manage the financial institution that provides savings, credit, and financial management services at nonexploitative terms to the poor.

Membership eligibility is usually defined in terms of some common affiliation, such as employment or residence. All members are owners of the enterprise and have equal privileges, opportunities, and responsibilities. Typically, a credit union only accepts deposits from and grants loans to members. All members are equal owners of the enterprise, and each has one vote in the election for committee members and the board of directors. Members of these elected bodies serve in an unpaid voluntary capacity.

Source: World Council of Credit Unions, www.woccu.org.

eral of the benefits of the regular banking system. Cooperatives continue to count for a very small share of the total financial system but have grown significantly in recent years (table 2.12 and figure 2.4).

Principal Players in Cooperative Finance

Cooperatives are formed for a wide range of activities in Brazil, and credit cooperatives rank third in importance in number of cooperatives and of employees but second in number of members (table 2.12). Non-credit cooperatives can act as channels for banking loans to their members, but only credit cooperatives are authorized to mobilize deposits and offer other financial services to their members. Credit cooperatives can take three forms: mutual credit, rural credit, or Luzzatti. *Mutual credit cooperatives* can be formed by a minimum of 20 persons who share a common workplace or professional association. *Rural credit cooperatives* can be formed by people who work predominantly in agriculture or related activities in rural areas. Up until July 2003, only 10 *Luzzatti* or *open cooperatives* were operating in the country, and no new ones were being authorized. New regulatory measures introduced in July 2003 allowed for the creation of open-admission cooperatives again, under certain conditions.[50]

Table 2.12 Number of Cooperatives in Brazil, by Type

Type	*No. of institutions*	*No. of people ('000)*	*No. of employees ('000)*
Agroindustry	1,587	822.3	108.3
Consumption	189	1,467.4	7.7
Credit	1,038	1,059.4	20.7
Education	278	73.3	2.7
Special	7	2.1	—
Health	863	327.2	21.4
Housing	297	69.7	1.4
Infrastructure	187	576.3	5.4
Mining	37	48.8	—
Production	147	9.9	0.4
Tourism	5	0.2	—
Workers	2,391	322.7	7.4
Total	7,026	4,779.1	175.4

Note: — = not available.
Source: ABRACOOP, www.abracoop.com.br.

Figure 2.4 Capital, Deposits, and Loans of the SICOOB and SICREDI Cooperative Systems, 1998–2001

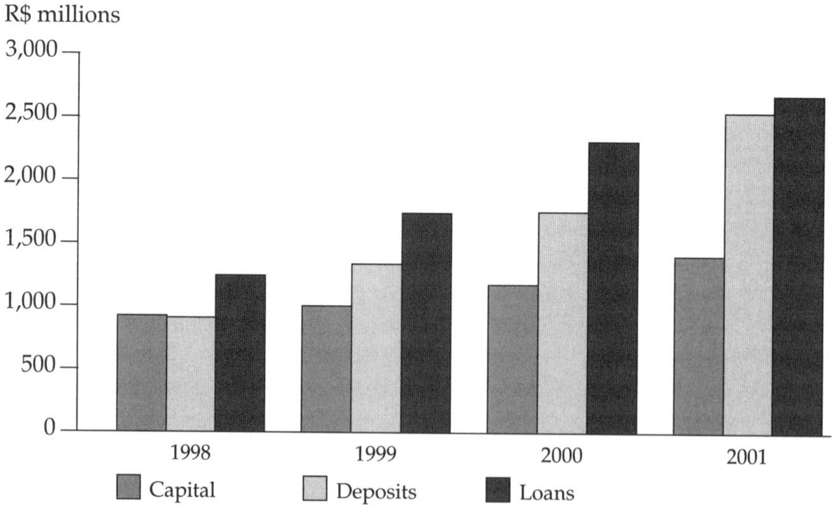

Source: SICCOB, www.bancoob.com.br, and SICREDI, www.sicredi.com.br.

What Are the Functions of a Central Credit Cooperative?

SICOOB identifies the following instructive list of purposes for constituting its central credit cooperatives, which is consistent with good practice in other countries:

- To promote integration among affiliated cooperatives
- To provide technical, legal, accounting, and financial assistance for operations and services
- To supervise single credit cooperatives
- To develop and coordinate training programs
- To redirect surplus resources from one cooperative to another
- To produce economies of scale for single cooperatives by centralizing services and administrative processes
- To seek lines of funding for onlending to affiliated cooperatives
- To help channel resources through BANCOOB
- To implement technical solutions for the system
- To establish product and service guidelines and ensure their implementation
- To enter into service agreements at a regional level
- To advise on the establishment of new cooperatives by guiding and accompanying the entire process, together with the Central Bank, as well as assisting with designing and equipping the new facilities
- To promote integration between credit cooperatives and other forms of cooperative.

Source: SICOOB, www.bancoob.com.br.

Central cooperatives are apex institutions for member credit cooperatives that operate at a state level and are owned by at least three member cooperatives. They serve to review standards applied by member cooperatives in such areas as accounting, loan origination, staffing, and facilities; facilitate flows of funds from cooperatives with surplus liquidity to those requiring additional resources; and assume some auxiliary responsibility from the Central Bank for supervision.

Because central credit cooperatives still lacked access to the payments system, cooperative banks were authorized in 1995 (CMN Resolution 2193 of August 31, 1995). Two such banks have emerged since then: Banco Cooperativo do Brasil (Cooperative Bank of Brasil; BANCOOB) and Banco Cooperativo SICREDI (Cooperative Bank SICREDI, BANSICREDI), owned by the central credit cooperatives in their networks, which act as regular commercial banks. This allows them to operate as correspondent banks for their respective networks and to offer a broader range of financial services than can be undertaken by the cooperatives alone.

Size, Composition, and Services Offered

In 2001, the Central Bank reported 1,306 credit cooperatives in Brazil. The Organização das Cooperativas Brasileiras (Brazil Cooperative Organization; OCB) provided data on 1,035 cooperatives, of which 670 are mutual credit cooperatives and therefore predominantly urban in nature, 355 are rural credit cooperatives, and the remaining 10 are Luzzattis. An alternative disaggregation from the three major credit cooperative systems in early 2002 indicates 769 in Sistema das Cooperativas de Crédito do Brasil (Brazilian Credit Cooperative System; SICOOB), 107 in Sistema de Crédito Cooperativo (Credit Cooperative System; SICREDI), and 33 in Cooperativa de Crédito Solidãrio (Mutual Credit Cooperative; CRESOL), plus 10 remaining Luzzatti cooperatives, or 919 credit cooperatives. In addition, Unicred operates a network of 400 credit cooperatives for medical doctors in 14 states, which has a working agreement with BANSICREDI for access to central clearing facilities (figure 2.5).

Despite numerical dominance by mutual credit cooperatives, at least in the case of SICOOB, the largest cooperative network, rural credit cooperatives have a considerably higher proportion of cooperative financial

Figure 2.5 Cooperatives in Brazil, by Type of Cooperative, 2001

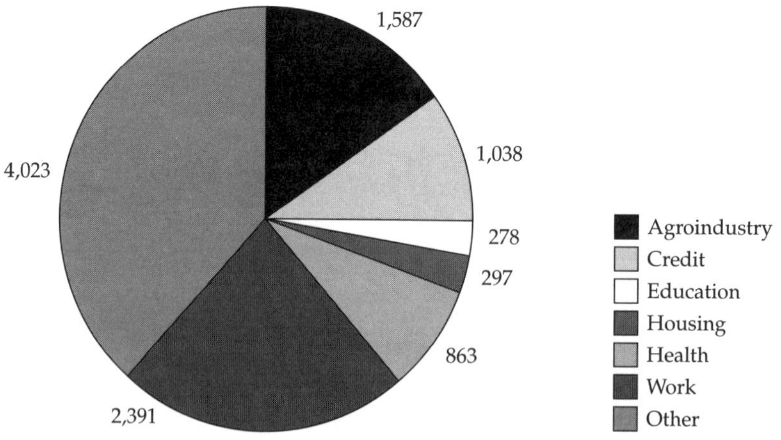

Source: Organização das Cooperativas Brasileiras, www.ocb.org.br.

An Introduction to CRESOL

The first CRESOL cooperative was founded in June 1995. With the establishment of an additional four cooperatives, a central cooperative (CRESOL-Baser) was set up in 1996 to support the system with norms, accounting, systems, training, and interaction with other players, such as banks, agricultural organizations, and national and subnational governments. The system grew from 920 members in June 1996 to 13,500 in December 2000, spread across 31 rural credit cooperatives operating in 100 municipalities in the three southern states of Paraná, Santa Catarina, and Rio Grande do Sul. These cooperatives are linked under the CRESOL-Baser central cooperative and supported by five microregional service units located across the three states.

The system provided approximately R$35 million in loans to its members in the 2000–2001 farming season. These amounts are substantially lower than those of SICREDI and SICOOB, but the CRESOL system, aside from being smaller, is also targeted to poorer and more rural clients than are the two bigger cooperative systems.

Source: Bittencourt and Abramovay 2001.

resources (around 70 percent). Taken together, credit cooperatives as a group account for one of every seven cooperatives in Brazil, ranking third behind agroindustry and worker cooperatives in number (figure 2.5). They also account for almost one-quarter of all affiliates of cooperatives. Nonetheless, membership in credit cooperatives, at slightly over 1 million, remains low at less than 1 percent of Brazil's total population and less than 3 percent of the working population.

Consolidated assets for SICOOB and SICREDI cooperative networks have risen substantially from 1998 to 2001 to over R$4.5 billion.[51] These assets are financed mainly through deposits, which rose from around R$900 million in 1998 to R$2.5 billion in 2001, and through liquid capital, which rose from some R$920 million to R$1.4 billion over the same period, with the difference funded by borrowing. The bulk of the resources went to finance loans to members, which rose from R$1.24 billion to R$2.68 billion.

Within the two networks, the respective apex cooperative banks (BANCOOB and SICOOB) account for 15–30 percent of all loans and 22–40 percent of all deposits. Deposits and loans grew remarkably between 1998 and 2001 (around 50–150 percent for deposits and 135–200 percent annually for loans). The two banks invest liquidity mobilized by member cooperatives, largely in liquid instruments issued by the National Treasury and by commercial banks. They also act as channels for public resources

Table 2.13 Distribution of Rural Credit, by Purpose and Lending Institution

	Credit (R$m)	*% share*	*Contracts ('000)*	*% share*
Banks	13,070	94.9	1,254	93.0
Working capital	8,426	61.2	979	72.5
Investment capital	2,265	16.4	258	19.2
Marketing credit	2,379	17.3	17	1.3
Rural credit cooperatives	710	5.2	95	7.0
Working capital	493	3.6	72	5.3
Investment capital	70	0.5	12	0.9
Marketing credit	147	1.1	11	0.8
Brazil	13,780	100.0	1,349	100.0
Working capital	8,919	64.7	1,051	77.9
Investment capital	2,335	16.9	270	20.0
Marketing credit	2,526	18.3	29	2.1

Source: Central Bank of Brazil, www.bc.gov.br.

to the cooperatives, notably from BNDES, to which the cooperatives do not have direct access.

In the area of rural credit, the presence of cooperatives is more important, reaching 7 percent of formal rural credit in 2000 (table 2.13). The sharp difference between their share of the rural market and of the overall market attests to the potential of cooperatives to reach more remote rural clients relatively more easily than banks. This can also be seen in appendix table A2.3, which clearly shows the presence of a few cooperatives in states in which there is virtually no presence for commercial and other banks or even for microfinance companies or finance companies. Their greater rural role probably also reflects the disbursement of government lines of credit at concessional terms to rural entities.

OUTREACH: GEOGRAPHIC AND BY INCOME LEVEL

Between them, SICREDI and SICOOB cover 18 states, with neither cooperative organization covering the Amazon states of Amazonas, Roraima, and Amapá or the Northeastern states of Maranhão, Piauí, Ceará, Alagoas, or Sergipe. With the exception of one state, Mato Grosso, there is no overlap between the states covered by SICREDI and SICOOB, so that member cooperatives are obliged to work under one or the other network, depending on the state (or establish a separate, smaller, and costlier network or work under the more restrictive regulations applicable to unaffiliated credit cooperatives).

In terms of outreach by income level, SICREDI estimates that 3–4 percent of credits are large, less than 20 percent are medium, and the vast

Table 2.14 CRESOL Membership, by Farm Size and Annual Income, 1999

Average area per member (ha)	*% members/ segment*	*Average area (ha)*	*Annual income per member (R$)*	*% members*
			Under 2,000	47.5
0.0– 10.0	32.4	7.8	2,001–4,000	18.5
10.1– 20.0	42.3	15.8	4,001–6,000	7.4
20.1– 30.0	12.0	24.7	6,001–8,000	10.7
30.1– 40.0	6.7	35.2	8,001–10,000	5.5
Over 40.0	6.6	56.4	10,001–12,000	5.3
			Over 12,000	5.1
Total	**100.0**	**18.3**	**Total**	**100.0**

Source: Bittencourt 1999.

majority are small, where 'small' refers to eligibility criteria used for access to PRONAF D loans (namely, less than R$30,000). A 1999 study of the CRESOL rural cooperative network offers more detailed data on the membership by farm size and by income level (table 2.14).

In particular, as of that year, 95 percent of CRESOL members earned incomes of under R$12,000. This clearly is a lower income strata than the larger cooperative networks. Three-quarters of members have average areas under 20 hectares.

Services Offered

The financial services that credit cooperatives can offer depend on whether or not they are affiliated with a cooperative network with central credit cooperatives and a cooperative bank.[52] Unaffiliated cooperatives are allowed to mobilize sight and time deposits from members, obtain national and international loans and grants, offer credit to members, place liquid assets in financial institutions, offer collection and custody services, and enter into agreements with other financial institutions to gain access to the check-clearing and settlement system and to correspondent banking services.

By linking with a cooperative bank, credit cooperatives are able to offer a broader range of services. For example, members of SICOOB and SICREDI issue credit cards, offer internet banking, issue trade credits including letters of credit, provide insurance (life, nonlife, and rural), and extend working capital and investment loans funded by public programs such as PRONAF and lines of credit under the BNDES (for example, FINAME, Programa Nacional de Recuperação de Pastagens Degradadas

[National Program of Recovery of Degraded Pastures; PROPASTO], Programa de Incentivo ao Uso de Correctivos de Solos [Program of Incentive for the Use of Soil Products; PROSOLO]). They are also able to facilitate forward sales, notably by coffee growers, through the Cédula de Produto Rural (rural bills of exchange; CPR) instrument.[53] Credit cooperatives cannot offer their members foreign exchange services, leasing, or housing finance.

Penetration of Brazil's Credit Cooperatives: International Comparisons

A comparison of the outreach of credit cooperatives in Brazil with that in other countries suggests that membership in Brazil is very low (table 2.15).[54] With around 1 million members in a population of 170 million, the penetration of cooperative finance remains below 1 percent of the total population and around 3 percent of the working population. Deposits in Brazilian credit cooperatives are less than 1 percent of total deposits in the banking system; the share of loans by credit cooperatives relative to total credit to the private sector is similar. This is very low compared to many countries in North and Latin America. Also, despite recent overall growth in credit union numbers, the performance of credit cooperatives affiliated with the World Council of Credit Unions (WOCCU) in Brazil has been virtually stagnant in the past five to six years (table 2.16). The low penetration rates of Brazilian cooperatives (when compared with other countries

Table 2.15 Credit Cooperatives in Brazil and Other Countries, 2001

Country	*Number*	*Members ('000)*	*% penetration ratio*[a]	*Savings (US$m)*	*Loans (US$m)*	*Reserves (US$m)*	*Assets (US$m)*
Brazil	423	467	0.6	201	191	24	285
Bolivia	15	102	4.1	50	45	7	62
Ecuador	332	1,481	35.3	162	143	54	220
Peru	175	349	4.6	226	178	19	271
Canada[b]	901	5,560	108.1	40,317	35,939	2,654	46,964
United States	10,355	81,586	57.9	449,013	330,894	55,910	514,691
Germany[b]	1,794	30,000	74.1	324,236	287,355	—	461,911
Spain	88	7,817	45.9	34,804	27,457	2,482	40,938

Note: — = not available.
a. Credit union members over economically active population, percentage.
b. Includes credit unions and other financial cooperatives.
Source: World Council of Credit Unions (WOCCU) Statistical Reports.

Table 2.16 Evolution of WOCCU-Affiliated Credit Unions in Brazil

Year	*No. of co-ops*	*Members ('000)*	*% penetration ratio*[a]	*Savings (US$m)*	*Loans (US$m)*	*Reserves (US$m)*	*Assets (US$m)*
2001	423	467	0.6	201	191	24	285
2000	423	467	0.7	268	255	33	381
1999	423	467	0.7	268	255	33	381
1998	368	800	1.1	63	187	36	352
1997	196	221	0.3	26	146	5	285
1996	435	435	0.6	101	213	178	475
1995	570	435	0.4	101	213	178	475
1994	564	450	0.5	34	115	115	226

a. Credit union members over working population, percentage.
Source: World Council of Credit Unions (WOCCU) Statistical Reports.

at similar levels of economic development), notwithstanding the long history of cooperative credit in Brazil and the relative depth of Brazil's overall financial system, suggest that regulatory factors played a significant role in retarding the development of cooperative finance in the country.

Financial Structure and Performance of Brazilian Credit Cooperatives

Some widely acknowledged common failings of credit unions in various countries have been avoided to a great extent by the large Brazilian cooperative networks. The common pitfalls of low deposit as well as low lending rates do not apply, as both deposit and lending interest rates in SICREDI and SICOOB are competitive with the banking system. Second, an effort has been made to maintain skilled staff. In SICREDI, around 60 percent of staff have tertiary-level education in relevant skills. SICREDI management has indicated that it intends to try to maintain salaries at levels that are competitive with private banks so as to retain skills. Third, considerable emphasis has been placed on systems, accounting, training, and standards.

Sources and Uses of Funds

Based on data from sample rural credit cooperatives in the SICREDI network, it appears that such cooperatives are fairly highly leveraged, at ratios at or just below the 10:1 limit. Deposits account for the bulk of financing, and borrowings from banks (interbank lines of credit) account

Dimensions of Outreach by Cooperatives in Various Countries

The proportion of the working-age population who are members of credit unions is already considerable in several countries. At the end of 2001, Dominica had the highest proportion of members to working-age population, 283 percent (due to multiple memberships), and the Caribbean as a whole had 49.6 percent. North America also has a high outreach of credit unions; Canada had a 30.4 percent proportion, and the United States, 57.9 percent. Credit unions in Europe play a very important role in the financial system. Members of credit unions in Austria and France are more than 100 percent of the working-age population; in the Netherlands, 97 percent; and in Germany and Hungary, around 75 percent. Spain and Italy also have very large credit unions and other financial cooperatives.

In the case of the United States, more than 10,000 credit unions with over $515 billion in assets serve more than 81 million people across the country. Credit unions have been rated first in customer satisfaction among financial institutions over a 10-year period, according to the *American Banker Newspaper's* annual customer satisfaction survey.

Source: World Council of Credit Unions, www.woccu.org, and National Credit Union Administration, www.ncua.org.

for another sizeable share (16 percent). Due to high liquidity requirements, 40–50 percent of resources are held as cash and bank deposits (with BANSICREDI), and around the same is onlent in credit operations to members, with rural credit accounting for slightly more than one-third of total credit. Fixed assets are kept to a minimum, at 3 percent of total assets. Within the capital account, reserves are more significant than member contributions or retained earnings. Around 40 percent of loans are personal loans, another 40 percent are working capital loans, and 20 percent are investment loans, with respective maturities averaging 90 days, 8 months, and 3 years. Off-balance-sheet items include custodial services, which can be popular.

At the central credit cooperatives, close to half of funds (48 percent at SICREDI) are kept liquid, around 40 percent is loaned, divided evenly between rural and nonrural credit, and the remainder is held as fixed and other assets. The discounting of public funds accounts for almost three-quarters of rural credit. On the financing side, deposits account for around 60 percent of resources, with most of these (80 percent) held as time deposits and the remainder as sight deposits. Loans and discounts account for just under 20 percent of funding, and the rest is capital.

Common Pitfalls of Credit Unions

- *Low deposit rates:* Deposit rates are often well below commercial bank rates, although because credit unions are typically riskier institutions, a competitive credit union deposit rate would normally exceed the bank rate. In the past, when credit unions have raised deposit rates to this level, deposit mobilization has often increased sharply, greatly expanding the outreach of the credit unions and their capacity to offer loans.
- *Low loan rates and little capitalization of profits:* Loan rates in Latin American credit unions are typically set so that very little or no profit is earned. Moreover, a large proportion of any profits that are earned is frequently paid out in dividends to members. Consequently, credit unions typically have little institutional capital for future expansion or to buffer negative shocks.
- *Opaque financial information and undisciplined financial practices:* Problems in this area include underreporting of loan delinquency, failure to write off overdue loans, overstatement of profits and capital by such accounting devices as deferring operating expenses or amortizing them over several years, and overstating asset values. Such practices render financial statements meaningless and raise risk perceptions.
- *Inadequate risk management:* Many credit unions believe that members have a right to borrow up to a certain multiple of share capital. Loan applications do not differentiate loan types. Loan collection efforts are often weak. Modern credit unions greatly relax or eliminate these share-multiple ceilings and seek detailed information to properly assess risks.
- *Low salary levels:* Credit union salary levels typically are set well below those paid elsewhere in the financial sector, which often results in low effort and morale, high turnover, and a general inability to recruit and retain high-quality staff. This frequently undercuts credit union performance and financial health.

Source: Westley 2001.

The two cooperative banks, BANCOOB and BANSICREDI, have some structural differences. The SICOOB system is larger than SICREDI in terms of members, but BANSICREDI has substantially larger assets than BANCOOB (their respective financial statements are in appendix tables A2.13 and A2.14). BANSICREDI, with slightly more than R$1 billion as of December 2001, essentially mobilizes resources through market operations (54 percent) and in turn places over 60 percent of its resources in the market. With a high share of nonrisk assets, its shareholders' equity is equivalent to only 4 percent of total assets. In the case of BANCOOB, net loans are the most important use of funds, reaching 37 percent compared to BANSICREDI's 26 percent of assets. On the liabilities side, deposits account for 37 percent of resources, compared to 17 percent for BANSICREDI. BANCOOB has a somewhat larger share of its liabilities in the form of long-term liabilities. Leverage is high, with BANCOOB's capital equivalent to just 6 percent of total resources.

In the case of CRESOL, lending was around R$35 million for the 2000–2001 cropping season, with Banco do Brasil financing R$20 million in PRONAF C and D loans; the BNDES financing R$9 million in PRONAF C, PROSOLO, PROLEITE (Programa de Incentivo à Mecanização ao Resfriamento e ao Transporte Granelizado da Produção de Leite; Program of Incentives for Mechanization, Cooling, and Transport of the Production of Milk), and other lines of credit; and its own funds supporting close to R$6 million in loans, divided into R$4 million for personal loans and R$2 million for producer loans.

Onlending and Deposit Interest Rates

Onlending by cooperatives appears to be at competitive rates for loans from free resources. SICREDI reports that loans to cooperative members using its free resources are at the CDI reference rate plus 4 percent to 12 percent (that is, about 22–30 percent, based on a CDI of 18 percent in June 2001). These can be personal loans, working capital, or investment loans. Lines of credit and rediscounts by the cooperative banks and central cooperatives to their member cooperatives are at interest rates that are adjusted daily according to liquidity and market conditions. For example, BANCOOB issues a daily rate sheet in its daily release called "Bom Dia BANCOOB."

Regarding deposits, cooperatives offer both sight and time deposits that are largely channeled to the cooperative banks. BANCOOB offers an overnight deposit rate to member credit unions of 90 percent of the CDI rate; an indexed deposit instrument for deposits offering a rate that starts at 90 percent of CDI for deposits under 30 days, rising to 100 percent of CDI for deposits over 120 days, and time deposits (certificates of deposit [CDs]) with pre- or post-fixed interest rates that are in some cases negotiable before their expiration. These are subject to withholding tax. Withdrawals before 30 days lead to imposition of the Imposto sobre Operações Financeiras (Tax on Financial Operations; IOF). Cooperative banks place their liquidity largely in Treasury instruments (Letras do Tesouro Nacional; Federal Treasury Bills) at the Sistema Especial de Liquidação e Custodia (overnight interest rate; SELIC) rate or in commercial bank CDs just above the SELIC rate.

Interest rates on publicly sourced funds for rural credit are consistent with their requirements typically for below-market interest rates. Most lines of credit stipulate 8.75 percent (for example, PROSOLO, PROLEITE,

PROPASTO), 11.95 percent for tractor modernization, or 1–4 percent on PRONAF loans.[55] To fund these, cooperative banks issue intrabank rural CDs to capture the directed rural credit of commercial banks, offering them between 6 percent and 8.5 percent. Where the rate to borrowers is below the cost of funds, as in PRONAF lines of credit, cooperative banks are the only private institutions that receive support through the 'equalization' scheme of the National Treasury.

In the case of PRONAF loans, the CRESOL system acts as a channel for Banco do Brasil to CRESOL members. Banco do Brasil receives a spread of 8.5 percent per year, together with a fee of R$13 per month per contract, as 'equalization compensation' from the Treasury for handling PRONAF loans. However, only 1.5 percent of this spread is passed on by Banco do Brasil to CRESOL, which is clearly insufficient when the latter must assume the credit risk in addition to administrative costs. CRESOL contends that were it to administer the PRONAF funds without Banco do Brasil as an intermediary, it could include technical assistance to producers within the spread that Banco do Brasil receives (Bittencourt 2001).

Loans funded by BNDES through its BNDES Automático or FINAME lines of credit (the latter are for private companies and rural producers who are purchasing domestically produced machinery and equipment) are at TJLP plus from 4 percent to 5.5 percent. BNDES charges the cooperative banks TJLP plus 1 percent, leaving the cooperatives with a 3 percent spread. With TJLP currently at 10 percent, the rate to ultimate borrowers is 14–15.5 percent.

Portfolio Quality

Overall, the delinquency rates in the vast majority of Brazilian credit cooperatives compare favorably with the private banking system, as well as with the prudential standards advocated by the WOCCU, namely of total delinquencies to total loan portfolio under 5 percent. Whereas loan delinquencies proved to be a problem in the 1960s and 1970s, and combined with other internal management and external (macroeconomic and regulatory) factors to cause the collapse of a number of cooperatives, loan delinquencies are apparently not a significant issue among cooperatives that are members of the two major networks—SICOOB and SICREDI. Atlantic Rating's review of BANCOOB in June 2001 notes that "BANCOOB has never experienced a delinquency since it opened for business."[56] The bank provisioned R$322,000 under loan loss reserves in the first half of 2001. Writeoffs totaling R$567,000 refer to accounting movements, whereas the effective loss within SICOOB is very low, around 1.5 percent. The cooperative banks are insulated by guarantees from the central cooperatives. Sound management information systems, incentives for cooperative directors and managers, and prudent loan origination and

Table 2.17 Classification of Assets for Banks and Select Cooperatives, by Level of Risk
(percent)

	Banking system	*Sample co-op bank BANCOOB*	*Sample state cooperative system: SICREDI-RS*	*Sample single cooperative: Encantado*
Categories AA or A	61.5	94.7	71.1	94.2
Category B	17.2	5.2	8.1	0.7
Category C	8.7	0.2	13.1	1.9
Category D	4.3	—	3.3	—
Category E	1.5	—	0.7	—
Category F	1.5	—	0.4	0.2
Category G	1.0	—	0.1	—
Category H	4.5	—	3.2	2.9

Note: — = not available. Banking system as of April 2002, BANCOOB as of June 2001, and SICREDI-RS and Encantado as of December 2001.
Source: Central Bank of Brazil 2002, www.bcb.gov.br; Atlantic Rating: BANCOOB—Banco Cooperativo do Brasil S.A., June 2001; SICREDI: Communications to Bank Staff, April 2002.

recovery procedures (including screening and pressure for recoveries that avail of the local cooperative spirit) help reduce credit risks at the local level (table 2.17).

In the case of CRESOL, too, delinquencies average about 5 percent, ranging from 3.5 percent for rural credit with its own loans and rising to 8 percent for personal loans, with a reduction to 2.6 percent to 6 percent after recovery efforts.[57] The delinquency rate is also around 5 percent for loans funded with public resources (such as PRONAF), although a portion are renegotiated to bring the delinquency rate down to 1 percent to 2 percent. Loan losses are substantially higher in a small share of CRESOL cooperatives where delinquencies are concentrated in a small number of borrowers, usually cooperative managers who diverted loan funds. Other early problems were excessive loan amounts per member or financing of high-risk activities and poor management information systems and accounting. CRESOL's liquidity was compromised by the need for member cooperatives to assume the credit risk and repay Banco do Brasil on behalf of delinquent members. Consideration should be given to reviewing the extent to which the relative market positions of Banco do Brasil versus smaller rural credit cooperatives explain their relative shares of the spread on PRONAF loans and what measures can be taken to better relate spread to credit risk and administrative expenditures on such public transfers.

PROFITABILITY

The profitability of the two cooperative banks in Brazil is low. The return on assets for BANCOOB was below 0.6 percent in 2000 and 2001, and in spite of high leverage, this converted into a return on equity of just 7–9 percent (that is, less than the rate of inflation). The returns for BANSICREDI were lower still, with a return on average assets of 0.3 percent and on equity of close to 6 percent. These rates compare to returns on assets at the same time of about 1.5 percent in the private banking system and on equity of around 20 percent.

On the other hand, these two banks are not designed to generate profits at the expense of their cooperative owners but rather to assist these to generate market returns and increase their coverage. Although BANCOOB generated a slightly higher profit than BANSICREDI, at the systemic level, profitability in the SICREDI system seems slightly higher than that in SICOOB. In particular, returns on equity averaged 22 percent for the SICREDI system as of December 2001, compared to under 10 percent for the SICOOB system, due in large measure to SICREDI's concentration in the profitable Southern and Central–West states, which have well-established rural producers (table 2.18 and figure 2.6).

The CRESOL system reported a loss in 2000 of R$20,000 on revenues of R$3.5 million and loans of R$35 million. The loss was attributed to having thin spreads to benefit members, subsidizing the establishment of new cooperatives, and covering the credit risks of members on public sector loans such as those of the PRONAF program. The system had produced small profits in 1996 (R$4,000 on revenues of R$189,000) and in 1997 (R$38,000 on revenues of R$526,000) (Bittencourt and Abramovay 2001).

A common factor depressing profits for all credit cooperatives is the absence of a central lender of last resort. This is because, in the absence of

Table 2.18 Key Financial Indicators for the SICREDI Cooperative System

State	*Equity*	*Deposits*	*Loans*	*Total assets*	*Profits*	*% return on average equity*
Rio Grande do Sul	211.7	1,061.4	747.7	1,317.4	40.6	23.7
Paraná	69.0	345.4	235.9	429.3	10.9	18.7
Mato Grosso do Sul	12.3	31.5	28.6	51.1	1.8	16.9
Mato Grosso	45.3	126.4	118.8	181.8	8.1	21.7
Total SICREDI	**338.4**	**1,564.8**	**1,131.1**	**1,979.5**	**61.4**	**22.2**

Source: SICREDI, www.sicredi.com.br.

Figure 2.6 Evolution of Profits and Equity for the SICOOB Cooperative System

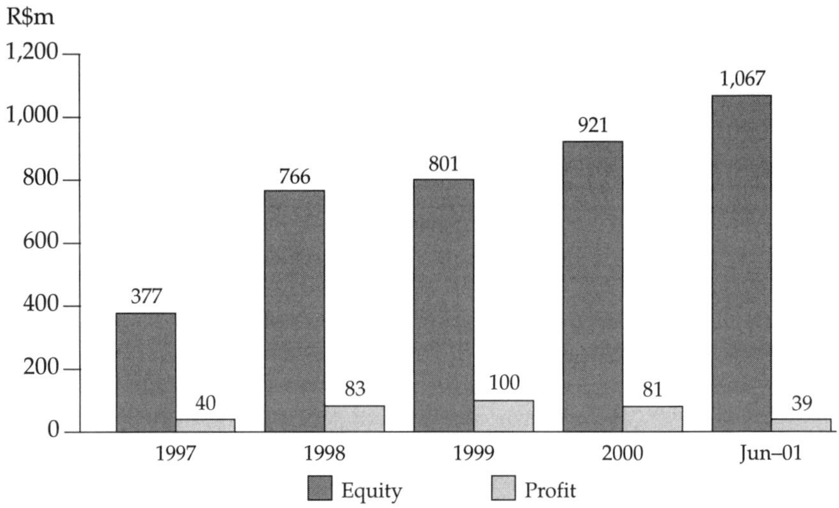

Source: SICOOB, www.bancoob.com.br.

a government-backed liquidity fund, or indeed of any central liquidity funds at the national level, cooperatives are obliged to autoinsure by maintaining a high ratio of liquidity to deposits, especially to sight deposits.[58] The 90 percent liquidity ratio on sight deposits results in a ratio of liquid to total assets well above the maximum of 20 percent advocated by the WOCCU and a low loan-to-deposit ratio, impeding an effective financial structure. Although exemption from income tax provides some relief for cooperatives, one way to compensate for relatively unremunerative returns on this large amount of liquidity could be to charge correspondingly higher interest rates on loans.

This is rendered less feasible through subsidized public programs in rural areas and through competition from banks in urban areas, which in turn, place a greater onus on cooperatives to cut administrative costs relative to banks, affecting their public image as well as their competitiveness in terms of staff salaries. Already, at slightly under 4 percent, personnel and administrative expenses for the SICREDI system in Rio Grande do Sul are indeed low by Brazilian banking system standards and also are at the low end of the 3–10 percent range advocated by the WOCCU.

An additional factor affecting not only profitability but also the viability of cooperatives in certain areas is membership restrictions. Clearly, banks are concerned that the exemption that cooperatives enjoy from IOF and income taxes would lead to 'unfair' competition if membership restrictions were to be lifted; on the other hand, there are areas of the country in which a restriction by location or by profession results in insufficient members to make cooperative banking viable. There is no clear answer to this. The temptation to adjust membership restrictions with a view to expanding access is high but may result in advantages to cooperatives purely from regulatory arbitrage and would foster the formation of separate and fragmented regulatory windows. It is not obvious that the members of such cooperatives would be the poor of these areas.

Legal, Regulatory, and Supervisory Framework for Credit Cooperatives

Legal Framework and Prudential Regulation

Until June 2003, credit cooperatives fell under the general law on cooperatives (Law No. 5764/71 of 1971), although as financial institutions, they are also subject to the general Financial Institutions Law No. 4549/64 of 1964 and the Resolutions of the National Monetary Council.[59] Just before the specification of prudential norms for SCMs, prudential guidelines and membership criteria for credit cooperatives were specified (CMN Resolution 2771 of August 30, 2000). Together with other new measures for microfinance, new regulations for credit cooperatives were also introduced in June 2003.[60]

Eligibility criteria for membership of credit unions in urban areas related to work or place of employment have been similar to those in closed cooperatives elsewhere. For example, in the United States, just as in Brazil, credit unions enjoy tax exemptions that commercial banks do not have, and therefore eligibility restrictions have been placed on membership of credit unions to avoid 'unfair' competition with banks.[61] Although the new regulations of June 2003 have somewhat reduced constraints on open-admission cooperatives, these are allowed only in thinly populated areas, where other financial services may be absent (CMN Resolution 3106 of June 25, 2003). Prudential regulations against credit risk were also specified, with limits on risk concentration through single-party exposure limits (credit to any member cannot exceed 10 percent of liquid capital for affiliated cooperatives or 5 percent for unaffiliated cooperatives), and limits on exposure to a member cooperative and at a central cooperative (less than 20 percent of liquid capital).[62]

The same resolution established minimum entry capital requirements for central cooperatives (R$60,000 for new institutions, rising to a minimum capital of R$300,000 by their fifth year of operations) and member cooperatives (R$3,000 at the outset, rising to R$60,000 over five years). In line with sound prudential principles, more stringent minimum capital requirements apply for nonfederated cooperatives (R$4,300 at the outset, rising to R$86,000 over four years). Nevertheless, these minimum capital requirements are very low, even by comparison to Brazil's microfinance societies and more so relative to other countries. Like SCMs, there are no ongoing capital adequacy ratios but instead limits to leverage (10 times liquid capital for single credit cooperatives that are members of a cooperative system and 5 times liquid capital for unaffiliated credit cooperatives). However, leverage ceilings are relaxed substantially for rural credit cooperatives that participate in the PRONAF program. The decision to relax leverage ceilings for PRONAF clients is not prudentially sound in light of the additional covariant risk exposure it creates for cooperatives among a clientele whose capacity to repay loans at market rates remains to be proven.

The most stringent requirements for Brazil's cooperatives are related to reserve requirements on deposits. Whereas cooperatives are not required to place such reserves with the Central Bank, they are obliged by central cooperatives to place 90 percent of sight deposits and 25 percent of time deposits in liquid instruments. Thus, loanable resources are substantially lower than for banks. This prudential requirement reflects the lack of access to deposit guarantees for cooperatives. Commercial bank deposits are insured by the deposit insurance fund of Brazil, the FGC, but the FGC does not cover deposits in cooperatives. With the introduction of new regulations in mid-2003, formal requirements for the extension of credit, based on deposits, have just been introduced for open cooperatives, which require a minimum of 50 percent of deposits to be used for credit.[63]

In the United States, there has been a separate deposit insurance fund for credit unions since 1970, known as the National Credit Union Share Insurance Fund (NCUSIF), which is built up with premia from credit unions to an amount close to 1.3 percent of deposits and backed by the full faith and credit of the U.S. government. In addition, a lender of last resort was established for U.S. credit unions in 1979—the Central Liquidity Facility. In the case of Brazil, apex commercial banks for each co-op network have been partially able to offer such services for cooperatives, through their own access to lender of last resort funds. In addition, SICOOB is considering establishing a networkwide deposit insurance system, most likely with a R$20,000 per account ceiling at a cost of R$0.03 per Real of insurance coverage. Four of the 15 central credit cooperatives in SICOOB already operate state-level self-insurance funds. Unlike the FGC or NCUSIF, these insurance funds do not have public backing; therefore, the risk will inevitably continue to be higher even if the funds are eventually consolidated at the system level, but this may prove to be a valuable first step to assess the viability of the fund before extending sovereign backing.

There is a clear case for providing incentives for the establishment of a liquidity facility for credit cooperatives. Credit cooperatives currently face high opportunity costs related to liquidity requirements, relative to commercial banks that are backed by the FGC. One option to be studied would be to encourage the establishment of a central liquidity facility for credit cooperatives that is privately managed by representatives of cooperatives, under Banco Central do Brasil (Central Bank of Brazil; BCB) supervision, and that enjoys clear, BCB-approved standards for liquidity support and is capitalized via a percentage of deposits. In turn, liquidity requirements on sight and time deposits could be eased, with the reduction in liquidity requirements related to the degree of capitalization of the facility. After evaluating the performance of the facility, consideration could be given to public backing for the facility.

Supervision

Credit cooperatives are supervised by the BCB, which approves applications for their establishment and appointments of boards of directors and establishes reporting requirements. Routine oversight, as a form of auxiliary supervision, is offered by all cooperative networks and has increased at the two main cooperative credit networks, SICOOB and SICREDI. These networks apply standards to varying degrees through their central credit cooperatives, which use moral suasion to enforce prudential standards. This moral suasion is of course backed by legal remedies in extreme cases, but more typically, standards are enforced through performance-related pay for cooperative managers, network-applied sanctions against the single cooperatives' directors in the event of noncompliance with guidelines, restrictions on credit to weaker cooperatives (for example, BANCOOB does not lend to member cooperatives with C ratings in its internal scoring system), and the ultimate sanction of expulsion of the cooperative from the network (while the ultimate sanction of the Central Bank is closure and liquidation).

Over the past five years, the Central Bank's confidence in the ability of all apex cooperatives, and notably, based on information collected by this study, SICOOB and SICREDI, to supervise their member credit cooperatives has clearly grown, due to the implementation of effective information systems and reliable reporting by the two networks, which allow for integrated supervision and benchmarking of financial performance. The two networks clearly differ substantially in terms of their philosophies, with SICREDI applying more rigorous harmonization of standards from loan origination guidelines down to the physical appearance of SICREDI-affiliated cooperatives' buildings. Moreover, although SICOOB affiliates have often conserved their earlier depository relationships with various commercial banks, SICREDI affiliates deposit their surplus funds exclusively in BANSICREDI. The differences in philosophies led member cooperatives in the state of Santa Catarina to disaffiliate as a group from SICREDI and join SICOOB.

As with banks, all loans of R$5,000 or more must be reported to the Central de Risco de Crédito, or central credit bureau run by the Central Bank.[64] Thus, clients who fail to repay one institution should be unable to obtain credit at others. Cooperatives can apply the same sets of policies regarding loan origination and enforcement as applied to other financial institutions. As in microfinance, cooperatives take advantage of the 'reputational knowledge and collateral' in terms of community spirit and knowledge of clients to ensure more effective screening of clients, as well informal sanctions to promote timely repayment of loans. Although SICREDI has enough information in its system to be able to design a credit-scoring system, it does not want to substitute for the personal knowledge that comes from the local operation of a cooperative venture.

Conceptual Issues in the Regulation and Supervision of Credit Cooperatives

Regulation

The distinctive characteristics of credit unions have induced regulators to introduce unique elements in the regulatory framework for closed or open common-bond credit cooperatives (Van Greuning, Gallardo, and Randhawa 1999). First, unlike banks, which are open to provide financial services to *any* person or enterprise, credit cooperatives restrict their operations to their members (closed credit cooperative) or those eligible for membership (common-bond credit cooperative). Therefore, it is argued that the public-interest motive for financial regulation and supervision is reduced to only those who are members of the cooperative. Nevertheless, a closed credit cooperative can be larger in asset size than a bank, as is the case in Peru, where the three largest credit cooperatives are larger in size than the smallest bank in the system. Therefore, selecting a criterion of being open or closed to regulate and supervise a credit cooperative can be misleading.

It is not uncommon to encounter, as in Brazil, more relaxed regulation in terms of entry capital, and in some cases more relaxed capital ratios (in the case of the United States). Reserve requirements at the Central Bank are not usually required, although credit cooperatives take deposits from their members. This is the case in Brazil and Peru. There is also a lack of access to deposit insurance. This increases the public perception that credit cooperatives are riskier institutions, although these institutions may manage more money from the public than open credit unions or even banks.[65] There is also no access to a liquidity facility.[66] Instead, central cooperatives or federations perform that duty, to a limited extent, as they are also financial institutions.

Credit cooperatives also commonly face several privileges and constraints with respect to other financial institutions. There are usually tax advantages, not only in Brazil but also in Germany, before cooperative banks became open: geographic restrictions on operations to level the competition between cooperatives and banks.[67] Commonly, credit cooperatives also suffer from instability of equity, as exit of a member from a cooperative can not only damage liquidity (withdrawing their deposits) but also solvency (by withdrawing contributions, the essential part in a cooperative's equity).[68] Problems of governance are much higher in credit cooperatives, both due to incapable management or abuse of position.

Conceptual Issues in the Supervision of Credit Cooperatives

There are two central and interrelated issues in this context: Which credit cooperatives should be supervised, and who should undertake this? Regarding the former question, it is argued that open cooperatives should clearly be subject to the supervision of a superintendency, the Central Bank, or other state agency. The question concerns closed or common-bond cooperatives. But criteria such as juridical form, being open or closed, or common-bond have generated inconsistencies, as some large credit cooperatives have been left out. A combination of size and openness, as used in Bolivia, Chile, Colombia, and Ecuador, is suggested. In Brazil, all cooperatives are supervised by the Central Bank. This may place a large burden on supervision capacity going forward.

To reduce supervisory costs, several countries have adopted methods of indirect supervision. These include, first, auxiliary supervision. The public agency in charge of the supervision of the financial system retains the responsibility of the supervision of credit cooperatives, but it is supported by private agents (federations or associations of credit cooperatives, banks, or central cooperatives), basically in the process of on-site supervision. The authority to intervene or sanction a credit cooperative remains in the public agency, which conducts regular reviews on the performance of the private agent. This is the case in Germany and the United States. Delegated supervision is an alternative. All supervisory functions are carried out by the private agent(s), even interventions and sanctions. However, the design of the regulatory framework remains in the public agency that also conducts reviews on the performance of the delegated supervision. This is the case in Peru and Costa Rica.

Lessons from Regulation and Supervision of Credit Cooperatives in Developed Countries

In Spain, the United States, Canada, and Germany, credit cooperatives are much more developed than in developing countries, not only by their outreach (measured as penetration ratios) but also by size in the financial system. A stable macroeconomic and political environment may have contributed, as well as the supervision and regulation applied to credit cooperatives by these countries. Potential factors could include the following:

- The United States and Germany have very strong and organized indirect supervisors of the cooperative sector. The National Credit Union Administration in the United States and the Regional Federations of Local Cooperatives in Germany are highly trained in the supervision of credit cooperatives, and both are under permanent inspection from the banking supervisors.[69]
- There is a clear delimitation of supervisory roles from representative roles in these indirect supervisors. In Germany, auditing and auxiliary supervision are conducted by regional federations, whereas their representation is done by two other federations, the DGRV (German Confederation of Credit Cooperatives) and the BVR (Association of German Popular Banks and Raiffeisen Banks). This reduces the conflict of interests inside the supervisor when it has to both supervise and represent the credit cooperatives.
- The regulation applied to credit cooperatives does not differ from the one applied to other financial institutions. This reduces regulatory arbitrage and provides incentives to fair competition, also reducing the public perception that credit cooperatives are riskier than banks.
- Credit cooperatives have also had access to liquidity facilities, deposit insurance, and credit bureaus, either establishing their own (deposit insurance and liquidity requirements) or using the same available for other financial institutions (credit bureau).

Suggestions for Brazil

Brazil should try as far as possible to apply similar financial regulations for credit cooperatives as for other financial institutions. Credit cooperatives, as financial institutions, whether they are closed, open, or common-bond, should be under the same standards of regulation applied to other financial institutions, to motivate competition and reduce their perceived higher risk associated with the lack to access to a liquidity facility, deposit insurance, and credit bureau. Certainly, some special features or credit cooperatives may differentiate their regulatory framework, such as the composition of their capital and their loan portfolios, but in general, regulations on solvency, credit risk, liquidity risk, market risks, and other aspects of financial regulation could be the same for credit cooperatives as for other financial institutions. Recent measures taken to ensure common capital ratios for cooperatives and banks are therefore a step in the right direction.

This also suggests a need to review regulations and incentives governing public rural credit programs channeled through credit cooperatives. Credit cooperatives are at their most effective when members feel considerable ownership of their cooperatives. When resources are perceived as coming from the state, particularly for disadvantaged populations, there are strong incentives not to repay. Policies, such as those that doubled the leverage permitted in the event of financing using public rural credit programs such as PRONAF, simply reinforced incentives that can undermine the cooperative spirit and the sustainability of the cooperatives. These regulations run counter to what is in general a prudent regulatory framework and the removal of such policies under a new regulation introduced in 2003 is most welcome (CMN Resolution 3106 of June 25, 2003).

Direct supervision of the entire cooperative network would strain supervisory capacity, and the present delegation of supervision appears to have many advantages. In the future, a clearer delineation of duties between the Central Bank and the central cooperatives may be desirable. A prudent balance must be maintained between direct and delegated oversight of credit cooperatives. The relatively low capital standards that facilitate broad access to cooperative financial services can also imply a proliferation of small formal financial institutions, with high costs to the supervisory entity, particularly in a country the size of Brazil. For example, in one Asian country, rural banks account for only 2 percent of banking system assets, yet they outnumber commercial banks by more than 20 to 1, and as a group they absorb one-third of banking regulators. Recent regulatory changes permitting open-membership cooperatives, and conversions to such structures by existing cooperatives, could lead to a potential expansion in numbers of cooperative members. To avoid high costs of supervision and the attention of a large share of Central Bank supervisors to a small share of systemic assets and systemic risks, it is important to continue to strengthen capacity for prudential oversight among cooperative networks, particularly through strengthening systems, accounting standards, and transparency in reporting, and to continue gradual extension of delegated supervision to cooperative networks that meet Central Bank standards of oversight while trying to avoid the conflict of interest of these networks who at the same time supervise and represent credit cooperatives.

Another way to supervise the many credit cooperatives in Brazil is to adopt hybrid supervision, combining criteria of size and openness, in which a few credit cooperatives would be under the direct control of the Central Bank, while the rest, a large number of small credit cooperatives, would be under delegated supervision of the cooperative networks or other third party.

Annex 2.1: Microfinance and Technology

All forms of microfinance institutions have greatly benefited in recent years from a series of technological innovations that have expanded the outreach, enhanced the productivity, reduced costs, and expanded the product range of microlending and lending to the poor. Yet with each there are also limits to their usefulness in terms of substituting for conventional lending techniques. This annex briefly describes some such technological innovations, discusses their advantages and limitations, and presents examples of their recent applications in microfinance.[70]

Automation and Computerization in Microfinance

Handheld Computers and Personal Digital Assistants (PDAs)

Handheld computers and PDAs that can be connected by modem to central management information systems allow a microfinance institution to deal with the geographic dispersal of clients by taking the office or evaluation techniques to the field. They allow loan officers to record client data, upload applications from the centralized database, and conduct quick and automated credit analysis. The accuracy and efficiency of lending decisions are enhanced, while processing time and costs are greatly reduced. The time savings increases loan officer capacity, which is a leading indicator of efficiency and, hence, returns.

Unlike traditional banks, microfinance institutions do not make loans based on revenue or collateral alone but also look at references from customers and neighbors, in addition to the loan officer's own perception (Beebe 2000). Although handheld computers are a powerful tool for making microloans, they will never replace loan officers. The personal knowledge or client relationships of loan officers or of loan groups remains integral to the lending process.

ATMs and Debit Cards[71]

ATMs are cost-effective means of providing financial services, because they increase geographic outreach, maximize hours of operation, and reduce employee costs, as human tellers do not have to conduct the transactions. The ATM option is especially cost effective for geographic targeting within poor pockets in city locations; maintaining ATMs in geographically remote areas has limits on cost-effectiveness just as bank branches have, due to needs to service machines and install infrastructure. The use of conventional ATMs may also be limited in some low-income contexts due to illiteracy or intimidation by technology. To promote the uses of ATMs among the poor, they have been customized in many countries. For instance, in Bolivia, special ATMs capable of overcoming language barriers and illiteracy and with functional simplicity have been developed. Instead of entering an identification number to access their accounts, customers place a finger in the given location to enable the machine to detect the fingerprint and identify the client. After the identification stage, a friendly voice welcomes customers in their native language and directs users through the desired transaction, through touch-activated screen icons based on pictures and symbols.[72] ATMs have been particularly popular for transmission of funds to rural pensioners who otherwise paid check-cashing fees to merchants. They reduce theft of checks, fraudulent claims, and transaction costs for the recipient. Provincial governments in some countries award contracts to cross-subsidize this marginally profitable service.

Smart Cards

Smart cards are ATM cards with an embedded microprocessor chip that can be used to complete financial transactions. A smart card resembles a credit card in size and shape, but unlike a normal credit card, which is a simple piece of plastic with a magnetic stripe, the smart card contains an embedded microprocessor chip that can hold up to 800 times the information of a magnetic stripe, including personal information (for example, identification via biometrics) and consumer information. It can function as a debit card or credit card, store account information for several financial products, and be programmed to hold and transfer money (Campion and Halpern 2001). The user can preload a certain amount of money into the card. Vendors that accept smart cards can pass the card through a reader that immediately transfers the appropriate amount into their accounts.

Where infrastructure exists, smart cards can pay for public transportation, goods, services, items from vending machines, loans, telephone calls, and other consumer goods. Because they hold customer account information and personal details, smart cards are more secure than ATM or credit cards. Smart cards, if programmed, can offer an unprecedented level of security with fingerprint imaging. Unlike debit cards and ATMs, which require expensive terminals and reliable telecommunications, smart cards can function off-line with battery-powered readers without a permanent network connection.

For microfinance, smart cards improve efficiency through card security and bulk electronic settlement routines that produce accurate accounts, provide a fully transparent and tamper-proof electronic audit trail, and reduce central accounting time. Similarly, this encourages merchants' participation because they benefit from reduced cash handling. The improved efficiency and the low price suggest that smart card technology will become more important in the transactions of poverty-oriented programming, but it is premature to predict the types of products that will be developed in the future.

Credit Scoring and Riskmetrics[73]

Credit scoring is used by lenders to help them calibrate the credit risk of loan applications. Information such as income, bill-paying history, late payments, past records on loans, and age are collected, aggregated using a statistical program, and then compared to the credit performance of consumers with similar profiles. Credit scoring models are being used extensively in microfinance. A typical microfinance model may take into account past repayment records, levels of indebtedness, the length of time a customer has been borrowing, net family income, net business income, whether the applicant rents or owns his or her house, and place of business, among others. However, to be able to make accurate decisions, credit scoring models require information that may not be easy to come by with microclients, especially in countries where comprehensive credit histories from credit bureaus and collection agencies are scarce, as in most developing countries (Schreiner 2000). Even in advanced countries, such as the United Kingdom and United States, credit scoring methodologies are often not applied to new small business entities, which have little prior credit history.

Beyond credit scoring, there are comprehensive risk management tools for extending microcredit that attempt to minimize unnecessary exposure to underperforming loans and capital losses. Two Mexican financial institutions currently using such risk management tools, perfected by a Spanish company, AIS, are Nacional Financiera and Financiera Rural (formerly Banrural).[74]

Telecommunications and the Internet[75]

Telecommunications, particularly the internet, have a huge potential to alleviate poverty. The internet promises to make virtually unlimited amounts of information accessible from anywhere in the world and to defy traditional borders and boundaries by allowing people from various countries, communities, religions, and ethnicities to exchange ideas openly and instantaneously. Making true the potential of the internet, however, poses enormous challenges. The greatest challenge by far is overcoming the so-called 'digital divide,' the disparity between those with access to information and communication technology versus those without. In the developing world, a computer is a luxury, and even phone lines and electricity are not always available. Although the average OECD country has approximately 11 times the per capita income of a South Asian country, it has 1,036 times as many internet hosts, 40 times as many computers, and 146 times as many mobile phones (World Bank 2002e).

The most promising developments seem to be happening in finding alternatives to landline dial-up access. Wireless networks can be set up at a much lower cost than landline networks. In impoverished areas where isolation and poor infrastructure are often the norm, cell phone use can play a crucial in enhancing the social and economic development. Cell phones have been particularly helpful for enhancing markets for microentities; women in rural areas can use cell phones to make sales calls, to order supplies, or to check commodity prices in the city to negotiate better prices for their crops. In Kenya and in India, fishermen have used cell phones to determine catch prices at different ports so that they can direct their returning trawlers back to the most profitable locations. In Bangladesh, thanks to the Village Phone Program, several thousand villages have access to cell phones through Grameen Telecom, a subsidiary of the Grameen Bank. Loan repayments for phones are in accordance with Grameen Bank procedures.

Examples of Applications of New Technologies in Microfinance

Debit Cards: Banco ADEMI

Banco ADEMI is a large microfinance institution and one of the most profitable banks in the Dominican Republic. Banco ADEMI offers its own plastic payment system, the ADEMI+ debit card (Campion and Halpern 2001). Under this scheme, the debit card is linked to a new loan product, the Prestamo con ahorro (loan with savings). When a customer applies for a loan up to RD$200,000 (US$12,500), he or she agrees to deposit 10 percent of the loan value into a Banco ADEMI savings account and to allow the bank to automatically withdraw future loan payments from that account. In exchange, Banco ADEMI authorizes loan amounts 10 percent higher than otherwise. The additional loan funds are then placed in savings at the time of the loan disbursement. The funds are not specified as a loan guaranty because the customer can withdraw them at any time. However, the customer must keep the savings account open throughout the loan cycle, which implies maintaining sufficient funds to cover loan payments and a minimum balance of RD$100 (US$6.25). On opening the savings account, Banco ADEMI issues a debit card to the customer to make deposits or withdrawals from the account from any ATM in its network (Campion and Halpern 2001).

CREDIT CARDS FOR FARMERS: KISAN

The Kisan credit card scheme was introduced in India in 1998 so that farmers could gain easy access to credit for working needs in their agricultural operations. It as been opened to all farmers who are prepared to borrow above a threshold of Rs5,000 (around US$100), who have not defaulted in repayment of loans in the past three consecutive years, and who have a minimum of five acres of irrigated land. The credit limit is set on the basis of land holding, the value of the crop cultivated, and income. Farmers can get loans up to five times the annual farm income or 50 percent of the value of the land as collateral, whichever is lower.

Kisan credit card scheme participants are given a credit card and a checkbook and are issued a passbook incorporating identity and transaction details. Revolving credit is extended with unlimited withdrawals and repayments within the overall ceiling; no loans should remain outstanding for more than 12 months. These repayment conditions provide much-needed flexibility to farmers. Kisan cards are valid for three years, subject to an annual review based on performance.

Participating commercial banks, regional rural banks, and cooperative banks provide the Kisan cards to the farmers. The scheme has gained popularity, and its implementation has been taken up by 27 commercial banks, 373 district central cooperative banks/state cooperative banks (two-tier structure), and 196 regional rural ranks throughout India. As of November 30, 2001, 20.4 million credit cards involving credit sanctions of around US$ 7.5 million had been issued. Cooperative banks accounted for 66 percent of Kisan credit cards, followed by commercial banks (27 percent) and regional rural banks (7 percent). Personal insurance coverage for accidental death or permanent disability has also been finalized, which offers protection to creditors.

However, according to the Reserve Bank of India (RBI), the success of the credit card scheme is debatable from some points of view. On the whole, the scheme has been well received by farmers in terms of timeliness, hassle-free operations, and adequacy of credit. On the other hand, relatively few farmers can get Kisan credit cards. Many who could benefit from the scheme do not possess land or title or are simply illiterate and unaware that such a scheme exists. There is an unfortunate absence of any village survey by banks to identify and target eligible farmers. Another key drawback of this scheme is its fungibility. Indeed, the State Bank of India has recently found that most farmers are using the Kisan cards for purchase of consumer durables instead of farm inputs. This practice could lead to more unproductive indebtedness.

HANDHELD COMPUTERS, PDAS, AND SMART CARDS: SWAYAM KRISHI SANGAM

Swayam Krishi Sangam (SKS) is a relatively successful microfinance institution in one of the poorest drought-prone regions of India. It was founded in 1997 and works with solidarity groups (sangams) of very poor women, with a mission of sustainability. It provides loans, savings, insurance, and other financial services to its customers. Service delivery, including loan disbursement, savings withdrawals, payment-due collections, and proposal making, would occur during solidarity group meetings and used to be very time consuming, as all transactions were recorded manually. Moreover, meetings could take place only within a

Table A2.1.1 SKS Real and Anticipated Time and Cost Savings *(US$ and minutes)*

	Anticipated time savings		*Real-time savings (with 2 centers)*	
Time savings—activity	*Manual system*	*Smart card system*	*Manual system*	*Smart card system*
Pledge and attendance	2	2	2, 3	2, 3
Cash collection and counting	8	8	4, 11	4, 11
Recording collection sheet	10	0	4, 6	—
Recording member accounts	30	10	10, 16	6, 8
Loan proposals/discussion	10	10	2, 10	2, 10
Total	**60**	**30**	**24, 46**	**14, 32**

Cost savings—item	*Manual system*	*Smart card system (expected)*	*Smart card (actual)*
Printed material	4,143[a]	1,316[b]	1,316
Smart cards (800 groups)	—	2,667	2,000
7 handheld computers	—	4,669	1,400
7 handheld printers, $111 each	—	777	—
Staff, $4,867 each	58,670 (10)	38,135 (6.5)	38,135 (6.5)
Travel, $1,333 per staff	13,330 (10)	8,664 (6.5)	8,664 (6.5)
Total	**76,143**	**56,229**	**51,515**
Total savings		**19,906**	**24,628**

Note: — = not available.

a. Passbooks = $3,556 and collection sheets = $587.

b. Receipts = $889 and monthly statements = $427.

Source: Campion and Halpern 2001.

small window of time early in the morning, as the rest of day is spent working in the field.

To increase the effectiveness of microloan delivery, SKS has developed a technology based on smart cards and handheld computers to automate approval, disbursement, and collection. SKS provides each group member a smart card that is read by a card reader on the loan officer's handheld computer, which displays the information contained and allows a synchronization of information between the computer and smart card once transactions are completed. After meeting with all the groups, the loan officer returns to the SKS office to synchronize and update the branch computer with the new data on the computer. SKS affirms that this technology has significantly lowered SKS's cost of operation, even beyond anticipation.

The financial sustainability of microfinance institutions like SKS has continuously been under strain—not only due to their clients' generally small loan portfolios but also due to the high travel costs to reach clients in their remote villages. With the new technology, the need for sangam managers to manually enter transactions into the passbook is eliminated. Thus, staff can cut down sangam meeting times and service more groups while reducing the risk of fraud and error. The time and cost savings can be productively used for scaling up the SKS microfinance activity.

BASIX and the Sudama Project

BASIX, a leading microfinance institution in India, focuses its operations on addressing the tiny credit need of low-income borrowers, often located in remote villages, and ensuring commercial viability of their ventures. Its most popular products among the poor involve tiny transactions of, say, Rs10 (US$0.20) in regular intervals. These could be weekly savings and or weekly repayments of small amounts. Small daily savings are also popu-

Table A2.1.2 BASIX

	1999–2000
No. of branches	10
No. of staff	79
No. of active borrowers	12,626
Loan portfolio outstanding (US$'000)	2,592
Average loan balance (US$)	208
Depth (%)	56
Operational self-suficiency (%)	77
Financial self-suficiency (%)	65

Source: www.basixindia.com.

lar. Borrowers are issued smart card technology–based Sudama cards, which act as identification cards and electronic loan books. The card itself is issued for a fee on registration and repaid in small installments. Once the payments for the card fee have been completed, the borrower becomes eligible for a loan. Cards are read at the BASIXPOT, or BASIX Point of Transaction, by a service agent with a computer equipped with a smart card reader and modem. Information is securely transferred to the BASIX unit server each evening with a call, which takes about 1 minute and costs less than US 5 cents. The agent uses the local bank for collections and disbursement of loans. He or she works on commission linked to the nature and number of transactions, the number of new borrowers registered, and the quality of the portfolio.

Once the new product was introduced, the agents in one location (Pala Sammudra) registered 70 new borrowers in one month and cut costs to one-third, and it has enabled its microcredit operations to work with poor borrowers spread over a large rural area. This project was partly funded by a Technical Assistance Facility of the IFC.

Postal Services and the Internet: South Africa's PiTs

PiTs, or public information terminals (internet kiosks), a joint project between the South African Department of Communications and the South African Post Office, were introduced in 2001 as a means of using the vast rural reach of the South African Post Office network to address the financial needs of low-income and rural citizens (Annamalai and others 2004). In 2001, South Africa had a population of 40 million that were serviced by South Africa Post Office in more than 2,700 outlets and 5,500 service points. More than 100 rural post offices had PiTs installed, providing internet access to more than 20 million people living in rural areas. The post office plans to install an additional 600 PiTs in 2002–2003, with the eventual goal of installing about 5,000 PiTs.

PiT kiosks are installed with an easy-to-use touch-screen interface, speakers, microphones, and web cam. They are extremely user friendly, with universally recognized icons to overcome the constraint of illiteracy. Post office staff have undergone extensive training to assist customers on the usage of PiTs.

Electronic banking services offered at the PiTs will provide SMEs and microenterprises greater access to financial services. Encryption technologies, such as biometric thumbprint and retina recognition, will be used to ensure banking security. Within the next two years, the post office also plans to offer e-finance services to SMEs in the underserved parts of South Africa. PiTs will offer SMEs access to electronic financing in their own local communities by providing an infrastructure for firms to apply for loans from all 26 competing banks in South Africa.

Annex 2.2: BNDES MFI Portfolio Analysis

Correlation Analyses

Attempts to separate the sample between institutions that received repeated lines of support from the BNDES and those that are still first-time clients do not suggest a significant difference in behavior between these groups. There is, however, some positive correlation between percentages in arrears and numbers of clients, as well as numbers of active credits, suggesting that, as some institutions grow, control over portfolio quality may suffer. Correlation between arrears and numbers of credits is 0.37, correlation between arrears and active clients is 0.33, and correlation between arrears and loan size is –0.21. There is also some negative correlation with loan size, suggesting that those microcredit institutions that concentrate on somewhat larger borrowers have a better portfolio quality. One of the best performers, with loans in arrears from 1 to 2.4 percent, had loans around three times the average for all MFIs in this sample.

Portfolio Growth Estimation

Over time, the total active portfolio of microcredit institutions that received funds from BNDES has grown from R$16.4 million in 1998 to R$31.7 million in 2000 and R$33.9 million in June 2001. But also, the number of institutions that received funding from BNDES has grown from 16 in 1998 to 31 in 2001. Average portfolio size, as discussed above, rose erratically over this period, from R$0.8 million to R$1.1 million per institution per year.

Attempts to determine whether the growth behavior of BNDES client institutions has been dynamic over time were analyzed by fitting a statistical growth trend to this array, as follows:

$$P_{it} = P_{i0} \, [\, e^{rt + b(\Delta X_{it})} \,],$$

where P_{it} is the active portfolio for institution i in period t and X_{it} is a vector of other control variables as described below, to include

The institution's default rate
The number of credits offered by the institution
The average loan size offered by the institution
The number of active clients catered to by the institution.

The linear transformation of the model resulted in a GLS regression:

$$lnapch = B_1(time) + B_2(crgrch) + B_3(avlnch) + B_4(wdfch)$$

where the variables were defined as

lnapch	$ln(P_{it}–P_{i0})$, the dependent variable
time	number of periods over which the panel of observations was based

crgrch change in the number of credits being granted during this period (current to base)

avlnch change in the average loan size of the institution during this period (current to base)

wdfch change in the weighted default rate of the institution during this period (current to base); the weights were the contributing proportion of each institution in each period to the overall active portfolio.

The results of the pooled cross-sectional time series GLS regression reveal a statistically significant coefficient of time of (0.116) for the half-yearly continuous compounding rate. Hence, the annual growth rate will be around 0.22 (or 22 percent) and is statistically significant. Change in average loan size and number of credits granted have both positive and significant coefficients. The effects of growth of default rate, number of credits and average loan size, and number of active clients on the dependent variable (the growth of active portfolio) are controlled for at the level of individual institutions. The results denote an average annual nominal rate of growth of around 22 percent for any given institution, suggesting that, even apart from the growth in the number of institutions, individual institutions do also show some tendency to grow over time.[76] Discounting for inflation, real rates of growth would be in the range of 16–18 percent (based on a coefficient of +0.116 for every six months, which is statistically significant after controlling for other influences captured through X_{it}). Average annual consumer inflation rates from 1996 to September 2001 ranged between 9.5 percent and 1.7 percent and were largely in the range of 5–7 percent over most of the period in question.

The other statistically significant coefficients are those for a change in number of credits granted (coefficient = 0.0001) and for change in average loan size (coefficient = 0.0003). The variable weighted default rate within X_{it} is, however, not significant.

Default Rate Trend Measures

Average rates of loans in arrears over 30 days for all BNDES clients, according to BNDES data, have fluctuated over time, between around 3.5 percent and 8.4 percent. In June 2000, loans in arrears averaged 6.12 percent for all 31 clients. Again, variations between institutions are large, and eliminating the two worst performers reduced this dramatically to 4 percent. Variations over time, even within the same institution, are sharp; at some times, bad loans have risen to one-quarter or one-third of total portfolio, only to apparently largely recover six months to one year later. To test for any improvements in performance over time, the model below investigates if there is any trend over time in default rates, through the specification:

$$WDF_{it} = WDF_{i0} \, [\, e^{rt + b(\Delta X_{it})} \,]$$

where WDF_{it} is the weighted default rate for institution i in period t and X_{it} is a vector of other control variables that include

The number of credits offered by the institution
The average loan size offered by the institution.

The linear transformation of the model resulted in a GLS regression:

$$lnwdfch = B_1(time) + B_2(crgrch) + B_3(avlnch)$$

where the variables were defined as

lnwdfch	$\ln(WDF_{it} - WDF_{i0})$, the dependent variable
time	number of periods over which the panel of observations was based
crgrch	change in the number of credits being granted during this period (current to base)
avlnch	change in the average loan size of the institution during this period (current to base).

The results suggest a coefficient of time of 0.059 as the half-yearly continuous compounding rate. Hence, the annual (positive) growth rate will be around 0.12 (or 12 percent) and is statistically significant. Change in average loan size and change in number of credits have nonsignificant coefficients. Including the change in active portfolio as an explanatory variable did not add any explanatory power to the model.

3
Downscaling Private Banks

Brazil's 175 private banks represent by far the majority of its 191 commercial banking institutions in numbers, and also in the provision of broad aggregates of financial services. Their role in deposit and lending activity has grown to a dominant position over the last decade, from 42 percent of total deposits in 1994 to 52 percent in 2001, and from 44 percent of total loans to 56 percent over the same period. Four of these private banks are substantially larger than the others: Bradesco, with 9 percent of total banking assets in June 2001; Itaú, with 7 percent; Santander, with 6 percent (via their acquisition of Banespa); and Unibanco, with 5 percent. Nevertheless, Brazil's two large public retail banks, Banco do Brasil and Caixa Econômica Federal, still account for close to 40 percent of deposits (20 and 19 percent, respectively, in December 2001), and the three federal banks (Banco do Brasil, Caixa, and the wholesale bank, BNDES) account for around 31 percent of total lending, or 14 percent, 6 percent, and 11 percent, respectively.

To what extent do these private banks 'downscale' their services—that is, contribute to the provision of financial services for the poorer segments of Brazil's society? This issue is investigated in this chapter along several dimensions. First, the role of private banks in the provision of small-deposit and small-loan services is examined, and conditions for opening of bank accounts in terms of initial documentation, minimum deposits, and ongoing fees for services are evaluated. Next, delivery channels presently used are discussed, from branches to ATM services and correspondent banking. Third, the role of new technologies in the provision of financial services to smaller and less affluent clients is discussed, assessing the present use of such technologies in Brazil, and offering examples from other countries. Finally, policies affecting the banking system as a whole that could differentially affect the willingness to engage with smaller clients are acknowledged, although the detailed discussion of these factors is left to chapter 7 of this study. The annex to this chapter discusses downscaling policies and practices developed or identified by a Chicago bank.

Several factors in the macroeconomic and regulatory environment reduce the incentives for outreach to small borrowers, and these are compounded by the shortcomings of the legal framework and infrastructure for the provision of financial services. Nevertheless, there are measures banks can adopt to increase their outreach to the poor, through partnerships with other institutions, through special services and windows, and through the use of more-appropriate technology. Key findings to emerge from this chapter are:

- Commercial banks in Brazil already play a significant role in the provision of financial services to small clients. As such, the scope for further expansion is promising. Small transaction size does not appear to be an absolute barrier for private banks in entering this segment.
- There is, however, a high degree of segmentation in the types of banking services that private banks wish to provide. On the deposit side, they are more likely to enter the possibly more lucrative segments of the market (sight deposits or, in other words, current accounts), where client remuneration is minimal or is much lower than the prevailing interbank rates (special savings deposits). This appears to be the case despite the directed credit requirements placed on these categories of deposits. Private banks are not keen to serve the term deposit needs of small clients, which are remunerated at rates close to the interbank rate, presumably because the advantages of term deposits, when compared to safe assets such as government securities, decline. Thus, transaction-based needs and needs for safe stores of value are met, although needs for returns and investments are served less. There is considerable variation among the individual business plans of private banks in outreach, whether the banks are wholly national or partly foreign owned.
- The important corollary to this finding is that public banks are not the principal providers of services to small account holders; however, they do provide services in this segment to those account holders who are more interested in investments and returns through term deposits, rather than to those whose needs are based on transactions or safe stores of value. Low-income clients do not show a strong preference for public banks.
- Fees for a basic package of banking services in Brazil do not appear high, but they could nevertheless constitute a significant proportion (1 to 2 percent per month) of the income of a less-well-off individual. In terms of institutional variation of transaction costs, although average fees for private and especially foreign banks may be higher than federal banks, the difference is not significant. Some large private banks are as competitive in prices and service range as federal banks, and, in some instances, federal bank service fees may be higher. Transaction fees appear to be a greater obstacle for personal banking services than for the provision of credit to enterprises; high interest rates are the most important factor for enterprises, especially small enterprises.

- Some specific banking services appear to be more uniformly available across different banks (such as ATM use and debit card facilities), although others are less likely to appear in basic packages of services without extra charges, and may be more competitively priced across institutions (checking facilities, overdraft facilities, provision of printed statements, and debit orders).
- The choice of delivery channels appears to be affected by regulatory requirements that raise the costs of establishing banking services, especially bank branches. The growth of correspondent banking has been partly in response to these, but correspondents also help to spread fixed costs. In future, competition in correspondent franchises and further broad-basing of their services (for example, including government bond distribution) could help to ensure that their competitive edge is maintained. But also, prices of other types of services such as bank card networks may also be affected by limited competition in their provision. Differentiated solutions are required to address these issues.
- New technologies based on phone connectivity (telephone and internet based) are widely used in Brazil but not for services to the lower-income segments of the population. Teleconnectivity in Brazil is relatively low in average terms, although there are many well-to-do who use internet banking. Many countries, including Brazil, are making a conscious effort to encourage more universal access to and use of telecommunication services through nondistortive targeted subsidies; several examples of good practice are available.
- A number of good practices have been identified by banks in other countries to promote the downscaling of their business, which could be considered by banks in Brazil. A first group of such practices depends on the development of appropriate products; a second approach rests on the development of partnerships with microfinance institutions, community organizations, and so forth; and a third rests upon image differentiation.
- Financial institutions will find success in downscaling difficult in the absence of both staff commitment at the most senior levels as well as appropriate staff training.
- Financial training of the target population would be greatly beneficial and can be delivered in combination with outreach programs.

The analysis of this chapter was undertaken, in large part, prior to the introduction of new measures in Brazil affecting the role of the banking system and access to financial services. These measures do not affect the analysis of the situation prevailing in Brazil, although there are implications for future policy. The new measures are summarized below, and references to these policies are included in subsequent text.

Expanding Access to Banks in Brazil: New Measures Introduced in 2003

New Basic Bank Accounts

CMN (National Monetary Council) Resolution 3104 of June 25, 2003, and CMN Resolution 3113 of July 31, 2003, establish new 'special deposit' accounts for sight deposits, which will offer a basic package of bank services. These services are free of charge up to certain transaction limits. No charges are made unless the account holder makes more than four withdrawals a month, gets more than four statements a month, or makes more than four deposits. The simplified accounts will not offer checking facilities, and all withdrawals will be by card only. Balances will be limited to R$1,000.

Conditions for opening a bank account are simplified, without the need for proof of income. Opening a simplified account will, however, still require a taxpayer/individual identification number and an identification card, along with other basic personal information. Such accounts can be used for making public payments. Financial institutions offering such accounts will include multiple banks, commercial banks, and the Caixa Econômica Federal.

Low-Cost Microcredit Loans

Law No. 10735 of September 11, 2003 (formerly Provisional Measure No. 122 of June 25, 2003), and CMN Resolutions 3109 and 3128 of July 24, 2003, and October 30, 2003, respectively, create additional measures that expand the opportunities for microfinance loans destined for low-income earners and small businesses. Interest rates on such loans will be capped at 2 percent per month. Loans will be limited to R$600 for individuals and R$1,000 for small business. Terms will be no less than 120 days (terms can be smaller as long as rates are adjusted accordingly). Fees for accessing credit are not to exceed 2 percent of the loan amount for individuals and 4 percent for small business. Credit will be offered to individuals with simplified accounts (with maximum deposits of R$1,000), low-income individuals, and enterprises (with maximum deposits of R$10,000). Such transactions must be made through institutions such as microfinance societies (Sociedades de Crédito ao Microempreendedor [SCMs]) or via bank loans (direct or onlent).

Obligatory Lending and Bank Reserve Requirements

According to the same regulations, such microfinance loans will be funded by an earmarked 2 percent of the sight deposits of banks. Microlending may be undertaken directly or onlent via other financial institutions. If such loans are not made, banks have to increase their unremunerated reserves at the Central Bank by a corresponding amount.

Payroll Loans—Automatic Deductions from Bank Accounts
Provisional Measure No. 130 of September 17, 2003, introduced payroll loans. Employees can authorize the automatic payment of loans, financings, and leasing contracts direct from their pay check. Authorized payments will be limited to 30 percent of the total amount.

Expanded Correspondent Banking
CMN Resolution 3110 of July 31, 2003, expands the outreach of correspondent banks, authorizing them to offer many banking services such as opening accounts (sight deposits, savings deposits, term deposits, and investment funds) and payment and credit facilities. Central Bank authorization will be required for entering into such contracts.

Deposit Services: Small Clients and Special Savings

For most small clients, especially for individuals or households not engaged in entrepreneurial activities, the most important financial service is the deposit of liquid assets and cash wealth. The extent to which private financial institutions are engaged in the provision of deposit services is investigated below and compared with the role of public banks in the provision of deposit services.

Deposit Structure: An Overview of Aggregate Deposits

Looking at the composition of aggregate deposits for all banks in Brazil, a first finding is that, in terms of deposit type, the overwhelming majority of clients in Brazil's banking system (totaling almost 97 percent of all clients) hold their money in the form of either unremunerated sight deposits or special savings deposits *(caderneta de poupança).* Special savings deposits are remunerated at rates below the prevailing overnight rate and are sometimes negative in real terms (figure 3.1).[1]

Only a relatively small number of clients (3.3 million persons or 3.1 percent of all depositors) hold term deposits, which, however, amount to a huge proportion—R$128.9 million (41.2 percent)—of all deposits by value. Thus, the role of banks in the provision of services to depositors in the form of sight or special savings deposits accounts is more important, in terms of client access, than aggregate deposits or, even more clearly, term deposits.

Figure 3.1 Interest Rates for Special Savings Deposits and Term Deposits, 1999–2002

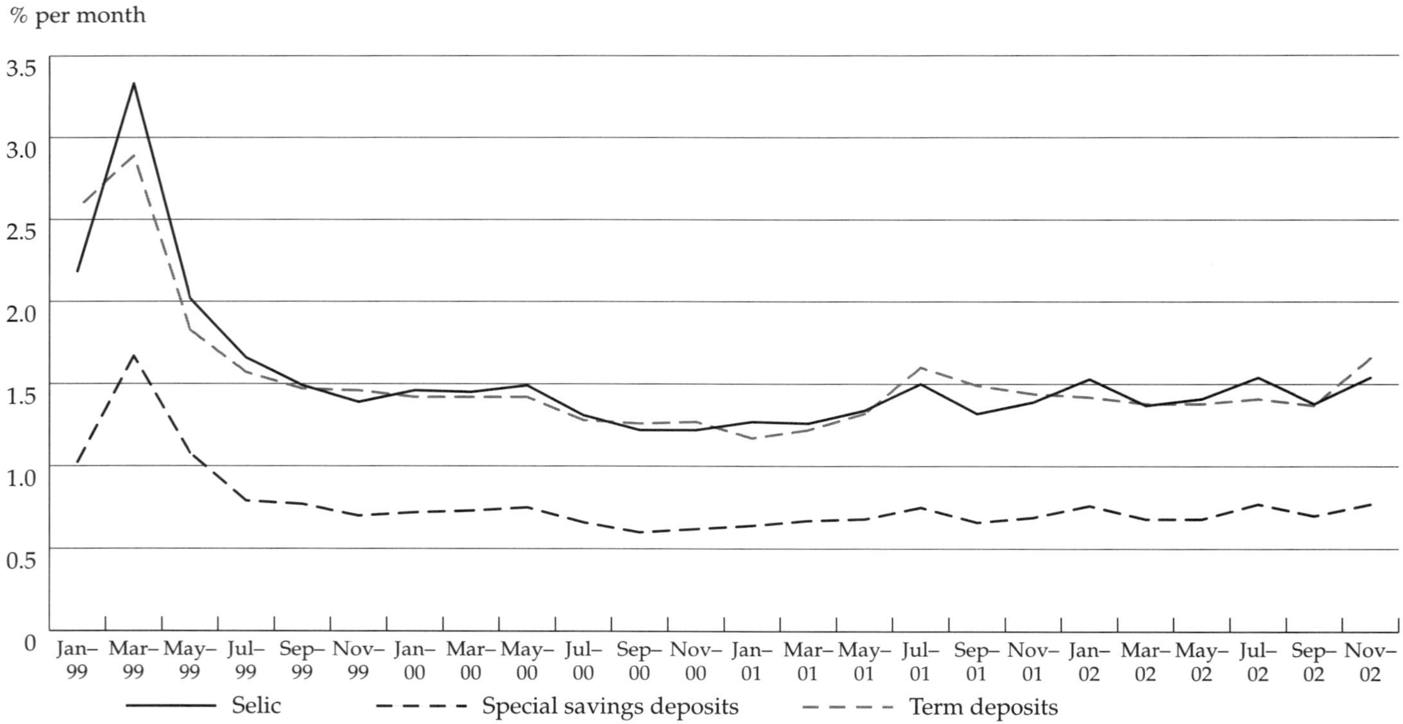

Source: World Bank staff calculations based on data from the Central Bank of Brazil.

The second observation is that private banks are already very active in provision of services to large numbers of clients, in the form of sight deposits, in particular, and also special savings deposits. However, with regard to the more highly remunerated term deposits, private banks deal with a relatively small number of large depositors. There is a striking difference in the composition of term deposit services between public and private institutions: 75 percent of term deposits, in value, are held by private institutions, but these account for only 25 percent of term deposit clients. The converse holds true for public banks. By contrast, for sight deposits, private banks serve a larger number of clients than public banks (59.5 percent) and hold more than half the total value of deposits (54.5 percent). For special savings deposits, these ratios are lower, but private banks still hold a larger proportion of total clients (44.7 percent) than total deposit value (42.6 percent). The inference is that private banks do not hesitate to provide services to large numbers of small account holders, provided the deposits are lucrative (as in the case of the unremunerated sight deposits). For deposits where reimbursements are much higher, such as term deposits, private banks prefer to focus on larger clients (figure 3.2).

The average size of client accounts in public banks is around the same as in comparable private banks (table 3.1). Public banks taken together have a larger share of total clients (51.4 percent) than total deposits (43.1 percent)—a difference of around 8 percent—and thus somewhat smaller average deposits per client, or R$2,800, compared to R$3,900 for all private banks. But the larger average account size of private banks is considerably influenced by some foreign-controlled institutions that appear to focus on high-net-worth clients. The apparent public bank advantage with small-account clients is reversed if similar large retail banks, public or private, are compared. Thus, the average deposit size in Banco do Brasil, at R$2,400, is not very different from the average size in the private banks, Bradesco and Itaú (R$2,500), and average deposits in the Caixa exceed this, at R$3,200. Looking at sight deposits, the average size in the largest private banks is below that of the public banks (R$1,100 and R$900, respectively), in contrast with R$1,300 in Banco do Brasil and R$1,700 in the Caixa. Bradesco retains the lowest-size ranking with regard to special savings deposits as well (R$1,800, compared to R$2,700 and R$2,400 at Banco do Brasil and the Caixa, respectively).

Deposits below R$5,000

The findings above suggest that private banks play an active role in some segments of the deposit market that serve the largest numbers of clients, and also that their intake of deposits in these segments is similar to that

Figure 3.2 Structure of Aggregate Deposits, December 2001

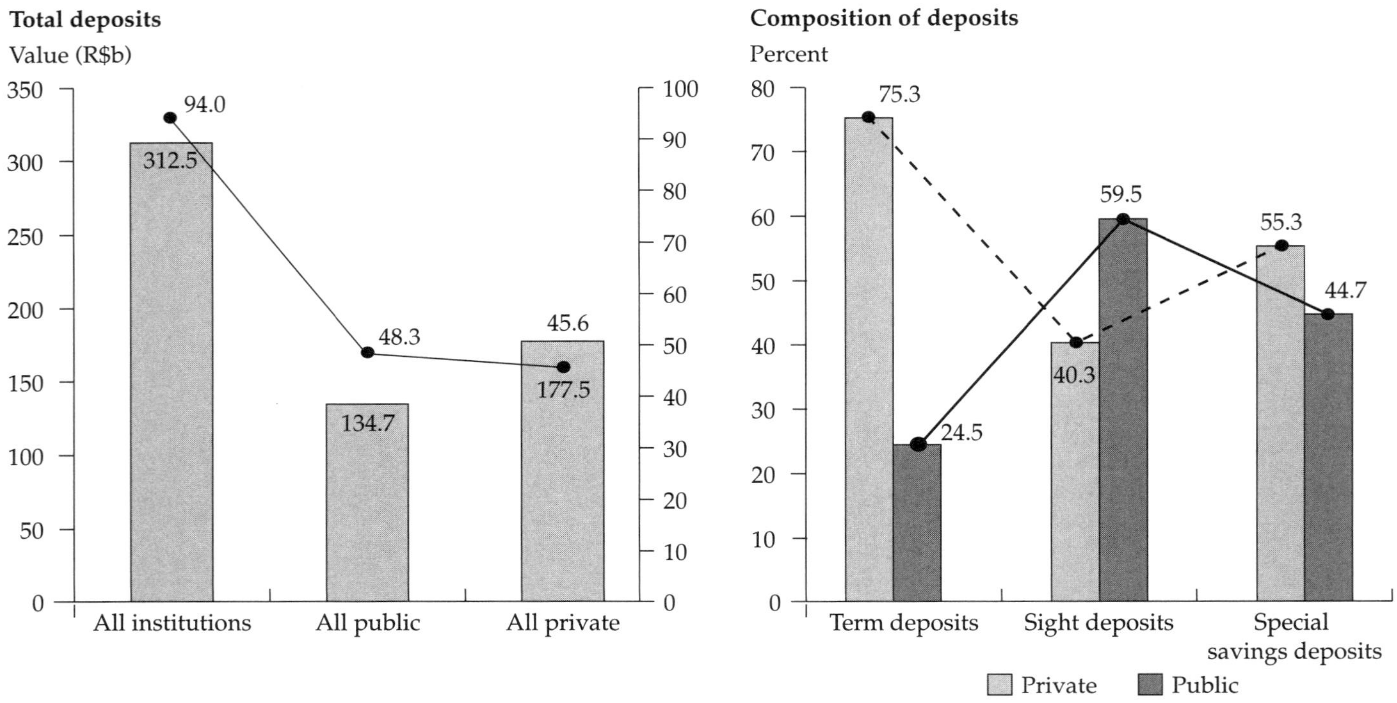

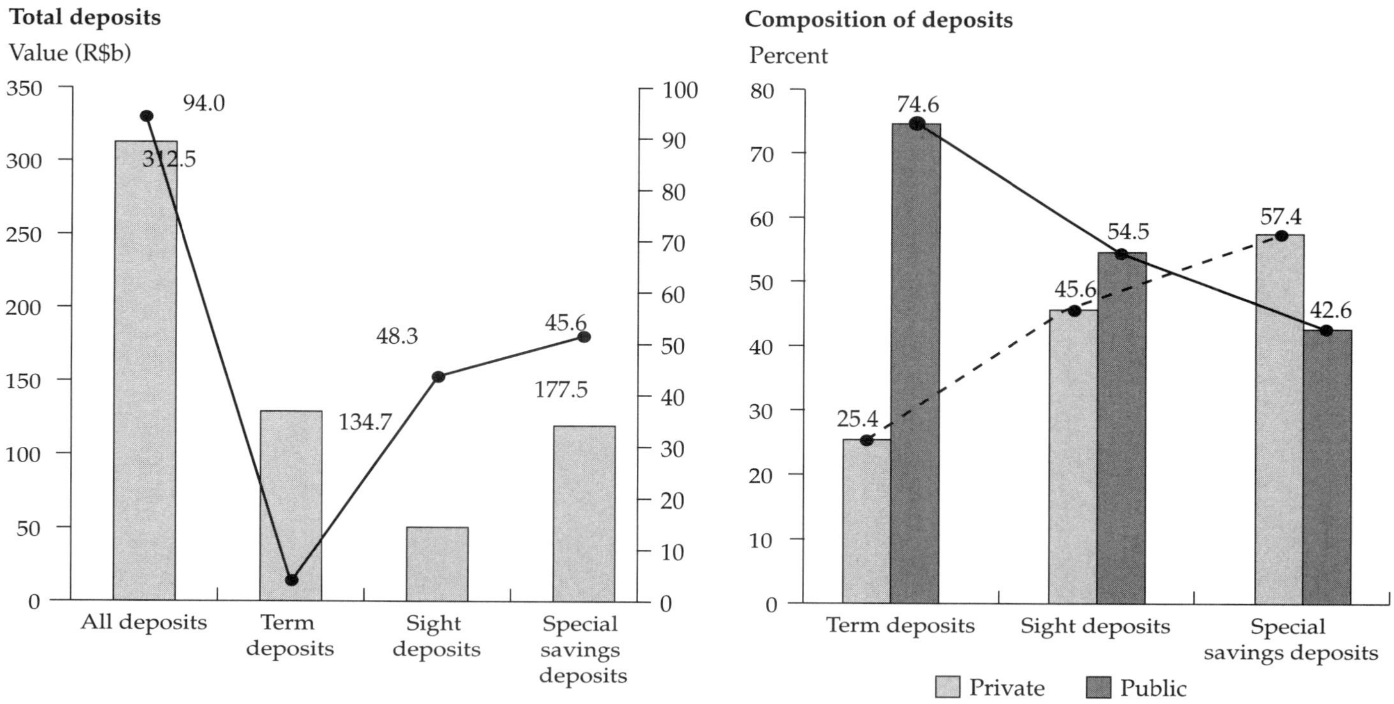

Source: World Bank calculations based on data from the Central Bank of Brazil–Fundo de Garantidor de Créditos (FGC).

Table 3.1 Structure of Deposits by Type and Institution, December 2001
(average deposit per client, R$'000)

Banks in Brazil	*All deposits*	*Term deposits*	*Sight deposits*	*Special savings deposits*
All institutions	3.3	38.8	1.2	2.3
All public:	2.8	13.1	1.3	2.4
o/w Banco do Brasil	2.4	10.0	1.3	2.7
Caixa[a]	3.2	..	1.7	2.4
All private:	3.9	118.1	1.1	2.2
o/w national				
Bradesco	2.5	77.5	1.1	1.8
Itaú	2.5	5.3	0.9	3.0
o/w foreign participation				
Unibanco	3.3	646.7	0.3	3.4
o/w foreign-controlled				
Santander	5.0	272.0	1.2	3.4
HSBC	4.0	555.6	2.2	1.5
ABN AMRO	2.8	73.3	2.8	1.9
Sudameris	10.5	214.3	3.5	1.1
BBV Banco	6.6	1,700.0	1.0	1.4
o/w foreign				
Citibank	16.5	2,500.0	8.3	12.3

Note: .. = negligible.
a. Caixa has a negligible role in term deposits.
Source: World Bank calculations based on data from the Central Bank of Brazil.

of the public banks. Does this also remain true for smaller-size deposits? In the second stage of analysis of deposit behavior for different institutional categories, deposits below R$5,000 are examined specifically. The broad message to emerge is that the significance of private banks for deposits below R$5,000 remains largely unchanged compared to their role in total deposits (figure 3.3 and appendix table A3.2).

In terms of numbers of clients, the share of private banks in this segment remains at 49 percent; there is a small decline in value (57 percent to 53 percent), suggesting, in combination with the stable share of numbers of clients, a somewhat greater concentration on smaller depositors. Private bank share in clients for sight deposits of less than R$5,000 is close to its share in total sight deposits (around 60 percent), with a marginal decline in value, and the share of clients in special savings deposits is also stable (at 45 percent) for deposits of all sizes compared to those below

Figure 3.3 Structure of Deposits below R$5,000 by Type, Institution, Numbers of Clients, and Value, December 2001

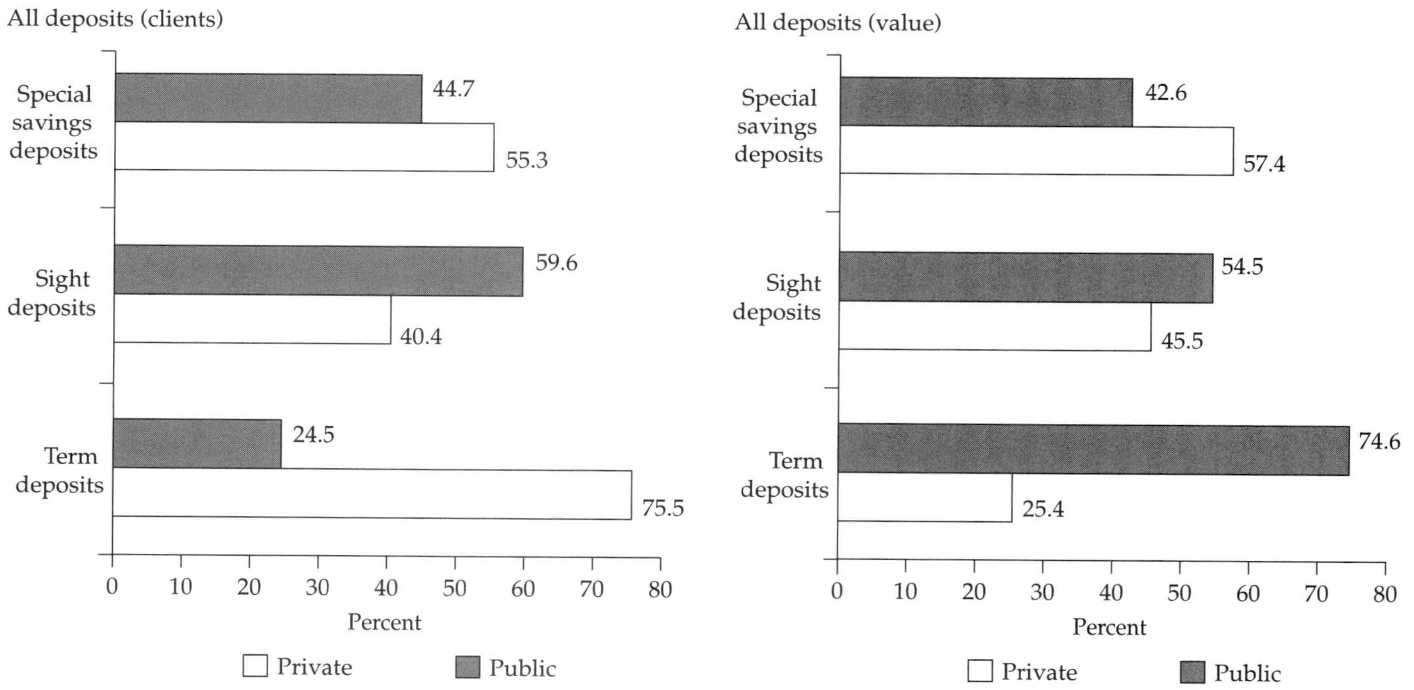

(*figure continued on next page*)

Figure 3.3 *(continued)*

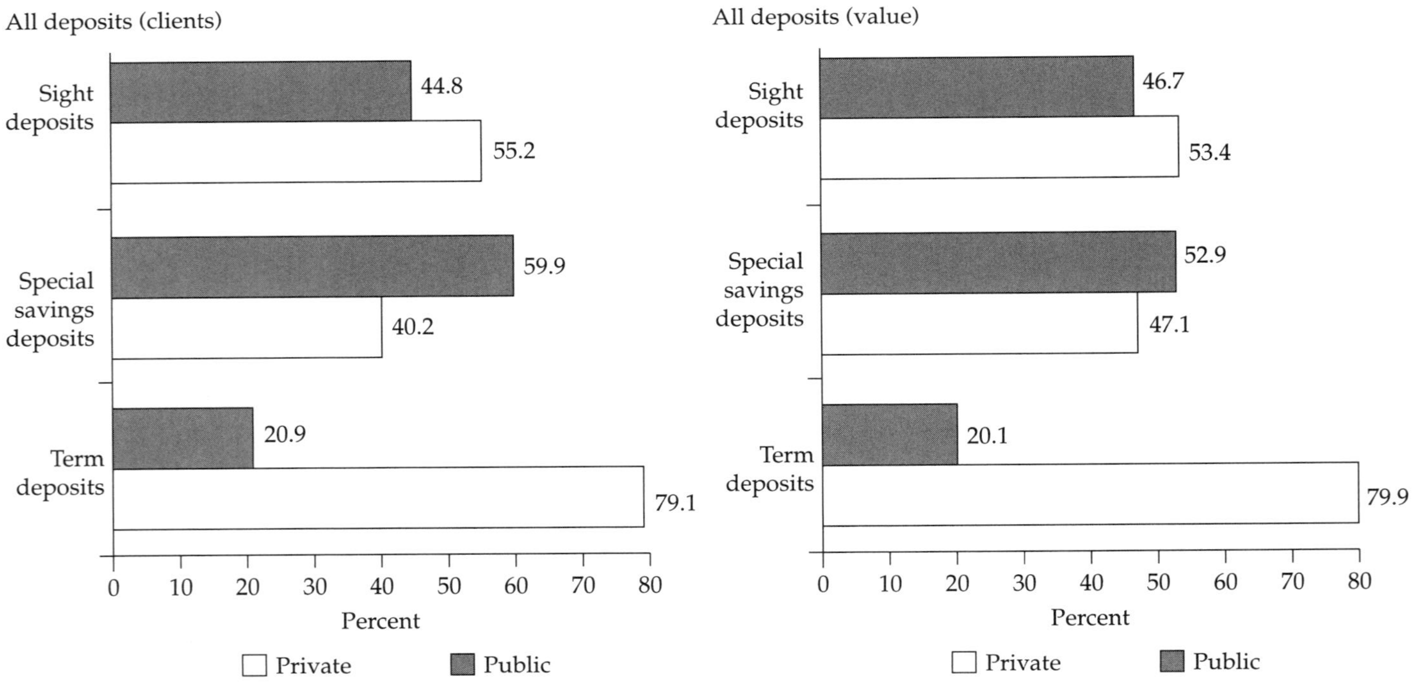

Source: World Bank calculations based on data from the Central Bank of Brazil–Fundo de Garantidor de Créditos.

R$5,000 (with a small increase in value from 43 percent to 47 percent). Data on individual institutions also reveal largely stable behavior for sight and savings deposits for the larger public and private banks.

Finally, the behavior of banks with regard to deposits in the smallest-size categories is examined. Included in the four size categories defined below are deposits below R$100 and three additional size categories below R$5,000. These data are available only for sight deposits and special savings accounts.

These data reveal, surprisingly, that for unremunerated sight deposits, private institutions dominate the provision of services in the smallest-size categories in numbers of clients (63 percent) and also value of deposits (87 percent). However, for (remunerated) special savings accounts, the private share declines to 43 percent of clients and 46 percent of value in the smallest-size categories. As deposit size categories increase, ratios of public and private provision of services stabilize, converging to the totals for all deposits below R$5,000 (figure 3.4 and appendix table A3.3). There are also strong differences between institutions, revealing that these are market segments that certain institutions choose to specialize in. Among private players, Unibanco accounts for 70 percent by value of the deposits below R$100, although only 21 percent of clients. Itaú and Bradesco take smaller deposits: both have client shares of around 17 percent and value shares in the range of 5 to 6 percent. For special savings deposits, the dominance of Caixa is clear: 30 percent of clients and value. However, the roles of the private bank, Bradesco, and the public Banco do Brasil are similar, with 18 and 17 percent, respectively, of clients; though Bradesco has a somewhat higher share of savings accounts by value—21 percent versus 13 percent for Banco do Brasil, suggesting somewhat larger account sizes within this size category.

In sum, private banks are very significant players today in the provision of deposit services to even the smallest clients, and they are aggressive in terms of presence in the more lucrative segments of these markets, with deposits (notably sight deposits) remunerated at a lower rate. Some private banks (Bradesco and Unibanco) have a major presence in special savings deposits for the smallest segments, although Caixa remained the dominant player. Provided returns are sufficient, therefore, barriers in establishing and maintaining small accounts do not appear to be an obstacle.

As a caveat, however, small deposit size does not necessarily imply low-income clients, although a correlation would be expected. To the limited extent that data are available on client income, they suggest that the proportion of low-income clients would be smaller than the proportion of small depositors. One large bank, for instance, has 5 percent of its deposits below R$10,000, but only about 1 and 2 percent, respectively, with indi-

Figure 3.4 Structure of Sight and Special Savings Deposits from R$1,000 to R$5,000, December 2001

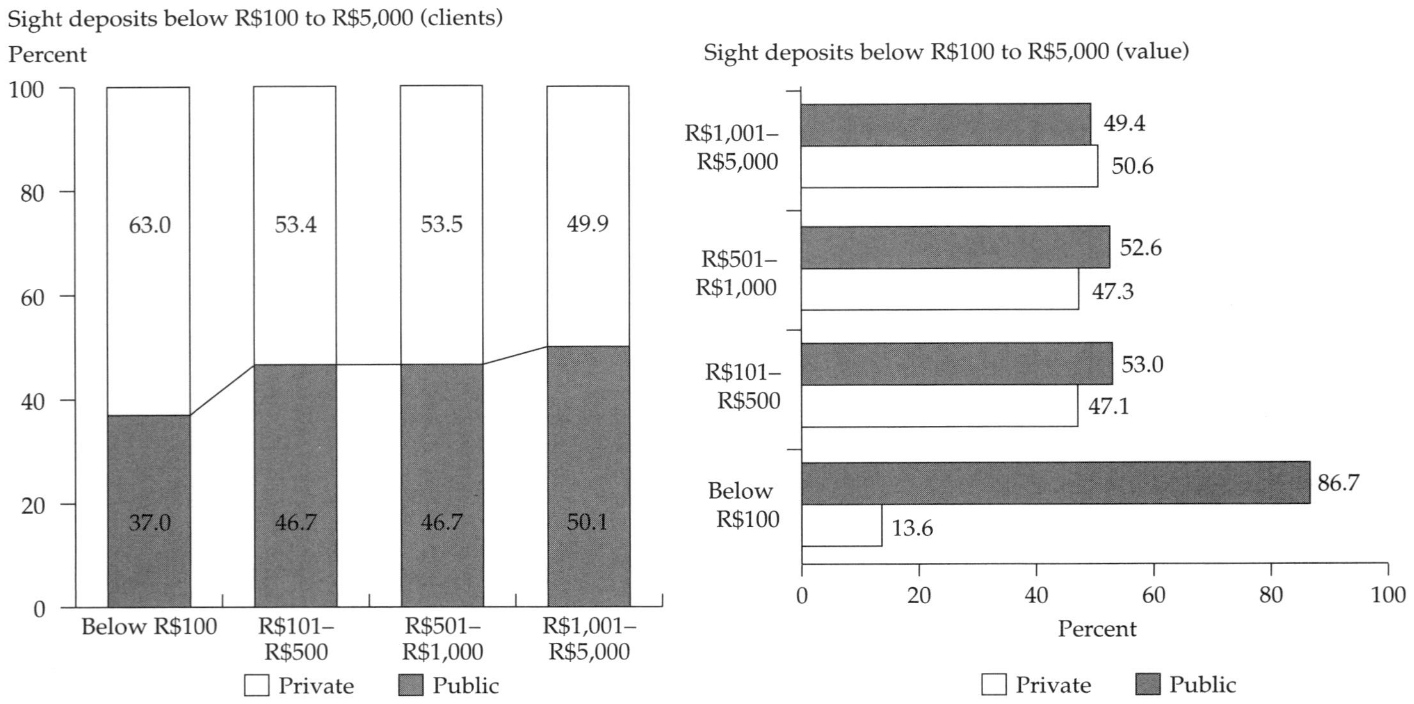

Special savings deposits below R$100 to R$5,000 (clients)

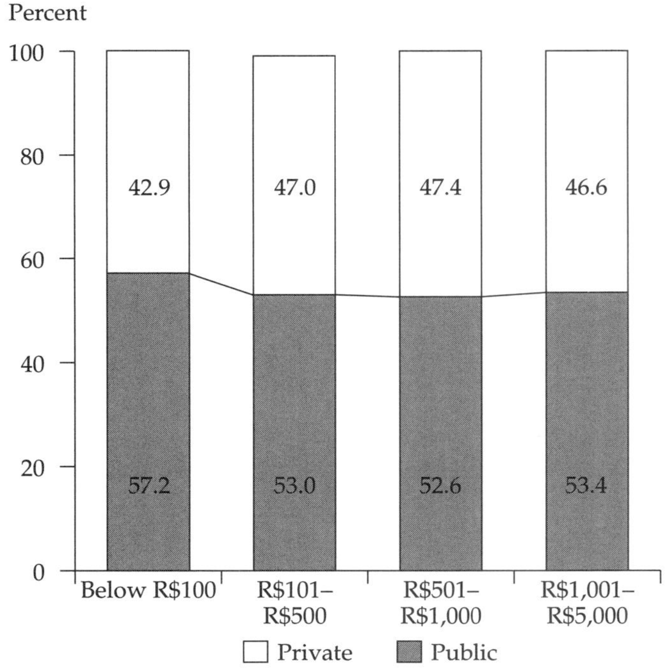

Special savings deposits below R$100 to R$5,000 (value)

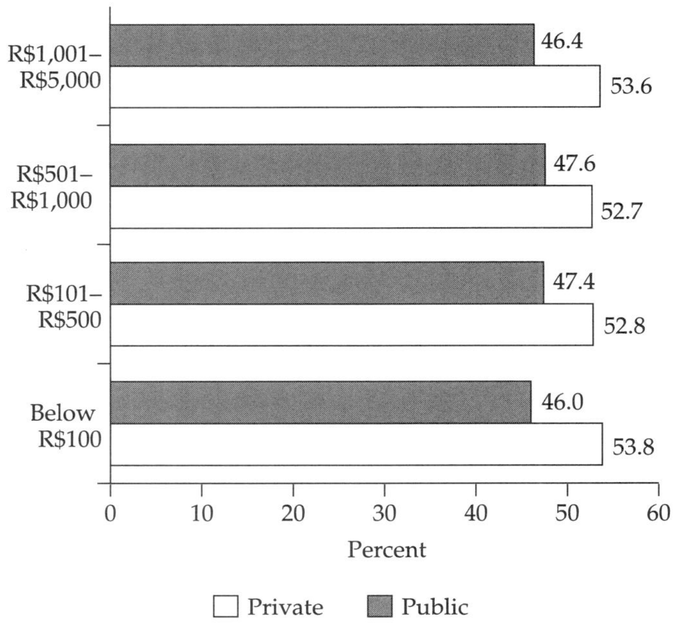

Source: World Bank calculations based on data from the Central Bank of Brazil–Fundo de Garantidor de Créditos.

viduals in the lowest two income classes, E and D, compared to 7 percent with middle-income individuals in class C, and 11 percent with middle-market companies.

Only limited data are available in the present study on the income levels of small depositors, based on information provided by banks. These data suggested that the very poor have a higher deposit-to-loan ratio than richer individuals. The average deposit balance held at banks by their class E customers fluctuates between four and six times the amount of outstanding loans they have. This compares to an average ratio of two to three for all other customer classes. Most of this balance is in special savings accounts. In some banks, the average deposit of a class E individual could be as high as about R$2,000 (US$900), a comparable level to the average for class B individuals. Classes C and D tend to have lower deposit balances, varying between R$400 and R$1,000 on average.[2]

The Client's Perspective: Demand for Bank Accounts and Deposit Services

The extent to which services are actually provided is not a measure of the difference between desired and actual levels of services. To gauge the gap between supply and demand of banking services in general and deposit services in particular, and also to assess the extent to which the services actually provided conform to client needs, the information above has been supplemented by the evidence from the survey of access to financial services in urban areas, discussed in chapter 1 of this study.

Results confirm that a gap between demand and supply does exist.[3] Although a large proportion of the 2,000 persons surveyed in urban areas of Brazil already have some form of bank account (43 percent, or around 850 persons), of the approximately 1,150 persons who do not have an account, two-thirds state that they would like to have an account (table 3.2). It also appears that demand is primarily for 'store of value' and transaction purposes and not for returns, because the primary reason cited for wanting a bank account is 'security.' Additional reasons suggest a dominance of needs for 'other financial services' (presumably services such as transactions or payments), particularly in the cases of current or special savings accounts. Rates of return are not considered an important reason, except for those with term deposits. In the case of current accounts and special savings accounts, lower transaction costs are also cited. These responses would suggest that the dominance of current and special savings accounts in small deposits reflects both client needs and the banking sector's interests.

Table 3.2 Three Main Reasons for Wanting a Bank Account

	Primary reason		*Secondary reason*		*Tertiary reason*	
Reason	*Frequency (nos.)*	*Cum. freq. (%)*	*Frequency (nos.)*	*Cum. freq. (%)*	*Frequency (nos.)*	*Cum. freq. (%)*
Any account type						
Security	883	65.9	113	18.3	52	12.9
Other financial services	128	75.5	214	53.0	84	33.7
Transactions w/ lower costs	73	80.9	116	71.8	53	46.8
Attractive rates of return	57	85.2	54	80.6	106	73.0
Others	199	100.0	119	100.0	109	100.0
Valid cases	(1,340)		(616)		(404)	
Current accounts						
Security	215	70.5	27	18.8	16	15.5
Other financial services	30	80.3	35	43.1	30	44.7
Transactions w/ lower costs	19	86.6	51	78.5	14	58.3
Attractive rates of return	3	87.5	6	82.6	13	70.9
Others	38	100.0	25	100.0	30	100.0
Valid cases	(305)		(144)		(103)	
Special savings accounts						
Security	259	73.2	29	18.7	26	24.8
Other financial services	18	90.4	30	78.1	19	74.3
Transactions w/ lower costs	24	79.9	39	43.9	11	35.2
Attractive rates of return	19	85.3	23	58.7	22	56.2
Others	34	100.0	34	100.0	27	100.0
Valid cases	(354)		(155)		(105)	

(table continued on next page)

Table 3.2 *(continued)*

Reason	*Primary reason*		*Secondary reason*		*Tertiary reason*	
	Frequency (nos.)	*Cum. freq. (%)*	*Frequency (nos.)*	*Cum. freq. (%)*	*Frequency (nos.)*	*Cum. freq. (%)*
Term deposits and investment accounts						
Security	235	67.7	20	15.0	23	23.2
Transactions w/ lower costs	35	77.8	40	45.1	21	44.4
Attractive rates of return	29	86.2	43	77.4	29	73.7
Others	48	100.0	30	100.0	26	100.0
Valid cases	(347)		(133)		(99)	

Source: World Bank survey of access to financial serices in urban areas in Brazil undertaken in 2002.

New Possibilities for Small Savings Other Than Deposits: Retail Bonds

To the extent that savers or account holders desire higher returns, new channels for small savings instruments through the direct purchase of retail government bonds are worthy of a mention. Sales of such bonds can be made through the internet under the Treasury Direct program. Closely modeled upon the program of the same name in the United States and widely used in a number of OECD countries, such retail debt sale programs have the double advantage of allowing a safe savings vehicle for small savers, remunerated at market rates, while at the same time allowing the government more efficient mechanisms for tapping local debt markets.[4] These schemes permit small investors with as little as R$200, or less than US$100, to invest in a low-risk, high-return investment with relatively high liquidity. By investing via the internet, costs involved are lower. The maximum amount allowed is R$200,000 per month. Prior to this, only banks, bond dealers, and other financial institutions registered in the Sistema Especial de Liquidacão e Custodia (SELIC) with a minimum amount of R$50,000 could purchase government bonds.

In its first two months of operation (January 2002 to March 2002), more than 31 percent of investors involved invested less than R$1,000, and almost two-thirds of all investors invested sums below R$5,000. More recent data offer the average transaction size rather than the detailed breakdown by size category. These suggest that average transaction size has increased progressively over time (table 3.3). Thus, although in prin-

Table 3.3 One Year of Treasury Direct Retail Bond Sales in Brazil, January 2002 to January 2003

Month	*Monthly sales (R$m)*	*Average value per transaction (R$'000)*	*Investors registered (nos. '000)*
January	5.9	6.3	2.4
February	7.0	8.0	3.0
March	6.3	7.7	3.4
April	3.3	7.4	3.6
May	3.2	7.2	3.8
June	2.7	7.2	4.0
July	4.2	7.1	4.4
August	5.1	7.4	4.6
September	6.2	7.7	4.8
October	11.0	8.3	5.0
November	9.9	8.7	5.3
December	12.2	9.0	5.6

Source: National Treasury, Brazil.

ciple very small deposits can be accepted, it appears that in practice average deposit size is several multiples of the minimum size. This suggests that efforts could be made to raise the publicity of the program to the attention of the smallest savers or increase the involvement of distributing financial institutions to use branch outlets or bank correspondent outlets.

Credit Services: Provision of Small Loans

Banks in Brazil offer a wide variety of loan products to businesses, including, in principle, the full range of products that could be of interest to lower-income groups. The issues are: To what extent are bank services targeted toward these groups, under what conditions, and at what price? The following sections investigate the extent to which bank credit is made available to small borrowers and lower-income groups.

Provision of Small Loans

The choice of products offered to each segment depends on the probable value added each customer segment would generate with each product. Evidence suggests that consumer loans are the most profitable products among those of interest to low-income individuals. By contrast, banks find that carrying out payment transactions with lower-income borrowers is not profitable because of the high administrative costs compared to the margin. However, the cost of carrying transaction services could be lowered by the use of new delivery channels, as discussed later in this section.

Data on small loans cover loan value and loan size, but not the number of clients served by an institution or market segment. In terms of the aggregate value of funds, it is not surprising that Brazil's largest commercial banks, both public and private, are the main providers of small loans, followed by nonbank finance institutions. In November 2001, banks provided a total of R$39 billion (US$17 billion) in loans below R$5,000 (US$2,150), with an average size as low as R$400 for some banks (US$180) at the then prevailing exchange rates. Nonbank finance institutions provided another R$5 billion (US$2 billion), while microfinance institutions provided only R$0.1 billion (US$43 million) of loans, with an average size of R$1,087.

One public bank, Banco do Brasil, provides 14 percent of all loans below R$5,000. The bank estimates that the average size of its consumer loans was R$1,100 in 2001 (less than US$500), placing it in direct competition with microfinance institutions. Banco do Brasil is followed by Brazil's other large banks: Bradesco, Caixa Econômica Federal, Itaú, and ABN AMRO, each with 6 to 8 percent in each market.[5] Unlike deposits, foreign banks play a significant role in the small-loan market, with a total market

Table 3.4 Share of Brazil's Commercial Banks in the Small-Loan Market in Terms of Loan Value, November 2001
(R$'000)

		% share in loan size category				
Bank	*Ownership*	*0–5*	*5–10*	*10–25*	*25–50*	*Above 50*
Private Brazilian banks		40	31	24	26	31
Public banks		34	33	46	52	48
Foreign banks[a]		26	36	30	22	21
Ten largest players in the market for loans below R$5,000						
Banco do Brasil	Public, federal	14	16	15	15	10
Caixa	Public, federal	8	8	18	28	2
Bradesco	Private	8	6	7	10	8
Itaú	Private	7	5	3	4	5
ABN AMRO	Foreign	6	9	6	4	2
Unibanco	Private, mixed	4	4	3	2	5
Santander (Banespa)	Foreign	3	2	2	3	1
Lloyds TSB	Foreign	3	0	0	0	0
HSBC Brasil	Foreign	3	3	2	3	1
Nossa Caixa	Public, state	2	1	1	1	0
Total 10 largest players		58	54	57	70	34

a. With foreign control.
Source: Central Bank of Brazil, Credit Risk database.

share of 26 percent in the market for loans below R$5,000 and 36 percent for loans below R$10,000 (table 3.4).

Since Caixa's restructuring in 2000, private banks dominate the small-loan market in volume of loans. The share of public banks in the small-loan market was substantially higher in 2000 before Caixa's balance sheet was restructured and a large part of its loan portfolio sold or written off. As a result, Caixa's share of the loan market segment below R$25,000 (US$10,700) dropped from a dominant 38 percent to 11 percent. Caixa is now in second place after Banco do Brasil, which accounts for 15 percent of loans in this segment. The small-loan market thus has become more competitive, and private commercial banks have become the largest players, with 63 percent of all loans in this segment, while public banks have dropped from 61 to 37 percent (table 3.5).

However, follow-up discussions with the banks in question and an analysis of their credit data suggest that a large part of small loans is not provided to lower-income borrowers. Detailed data available for some banks suggest that the majority of their small loans are borrowed by mid-

Table 3.5 Recent Evolution of Bank Shares in the Small-Loan Market, December 2000 to November 2001
(% shares)

		Loan size R$'000			
Bank	*Ownership*	*0–25*	*Above 25*	*0–25*	*Above 25*
		December 2000 (%)		*November 2001 (%)*	
Private Brazilian banks		22	28	33	30
Public banks		61	50	37	49
Foreign banks		17	21	29	21
Ten largest players in the market for loans below R$5,000					
Banco do Brasil	Public	9	10	15	10
Caixa	Public	38	14	11	3
Bradesco	Private	6	7	7	8
Itaú	Private	3	4	6	5
ABN AMRO	Foreign	3	3	7	2
Unibanco	Private mixed	2	4	4	5
Santander (Banespa)	Foreign	1	5	3	1
Lloyds TSB	Foreign	0	0	1	0
HSBC Brasil	Foreign	2	1	3	1
Nossa Caixa	Public	1	1	2	0
Total 10 largest players		65	49	59	35

Source: Central Bank of Brazil, Credit Risk database.

dle-income individuals and middle-market businesses. In the case of one large bank, for instance, 11 percent of its loans are below R$5,000. However, only 1 percent of its outstanding loan portfolio is to individuals in class E, and 2 percent to class D, while 10 percent goes to middle-class clients in class C and 9 percent to middle-market enterprises. Data on the number of clients served for different types of loans and within lower-loan-size groups would be desirable to supplement this conclusion.

For most large Brazilian banks, the small-loan segment is important. For the 10 Brazilian banks with the largest volume of loans below R$5,000 (tables 3.4 and 3.5 above), these loans represent 24 percent on average of their total loan portfolio. By comparison, all other loan size categories represent less than 10 percent each of their total loan portfolio. Clients with loans below R$5,000 account for a significant part of their clientele, and those with loans below R$10,000 for another very large *tranche*. There are also some smaller banks with a focus on low-income clients, such as Banco BBM, which provides working capital financing to small businesses, backed by their receivables.

Some banks channel their loans to lower-income clients through specialty finance subsidiaries. For several private banks, activities with low-income clients are concentrated in dedicated subsidiaries with a focus on consumer lending. This enables the banks to maintain their image vis-à-vis their middle- and high-income clients, and to present themselves with a friendlier face to lower-income clients. For instance, although Unibanco has only 1 percent of its loan portfolio with individuals in class E and a similar percentage in class D, Fininvest, its consumer finance subsidiary, has 11 and 28 percent, respectively, in those categories. In terms of their client base, individuals in classes D and E constitute only 10 percent of Unibanco's clients but 54 percent of the clients of Fininvest (table 3.6).

Many specialty finance companies dedicate their activities to lower-income populations. Large nonbank finance institutions in Brazil, such as Fininvest and Panamericano, are consumer finance specialists that dedicate their activities to such clients. These institutions play a much more limited role in terms of volume than large banks, but are significant players in the small-loan market compared to microfinance institutions (table 3.7).

Table 3.6 The Importance of Small Loans for the 10 Largest Brazilian Banks, November 2001
(value and % share)

	Loans below R$5,000		*Loans between R$5,000 and R$10,000*	
Bank	*Volume (R$m)*	*% of total portfolio*	*Volume (R$m)*	*% of total portfolio*
Banco do Brasil	6,095	13	3,368	7
Bradesco	3,697	11	1,209	4
Caixa	3,608	17	1,687	8
Itaú	3,260	16	1,164	6
ABN AMRO	2,506	20	1,952	15
Unibanco	1,864	11	797	5
Santander (Banespa)	1,508	28	504	9
Lloyds TSB	1,337	73	neg.	0
HSBC Brasil	1,308	19	675	10
Nossa Caixa	997	35	298	10
Total/average	26,179	24	11,654	7

Source: Central Bank of Brazil, Credit Risk database.

Table 3.7 Nonbanks with a Significant Market Share in the Small-Loan Market, November 2001

Banks	*Specialty*	*Loans below R$10,000 (R$m)*	*% of total loan portfolio*
Fininvest	Consumer finance	1,274	94
Bradesco	Small business finance	1,001	100
Finaustria	Car financing	769	78
Itaú Leasing	Leasing	625	49
BV	Car financing	457	63
ABN AMRO commercial finance	Small business finance	380	44
Bandeirantes	Small business finance	118	20
Pernambucanas	Consumer finance	117	100
Panamericano	Consumer Finance	105	85
Lloyds TSB Leasing	Leasing	68	93
Total/average		5,070	72

Source: Central Bank of Brazil, Credit Risk database.

Small Transactions versus Transactions with Low-Income Clients

The above analysis suggests that obstacles to lending to lower-income individuals or to collecting their deposits do not necessarily lie in the small size of the transactions. In the case of deposits, it has been demonstrated that initial and ongoing transaction costs associated with small deposit intake and monitoring are less significant than interest rate differentials on different types of deposits. In the case of loans, profitability depends not only on initial and ongoing transaction processing costs but also on the default risk associated with each class of borrower, the cost of assessing such default risk, and the potential to set lending rates that adequately reflect these costs and risks. Key elements of initial (entry) and ongoing (per transaction) costs and prices are investigated below. Alternative delivery channels are then examined, because these costs vary significantly with the delivery channel chosen.

Entry Requirements, Prices, and Transaction Costs

If banks are prepared to offer services to small clients, what are the reasons that hold back such clients from opening bank accounts? A variety of factors could be possible.

Entry Requirements: The Client's Perspective

From the point of view of the individual, requirements for opening an account may have been too stringent. Until recent changes introduced in 2003, opening an account required proof of identity, income, clean credit records, references, and, in the case of prospective borrowers, collateral. Also, the prices and conditions at which services were offered by banks could have been unattractive for less-affluent clients. Implicit or explicit high prices could include, for example, high initial deposits or high minimum balances, high ongoing maintenance fees, or high fees per transaction. Unattractive conditions could include inconvenient locations or hours of service, or even behavior toward unaccustomed clients that could have been perceived as overwhelming or unwelcoming.[6]

Finally, it is also possible that there has been limited interest in having a bank account among some persons who are very poor, and for whom the need to store value is not important.[7] A partial investigation of the importance of these issues was investigated in the World Bank 2002 survey of access to financial services in urban areas of Brazil. Information was also obtained from individual banks on entry requirements for bank services and the pricing of such services, and Central Bank data on the pricing of services were also evaluated.

Results from the World Bank survey suggest that both sets of reasons have discouraged the opening of bank accounts. Perceived levels of minimum funds needed to use banking services, entry requirements for documentation and references, and the costs and fees of service provision have affected potential client behavior (table 3.8). Official regulations pertaining to requirements for opening an account have been, until recently, onerous and diffuse, and added to these were the requirements that most banks demanded in practice.[8] Official requirements included an identity card, proof of address, and a taxpayer individual identification number (Cadastro de Pessoa Física [CPF]).[9] Such requirements still prevail for accounts other than the new basic accounts for low-income persons.

On standard accounts, the branch manager's signature was required to attest to the validity of the documents. Not only did this make a branch visit necessary, but it also implied that the manager would be personally liable in cases of misinformation. This made managers reluctant to vouch for individuals perceived to be risky. According to standard requirements, financial institutions can open accounts for persons with negative information in credit bureaus, but may not furnish checkbooks if they have issued checks drawn with insufficient funds. However, beyond these, many banks require clean credit records, proof of income and minimum income levels, and minimum initial deposits. Banks with these require-

Table 3.8 Survey on Access to Financial Services in Brazil: Reasons for Not Having a Bank Account

	Primary reason		*Secondary reason*		*Tertiary reason*	
Reason	*Frequency (nos.)*	*Cum. freq. (%)*	*Frequency (nos.)*	*Cum. freq. (%)*	*Frequency (nos.)*	*Cum. freq. (%)*
Group 1—client characteristics						
Don't have enough money	817	93.3	45	21.3	31	25.4
Don't have the right documents	22	95.8	83	60.7	12	35.2
Don't know how to open an account	13	97.3	29	74.4	25	55.7
Need more references	12	98.6	21	84.4	32	82.0
Bad credit history	8	100.0	19	93.0	18	97.0
Hostile bank environment	4	100.0	14	100.0	4	100.0
Valid cases	(872)		(197)		(118)	
Group 2—bank characteristics						
High fees	125	42.2	40	31.5	9	11.0
Transactions take too long	63	63.5	17	44.9	15	29.3
Fear losing money	50	80.4	17	58.3	15	47.6
No bank close by	24	88.5	13	68.5	6	54.9
Bad service	23	96.0	24	87.0	24	84.0
Bank hours inconvenient	11	100.0	16	100.0	13	100.0
Valid cases	(285)		(111)		(69)	

Source: World Bank survey of access to financial serices in urban areas in Brazil undertaken in 2002.

ments have included the publicly owned federal banks, where these minimum deposits have been no lower than comparable private banks.

Brazil's banks have usually applied a credit-scoring methodology to all account applicants and defined ex-ante what products the account holder could have access to. Applications for these products could then be sent on-line or via an ATM. The only accounts that could be opened without credit scoring were the *caderneta de poupança* or passbook savings deposits. Persons unable to provide all the above information were sometimes deemed to be ineligible by these methods. In addition, for loans to individuals, institutions have required a minimum salary level, or a cosigner or guarantor. Minimum salary levels for loans have been higher for banks than for consumer loan agencies or nonbanks. There has, therefore, been scope for simplification of conditions required for the opening of an account. Recent measures introduced by the government establishing simplified accounts for individuals are in broad terms a step in the right direction.

Nonbanks or consumer credit agencies (such as merchant or store credit) have apparently shared most of these requirements, with one key difference—less importance has been given to the credit record, which they usually do not require or check. However, supermarket chains and large stores that issue credit cards in their name do require credit checks as well as the minimum salary, although minimum salary levels can be much lower than at banks, at levels (such as R$150 to R$270) below the prevailing minimum salary in 2001 of around R$180.

Pricing of Banking Services for Individuals and Households

A first measure of the extent to which the prices or costs of bank services may have been considered high by some client groups can be gauged from table 3.9, which lays out the costs of provision of basic bank services associated with a sight deposit. Fees detailed in this table are on a per-service basis. The data suggest that monthly fees, although low in absolute terms, may nevertheless have been expensive for a low-income client. Fees that ranged from R$3 to R$5 for monthly services could constitute 1.5 to 2.5 percent of an individual earning R$200 per month, which is the cutoff level for the first quintile of our sample and exceeds a monthly income at the minimum wage of R$180 per month.

A second and possibly more realistic measure of bank fees is the cost of provision of a basket of services. Most banks provide their services in this manner, offering two or three standard combinations of services to clients in broad categories of service needs. Thus, Itaú offers three broad packages: an electronic package, a basic package, and an all-inclusive package.

Table 3.9 Fees and Requirements for Sight Deposit Services at Key Brazilian Banks, 2002

		Financial institutions				
		Public		*Private*		
Documentation necessary to open an account		*Caixa Econômica Federal (CEF)*	*Banco do Brasil (BB)*	*(BANERJ)–Itaú*	*Banco Real ABN AMRO bank*	*Bradesco*
Identity card		Yes	Yes	Yes	Yes	Yes
Taxpayer number		Yes	Yes	Yes	Yes	Yes
Proof of residence		Yes	Yes	Yes	Yes	Yes
Proof of income		Yes (R$800)	Yes (no min.)	Yes (R$750)	Yes (R$300)	Yes (R$900)
Initial deposit		500	No	No	50	No
Fees per service (R$)						
Service fee	Monthly	4	4	4.5	3	5
Statement	Per transaction	0.9	1	0.9	0.8	1.3
Account balance	Per transaction	0.6	Exempt	Exempt	0.6	Exempt
Card service fee	Monthly	Exempt	1.5	Exempt	Exempt	Exempt
Card Issue	Event	3	Exempt	Exempt	Exempt	Exempt
Checkbook	Event	6	5	Exempt	4.5	6
Transfers[a]	Event	9	9	10	11	9.8

Note: Option 1: Specific fees are charged for each transaction. Option 2: Packages of services are offered, for a single monthly fee, for a package of predetermined services (appendix table A3.4).

a. Refers to credit order documents or credit transfers, which are used to make transfer of funds between different accounts in the same or different banks.

Source: Bank information through websites and site visits.

ABN AMRO also offers three broad standard baskets and the public banks, Banco do Brasil and Caixa, each offer a basic as well as a special package (appendix table A3.4). Basic baskets of services have similar monthly charges; Caixa and Banco do Brasil, the two public banks, offer service packages of R$3.00 and R$3.50, respectively, while services from private banks begin at the same level (R$3.50 in Bradesco) and somewhat higher at ABN AMRO (R$4.00) and Itaú (R$6.00). The difference between basic and more expensive service packages appears to lie in services such as the number of withdrawals, the provision of monthly statements, and, significantly, checking services and overdraft *(cheque especial)* facilities.

Packages offered by some private banks such as Bradesco appear competitive compared to the public banks, and there is little to choose between them. However, other private banks in table 3.9 prefer to scale prices of some services based on the volume of transactions. In addition (and not cited in the table), most banks offer volume discounts on service fees, based on overall deposit size. As deposit size increases, monthly maintenance costs decrease and finally disappear. Although this is logical from the point of view of scale economies for the bank, it is regressive from the point of view of small consumers.

For standard accounts, per-transaction prices, too, can be expensive for the poor, especially for some transactions. To open an account, registration of client information (including the client *cadastro* or tax registration number) is required and is regularly updated by some banks. Many institutions charge an initiation fee for this service, and some require fees for the ongoing updating of client information. The average cost of this service was R$31 in February 2002 (with a range varying from R$0 to R$270), and the average cost of a credit history check was R$21 (with a range from R$0 to R$300). The average cost of opening a current account was R$14 (with a range from R$0 to R$30). This meant that it is possible to open an account at no cost in some banks, but that the average cost is R$66, nearly 37 percent of the minimum wage. The average cost of a credit assessment is R$105 (with a range from R$0 to R$800), or nearly 60 percent of the minimum salary. Charges for checking and overdraft facilities *(cheques especial)* are particularly high, especially in terms of interest rates charged for the latter. Overdraft facilities may be accessed by debit cards with preapproved overdraft limits, which is a key factor in their popularity from the clients' perspective. Another reason on the supplier side may be that problems associated with the recovery of formal loans do not apply to overdrafts.

Interest rates are very high for those categories of lending important to small consumers and to small entrepreneurs, especially overdrafts. Loans on overdrafts represent the overwhelming proportion of bank credit—72 percent of new lending to individuals in December 2002 and more than 45 percent of new loans to enterprises. Moreover, the percentage of new lending that consists of overdrafts is much higher than the stock of all loans (13 percent of outstanding loans to individuals and around 29 percent of loans to enterprises), and the interest rate on this category of lending is very high, up to as much as 160 percent on an annualized basis (table 3.10).

Moreover, overdrafts and other expensive categories of loans form a large proportion of new loans. Overdrafts as a part of outstanding loan stock are growing particularly fast for enterprise overdrafts. Vehicle and personal loans are the most rapidly growing categories for personal loans (figure 3.5).

Apart from overdrafts, debit card services are cheap to provide and they are the most common product used by lower-income clients. All the baskets of services offered (appendix table A3.4) include one debit card for an account holder. Brazilian banks interviewed indicate that up to 60 to 85 percent of their clients in classes D and E have debit cards with preapproved overdraft limits, against only 20 to 40 percent of clients in classes A and B. By contrast, about 20 percent of clients in classes A and B have a credit card, compared to less than 5 percent of class D and E clients. Nearly 95 percent of the outstanding loan balance of class E individuals on average comes from an overdraft rather than a formal loan. For classes C and D, the percentage remains high at around 80 percent.

Under the new arrangements, a basic basket of services is now offered free of charge to low-income consumers. Such baskets offer limited services and do not include check-writing facilities. These resemble, in many respects, basic accounts offered in many other countries, and as such are a welcome development. However, in Brazil such accounts are offered entirely free of charge, which may make their sustainability difficult, as well as expensive and unattractive for sponsoring financial institutions. A second unusual feature is the offering of low-cost loans to the holders of such accounts.

Pricing of Banking Services for Small Enterprises

In contrast to individuals, banking services sought by small entrepreneurs are primarily credit, and interest rates are perceived as the key constraint to access. A study conducted by the World Business Environment Survey (Batra, Kaufman, and Stone 2003) on a sample of 201 Brazilian firms of various sizes showed that the high level of interest rates is perceived as the main operational and growth constraint by companies in Brazil, followed by collateral requirements. These two factors have been more important in Brazil than in other Latin American countries or elsewhere

Table 3.10 Interest Rates, Outstanding Stock, and New Loans to Consumers by Loan Type (Free Credit), December 2002

Loans	*Average annual interest rate*[a]	*Outstanding loans*		*New loans*		*Delinquency (% more than 90 days)*	*Average maturity (days)*
		R$m	*%*	*R$m*	*%*		
Loans to individuals							
Overdrafts	163.9	8,545	13.2	13,555	72.4	8.4	21.0
Personal	91.8	24,601	38.0	2,480	13.2	8.6	220.2
Vehicles	55.5	26,933	41.7	1,708	9.1	2.9	517.1
Other fixed assets	80.7	4,579	7.1	989	5.3	11.4	165.5
Total		64,658	100.0	18,731	100.0		
Loans to enterprises							
Overdrafts	77.3	20,247	29.3	16,595	45.6	1.6	22.5
Discount of duplicates	56.1	6,045	8.7	4,458	12.2	4.4	31.6
Working capital	42.3	29,562	42.8	9,035	24.8	3.4	238.3
Fixed assets	43.0	4,278	6.2	9901	2.7	1.8	257.9
Vendor	32.9	7,852	11.4	3,573	9.8	0.4	70.1
Hot money	52.0	619	0.9	1,341	3.7	4.7	10.1
Promissory note	50.9	520	0.8	424.2	1.2	2.2	34.3
Total		69,123	100.0	36,416	100.0		

a. Average interest rates weighted by outstanding loans until May 2000 and by daily average of new loans since May 2000.
Source: Central Bank of Brazil.

Figure 3.5 Credit Operations with Nonearmarked Funds, July 2000 to December 2002

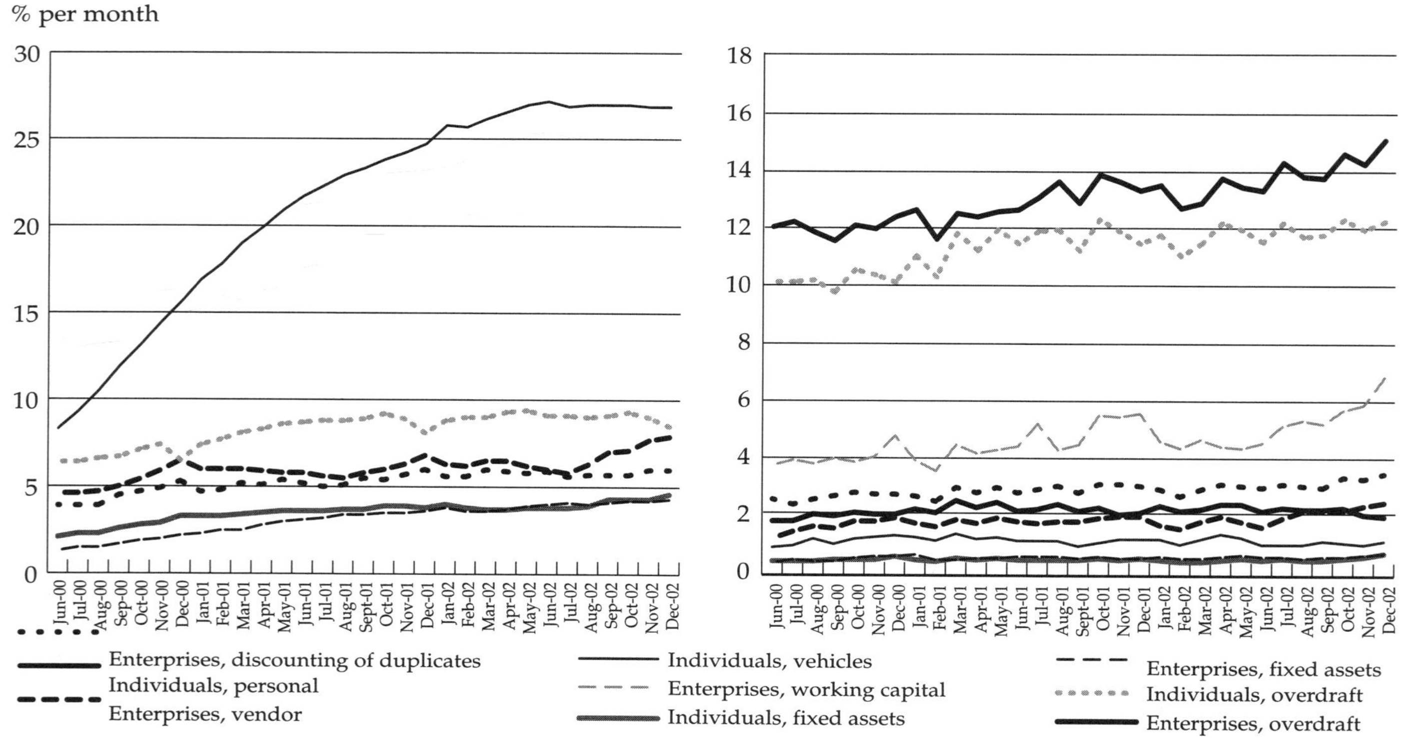

Source: World Bank staff based on Central Bank of Brazil data.

in the world. And for small firms, interest rates are an even stronger constraint than for larger firms (table 3.11).[10]

By contrast, bank transaction fees appear reasonable to microbusinesses and small companies. Most banks charge lower service fees for small enterprises. Bank registration costs average R$52 for enterprises, account opening fees are R$15, credit checks average R$29, and loan processing fees average R$140. Obtaining a loan backed by receivables is much more expensive (about R$600).

An additional source of information on the links between bank fees and type of institution, provided by the Central Bank, suggests, in contrast to the observations above, that on average, federal banks may be significantly cheaper than private and foreign banks (table 3.12). The difference varies from 20 percent to open a current account to nearly 200 percent for a credit file analysis. But these averages for all banks within each category may be influenced by those private or foreign banks targeted at high-net-worth individuals. Comparisons of the largest private and public banks, undertaken above, reveal similar outcomes. And the data below support the finding that the highest prices charged by some federal banks are in line with average private bank prices. Foreign banks tend to be more expensive than private national banks.

Table 3.11 Constraints to Enterprise Operations and Growth: An International Comparison

		Rating of specific constraints				
Firms	*Is financing a constraint?*	*High interest rates*	*Collateral require-ments*	*Access to long-term loans*	*Banks lack loanable funds*	*Access to lease finance*
All firms						
Brazil—all firms	2.69	3.71	2.91	2.90	1.81	1.71
Latin America	2.86	3.57	2.79	2.91	2.22	2.08
Upper-middle-income countries	2.69	3.41	2.37	2.54	1.83	1.71
OECD	2.35	2.65	2.25	1.80	1.59	1.68
Brazilian firms by size category						
Small firms	2.47	3.79	2.76	2.54	1.73	1.88
Medium firms	2.82	3.73	3.00	3.00	1.84	1.74
Large firms	2.33	3.53	2.64	2.76	1.72	1.45

Note: Ratings are as follows: 1 = no obstacle, 2 = minor obstacle, 3 = moderate obstacle, 4 = major obstacle.
Source: World Bank, 2001m.

Table 3.12 Average Transaction Costs by Type of Bank in Brazil

	Price per transaction (R$)								
	Federal banks			*Private national banks*			*Foreign banks*		
Transaction by individuals	*Min.*	*Avg.*	*Max.*	*Min.*	*Avg.*	*Max.*	*Min.*	*Avg.*	*Max.*
Client cadastre	0	15	20	0	31	270	0	34	250
Credit history check	0	10	15	0	12	30	0	16	80
Current account opening	0	9	10	0	12	30	0	20	30
Debit card	0	0	2 p.m.	0	0	3 p.m.	0	0	6 p.m.
Overdraft facilities	0	15	30	0	31	200	0	21	100
Credit granting	15	38	150	0	113	500	0	88	400

Note: p.m. = per month.
Source: Central Bank of Brazil, February 2002.

Table 3.13 Transaction Cost Comparison, Banks and Nonbanks

	Price per transaction (R$)					
	All banks			*NBFIs*		
Transaction by individuals	*Min.*	*Avg.*	*Max.*	*Min.*	*Avg.*	*Max.*
Client cadastre	0	32	270	0	45	130
Credit history check	0	21	300	0	135	300
Current account opening	0	14	30	n.a.	n.a.	n.a.
Debit card	0	0	6 p.m.	0	0	20 p.a.
Issue of special checks	0	26	200	n.a.	n.a.	n.a.
Credit granting	0	105	800	0	139	800

Note: n.a. = not applicable; p.a. = per annum; p.m. = per month.
Source: Data provided by the Central Bank of Brazil to World Bank Staff, February 2002.

Finally, it is worth noting that nonbank financial institutions (NBFIs) are generally more expensive than banks. On average, it costs R$45 to become a client of an NBFI and obtain a debit card equivalent to one minimum salary, compared to R$32 for all banks. A credit history averages R$135, compared to R$21 for all banks (table 3.13).

Delivery Channels: Branches, ATMs, and Correspondent Banking

Bank fees and transaction prices discussed above are affected by the real costs of delivery of services, by the risks associated with the provision of specific types of services to different categories of consumers, and by the contestability of entry of other banks into each market segment. The present section evaluates the role of different modes of delivery of services in terms of their possible contribution to the expansion of outreach. More widely used traditional channels are discussed in the present section, such as bank branches, ATM networks, and correspondent banking services. The relative provision of these services is described in table 3.14. New techniques for delivery of services, based on internet and phone technology, are discussed in the following section.

Brick and Mortar Institutions: Bank Branches

Bank branches are the most traditional and still are the most important channel for the provision of financial services in Brazil. Bill payment is still conducted mostly through branches because the postal system is perceived as less reliable. As discussed in the first chapter of this study,

Table 3.14 Types of Distribution Channels Used by Different Bank Groups

Bank	*Branches*	*Outposts*	*ATMs*
Public banks	6,556	4,054	3,317
Private domestic banks	6,147	2,415	7,471
Foreign banks	3,693	2,837	1,887

Source: Central Bank of Brazil 2000b.

Brazil's banks serve a much higher number of inhabitants per branch than in developed countries, but service levels are above average compared to other developing countries. Brazil has more bank branches relative to population than other Latin American countries or other large developing countries. Measured relative to GDP, its bank branch intensity is lower than Colombia, India, and Indonesia, which are all poorer than Brazil, but the two latter are much more densely populated. Branch intensity relative to GDP in Brazil is higher than in Chile or Mexico, although both are richer than Brazil. It is true that regional distribution of bank branches differs widely, with less service in the North and Northeast, but these are in large measure explained by differences in population density and regional GDP and, thus, by differentials in personal income.

In any event, the provision of bank branch services is expensive, and expanding branch networks in underserved regions is not a profitable strategy. Banks agree that the high labor, security, and capital costs associated with branch opening make it unprofitable to attend to poor people in remote areas through new branch services.

Banking Correspondents

The high fixed costs of establishing a bank branch are raised disproportionately by a series of security regulations, labor laws, restrictive hours, and so forth. In response, from the late 1990s, Brazil's banks began to develop physical outlets for their services that are not considered to be bank branches. Since March 2000, such 'correspondent banking' agreements have been officially recognized, and there has been a dramatic increase in the number of financial institutions entering into correspondent arrangements, as well as in the number of correspondent outlets, in the last two years (table 3.15).[11] Correspondents include nonfinancial legal entities such as convenience shops and supermarket chains and, more recently, post offices, largely for the provision of basic payment, deposit, and simple cash withdrawal transactions to a wider public and particularly to low-income populations.

Costs of Maintaining Bank Branches in Brazil

Security Costs
Law No. 7102 of June 1983 of the Ministry of Justice requires all financial outlets of public and private banks, savings banks, credit societies, and savings associations (defined as branches where movements of funds occur) to implement security measures, including the provision of (1) trained armed guards; (2) an alarm enabling communication with another branch of the institution, a security company, or the police; and (3) a camera, or a blinded cabin with a permanent armed guard, or other equipment to delay the actions of criminals.

Transport Costs
The law also requires that transportation of funds should be undertaken by professionals or specially trained staff from the financial institution approved by the Ministry of Justice. For sums of more than R$7,000, a regular vehicle may be used but with two armed guards. Beyond R$20,000, a special vehicle is required.

Labor Costs and Restrictions
The Bankers Union Agreement imposes a maximum of six hours of work five days a week for nonmanagerial bank employees (but this also tends to serve as a minimum, requiring branches to be open sometimes for long periods, sometimes with little work to do). Overtime must be paid for extra hours. Labor costs are high and salaries are negotiated with a union of bank employees. In addition, social contributions and taxes allegedly amount to around 83 percent of salaries. Of these, 59 percent are taxes, 11 percent social security contributions, and 12 percent are additional benefits (insurance and so on).

Capital Requirements
An additional Bank for International Settlements (BIS) ratio capital requirement of 2 percent is required per branch established in São Paulo and Rio de Janeiro and 1 percent per branch located elsewhere in Brazil.

Other Costs
Brazilian law also requires disabled access in all branches.

The best-established of these chains is run by Caixa, the giant public sector bank, which has a monopoly franchise on the network of about 8,000 lotto game outlets spread across the country. In addition, Caixa is establishing new relationships with 2,400 correspondents, with the objective of being present in all 2,000 municipalities where it currently had no

Table 3.15 Correspondents in Brazil, 2001 and 2002

Institution	*12/31/2001*	*11/30/2002*	*Projections for 2003*
Number of contracting institutions	52	68	n.a.
Banks	42	53	n.a.
Finance companies	10	15	n.a.
Total correspondent points in Brazil (nos. '000)	14.1	23.9	n.a.
Lottery shops (nos. '000)	8.9	9.0	9.0
Post offices (nos. '000)	n.a.	2.0	5.4
Others (nos. '000)	5.2	12.9	n.a.

Note: n.a. = not applicable.
Source: Central Bank of Brazil.

outlets. As a result, by June 2002, Caixa expected to be present in all municipalities of Brazil with at least one correspondent banker offering payment and deposit services. Payment transactions worth R$65 million are made each year through Caixa's lotto game outlets, of which 55 percent are worth less than R$40 each (US$16). Caixa Econômica Federal, which runs the Casa Lotérica chain, estimates that the average cost of a bank transaction at a correspondent bank is only a fourth as much as at a branch.

The most significant expansion of correspondent banking services prior to 2003 was the creation of postal service correspondents, through the auction by the government, in August 2001, of the postal franchise. It was awarded to Brazil's largest private bank, Bradesco, for R$201 million (US$81 million), which won the exclusive right to distribute financial services through the 5,532 agencies of the Brazilian post office, ECT (Empresa Brasileira de Correios e Telégrafos). The contract has a maturity of five years, which begins when each post office agency will be connected to Bradesco. All agencies are expected to be operational by 2004. The concession will therefore last at least until 2009. It can be renewed without a fresh bidding process. Under the terms of its contract, Bradesco has undertaken to connect agencies located in municipalities without banking service on a priority basis. ECT has a greater relative presence in the poor Northeast area of Brazil than the banks. Bradesco will be allowed to distribute basic financial services through the ECT, such as payment and account transaction services, in exclusivity. The post office is present in 1,738 municipalities without a bank (table 3.16).[12]

Bradesco hopes to gain some 3.5 million new current account holders in two years from the post office client base. These clients would bring Bradesco's current client base of 11.8 million current account holders to 15.2 million. Through the post office, Bradesco intends to target low-

Table 3.16 Geographic Coverage of the Banking System and the Postal Network

	Banking system		*ECT*			
Region	*No. of branches*	*% total banking system*	*No. of outlets*	*% total system*	*GDP per capita (US$)*[a]	*Population (nos. million)*
North	563	3.4	416	7.9	2,219	12.9
Southeast	9,108	54.6	1,746	32.9	5,057	72.3
Central–West	1,208	7.2	485	9.2	3,380	11.6
Northeast	2,377	14.3	1,677	31.6	1,701	47.7
South	3,415	20.5	975	18.4	4,358	25.1
Total	16,671	100.0	5,299[b]	100.0	3,680	169.5

a. Data from IBGE (2000).
b. Includes only agencies that are planned to sign an agreement with Bradesco.
Source: Lehman Brothers.

income individuals, especially in remote areas, who otherwise could not be targeted profitably even using ATMs. Bradesco may also transfer some of its existing clientele to the post office to reduce the cost of serving them. The current agreement covers the following services: demand deposits, savings deposits, check cashing, bill payment, remittance operations, and collections. Bradesco undertook to start working with about 1,000 post office agencies established in the Northeast in order to fulfill its contractual obligation to start with the poorest regions of Brazil. On April 5, 2002, Bradesco opened its first 27 Postal Bank branches, with one for every state in Brazil, including the Federal District. According to the original timetable, 3,000 branches were to be opened by the end of 2002, and in practice, 4,000 branches had been reported open by end-January 2004.

With the ECT network of Bradesco and the Casa Lotérica franchise, all municipalities in Brazil will have access to at least one bank, and sometimes two, for basic financial transactions (payment, and account deposits and transfers), when these two networks are fully operational. Both institutions plan to extend the services offered by these networks to opening of accounts and credit granting, but several identification and security issues still need to be resolved.

Other large banks in Brazil are increasingly establishing associations with local distributors to reach out to the general populace. The Central Bank estimated at the beginning of 2003 that there were about 1,500 correspondent outlets in use in Brazil, excluding the Lotéricas and the post office. At that time, Banco do Brasil, for instance, had recently signed a correspondent agreement with a supermarket chain in Rio de Janeiro, and

ABN AMRO had entered into an agreement with a 24-hour drugstore chain in Fortaleza. Many poor beach vendors in Fortaleza use these facilities to make deposits or payments at night. Unibanco's subsidiary finance company, Fininvest, has signed agreements with the supermarket chains Magazine Luiza and Globex's Ponto Frio through which it can distribute consumer loans to customers in the stores. Through these three outlets, Unibanco reaches some 7 million people in lower-middle and low-income groups, mostly in the South and Southeast of Brazil.

However, the Fininvest agreements (and some other retail financial arrangements) are not considered correspondent banking agreements because Fininvest deploys its own employees in the store, instead of using the store's employees. This is more costly than a correspondent agreement given the relatively higher labor costs of Fininvest's own employees. But employees of Fininvest, which is a nonbank finance company, are likely to be less costly than those of its parent, Unibanco, because they are not subject to the same labor laws. Nevertheless, there are still savings in fixed costs relative to establishing a branch.

One reason cited for bank reluctance to further expand correspondent networks is the fear of labor union complaints, because union leaders consider that correspondents should be subject to the same labor laws as bank employees. Threats of court action have been made, and banks believe that the court system in Brazil would tend to favor labor over employers, and potential indemnities could be costly.

In addition, correspondent agreements are profitable in small cities and remote areas, given the high cost of using supermarket space and installing the required technological connections, if the number of daily transactions is small. In addition, negotiating separate agreements with small chains with only a local presence in smaller cities could be difficult and costly. The extent to which the dramatic growth in correspondent agreements witnessed over the last two years can be sustained remains to be seen. Future agreements could remain limited in size and presence mostly to large cities.

To conclude, banking correspondent arrangements have a significant niche role in Brazil, but this is at least partly the result of regulatory costs imposed on bank branches. If the legal footing of correspondents is not clearly established to be independent of banks, this advantage could be eroded. Nonbank finance company arrangements with retailers represent the next level of outreach. The expansion of the major distribution networks of Caixa and Bradesco represents the most important correspondent chains to date and highlights the importance of outlets such as post offices and lottery shops.

The possibility of permitting some competition in the award or at least renewal of the franchise of such chains could help to ensure their future competitiveness. The attribution to Bradesco of the right to distribute banking products through the branches of the post office resulted from a competitive process. However, the decision to grant it an exclusive right over the entire network ended up limiting potential competition in some municipalities with no other financial service provider. Post office franchises awarded in many other countries are subject to periodic challenges at the time of both contract award and renewal.

Bank Automated Teller Machines

Private Brazilian banks attempt to use segmented delivery channel strategies, matching the cost of reaching certain segments of customers with the value added they generate. Lower-cost technology, particular ATMs, is popular for reaching poorer and potentially lower-value-added individuals. Access to automated teller machines has increased substantially over the last five years (from about 5,000 in 1996 to more than 16,000 in 2001) in all regions of Brazil, although service may again be biased in favor of the Southern regions (appendix table A1.2).[13] Fifty-nine percent were in the Southeast, compared to only 4 percent in the North. In terms of ATMs per inhabitant, the Southeast, Central–West, and South of Brazil are clearly the best served (figure 3.6). But adjusting for differences in levels of economic activity, regional differentials are less distinct. The Northeast of Brazil actually has a fairly high density of ATMs relative to GDP per capita, while ratios for the South and Central–West are low. However, the Southeast is still clearly the best-off region, even adjusting for income differentials, whereas the North is clearly the worst off.

Overall ATM coverage at four per 10,000 inhabitants is high in Brazil, even compared to more mature markets such as the United States (which has two ATMs per 10,000 inhabitants), based on its 10 largest networks. Moreover, ATM growth has stabilized in the United States but is still growing in Brazil (table 3.17).

Apart from correspondents, automated teller machines have been the main means for banks to reach lower-income populations. Itaú estimates, for instance, that 68 percent of its consumer loan applications are made at ATMs. The cost of processing such applications is less than 1 percent of the cost of the same transaction made at a branch. Banco do Brasil estimates that 78 percent of all its transactions are made at ATMs, with a daily value of R$40 million (US$18 million). Fininvest, whose client base includes mostly people in classes C, D, and E, calculates that clients in classes D and E use ATMs twice as often as the telephone, whereas customers in class C are indifferent.

Despite efforts to continue expanding networks, however, coverage remains partial. Further expansion of ATM networks to increase the out-

Figure 3.6 Regional Distribution of ATMs Relative to Population and Income in Brazil

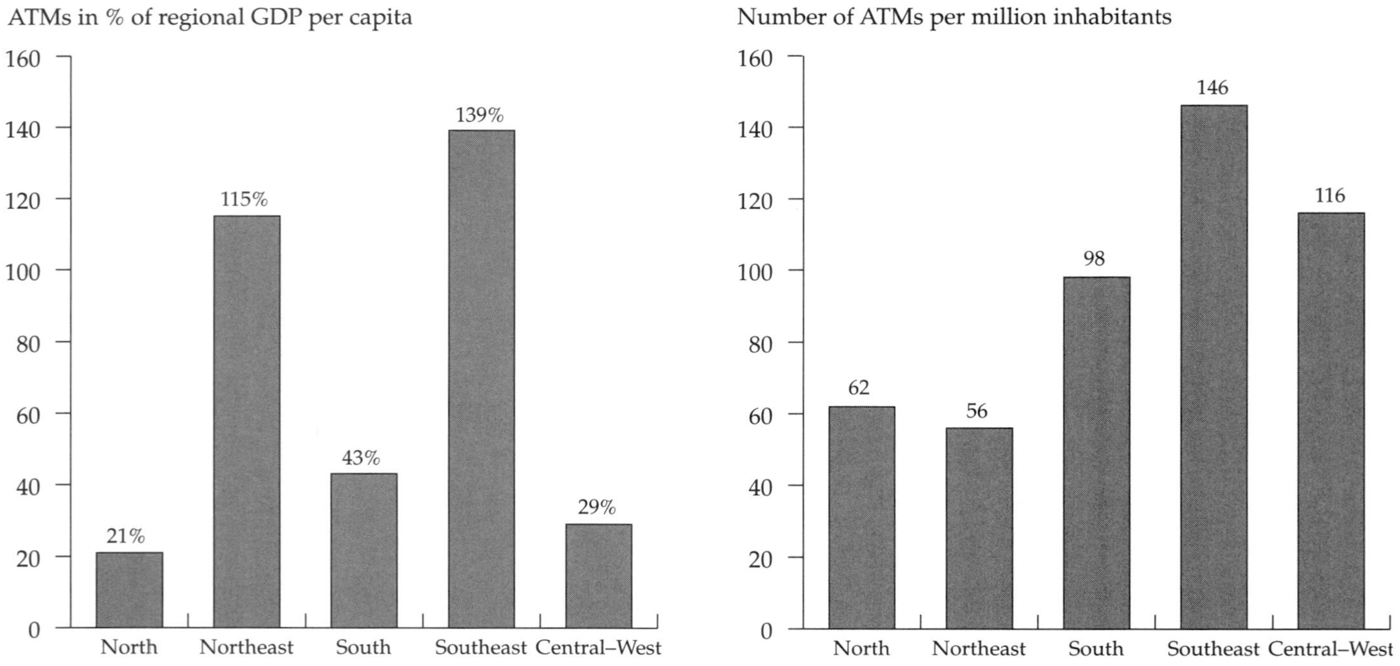

Source: World Bank staff estimates.

Table 3.17 ATM Fleet in the United States and in Brazil

United States			*Brazil*	
Largest ATM fleet owners	*2001*	*2000*	*Six largest ATM fleet owners*	*2001*
Bank of America	12,000	14,000	Banco do Brasil	31,922
American Express	8,700	8,600	Bradesco	18,940
Wells Fargo Bank	7,708	6,500	Caixa Econômica Federal	12,052[a]
Bank One Corp.	6,055	8,500		
US Bancorp	6,023	3,600	Itaú	11,375
CIBC	4,314	4,324	Unibanco	6,160
Total top 10			Santander (Banespa)	985
(including these 6)	57,395	58,215	Total these banks	81,434

a. This figure totals the agencies and service outposts (PAB, PAE, lottery houses, banking correspondents, and so on), and serves as a proxy for the total number of Caixa's individual ATMs.

Source: Card Industry Directory (2002) for the United States; individual bank data for Brazil.

reach of private banks in lower-income segments may not be profitable. Expanding networks to small cities or rural areas would create large money transportation costs and pose severe security issues. Banks estimate that 4,000 to 5,000 daily transactions are required to make an ATM profitable. Such levels would be nearly impossible to reach in small cities, and even less so in remote areas.

The issue of competition in ATM provision is important. Today, most banks in Brazil have their own ATM networks. Sharing ATMs could facilitate the profitable expansion of these networks in remote areas. But large infrastructure sunk costs create barriers to entry and reduce competition. Some large banks are reluctant to share their ATM networks because of their sunk costs. Banks argue that ATMs are sales points and therefore are proprietary and should not be shared. In most other countries, however, ATMs are shared. This resistance to sharing creates an enormous barrier to entry for other banks that would like to develop services to lower-income populations but do not have an extensive ATM network. Increasing competition would improve efficiency. It is not clear that replication of the same infrastructure by competing financial service providers is really in the interest of final consumers, particularly in sparsely populated areas of very low income.

Costs would likely be lower and entry easier with more sharing of existing infrastructure. In addition, reduced sunk costs would likely reduce bank spreads.[14] Banks with large existing networks could consider charging fees to other banks for widening the use of their networks. An investigation of the competitive compatibility of the present system could also be considered. As in the case of the exclusive award of the postal franchise, infrastructure sharing could limit long-term competitiveness in service provision.

An inadequate retail payment infrastructure also contributes to reducing competition and increasing the costs of small-value transactions. Today in Brazil, small-value transfers are dealt with in a highly decentralized manner. Banco do Brasil clears checks through the COMPE (Centralizadora da Compensação de Cheques e Outros Papéis; Central Settlement System of Checks and Other Papers) payments system; the Banco24Horas network clears electronic checks; and credit cards are cleared and settled over two separate switching systems (Redeshop, held by Credicard, and Visa Net). Several other small systems compete to clear electronic funds transfers for retail payments. Commercial banks in Brazil are currently establishing the SIP system (Sistema Integrado de Pagamento; Integrated Payment System) for clearing and settling payments, in parallel with the new Real Time Gross Settlement (RTGS) system for large-value payments. These arrangements and their links to the new RTGS system need to be evaluated from the vantage point of how consistent they are with proper competition policy. Such reviews have been made in other countries such as Canada, South Africa, and the United Kingdom.

New Technologies: Use of the Internet and Phone Banking

Developments in new technologies for information collection, storage, processing, and transmission could potentially have a strong influence on bank costs in at least three important ways. First, they can lower costs by substituting computers for paper-based and labor-intensive methods of transactions accounting and internal operations. Second, they could reduce personnel costs at the teller level; for example, through automated teller machines, telephone banking, and personal computer banking, enabling institutions to reach a wider geographic base. Third, on the credit side, institutions can greatly increase the efficiency and decrease the risks of providing credit services by using credit-scoring models.[15] The possibility of remote access of these technologies could eventually reduce the strategic importance of branches and ATMs.

High inflation and high labor costs have provided incentives for banks in Brazil to develop such technologies. Surveys by private banks and the Central Bank suggest that costs of delivery are lowest for internet transactions, followed by ATMs, then branches. Transaction costs, too, usually are commensurately lower. Although the internet would be the most profitable channel to reach out to lower-income clients, connectivity and fixed costs are obstacles. Brazilian banks find that nearly all of their internet clients belong to the richest social classes. Efforts to provide cheap financing for the purchase of personal computers and to offer free internet access have not met with large success, or have not been targeted at the appropriate income segments.[16]

Surveys indicate that a much wider range of persons, in terms of per-capita income, own cell phones than computers, and a greater proportion of low-income bank clients use phone banking rather than internet banking. Phone users are forecast to grow much faster than internet users. Moreover, the voice-activated methodology of phone-based systems may be easier for less-sophisticated clients. But, again, both the cost of the instrument and connectivity remain large obstacles.

Telephone Banking

The telephone may allow banks to better penetrate lower-income segments. Some surveys have indicated that the income distribution of cell phone owners is much wider than for computer owners, and the cost of a cellular phone call is much cheaper than in many other countries in the world (figure 3.7).

Brazil's phone industry appears to be quite competitive, with at least two operators for fixed and cellular lines in each region, and two national providers for long distance and international calls. Cellular phone charges have fallen significantly, from US$0.77 per three minutes in 1998 to US$0.24 in 2000. An equivalent fixed-line call is much lower, at around US$0.04.

Although these fees are in line with, and even slightly lower than, those in many other countries, they represent a higher proportion of Brazil's GDP per capita. Connection charges represent about 0.75 percent of the GDP per capita of the poorest Northeast region (compared to 0.05 percent in most of Europe) and monthly subscription fees about 0.5 percent (compared to 0.05 percent in most of Europe). They represent a very high 9 percent and 6 percent, respectively, of the minimum salary. In addition, the subscriber has to pay the cost of the phone itself, an activation fee of about US$6, and a monthly subscription fee of about US$11. Most banks charge a monthly fee ranging from US$0.80 to US$2.00 for phone banking. The relatively high cost of a telephone line is also a factor.

Brazil, like many developing countries, has a Universal Access Plan for telecommunication services, and the government is investing some US$600 million a year in building out telecommunication infrastructure in underdeveloped areas. Effective penetration will depend as much on the nature of the regulatory regime adopted, including tariff structures, as on the installation of physical infrastructure (figure 3.8).

Figure 3.7 Bank Transactions and Cellular Phone Costs in Brazil and Other Countries

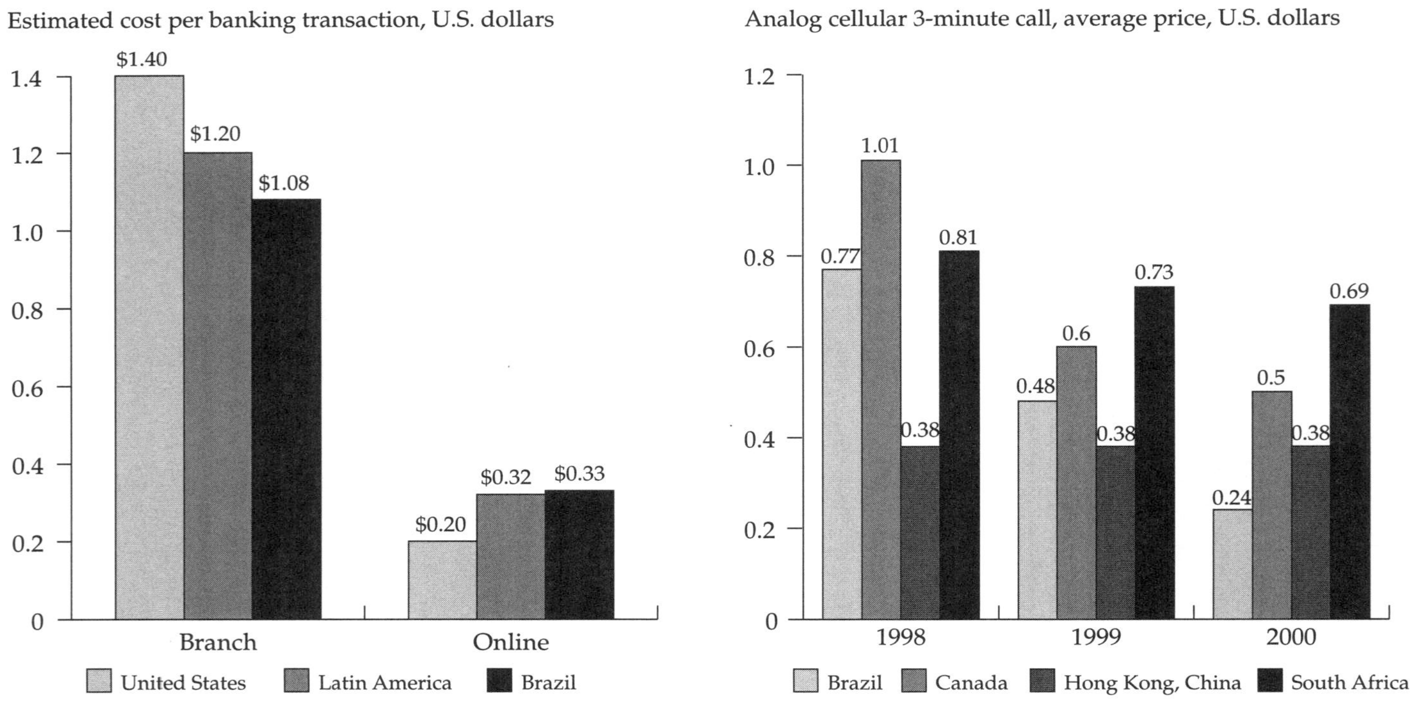

Source: World Bank, Tower Group Research.

Figure 3.8 Teledensity and Gross Domestic Product per Capita and Telecommunications in Brazil and Other Countries

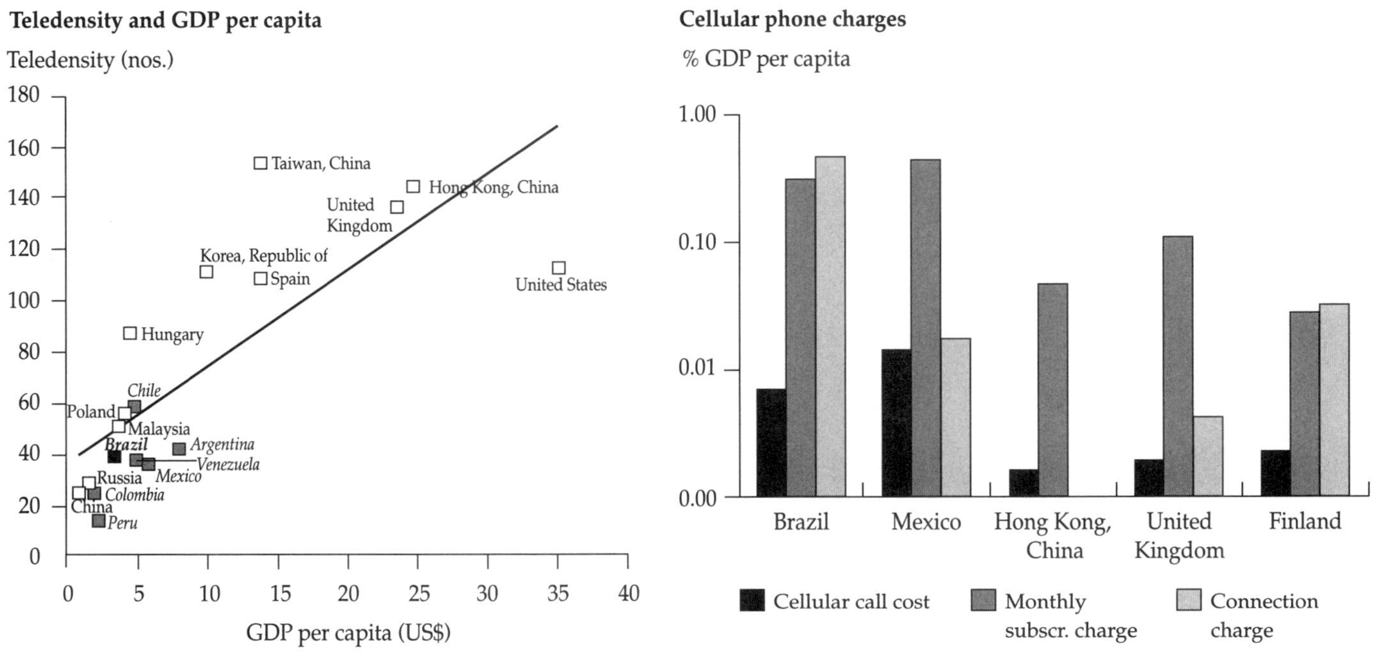

Note: Teledensity is defined as the total number of telephone subscribers per 100 inhabitants (2001). GDP per capita (US$) (2000).
Source: International Telecommunication Union database.

Financial Services and Universal Telephone Access

The provision of financial services via the internet or the telephone depends critically on their cost, but these in turn are substantially influenced by the structure of tariffs and government regulatory practice toward the sector. The value of the widespread availability of phone services is a recognized principle and good practice among telecommunication regulators today, and is described in terms of universal service (connectivity of all households, mostly applicable to developed countries) or universal access (reasonable availability of at least public phone services to all persons, mostly applicable to developing countries). The principle of universal service has been widely studied.

There are various approaches to universality policies, which have their benefits and drawbacks. (1) Market-based reforms, including privatization, competition, and cost-based pricing, have been successfully used, especially in industrialized countries, and teledensity levels did not decrease. But privatization and competition alone will not expand service to uneconomic areas. Other practices for improving phone access have included (2) mandatory service provision or (3) cross-subsidies. Mandatory provision can be effective, especially if applied to newly licensed or newly privatized operators but it may place the burden on a subset of operators and could be used as a rationale to limit competition elsewhere. Cross- subsidies are the traditional approach between different classes of services (interservice subsidies) or between regions (intraservice cross-subsidization with geographic tariff averaging). There is an implicit subsidy from urban to rural users. Today, it is increasingly recognized that such practices could promote inefficiency, depressing demand for higher-class services such as international or internet, and limiting the subsidy to existing users. These subsidies constitute a hidden form of taxation that could be anticompetitive.

A modification of traditional cross-subsidization that fits in with a competitive market regime is (4) an access deficit charge (ADC) scheme. In this case, other operators also contribute to the cross-subsidization of services provided by a given operator to provide local services. A number of regulators, such as in Australia and Canada, have modified their ADC regimes by targeting subsidies to finance only high-cost or low-income subscribers. However, these, too, could be potentially anticompetitive, and countries such as the United Kingdom have now abolished ADCs altogether. The approach regulators consider the most efficient and least distorting today is (5) universality funds. Such funds cover revenue from a variety of sources, including general government revenues, interconnection charges, and levies on all telecommunication operators. These funds are then used to target high-cost areas and/or low-income persons. Best practice for rural telecommunications is presently considered to be an investment subsidy awarded in a bidding process to private operators, rather than an operational or tariff subsidy.

Examples of good practice in the region include Chile and Peru. Chile began by introducing market-based competition with the privatization of its phone system, followed by public budgetary funding to provide targeted financial subsidies to those lacking access. Peru's universal access policy began with a new regulatory framework promoting privatization and private sector participation, but also establishing an access fund, which levies a 1 percent charge on gross telecommunication revenues. Chile's telecommunication regulator, FITEL, establishes criteria to select those localities in rural areas or high social interest areas where it will fund service expansion. But FITEL does not provide subsidies for subscribers directly or funding for localities that already have access.

Access in poor areas has usually been attempted through telecenters, which provide public access to information and communication services. These could include phone, fax, low-speed dial-up internet, and other services such as printers, copiers, and scanners. Successful telecenters are often combined with other services and are run by private entrepreneurs who can adapt and develop local business plans. One example of a telecenter offering financial services in Brazil is the POPBANK, established at São Paulo bakery chains. Conversely, examples of banks supporting the development of phone services in the poorest countries and areas include the Grameen village phone in Bangladesh, where a Grameen Bank member (often a woman) uses funds provided by the bank under its lease-purchase arrangements to buy a cellular phone, and then uses the phone to provide phone services to village members. Grameen Telecom coverage is provided by a fiber optic cable network along the railway network. Operators are selected with the same care as microcredit providers. But GSM cell phone technology is a high-cost solution for universal access in rural areas and may only be possible because of the current regulatory practices, which are not efficient in many ways. Even so, it is not viable for inexpensive e-mail, internet, or data connectivity. Wireless local loop technologies may be a cheaper option for rural networks than GSM cellular phones. The government also has card phones installed in some towns, with lower tariffs than the village phone. The long-run future of the Grameen village phones is still unclear.

Source: World Bank 2000e; World Bank 2001i; World Bank 2003.

Overall teledensity in Brazil is, however, low by international standards, and in particular for lower-income populations. At the end of 2001, there were about 45 million fixed telephone units and 30 million cell phones in use in Brazil, for a population of about 170 million. But a large number of these telephones are used by offices, and many rich families have more than one phone. A study in São Paulo in 1999 showed that 98 percent of the highest-income-bracket individuals owned a phone, compared to only 8 percent of the lowest bracket. And on a per unit of population basis, international comparisons confirm that overall connectivity is low in Brazil compared to developed or emerging economies, and is also lower than in large neighboring countries. Therefore, like the internet, Brazilian banks have not yet used phone banking to reach out to lower-income people, although the potential may be larger (figure 3.9).

Internet Banking

The Central Bank of Brazil estimated that at end-2002 the average banking transaction using the internet costs R$0.24 (US$10 cents), compared to R$0.33 (US$13 cents) for dialed-line banking services and R$2 (US$80 cents) for transactions at a branch. Estimates by Tower Group Research confirm these wide savings.[17] Brazil's largest banks have all developed extensive internet-based activities, and comparisons with Asia's emerging economies based on survey evidence suggest that a higher percentage of users in Brazil make extensive use of new technologies (figure 3.10). Brazil's banks are even succeeding in closing the gap with the United States in terms of internet penetration among clients (figure 3.11). Whereas the use of computers and the internet in Brazil for recreational and leisure activities is lower than in the United States, for purposes of work and services such as banking, Brazil scores better than the United States, at least among the connected segment of the population.

However, huge disparities in access to internet services limit the use of this technology to extend financial services to the poorer segments of the population. The Central Bank revealed that only 10 million people (or 6 percent of the population) own a personal computer and 8 million use the internet. An estimated 90 percent of the 8 million internet banking users belong to high-income classes.[18] Only about 4 percent of total individual bank clients used internet banking in 1999 and only 10 percent of corporate users. Access is in part limited by supply, because the smaller Brazilian banks do not have websites, but also because of low connectivity, especially in rural areas, although this is growing rapidly. And buying a computer is out of reach for most of Brazil's poor. Unless products offered and internet access channels are modified, it will be difficult to use this technology for large-scale popular outreach.[19] And growing internet security concerns would also have to be addressed.[20]

Figure 3.9 Main Telephone Line, Cellular, and Internet Penetration in Brazil and Other Countries

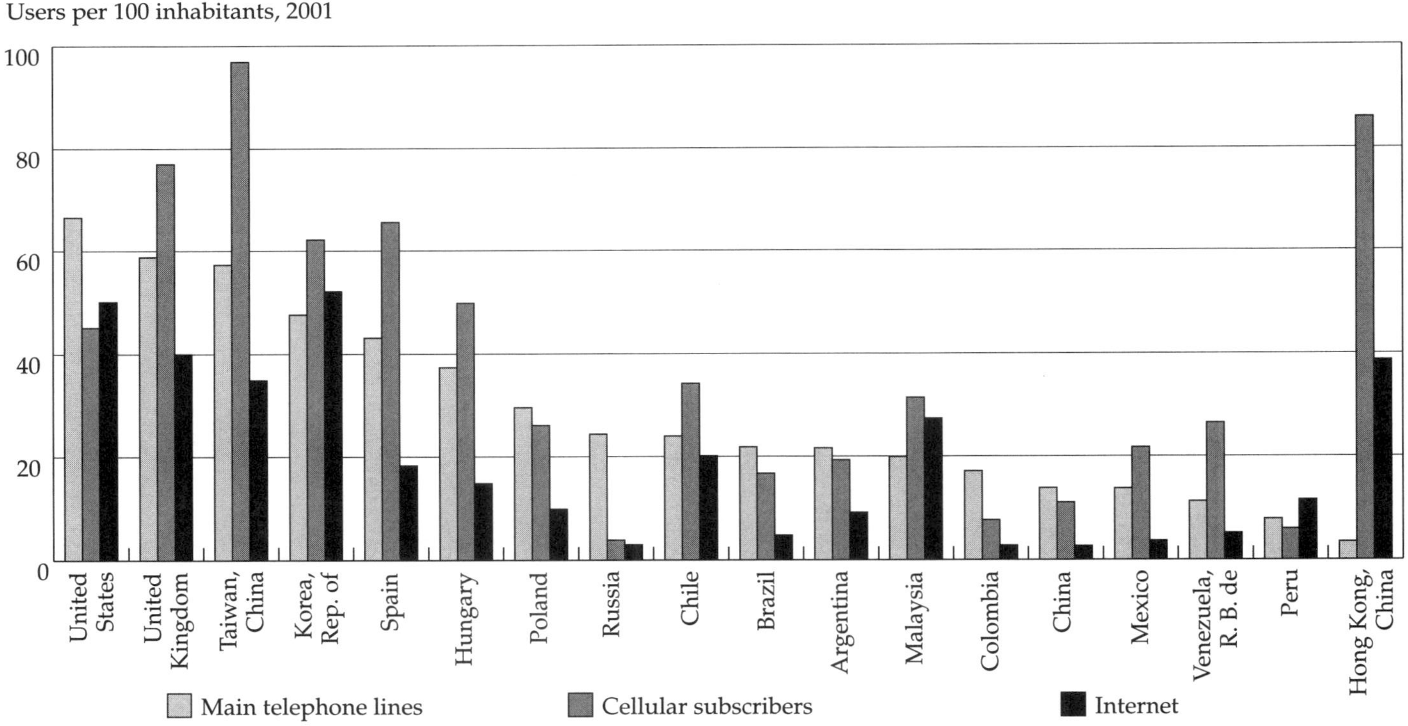

Source: International Telecommunication Union, www.itu.int/ITU-D/ict/.

Figure 3.10 Online Internet Banking in Brazil and Asia

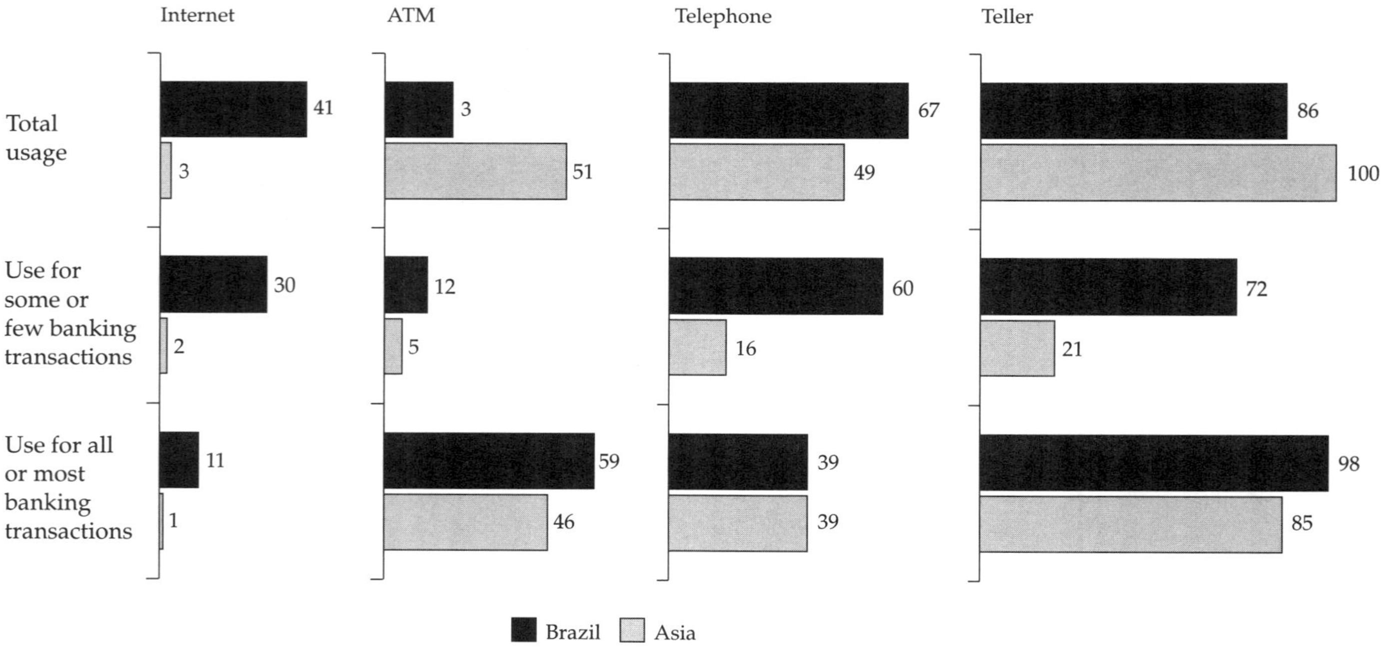

Source: World Bank staff estimates.

Figure 3.11 Internet Use and Online Banking in Brazil and the United States

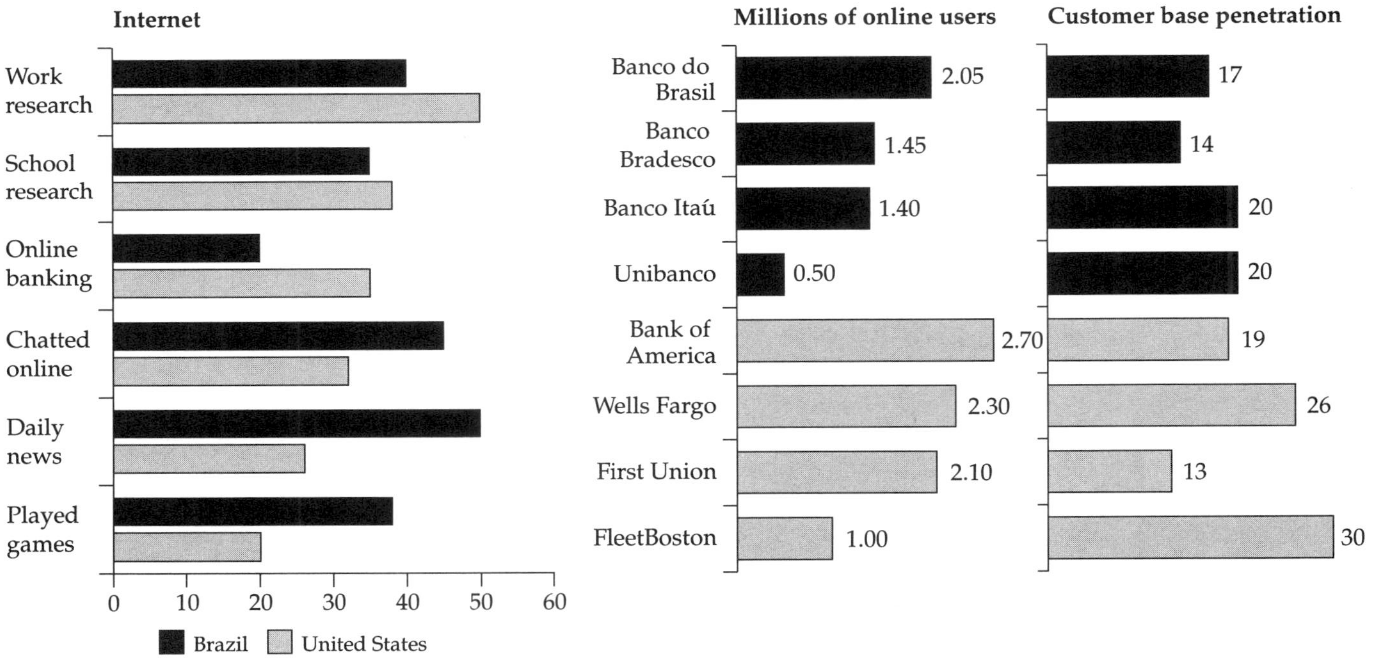

Sources: Credit Suisse First Boston; McKinsey; World Bank staff estimates.

Downscaling of Banks Elsewhere: What Can Banks Do?

What have banks in other countries done to achieve downscaling? In some countries, the government has instituted special schemes to promote access through the banking community. These forms of government assistance are discussed in chapter 7 of this study. There are also measures banks can take themselves. Typically, banks are more motivated to enter the markets of the 'unbanked' in environments that are more competitive and where the growth of credit services is the main vehicle of growth for the financial system.

These approaches have several identifiable elements, which are sometimes present exclusively and sometimes in combination. These include, first, the adoption of new technological platforms more suited to microlending, or to serving a community with the profile of the 'unbanked.' A second common element is the building of partnerships with microfinance institutions, nonbanks, correspondents, or NGOs. Other elements are to use image differentiation and adopt special programs of outreach. Examples of these practices are described below.

Downscaling through Partnerships

In South Africa, outreach by the formal banking community has been encouraged by the government, although there are no explicit legal requirements. Moreover, competition in the banking industry is immense and domestic growth opportunities are scarce (Moody's 2001). Commercial banks have chosen different ways to grow into this market; through joint ventures, acquisition of existing microlending institutions, correspondent-type low-cost retail chain branches, and the introduction of new products such as smart cards (table 3.18).

Alliance of Standard Bank and African Bank: Partnership and New Technology

The most successful partnership in South Africa has been the alliance of Standard Bank with African Bank, which illustrates the advantages of a regular bank teaming up with a microlending group to extend its outreach to small clients.[21]

Standard Bank's E-Plan takes advantage of the relative strengths of the two institutions: the strong technology platform and credit-scoring techniques of Standard Bank and the familiarity and outreach to the black community of African Bank. The revenue is split 60:40 between Standard Bank and African Bank. Potential E-Loan customers are required to have

Table 3.18 Downscaling through Partnerships by Commercial Banks in South Africa

Standard Bank	Entered into cooperation with African Bank, leading micro-lender in South Africa, to provide African Bank loans through AutoBank E centers. This electronic banking service targets low-end customers and does not have a minimum income requirement, but customers need to have regular income streams. African Bank offers Standard Bank's microlending products and carries out credit approval and collection functions. Both banks increased their customer base for microloans, and Standard Bank leveraged off African Bank's expertise in microlending.
ABSA	Acquired FBC Fidelity Bank and merged it into its own People's Bank to offer banking services to the 'underbanked' mass market, emerging middle class, and small and medium enterprises.
Nedcor	Cooperation with JD Group, furniture retailer.
	Acquired 50 percent of Pick'nPay's (online grocery) financial services arm for credit card and transactional business.
	PepBank—small outlets in PepStores across South Africa to provide banking services to those who have been excluded from formal banking through low-cost transaction services.
BoE	Bought Credcor, a retail finance company using proprietary credit assessment techniques to provide finance, mainly in the retail consumer credit arena, through a network of retailers but also directly through its outlets.
	Inherited 33 percent stake in Saambou bank, another pioneer in the industry, through the acquisition of Fedsure. Saambou has increased its exposure in the market significantly (up to R2 billion from R80 million two years ago), using its network of agents.
Investec	In addition to the cooperation with Standard Bank, African Bank formed an alliance with Edcon Group to expand its distribution network.

Source: Moody's; media articles; bank web pages.

a paycheck and a direct-deposit account with Standard Bank for at least three months (African Bank does not take deposits).

The success of the product may be traced to a series of factors. First is the automation of all transactions. After an initial application and interview with a branch employee, customers complete all financial transactions, including rolling over their loan, at the ATM machines in Standard Bank 'E-Branches,' which cuts the cost of providing numerous, low-value transactions. Second, the Bank has real-time access to the borrower's account information, and can withdraw loan payments electronically when paychecks are deposited. Thus, loan defaults have been very low, at about 2 percent. Third, interest rates are very high at about 75 percent a year, because this category of borrowers has limited financing options. Also, automated credit-scoring techniques are used, using a Standard Bank proprietary credit model and the customer's deposit-account information to 'score' the customer and give immediate loan approval or rejection. Standard Bank also checks the MicroLenders Credit Bureau for any unreported outstanding loans.

Overall, the E-Plan is an important source of consumer microcredit in the black community in South Africa and is a first step in offering formal banking services to an 'underbanked' population. The provision of microcredit through banks is an improvement over microlenders because interest rates, though high, are lower than microlender rates (which generally exceed 200 percent annually). Although the current product offering is small and limited to consumer loans, there is the potential for customers to build credit histories that could lead to great consumer and commercial credit.

The South African examples illustrate the importance of the enabling environment in two specific areas. First is the value of widely available and easily accessible credit information for microlenders, retailers, and both small and large banks. This credit information is available because of the presence of leading international bureaus such as Equifax and TransUnion, which compete on price and services such as various end-user products like credit-scoring models (to banks and retailers) and customer reports (to microlenders). The role of credit bureaus in Brazil is discussed in greater detail in chapter 6 of this study.

A second factor is the increase in competition, which has created pressures for the largest banks to move downscale. Nevertheless, there is a perception that the costs of some financial services in South Africa are high because of insufficient competition. South African authorities have conducted a major analysis on access to financing for small and medium enterprises, which takes a systemic look at competition issues across payment, savings, and credit-related services in South Africa. One of the conclusions of the report is that "the problem is not so much the availability of [debt] finance as such for small enterprises, but rather inefficiencies in the provision of financial services to such users due to competitive factors such as barriers of entry of potential new providers" (Falkena and Reserve Bank of South Africa 2002). Many of its conclusions are along the lines of a similar study on competition in financial services undertaken two years earlier in the United Kingdom (Cruickshank 2000; Falkena 2002). This illustrates again the desirability of looking in greater detail at the role of competition issues in the downscaling of financial services in Brazil.

PERU AND BOLIVIA

In Peru, three of the largest banks in the financial sector have substantially higher participation in the financing of microenterprises than the overall banking system.[22] Banco Wiese Sudameris was one of the first commercial banks to enter microfinance, and has been followed recently by Banco Continental BBV and Banco de Credito del Peru. Smaller banks and finance companies like Banco de Trabajo, Financiera Solución, and Financiera Daewoo have changed their focus from consumer loans to microloans.[23] In Bolivia, Banco del Credito de Bolivia increased its presence in microfinance, and Banco Económico also has a much higher share of its portfolio in microloans than the rest of the banks in Bolivia. The Bolivian banking system is not as concentrated as in Peru, but Banco de Credito is one of the largest Bolivian banks, and Banco Económico is a medium-size bank (table 3.19).

Commercial banks are the second largest investors in regulated microfinance institutions in Peru, predominantly through their financing of CMACs (Cajas Municipales de Ahorro y Credito; municipal savings and loan offices) and, to a lesser extent, their participation in EDPYMEs (Empresa de Desarrollo de la Pequeña y Micro Empresa; regulated microfinance institutions). The high number of closed CRACs (Cajas Rurales de Ahorro y Credito; rural savings and loan associations) precludes banks from financing these types of institutions (tables 3.20 and 3.21).

Besides funding microfinance institutions, commercial banks have established partnerships by investing in the capital of microfinance institutions. Banco Wiese Sudameris owns 6 percent of Mibanco. Some banks have established or reorganized existing financial institutions following acquisition or change of control. This is the case of Financiera de Credito in Peru, which is fully owned by the same holding company that owns Banco de Credito. Originally focused on the market of consumer loans, in recent years, Financiera de Credito has become one of the largest providers of microloans in Peru. In Chile, Banco Santander bought a finance company that had already established a strong microenterprise credit program within its consumer loan portfolio. This finance company, BANAFE, is the leading supplier of microcredits in Chile (Christen and Drake 2001).

Table 3.19 Banks and Finance Companies in Microfinance, Peru and Bolivia

	Microenterprise loan portfolio					
	2000[a]		*2001*		*June 2002*	
Institution/country	*Amount (US$m)*	*Share*[b] *(%)*	*Amount (US$m)*	*Share*[b] *(%)*	*Amount (US$m)*	*Share*[b] *(%)*
Peru						
Banco Continental BBV	9	0.4	114	6.0	109	5.6
Banco Wiese Sudameris	45	1.6	33	1.2	28	0.8
Banco de Credito del Peru	18	0.6	23	0.7	27	1.0
Banco del Trabajo	2	1.7	40	34.3	51	37.0
Mibanco	34	91.4	47	75.8	51	68.4
Other banks	15	0.1	3	0.0	5	0.1
Total all banks, Peru	123	0.6	261	1.7	271	1.7
Financiera Daewoo	15	70.1	11	71.8	10	73.3
Financiera de Credito	29	55.7	49	72.1	54	76.3
Other finance companies	0	0.0	0	0.0	0	0.0
Total all finance companies, Peru	44	22.6	60	24.1	64	24.6
Bolivia						
Banco Solidario	56	78.1	56	68.7	50	63.0
Banco de Credito de Bolivia	43	9.2	111	28.4	54	15.2
Banco Económico	12	5.9	10	4.7	8	4.2
Total other banks, Bolivia	12	0.5	9	0.4	10	0.4
Total all banks, Bolivia	123	3.7	186	6.2	122	4.3

a. For Bolivia, the information is from June 2001. For the other cases, the information is from the end of the year.
b. Share in total loan portfolio of each financial institution listed.
Source: Superintendência de Banca e Seguros (SBS) and Superintendência de Bancos e Entidades Financeiras (SBEF).

Downscaling: A New Image for a Different Community?

Successful banks that have extended their outreach to the underserved emphasize the importance of image differentiation and the use of different channels of service delivery for different client groups. One recently cited example in the United States is Mitchell Bank, a small bank that has focused on the 'underbanked' community of immigrant teenagers in the suburbs of Milwaukee. Its service branch, located in a low-income district, is run by students who earn credit toward their graduation require-

Table 3.20 Other Latin American Banks and Finance Companies in Microfinance

Country	*Banks and finance companies*
Honduras	Banhcafe (L), Banco del Comercio (L), Aval-Card
El Salvador	Banco Agrícola (L), Banco Salvadoreño (L)
Ecuador	Banco de Pichincha (L), Banco Solidario (S)
Argentina	Banco Balcarce (L)
Guatemala	Bancafe (L),
Chile	Banco del Desarrollo (L), Banco Santander (L)
Paraguay	Banco Multibanco (L), El Comercio Financiera, Financiera Familiar, Visión de Finanzas
Haiti	Bank de l'Union Haitienne (L), Sogebank (L)
Guyana	Bank of Nova Scotia (L)
Panama	Multicredit Bank (L), Mibanco (S)
Dominican Republic	Banco de Desarrollo Unificado (S)
Mexico	Credito Familiar
Colombia	Financiera Compartir

Note: L = large; S = small.
Source: Valenzuela 2001.

Table 3.21 Sources of External Financing for Peruvian Microfinance Institutions, December 2000

(nuevos soles millions)

Microfinance institution	*Development financial company*	*Banks*	*Other sources*	*Total*
EDPYMEs[a]	22.8	6.5	40.2	69.5
CRACs[b]	106.1	3.9	13.7	123.7
CMACs[c]	85.5	89.1	17.1	191.7
Mibanco	57.0	0	7.0	64.1
Total	271.4	99.4	78.1	448.9

a. Empresa de Desarrollo de la Pequeña y Micro Empresa.
b. Cajas Rurales de Ahorro y Credito.
c. Cajas Municipales de Ahorro y Credito.
Source: SBS.

ments while working under adult supervision. At least 90 percent of its customers have never had a bank account before. One indicator of its successful outreach is that many parents of students now deposit their pay checks there. Another key element in their strategy is the establishment of ties with community organizations such as schools and clubs. Another U.S. bank, First Bank of the Americas, has linked up with church networks serving immigrants. Such channels could also be used for financial education programs. First Bank has hired a Spanish-speaking marketing consultant who addresses churchgoers about the dangers of money lenders and the benefits of established banking organizations supported by the church or community leaders.[24]

Some financial institutions in Brazil are very aware of the role of image differentiation; Unibanco points to its consumer finance company, Fininvest, a 100-percent-owned subsidiary, as an example of its product differentiation strategy. Fininvest focuses on consumer credits and personal loans, and had more than R$8 million in current operations in 2002 and 109 branches. Unibanco also offers these financial products through its 50:50 joint venture companies, Ponto Frio and Luiza Cred, which operate through store chains of 358 and 126 stores, respectively. Among the benefits of using such companies, the bank cites reduced client acquisition costs, cross-selling opportunities, specialized credit expertise for low-income segments, and appropriately tailored financial products (presentation of Unibanco at the World Bank Seminar on Access to Financial Services, February 2003).

Products successfully used for outreach include payroll card programs given to employers, who then put funds directly into the accounts of employees, typically teenagers or immigrants. The employees are then able to use debit cards to operate these accounts, co-branded by popular names such as Visa. Check-writing or credit facilities are not included, thus limiting the banks' risk and helping to reduce the conflicts between the marketing and risk-control departments of banks in terms of accessibility versus fiduciary responsibility. For immigrant communities, another popular device has been dual ATM cards, which allow a party in the United States to deposit funds that could be withdrawn by a recipient abroad, as an alternative to expensive wire transfer services. Designated community banks such as the First Bank of America, in Chicago's Hispanic district, have the support of the U.S. Treasury in their basic loan programs aimed at the previously underserved.[25]

There are also examples of more relaxed entry requirements. Thus, some banks in the United States tacitly acknowledge the cards issued by Mexican consulates, the *matricula consular,* regardless of legal status, as proof of identity.

Finally, government programs to boost access in the United States have gained ground. Legislation was recently passed requiring all federal payments to be made electronically, which exposed the large numbers of 'unbanked.' The Treasury Department has set up a new Office of Financial Education, which has launched a pilot program called First Accounts, operating in 26 states, designed to bring 35,000 persons into the banking system for the first time (chapter 7 has details).

Suggested Good Practice in Downscaling

Largely because of the Community Reinvestment Act and its various modifications, interest has been keen in the United States among analysts and academics to examine 'what works' in terms of effective outreach. One practiced observer has proposed a menu of five key elements for any strategy for bringing the 'unbanked' into the financial mainstream:[26]

1. *Open specialized bank branches that provide commercial check-cashing outlet (CCO) services.* These outlets should be conveniently located for lower-income households and should provide fee-based check-cashing services in addition to traditional consumer banking services. Opening such outlets serves three purposes. By offering check-cashing services in a bank branch, the bank builds a relationship with its check-cashing customers. The establishment of the outlets also is a recognition that many check-cashing customers are likely to be slow to open deposit accounts. And check-cashing fees provide new sources of revenue for banks with branches in lower-income areas, which often report that it is difficult to cover the costs of these branches with traditional services. In Brazil, the opening of bill-paying outlets such as the Caixa's Lotéricas may serve a similar purpose—a proportionally smaller part of payments are received in the form of checks. Additional emphasis on check cashing could, however, be added.
2. *Offer starter or basic bank accounts that have low minimum-balance requirements, cannot be overdrawn, and include low-cost money orders for making long-distance payments.* In addition to check-cashing services, the outlets should offer traditional deposit accounts and low-cost, low-minimum-balance savings accounts that give account holders the option to buy money orders for long-distance payments. Brazil's banks have offered such minimum packages of services, and recently new regulations have led to a reduction to zero, for the client, of the cost of a basic account, which has also been combined with a simplification of eligibility and entry documentation.
3. *Offer accounts specifically designed to help people accumulate savings.* Savings-building accounts should entice customers to save systematically. The accounts should include features such as financial penalties for closing savings accounts, and automatic but low periodic transfers to savings accounts. In Brazil, these would be different from the current passbook savings accounts, which have the benefit of flexibility and low entry requirements but which do not remunerate the depositor at market rates or help to develop good savings practices.
4. *Offer deposit-secured emergency loans to individuals whose credit histories make them ineligible for traditional mainstream credit.* In this scheme, col-

lateral could be the balance that a member has accumulated in a savings-building account. For individuals without savings, the outlets might consider working with a third party, such as a not-for-profit community-based organization, to raise funds. The new provision for simplified microloans is a step in this direction. However, it is proposed that the present recommendation would expand such loans to include collateral defined more broadly and also include persons with limited or impaired credit histories.[27]

5. *Seek community-based organizations and offer financial literacy programs.* The value of community partnerships has been widely acknowledged in microlending; it could also be incorporated into the downscaling of mainstream banking. Partnerships with such groups help promote outlets to the community. Such outlets can also leverage the community organization's partnership to conduct financial counseling programs. Such an outreach-based strategy is preferable to the traditional approach for several reasons: it attracts the 'unbanked' into bank branches, it offers the 'unbanked' services especially designed to meet their needs, and it helps the 'unbanked' to become traditional bank customers. In the United States, community partnerships are appealing to banks because delivering financial services to lower-income community organizations counts toward bank Community Reinvestment Act obligations, while offering the banks some additional credit quality protection and hence a less-risky rate of return on their investment.

Annex 3.1:
Bank Downscaling: One Bank's Viewpoint

This annex provides an overview of successful practices in commercial bank downscaling to low-access groups, as perceived by a commercial bank in the United States with considerable practical experience in this area, ShoreBank of Chicago, which has been noted for its successful outreach in the poor and minority neighborhoods of urban Chicago.[28] ShoreBank now has partnerships with institutions in other countries, especially Eastern Europe and also Latin America, that are aimed at promoting access for the poor and for persons in remote locations or in minority communities. It has developed programs of overseas outreach, which are also touched on in this annex. ShoreBank seeks to identify appropriate retail products for individuals and for small enterprises and microbusiness, and also to develop successful market outreach strategies, all of which are discussed below. Within these contexts, sound principles of client selection and evaluation are presented.[29]

Retail Products

The following are some retail products identified by ShoreBank that promote access to financial services by poor or disadvantaged individuals or small enterprises.

Products for Individuals

Get Checking is aimed at individuals who have never had an account or who have mishandled a checking account in the past. It began in 1998 in Wisconsin as a partnership among financial institutions, community-based financial educators, and an eFunds Corporation (the owner of ChexSystems). Participants must undergo six hours of instruction and training in checking and savings accounts at a cost of US$35 for course materials. Upon completion and after passing a test, participants receive a certificate that guarantees the right to open an account, provided previous credit or account problems have been resolved. Participating banks waive the ChexSystems report requirement when opening an account. This is an important feature of the program, because most banks block the opening of accounts for a period of five years to those who have had a negative ChexSystems report.

As of December 2001, 1,012 individuals had participated in the classes and 914 received certificates. Nearly 75 percent of participants were below 35 years of age, and 79 percent listed their race or ethnicity as African American, Latino, Asian, or other. Eighty-eight percent of participants had incomes 80 percent or less of the Milwaukee County median. Today, Get Checking is offered in 37 locations across the country. For example, as of June 2002, Wells Fargo Bank Wisconsin, which played a major role in developing the program, had opened 85 checking accounts and nine savings accounts for program graduates. US Bank was the first bank to offer the program nationally in 2002 (Williams and Nieman 2003).

In terms of applicability in Brazil, such a program could help those who have been on a negative list at Serasa or other credit reporting systems. The participation of the credit reporting agency itself together with the banks is noteworthy, as is the incentive-compatible structure, which requires applicants to purchase course materials, thus, reducing moral hazard.

Payday alternative loans are a high-cost source of emergency cash for low-income individuals. Payday lenders (often check-cashing companies) provide loans to individuals based on future paychecks. These loans are also known as 'cash advance loans' or 'post-dated-check loans.' The fees and interest charged during the 14-day lending period between paychecks translate into annual percentage interest rates as high as 300 percent or more (State of California 2001). This expensive payday debt can accumulate quickly. The borrower profile would be someone with a poor credit history or outside of the formal financial system.

North Side Community Federal Credit Union in Chicago has developed a new product within the last year, the Payday Alternative Loan (PAL), to help those who have accumulated payday debt get out of the trap. It is a US$500, six-month loan made at 16.5 percent APR. PAL is approved automatically and funded immediately for any community resident who has an income of more than US$1,000 per month, regardless of credit history. The credit union seeks repayment from payroll deductions to reduce delinquency and charges an application fee. Research concerning the clients who have used the product indicates that 16 percent had filed for bankruptcy in the past three years and that they had an average credit score of 548 (only 14 percent had a credit score above 600). The credit union reports all repayments to the credit bureau to help members build positive credit histories, and partners with a financial literacy provider. The product is currently in the pilot and testing stage, but to date, 523 loans have been made; whereas delinquencies are common, writeoffs are minimal.[30] The product will break even under the best of circumstances, but it provides an important entry to financial services to low- and moderate-income individuals. Note that the use of positive credit histories is especially noteworthy in the Brazilian context, where positive credit history is limited.

Extra Credit Savings Program. In 2000, ShoreBank launched an initiative at two of its branches in Chicago aimed at bringing low-income new depositors into the financial system through partnerships with the Center for Law and Human Services (CLHS).[31] ShoreBank offered its space on nights and weekends for CLHS to process tax returns of low-income individuals for free. Most of these low-income working households were eligible for the earned income tax credit, a refund worth as much as US$4,000. The program arranged for the opening of accounts at ShoreBank for the direct deposit of tax refunds to the new accounts. Over two years, the program attracted 202 new accounts and more than US$200,000 in deposits. Twenty of the new account holders also opened savings accounts, checking accounts, and certificates of deposit. Although 63 percent of the accounts were spent within two to three months of participation in the program, 14 percent continued to use their accounts for savings and the remaining 22 percent for transactions. More than 70 percent of respondents in a follow-up interview said the account changed the way they used their tax refund and helped them save more than they would have without the account (ShoreBank 2001).

Although this program was instituted on a small scale and centers around a specific aspect of the U.S. tax system, it points to the potential for building access to financial services through establishing accounts for electronic payments of any kind, including paychecks or remittances. It also provides an example of a successful partnership between a community financial institution and a nonprofit community group.

Remittances have received much attention in recent years as a profitable new product for commercial banks, such as Citigroup, Wells Fargo, and Bank of America. This profitable niche for transfers and foreign-exchange fees, estimated at between US$900 million and US$1.8 billion annually, has been dominated by Western Union (Krebsbach 2002). An example of a new remittance product is Bank of America's SafeSend, a wire transfer service that can be accessed from 20,000 ATMs in Mexico using a SafeSend card sent to the user via courier, with a transaction cost of US$10. Bank of America views the remittance product as a means of capturing new Hispanic clients (39 million in the United States). Currently, 37 percent of those who have signed up for SafeSend have opened other accounts. The bank expects to receive no less than 80 percent of future growth in retail banking from the Hispanic market. Only 58 percent of Hispanics have checking accounts, versus 93 percent of non-Hispanic whites (Tully 2003).

Mexicans in particular are gaining greater access to the financial system in the United States with the matricula card, the certificate of consular registration offered to Mexican nationals by the consulate of Mexico (Williams and Nieman 2003). The matricula provides an acceptable form of identification for opening bank accounts, and thus moves savings from under mattresses into bank accounts. As an outreach strategy, Bank of America has been actively marketing to Mexicans as they wait in line at the consulate for their matricula document (Tully 2003). The growth of the remittance business can also be used to attract more clients to the financial services sector in the countries of the recipients, as they use ATMs to gain access to their funds. Remittances form a relatively low part of financial receipts in Brazil, in contrast to other countries in the Latin America region.

Products for Small Business and Microenterprises

Term loans of up to one year. Commercial banks typically have entered low-access markets with pilot products offered through test branches, later expanding their product offerings as profit and performance indicators demonstrate market potential. Demonstration effects can be powerful in this context. Loans with a term of up to a year are the most standard product for entering this market niche. Long-term loans to small enterprises in certain neighborhoods were rare in the late 1960s, when one of the founders of ShoreBank first made a loan to a minority-owned McDonald's franchise in the urban core of South Chicago. At the time, this was considered a highly risky transaction by mainstream banks, given the location of the business and the structure of the McDonald's franchise agreement. Today, however, these loans are readily underwritten and later securitized by mainstream banks.

This process has been facilitated also by readily available credit bureau information, although borrower credit histories in the low-access market may be unfavorable. Income tax returns are also widely available, and many customers have established account relationships in the bank where they apply for a loan. Although some banks, such as Wells Fargo and Bank of America, have developed credit-scoring models for term loans to small businesses, traditional credit analysis is still employed by many banks. Credit-scoring models may improve efficiency and allow banks to reach a greater number of clients, but they also may exclude potentially viable borrowers or fail to identify a future default.

ShoreBank has explored developing a scorecard for loans below US$150,000, but has chosen to rely on its traditional analysis process to avoid disqualifying potential borrowers outside the realm of a traditional scorecard. ShoreBank's lending methodology is a rigorous underwriting process, using all available information on the company, its owners, and affiliate companies. Efficiency is reached by streamlining the application processes so that documentation requirements do not overwhelm clients; by combining these with seasoned lenders with the ability to quickly assess a potential deal, based primarily on cash flow projections, market potential, skill level, and character of the management team; and by adjusting the depth of analysis for new versus repeat borrowers and for loan type—trade, production, or start-up lending.

Consistent monitoring of the outstanding small-business portfolio is a significant factor in success. Although ShoreBank may have a higher level of delinquencies than its peers (banks with similar asset size), suggesting higher risk-taking, it also has higher writeoffs. Monitoring includes quarterly collection of updated financial information, site visits, and tracking of performance against projections. ShoreBank has incorporated a risk rating system to inform management of asset quality. In its partnerships overseas, ShoreBank encourages similar quarterly monitoring to look for changes in management, observe the flow of business, and check the presence and condition of collateral. Structuring frequent, even monthly, payments prevents the entrepreneur from spending available cash for loan repayments on other business needs; also, these payments serve as an opportunity to visit the client.

ShoreBank contrasts the effectiveness of its continued personal involvement as an early warning system with the lower monitoring of most mainstream banks, which rely more heavily on credit-scoring methodologies. In developing markets, where credit bureau information is scant and small businesses lack substantial track records, credit analysis is more labor intensive in terms of data collection. ShoreBank Advisory

Services has been working to adapt a partial scorecard on a pilot basis with some of its partner banks in Eastern Europe. Banorte in Mexico has adopted a 'mini-scoring' model for its small-business portfolio. Although Banorte can make a credit decision in two hours based on the scorecard output, it spends days collecting the necessary information for the scorecard. The scorecard automatically excludes companies with less than three years of experience.

Beyond intensive due diligence, ShoreBank has always sought to use government or other guarantees to 'limit the risk,' via guarantee programs and cooperation with state economic development agencies. This demonstrates the importance of third-party guarantees and guarantee programs such as those of the Small Business Administration (SBA) in small-business loans in the United States. When ShoreBank first began lending to small businesses in the early 1970s, nearly 100 percent of their small-enterprise loans were term loans guaranteed by the SBA. ShoreBank actually limited its offering of other loan products, such as credit lines, to small enterprises until the mid-1990s, because of the importance of the SBA guarantee as the secondary source of repayment. ShoreBank leveraged these guarantee programs to further its outreach, and was a substantial user of the state-run Illinois Capital Access Program. Guarantee programs can thus be a useful tool in broadening access to credit.

ShoreBank has also leveraged third-party guarantees from individuals and enterprises to make deals happen. The bank has worked with state and local grant programs, or mezzanine funds, to structure multilayered financing packages for its clients. This pulling together of multiple sources of financing helps to mitigate risk. However, these deals involve considerable coordination effort on the part of the lender. Also, guarantee programs, though very important in small-business lending in the United States through the 1990s, may not work in the same manner internationally. Some of the concerns voiced by donors are that guarantees would take the place of rigorous credit analysis. Banks have expressed concern that guarantee programs would add additional layers of bureaucracy and in the end are not worth the effort. It would be interesting to review the performance of guarantee programs, such as the United States Agency for International Development (USAID) Development Credit Authority, outside of the United States.

Loans to start-up companies. Loans to newly established companies, or start-ups, are in a higher risk category. Whereas the entrepreneurs may have a track record, their businesses do not. Few banks are willing to take on this risk without third-party guarantees. ShoreBank makes loans to start-ups if owners contribute a significant amount (30 percent) to the total project, and if the business is an intrinsically sound and profitable proposition. These loans are almost always backed by SBA or other guarantees. Typically, start-ups are candidates for nonprofit loan funds or for venture capital–type financing through the SBA's program or other community development venture capital funds.

In Eastern Europe, Shorebank Advisory Services has partnered with local banks to structure financing packages to start-up businesses without guarantee programs. Erste Bank in Austria, owner of Ceska Sporitelna in the Czech Republic, has established specialized branches in Austria to process loan applications to start-up companies, where skilled loan officers with small-business consulting experience connect these borrowers to training and small-business support. Rejection rates are high (80 percent or higher), but this provides an opportunity to work with promising growing companies. Erste is planning to start such a program in the Czech Republic. Start-ups also require heightened vigilance in monitoring. In many cases, start-ups involve construction and equipment installation, and lenders should perform on-site visits at milestones identified during the analysis process, such as the delivery of equipment. Sales targets, cost projections, and margins should be monitored against projections, with financial updates on a monthly basis.

Credit lines are typically extended to small enterprises to increase working capital through their primary accounts. Although they can be unsecured, they are more often secured by accounts receivable or inventory, rather than fixed assets. ShoreBank did not initially offer credit lines because of the weak collateral position and the costs of linking outstandings with specific inventories or receivables. Now, a greater percentage of ShoreBank borrowers receive credit lines. Many banks provide credit lines as part of a suite of products for small and micro clients. For example, Ceska Sporitelna in the Czech Republic has developed the 'Profit Program,' a bundle of products targeting microenterprises and small businesses that incorporates a special direct-deposit account, a credit card, and a credit line of US$3,000 to US$6,000.

Credit lines are typically higher priced than term loans and thus are a more expensive but more convenient option for the borrower. Fees for credit lines can be higher because of increased maintenance costs for the bank. However, in some environments, taking receivables or inventories as collateral may be difficult to document or enforce. This partly explains the huge differentials in interest rates of lines of credit and term loans, in Brazil and elsewhere. Approval procedures may be relatively easy; commercial banks often base their approvals on account balances and collateral appraisal alone.[32] Servicing for credit lines frequently involves additional monitoring of collateral if linked to accounts receivable or inventory levels.

Credit may also be extended through corporate or personal credit cards. Corporate credit cards are now a basic product offered to small businesses at banks of all sizes in the United States. In Eastern Europe and Latin America, they are being offered increasingly to small-business clients as well. Personal credit cards are available for smaller loans. Finally, an overdraft entitles account holders (retail or commercial) to exceed account balances for fixed periods at a rate of interest comparable to a credit card. These loans serve as emergency funding, like credit cards, for companies experiencing temporary cash shortages. They are typically smaller in size than a credit line and are not secured. Often, the primary consideration in qualifying for an overdraft is the average account balance. Amounts granted are linked to income or revenue levels. Again, like a credit line, this product is more costly to the borrower than traditional debt, but the processing is instantaneous if the customer qualifies for the product.

As in Brazil, where the *cheque especial* overdraft is popular, consumer overdrafts have been controversial because it is sometimes not immediately apparent to account holders that they have slipped into an overdraft situation and are faced with mounting fees or interest charges. As with credit lines, overdrafts are frequently approved based on a credit-scoring type of approach, or simply account balances. For example, TBC Bank in Georgia, Eastern Europe, has been offering overdrafts to individuals and businesses based on individual income levels (limited by two times the monthly salary), or up to US$50,000 per company. Monitoring for overdrafts is typically a matter of tracking account balances and receipt of periodic financial reporting. Because these loans are unsecured, rates are high to compensate for this higher risk.

Gold-collateralized lending or pawn lending through banks. Some commercial banks in developing economies have entered into 'gold pawn lending' to microenterprises, traditionally a microfinance institution product. TBC Bank in Georgia has recently launched this product to microenterprises. The new service provided in these loans is storage and security of the collateral, including high-value collateral. Loans are provided in the range of US$25 to US$250, based on the appraisal of the collateral alone at a rate of 36 percent a year. The benefit for the borrower is rapid disbursal. The benefit for the bank is its ability to attract new customers to the bank that might not qualify for consumer or business loans based on income-generation capacity. The downside is the high administrative costs for the pawn lending in appraising and storing the collateral.

In developed economies, this niche is occupied by pawnshops, check-cashing services, and other issuers of urgent cash. These products would be utilized by consumers with low or no credit scores, or by the undocumented. In the absence of positive credit history, these loans offer low-access individuals an alternative to traditional bank financing and an entryway into the financial system. They can be offered along with other microfinance or consumer-lending products to complete market coverage. However, this is an expensive option for the borrower and is costly for the bank to administer. Such lending lies largely outside the banking sector in Brazil, although interest rate spreads are high.

Other products for businesses. ShoreBank and other banks with a focus on the microenterprise and small-business segment have broadened their product offerings to better serve their customers and generate fee income as they face increased competition. By offering bundled products and services, the bank reaches new customers and provides convenience and savings to its clients. In recent years, ShoreBank has developed several products targeted at its core small-business customers. These include Small Business Checking (for businesses with a low monthly volume of deposits and checks), Sweep Accounts, and Zero Balance Checking, which enables businesses to track expenses and monitor costs by department, location, and type of expense.

Alpha Bank in Romania has a goal of providing at least four products for any type of customer, including small businesses. They believe this solidifies the relationship with the client, making it more difficult for customers to switch to another bank. One of the products Alpha Bank has marketed to employees of small businesses is the Employee Credit Card, which is an overdraft credit limit for employees with direct-deposit services. The use of funds is flexible, and the limit generally increases over time based on the employee's salary.

Outreach Strategies and Marketing

Banks embarking on a new product or downscaling for the first time need an outreach strategy. One approach is to leverage partnerships with community organizations, for-profit businesses, or state, national, and multilateral programs to generate wider outreach. Another is to establish collaboration with microfinance. Banks can learn the culture of the microfinance borrower from the MFI, while the microfinance institution (MFI), receives financing from the bank and benefits from the bank's branch networks and infrastructure, as discussed in chapter 2 of this study. Fundamental to both is the recognition that success depends on attracting and retaining a solid customer base within the target market that generates profits for the bank. Those banks with a winning customer outreach strategy in this segment will ultimately shape the market.

A first hurdle sometimes faced by commercial banks is their negative market perception among potential clients. Banks, especially older, well-established banks, may be viewed as unsympathetic to the needs of small businesses, requiring excessive documentation and collateral coverage, and lacking interest in small customers. Outreach requires that the bank dismantle this image. Approaches and principles to this end are discussed below.

Selecting the appropriate staff to reach out to low-access customers is the first critical element of outreach. Staff working in this area should have the desire to service this market segment and an ability to work with clients with low levels of education and financial sophistication. Prior work experience in a small business, or through small-business support services, is advantageous. Extensive work experience in traditional commercial lending can be detrimental, given that microenterprise and small-business finance may strike these lenders as too risky or too small for the trouble. Specialized training in analyzing microenterprises and small businesses can be beneficial, not only to improve the quality of credit analysis, but also to appreciate the particular characteristics of this market segment.

Hiring staff from the target communities helps to break down cultural barriers and ease the interaction with potential clients. For example, ShoreBank hired many African American lenders to work with businesses in its urban 'footprint' in Chicago, Cleveland, and Detroit. When traditional banks were not welcoming to minority entrepreneurs, ShoreBank projected an image of commitment to the local community. In Brazil, this could mean hiring persons from those urban areas and disadvantaged communities where financial access is to be expanded.

A high level of customer orientation among all levels of bank staff is another essential tool in serving low-access communities. This is frequently an area of weakness at traditional commercial banks. If service issues are not addressed prior to a sales effort, new customers will be repelled by their banking experience. Customer service among low-access clients entails basic concepts such as courtesy, client-needs assessment, and service recovery in the case of complaints. In addition, customer service entails an ability to work with clients who have an innate distrust of banks, or a low level of education. Therefore, specialized training in both customer service and cultural sensitivity is recommended.

A fundamental structural change implemented by banks active in downscaling to low-access segments is the creation of specialized divisions to target these segments. Many banks working with small businesses in the United States have established separate microenterprise and small-business lending departments with dedicated loan officers and resources. This allows for recruitment of appropriate staff and application of appropriate loan methodology. Large banks often choose to deliver products to microenterprises and small business throughout the bank. Although this gives a national bank the ability to reach all areas where it may have branches, not all lenders may have the skills or desire to work with this segment, and some may not actively promote the products. Having a department head or internal champion responsible for products to this segment is essential to facilitate growth of these products.

Another example of an innovative approach to organizational structure is the establishment of specialized start-up branches by Erste Bank of Austria. By focusing lenders with higher-level skills on analyzing and servicing start-up businesses in one location, the bank will serve this niche segment more efficiently and mitigate risk. Yet another innovation is the creation of mobile sales forces and separating lenders from the sales forces. The dedicated mobile sales force travels to potential commercial and retail clients, including outlying rural areas. This leaves lenders more time to concentrate on loan appraisals, thus addressing the issue that good lenders are not necessarily good salespeople, although many lenders have volume targets and are expected to engage in direct marketing.

Similarly, client relations are better maintained by separating the collection department from lending. Banorte in Mexico has established special call centers to deal with delinquencies beyond 30 days on their small-business loan portfolio. This provides lenders with another resource should their customers have delayed repayments. The phone call from a different department allows the lender to continue to play the role of supportive partner, while collections can place additional pressure on the client if needed.

Moving downscaling to the retail lending department of a bank is another possibility. At Ceska Sporitelna, businesses with more than US$800,000 in annual sales are handled by the corporate division, and anything below that amount is retail. Staff are differentiated along these lines as well. Alpha Bank in Romania and TBC Bank in Georgia have actively been shifting their focus to retail products as competition in the banking sector has increased. Both banks have developed new retail products, such as 'gift cards,' special accounts for children, offers of free safe deposit box services with new accounts, and so forth. This retail approach helps these banks in Eastern Europe reach previously 'unbanked' populations.

Another outreach strategy has been the use of specialized products or programs to attract new customers. For example, the Profit Program developed by Ceska Sporitelna, in which a credit line of US$3,000 to US$6,000 is offered to existing clients of the bank, has attracted new lending business for the bank. Many of these customers previously had a non-borrowing relationship with the bank and had not applied for a loan because the process was too onerous and bureaucratic. TBC Bank uses the gold-collateralized loan product to reach new retail customers in outlying areas and compete with informal lenders. TBC is also currently developing a loan product for farmers of vineyards in rural areas, which it hopes will attract a new subset of customers to the bank.

Banks can further enhance their outreach potential by building partnerships and alliances with grassroots organizations, for-profit businesses, nonprofits, and NGOs. ShoreBank staff have traditionally participated on boards of local nonprofit organizations and church groups. ShoreBank's holding company structure lends itself to these partnerships as well. In each community in which it operates, ShoreBank has a commercial bank, nonbank loan funds, nonprofit business development services, and real estate development corporations. The group of ShoreBank banks works in partnership with the nonbanks, typically in cases where collateral coverage is insufficient to provide the total financing package needed by the business. These alliances allow ShoreBank to offer greater access to financing to viable businesses. ShoreBank and other commercial banks in the United States have also partnered with providers of financial literacy training and free tax return compilation to bring low-income account holders into the bank.

Similarly TBC Bank in Georgia has provided financing to the microlending activities of FINCA (the Foundation for International Community Assistance), and has held a stake in the European Bank for Reconstruction and Development (EBRD)—and the International Finance Corporation (IFC)—sponsored Microfinance Bank (which TBC recently sold). It started partnering with FINCA by virtue of a long-term account relationship FINCA had with TBC. TBC also saw this as an opportunity to place funds profitably. Ownership in the Microfinance Bank allowed TBC to learn more about the sector. Banorte in Mexico and Alpha Bank in Romania have partnered with car dealerships and other providers of retail goods and services to gain access to new clients and markets.

In a highly competitive banking environment, most banks find it necessary to engage in direct marketing and cold calling to potential customers. Direct marketing efforts may involve hosting events for entrepreneurs in partnership with the local mayor's office, sponsorship of small-business training seminars, visits to trade shows and open-air markets, and other approaches. The Bank of America example above, in which employees handed out brochures and coffee to Mexicans waiting in line at the consular section to receive their Matricula identity card, is another type of direct marketing. Most banks also engage in some form of mass media advertising, whether through radio spots, newspaper articles and advertisements, or sponsorship of local community activities. Advertising and marketing efforts are most successful when the product is well defined for the target group.

Some banks have chosen to target low-income or microcustomers through special-purpose entities. If initial market research has shown that the bank image is negative, rather than expending resources to improve the image, the bank creates a new arm. For example, Banorte in Mexico has chosen to launch its microlending below US$6,000 through a special-purpose entity. Some of the bank infrastructure will be used, but in most cases the client will not be aware that Banorte owns the entity. The primary reason is the negative image of the bank in this market as a result of the peso crisis in the 1990s.

Although the financial institutions may differ in location, asset size, and motivation for downscaling, all agree that commitment at the highest levels of the organization to reach these markets is critical. Efforts needed are not sustainable to scale unless top management makes it a priority.

Finally, and to summarize, other key factors of success in bank downscaling include the extent to which the product addresses an unmet demand, the rigor of the lending methodology, the quality of the staff, pricing, and the effectiveness of the outreach strategy.

4
Partnering Nonbanks

Introduction

To what extent can financial institutions other than banks contribute to financial access for the underserved? An examination of the institutional distribution of the assets of the financial system indicates a heavy concentration in the banking system. Between 90 and 95 percent of total financial assets in the past five years are in banks, in contrast to only 3 to 4 percent in finance companies and leasing companies taken together and around 2 to 3 percent in all other financial intermediaries (table 4.1 and appendix table A1.3). But these data may overemphasize the importance of the banking system. Banking system assets as represented below consolidate data for Brazil's multiple banks, and to the extent that departments of these banks also engage in non-bank activities, these would be reflected under bank assets.[1]

As discussed in the previous chapter, several credit instruments other than 'plain vanilla' bank loans are used increasingly by both individuals and enterprises.[2] These include, particularly, overdrafts, credit cards, and vehicle loans for individuals (these accounted for 11 percent, 6 percent, and 35 percent of outstanding loans to individuals, respectively, as of December 2002, and 55 percent, 10 percent, and 7 percent of new loans

Table 4.1 Financial System Assets, by Institutional Type

Percentage of total assets	*Dec. 1995*	*Dec. 1996*	*Dec. 1997*	*Dec. 1998*	*Dec. 1999*	*Dec. 2000*	*Dec. 2001*
Banks[a]	91.40	90.25	91.42	90.67	91.58	93.08	93.64
Multiple banks	53.31	52.76	52.10	47.10	50.76	52.61	69.10
Cooperatives	0.20	0.25	0.31	0.41	0.54	0.62	0.75
Finance companies	0.29	0.59	0.52	0.41	0.53	0.71	0.49
Leasing companies	3.33	3.36	4.17	5.24	5.42	3.87	3.29
Other financial intermediaries[b]	4.78	5.55	3.58	3.27	1.93	1.72	1.83

a. Includes multiple banks, commercial banks, national savings banks, development banks, and investment banks.

b. Includes housing finance entities, securities markets brokers and dealers, and foreign exchange dealers.

Source: Central Bank of Brazil.

contracted, respectively). Enterprise financing also makes considerable use of overdrafts (15 percent of outstanding loans and 30 percent of new loans), and although smaller in volume, the discounting of commercial invoices, or 'duplicatas' (4 percent of outstanding loans and 8 percent of new loans) as well as the provision of vendor credit (around 6 percent of new or outstanding credit) (figure 4.1).[3]

Some of these instruments are closely associated with and move in parallel to other forms of financing that lie outside the banking system. For example, the rapid growth of the discount of duplicatas (commercial invoices) by commercial banks is significant. However, the activities of factoring companies, which are the main providers of credit through the purchase of receivables, are not included among data on financial institutions, as factoring is deemed to be a purely commercial activity. In addition to the discount of invoices, included in credit data, which amounted to around R$6 billion in 2001, the estimated factoring portfolio at the end of 2001 was R$27 billion, and factoring represented an estimated 2.3 percent of Brazil's gross domestic product (GDP). These figures indicate that factoring companies may have a significant role in providing access to financial services, indeed particularly for smaller enterprises that may face difficulties in obtaining conventional bank finance. The purchase price of receivables through factoring companies is higher than the interest rates applied by banks for the discounting of invoices. Thus, at the end of 2001, the nominal interest rate applied was 50.1 percent for invoices discounted at banks, while the implicit average 'purchase factor,' real and effective, was 58.2 percent.[4]

On the consumer credit side, vehicles credit and credit card loans both have shown an upward trend (table 4.2). These activities are also associated with leasing companies and consumer finance companies. Indeed, the clear upward trend in vehicles credit is due in part to the decrease of leasing activity over the past few years, as discussed further below. Credit cards receivables are included in the statistics above only to the extent that these may be refinanced by banks.[5] Finance companies' portfolio was 0.4 percent of GDP, amounting to R$4.4 billion in value, compared to an aggregate consumer credit portfolio of R$70 billion for the entire financial system.[6] And Brazil's outstanding leasing portfolio represented 1 percent of GDP at end-2001, with a portfolio of R$11.6 billion.[7] Information about trade finance is dispersed, making it very difficult to estimate a global figure for this form of financing.

Given the significance of these activities, the present chapter examines their contribution to financial access, especially for small-scale enterprises and for low-income consumers, and assesses the potential for an expanded contribution.[8] This chapter suggests that the weak bankruptcy and secured transaction laws that complicate the use of collateral in Brazil

Figure 4.1 Loans to Companies and Individuals in Brazil, by Instrument

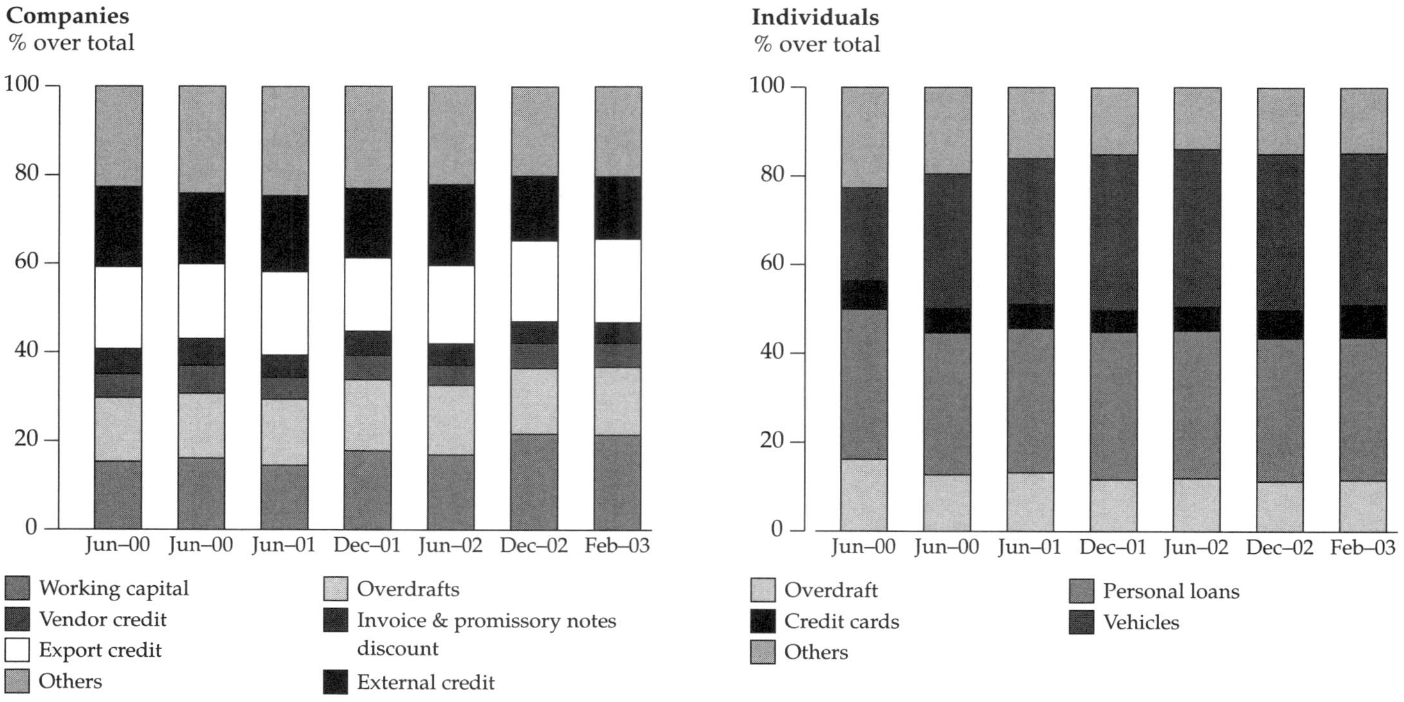

Source: Central Bank of Brazil; appendix tables A4.1 and A4.2.

Table 4.2 Finance, Leasing, and Factoring Companies in Brazil, December 2001
(R$ billions)

	Finance companies	*Leasing companies*	*Factoring companies*
No. of companies	39	71	717
Total loans	4.6	11.6	27.4
Total assets	5.4	36.8	—
Total deposits	2.9	2.5	—
Total net worth	1.2	8.3	1.4
Average total loans by company	0.119	0.163	0.038
Average total assets by company	0.139	0.518	—
Average total deposits by company	0.076	0.034	—
Average total net worth by company	0.030	0.116	0.002

Note: — = not available.
Source: Central Bank of Brazil.

create incentive for forms of financing (for example, factoring, leasing, trade finance) other than straightforward credit, which reduces risk by securing repayments against accounts receivable or by maintaining title and using self-executable legal instruments. In addition, these institutions do not face many of the high costs of entry of banks, and some non-banks such as factoring and finance companies are better equipped to handle the high operating costs for small-scale clients. As such, they could have an important role, although factoring and trade financing provide only working capital and cannot meet investment needs. Leasing could potentially contribute to investment finance but has been used little for this purpose.

The contributions of these sectors have been below their potential, in part because their own legal underpinnings are fragmented and sometimes challenged as to their legitimacy. Also, from a practical point of view, their distinguishing characteristics are not always evident in the services they provide. Factoring does not have a law governing its services, and the treatment it has received in civil litigation has sometimes been perceived as arbitrary. In both leasing and factoring, there remains confusion between these specialities and normal bank credit. Thus, in the case of leasing, it is sometimes concluded that leases are essentially similar to loans; also, distinctions between financial and operational leases are sometimes unclear. In the case of factoring, the discounting of invoice or predated checks is considered at par with the purchase of receivables. Until a mature distinction regarding these novel contracts is established, it will be hard to expand the growth of these industries in Brazil.

Nevertheless, there is scope for an increase in the services these industries offer to improve access to financial services. Key findings are summarized below.

- There is a sizeable real contribution of the factoring industry to the provision of services to small enterprises today, which could be strengthened and legitimized to extend its outreach.
- At present, the distinction between genuine factoring and the discounting of invoices or checks is not sufficiently clear in practice. Consolidation of the dispersed legal framework of the factoring industry could contribute toward this. A proposed draft law on factoring has been pending in Congress for years. Its final passage would be beneficial to the industry.
- The legal framework should also clarify distinctions between recourse financing and non-recourse financing by factors. Financing with recourse, although not forbidden, has not been recognized in legal jurisprudence. Lack of recourse in cases of fraudulent transactions by clients is costly for factoring companies.
- The tax treatment of factoring needs investigation. At present, they are subject to all financial transaction taxes as well as to commercial taxes. A case has been pending in the Federal Supreme Court to resolve this.
- Permitting factoring companies wider access to finance, for example, through the issue of commercial bills or debentures, as permitted elsewhere, could be explored. This could be eased if the proposed draft law is passed.
- Finally, international factoring could be eased by the relaxation of certain restrictions against holding foreign-currency accounts.
- Leasing today is an activity mainly for large firms, where the obsolescence of equipment or contracting of maintenance for operational leasing makes this an attractive option for investment financing. For individuals, leasing has been used largely by those who are 'better off,' primarily to acquire vehicles. Leasing is largely beyond the domain of the less-well-off segments of consumers, or small firms, and thus today are of limited immediate importance in terms of expansion of access.
- The legal framework for leasing is fragmented, and for many purposes, leasing falls under the Civil Code. As of mid-2003, a dedicated leasing law was under preparation and was due to be submitted to Congress. This will be important in terms of clarifying the framework for leasing operations.
- The leasing industry has fluctuated markedly in Brazil in the past decade. Regulatory arbitrage in the tax system has considerably influenced the development of the leasing industry and contributed to its boom, especially in consumer vehicles leasing, in the latter 1990s. Fur-

ther changes in the tax system, together with the impact of devaluation on dollar-indexed loans, and also judicial activism that tended to shelter the lessee led to its subsequent contraction and to the move away from individual leasing by lessors.

- The relatively slow growth in leasing of machinery and equipment has also been ascribed to the availability of alternative sources of finance (such as FINAME credit lines of the Banco Nacional de Desenvolvimento Econômico e Social [National Bank for Economic and Social Development; BNDES]), which are longer in term (three to five years).
- Leasing has tax advantages for the lessor due to provisions for accelerated depreciation of leased assets at around 30 percent per year. Leasing also has potential tax advantages for the lessee due to the writeoff of periodic payments against income. But it may be difficult for smaller firms to benefit from this without using more complex tax forms ('lucro real,' or actual income), which permit itemized deductions, instead of the simplified tax forms based on standardized deductions and estimated income ('lucro presumido').
- The tax regime for leasing was also made more complicated by the treatment of residual value. If low, leases were sometimes not recognized but treated as loans. The industry sought legal clarification, and in 2003, the Superior Court of Justice (Superior Tribunal de Justiça) clarified the use of residual value in leasing contracts to include all payments, irrespective of the timing of such payment during the life of the contract. It will considerably influence the extent to which the industry regains its attractiveness.
- Leasing has an accounting advantage in Brazil, as financial leases are booked as operational leases, thus allowing capital goods acquisition without raising the gearing (indebtedness) ratio. However, this accounting treatment is unorthodox.
- Overall, a review of the accounting framework of the leasing industry should be undertaken to (1) clearly distinguish between loans and lease as well as between financial and operating leases, (2) examine the possibility of permitting write-offs against income for small firms, and (3) harmonize accounting methodology with international practice.
- Partnerships between financial intermediaries and commercial companies could constitute a feasible alternative to promote operational leasing for smaller enterprises. This would be promoted by more competition in the industrial segments, which could constitute the lessees.
- Finance companies, which have the advantage for the consumer of easier access than bank accounts, are an important alternative for consumer credit at low- and medium-income levels.

- For financial institutions, they offer an avenue for product differentiation as well as lower-cost funds, as there are no reserve requirements.
- Access to funding is tight for those finance companies that operate independently, as they are not deposit-taking institutions. However, most of their services could today be provided by multiple banks.

Factoring

Factoring in Brazil: Evolution and Development

Factoring, known in Brazil as 'fomento mercantil,' is a service activity that includes ongoing advisory work on credit, risk, accounting, inventory, and working capital management, in tandem with the irrevocable purchase of credit rights, in the form of receivables that arise from the sale of goods or services with a typical maturity of 30 to 60 days. The factoring company assumes the insolvency risk associated with these credit rights.[9] Factoring must be based on commercial sales and is governed by Brazil's Civil Code.[10] It can be conducted only with 'legal persons' or enterprises and not with individuals. Real estate, as in international practice, is also excluded. The most common accounts receivable are duplicatas (commercial invoices), which account for almost 90 percent of all factoring receivables (see below). Others are bills of exchange, bills of lading, warrants, promissory notes, checks, and pre-dated checks (which can be used only if they originate from mercantile sales).

There are an estimated 720 known factoring companies in Brazil, which provide services to more than 65,000 small and medium enterprises (end-2001).[11] Eighty percent of these enterprises belong to the industrial sector, with a monthly turnover of around US$1 billion. Brazilian enterprises obtained about US$10 billion (R$27 billion) as creditor rights resulting from mercantile sales, representing 6 percent of all domestic sources of financing in 2001. This figure constitutes an impressive increase of around 50 percent over 1998 (US$7 billion, R$19 billion). Factoring companies had more than 6,000 employees and were estimated to provide another 710,000 indirect employment opportunities. Thus, factoring is a sizeable industry in Brazil and an important source of finance for a number of firms.

Brazil's factoring companies are located mainly in the Southeast (51 percent), South (21 percent), and Northeast (17 percent), with more than 250 in the state of São Paulo alone (appendix table A4.5). As shown in table 4.3, factoring firms tend to have no more than 8 to 10 employees in any part of the country, but the average portfolio handled per employee tends to be much larger in São Paulo (around R$8.5 million) than the national average (R$4.4 million), while the Northeast states of Piauí,

Table 4.3 Factoring Companies in Selected States and Regions in Brazil, 2001

	Summary statistics							*Key ratios*				
	Nos.	*Net worth (R$m)*	*Portfolio (R$m)*	*% delinquency*	*No. employment*	*No. of clients*	*Average employment factoring companies*	*Average client firms/ factoring companies*	*Average portfolio, factoring companies*	*Average net worth, factoring companies*	*Average portfolio employee*	*Average client firms/ employee*
São Paulo	255	908	18,597	3.0	2,190	18,050	9	71	72.9	3.56	8.49	8.2
Rio Grande do Sul	74	203	2,598	3.2	670	8,100	9	109	35.1	2.74	3.88	12.1
Rio de Janeiro	79	56	1,472	3.7	605	4,850	8	61	18.6	0.71	2.43	8
Ceará/Piauí/ Maranhão	38	23	577	4.1	310	4,750	8	125	15.2	0.61	1.86	15.3
Total, all states	717	1,406	27,397	3.8	6,186	66,070	9	92	38.2	1.96	4.43	10.7

Source: Estimates based on data from ANFAC; appendix table A4.5.

Maranhão, and Ceará have ratios of around R$1.9 million per employee. In terms of average numbers of firms per employees, however, the reverse applies; factoring companies in São Paulo handle around 8 firms per employee, while in the Northeast, each employee deals with an average of 15 firms (or 71 firms per factorinng company in São Paulo compared to 125 in the Northeast). These figures illustrate the much smaller clients that such firms have in the Northeast. In national terms, following some consolidation, two broad groups of factoring companies have emerged: (1) large, conglomerate-affiliated companies and (2) smaller, independent companies that specialize in funding smaller accounts and servicing smaller clients.[12]

Factoring companies serve a broad spectrum of sectors (figures 4.2 and 4.3). The industrial sector accounts for 65 percent of overall activity, the commercial sector for another 20 percent, and the services sector for 15 percent. The overall delinquency ratio for receivables is estimated to be around 3.8 percent, although this figure could be an underestimate because firms use credit recovery techniques, such as discounts, to receive, at least in part, past due credit that may not be declared delinquent.

Pricing Interest Rates and the Purchase Factor

The cost of a factoring operation has two components: (1) a fee for the provision of services and (2) the price, or the 'purchase factor,' for the purchase of receivables. The fee for the provision of services is fixed ad valorem.

There is an important conceptual difference between interest rates and purchase factors, although they are closely associated. *Interest* is the remuneration of capital for the time during which it is used in a credit operation. The *purchase factor* is the price paid for the sale of a credit right. Factoring companies use as a base the 'factor ANFAC' (Associação Nacional das Sociedades de Fomento Mercantil; Brazilian Factoring Association) to quote the price of factoring services in Brazil. The factor is published daily and varies with the money market or certificado de depósito bancário (bank certificate of deposit; CDB). The components of the factor ANFAC include the opportunity costs of resources, assessed in terms of the CDB rate, operational costs, taxes, and expected profits. The purchase factor varies with industry conditions and the creditworthiness of the customer.

As an illustration, the purchase factor was more than twice the interbank lending rate in February 2003, at 4.4 percent per month (67.7 percent per year equivalent), compared to the prevailing CDB interest rate of 1.83 percent (25.7 percent per year equivalent).[13] As expected, this was also higher than the prevailing average bank discount rate for commercial invoices, which was 58.5 percent per year at the same time. Factoring

Figure 4.2 Evolution of the Portfolio of Factoring Companies Associated with ANFAC

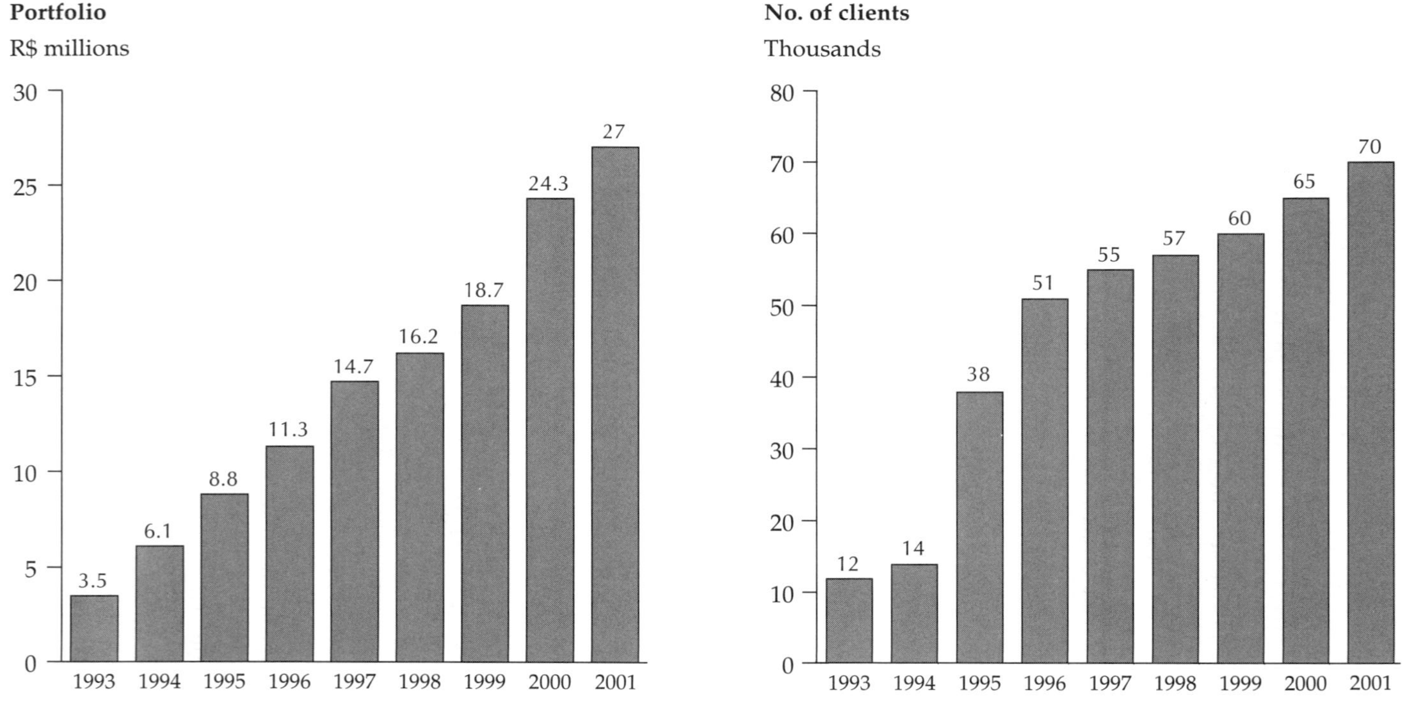

Source: ANFAC.

Figure 4.3 Factoring Companies' Portfolios, by Sector, 2000–01

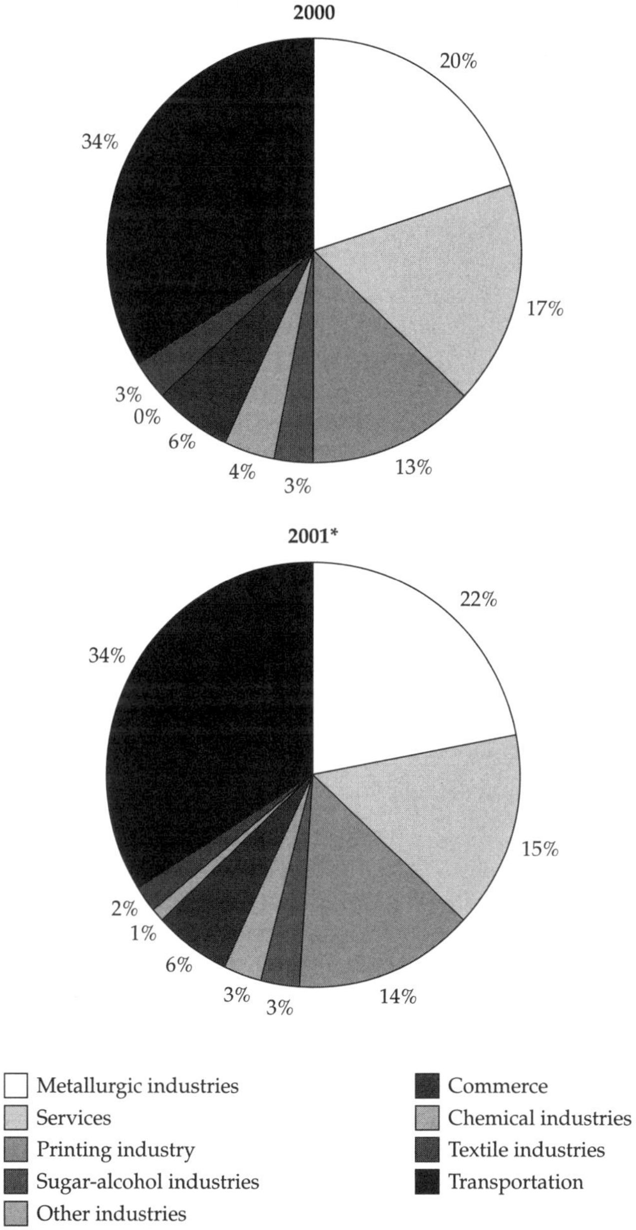

Note: * = preliminary.
Source: ANFAC.

companies point out, however, that this rate is effective and final, while banks' effective interest rates are higher, as other bank charges are added to the rate, such as a credit issuance fee, a price for receivables, overheads, retention of a percentage of the loan's value, product sales, and so forth. However, many of the factor's clients may not be able to obtain lower rates through bank discounts or any other formal financing.

As shown in figure 4.4, the spread between the purchase factor and the bank discount rate for commercial invoices showed some downward tendency over time, from mid-2000 to mid-2002, although there was some fluctuation in this trend over the past year. The spread relative to the CDB has declined more consistently. Both suggest improved competitiveness in the factoring business.

FACTORING VERSUS BANK SERVICES—CONTRAST AND COMPLEMENTARITY

There are several respects in which factoring activities differ from the provision of bank credit. Typically, factors provide a bundle of services to their clients, and forms of factoring can vary from the most basic to more complex bundles of services. Under conventional factoring, the merchant client receives a cash payment at a discounted price for the sale of credit rights to the factoring company. Under trustee factoring, the factoring company provides the additional service of managing the merchant's cash flow. More sophisticated arrangements also exist, such as raw material/input factoring, in which the factoring company guarantees the purchase of the product to the supplier, with first claims for its merchant. Factoring companies manage their credit risk through traditional credit information services available in Brazil, complementing traditional credit analysis with personal contact with the sellers to gain knowledge of their business practices, such as the timeliness and product quality, and their market.[14] The factor must also verify the authenticity of documentation directly with the buyer to ensure that sales are legitimate and protect itself against false trade documentation.

Thus, factors can play an important role for SMEs, not only as buyers of receivables but more importantly as supporters in strategic decision-making, providers of accounting and marketing knowledge, and also providers of knowledge of cash flow and inventory management. The factoring company and the factor have a tight interdependence of interests; thus, there are incentive-compatible objectives that help overcome problems of information asymmetries that SMEs encounter with banks. Factors operate very close to their clients, as they are assuming important credit risk and need effective credit information about the merchants' clients.

The purchase of receivables is normally on a nonrecourse basis and without any pledge or collateral. The factor buying the merchant´s credit

Figure 4.4 Evolution of Purchase Factor, Interest Rates, and Spreads in Brazil, July 1994 to February 2003

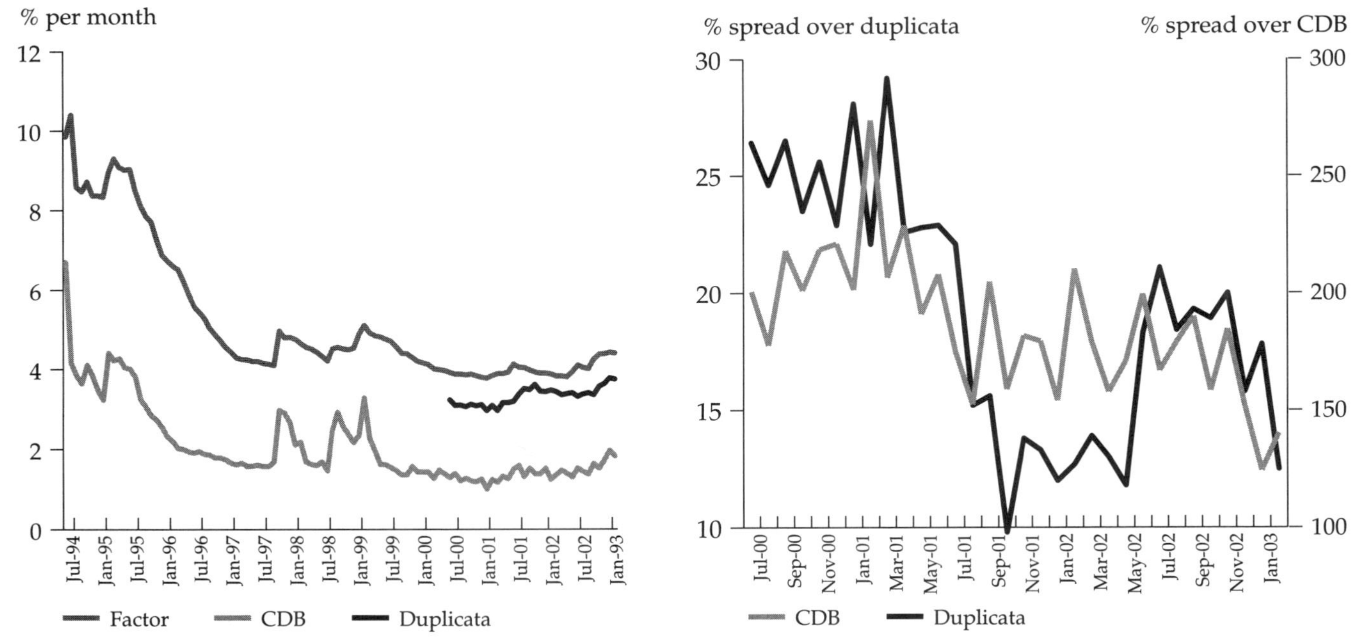

Source: ANFAC.

Commercial Invoice Duplicates

Duplicatas are a truly Brazilian form of accounts receivable, created to satisfy the requirements of Article 219 of the old Commercial Code, according to which, "In commercial sales, the seller is obliged to present to the buyer the invoice and duplicate [*duplicata*], one for the seller and one for the buyer. If an invoice is not presented, the sale is assumed to be a cash operation (Article 137)."

The consequent creation of the duplicata as a commercial credit instrument arose from the body of implementing regulations for this provision (Law No. 187/36 granted the duplicata the status of a credit title; Law No. 5474/68, governing commercial sales, modified this to permit the circulation of this title). Duplicatas are issued by sellers to buyers and are the only credit instrument that can be used by sellers to register the commercial sale of products and services. They are, therefore, deemed to be causal credit instruments, as they can be issued only to represent the commercial sale of products and services.

Provided it is appropriately signed by both parties, a duplicata is in principle an auto-executable credit instrument (see chapter 6). Lenders do not need to pursue a cognition suit and can directly enter an execution suit after filing a protest for nonpayment with a notary public.

receivables makes a credit evaluation in advance and assumes all risk of nonpayment. Factoring companies purchasing receivables do not have the same rights as banks. Sellers transfer their credit risk to factors as they buy the receivables. Banks, on the other hand, may charge the seller when the buyer does not pay, as they lend to sellers and use the receivables as collateral. The only exception is when the buyer does not pay because the contract was not fulfilled or the receivables are false.[15] A factoring operation is thus different from a credit operation and, by law, factoring companies cannot carry out operations exclusive to financial intermediaries.[16] One consequence is that factors typically have a closer acquaintance with their clients' business and also make more efforts to undertake detailed credit risk assessments than would be typical for a bank.

Factoring companies cannot normally receive resources from third parties but have to operate with their own resources. Thus, for example, factoring companies cannot take deposits or issue bills of exchange. Factoring companies point out that in other countries, the issue of commercial paper or of debentures has been more readily admitted.

Factoring is an important player in both the provision and use of credit information systems, as both user and provider of information. Factoring normally uses the negative credit information systems of the two princi-

Table 4.4 Differences between Financial Intermediation and Factoring

Financial intermediation	*Factoring*
Credit operations	No credit operations, but purchase of credit rights (receivables)
Obtains funds from the public to invest in credit operations by means of financial intermediation	Only operates with resources not collected from the public; no financial intermediation
Remuneration consists of interest rates for the use of capital during a period of time	Remuneration does not have an interest rate or discount rate but the payment of a price for the sale of services and the purchase of credit rights
Needs authorization from the Central Bank (Law No. 4595/64) to operate	Is not a financial intermediary; a commercial activity that only operates with legal persons; does not require authorization from the Central Bank
Operates with legal persons and individuals	Only operates with legal persons or professionals that are considered to be legal economic entities
Profits are generated by means of a spread between financing and credit interest rates	Price includes all cost items (market interest rate, operational costs, taxes) and the expected profit and risks.

pal private credit bureaus of Brazil, SCI (Segurança ao Crédito e Informações; Credit and Information Security) and SERASA. Factoring companies are both users and producers of information. As of May 2003, ANFAC, together with SERASA and Equifax, has had an ambitious project for the creation of a dedicated information database on members' risks, to cover the 70,000 of factoring enterprises.

As a result of these differences, factoring has several benefits over funding from bank loans (table 4.4). First, funding can be obtained more rapidly. Second, for the provider of credit, the exposure is limited to the amount of invoices issued to the seller, and the creditworthiness of the seller is less important. Third, this allows for companies in legal difficulty to borrow from factors, because factoring depends on the creditworthiness of the seller's customers. On the contrary, banks do not have an incentive to lend to firms in financial distress, as this could imply a higher risk classification of the loan and would mean higher capital requirements. Under the prevailing bankrupcy law, unlike factors, banks have not been permitted to operate with companies in receivership. Fourth, it is clear that factoring will have considerably higher implied rates of interest than bank loans, but this can be explained largely by the composite nature of services provided, the need for much closer client scrutiny and knowledge, and the limited sources of finance available to the factor, who must rely largely on internal resources.

Because of high implicit interest rates, factoring companies in Brazil are vulnerable to legal challenges due to the provisions of the Usury Law. This challenge to their legitimacy serves to further raise their costs of service provision and the purchase of receivables. Technically, until January 2002, interest rates were capped at 12 percent per annum under Brazil's Usury Law of 1933. Although it does not remove a cap on interest rates, the new Civil Code caps these at the rate of servicing charges on overdue Treasury paper (Law No. 10406 of January 10, 2002). Although an exemption from the restrictions of this law was largely obtained for all entities that are part of the national financial system, factoring, being deemed a commercial activity, falls outside the safe territory of other providers of finance. Factoring companies point out that they do not charge interest, as their acquisition of receivables constitutes an outright sale. However, the implicit factor or interest rate equivalent can be easily calculated, and thus factors have often been the subject of disputes in the court system, due to their charging of 'usurious' interest rates. This may also explain the small size of Brazil's factoring firms in an international comparison; Brazil's more than 700 factoring companies are ahead of even the United States in numbers, which has less than 300 such entities, but the U.S. firms have a total portfolio value around 10 times as large as in Brazil (appendix table A4.7).

These challenges to the legitimacy of factoring are compounded by suspected illicit activities of some firms, which have been known in particular to offer services outside their legal scope, for example, deposit-taking or loan provision. One of the main objectives of ANFAC, the factoring company trade association, is to delimit factoring from other activities, sometimes illegal, of financial intermediation, without the required approval of the Central Bank, or grant loans at usurious interest rates under the name of 'factoring.' ANFAC has agreed on a model of factoring contract (contrato de fomento mercantil) to be used by its associates, has issued a *Code of Ethics* (*Código de Ética e Auto-Regulação*), has approved a set of General Rules for Factoring Operations[17] (Regulamento Geral das Operações de Fomento Mercantil) and, in 1999, reached a Technical Cooperation Agreement (Acordo de Cooperação Técnica) with the Economic Law Secretariat of the Ministry of Justice (Secretaria de Direito Econômico do Ministério da Justiça). The agreement has three basic objectives: (1) to recognize and preserve factoring as a means of supporting productive activities, (2) to protect affiliated companies by means of a 'qualification and quality' certification, and (3) to establish a system of technical cooperation with the Federal public administration to prevent the emergence of illegal activities under the guise of factoring. ANFAC has been petitioning strongly for a specific factoring law to help eliminate illegitimate activities and protect its members.

International Factoring and International Comparisons

International factoring in Brazil is undeveloped, especially relative to the large size of the domestic factoring sector (table 4.5). The most significant obstacle to the development of international factoring is that factoring companies in Brazil are not allowed to hold foreign-currency accounts. Thus, they are not able to make advances to the exporter in the currency of their invoices, which introduces exchange rate risk. It would thus be difficult to serve the export community without involving commercial banks. If conditions for permitting international factoring could be eased, export companies could reduce their risks. Italy and the United Kingdom have extensively used factoring to involve SMEs in export activity. In Latin America, countries such as Mexico have also begun to engage in international factoring. In contrast, in Brazil, exports are carried out by big companies with more access to financial services from conventional financial intermediaries.

By 2002, factoring operations were carried out in more than 50 countries, with an estimated total worldwide factoring value exceeding US$640 billion. It was estimated that approximately 90 percent of revenues came from service provision charges and only 10 percent from the purchase of receivables. The important recent growth of factoring is in part provoked by increasing competition among merchants who wish to offer better payment conditions to their clients without expanding their own working-capital needs. It constitutes a way to introduce products in international markets that otherwise would imply high credit risk.

Brazil's Factoring Regime: Regulation, Supervision, and Tax Treatment

Brazil's laws provide a framework for factoring, although it is fragmented and sometimes lacks clarity. The question of whether factoring is a financial or commercial activity was unclear before 1988. This was clarified by Circular 1359/88, which clearly recognized factoring as a commercial activity to be regulated by commercial law.[18] The specific characteristics of factoring call for a clear legal framework, but today, this is dispersed and incomplete. A draft law (230/95) that seeks to clarify the operational

Table 4.5 Comparison of Factoring Turnover in Brazil and Selected Other Countries, 2000
(US$ millions)

	No. of companies	*Domestic*	*International*	*Total*
Total Europe	435	378,705	35,678	414,383
of which				
France	39	48,250	4,200	52,450
Germany	15	18,660	4,823	23,483
Italy	45	105,000	5,000	110,000
Spain	19	18,870	630	19,500
United Kingdom	70	117,700	6,070	123,770
Total Americas	1,114	139,671	4,578	144,249
of which				
Argentina	5	1,700	15	1,715
Brazil	703	12,000	12	12,012
Chile	25	2,525	125	2,650
Mexico	13	4,970	60	5,030
United States	293	116,000	4,000	120,000
Total world	1,689	596,729	44,843	641,572

Source: Factors Chain International 2001; appendix table A4.7.

and legal framework for factoring has been pending in the Congress for approval for a long period.[19] The law was approved by a commission of the Senate in December 2002. However, several amendments were proposed after the new Congress was reconstituted in 2003, and these are still under discussion. Prospects for the supplementary vote needed in Senate to clear this are indefinite.

The framework for oversight for factoring companies, as commercial companies, is limited. Unfortunately, this situation has been used by some companies to undertake financial intermediation activities under the name of 'factoring.' Draft law 230/95, besides trying to establish a specific legal framework for factoring, supports the creation of a regulatory agency with limited powers. ANFAC has also agreed to enter into a Technical Cooperation Agreement with the Economic Law Secretariat of the Ministry of Justice , which would provide a certificate of qualification and quality to those factoring companies affiliated with ANFAC that comply with the agreement.

In practice, there is no clear distinction in factoring laws in Brazil between financing without recourse and financing undertaken on a recourse basis (accounts receivable financing). In Brazil, financing on a recourse basis is undertaken through a pro solvendo[20] clause in factoring

A Framework of Control for Factoring Activities?

One frequent allegation against factoring companies is that they undertake functions of financial intermediation without authorization. The law governing financial crimes (Law No. 7492/86, "Crimes contra o Sistema Financeiro Nacional") considers criminal those actions in which an institution acts as a financial intermediary without Central Bank authorization. There are also protections against this in Law No. 4595/64, the basic Financial Institutions Law. Despite this, 'false' factoring companies are encountered, which illegally offer remuneration by means of deposit-taking and bond issuance. Some factoring companies offer a menu of services that include both lending and factoring, and thus it is difficult to separate legitimate and less legitimate activities.

Another allegation faced by factoring companies is that some lend at 'abusive' interest rates or extort unfair fees from clients. These allegations are largely based on the old Usury Law of Brazil, which capped real interest rates at 12 percent per year and which financial institutions are not bound by. As nonfinancial enterprises, however, the protection against such allegations for factoring companies, which lies in the purchase of receivables rather than on the charging of interest, is sometimes questioned. Medida Provisória (MP) 1820/99 (reissued as MP 2172/2001) echoed the principle of avoiding excessive interest charges. It is not clear to what extent such activities are really illicit or extortionate. Some factoring companies are now seeking conversion to SCMs (see chapter 2 of this study) to avoid allegations of illicit lending activities and to obtain protections against allegations of usury.

contracts, which allows for the repurchase of receivables by the merchant in case of debtor insolvency. In 1989, after seven years of factoring activity in Brazil, the factoring contract evolved from a cession of credit to a commercial contract, which, however, included some restrictive clauses affecting recourse financing. This contract can be voluntarily altered by the parties if all legal prerequisites are fulfilled. It was deemed in an appeal to the Conselho de Recursos do Sistema Financeiro Nacional (a high-level appeal committee for all financial sector issues) that there is no regulation in the Brazilian legal framework that prohibits the pro solvendo clause.[21]

Tax Regime

To what extent does the tax regime for factoring companies differ from the framework for banks? Does this constitute any advantage or disadvantage for such companies?[22] First, factoring companies, unlike banks, do not pay interest, as there are restrictions against their access to funds from third parties in the market. Thus, they cannot deduct from their income any interest expense, and taxes affect them more heavily. This tax burden is passed to clients as the additional costs of factoring services. Second, as they undertake commercial transactions to purchase receivables, the tax note, invoice, and duplicata (credit right) associated with such sales must be issued. The commercial transaction is subject to the Imposto de Circulação de Mercadorias. Law No. 5474/68 (Article 20) allows service providers to issue invoices and commericial invoices representative of their rights. Next, the service provider is subject to a tax on services, the Imposto sobre Serviços (Tax on Services; ISS), which is locally collected with a tax rate varying from 0.7 percent to 5 percent, depending on location. Sometimes, factoring companies are asked to collect the ISS on overall revenue (service provision plus revenues from purchase of receivables). An additional charge, the COFINS (Contribution for the Financing of Social Security) tax, does not take into account the dual nature of factoring activities, and the tax base includes both the revenues for service provision and the revenue for receivables purchase.[23] Until recently, the COFINS tax, as well as another indirect tax, the PIS (Programa de Integração Social; Program of Social Integration), were also cascading taxes, with implied double taxation; however, recent legislative modifications in 2002 and 2003 have alleviated this.[24]

Third, factors are taxed in the same way as banks in terms of financial transaction taxes. Another indirect tax, the Imposto sobre Operações Financeiras (Tax on Financial Operations; IOF) on financial transactions, which was established by Law No. 9532/97 for credit operations of financial intermediaries, includes factoring companies in its scope (Article 58), although factoring companies are not financial intermediaries. Moreover, factors complain that they should be exempted from the IOF tax. On the other hand, credit transfers (cessão de créditos) between financial intermediaries or between financial intermediaries and leasing companies are not subject to the IOF (Decree 2219/97, Article 8, VII), and factors do not benefit from this. These appear to be contrary to principles of equality of tax treatment.

Factoring: Summary and Key Issues

Factoring is an important alternative to the banking sector for the financing of small and medium enterprises. Given difficulties of entry into the formal banking system, factoring companies have found an important market niche. It is currently a key, if not the main, source of finance for SMEs. Factoring companies work at a much smaller scale than banks, in close association with the creditor. Thus, factoring companies are able to perform a credit risk assessment based on a day-to-day working relationship rather than on financial statements.

Weak bankruptcy and secured transactions laws generate difficulties in the use of collateral in Brazil and create special incentives for forms of financing such as factoring. In general, firms receive financing contingent on their future expected cash flows. Accounts receivables are already expected cash flows and, thus, a company eliminates its clients' business risks through factoring. However, factoring can only provide financing for working capital needs and not for long-term investments.

Factoring enables quick but costly access to financing. But alternatives such as bank credit based on the discount of invoices is not much cheaper, and bank credit in the guise of personal or consumer overdraft facilities are more expensive. Although there are some provisions for credit through public banks such as the FINAME programs of the BNDES for small and medium enterprises and considerably smaller volumes of credit offered by public bodies such as SEBRAE (Brazilian Services to Support Micro and Small Enterprises), a government agency for fostering small-enterprise development, these funds can be obtained only after a bureaucratic process that takes much longer than financing provided by factoring companies. If forthcoming, these other sources of finance can constitute a complement to factoring in the sense that they can be used for long-term investment purposes, while factoring remains a flexible alternative for working capital financing.

Factoring in Brazil has to trade off adequate demand for services it provides against the mitigation of risks by offering recourse financing. One of the key elements of the demand of factoring services is the decrease of nonpayment risk for merchants. Factoring companies are in a privileged position regarding merchants' client credit information. But, with nonrecourse financing (that is, pro soluto), factoring companies bear all the nonpayment risks. In addition, they can finance their activities only with their own resources, funds from partners or shareholders, or bank lines of credit. The combination of those elements could require some recourse financing to alleviate factoring companies' exposure. However, recourse financing requires a very clear and comprehensive legal and supervisory framework that is currently missing in Brazil.

A consolidation of the dispersed legal framework and clarification of factoring with and without recourse is needed. As mentioned before, the legal framework for factoring is dispersed, and the consolidation efforts currently under way are welcome. The legal framework is now unclear with regard to distinguishing between factoring with or without recourse, although there are no impediments to this in the new Civil Code, and jurisprudence has been established that receivables purchase with recourse is a legal activity. This is also normal in other countries. As indicated in the paragraph above, a combination of both could be important for balancing risks, and a clarification could lower costs to the client.

Factoring companies would also benefit greatly if it could be clarified that the usury code would not apply to their legitimate factoring activities. Some allegations of high interest rates charged are clearly due to the continued role played by this now-outdated regulation.

Some structure of oversight may also help to achieve this. Currently, there is no framework of oversight for factoring other than the self-regulatory adoption of the ANFAC *Code of Ethics*. Factoring still has a low public image due to its sometime association with illegal activity and usury. Some closer scrutiny by such an entity of factoring companies that undertake illicit financial intermediation may be useful. However, it must be recognized that, in most countries, factoring would not be subject to the formal supervision needed for deposit-taking financial sector entities, and, thus, care should be taken to structure oversight, bearing in mind the recognition of the contractual and commercial status of this industry. The difficult decision following this is what form of agency could be involved. Supervision of the form undertaken by the Central Bank for financial institutions is not appropriate, nor would it be normally permitted, yet a new agency established for this purpose, even if minimal, could be very costly.

To take advantage of synergies, many factoring companies are associating with microfinance institutions or are even converting to such institutions. There are several advantages to being associated with a microfinance institution: achieving a mantle of respectability by signaling its regulated nature, access to financing, reduction of administrative costs, and use of the client's databases. Some microfinance institutions, the Sociedades de Crédito ao Microempreendedor (microcredit companies; SCMs), are supervised by the Central Bank, as they are considered financial intermediaries, which would confer on factoring companies the status of being 'regulated.' Moreover, SCMs have access to BNDES and multilateral bank financing in addition to their own resources. Owners of factoring companies may also be owners of SCMs and although this does not permit a direct contribution to capital, it can still help to lower shared overhead and enables the sharing of credit information and the establishment of a common collection structure. As of mid-2003, several factoring companies were known to have the same owners as SCMs.

Finally, a simplification of the tax treatment for factoring would contribute to diminishing factoring costs. Almost 25 percent of the 'purchase factor' is due to taxes. The other components are estimated to be opportunity cost (25 percent), risk and profit (25 percent), and operational expenses, including collection expenses for the remaining 25 percent.

Leasing

Origin, Concept, and Evolution

Leasing, known as arrendamento mercantil, accelerated in Brazil from the 1970s, when its core legal framework was also established.[25] Initially consisting largely of government leasing to finance huge civil construction projects, with a limited number of large domestic and foreign banks as lessors, it expanded and diversified in the 1980s when additional banks entered the leasing business. Private companies began to consider leasing as an alternative for long-term investment financing. Leasing to individuals accelerated only at the end of the 1980s and 1990s, with the boom of vehicles leasing.[26]

Leasing is a contract giving the right of possession and use of an asset for an specific period of time in exchange for a flow of payments that cover the asset redemption, financial costs, and taxes plus the lessor's return.[27] When a lease is terminated, the leased asset reverts to the lessor, but the lease agreement can give the lessee the option to purchase the asset or take on a new lease based on the residual value of the asset. Leased assets can include real estate, vehicles, machinery, equipment, and generally any asset able to generate returns. Leasing differs from renting because the asset is gradually redeemed and because there is an option to buy the asset for its residual value. It is different from other forms of financing, as the client receives the asset and not the funds and because during the duration of the lease the ownership of the asset remains with the lessor.

Both financial and operational leases are recognized in Brazil (table 4.6). A *financial* lease is designed for the use of a lessee-specified asset for a long period of time, while an *operational* lease is designed for the use of an existing asset for a short period of time.[28] Financial leasing transfers to the lessee all risks associated with the use of the leased asset. Most financial leases are arranged for new assets. The lessee identifies the asset, arranges for the leasing company to buy it from the manufacturer, and signs the contract with the leasing company. Operational leasing has two components: (1) the financing of the asset and (2) the provision of services (for example, maintenance of the equipment, technical assistance, insurance). In both type of leases, the lessee could be a legal person or an individual.

The tremendous growth of leasing after 1994 followed the macroeconomic success in bringing down inflation, which made it possible to enter into longer-term financial contracts. The boom was sectorally reflected in increased leasing to individuals, mostly for vehicles, despite a parallel decline in leasing to the government, possibly a reflection of client privatization. Leasing volume peaked in 1998, just before the devaluation of the Real, and declined thereafter, back to the level of 1995 by 2000.

Table 4.6 Summary of Characteristics of Financial and Operational Leases in Brazil

Characteristic	*Financial lease*	*Operational lease*
Payment	Payments and other charges are enough for the lessor to (1) recover the cost of the leased asset and obtain a return on the funds invested and (2) freely negotiate the option price of the asset.	Payments and other leasing charges cover the full cost of making the asset available to the lessee; the present value of payments must not be greater than 90 percent of the cost of the asset.
Minimum term	The term of the contract is calculated based on the economic life of the asset; the minimum term is 24 months for assets with an economic life equal or less than five years and 36 months for assets with an economic life of over five years. If these terms are not respected, the transactions is considered a commercial sale.	Ninety days or less than 75 percent of the economic life of the asset, whichever is shorter.
Option to buy	For the lessee, the interest in acquiring the asset can only be executed at the end of the lease contract. The price may be negotiated at contract signature (VRG; price limit: 1–95 percent of the asset cost) or market value at the end of the contract. In the latter, the residual value of the asset is excluded from the calculation base for periodic payment.	Normally, the lessee does not intend to buy the asset, and there is no obligation of a residual payment. However, the lessee may acquire the asset at its market value (Resolutions 2309/96 and 2465/98). There is no VRG.
Services	Maintenance, technical, and operating services are not provided by the lessor.	Maintenance, technical, and operating services may be provided by the lessor.
Option to cancel	The lessee does not have an option to cancel the contract.	The lessee has an option to cancel the lease under the conditions established in the contract.
Asset characteristics	The lessor must acquire the asset according to the specifications of the lessee, exclusively for the leasing operation.	Asset already exists.

Regulatory arbitrage in the tax system has considerably influenced the rises and declines of the leasing industry. The boom in leasing in the late 1990s was significantly also a reflection of the increase of the financial transactions tax (IOF) in May 1997, which rendered leasing more attractive to individuals compared to consumer credit. Consumer credit is subject to the financial transactions tax IOF, while leasing is subject to the tax on services, the ISS. The IOF rate rose from 6 percent to 15 percent of sales value, while the ISS on leasing transactions varied between 0.25 percent to 0.5 prcent of all transactions. This unequal treatment provoked a tax-motivated expansion of leasing activity in the vehicles sector, which, however, declined again due to the reestablished greater equality of tax treatment.

By 1999, the IOF rate declined to 1.5 percent. Meanwhile, new regulations introduced in June 2002 have tried to establish uniform rates for the ISS for leasing across different areas, with a 2 percent minimum to 5 percent maximum rate (Constitutional Amendment No. 37 of June 12, 2002). Preference has swung once again in favor of consumer credit. Moreover, the minimum term of a leasing contract is 24 months, compared to 6 months for consumer loans, which also reduces the attractiveness of leasing in periods of macroeconomic uncertainty. Besides, with direct consumer credit, the ownership and title of the vehicle remain with the consumer, while in leases, the title stays with the lessor.

The steep decline of leasing in 1999 was partly due to macroeconomic events; some leases were dollar denominated or indexed, due to the nominally lower interest rates. With the devaluation of 1999, many lessees suffered difficulties and leasing portfolios shrunk.[29] By 2001, leasing in domestic currency (pré-fixados) represented almost 85 percent of total contracts. Less than 5 percent were indexed to the dollar (4.4 percent), while contracts indexed to domestic rates represented another 11.5 percent (figure 4.5).[30]

Currently, there are around 65 leasing companies or institutions with leasing portfolios in Brazil. Brazilian enterprises obtained about US$5 billion in 2000 from leasing companies, representing around 3 percent of domestic enterprise financing. A large proportion of the top 10 leasing companies include subsidiaries or affiliates of Fiat, Ford, and Daimler Chrysler, although some computer equipment leasing companies (such as IBM) are also present. The 10 largest leasing companies accounted for 70.6 percent of the present value of leasing assets in February 2003 (appendix table A4.6). In terms of asset type, vehicles leasing represented 57.5 percent of total leasing; machines and equipment, 25.5 percent; technology and equipment, 12.3 percent; and others, 4.7 percent by February 2003 (figure 4.6). As observed, there have been dramatic shifts in the asset composition of the leasing industry in the past decade, with the boom and subsequent decline in consumer vehicles leasing.

Figure 4.5 Evolution of the Leasing Portfolio and Operations in Brazil, by Type of Asset, 1990 to February 2003

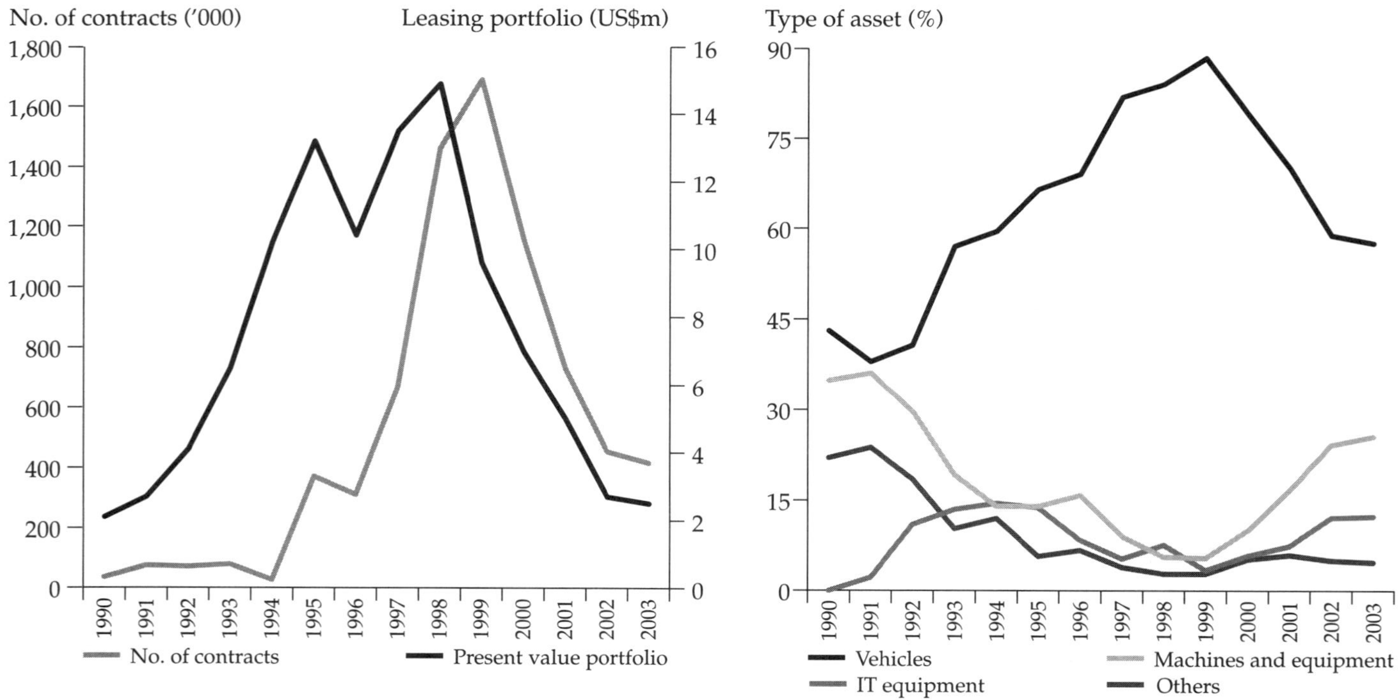

Source: ABEL

Figure 4.6 Types of Indexation in Leasing Contracts in Brazil, 1998 to February 2003

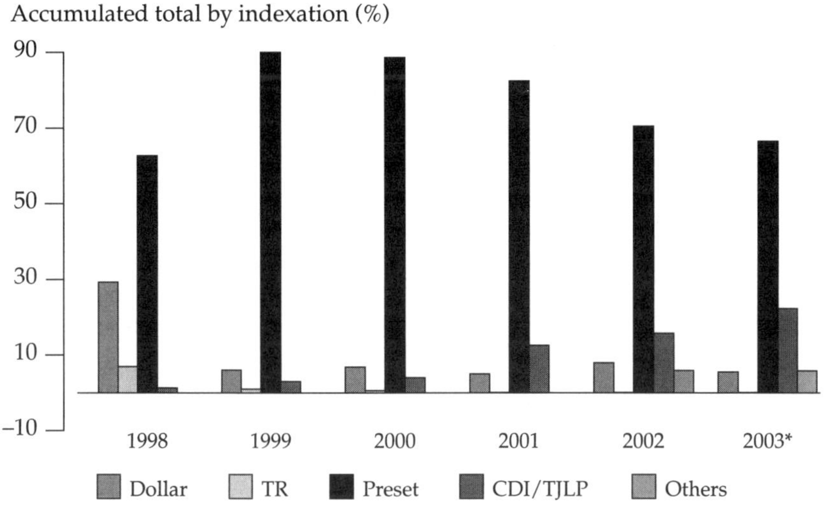

Note: * = preliminary.
Source: ABEL.

In terms of lessee sectors of activity, the service sector showed a big increase over individual leasing from 2001, increasing from 31 percent to 39 percent of activity, while individual leasing declined from 29 percent to 19 percent as vehicle purchasers began to move toward direct consumer credit and away from leasing (figure 4.7).

By international comparisons, Brazil's leasing industry had attained sizeable proportions by 1999, before devaluation (table 4.7). The experience of developed countries suggests a potential for the growth of leasing activity in Brazil, especially operational leasing, or the provision of a service together with adequate maintenance for its efficient use. Effective demand for operational leasing appears to lie mainly in the chemicals, pharmaceuticals, and consumer goods sectors.

International Leasing

International leasing (that is, with a foreign lessor) in Brazil, limited to airplanes in the 1980s, grew in importance in the 1990s.[31] The lessee is considered the importer of the assets if acquired from abroad and, thus, is responsible for the payment of tariffs, freight and insurance, and taxes. Lower nominal interest rates for the lessee have been the attraction,

Figure 4.7 Evolution of Leasing Operations, by Sector, 1993 to February 2003

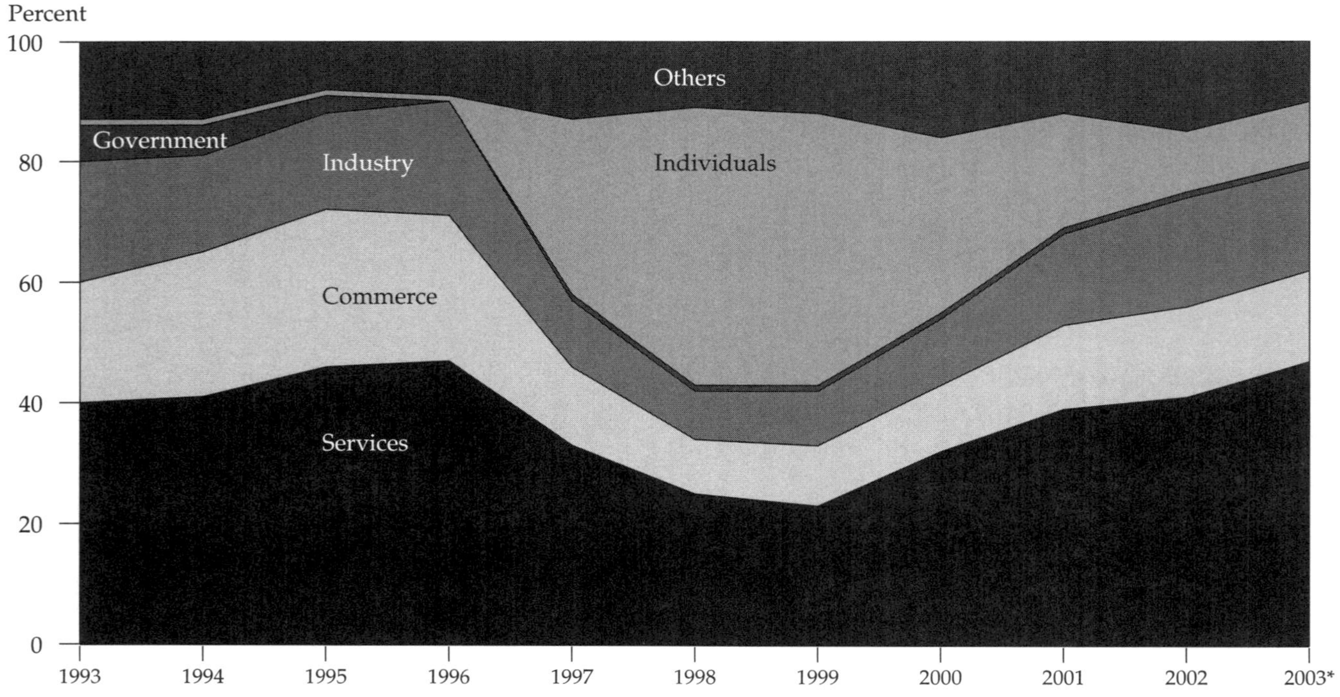

Note: * = preliminary.
Source: ABEL.

Table 4.7 Present Value of Leasing Contracts in Brazil and Other Countries, 1999
(US$ billions)

Countries	*Value*
United States	183,000
Japan	63,000
Germany	37,000
United Kingdom	20,000
France	18,000
Italy	13,600
Brazil	**13,300**

Source: Data provided by ABEL.

together with longer terms. The foreign lessor is also exposed to 'country risk.' International leasing grew in importance from 1996, facilitated by a faster approval process at the Central Bank[32] and a more open balance of payments capital account. International operational leasing has been extensively used for airplanes and also for medical equipment. Other sectors that recently have been active in international leasing in Brazil are power, telecommunications, and infrastructure.

It therefore appears that leasing is an activity mainly for large firms, in which the obsolescence of equipment or the contracting of maintenance for operational leasing makes this an attractive option for investment financing. For individuals, too, leasing appears to be used largely by those who are better off, primarily to acquire vehicles. Thus, leasing today is therefore largely beyond the domain of the less-well-off segments of consumers or small firms.

Legal and Supervisory Framework and Tax Treatment of Leasing

Leasing regulation is fragmented. Law No. 6099/74 defines the tax treatment of commercial leasing, and Law No. 7132/83, which altered Law No. 6099/74, empowered the Central Bank to supervise this activity. As the industry evolved, new resolutions in the 1990s allowed for operational leasing (Resolution 2309/96) and introduced leasing export (Leasing Exportação) with lessees abroad, as a form of 'export' of Brazilian assets.[33] A recent Circular (3036/01) introduced more flexibility in leasing contracts to permit seasonal variations in periodic payments and the lessee's payment capacity. Additional regulations are detailed in appendix table A4.8 and the website of the Associação Brasileira das Empresas de Leasing (ABEL; Brazilian Leasing Companies Association). A dedicated leasing law is under preparation and is due to be submitted to Congress. However, this will take a couple of years to be voted on.

Leasing is a financial activity and is, thus, subject to Central Bank supervision. Lessors must be leasing companies organized as corporations or multiple banks (with a leasing portfolio) or other financial institutions authorized to operate a leasing portfolio. Leasing companies are therefore subject to entry conditions, including minimum capital requirements as established for financial institutions, as well as prudential regulations.

Until recently, prudential regulations on concentration limits that imposed a 25 percent exposure limit to a specific client did not aid the commercial flexibility of this industry. If the primary client of a company is the government (as was historically true for a large part of leasing activity), this rule could be very limiting. Recent modifications to the regulations, however, have eased this.[34]

Tax Regime and Accounting Treatment

Leasing operations may provide tax shields for enterprises because payments are treated as expenses and may be deducted from taxable income. However, individuals cannot deduct lease payments as operational expenses. Also, a 30 percent accelerated redemption of the leased asset to the lessee is permitted, which could aid the distribution of profit flows. Leasing activity is subject to the expected taxes: the service tax ISS, which must be collected in the location where the services were provided. This creates difficulties due to the diversity in ISS rates in different locations and for different economic activities, varying from 0.25 to 5 percent. Leasing is also subject to the federal social contribution tax (Contribuição Social sobre o Lucro; CSSL) and to the social security tax (COFINS) as well as to another social tax, the PIS.

Under conventional accounting practices, leasing also has an accounting advantage in Brazil, as it does not increase a firm's indebtedness ratio. Most leases are recorded as operating leases even though most contracts are capital leases. Thus, lease payments are expensed as incurred, and the lease obligation is not recorded as a liability against capital. Goods leased are accounted for as assets of the lessor, similar to financial leasing. The lessee is therefore able to finance the purchase of the asset without increasing its indebtedness ratio. This accounting treatment is not in line with international standards, in which leases analogous to a financed purchase of an asset are classified as capital leases, and the leased asset and the lease obligation are recognized on the balance sheet.[35]

The Scope forExtension of Leasing

For many products, especially those with high obsolescence, operational leasing may be more appropriate than financial leasing. Moreover, the tax treatment is more favorable for legal persons. This is because in financial leases, the residual value is not deductible, while in operational leases all payments by the lessee are deductible.[36] Lessees also have the flexibility to terminate the contract with two months' notice. Yet true operational leasing in Brazil is limited, and currently, almost all leasing contracts signed in Brazil are de facto financial leases.

This can be explained by a combination of several factors. First, most of the finance providers in leasing contracts are financial intermediaries who lack the interest and expertise in the commercial aspects of leasing, in particular, pricing the residual value of leased assets.[37] Financial intermediaries thus try to avoid the market risk of retaining the leased asset. Second, the lessee's rights of termination in operational leases increases the lessor's exposure to market risk related to the residual value of the leased asset in addition to the normal credit risk related to the creditworthiness of the lessee. Third, the lack of secondary markets for leased assets also impedes the development of operational leasing and makes the pricing of assets even more difficult. Fourth, this may reflect limited competition in the manufacturing industries; in highly competitive environments, commercial companies use operational leasing to help the sale of their products, even if they have to undertake more risks.[38] Fifth, financial intermediaries can access financial resources more cheaply than commercial companies, which tends to further limit the role of real commercial companies in the business. Finally, on the demand side, a cultural preference in favor of ownership is sometimes alluded to, which may also create a preference for financial leasing.

Partnerships between financial intermediaries and commercial companies could constitute a feasible alternative to promote operational leasing. On the one hand, financial intermediaries have cheaper access to financial resources than commercial companies and better access to potential clients' credit information. On the other hand, commercial companies know how to price used assets, have better access to secondary markets (if they exist), or (if not) have the capacity to create them through remarketing activity and better access to potential clients.[39] Increasing competition between supplying enterprises could foster the emergence of these partnerships and promote the emergence of operational leasing, which provides comprehensive services of maintenance and technical assistance in addition to financing. In Brazil, sectors that offer financial leasing sometimes accompany these contracts with a service provision contract, if necessary. Broad-basing this partnership to include a wide spectrum of financial institutions could create the basis for offering operational leasing to small clients.

The sometimes arbitrary treatment accorded to lessors at the time of the depreciation of the Real, and the court judgments in favor of lessees, also led to a loss of faith in the leasing industry and its consequent contraction. The deleterious effects of this form of judiciary activism are discussed further in chapter 6. As mentioned above, the depreciation of the Real in 1999 led to difficulties for many lessees, as many vehicle leasing contracts were indexed to the U.S. dollar.[40] Court rulings determined that these contracts were no longer pegged to the U.S. dollar, and lessees paid the rest of the lease according to arbitrarily defined dollar values, except in cases in which the lessor obtained foreign resources to finance the acquisition of the asset. Some rulings of the Superior Tribunal de Justiça overruled contractual clauses, stating that leasing payments indexed to the dollar constituted an 'excessive' burden for the lessee (based on the Código de Defesa do Consumidor), and substituted the indexation with the consumer price index (Índice Nacional de Preços ao Consumidor), even though this is not a financial index and does not take interest rate evolution into account. In most cases, renegotiation of the contracts with better conditions for the lessee were agreed. This inability to adequately manage risks for the lessor has been a principal cause of the current drop in individual leasing, in particular.

The distinction between leasing contracts and normal commercial sales is sometimes blurred. The Treasury has deemed some leasing operations to be normal commercial sales due to low residual values for the leased asset, indicating that the real purpose of the operation could be tax evasion. But this conclusion has been contested and overturned in some cases in the courts of the Primeira Turma do Superior Tribunal de Justiça and Câmara Superior de Recursos Fiscais. Lack of clarity in treatment is another factor impeding the development of this industry.

Prepayment of the guaranteed residual value (VRG) sometimes has created difficulties for the repossession of the leased asset in cases in which the lessees failed to pay. This has been an important problem in the vehicles sector. In Brazil, lessors in the vehicles sector have accepted traded-in vehicles from the client as a down payment on the new purchase. However, until very recently, leasing contracts could not include a down payment, so it was considered a prepayment of the VRG and, thus, legally regarded as an anticipated purchase option. In these cases, the operation was not considered to be leasing but a normal financial operation for the purchase of an asset and, thus, subject to the alienação fiduciaria process in case of repossession. This process usually takes longer than the repossession in the case of a leasing operation, as the ownership of the asset remains with the lessor.[41] However, a recent court ruling recognized the claim that leasing laws were to apply in such cases. The leasing industry is challenging this in the courts and is awaiting the decision of a pending case before the Justiça, which could resolve this.

Consumer Finance for Individuals and Trade Finance for Enterprises

Consumer Finance Companies

Finance companies (financeiras) are special-purpose nonbank financial institutions referred to in the regulation as SCFIs (Sociedades de Crédito, Financiamento e Investimento; credit, finance, and investment companies). Their activities are subject to regulations for direct consumer credit, most frequently used for installment purchase of consumer goods but also used for vehicles, letters of credit, and refinancing of credit and real estate. Finance companies were originally permitted a wider range of activities, including the financing of trade and, to some extent, construction financing. Their activities were progressively limited in scope during the 1960s and 1970s, to restrict them from taking on the more broad-based intermediation permitted to banks.[42] It is not, therefore, surprising that finance companies are a relatively small segment of the financial system, and their operations have not grown significantly despite the recent boom of consumer lending (figure 4.8). At the end of 2001, finance companies had a portfolio of R$4.4 billion compared to an overall R$70 billion consumer credit portfolio for the entire financial sector. The number of finance companies in Brazil is small, at around 40 over the past two to three years. Like factoring companies, they are mainly concentrated in the state of São Paulo, where more than half the country's finance companies have been located. The others are distributed among 9 other states, leaving 17 states without any finance companies (appendix table A4.3).

The access of such companies to finance is limited; finance companies may not accept deposits or issue commercial invoices or promissory notes. Finance companies may, however, raise financing through assignment of credits (cessão de créditos) to banks and increasingly have obtained capital from their associated banks. Since 1988, when Brazil introduced universal banking, its bank conglomerates (bancos múltiplos) have also engaged in consumer credit, and many finance companies were absorbed into such banks (Resolution 1524 of September 21, 1988). This allowed diversification of their credit portfolio and permitted them to obtain financing through term deposits (which can be issued only by banks). But, many multiple banks are now directly engaged in the consumer credit portfolio, which imposes a higher regulatory burden for finance companies without the benefits of diversifying their portfolios.

Figure 4.8 Finance Companies' Role in Consumer Credit in Brazil

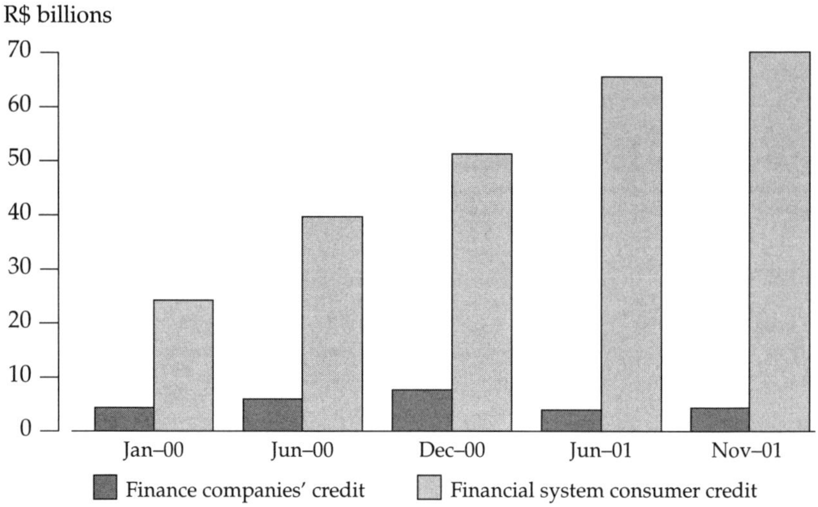

Source: Central Bank of Brazil.

With the launch of the new payments system in April 2002, finance companies claim that costs have increased further, as all banks are direct participants, while finance companies must use their services.

For banks, however, it can still be an advantage to use their finance company subsidiaries for a portion of their consumer lending. First, because finance companies are not deposit-taking institutions, they are not subject to the reserve requirements of banks and can, thus, lend more cheaply, without the burden of this implicit tax. Second, they can access clientele whom banks would find it difficult to accept, given the stringent entry requirements for the opening of bank accounts. Thus, finance companies can also serve the objective of providing a diversified image and product for lower-income consumers, with a dedicated brand name and marketing techniques and different entry requirements. Finally, a large proportion of finance companies' consumer credit assets are secured by liens, under the alienação fiduciaria em garantia system, and creditors may take possession of the asset and sell it in case of nonpayment. This has been particularly successful for automobiles, although more difficult to impose on other consumer durables due to the absence of clear title and ownership registration. Such assets can therefore be sold by their owners when the execution of a guarantee is required.

Finance companies have therefore lost some of their original rationale, which was clearer in the years before multiple banking. Their continued role is largely due to regulatory distinctions in reserve requirements (which are not required due to their non-deposit-taking nature) and in entry requirements, both of which can lower lending costs, but this has to be counterbalanced by possibly increased service costs, recently, for the use of the payments system. Another role played by finance companies is in aiding product and market differentiation to serve different market segments. The principal difficulty impeding the growth of the finance companies' business is the high costs of funding, given their lack of access to deposits, which has also acted as a disincentive to the continued survival of independent small-scale finance companies. In addition, they face high costs originating in a high proportions of nonperforming loans, which require provisioning.

Finally, finance companies also have to face the challenge of the persistently high informal economy. Post-dated checks are a better accepted instrument in the Brazilian market than bills of exchange, which can also be discounted at banks, which is an advantage in terms of capturing the consumer credit business.

Brazil's finance companies enjoy the benefit of a trade association, ACREFI (Associação Nacional das Instituições de Crédito, Financiamento e Investimento; National Association of Credit, Finance, and Investment Institutions), established in 1958 to promote their objectives.[43] ACREFI has 61 associated members, including 'pure' finance companies as well as those that have been transformed into or absorbed by multiple banks.

Trade Finance and Vendor Credit

Vendor or supplier credit, used to finance sales, is the least expensive form of credit, with one of the lowest default rates. As indicated in figure 4.1, vendor credit has represented a stable proportion of finance to enterprises, averaging around 5 to 6 percent. Products are sold on credit by the seller who receives cash back from the bank. The seller transfers its credit to the bank, which charges an intermediation fee, pays the seller, and finances the buyer. Apart from the elimination of credit risk, the seller is able to offer a more competitive price based on reduced working capital costs and a smaller receivables account. As financing costs are excluded from the invoice price, the seller also has the advantage of lower value-added taxes. Vendor credit averaged 72 days of financing in December 2000, a term longer than the usual 30 days granted by suppliers. Transactions may be with fixed interest rates (30–90 days), floating interest rates (120–360 days), or exchange rate indexed (90–180 days). Vendor credit is executed through three instruments: (1) a contract to open a line of credit between the financial institution and the seller; (2) a contract among the financial institution, the seller, and the buyer; and (3) documents corresponding to each credit transaction. Collateral, such as promissory notes, is generally required. Although some companies use supplier credit as their favored way of financing working capital, this is not usual. The availability of such credit would depend on the creditworthiness of the potential creditor.

New forms of finance through the discounting of credit card receivables are also emerging. Although genuine credit card use is still limited in Brazil (as most cards are, in fact, debit cards or payable in full every month), retailers can discount credit card receivables in banks or at credit card companies. Receivables in this case may not be represented by certificates but by a book entry note, which may make this less secure from the point of view of legal recovery.[44] There is, however, growth potential for this form of financing.

Another emerging alternative form of financing is through franchises. In this case, the franchiser provides not only the brand name and products, as is common in other countries, but also financing for the retailer for terms that vary between 45 and 90 days. This is a relatively new form of financing in Brazil, which began in the past decade.

Finally, there are specialized channels for trade finance for export promotion incorporated into the formal credit market. Although not explored in detail here, they are briefly described in the present section. As shown in table 3.10 and figure 4.1, trade finance forms a relatively large part of total enterprise finance in Brazil, amounting to around one-third of outstanding loans and 10 to 15 percent of new loans. In Brazil, there are two formal instruments to promote export activities; the Adiantamento de Contrato de Câmbio (Advance on Exchange Contract; ACC) and Adiantamento de Contrato de Exportação (Advance on Exportation Contract; ACE). Programs associated with these are based on receivables expected from exports and are, thus, similar to export letters of credit. ACCs are extended for terms of up to six months, while ACEs are for up to two years. These credit facilities are open only to well-established businesses and, especially in the case of ACEs, require the exporter to have good credit records. Thus, present forms of export financing favor established businesses and suggest, however, that there may be good opportunities for international factoring to promote export activities for start-up or small firms that do not have easy access to financial services.

5
Channeling Rural Finance

A large part of the issue of financial access that has occupied the attention of policymakers in Brazil has been the problem of access to specialized financial services in sectors where it has been particularly difficult to attract private finance. Two areas of the financial system that stand out in this context are rural financial services and access to housing finance. A substantial part of the system of targeted or earmarked credit, which has existed for decades in Brazil, arose because of the need to address these specialized credit needs. The present chapter examines the evolution of one of these areas: rural finance. The chapter evaluates the rationale for and cost of the present system and discusses other options for meeting these needs.[1]

Specialized Finance and Directed Credit in Brazil

Many have pointed out that rural finance faces special difficulties and thus merits special solutions. There are, first, geographic issues of access in remote rural areas. These are combined with typically high rates of poverty, lower population densities, isolated markets, highly covariant risks, limited opportunities for risk diversification, sharp seasonal variations in income and in the demand for and supply of financial resources, and lack of traditional collateral. All these factors result in high transaction costs and higher perceived risk in providing financial services in rural areas.[2] It is argued that, as a result, credit to rural markets is 'rationed' in the sense that lenders tend to limit quantity, even if prices are flexible.

Traditionally, governments have tended to address the challenges of rural financial intermediation via some combination of the following policies: sectorally directed credit (quantity controls), combined with lower-than-market interest rates (price controls), and budgetary or off-budget support, often funneled through publicly owned banks, with the volume of agricultural credit disbursed as the key performance indicator.[3] Although governments have succeeded in thus channeling substantial resources to rural areas, there has been less emphasis on loan recovery and institutional sustainability, on serving nonagricultural rural activities that can help to spread risks, or on strengthening intermediation by mobilizing rural savings. Such traditional interventions have often resulted in poor loan portfolios and institutionally unsustainable rural financial institutions, leading to costly failures arising from incentive problems and poor governance.

Brazil's response to the challenge of rural finance has been similar to those described above. In Brazil, as in many other countries, selective or directed credit has been channeled largely through public financial entities, either directly or through onlending arrangements with private financial entities. Brazil's largest banks, the Banco do Brasil and the Caixa Econômica Federal, have served as the primary vehicles for channeling credit to the rural and housing sectors, respectively. There are also mandated private sector programs for directed credit: 25 percent of unremunerated demand deposits must be devoted to rural finance, and 65 percent of passbook savings deposits are earmarked for housing loans.

Directed credit shrank after mid-2000, following the government-financed restructuring of the federal banks that removed a substantial volume of directed credit from their books in exchange for government debt. But despite the decline from about 54 percent of total credit in June 2000 to about 38 percent in March 2002, directed credit remained high, and the proportions going toward housing and rural credit also remained high (figure 5.1). Both banks suffered in differing degrees from problems with their loan portfolios and less-than-adequate attention to operational efficiency, resulting in the portfolio quality difficulties that eventually led to their recapitalization in June 2001.

In Brazil, the provision of large volumes of directed credit has been sustained over time partly because of the financing of such credit by off-budget taxes, such as the Fundo de Garantia do Tempo de Serviço or indemnity fund (FGTS) and the Fundo de Amparo ao Trabalhador or Workers' Support Fund (FAT), and by earmarked constitutional funds, thus representing an implicit tax on the beneficiaries of these funds. As discussed further below, a large part of this directed credit has failed to meet intended targets, with better-off farmers, for example, capturing much of the subsidies rather than the poorer groups for whom the subsidies are intended. In agriculture, the largest 2 percent of the borrowers received 57 percent of the loans, while the smallest 75 percent of borrowers received only 6 percent of credit.[4]

Apart from such questions regarding the appropriateness of the targeting of directed credit, the present system of directed credit is expensive to sustain. In 2002, volumes of free credit and directed credit amounted to around R$212 billion and R$143 billion, respectively. According to one set of estimates based on simplified assumptions, assuming all directed credit is at the Taxa de Juras de Longo Prazo (TJLP) or long-term interest rate, and assuming all free credit is at the SELIC (Sistema Especial de Liquidação e Custodia; interbank) rate, which is a lower bound, the gov-

Figure 5.1 Trends and Composition of Directed Credit, 2000–02

Free and directed credit

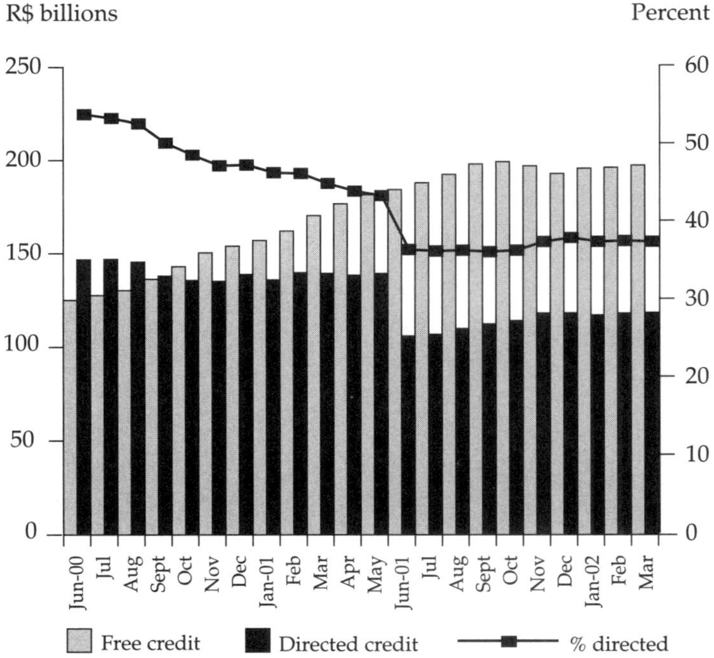

Composition of directed credit

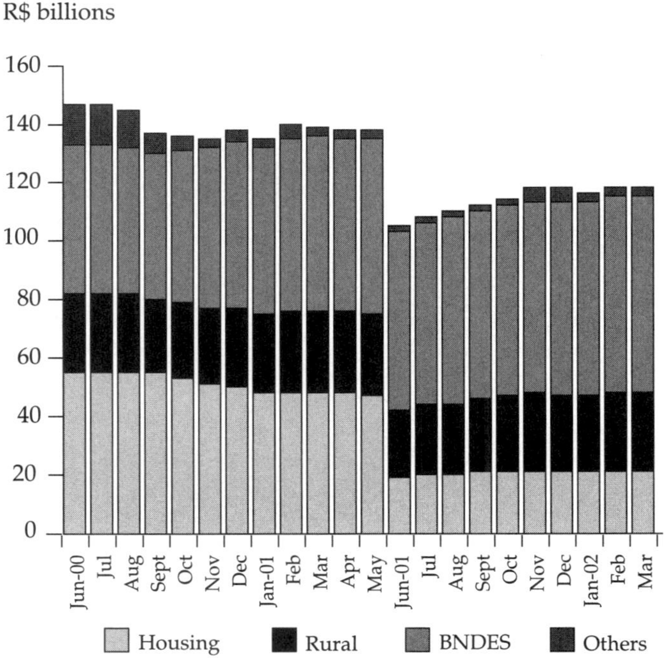

Note: BNDES = Banco Nacional de Desenvolvimento Econômico e Social.
Source: World Bank staff based on data from the Central Bank of Brazil.

ernment financial outlay involved would amount to around R$18.6 billion or some 5 percent of total credit. Even if we refine this estimate, separating the volumes of rural and housing credit and credit channeled through the National Development Bank (the Banco Nacional de Desenvolvimento Econômico e Social or BNDES), adjusting interest rates, and adding a spread for BNDES lending, the broad parameters of the subsidy element involved remain unchanged.[5] These are conservative estimates. An attempt to calculate the full subsidies in only the National Program to Strengthen Family Agriculture (Programa Nacional de Fortalecimiento da Agricultura Familiar [PRONAF]) estimated the subsidies at R$1.1 billion, as discussed later in this chapter.

The next three sections of this chapter describe the present system in Brazil and evaluate its efficiency. This is followed by a discussion of broad approaches to widen access based on newer international paradigms.

The principal findings and conclusions of this chapter are presented below.

- The Brazilian rural financial system today, contrary to best practice, has limited outreach at high cost instead of mass outreach at low cost. Most rural households have no access to formal financial services. Credit remains highly concentrated, with three-quarters of all clients receiving less than 6 percent of credit, while the top 2 percent of contracts accounted for 57 percent of all credit.
- Public sector programs and institutions play a predominant role in the national rural credit system, and these have crowded out the private provision of credit at market rates. Freely provided private sector resources have declined to as little as 5 percent of formal rural credit.
- Brazil needs to implement a gradual but credible transition program to market-determined interest rates on all rural credit and savings. Although overnight removal may create at least a transitory decline in the allocation of resources to the rural sector and may not be politically acceptable, steps to mitigate the effects can be taken. (1) There could be increases in subsidized rates on the most heavily subsidized programs, notably PRONAF, whose enormous, timely repayment rebates result in highly negative nominal interest rates. (2) Phased rates could also be applied to the 25 percent directed lending requirement. (3) Although the special privileges of the Banco do Brasil, in the form of the equalization payments for administering subsidized funds, have been ended, other financial institutions could be encouraged to compete actively for this role.
- In parallel, remaining subsidies can be explicitly monitored and budgeted and refocused away from interest rates to transaction costs. Subsidies have largely been captured by well-to-do farmers and

nonfarming corporations, for whom there is no justification for a credit subsidy on either equity or efficiency grounds. The net impact has been to inflate rural land prices, because subsidies are capitalized into the value of land. Another effect of subsidies has been to promote a more regressive rural income distribution. There is an urgent need to apply a more uniform approach in applying lending interest rates in such programs, because ultimately public funds finance both the relatively efficient and largely self-sustaining programs like CrediAmigo and the highly subsidized programs like PRONAF.

- Brazil can try to address information and insurance constraints to reduce risks in rural lending. The potential is good for advancing a range of related financial instruments for risk management: price risk management for agricultural commodities, area-based index insurance, and warehouse receipts. These instruments allow farmers to increase their specialization and adopt higher-risk, higher-return production strategies.
- In a wider context, strengthening rural finance requires attention to the same issues as those affecting overall financial intermediation: addressing issues of high spreads, high administrative costs, and relatively high profits for banks operating in Brazil versus in comparable economies, combined with high financial sector taxation.
- Finally, Brazil could benefit from greater support to innovation and research in rural finance.

Overview of Rural Finance in Brazil

Basic Model and Volumes of Overall Credit

The Brazilian agricultural finance system has witnessed some significant changes in the last decade. Much of the budgetary support that was given to the sector in the past has been removed in recent years, and price supports to agricultural produce, and the resulting storage costs borne by the government, have either been eliminated or reduced substantially. However, agriculture still benefits significantly from concessional credit through both budgetary and earmarked off-budget sources. This credit is channeled substantially through three federal banks, especially Banco do Brasil, as is directed or mandated credit, and is subject to both quantitative and price controls.

Directed credit is implemented via a 25 percent mandatory lending requirement on all demand deposits in the banking system, which can either be deposited with the Central Bank without remuneration or used for lending to agriculture at controlled interest rates.[6] Ceiling lending interest rates set by the government were highly negative in real terms

Figure 5.2 Nominal and Real Interest Rates in Rural Credit in Brazil, 1995–2001

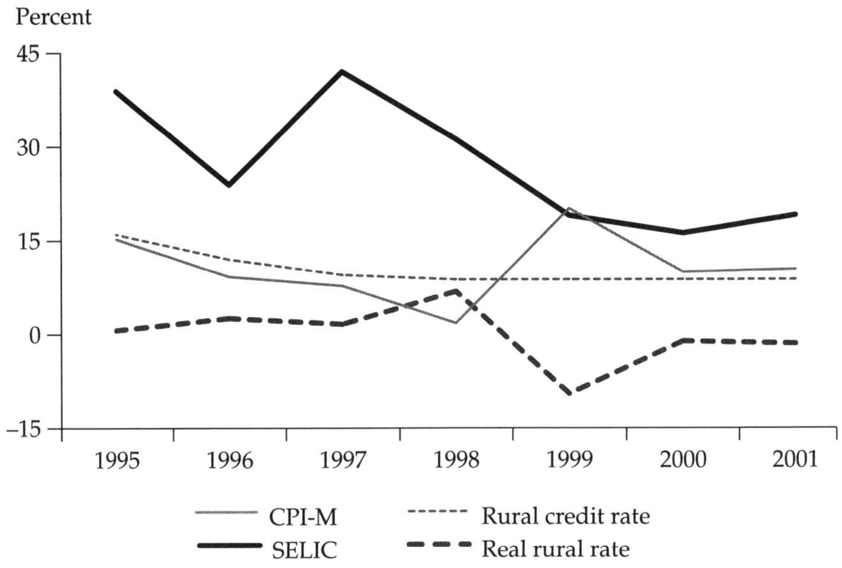

Source: Central Bank of Brazil.

prior to the Real Plan in 1995, as inflation soared above 1,000 percent. However, recently, with an exception in 1998, rates turned positive for a brief period in the late 1990s, although they remained substantially below reference market rates such as the SELIC rate (figure 5.2). Thus, the present agricultural credit system broadly follows the 'traditional' model outlined above.

In terms of total volume, over time there have been sharp variations in the amount of credit provided to agriculture. In real terms, volumes of credit were as high as R$51.7 billion in 1975, declining to a low of below R$5 billion in 1993. Real credit rose again thereafter, to R$13.8 billion by the end of the decade for the 2000 crop season, and further to R$21 billion in 2002. Although still substantially below their peak (figure 5.3 and table 5.1), a new upward trend may be emerging.

Principal Players: Demand for Rural Finance

On the demand side, close to 20 percent of Brazil's population, or approximately 35 million people, and an estimated 4.8 million rural establish-

Figure 5.3 Credit Flows to Agriculture: Reductions with Fluctuation, 1969–2002

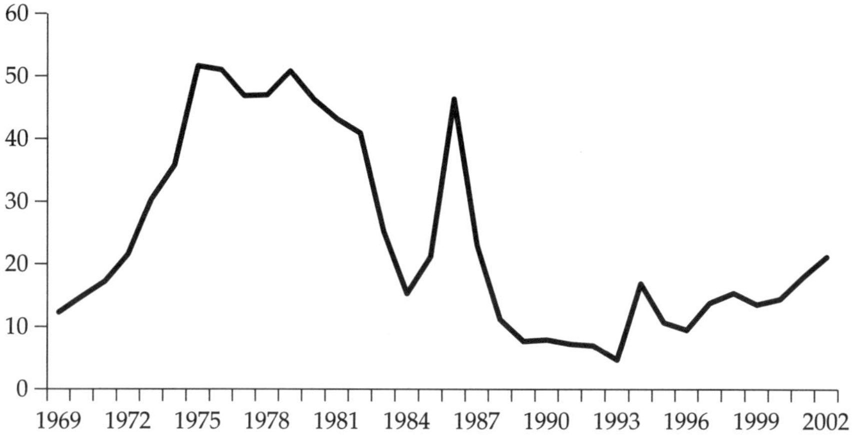

Note: In millions of constant 2001 Reais, deflated by IGP–DI index.
Source: Central Bank of Brazil 2001a.

Table 5.1 Aggregate Credit to the Rural Sector in Brazil, 1969–2002

Year	*Value (R$m)*	*Year*	*Value (R$m)*	*Year*	*Value (R$m)*
1969	12,297	1981	43,170	1993	4,713
1970	14,796	1982	40,910	1994	16,889
1971	17,206	1983	25,275	1995	10,690
1972	21,562	1984	15,286	1996	9,493
1973	30,364	1985	21,174	1997	13,809
1974	35,827	1986	46,348	1998	15,364
1975	51,667	1987	23,008	1999	13,556
1976	51,042	1988	11,198	2000	14,433
1977	46,851	1989	7,711	2001	17,942
1978	46,979	1990	7,936	2002	21,170
1979	50,835	1991	7,271	n.a.	n.a.
1980	46,289	1992	6,988	n.a.	n.a.

Note: n.a. = not applicable. In millions of constant 2001 Reais, deflated by IGP–DI index.
Source: Central Bank of Brazil 2001a.

Table 5.2 Concentration of Agricultural Landholdings in Brazil
(percent)

Size (hectares)	*Farm units*	*Total area*
0–10	49.43	2.23
10–50	31.20	9.97
50–100	8.24	7.76
100–500	8.47	23.57
500–1,000	1.23	11.36
Above 1,000	1.43	45.11
Total	100.00	100.00

Source: Kessel 2001.

ments, or farm units, constitute the client base for rural financial services. Brazil has an extremely skewed land distribution, with the wealthiest 1 percent of farmers accounting for 45 percent of landholdings and the poorest 50 percent of farmers holding just 2 percent of agricultural land (table 5.2).

There are also significant regional distinctions in the rural clientele. The northern Amazon region has limited agricultural potential and small, scattered populations; the semiarid Northeast region has the highest concentrations of poverty, particularly among inland smallholdings producing nontradable crops; the Central–West region is characterized by large landholdings with a heavy emphasis on production of Brazil's main crop, soy, for export; the Southeastern region includes the wealthier state of São Paulo, with an agricultural hinterland for Latin America's largest city and the less-wealthy states north of São Paulo; and the South includes three states that account for close to 50 percent of Brazil's agricultural GDP, and has the longest tradition of cooperative organization in Brazil.

Principal Sources: Credit Supply

The principal sources of funding for rural credit include (1) mandatory lending of 25 percent of all demand deposits; (2) private bank resources (deposits and borrowings) freely lent to the agricultural sector; (3) the rural savings (*poupança*) program of federal banks, whereby rural savings are channeled to rural credit; (4) the Workers' Support Fund or FAT (Fundo de Amparo ao Trabalhador); (5) constitutionally mandated allocations of taxes to rural credit in the Northern, Northeastern, and Central–West regions (Constitutional Funds or FCOs [Fundos Constitucionais]); and (6) resources from the National Treasury.[7] As of November 2001, the total outstanding loan portfolio for agriculture amounted to about R$26.7 billion, equivalent to 8 percent of the loan portfolio of the banking system, and to 33 percent of agricultural GDP, which was close to R$80 billion for 2000 (figure 5.4).

There have been marked changes in the relative share of resources provided by different sources of funds (table 5.3 and figure 5.5). In 1995, Treasury resources accounted for more than 20 percent of total credit extended, but by 2000, the Treasury's share of lending had declined to zero, although there was a small reemergence in 2001 and 2002. Similarly, free resources of banks accounted for close to 20 percent of total financing of the sector in 1995 but remained at around 5 percent between 1998 and 2002. On the other hand, the share of the banks' obligatory resources, or, in other words, the 25 percent of the value of demand deposit accounts earmarked to finance agriculture, increased from around 20 percent in 1995 to more than 50 percent in 2000 and 59 percent in 2001, declining somewhat to 53 percent by 2002.

This suggests that the growth of lending to the sector has been related to the growth of demand accounts in the banking sector. This is noteworthy because much of the subsidy embedded in this arrangement is left with the financial institutions, which are able to choose the best and most risk-free borrower. Thus, subsidies do not necessarily reach targeted small producers. Funding from rural savings fluctuated between 10 and 19 percent between 1998 and 2002. The share of BNDES/FINAME increased somewhat, from 4.1 percent in 1998 to 7.2 percent in 2002, and there has been some increase in the share of the Constitutional Funds (from 2.7 percent to 4.7 percent).

Public Programs and Federal Banks

The principal financial institutions involved in rural agriculture have been the three federal banks: the Banco do Brasil, which operates nationally, and the Banco do Nordeste and Banco da Amazônia. Private banks play an important role in channeling public funds and the mandatory allocations of their demand deposits to agriculture, and in certain rural areas, particularly in the South, they mobilize deposits for lending in urban areas.[8] Credit cooperatives, which were discredited and almost disappeared entirely during the 1980s, are making a gradual comeback, as discussed in chapter 2. Production cooperatives act as channels for loans to their members, but they are not allowed to mobilize deposits. Microfinance is insignificant in the rural sector, and traditional moneylenders play a minor role, although they can be important for poorer rural households, particularly before the harvest. Another growing source of finance is trade credit and supplier credit from local merchants, fertilizer companies, and wholesalers. These sources frequently provide credit for prearranged sales, especially through the bills of exchange or CPRs (Cédula de Produto Rural), described below.

Figure 5.4 Flow of Funds under the National Rural Credit System

Sources of funds →	*Intermediaries* →	*Programs/types of credit* →	*Beneficiaries*
1. Mandatory bank funds	1. Banco do Brasil	1. Nonspecific lines of credit	1. Individual agricultural producers operating family farm
2. Noncontrolled bank resources	2. Banco do Nordeste	2. PRONAF	2. Large-scale farm enterprises
3. Constitutional funds	3. Banco da Amazônia	3. Crop-specific or input-specific lines of credit	3. Members of credit cooperatives
4. Workers' Support Fund (FAT)	4. State banks		4. Agroenterprises
5. Rural savings (Poupança Rural)	5. Private banks		
6. Treasury resources	6. Credit cooperatives		

Source: Bank staff.

Table 5.3 Sources of Finance for Rural Credit in Brazil, 1995–2002
(R$ millions)

Sources	*1995*	*1997*	*1998*	*1999*	*2000*	*2001*	*2002*
Freely allocated resources	1,710.4	591.8	522.4	581.3	651.8	722.4	1,159.4
Obligatory resources	1,389.7	4,417.4	4,538.5	4,887.7	7,137.6	10,577.9	11,832.6
Rural savings	3,848.4	828.7	1,450.2	2,218.9	1,976.1	1,851.9	2,827.7
FAT—Workers' Fund	0.0	1,813.2	1,946.7	1,931.7	1,751.1	1,789.4	2,283.5
Constitutional Funds	962.1	555.0	1,039.1	914.5	806.4	1,084.4	1,544.6
BNDES/FINAME	—	332.6	516.8	595.9	779.6	1,082.2	1,623.5
FUNCAFÉ[a]	—	354.5	617.3	571.4	296.4	194.7	501.8
National Treasury	2,138.0	148.1	185.4	13.7	2.6	289.1	376.6
INCRA/PROCERA[b]	—	45.6	124.3	37.4	4.3	273.0	214.8
Other sources	641.4	752.6	503.1	239.6	373.6	77.0	78.9
Total	10,689.9	9,839.5	11,443.8	11,992.1	13,779.5	17,942.1	22,443.3

Note: — = not available.
a. FUNCAFÉ is the coffee support fund or Fundo de Defesa da Economia Cafeeíra.
b. INCRA is Instituto Nacional de Colonização e Reforma Agrária; PROCERA is the Land Reform Program.
Source: Santo 2001; Central Bank of Brazil 2000, 2001. (See appendix tables A5.1, A5.1a to A5.1e, and A5.3 for further details.)

Figure 5.5 Sources of Funds for Agricultural Credit: Increased Obligatory Lending

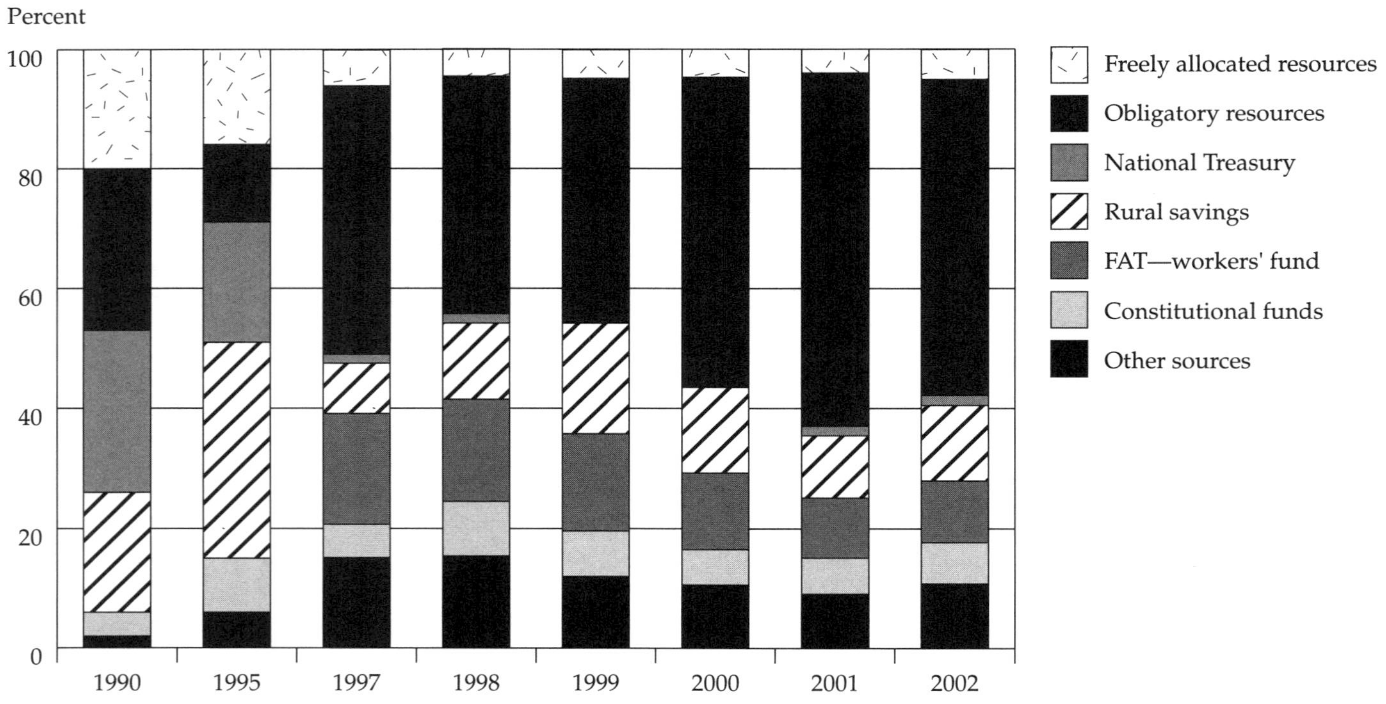

Source: Kessel 2001.

Banco do Brasil and Rural Credit

Banco do Brasil is the largest provider of rural credit in Brazil, particularly of small-farmer credit through the PRONAF program, and it also administers a series of other agricultural funds such as PRODECER, or FUNCAFÉ, funded by earmarked taxes. Banco do Brasil is therefore a key player in increasing access to rural finance. With total assets of R$157 billion, a domestic distribution network of 8,300 branches and service centers, more than 32,000 ATMs, and almost 90,000 staff as of September 2001, the state-owned Banco do Brasil is by far the largest bank in Latin America. On the other hand, a large share of its assets is kept in liquid investments, and only R$40 billion is dedicated to credit operations, of which R$11.5 billion is classified as rural and agribusiness loans. With shareholders' capital of only R$8.2 billion, Banco do Brasil is highly leveraged by Basle standards, and yet its return on equity is relatively low, at 12 percent as of the third quarter of 2001. The total deposits of R$73 billion account for less than half of total liabilities and net worth, and almost one-quarter of liabilities are obtained via open market funding. Personnel and administrative expenses are relatively high, amounting to 5.5 percent of credit operations as of September 2001, while provisions amount to 6 percent of the loan portfolio.

There has been a proposal to increase private equity participation in Banco do Brasil. The proposed listing on the Novo Mercado may not substantially improve governance because minority private shareholders cannot have a seat on the board of directors, and international evidence suggests that they are unlikely to have an impact on a public bank's performance. Private participation would have to be greater to have a real impact on governance. Banco do Brasil does have a well-established banking franchise, but its sustainability depends on reducing its high-cost and nonperforming loans. Banco do Brasil relies more heavily on deposits than do Caixa and BNDES, but these include deposits from special funds. A substantial share of its deposits in 2001 came from special deposits, including R$13 billion from judicial deposits. About 7 percent of Banco do Brasil's funds in 2001 came from Constitutional Funds and onlending from BNDES, FINAME, Caixa Econômica Federal, and other financial institutions. Banco do Brasil is the Treasury agent for the Central–West Constitutional Fund, FCO.

Source: Central Bank of Brazil, staff discussions.

Banco do Brasil has maintained its predominant role with more than 4,200 branches nationwide, accounting for 61 percent of loans granted and 43 percent of the credit extended, with an average loan size of R$6,700 in 2000. Other federal and state banks together accounted for around 17

Inconsistent Public Support: PRONAF versus CrediAmigo

PRONAF, a national program to strengthen family farming, started operations in 1995. It benefits agricultural producers who rely on family labor by allowing them to borrow cheap funds at an interest rate of from 1 to 4 percent, which was negative in real terms in 1999. The maximum loan amounts under this program are R$5,000 for working capital and R$15,000 for investments in fixed assets. The program's volume of lending has grown and accounted for about 16.3 percent of total agricultural lending in 1999, compared with about 13.1 percent in 1998. Banco do Brasil is its main implementing agency, extending R$0.87 billion in PRONAF loans in 1999, benefiting about 450,000 families. Loans averaged R$2,000 each. The plans for 2000 indicated similar amounts. The resources for PRONAF come from the FAT program, and the Ministry of Finance covers the difference between the actual cost and the low lending interest paid by the borrowers.

According to Banco do Brasil, its PRONAF loan collection performance is about 97 to 98 percent. With these high repayment rates, PRONAF is considered successful in an environment that has become used to poor financial discipline and low loan recovery. But the low lending interest rate should be a matter of concern, because nothing seemed to justify lending at negative real interest rates in 1999, when the lion's share of the farming households had neither access to formal credit nor a chance to obtain it in the foreseeable future. Setting the lending rate higher would have allowed, other things remaining equal, the expansion of lending to this clientele, because the accumulation of interest revenue would have made the program more financially independent and less susceptible to reductions in budgetary allocations, which were needed to continue financing the program. The low lending interest rate can be contrasted to that of CrediAmigo, discussed in chapter 2 of this study, which charges much higher interest rates.

In 2002, PRONAF realized 965 million contracts for a total of R$2.3 billion. PRONAF also extends loan guarantees. It is now pioneering the introduction of rural credit through magnetic cards for proven good borrowers. PRONAF has begun to accept certificates of borrowing capacity extended by third parties, such as technical assistance organizations or labor unions. Although it is true that microfinance is used with nonagricultural activities and personal loans, and PRONAF is also used for agriculture, current expenditures, and investments, there is a need to apply a more uniform approach in applying lending interest rates in such programs, because ultimately public funds finance them both. Many clients of CrediAmigo are poorer than PRONAF's clients.

percent of total loan contracts but only 9 percent of total credit. In contrast, private banks accounted for 15 percent of contracts but 43 percent of credit extended in 2000, with an average loan size of R$28,600, about four times larger than the average Banco do Brasil loan amount (appendix table A5.6). Credit cooperatives, with average loans of around R$7,500 each, accounted for 5 percent of loans and 6 percent of credit extended in 2000.

A large proportion of funding channeled by public and private banks to the rural sector is earmarked through a series of special programs (figure 5.4 and appendix table A5.2). The key programs are PRONAF, launched in 1994, and a series of crop-specific programs channeled through the second-tier national development bank, BNDES, for products such as coffee, milk, cashews, wine, ornamental horticulture, and aquaculture, and for modernization of the tractor fleet. The underlying purpose of some of these programs is to provide income support. PRONAF is more a social or income-support-oriented program than a commercial program.

Loan terms to agriculture are highly preferential, with a standard rate of 8.75 percent for most lines of credit using mandatory funds (appendix table A5.7). Interest rates reach 10.75 percent for tractor loans of more than R$250,000 under the MODERFROTA program and 11.95 percent for equipment purchase or maintenance loans under a Resolution of the National Monetary Council 2662, October 28, 1999. On the other hand, family farm loans under PRONAF range from 1 to 4 percent (table 5.4), with substantial timely payment incentives for some categories of clients, although mandatory life insurance and compensatory balances can raise the costs to farmers to 9 percent. Finally, agricultural loans in arrears prior to 1995 have typically been renegotiated at rates of 3 percent over 25 years.

In 2002, a change was introduced in the PRONAF program to permit the use of directed credit, the 25 percent of the value of demand accounts, in financing PRONAF lending. However, if used for loans to PRONAF, only 80 percent of this amount can be counted against the 25 percent mandatory requirement. Thus, PRONAF is entitled to use up to 31.25 percent of the value of demand accounts as a low-cost source instead of the 25 percent for a regular agricultural loan, or 25 percent × [1/0.8] = 31.25 percent. This change is reflected in the reversal of the stagnation of PRONAF volumes of lending in recent years (figure 5.6).

These rates compare with market lending rates of 18 to 25 percent for agricultural loans provided by banks and cooperatives in 2002, using freely allocated resources. Typical corporate lending rates outside agriculture were then around 18 percent and reached 55 to 60 percent for consumer credit. This compared with inflation of 9.5 percent in 2001, an interbank rate (SELIC) of around 19 percent, and deposit rates of 10 percent. With regard to repayment periods, two-thirds of all credit is sea-

Table 5.4 PRONAF Low-Cost Loans to Family Farms

Category	*Target clientele*	*Loan amounts*	*Nominal annual interest rate (%)*	*Other loan terms*
Investment: Group A	Agrarian reform beneficiaries with no earlier investment loans	R$4,000–R$12,000	1	One-time only; 40% rebate for timely repayment; <10 years with <5 year grace
Investment: Group B	Farmers and rural workers in th Northeast Region with income <R$1,500	<R$500	1	40% rebate for timely repayment; <2 years with <1 year grace
Investment: Group C	Income between R$1,500 and R$10,000, no employees	Seasonal: R$500–R$2,000 Investment: R$1,500-R$5,000	4	Same as above; R$200 rebate for timely repayment of seasonal loan, 25% for term loan; Investment loans: <8 years with <5 years grace
Investment: Group D	Income between R$10,000 and R$30,000; <2 employees; <4 rural farm modules land size;[a] owner lives on/near farm	Seasonal: <R$5,000 Investment: <R$15,000	4	Investment loans: <8 years with <5 years grace; 25% rebate for timely repayment of investment loans

a. A rural farm module varies by region, from 18 hectares in the South to 75 hectares in the Northeast.
Source: Ministry of Agricultural Development 2000; Central Bank of Brazil 2000a.

Figure 5.6 Rural Credit from PRONAF

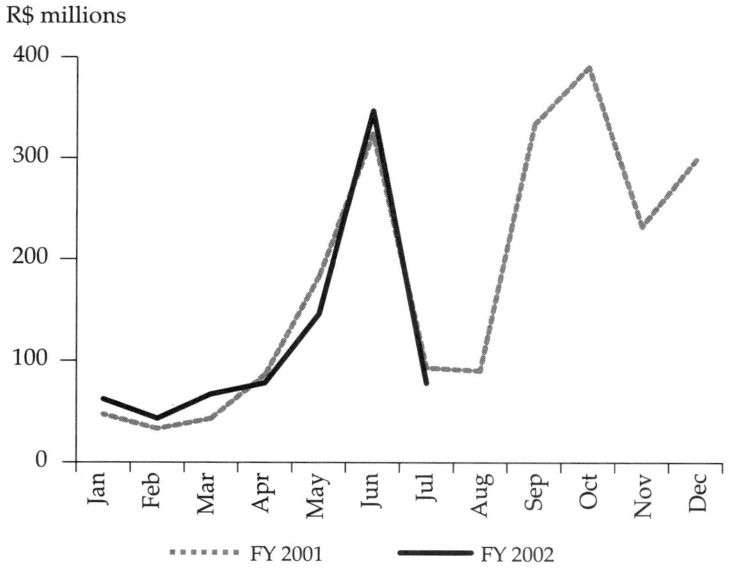

Month	*FY 2001*	*FY 2002*
January	47	62
February	33	43
March	43	67
April	86	78
May	183	146
June	324	347
July	93	78
August	90	—
September	334	—
October	390	—
November	232	—
December	298	—

Note: — = not available.
Source: Central Bank of Brazil (Somente Exigibilidade Bancária), Banco Cooperativo do Brasil (BANCOOB), Banco Cooperativo SICRIDI (BANSICREDI), Amazonia Bank (BASA), Banco do Brasil (BB), Banco do Nordeste do Brasil (BNB), and BNDES; Ministry of Agricultural Development: www.pronaf.gov.br.

sonal, mostly contracted in July through September of each year, and repayable by June. Repayment periods on investment credit range from five to eight years, with two to three years' grace.

Rural Savings

Banks are not required to distinguish rural from urban savings mobilization, and thus, this breakdown is not available. However, one savings program of note is the Poupança Rural program, operated by the federal banks Banco do Brasil, BNB, and BASA. In the case of Banco do Brasil, savings mobilized in rural areas are channeled back into rural credit, contributing almost R$2 billion in resources for rural credit programs in 2000. By 2002, rural savings rose further to R$2.8 billion, but accounted for a smaller share, or 12.6 percent, of rural credit. Deposit rates were low, fixed at a benchmark index rate in 2001, using the taxa de referência or TR, itself at around 2 percent, plus 6 percent, to arrive at a rate of 8 percent.

Private Banks and Supplier Credit

Private banks must assign their mandated 25 percent of deposits to any agricultural clients who apply, and as a result, they choose to lend to the largest and least risky agribusinesses that meet the criteria, thus minimizing transaction cost and credit risk. They can thus share the grant element that is embedded in a loan with the borrowers. This grant element is reflected in a formal ceiling to the lending interest rate of 8.75 percent per year, compared with much higher free market rates. Actual effective lending rates are determined by the bargaining power of the creditors and the borrowers. In some cases, effective lending rates can be substantially higher than the formal lending rate, by requiring compensatory balances or through fees and commissions or a variety of other means. Smaller clients with little bargaining power are less protected against such higher effective lending rates.

Data indicate that some small clients have gained access to credit extended by private banks, particularly where credit risk has been substantially reduced through association with a larger, better-established intermediary. The examples are small diary farms that sell milk routinely to Nestle, or clients of John Deere, financed by Unibanco. Itaú similarly finances small tobacco growers who sell to a large buyer, Sausa Cruz. In such cases, the relationship with the lender is backed by a formal credit guarantee extended by the large supplier or purchasing firm or by the informal reputational collateral of such clients, who would have too much to lose if they defaulted because of the impact upon their relationship with their buyers.

Among private banks, Bradesco claims to be the main lender to small farmers. It lends in amounts not exceeding R$30,000 to R$40,000 per farmer, and its agricultural loan portfolio accounts for about 10 percent of its total loan portfolio. Bradesco's total outstanding agricultural loan portfolio exceeds the floor of 25 percent of its outstanding demand accounts, thereby indicating a use of free resources in lending to the agricultural sector. Bradesco also onlends a substantial part of its agricultural lending to cooperatives, which onlend to their members. All private banks surveyed maintain that loan losses on agricultural lending are relatively low compared to loan losses in other sectors. As with microfinance lending through CrediAmigo, this suggests that heavily subsidized financial resources are not essential to mitigate credit risk associated with agricultural lending.

Private banks complain about the preferred status enjoyed by the federal banks and cooperative banks that benefit from the government's 'equalization' payments, which operate on a 'cost-plus' basis in the implementation of the various directed credit programs through, for example, the Constitutional Funds. Private banks underscored that they could increase their agriculture lending if they could similarly gain access to such equalization payments.

Bills of Exchange: Cédulas de Produto Rural

An important phenomenon in recent years has been the expansion of the CPR, which is a contract issued by rural producers, whether individuals, cooperatives, or associations. It represents an obligation of the producer to deliver a given quantity of a product, of a specified quality, on a given date. The CPR involves a forward sale as well as a hedging mechanism to ensure a given price for the producer.[9] Banco do Brasil began promoting the rural *cédulas* partly as a response to the sharp decline in the volume of the formal agricultural lending in Brazil witnessed in the latter 1990s.[10] Now, much of the volume of CPR transactions is handled outside the formal agricultural credit system. In particular, agroindustry, with its generally better information on producers and better access to financial markets, has become an important supplier of credit to the primary agricultural sector through this mechanism, which has expanded rapidly, reaching an estimated R$6 billion compared to overall formal credit programs of around R$13.8 billion in 2000. Banco do Brasil continues to play a significant role in extending the use of CPRs and guaranteed about R$800 million in CPRs in 2001, which it expected to increase to R$1 billion in 2002.

An important reason for the rapid growth in CPRs has been their legal advantages as self-executable legal instruments: there is no need for legal cognizance of the suit before execution of debt recovery can begin. The CPR instrument is confined to agricultural products and to individual producers only, so agricultural enterprises that produce primary products

Cédulas De Produto Rural: Bills of Exchange for Rural Products

The CPR is a title created to serve as an instrument for private agricultural financing. The CPR can be issued by the rural producer, its associations, or cooperatives, and it represents an obligation of the rural producer to deliver a given quantity of a product at a specified quality on a given date. Rural *cédulas* began in 1994, partly as a response to the sharp decline in the volume of formal agricultural credit lending in Brazil and with the recognition of such instruments in the financial system as a whole. The delivery is anchored in the existence of a clearinghouse for liquidation of the contracts, and a performance bond that the merchandise will actually be delivered as specified in the contract

The development of the CPR as an instrument to add liquidity and provide forward contracts was supported by law in August 1994. The CPR also serves as a hedging mechanism and, since its inception, has gained momentum particularly with respect to soybeans and coffee. With respect to the specific conditions in Brazil, the CPR provided a sorely needed financial and hedging instrument that partially assisted in compensating for the decline in agricultural lending. The CPR was by far a better device than the inefficient barter mechanism that gained momentum when the reduction in formal credit to agriculture took place. The Banco do Brasil has estimated that the accumulated value of CPRs sold has been in the range of R$5 billion over 1995 to 2000. The Banco do Brasil charges 0.65 percent per month for guaranteeing a CPR.

cannot benefit from it. Researchers from the University of São Paulo estimate that about 80 percent of such transactions are contracted without a bank guarantee and that the average contract duration is about six to eight months long. The most popular commodities contracted through CPRs are coffee, soy, corn, rice, beef, and, recently, milk.

Brazil's futures market exchange, Bolsa Mercantil de Futuros (BM&F), is presently planning to introduce trading of CPR contracts in the secondary market. A typical CPR is used to finance inputs, and they are estimated to be financing up to 30 percent of expected sale value of the produce. Effective lending interest rates are difficult to determine because the selling price is often set below the market rate. Guarantees for CPRs are extended almost exclusively by Banco do Brasil, but some other banks and at least one insurance company are presently considering entering this lucrative market.

Finally, authorities pointed out that private contributions to agricultural credit are also increasing through such channels as agroindustrial producers and suppliers' credit.

Agricultural Insurance

Rural agricultural insurance has until recently enjoyed low private participation. Premiums related to agricultural insurance in 2001 accounted for only 0.3 percent of total premiums received by the insurance sector (table 5.5). Brazil's insurance sector was relatively underdeveloped in terms of premiums per capita, at $75, or in premiums as a share of GDP, at 3 percent, when compared to other countries in Latin America.[11] Only 3 percent of cultivated agricultural land was estimated to be covered by insurance. Moreover, more than half of all premiums received by private insurers, of which 64 percent were for agricultural insurance, were on policies written in São Paulo. A further 11 percent were received from the three southern states of Rio Grande do Sul, Santa Catarina, and Paraná, where 27 percent of premiums were for agricultural insurance. Coverage was negligible in the remainder of the country.

Table 5.5 Agricultural Insurance Relative to the Total Insurance Market, 2001
(R$ millions)

	Geographic distribution					
Type of insurance	*São Paulo*	*Rio de Janeiro*	*South*	*Other states*	*Total*	*Distribution (%)*
Agriculture	39.9	2.2	16.2	22.8	81.1	0.3
of which private insurance	–20.0	–2.0	–13.8	–0.9	–36.7	(0.1)
Automobile	3,098.9	749.4	928.4	1,458.6	6,235.4	24.7
Health	3,307.3	1,231.2	289.4	1,238.3	6,066.3	24.0
Life	2,258.7	487.8	597.7	933.1	4,277.2	16.9
Civil liability	1,207.2	184.2	411.0	489.7	2,292.0	9.1
Fire	761.1	273.7	221.3	220.4	1,476.4	5.8
Other	2,425.4	982.6	438.9	1,017.8	4,864.7	19.2
Total	13,098.5	3,911.2	2,902.8	5,380.7	25,293.2	100.0
Distribution (%)	51.8	15.5	11.5	21.3	100.0	

	Distribution of agricultural premiums collected by the private insurance industry (%)					
State	*São Paulo*	*Paraná*	*Rio Grande do Sul*	*Rio de Janeiro*	*Santa Catarina*	*Others*
Participation (total premium)	64	12	9	8	6	1

Note: States of the South include Paraná, Rio Grande do Sul, and Santa Catarina.
Source: FENASEG and SUSEP.

Government initiative in this area faltered in the 1960s with the collapse of the National Insurance Company, but began again in 1973 with PROAGRO, the Guarantee Program for Agricultural Activity (Santo 2001). This program provided credit guarantees rather than income or crop insurance and, until the mid-1980s, was mandatory for beneficiaries of agricultural loans. By the late 1980s and early 1990s it had losses of R$150 million per year, and coverage had to be sharply curtailed. Premiums were raised substantially in the early 1990s, from, for example, 6 to 11.7 percent for nonirrigated rice and beans. Since the mid-1990s, the program has had limited coverage, with only 1.5 million contracts over five years, and has been subject to more stringent criteria. However, it has now obtained an excess of premiums over indemnities to produce cumulative profits over five years of R$6 million on premiums of R$60 million.

In 2002, the government tried to initiate a program of public support for insurance premiums. Brazil's authorities point out that substantial public support has been extended to agricultural insurance in developed and developing countries for support to both premiums and catastrophic event coverage.

Private parties in Brazil are also aware of the advantages of new forms of agricultural insurance through put options and through index-based yield insurance, although the government has not so far been tracking these possibilities. Pilot programs are under implementation by Banco do Brasil, such as put options on commodities, with technical assistance from the Australian bank, Macquarie, and by Portoseguro, which provides index-based yield insurance. These programs are discussed further below. Private banks have a particular interest in such instruments, pointing out that such insurance could increase their lending, particularly to small producers, because it reduces credit risk. Banco do Brasil is providing extensive training to selected staff on these new methods. Banco de Brasil also owns about 60 percent of an insurance company, Alliansa, that could assist in introducing such instruments and enable their joint marketing with traditional lending instruments.

Portoseguro is a private insurance company that introduced agricultural insurance in its product range in 1998. Portoseguro does not receive government support but pointed out that federal and state policies toward insurance can strongly affect the demand for such new products. In 2000, the state of Rio Grande do Sul paid 90 percent of the insurance premiums of small farmers with holdings of less than 5 hectares. This scheme covered about 25,000 small-scale beneficiaries and generated R$2.5 million in premiums, or about R$100 per farmer. Coverage was purchased primarily for corn and wine grapes. Indemnity payments, however, far exceeded the premiums received and amounted to R$4.1 million. Portoseguro would have to increase the premiums to avoid further losses. It is not clear, however, whether the state government will continue to subsidize the scheme and, if so, to what extent. The degree of state support will substantially influence future services offered. In 2001, Portoseguro collected some R$12 million in agricultural insurance premiums.

Portoseguro estimates its share at one-quarter of total agricultural premiums collected by the Brazilian insurance industry, which it estimates at some R$50 million per year, covering an insured value of about R$500 million with premiums in a range of 8 to 12 percent of the value of assets insured. According to their estimates, premium income related to agriculture insurance, including agroindustry, accounted for about 0.125 percent of total premiums collected by the Brazilian insurance industry. Portoseguro also provides a 'delivery insurance' of raw material to the sugar industry, where the premiums range between 0.5 to 3.0 percent. So far, Portoseguro has not penetrated the business of guaranteeing CPRs, where Banco do Brasil remains the main and almost the sole player.

Portoseguro has provided index-based insurance to corn, soybeans, and wheat in the last two years. For soybeans, the index-based insurance is related to the quantity of rainfall within the crucial 60 days starting one month after the planting. The premium ranges between 2 and 15 percent of the estimated normal sale value. Some form of government subsidy for this was clearly hoped for. According to Portoseguro, private banks often require insurance as a prerequisite to the approval of a loan, thereby enhancing the agricultural insurance business (table 5.6).

The Salient international reinsurance companies of Munich Re, Swiss Re, and Partner are active in the reinsurance business and were recently allowed to perform in all areas where IRB (Instituto do Reseguros do Brasil) is not performing. Portoseguro reinsures about 85 percent of its insured value with the international reinsurers.

Cosesp is an insurance company owned by the state of São Paulo, and its activity is limited to the state of São Paulo. The company's main source of income and activity is life insurance. Cosesp is not involved in index-based insurance, but about 5 percent of premiums collected are generated from broad-based agriculture insurance. On average, the agricultural insurance premium is 5 percent of the value of the produce, and it ranges between 1.5 and 12 percent of the insured value. The administrative cost exceeds 20 percent of the value of the premium.

High administrative cost characterizes traditional crop insurance, which requires monitoring of specific damage in individual plots. Such high administrative costs constitute an impeding factor, which limits the social value added embedded in traditional crop insurance programs. By contrast, index-based insurance programs do not require any individual monitoring of plots and related damages, and, therefore, the administra-

Table 5.6 Agricultural Insurance in Brazil: Basic Information and Volume of Premiums/Losses

Basic information (2001)	*Item*
Number of contracts	38,842
Amount insured	US$329.3 million (R$990 million)
Premiums	US$17.4 million (R$52 million)
Average tax/fee	5.29%
Area covered	1.3 million hectares
Area planted[a]	46.2 million hectares

	Volume of premiums/losses (from June 1999 to May 2002)		
Company	*Total premiums (R$ millions)*	*Retained loss (R$ millions)*	*Participation (%)*
Cosesp	63.7	32.8	56
Porto Seguro	18.9	5.8	17
Brasil	17.3	5.0	15
Excelsior	9.4	2.7	8
Total	112.8	48.8	100

a. Only 2.8 percent of the area planted is insured.
Source: DETEC or Departamento Técnico Atuarial.

tive cost involved is much smaller. Cosesp's management has started to study the subject of index-based insurance but has not started to sell index-based policies.

A final note in this consideration of agricultural insurance is the secondary market for insurance instruments. Brazil's futures market exchange, the BM&F, indicated an interest in the new insurance instruments. According to BM&F management, the government has decided to support coffee producers in light of the falling coffee prices by selling coffee put options dated March 2004. However, most of Brazil's coffee contracts are traded in New York, and coffee contracts traded in Brazil amount to only about 12 percent of the volume of coffee contracts traded in New York. Coffee accounts for about one-half of the total volume of commodities traded on the BM&F.

Because the annual value of coffee grown by small farmers is often below R$5,000 per household, which is the lowest value for standard coffee contracts traded on the BM&F exchange in São Paulo, it would be prohibitive to sell put options as separate, small-denomination products to small producers. However, by coupling a put option as a joint product with credit and other financial products, transaction costs could be reduced significantly for the creditor and the rural producer alike. For creditors, the resulting synergy of credit enhancement would provide both fee-based revenue and a better-quality loan portfolio. Further benefits arise when there is a secondary market for the options instruments, such as for CPRs, allowing for repricing of risks during any time in the cropping season, and for the participation of a broader range of investors in financing rural production. This is the direction in which the BM&F of São Paulo is heading. The existence of a clearinghouse for liquidation of the contracts and a system of performance bonds so that the merchandise will actually be delivered as specified in the contract are prerequisites for success.

Analysis of the Present System of Agricultural Credit

Brazilian agriculture has achieved some important successes over the past decade, sharply increasing production and productivity across a wide range of products and establishing Brazil as a major competitor, not only in more traditional products, such as coffee, but also in newer ones, such as soy. At the family farm level, PRONAF has managed to extend credit to hundreds of thousands of lower-income farm families previously outside the formal credit system, and has reportedly achieved solid repayment rates in excess of 90 percent. On the other hand, it is difficult to argue that the successes achieved by Brazilian agriculture can be attributed to the national rural credit system, and the outreach achieved by PRONAF has come at an extremely high cost, which is reflected in rebates of 25 to 40 percent of principal on loans at only 1 to 4 percent interest. More generally, a review of experience with rural credit programs in Brazil suggests that they have generally fallen short of best international practice, and that reforms could help to upgrade the coverage and sustainability of the system.

Output Levels and Credit

A first observation is that the increases in agricultural production and in productivity are not correlated with the volume of agricultural credit. In particular, productivity and production have increased significantly in recent years, even as formal agricultural credit has fallen sharply (figure 5.7 and table 5.7). As credit per hectare declined from R$390,000 to R$90,000 during 1979–99, and credit per ton of production fell even more steeply from R$350,000 to R$40,000, productivity of grains soared from 1,500 to almost 2,500 kilograms per hectare (Kessel 2001).

This conclusion requires some caveats. First, data reflect formal credit and do not include, for example, credit such as that provided by agro-

Figure 5.7 Agricultural Production and Formal Agricultural Credit

Index of growth in rural credit and grains production (1967 = 100)

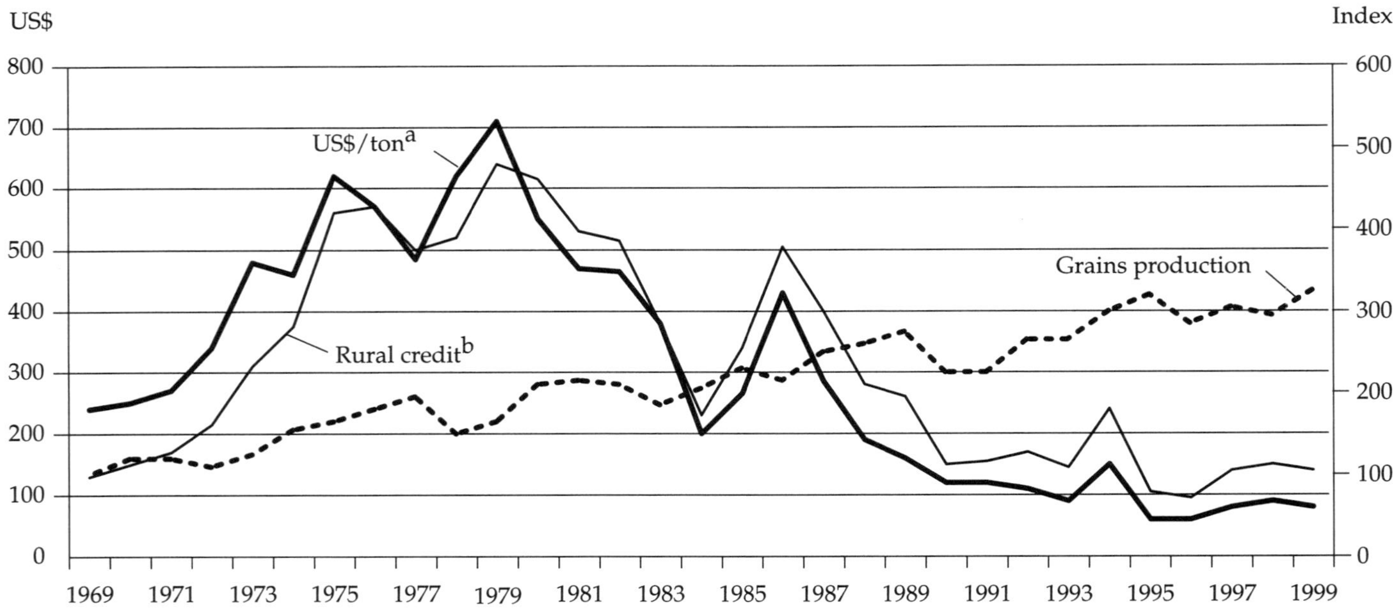

a. Nominal credit values were adjusted by the general price index for domestically available goods, then converted by the average 1999 exchange rate of R$1.8428/US$1.

b. Credit per ton of grains produced (US$).

Source: Central Bank of Brazil, as reproduced in Kessel 2001.

Table 5.7 Rise in Agricultural Productivity and Decline in Formal Agricultural Credit

Year	*Productivity (tons/ha)*	*Average loan amount (R$'000)*	*Amount per hectare (R$'000)*	*Amount per ton (R$'000)*
1979	1.49	22.2	389.8	350.0
1986	n.a.	8.0	312.4	229.6
1994	1.95	24.2	179.5	90.3
1999	2.48	7.2	90.7	40.9

Note: n.a. = not applicable.
Source: Kessel 2001.

industry through *cédulas,* estimated to be substantial and growing. Changes in the relative share of these forms of credit over time are also not reflected. Second, for many years, agricultural credit was diverted to nonagricultural activities in almost unprecedented amounts when compared with other countries. For example, the value of wheat financed in 1979 was 25 percent higher than the value of wheat produced. Loans for agriculture were always in high demand, because they came with highly subsidized interest rates as well as the expectation, and frequent practice, of debt forgiveness, which, of course, generated further expectations to benefit from 'more of the same' in the future. Waivers of loan indexation and rescheduling of agricultural debts at much more lenient terms made the ownership of an agricultural loan a remarkably highly remunerative and rewarding asset. This in turn is reflected in the close correlation between land prices and credit (figure 5.8), with the subsidy capitalized into the value of land, as has occurred elsewhere—in the case of sheep farming in New Zealand, for example.[12]

During the past four decades, there have been repeated experiences of debt forgiveness for agricultural loans. The last major programs were after the 1994 economic crisis, again in 1999, and then, substantially, in 2001. When forgiveness of credit through public sector institutions is coupled with limited progress on enforcement systems, a culture of nonpayment ensues and the rural credit system lends itself to use for political purposes. Appropriate sanctions and incentives are essential to ensure sound credit discipline and thereby more sustainable programs with greater coverage. In the PRONAF program, the incentives to repay on time are so disproportionate in relation to the loan amount that a farmer can borrow R$100, repay only R$60, and be considered a performing borrower. In this case, the incentive would appear to institutionalize and reinforce unviable lending rather than bring about a situation in which the private sector can service these clients with its own resources.

Figure 5.8 Correlation of Volume of Credit with Land Price Value

Index of growth in rural credit and grains production (1967 = 100)

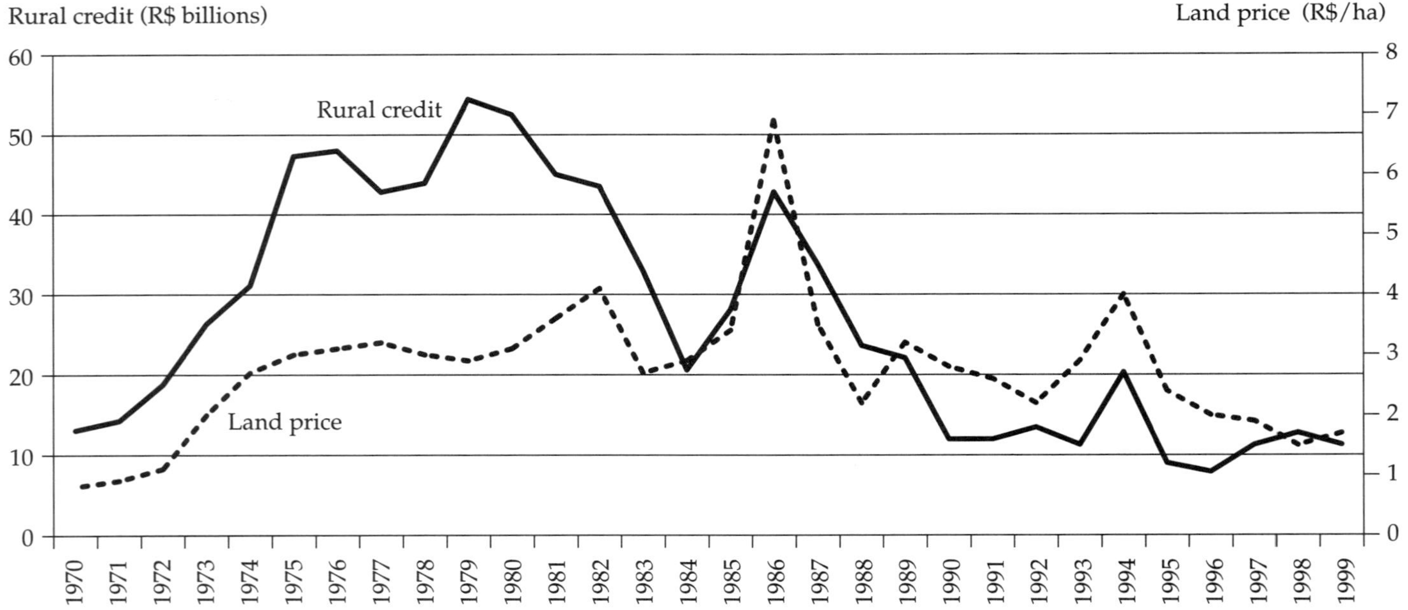

Source: Fundação Getulio Vargas and Central Bank of Brazil, as reproduced in Kessel 2001.

Outreach

Outreach to the poor remains limited. Although one-quarter of all demand deposits in Brazil are supposed to be made available for agricultural lending, data indicate that less than a third of farming households in Brazil have access to formal credit, with 1.35 million contracts written in 2000 for 4.8 million households (Central Bank of Brazil 2000a; Ministry of Agricultural Development 2000). Credit also remains highly concentrated, with three-quarters of all clients receiving less than 6 percent of credit, while the top 2 percent of contracts account for 57 percent of all credit (figure 5.9).[13] This distribution of credit by size of contract partly reflects the skewed distribution of land.

Figure 5.9 Distribution of Agricultural Credit by Contract Size

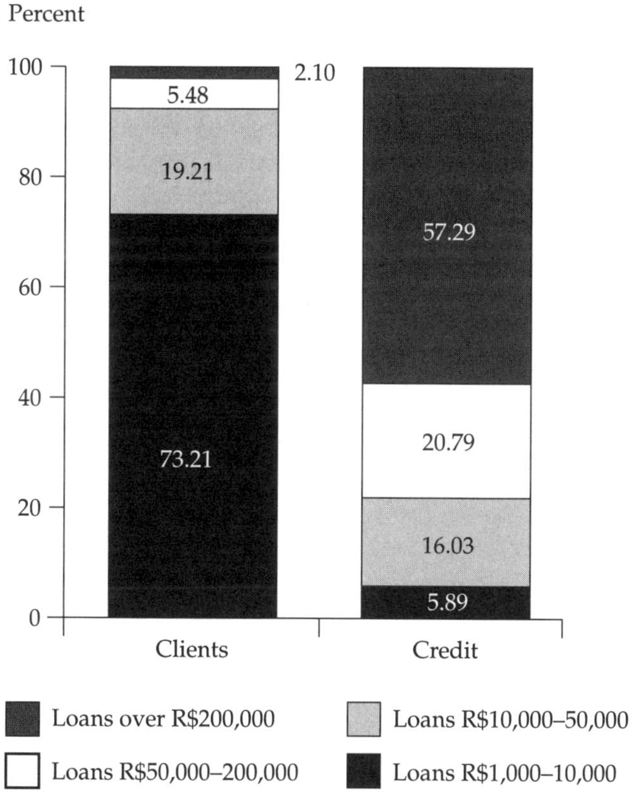

Source: Central Bank of Brazil 2000a; Kessel 2001.

The difficulties are particularly great in Northeast Brazil, where the average farm income is a third to a fifth of other regions; almost 60 percent of farm units are under five hectares, compared to at most 25 percent elsewhere; one in five farmers is a squatter; and barely 2 percent of farmers receive technical assistance, compared to almost 50 percent in the South (table 5.8). Thus, family farms in the Northeast accounted for 42 percent of holdings, but just 10 percent of area cultivated, 6 percent of production, and less than 4 percent of financing.

Of the 4.8 million farms identified in the 1996 agricultural census, 4.1 million were family farms, with less than 15 rural 'modules' of land, or the equivalent of less than some 300 hectares in the South and less than approximately 1,100 hectares of land in the North. Family workers outnumber nonfamily employees. Of these 4.1 million, the wealthiest 1.3 million have 15 percent of all farm land but account for 31 percent of production. These are among the most productive farmers in Brazil (Binswanger, Deininger, and Feder 1993; Ministry of Agricultural Development 2000). The next 1.1 million account for only 5 percent of production, and the remaining 1.6 million subsistence farms account for just 2 percent of total production. At the landowner farm level, 700,000 farms account for 70 percent of land but produce 63 percent of total production. This group includes about 90,000 highly profitable ventures and a large number of undercapitalized estates that are not efficient producers.

The viability of commercial bank lending to the bottom 2.7 million farms in terms of production is questionable, although there may be scope for lending through credit cooperatives and production cooperatives. Nonetheless, small-scale savings mobilization is likely to be feasible for many underserved clients in this group. Alternative assistance through infrastructure support or improved dissemination of low-cost techniques for enhancing production may be suitable. In Northeast Brazil, social security transfers constitute an important safety net for residents of many of the poorest communities. The top 1.3 million or so family farms do have a fairly high degree of coverage, particularly in the South, but it is essential to ensure that this is deepened, through savings, credit, and CPR-style insurance, to avoid their slippage into the lower-income categories. At the landowner farm level, it is believed that there is a very high degree of penetration of credit, which, therefore, means that credit is allocated to a large number of farms that are substantially less-efficient users of those resources than the top end of family farms that have more constrained access to financial services. The credit subsidies implicit in the below-market interest rates provide incentives for larger farmers to capture these resources, in many cases, allocating them to less-efficient investments.

The subsidy does not reach the poorest farmers. Controlled interest rates on directed agricultural lending are unattractive because they typi-

Table 5.8 Brazilian Farm Units, Area, Gross Value of Production, and Total Financing

Enterprises	*Farm units ('000)*	*Share (%)*	*Area ('000 ha)*	*Share (%)*	*Product. (R$'000)*	*Share (%)*	*Financing (R$'000)*	*Share (%)*
Family enterprises	4,139	85.2	107,768	30.5	18,118	37.9	938	25.3
of which Northeast	2,055	42.3	34,043	9.6	3,027	6.3	134	3.6
Central–West	162	3.3	13,691	3.9	1,123	2.3	95	2.6
North	381	7.8	21,861	6.2	1,353	2.8	50	1.3
Southeast	634	13.0	18,745	5.3	4,039	8.5	143	3.9
South	908	18.7	19,428	5.5	8,576	17.9	516	13.9
Business enterprises	555	11.4	240,042	67.9	29,140	61.0	2,735	73.8
Other	166	3.4	5,801	1.6	539	1.1	34	0.9
Total for Brazil	4,860	100.0	353,611	100.0	47,797	100.0	3,707	100.0

Source: Ministry of Agricultural Development 2000.

cally fail to cover the cost of borrowed funds, loan administration, loan loss provisions, and a normal profit margin. The incentive for private banks, therefore, is to allocate a large portion of their mandatory lending at 8.75 percent to public banks or to large agricultural enterprises. The five largest private banks concentrate 80 percent of their agricultural lending among 10 percent of their borrowers, while the smallest 50 percent of borrowers account for only 4 percent of credit extended.

In the case of private bank loans to agroindustrial enterprises or large farms, the subsidy is split with the borrower in the form of mandatory compensating balances or the joint sale of other financial products and services priced above their usual price. Those enterprises may extend credit to primary agricultural producers, but only at market rates, so that the subsidy is split between the banks and the agroindustrial enterprises and almost never reaches the intended beneficiary. In some alleged cases, credit providers directly require borrowers to bid for below-market resources through side payments to the credit officer and thereby capture a portion of the subsidy.

The dilemma of subsidized credit programs in many countries is the tradeoff between serving more clients from the target group by spreading budgetary resources more thinly and thereby ensuring greater access, or providing a larger interest rate subsidy to fewer participants in the credit program. International best practice suggests that improving access should be given priority. For example, studies by Townsend and others (1997) in Thailand pointed to increased social returns from access to financial services that were over and above what could be assessed based on results of the financial institutions involved. In particular, in the Thai context, Townsend and others found that access to such services explains an 'additionality' of 7 percent in lifetime wealth accumulation by borrowers and savers relative to control groups with no access. In addition, Townsend and Yaron (2001) found that prior to the 1997 East Asia crisis, the annual value, or the cost recovery factor, of the incremental wealth of Thai farmers with access to financial services exceeded the annual subsidy to the Bank for Agriculture and Agricultural Cooperatives of Thailand (BAAC), which was providing that access.

Once it is agreed that the issue is to expand the access to credit, the choice becomes clear. Money spent on subsidizing lending interest rates to the ultimate clients reduces the scope and number of clients who could have gained access to formal financial services. Brazil has made some progress in curtailing the volume of directed, subsidized credit, and the spread between market and subsidized rates has narrowed as market rates have fallen (figure 5.10), but there is an urgent need to ensure further progress and to provide an enabling environment for the promotion of rural financial markets that operate according to principles of efficiency

Figure 5.10 Narrowing Spread between the SELIC Rate and the Controlled Agricultural Interest Rate

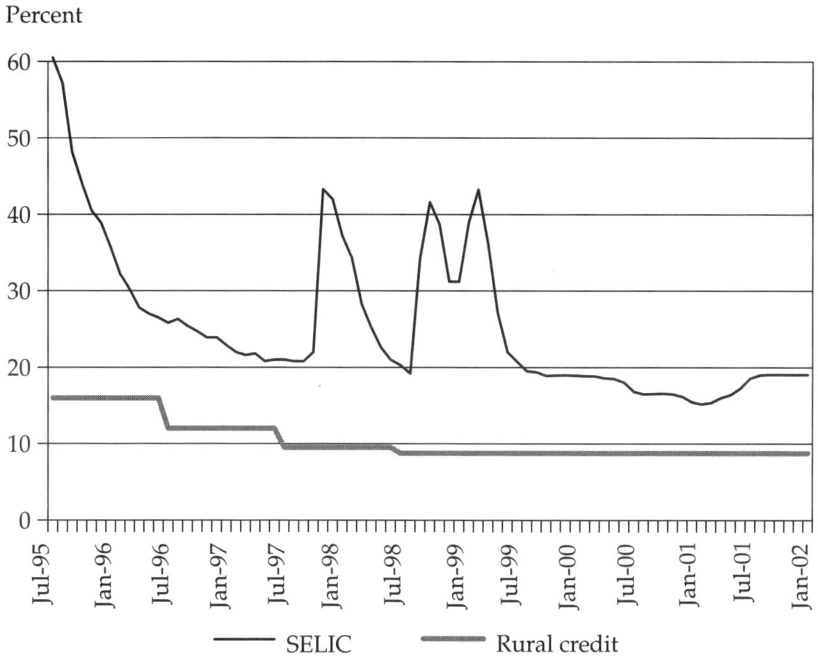

Source: Central Bank of Brazil.

and outreach that run counter to the present agricultural credit system in Brazil.

Disaggregation of Subsidies and Estimation of Subsidy Dependence

The subsidy system has several components. Apart from (1) the obvious opportunity cost of providing resources to lending institutions at a below-market rate for onlending to agriculture, there is also (2) the cost of making up the difference between these rates and the minimum rate required for lenders to break even (this difference is known in Brazil as *equilização,* and is explicitly funded in the budget for some programs). Other components include (3) the opportunity cost of below-market returns to capital for the lending institutions providing rural credit, even assuming solid recovery rates on loans; (4) the cost of write-downs of loans and capital because of poor repayment rates and debt forgiveness; and, finally, (e) the public cost of credit guarantee mechanisms used to indemnify private creditors who are not repaid by borrowers.[14]

To illustrate the first of these, with the SELIC rate at around 19 percent in late 2001, budgetary funds (or Constitutional Funds) and Workers' Support Funds (FAT) were being provided to lending institutions for rural credit programs at the TJLP of about 11 percent, implying a cost to government of 8 percent on the amount provided.

To illustrate the workings of the equalization scheme, if, for example, Banco do Brasil uses FAT resources obtained at a TJLP rate of 11 percent to onlend at 8.75 percent, it receives the difference of 2.25 percent from the Treasury. However, it also receives an account maintenance fee for public credit programs of around R$130 per account per year, as well as a spread of around 8.5 percent to cover administrative costs and loan loss provisions. Banco do Nordeste receives a lower spread of around 3 percent, but its financial situation obliges it to request a higher spread of around 11 percent.

With regard to subsidies implicit in nonperforming loans, the capital of several state banks had to be written down because of both inadequate returns on performing loans and high levels of nonperforming loans. Federal banks have enjoyed repeated capital injections. On the nonperforming loan side, an indication of the costs can be obtained by discounting a fixed rate 3 percent loan repaid in even payments over 25 years, which were the typical restructuring terms for eligible nonperforming loans prior to 1994–95, at a market rate of 18 percent. At a concessional rate of 3 percent fixed for 25 years, the subsidy element turns out to be 70 percent compared with a hypothetical 25-year fixed-rate loan at 18 percent. Therefore, the costs of loan waivers and reschedulings have been substantial as well as highly regressive.

Finally, in the event of credit guarantees, a cost to government of R$150 million per year was cited above, which proved to be fiscally unsustainable. Estimates of the total subsidy undertaken for Banco do Nordeste suggested a lower bound for the subsidy dependence index (SDI) of 71 percent as of June 2001. That is, BNB would have had to increase its average onlending interest rate by somewhat less than double that average throughout the 2001 crop year to earn the interest revenues required to be self-sustaining (based on Sánchez and Zunic [2002]).

An approximate estimate of the subsidies involved in the PRONAF program was also undertaken. The principal source of funding for PRONAF is the FAT, which was provided at 11 percent in 2000, compared to a yield on bank certificates of deposit of 17 percent. Data indicate reimbursements to creditors by the Treasury equivalent to 15.5 percent of outstanding PRONAF loans. Assuming that reimbursements are to cover only the opportunity cost of the difference between the SELIC rate and the TJLP rate, the subsidy dependence of PRONAF would be around 442 percent, or the equivalent of 15.5 percent divided by 3.5 percent: the average onlending rate across categories of PRONAF clients.[15]

Additional consideration must be given to the rebates for timely payment, equivalent to 25 to 40 percent of principal. Although the SDI formula cannot be calculated if rebates are taken into account, because the denominator becomes negative with rebates that exceed the interest income earned on the original principal, the interest income that would need to be earned to cover the cost of the rebate can be estimated. Thus, on a loan portfolio of R$2.1 billion earning 3.5 percent, the subsidy amounts to around R$325 million before rebates or R$1.1 billion after rebates, or 50 centavos on every Real of credit provided. With seasonal loans with a duration of slightly less than one year, real discounts for timely payment are somewhat higher than the nominal 25 to 40 percent of principal when presented on an annualized basis.

Designing Rural Financial Systems: Principles and Experience

A general approach toward overall rural development, and consequently toward rural finance, first evolved in the 1960s, reflecting thinking in planned economic development. Under this now-traditional approach, the foremost aim was expanded output and enhanced productivity, and the principal means toward this goal was increased technology as embodied in the green revolutions. The adoption of subsidized interest rates was viewed as essential to ensuring adoption of new technologies, particularly because the majority of farmers were considered too poor to afford loans for superior inputs or for investments at market rates. To ensure that resources reached farmers at affordable rates, the traditional approach called for public intervention, either through lending by designated public banks or through mandatory and below-market loans from private banks. Brazil's system of rural finance reflected this thinking.

A new paradigm emerged in other countries in the early 1980s, notably in rural finance in East Asia and in urban microfinance in Latin America, that gradually has become mainstream thinking as evidence of success stories mounted.[16] The new paradigm has taken a more integrated approach to rural development, focusing on two key goals: expanded income and reduced poverty. It recognizes that the traditional approach may create distortions that preclude the achievement of these objectives. For example, in the Brazilian context, of the R$80 billion of annual agricultural production, less than R$13 billion is financed at subsidized rates, and a part of the subsidies is captured by intermediaries or nontarget beneficiaries. Loans are diverted to nonagricultural purposes, private creditors who can only afford to lend at market rates are crowded out, and the vast majority of farms fail to gain access to affordable credit. Ultimately, this blurs the linkages of formal credit and agricultural production or productivity.

The new approach to rural finance recognizes, first, that credit alone is not the answer: efficient rural finance is predicated on an integrated overall approach to rural development. Moreover, effective rural finance requires access to a range of efficient financial services, including the capturing of savings. There is an active role for government in establishing a favorable policy environment to facilitate the smooth functioning of rural financial markets, but a more limited role in direct interventions. Direct interventions need to be justified explicitly on market failure or poverty reduction grounds, while exhausting possibilities for market-driven solutions, and need to be evaluated continuously according to the two key performance criteria of outreach and self-sustainability. Government actions for improved rural infrastructure and human development are also important.

The case of intervention depends upon the extent to which there is still scope for the improvement of outreach and poverty alleviation through

Two Perspectives on Market Failure: The Argument for and against Intervention

Joseph Stiglitz (1994), writing on the role of the state in financial markets: "There *is* a role for the state in financial markets; it is a role motivated by pervasive market failures. In developing countries, market failures are almost undoubtedly greater than in the more developed countries....While limitations on markets are greater in less developed countries than in developed countries, so too, many would argue, are limitations on government. We have argued that government policies can be designed which are attentive to those limitations....What is clear is that a simple ideological commitment to financial market liberalization cannot be derived either from economic theory or be justified by an examination of a broad base of experience."

Timothy Besley (1994) on rural markets: "In summary, there may be good arguments for intervention, and some may be based on market failure. But as one unpacks each argument, the realization grows that, given the current status of empirical evidence on many relevant questions, it is impossible to be categorical that an intervention in the credit markets is justified. Empirical work that can speak to these issues is the next challenge if the theoretical progress on the operation of rural credit markets is to be matched by progress in the policy sphere."

efficiency enhancements, through changes in overall policy, and through improvement in the regulatory framework for the financial system to facilitate the workings of the market, or whether, in spite of a favorable policy environment and legal and regulatory framework, there is a case for direct intervention based on market failures. Even in such cases, the extent to which governments can address such market failures efficiently and cost-effectively continues to be debated, both in practice and in academic theory.

First Principles of the New Approach: An Efficient Enabling Environment

As pointed out in the opening chapter of this study, and echoed in chapter 7, the overall policy environment has to be considered prior to all other factors influencing access. Macroeconomic instability affects rural financial markets directly through monetary variables, such as real interest rates, or indirectly via its impact on bank willingness to extend credit. In the Brazilian context, macroeconomic distortions had pervasively detrimental impacts on the economy prior to the adoption of the Real Plan, which ushered in greater price stability and a flexible exchange rate regime. The price uncertainty engendered by high inflation rates contributed to enormous pressure on the government to absorb the costs of loans in arrears and to intervene in credit markets for sectors deemed to have a policy priority. In recent years, there has been greater macroeconomic stability, which has led to unprecedented opportunities for more efficient rural financial intermediation. Yet high borrowing requirements of the public sector reduce the willingness of private banks to lend, especially to sectors perceived to have greater risks.

In many developing countries, government policies have tended to favor industry over agriculture and urban over rural sectors. Such policies include, for example, usury laws that rule out the formalization of the small, risky, and high-cost loans typical in rural areas; underdeveloped legal and regulatory provisions regarding land titling and collateral for typical rural assets; pricing and exchange rate distortions that favor industry over agriculture; and infrastructure and human development policies that favor urban over rural areas. These policies reduce the profitability of agriculture and nonfarm rural enterprises and damage rural financial markets.[17]

Although a study of the 'eight pillars' in the Brazilian context lies beyond the scope of this study, working principles for creating an improved environment for rural development include establishing a more neutral trade regime between agricultural exportables and importables, removing nontariff barriers, ensuring market-determined exchange rates, reducing excessive industrial protection, shifting public investment priorities toward rural areas, and increasing participation in community development. These reforms, in which Brazil had made important advances in the past decade, will improve the efficiency of the rural sector and enable rural communities to earn a higher return on their investments.

Policies toward financial intermediaries operating in the rural sector need to reflect the fact that the public banks face the same prudential risks as other financial institutions. According primacy to the objective of achieving certain volumes of rural credit, whether on their own account or as administrators of earmarked government funds, has sometimes been at the expense of maintaining the overall financial soundness of these institutions. It is vital that the prudential supervision norms applied to private banks are rigorously applied to public sector banks as well. Heavy financial sector taxation affects rural lending, as do interest rate controls on the lending side, where all banks have been subject to an 8.75 percent ceiling interest rate on directed lending for agriculture. Financial sector taxation also applies to the cooperative banks, Banco Cooperativo do Brasil (BANCOOB) and Banco Cooperativo SICREDI (BANSICREDI). Equally, on the savings side, deposit rates are fixed, and banks are obliged to channel 40 percent of those resources to rural credit, albeit at freely determined interest rates. These factors suggest that considerable scope remains for enhancing rural financial intermediation through broader financial sector reforms.

The Legal Framework for Contract Enforcement: Rural Collateral

Lenders need a system where claims against property can be created, publicly established, or perfected and enforced. The more uncertain and expensive this process, the less willing lenders are to lend. Problems can arise in creating a mortgage or a claim on property, because of difficulties or costs associated with title, registration, or the absence of legal provisions for future interests. When perfecting a claim, there may be no clearly designated, easily accessible registries, and search costs may be high. Enforcement of mortgaged land or property can be costly, lengthy, and uncertain.

Other laws and regulations that constrain rural financial intermediation include exempt property provisions that prevent rural smallholders from using their smallholdings as collateral, and usury laws that rule out small loans from formal financial intermediaries. High spreads on free market mortgage rates in Brazil have been attributed, among other factors, to cadastral issues and guarantees, which are cited in one in seven

Expanding Rural Collateral: Improved Titling and Registration Systems

Low availability of collateral limits the availability of credit to the rural poor, and the difficulty of using land as collateral has frequently been related to the difficulty of proving title. New satellite-based global positioning system (GPS) networks for high-tech land titling have shaved years off the time it takes to get land titles, as demonstrated by CARE, a private aid organization, working on a pilot project of 11,900 acres with Salvadoran communities.

Carrying a radio transmitter that beams signals to the satellites, workers walk around the property, creating an extremely accurate map. The satellite information is fed into a computer. With that information, CARE advisers work with the community to decide how to divide the land into individual plots. Areas that are unsuitable for grazing or growing crops are then measured and divided. Because the GPS system is computerized, technicians are able to divide the land quickly, using laser beams to measure distances. The computer program can then print a detailed written description of each plot, a tedious job when done by hand. Not only does the clarification of ownership rights help in providing collateral, but, more fundamentally, it provides security of tenure and permits workers to invest in and work on their land, once ownership rights are clear.

Registration is as important as titling. In Bolivia and Peru, the government delivered title through an agrarian reform law that delivered special deeds to land. But these deeds were not registered in the real estate registries specified for that purpose in the Civil Code. Consequently, when a lender went to register a mortgage against a property, there would be no record of ownership and no property against which to register the mortgage. Such a title is sufficient to give the possessor some security of tenure because legal processes would probably fail to dislodge the occupier. But the system will not permit lenders to use the land as collateral because there is no feasible way to enter the mortgage.

Source: Farah 1996; Fleisig and de la Peña 1996.

cases, according to a survey of lenders by the National Agricultural Confederation. High spreads are also caused by difficulties in the enforcement, rather than creation or perfection, of guarantees. The advantage of the rural *cédula,* which explains their rapid growth from zero to R$6 billion since the law on these instruments was passed in 1994, is their precedence over other legal contracts.[18]

The legal, regulatory, and institutional changes needed to expand access to credit through enhanced use of collateral in rural areas include land titling and registration as well as more generously defined laws on

Expanding the Range of Collateralizable Assets: Warehouse Receipts and Inventory

'Warehouse receipts' refer to the practice of depositing a finished good or agricultural product in a warehouse and receiving a receipt certifying deposit of the good. The receipt can then be used as collateral, with the advantage that the collateral has a high commercial value and can be easily liquidated. Three parties are involved in the transaction: the farmer, who takes his goods to the warehouse; the warehouse operator, who classifies the goods and determines their value; and the bank or microfinance institution (MFI), which issues a loan based on the receipt issued by the warehouse operator.

To ensure a successful warehouse receipts program, it is important to ensure that there is discipline and trust in the warehouse, that operations are on a sufficiently large scale, that there is a thorough understanding of annual price cycles that permits proper valuation and pricing of a stored product at any given moment, and that the product is handled properly, with appropriate oversight.

Creditors gain from warehouse receipts by decreasing their risk, by reducing seasonal price variability, and by increasing liquidity. The drawback to warehousing is the cost of working with or establishing a warehouse. Entrepreneurs gain from warehousing by increasing profitability, price transparency, and food stability. The drawbacks for entrepreneurs are the increased tendency toward speculation associated with warehousing, the shortage of small-scale drying or preservation technologies for agricultural products, an unreliable supply or shortage of storage chemicals, and the costs associated with transporting goods to the warehouse.

Source: Bass and Henderson 2000.

secured transactions to allow for a broader range of collateralizable assets such as accounts receivables, farm equipment and durables, and warehouse receipts. Other changes needed include lowering foreclosure costs; drafting specific, clear, and limited homestead provisions; and judicial reforms.

Thus, measures to improve each stage of the process of creation, perfection, and enforcement of loans can serve to increase the supply of credit and reduce spreads and funding costs for Brazilian business, including in the rural sector. They therefore merit further study to guide policy reforms. In other countries, these have produced gains that have been estimated at several percentage points of GDP, although the costs of such legal reform programs are usually remarkably low (Fleisig and de la Peña 1996).

Information Barriers

Even if the enforcement of credit rights is complicated, denial of future credits to delinquent borrowers can be a powerful mechanism for encouraging timely payment. The importance of credit histories and credit information systems in this context is critical. In this regard, Brazil has begun to make important advances, both through the Central de Risco administered by the Central Bank, which covers all loans above R$5,000, and through private credit bureaus, such as Serasa. Nonetheless, information barriers will continue to be important for new entrants into the formal financial system who have yet to establish a recorded credit history.

Possible solutions for this problem could involve start-up subsidies to defray a portion of transaction costs for new lenders working with poorer clients with no prior borrowing history. These start-up subsidies should be phased out over a given time period, such as three to five years, and be at least in part performance related. For example, the subsidies should be based on progress measured against an indicator of outreach. Finally, other sound schemes for enhancing microcredit could also be applied, such as lending through self-help or community-based groups to take advantage of social collateral, step-lending with rapid and frequent repayment, and other principles as discussed in chapter 2 of this study. New technologies can also be brought to bear in order to reduce transaction costs and easily manage information on small financial transactions.

Assessing the Merits of Direct Interventions in Rural Credit and Savings

Although much can be done to create a favorable environment for rural finance, there may be a case for direct interventions on grounds of identified market failures, or in the event that markets are considered relatively efficient but unable to redress imbalances in incomes produced by the market, to directly reduce poverty. In the latter case, a decision to intervene should begin with a poverty assessment to characterize the poor and their binding constraints, and consider whether market-based solutions can redress the concerns. In the event that market solutions are judged inadequate, direct interventions in rural financial markets need to be weighed against alternative interventions such as targeted food support, social insurance, employment generation, and investments in infrastructure or human development.

Where direct interventions, whether through public institutions or support to private intermediaries, are undertaken in rural financial markets with poverty reduction as the justification, these interventions should still involve market-based interest rates to be paid by ultimate clients, although they can be combined with, for example, matching grants for community-based funds, support for social intermediation, or start-up subsidies for innovative savings and credit programs. Brazil's own experience through programs such as CrediAmigo, supported by Banco do Nordeste, indicates the potential of poverty-oriented interventions that have been conducted in a sustainable manner and adopt best practices in microfinance (chapter 2). A framework was introduced in the early 1990s for assessing the performance of rural financial institutions that has gained wide acceptance. It proposes two primary criteria, outreach and self-sustainability. Those rural financial institutions that provide a broad range of services to the target clientele in an efficient manner are likely to have the desired impact of expanding incomes and reducing poverty.

Outreach is measured by several indicators, such as number of clients, the average loan size as proxy for income level, and the percentage of female clients. Self-sustainability is assessed by calculating the subsidy dependence index, which indicates the percentage by which the prevailing average onlending interest rate would have to increase to make it self-sustainable or subsidy independent (Yaron, Benjamin, and Piprek 1997). There have been few attempts so far to assess Brazil's rural financial institutions on the basis of their outreach and self-sustainability, with the exception of Kessel (2001). The subsidy dependence index also indicates the cost to society of subsidizing such a financial institution, measured against its interest earned. Furthermore, calculations of this index facilitate evaluations of the use of subsidies in rural financial institutions versus alternative uses for society. The main factors that contribute to self-sustainability are adequate onlending rates and interest rate spreads, high rates of loan collection, high levels of savings that are mobilized efficiently, and low administrative cost.

Developing Insurance Services in Rural Areas

Rural producers face two principal risks: the price and the quantity of their production. Taken together, these determine their incomes. In light of their limited ability to absorb or spread such risks, rural producers will opt for low-risk, low-yield patterns of production in the absence of an adequate insurance system. This in turn will perpetuate their poverty or at best retard their growth in income. Moreover, where prices are liberalized and markets opened to international competition, the risk that results from exposure to volatility in international prices can lead to a backlash against liberalization and pressures for state intervention to close markets or support prices, either of which can be extremely expensive for domestic markets. Therefore, mechanisms that allow farmers to share the price risks, as well as a large share of production risks, can be welfare enhancing, particularly for poorer farmers whose ability to address these risks is especially constrained.

Well-designed schemes have two additional advantages: first they enable farmers to feel more comfortable to specialize in production, which is extremely important to facilitate the adoption of more-advanced, high-risk-return technologies. Second, by reducing variance in producers' incomes, they reduce risks for creditors, enabling lenders to provide more credit at lower interest rates. Well-designed insurance products can substitute for more traditional forms of collateral and thereby allow creditors to lend to small-scale farmers who would otherwise be considered bad risks and have no access to credit.

Strategies have been tried in the past to manage commodity price risk, such as international commodity agreements for tin and rubber, marketing boards for cocoa and cotton in various Western African countries, and price controls such as seasonally invariant grains prices in Mexico in the 1980s. These strategies have proved to be largely ineffective. In a vast number of cases, they have simply proved to be a substantial tax on producers and have therefore depressed production. Many developing countries have, therefore, moved toward a policy framework of liberalized trading environments to enhance producer incentives and improve the efficiency of the commodity marketing sector. Nonetheless, there are two areas in which recent innovations appear fruitful. The first is modern commodity price risk management mechanisms such as the CPRs, or a joint product of a loan with a put option on the price of the commodity concerned; the second is area-based index insurance.

Put options allow producers to set a market-determined floor to the price they can expect to receive at the end of a crop season. Because the annual value of commodities grown is often below R$5,000 per household, which is the lowest value for standard coffee contracts traded on the BM&F exchange in São Paulo, it would be prohibitive to sell put options as separate, small-denomination products to small producers. However, by coupling a put option as a joint product with credit and other financial products, transaction costs can be reduced significantly for the creditor and the rural producer alike (figure 5.11). Moreover, creditors are able to take advantage of the synergy created between insurance components and credit enhancement in more than one way, because the joint product not only provides an additional source of fee-based revenue but also improves the quality of the loan portfolio by eliminating or reducing unwilling defaults.

Further benefits arise when there is a secondary market for the options instruments, allowing for repricing of risks during the cropping season and for the participation of a broader range of investors in financing rural

Figure 5.11 Integrated Credit and Insurance Products: Suggestions for Efficiency Gains

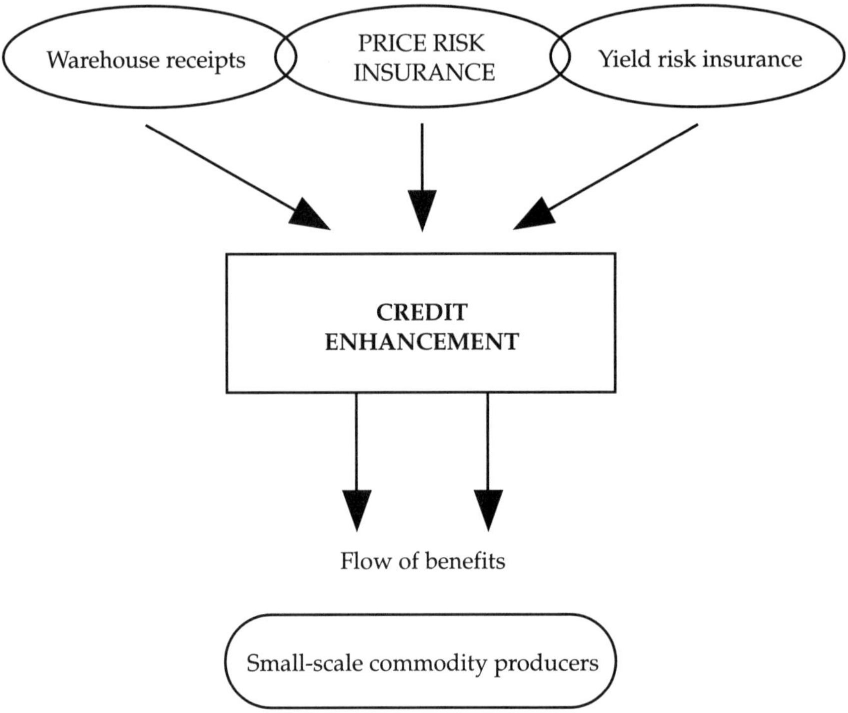

Source: Yaron 2000a.

production. This is the direction in which the BM&F of São Paulo is heading. The existence of a clearinghouse for liquidation of the contracts and a system of performance bonds so that the merchandise will actually be delivered as specified in the contract are prerequisites for success.

Area-based index insurance provides an incentive-compatible alternative to standard crop insurance schemes to help farmers mitigate production risks. Area-based index insurance is in some ways similar to a lottery, with contracts involving payment of an actuarially calculated premium, like the purchase of a lottery ticket, that result in a payout under the scheme in the event of specific clear outcomes. Such outcomes might be, for example, when a given number appears, such as rainfall below a given critical quantity during a specific predetermined period, say 30 days, of the cropping season, or when yields over a given area, but not on a spe-

Drought Insurance Proposal: Area-Based Index Insurance

Drought devastates the welfare of many poor people. It ought to be insurable. But to design effective drought insurance, several objectives must be met.

First, the insurance must be readily accessible to all kinds of households: small and large farmers, landless laborers, shopkeepers, agricultural merchants, and processors and artisans. This means that insurance contracts cannot be tied solely to crop or livestock production. Second, the insurance must be affordable, particularly by poor people. This implies that administrative costs must be kept very low, and that only rare drought events, say in 1 or 2 years out of 10, can reasonably be insured. Third, because drought damage within a region tends to be highly covariate, drought insurance will be financially viable only if a mechanism exists to spread the risk beyond the insured region. In a large country, this might be achieved by insuring many regions, particularly if these have low or even negatively correlated rainfall patterns. But more generally, it is necessary to establish arrangements for reinsurance or contingent loans with the government or with private banking and insurance.

The drought insurance proposed here would be weather station specific, with rainfall monitored from satellites. All persons insuring against drought at a specific station would pay the same premium and receive the same indemnity per dollar of insurance. Indemnities should be paid whenever the station's cumulative rainfall for some specified period of the year, say an agricultural season, fell below an agreed 'drought' level of, for example, 70 percent of average. Premiums would be calculated on the probability of a drought occurring, on the size of the indemnity to be paid, and on administrative costs. For example, for a station faced with a 1-year-in-10 drought and an insurance administration cost of 10 percent, a $1.00 insurance ticket would pay out approximately $9.00 in the event of a drought. This would be the expected premium collected over 10 years minus the 10 percent administrative cost. The calculation is approximate because no allowance has been made for expected interest earnings on accumulated premiums held by the insurer, for reinsurance costs, or for the need to build a financial reserve.

Drought insurance tickets could be marketed rather like lottery tickets, employing low-income people to sell the tickets on commission. Unlike standard insurance, however, all ticket holders for a given weather station would receive an indemnity in a drought year, but no indemnity in non-drought years. If the scheme were managed by a commercial bank, the indemnities could be issued through local branch offices after being announced in the local press and on radio and television.

(box continued next page)

(box continued)

Because all participants would pay the same premium and receive the same indemnity, drought insurance avoids all moral hazard and adverse selection problems. Because the insurance does not require any contract writing with individuals, or any field inspections or loss assessments, administrative costs could be kept very low, at perhaps 2 to 3 percent of the ticket value. These features could make the drought insurance an attractive proposition for reinsurance in the international market, and in this way, overcome the covariate risk problem of regional droughts.

To be most beneficial to rural households, the drought insurance should be sold freely to all types of people. People should be able to purchase insurance from any insured weather station, so that they can exploit less than perfectly correlated drought risks to tailor insurance portfolios to better match their own individual risk. Private firms might even offer such portfolio insurance. The emergence of secondary markets should not be discouraged, so that cash-short individuals could obtain their indemnities earlier in a drought year, perhaps at a market discount.

Source: Adapted from Hazell (1995).

cific farmer's field, fall substantially below long-term average values. In years when the insured event occurs, all the insured people who purchased the insurance receive the same payment per unit of insurance, irrespective of the actual damage to their crops and income that resulted from the low rainfall or their individual yield. This instrument is designed to overcome the issues of moral hazard and adverse selection that presently plague the traditional insurance programs. Rainfall and area yield can be verified by independent systems that do not require the monitoring of each claimant for individual damages and indemnification.

This scheme has the advantage that, in addition to avoiding all moral hazard and adverse selection problems, it is inexpensive to administer, because there are no individual contracts to write and no on-farm inspections are needed. Also, the insurance can be sold to anyone and not only to farmers. It can and should preferably be sold to all those whose income is correlated with the insured event. It can easily be run by the private sector; and when unsubsidized, as it should be, it will only be purchased if it is considered less expensive or more effective than alternative risk management strategies. A secondary market for insurance certificates could emerge, which would encourage adjustments as the crop season develops, and it could relieve the government from the need to assist farmers in the event of severe droughts or a substantial decline in yields.

Conclusions and Recommendations

A first broad conclusion is that the Brazilian rural financial system today, contrary to best practice, has limited outreach at high cost instead of mass outreach at low cost. Although the ideal is a self-sustaining system that has broad coverage of target clients, the Brazilian rural financial system presently provides highly subsidized resources that reach only a minority of target clients. Despite channeling vast amounts of scarce resources through the system since the mid-1960s, most rural households still have no access to formal financial services.

Public sector programs and institutions still play a predominant role in the national rural credit system, and these have crowded out the private provision of credit at market rates. Freely provided private sector resources have declined to as little as 5 percent of formal rural credit. The system is driven by administrative allocation of funds to targeted programs. Interest ceilings imposed on publicly mandated programs, coupled with relatively weak loan enforcement by public creditors, crowd out private sector intermediaries. It is thus not surprising that the private sector limits its role with respect to supply of regular financial services, allocating most of its resources to larger clients and to such products as the rural *cédulas*, for which such policy distortions pose less of a problem.

Controls on the price of credit via interest rates are a major impediment to credit expansion. Brazil needs to implement a gradual but credible transition program to market-determined interest rates on all rural credit and savings. The dilemma is how to introduce appropriate policies and instruments when the overnight removal of a mandated system could create at least a transitory decline in the allocation of resources to the rural sector that may not be politically acceptable. Thus, the transition may require some continuation in the directed credit system but with substantial phased reductions in the level of subsidies concerned, allowing private banks to more freely adjust lending rates to reflect administrative cost and risk. This change would introduce immediate increases in subsidized rates on the most heavily subsidized programs, notably PRONAF, whose enormous, timely repayment rebates result in highly negative nominal interest rates.

Another area where phased rates could be applied is the 25 percent directed lending requirement. During a transition, the proportion of these resources that are subject to below-market interest ceilings could be reduced or interest rates could be raised toward market rates. The special privileges of the Banco do Brasil, in the form of the equalization payments for administering subsidized programs, have been extended to include other federal and cooperative banks.[19] Financial institutions could be permitted to compete for this role, with preference to those that require lower equalization or less subsidy.

In parallel, overall subsidies can be explicitly monitored and budgeted, and refocused away from interest rates to transaction costs to promote innovation and outreach in targeted, underserved markets. Systematic and regular application of tools such as the subsidy dependence index could achieve this objective. Brazil's rural credit subsidies result in crowding out of private creditors; also, in recent years, the cost of funding these subsidies has been borne primarily by the financial sector through mandated lending, rather than by the National Treasury. This has added to the already very large spreads that characterize financial intermediation and has driven up the cost of credit for 'nonpriority' sectors in Brazil.

In addition, the subsidies have been captured largely by well-to-do farmers and nonfarming corporations, for which there is no justification for a credit subsidy on either equity or efficiency grounds. The net impact has been to inflate rural land prices, because subsidies are capitalized into the value of land, and promote a more regressive rural income distribution. Yet within the same system, there is a best-practice program, CrediAmigo. This program charges clients monthly interest rates that are about equivalent to the annual interest rate on PRONAF loans, but CrediAmigo loans are much smaller than PRONAF loans and therefore presumably go to much less-wealthy clients. This program demonstrates that when a microfinance system is well designed, it is possible not only to reach the poor but also to do so with limited subsidy dependence. In view of the fact that ultimately public funds finance both CrediAmigo and PRONAF, there is an urgent need to apply a more uniform approach in applying lending interest rates in such programs.

Brazil can try to address information and insurance constraints to reduce risks in rural lending by strengthening the nexus between efficient insurance mechanisms and rural credit, and strengthening information systems to reduce credit risk. The Central Bank's credit information system represents an important advance in addressing information constraints that warrants further support. In addition, Brazil's rapidly growing use of instruments such as the *cédulas* represents an important risk mitigation effort that merits further strengthening through registries and secondary trading arrangements, as outlined in chapter 6.

There is good potential for advancing a range of related financial instruments for risk management: price risk management for agricultural commodities, area-based index insurance, and warehouse receipts. Each reduces clients' credit risk, allowing not only for better credit terms for existing clients, but also for the potential to lift a stratum of noncreditworthy clients to creditworthy status, which is particularly important for poorer rural households. These instruments allow farmers to increase their specialization and adopt higher-risk, higher-return production strategies. Brazil produces a large variety of agricultural products, and has one of one of the largest agricultural commodity liquid exchanges (BM&F) and a large state-owned bank active in agricultural lending: Banco do Brasil. This combination should facilitate the promotion of risk management instruments and substantially improve rural financial intermediation.

In a wider context, strengthening rural finance requires attention to the same issues as those affecting overall financial intermediation: addressing issues of high spreads, high administrative costs, and relatively high profits for banks operating in Brazil versus in comparable economies, combined with high financial sector taxation. Also, as addressed in chapter 6 of this study, specific legal and regulatory reforms need to be investigated to reduce the costs of creating, perfecting, and enforcing claims and thereby contribute to lower risks, reduced spreads, and more resources for onlending.

Finally, Brazil could benefit from greater support for innovation and research in rural finance. Numerous innovations have been introduced in rural financial intermediation in countries such as Bangladesh, Bolivia, El Salvador, Indonesia, Thailand, and Brazil itself during the past two decades, which warrant further development in the Brazilian context, as discussed in chapter 2. These innovations have been in such areas as delivery mechanisms like mobile banking and smart cards; social intermediation, as, for example, group lending, contract enforcement through peer pressure, increasing loan sizes over time, or relating them to savings; staff incentives such as profit-sharing; and loan monitoring through efficient management information systems.

Pursuing such innovations has almost always required state or donor support in the early phases of project implementation, because they tend to be below the social optimum. This situation could justify public intervention on pure efficiency grounds to shoulder some of the costs associated with the piloting of approaches that have proved successful in similar socioeconomic and cultural conditions elsewhere (annex 5.2). Such subsidies should be on a time-bound, declining basis and linked to progress on key performance indicators related to outreach to target clientele and increasing self-sustainability. Potential beneficiary institutions should include all those that can contribute to improved rural financial intermediation, such as nongovernmental organizations (NGOs), banks, credit unions, cooperatives, and financial corporations.

Annex 5.1
The Subsidy Dependence Index: Rationale and Calculation

The objective of the SDI methodology is to provide a comprehensive method of assessing and measuring the overall financial costs involved in operating a rural financial institution and quantifying its subsidy dependence.[20] The SDI methodology suggests moving away from overreliance on the financial profitability ratios of conventional accounting procedures in the financial analysis of rural financial institutions. The SDI method provides a public interest analysis of a rural financial institution's financial performance and its subsidy dependence. This type of analysis involves taking full account of the overall social costs entailed in operating a rural financial institution, including the full value of all subsidies received by the institution. The SDI makes explicit the subsidy needed to keep the institution or a specific program afloat, much of which is not reflected in conventional accounting reporting.

The proposed SDI is a user-friendly device that is simple to calculate because it does not require collecting detailed information on a rural financial institution's operational costs. The SDI is instrumental in (1) placing the total amount of subsidies received by a rural financial institution in the context of its activity level, as measured against interest income earned on its loan portfolio; (2) tracking its subsidy dependence over time; (3) comparing the subsidy dependence of different rural financial institutions that provide similar services to a similar clientele; and (4) indicating the matching grant amount that would be needed for the operation of a given institution. Thus, the numerator of the SDI is the subsidy granted by the society measured against the denominator of the SDI, namely the value of interest payments and fees paid by clients.

The SDI calculation requires the application of certain procedures as well as judgment, and consistency from period to period is more important than the absolute accuracy of the figures included in the SDI computation. The SDI is a ratio that measures the percentage increase in the average lending interest rate required to compensate a rural financial institution for the elimination of subsidies in a given year while keeping its return on equity equal to the approximate nonconcessional borrowing cost. The index assumes, for simplicity, that an increase in the lending interest rate is the only change made to compensate for loss of subsidy.

Calculating the SDI involves aggregating all the subsidies received by a rural financial institution. The total amount of the subsidy is then measured against its lending interest rate multiplied by its average annual loan portfolio, because lending is the prime activity of a supply-led rural financial institution. Although removal of subsidies received is not always politically feasible or desirable, measurement of any subsidy is always warranted, economically and politically.

Measuring the annual subsidy as a percentage of interest income of a given financial institution yields the percentage by which interest income would have to increase to replace the subsidies, and provides data on the percentage points by which its lending interest rate would have to increase to eliminate subsidies.

Computation of the Subsidy Dependence Index

The amount of the annual subsidy received is defined as:

$$S = A\,(m - c) + [(E * m) - p] + K\,,$$

where:

S = Annual subsidy received

A = Concessional borrowed funds outstanding (annual average)

m = Interest rate the rural financial institution would be assumed to pay for borrowed funds if access to borrowed concessional funds were eliminated

c = Weighted average annual concessional rate of interest actually paid by the rural financial institution on its average annual concessional borrowed funds outstanding

E = Average annual equity

p = Reported annual profit before tax (adjusted, when necessary, for loan loss provisions, inflation, and so on)

K = The sum of all other annual subsidies received by the rural financial institution (such as partial or complete coverage of its operational costs by the state.

$$\mathrm{SDI} = \frac{\mathrm{S}}{LP * i}\,,$$

where:

SDI = Index of subsidy dependence of the rural financial institution

S = Annual subsidy received by the rural financial institution (see above)

LP = Average annual outstanding loan portfolio of the rural financial institution

i = Weighted average yield earned on the loan portfolio of the rural financial institution.

The SDI by itself does not clarify how the subsidy was used and whether most benefits were accrued to clients or were consumed by an inefficient bureaucracy. The latter question, though important, requires far more detailed data and even then is often subject to interpretation. The advantage of the SDI is its simplicity, and as such it focuses exclusively on the intake subsidy, that is, the value of subsidy received by the rural financial institution. The SDI should be seen in some instances as a lower bound because full financing of rural financial institution activities is likely to be difficult at current market borrowing rates *(m)* if its financial performance is dismal. However, calculating this lower bound is vital for ascertaining either the institution's progress toward self-sustainability or the social desirability of its continued subsidy dependence.

An SDI of zero means that a rural financial institution has achieved full self-sustainability. An SDI of 100 percent indicates that a doubling of the average lending interest rate is required if subsidies are to be eliminated. Similarly, an SDI of 200 percent indicates that a threefold increase in the onlending interest rate is required to compensate for the subsidy elimination. A negative SDI indicates not only that a rural financial institution has fully achieved self-sustainability, but also that its annual profits, minus its capital (equity) charged at the approximate market interest rate, exceeded the total annual value of subsidies, if subsidies were received. A negative SDI also implies that the rural financial institution could have lowered its average lending interest rate while simultaneously eliminating any subsidies received in the same year.

Annex 5.2 Old and New Approaches to Rural Finance: Goals and Principles

Old approaches	*New approaches*
Primary goals	**Primary goals**
• Growth and income expansion, frequently pursued by introducing modern technologies with concessional credit.	• Growth and income expansion.
• Poverty reduction.	• Poverty reduction.
Working assumptions	**Working assumptions**
• Accelerated economic development requires controlled commodity and financial markets, such as control of food prices and interest rates.	• Accelerated economic development requires enhanced competition in goods and financial markets, for example, through flexible prices.
• Small farmers and rural entrepreneurs cannot pay commercial interest rates.	• Small farmers and rural entrepreneurs can pay commercial, market-related interest rates.
• Small farmers and rural entrepreneurs cannot save.	• Small farmers and rural entrepreneurs can and want to save.
• Access to concessional *credit* is essential to growth and poverty reduction.	• Access to nonsubsidized *financial services* is essential to growth and poverty reduction.
Role of government	**Role of government**
• Direct intervention in and control of the agricultural sector and of agricultural credit.	• Creating a favorable policy environment while minimizing direct intervention in and control of the agricultural sector and agricultural credit.

(annex continued next page)

Annex 5.2 *(continued)*

Mechanisms of government intervention: Policy environment	Mechanisms of government intervention: Policy environment
Eight pillars of urban-biased policies	*Introduce and maintain a policy environment to promote rural financial markets*
• Maintain an overvalued exchange rate to ensure a cheap supply of agricultural produce. • Control prices of agricultural products. • Levy excessive taxes on agricultural exports. • Excessively protect domestic industries of which outputs are used as agricultural inputs.	• Support macroeconomic stability through market-determined exchange rates. • Maintain a level playing field among economic subsectors, including the agricultural and rural sectors, and enhance competition. • Deregulate the financial sector and support a competitive environment.
• Enforce usury laws that, despite their good intentions, hamper the provision of financial services to the rural poor.	• Introduce legal, regulatory, and enforcement mechanisms that address the specific requirements of the rural population.
• Enforce laws and regulations that do not take into account the unique features and requirements of the rural economy.	• Eliminate urban-biased policies that discourage rural development and impede the development of rural financial markets.
• Underdeveloped legal and regulatory provisions regarding land titling and collateral for typical rural assets (land, crops, and farm implements) relative to urban assets (cars, durables, and homes).	
• Excessive taxes on agricultural credit.	
Direct rural financial interventions	**Direct rural financial interventions**
• Introduce legal ceiling on deposit and onlending interest rates.	• Remove ceilings on deposit and onlending interest rates: encourage market-determined rates.

- Establish state-owned rural financial institutions. Formal financial services to rural communities are mostly provided by these institutions.
- Provide financial services primarily to agriculture, discriminating against rural nonagricultural entrepreneurs.
- Focus on the provision of (agricultural) credit: savings in monetary instruments are discouraged in rural areas.
- Provide special benefits and concessional funds to state-owned rural financial institutions; subsidize onlending interest rates to their clientele to compensate for urban-biased policies.
- Cover loan losses of rural financial institutions and frequently bail out loss-makers.
- Support poorly administered crop insurance and credit guarantee schemes.

- Provide financial services through various rural financial institutions.
- Provide financial services to all rural entrepreneurs and not only to agriculture-related activities.
- Encourage domestic savings mobilization through the provision of savings facilities with positive interest rates.
- Revitalize and restructure rural financial institutions: encourage sound management principles.
- Privatize rural financial institutions or segments of their operations where appropriate; shut down inefficient and unsalvageable rural financial institutions.
- Support early innovators: provide seed capital and auction subsidies to new pilot or existing credit unions, NGOs, and other rural financial institutions that meet strict eligibility criteria and are capable of providing efficient rural financial services; partially cover start-up costs, which means take the 'infant industry' approach.
- Support institution building: assist in staff training, develop a management information system, conduct research, and disseminate information on successful institutions or practices in similar socioeconomic and cultural settings.

(annex continued next page)

Annex 5.2 *(continued)*

	• Extend limited subsidies to rural financial institutions to compensate for distortive policies, which are presently being removed; cap and gradually phase out subsidies. • Introduce adequately priced and well-administered crop insurance and review effectiveness of credit guarantee schemes.
Policy variables and outcomes	**Policy variables and outcomes**
• There is underinvestment in rural public infrastructure, for example, roads and water supply, and in rural human resources in, for example, education and health. • Subsidized interest rates are used primarily as a compensatory mechanism rather than an allocative one. • Subsidies mostly benefit the agricultural sector, and mainly the well-to-do, influential farmers. • Nonagricultural rural entrepreneurs have limited access to financial services: rural development slowed down. • Insufficient provision of savings facilities and artificially low deposit interest rates, because of interest rate ceilings, result in limited savings mobilization. • Rural financial institutions are dependent on rediscounting facilities, and donor and budget funds, to back their subsidized loan portfolios.	• Rural infrastructure and educational and health facilities are improved. • Positive real interest rates serve as an allocative mechanism. • Interest rates are sufficiently high to ensure sound spreads between lending and deposit rates. • All rural entrepreneurs have access to financial services. • Rural financial institution dependence on borrowed funds from donors and governments is reduced as domestic savings mobilization becomes the main source of finance: improved financial self-sustainability.

• Rural financial institutions do not enjoy autonomy: most operational decisions are dictated, such as onlending interest rates, cost of borrowed funds, and staff policies. • Special privileges are often extended to rural financial institutions, resulting in dependence on concessional funds, lack of competition, and no incentives to improve performance: rural financial institutions are often perceived as disbursement windows. • No commercial imperatives for (state-owned) rural financial institutions; management is not accountable for their performance; financial indiscipline and poor loan collection prevail.	• Rural financial institutions enjoy autonomy in introducing efficient operating methods, such as setting market-determined interest rates on loans and deposits, and implementing staff and client incentive schemes. • No special privileges are extended to state-owned rural financial institutions; a level playing field is maintained and competition among them is encouraged; access to subsidies, when warranted, is not contingent on a rural financial institution's ownership. • Institution building and financial discipline are encouraged through management's accountability for rural financial institution performance; poor loan collection is not tolerated. • Improved performance and productivity by rural financial institution staff is motivated by advanced performance incentive systems.
• Lack of staff incentives result in poor performance from unmotivated staff. • Rural financial institution performance is evaluated in terms of traditional financial profitability ratios (return on equity and return on assets), ignoring the cost of subsidies: the real cost to society of maintaining a rural financial institution is not known.	• Rural financial institution performance is evaluated in terms of outreach to its target clientele and financial self-sustainability, as measured by the SDI; these criteria enable the assessment of the real impact and cost of a rural financial institution.

Source: Yaron, Benjamin, and Piprek 1997.

Annex 5.3 The New Approach to Rural Finance: Indonesia's BRI–Unit Desas

Item	*Principal features*
Background	Established in 1984 as a vestige of the Indonesian Government's BIMAS (Mass Guidance) program of directed credit for rice intensification.
Operating philosophy	Broad rural financial intermediation, including both savings and credit services, on a for-profit basis.
Target market	Low income, rural population in general, rather than just agricultural borrowers.
Organizational structure	The Unit Desa System (BRI–UD) is an independent profit center within Bank Rakyat Indonesia (BRI), with substantial operational autonomy. Each Unit Desa or village bank, in turn, is an autonomous profit center within the BRI–UD system.
Management of information	BRI–UD has developed an extremely efficient management information system (MIS) based on a stand-alone, PC-based system installed in more than 90 percent of Unit Desas.
Pricing policies	Positive real interest rates on deposits, an internal surplus funds transfer price above the price of mobilizing deposits, and onlending rates that allow for full coverage of all financial and operational costs. In recent years, the nominal annual yield on loans has been around 32 percent versus financing costs of around 10 percent.
Savings mobilization	BRI–UD offers four demand and term savings instruments, with interest rates that vary with account size and liquidity, tailored on the basis of client demand surveys.
Lending approach	Loans generally have a maturity of one year, with monthly repayments, and are provided for any legal, rural, income-generating activity. Loan applications are processed in one week for new borrowers and less for repeat customers. Loans are

	extended on an individual basis, and collateral is strongly desired but not mandatory. Paperwork is kept to a minimum. BRI–UD uses smaller offices and mobile banking in remoter areas, and officers visit clients in these areas once or twice a week.
Incentives for staff	Ten percent of each unit's annual profit is distributed to that unit's employees based on their individual salary levels and on their performance in contributing to the unit's profits. These incentive bonuses are paid out early in the new year, and are capped at one-and-one-half-month's salary per employee.
Incentives for clients	Clients are prescreened based on available information gathered in the community from both clients' peers and from local leaders. Clients earn interest rebates of about 12 percent a year and access to larger loans if they repay on time. Staff incentives mean that clients are subject to more careful monitoring and enforcement of loans than under traditional government credit disbursement programs. Proper loan pricing means more selective investment choices and credibility of the bank.
Accounting policies related to loans in arrears	Conservative asset classification and loan loss provisioning: BRI–UD has a general loan loss reserve of 3 percent against all loans not yet due, plus 50 percent reserves against loans less than three months overdue, and 100 percent reserves against loans three months to one year overdue. Loans more than one year overdue are fully written off.
Funds management	The BRI system serves as a clearinghouse between cash surplus and cash deficit units, transferring resources between units at the internally set transfer rate.

(annex continued next page)

Annex 5.3 *(continued)*

BRI–UD's financial performance	With relatively little initial subsidization in 1984, BRI–UD became profitable within 18 months and has become a global leader in rural financial intermediation. It has more than 22 million depositors and 4.5 million borrowers. Around 96 percent of the units are profitable. BRI–UD has consistently earned returns on equity of more than 100 percent since the mid-1990s, and return on assets of more than 6 percent. BRI–UD would be fully self-sufficient even if it cut its onlending rate by half to around 18 percent.
Impact on clients	An early study (Sutoro and Haryanto 1990) of BRI–UD's borrowers found growth rates of 25 percent in real profits, 21 percent in household income, and 18 percent in employment per enterprise. And women had better access to banking service (25 percent) than is common in the Indonesian banking system (Reed and Befus 1993).

Source: Yaron and Benjamin 1998; Sutoro and Haryanto 1990; Reed and Befus 1993.

6
Installing Institutional Infrastructure

As discussed in chapter 1 of this study, the depth of credit markets as well as cost of such services are affected by institutional factors such as creditor rights and credit reporting, which are reflected in interest rate structures and spreads. Weak credit markets in Latin America have been traced in several studies to weak creditor rights, poor borrower screening, and insufficient creditor protection, which are all factors that can make credit scarce and expensive.[1] These are reflected in Brazil's extremely high interest rate spreads and in the high default and overhead costs embedded in these spreads. According to an analysis by the Central Bank, the large spreads charged by banks in Brazil could be divided (in August 2002) into administrative expenses (14 percent), taxes (29 percent), profits (40 percent), and the cost of default (17 percent).[2] Moreover, the share of default in spreads has shown some upward trend from mid-1999, rising from around 11 percent to 17–18 percent in 2002 (figure 6.1). These factors are important in explaining the overall small size of the credit market. This suggests that initiatives that reduce default, either by allowing creditors to better select borrowers or by reducing the willingness and ability of borrowers to default, would contribute to reducing spreads and expanding the volume of credit in the economy. By protecting creditor rights, forcing borrowers to abide by the terms of the loan contract, or guaranteeing the rapid and sure repossession of collateral in case of default, one encourages creditors to lend more and at lower loan spreads.[3]

The disproportionate impact of the rationing of credit due to debtor-oriented laws on certain types of borrowers, restricting their access to credit, or penalizing them with especially large spreads has been illustrated in studies on the United States. These have found that, in American states with debtor-oriented bankruptcy laws, credit tends to be channeled to high-asset households, with a reduction in the availability and amount of credit extended to low-asset households (Gropp, Scholz, and White 1997). Moreover, they have found evidence that low-asset households are charged higher interest rates on automobile loans in high-bankruptcy-exemption states.[4]

Credit reporting also strengthens credit markets. It enables lenders to screen applicants more accurately and efficiently and also provides bor-

Figure 6.1 Spreads in Bank Intermediation in Brazil

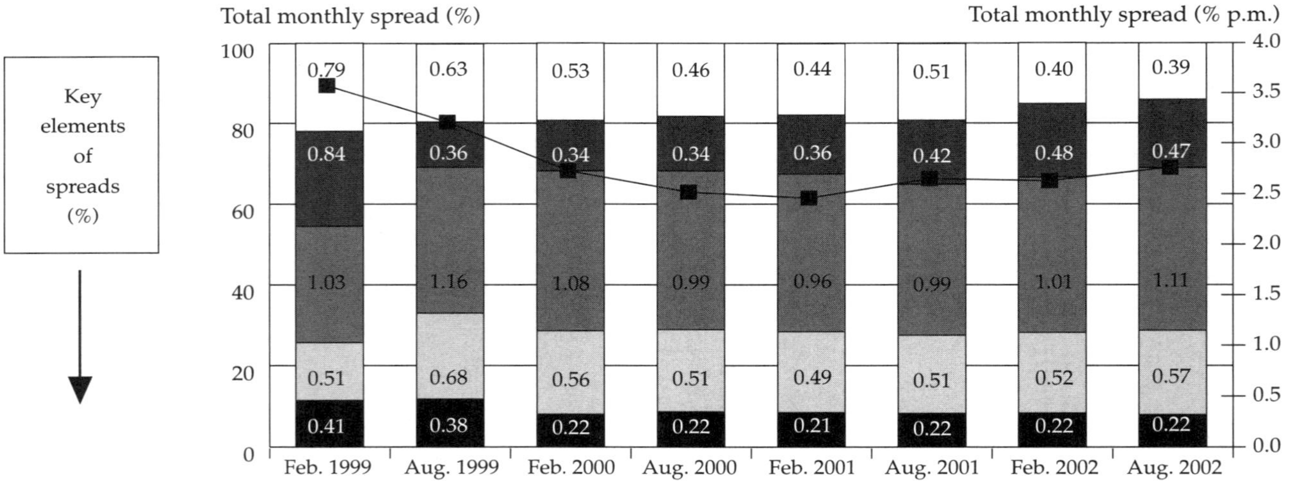

	Feb. 1999	Aug. 1999	Feb. 2000	Aug. 2000	Feb. 2001	Aug. 2001	Feb. 2002	Aug. 2002
Administrative costs	22.1	19.6	19.4	18.3	17.9	19.2	15.2	14.1
Default expenses	23.5	11.2	12.5	13.5	15.8	15.8	18.3	17.0
Net bank margin	28.8	36.1	39.6	39.3	37.4	37.4	38.4	40.2
Direct taxation	14.2	21.2	20.5	20.2	19.2	19.2	19.8	20.7
Indirect taxation + FGC	11.5	11.8	8.1	8.7	8.5	8.3	8.4	8.0
Total monthly spread (%)	100.0	100.0	100.0	100.0	100.0	100.0	100.0	100.0
Total monthly spread (% p.m.)	3.58	3.21	2.73	2.52	2.46	2.65	2.63	2.76

Indirect taxation + FGC
Direct taxation
Net bank margin
Default expenses
Administrative costs
Total monthly spread

Source: Central Bank of Brazil (2002c).

rowers with incentives to repay, as the 'reputational collateral' motivates them to maintain a good credit history for future transactions. It provides an incentive similar to physical collateral, especially because default in one institution is rapidly communicated throughout the system. Moreover, credit reporting also has a disproportionate effect on lower-income segments of the population. In the United States, where credit reporting is most developed, consumers in the lowest income quintile have seen the most dramatic increase in access to credit in the past 30 years, increasing their access to credit by more than 70 percent. Much of this increase has been attributed to the availability of credit information. Similarly, access to more accurate small-business credit information, including the linking of data on firm owners and their businesses, enabled the small-business credit market in the United States to expand rapidly in the 1990s. Credit reporting can contribute to both reductions in interest rates and increased lending volumes.[5]

This chapter discusses the importance of key institutional factors in credit market development pertaining to creditor rights and reporting in Brazil. The first part analyzes how creditor protection is defined in law and applied in practice, in terms of the enforcement of such rights by the judiciary. The second part discusses secured credit transactions, and the last part concludes with a review of credit information systems and credit screening in Brazil, evaluating these relative to other countries in the region.

Creditor Rights, Security Interests, and Access to Credit

The principal issues highlighted in this section regarding the legal and judicial protection of creditor rights in Brazil are[6]

- Substantive law is not very different from that in other French civil law countries and is generally perceived as adequate by creditors.
- However, legislative procedures are protracted, with recourse to successive appeals or injunctions, which diminish the value of legal protection.
- Judicial decisions on credit disputes are perceived to be pro-debtor, reflecting judicial social activism, sometimes to the disregard of what is established in the law or the contract. Consequently, jurisprudence and patterns of judicial behavior play a role as or more important than the law itself in regulating credit disputes.[7]
- Especially for small loans, judicial processes are avoided as far as possible due to the uncertainty, expense, and time-consuming nature of judicial processes. Instead, extrajudicial collection through collection

agencies is relied on, despite tax advantages in proceeding through the court system.

- The use of self-executable credit instruments that can help limit court procedures is also popular. However, these are more common for larger contracts than for small retail loans.
- Small-claims courts cannot be used for this purpose either, because only individuals can initiate causes in these courts. Instead, banks rely on the incentives provided by credit reporting and collection agencies and concerns about negative credit information to enforce repayment. For example, the widespread use of checks in Brazil, uncommon in many other Latin American countries, is due to the availability of timely data on bad checks.
- Finally, however, the most popular consumer loan products are not self-executable instruments (the overdraft facility or *cheque especial*). This is largely due to the formality of requirements for the recognition of a contracted loan (including signatures and witnesses). The ease of extending informal consumer loans through ATMs counterbalances for financial institutions the loss of their self-executable nature. Provisions for loan losses are reflected in higher spreads.

Legal Protection of Creditor Rights

When a debtor defaults and there is no simple and amiable resolution and collection, the loan goes to the credit recovery department. Extrajudicial collection starts at this point. Nonperforming debtors face heavy penalties, including large fees charged by collection firms. But court and lawyer fees are avoided by both parties. Eventually, debt negotiations take place with large discounts, even up to repayment of less than half of outstanding debt.

Creditors may choose judicial execution of debt if extrajudicial collection fails or because of the tax expense write-offs available if judicial collection is initiated. Law No. 9430 of December 1996 states that deductions against taxable profits of nonperforming loans are allowed for secured credits, for all values and for unsecured loans, above R$30,000, per operation due for more than a year, as long as judicial action has been initiated and maintained.

Procedures for judicial debt collection under the Civil Code depend on the type of credit instrument used. Self-executable securities can aid judicial recovery, as the debt is already recognized to exist, which eliminates one major step in the judicial procedure. The importance of using self-executable (or extrajudicial) securities becomes evident by noticing that the commonly used credit securities in Brazil are self-executable: the duplicata (a certified and negotiable copy of an invoice, a credit security

Judicial Procedures for Debt Recovery for Alternative Credit Instruments in Brazil

If the credit instrument used does not allow formal proof of the existence and value of the debt, recovery must begin with a *cognizance action,* and only after a favorable court ruling can the debt be considered executable. If the acknowledgment of a debt is challenged by the debtor, a standard cognizance action in Brazil could take several years. This is the main reason why creditors avoid following this type of procedure. Specific credit securities, known as *self-executable securities,* are defined such that they are automatically recognized as existent, so that the first step of filing for cognizance is not necessary. If a loan based on such securities is not paid, the creditor files a protest with the public registry (Cartório de Ofício de Registro e Protesto de Títulos) and can then proceed directly to an execution action. Banks usually structure larger personal loans and enterprise loans using such self-executable securities and would need to initiate a cognizance action only if the loan contract does not have an extrajudicial title, for example, for current account debts (overdraft, or *cheque especial*).

After the cognizance process, or with a self-executable security, the creditor proceeds to an *execution action.* The defendant then pays or names assets to pledge as a guarantee of payment. The court officer or the creditor may list assets for pledge if the debtor does not do so. The execution action is suspended until such assets are found. Although both a *secured* and an *unsecured* loan must go through this process, the existence of a guarantee ensures that there will be assets to pledge. Until such assets are identified, action is suspended. If the loan has a personal guarantee, the assets of the guarantor will be available. If a firm enters into a financial reorganization (*concordata*), a secured creditor's assets are automatically pledged. Pledged assets are auctioned, and the debt is paid off with the proceeds. Judicial debt collection thus depends crucially on the debtor having sufficient assets to cover payment, which is why banks often ask clients to list assets when opening accounts.

A debtor can also request an *embargo to the execution action,* arguing, for example, that interest rates are too high, that compounded interest rates have been applied (*anatocismo;* forbidden under the 1933 Usury Law), that the assets are essential to earnings, that job loss will result, or that the signature of contract was unauthorized.

An insolvent debtor enterprise may ask a judge to let him or her go into *concordata.* This does not affect the debts the firm has with its employees, the tax authorities, or secured and privileged credits (for example, those using the *cédulas de crédito*). But it suspends payments to unsecured creditors, including those who usually provide the firm's working capital, such as banks and suppliers.

(box continued next page)

(box continued)

Finally, the creditor may request that the debtor be declared bankrupt. However, the incentives to do so are not strong, as typically the little that is left over after paying for lawyers and court fees is barely enough to pay workers and the government, who have senior claims, let alone other debts. So, in general, banks prefer to help the debtor to get out of difficulties, often trading part of the debt for real assets at a substantial discount.

When a firm is declared bankrupt, all execution actions are halted, except for fiscal executions. The judge then nominates a *síndico* (usually the largest creditor) who will manage the company and analyze the quality of its assets and liabilities. Following this, the company is put either in reorganization, in which case management returns to its owner(s), or in liquidation. During liquidation all the assets of the bankrupt company are collected, sold at a judicial auction, and used to pay back its creditors (according to the quality of the credit and proportionately for credits of the same quality).

apparently existent only in Brazil), the bill of exchange, the promissory note, and industrial and commercial credit *cédulas*. A check is also self-executable.[8] The securing of credits with guarantees, pledges, or other means, although not affecting the procedure, also raises the likelihood of eventual recovery of funds, as it guarantees the existence of assets that could be used to pay off the debt.

Complaints about these procedures tend to be based not so much on content as on timing, due to the multiple possibilities of delay of cognizance and of execution through appeals and embargoes. There are also complaints about the politicization of judges' opinions and rulings, which tend to be biased in favor of those perceived to belong to the weaker sections of society, but such judgments also undermine confidence in the legal process. In terms of the content of the law, dissatisfaction is the most evident with regard to the bankruptcy process, which is the final form of judicially executed debt recovery.[9] However, the small claims that form the central focus of this study rarely proceed to this point.

Judicial Enforcement of Creditor Rights

Looking at judicial enforcement, a wide spectrum of difficulties have been printed out. The first principal problem is the slowness of the judicial process. This is demonstrated by two recent surveys. The first, a survey of businesspeople, shows that more than 90 percent believe that the judiciary performs poorly in terms of the speed of case resolution.[10] A second, this time of judges, revealed that more than 45 percent share this opinion.[11]

Judicial slowness harms credit markets in at least three distinct ways. First, it dilutes the credibility of the threat of judicial action to enforce creditors' rights. Even for small borrowers, the prospect of judicial collection is less threatening than negative information entering their credit report at the private credit-reporting bureaus, the Centralização de Serviços dos Bancos (Private Credit Reporting Bureau; SERASA) or the Serviço Central de Proteção ao Crédito (Credit Protection Service; SCPC) (see below).[12] Next, it creates perverse incentives for debtors to use the judiciary to postpone fulfilling obligations (that is, to delay repayments). Judges surveyed consider this practice to be quite frequent (60 percent of the time) in cases concerning credit operations, second only to tax cases and ahead of disputes related to rent of real estate, commercial transactions, and labor conflicts (table 6.1).

In addition, slowness greatly reduces the value of collateral, which often depreciates or disappears during the judicial process. This is one reason why collateral values often considerably exceed loan values. Fiduciary alienation in the case of vehicles has been an exception, but creditors have been reluctant to use this instrument for other credit contracts until there is a sufficient jurisprudence. Loans for cars carry a much lower interest rate than for *duplicatas* and a fortiori less than for consumer loans.

Table 6.1 Frequency with Which Private Parties Resort to Justice to Postpone Obligations, by Area of Law
(percent)

Area of law	*Very frequent*	*Somewhat frequent*	*Infrequent*	*Never or almost never occurs*	*Do not know/no opinion*	*No answer*
Tax	45.4	25.7	8.7	1.8	12.5	5.9
Credit market	32.7	27.5	13.8	3.8	15.9	6.3
Labor	25.4	18.6	20.0	18.8	12	5.3
Commercial	24.8	34.5	16.5	3.1	14.2	6.9
Real estate rent contracts	20.2	30.8	22.4	8.0	11.7	6.9
Consumer rights	8.6	17.5	33.5	21.3	13.4	5.7
Environment	8.1	17.9	29.8	20.0	17.9	6.2
Intellectual property	8.1	17.5	29.3	9.2	27.8	8.1

Note: The question read, "It is often argued that many people, firms and interest groups resort to the judiciary not to claim their rights, but to exploit the slowness of the judiciary. In your view, in which kind of cases is this practice more frequent?"
Source: Pinheiro (2001).

Time Taken for Judicial Actions in Brazil

In the case of judicial debt collection, the problem of slowness starts with *notifying* the debtor. Although small debtors are usually not hard to find, locating large debtors can take years. If a process is started without the debtor being notified, it will likely have to start once again, going through the same steps, if the debtor later shows up. This makes notification an essential step in any judicial collection and a major cause for delay in some cases.

Next, a *cognizance action* lasts, on average, five years, often with experts required to determine *loan value.* Interest is sometimes compounded on a daily basis, with daily interest rates of up to 20 decimal places. Once a decision is reached and the *execution action* begins, a dispute usually arises concerning the *value of pledgable assets.* Two years can elapse discussing the acceptability or value of the assets (debtors have offered public debt securities issued a century ago). The discussion about the acceptability and value of the assets can go up to the Supreme Court, with the case returning to the First Degree Court once this issue has been settled.

After determining the pledge, the debtor may present an *embargo,* which takes about six months to rule but could be much longer if the judge requests an expert opinion. Once a decision is reached, the debtor may then initiate another embargo action and this may go on successively until "all chances of defense are exhausted." Note also that the debtor may request a *negotiation* at any time during the process, and the creditor is then asked to participate in good faith. Once all embargoes are judged and a decision is reached, the debtor may still *appeal* to a higher court. In São Paulo, Brazil's financial center, the *Tribunal de Justiça* (appeals court) may take two years just to assign the case to a Second-Degree judge. An additional two years may pass until a decision is reached, and the debtor is again allowed to present embargoes. Generally, the entire process may take somewhere between 1 and 10 years, depending on the creditor's case and the skill of the debtor's lawyers.

A second general problem with judicial enforcement procedures today is the excesssive procedural formalism of the Brazilian judiciary, as confirmed by a majority (more than 51 percent) of the judges surveyed. The correct writing of the contract, detailing of guarantees, witnessing, and so forth are of fundamental importance and can be more important than the demonstration of good-faith intent. As discussed in the next section, guarantees and collateral not only require registration, but also the process of registration can require several supporting documents.

This procedural formalism also implies that some common forms of consumer and small-enterprise credit, such as the overdraft facility (*cheque especial*), which can be exercised at a bank ATM, are not recognized as self-executable instruments. These require borrower and creditor signatures, two witnesses, and specified loan value. In this case, the formalistic approach of legislation has not kept up with common methods of contracting loans in the present technological environment. This is also true of the *duplicata*. To be self-executable, the *duplicata* must be signed by the client who buys the good or service that originated it. In practice, however, banks simply provide a specific software to clients, in which the basic information on the *duplicata* is recorded. The law, however, still requires written documents, so that the certainty of the debt may be challenged in court.

Third, the cost of judicial collection is high. Lawyers hired by banks charge up to 20 percent of the value recovered, plus reimbursement of expenses. In São Paulo, the party that starts the case has to pay court fees of 1 percent of the value in question, plus 1 percent on appeal, plus 1 percent for the execution action. Creditors also have to pay to register documents, for debtor notification, and for the listing of pledgable assets. For small loans, judicial recovery is relatively costly to initiate. In contrast, collection agencies charge a success fee between 5 percent and 10 percent of the value recovered.

Fourth, creditors argue that a pro-debtor bias in judicial rulings weakens the protection of their rights established in the law. An often-cited view is that in many instances, the judiciary does not apply the law but rather seeks to do 'social justice.' An analysis of the politicization of judicial decisions through the survey of 741 judges mentioned above suggests that a fifth of the judges believe this to be frequent (table 6.2). For credit operations, the likelihood of such politicization is relatively high; around 40 percent of those surveyed believed it to be frequent or very frequent.

Even if this stance is more common in lower courts and can often be reversed by appealing to higher courts, it can significantly weaken creditor protection not least because of the costs involved in paying lawyers, court fees, and so forth. This sort of judicial activism explains why, when new legislation is passed to 'clarify' certain aspects of the law or to change the way judges tend to decide, creditors wait until a sufficient number of rulings establish the interpretation of judges before using new legislation.

Fifth and finally, other features of the judiciary affect the performance of credit markets. First, there are sizable differences among the judicial systems of the various states, and even inside a state, the quality of courts varies from one jurisdiction to another. Second, the judiciary, as any large institution, is not free from problems of corruption and political influence, which are perceived to be more likely to happen in some states than in others and to have the financial sector as a frequent target (Aith 2000).

Table 6.2 Likelihood of Judges´ Decisions Being Politicized, by Type of Cause
(percent)

Type of cause	*Very frequent*	*Some-what frequent*	*Infre-quent*	*Never or almost never occurs*	*Do not know/no opinion*	*No answer*
Privatization	25.0	31.4	17.5	5.5	11.9	8.6
Public utilities	17.9	32.5	20.9	7.4	13.0	8.2
Environment	17.1	28.2	22.1	10.9	12.4	9.2
Labor	17.0	28.1	25.9	12.0	10.7	6.3
Social security	14.7	31.3	27.1	9.6	9.3	8.0
Consumer rights	12.0	29.6	25.8	13.4	10.9	8.4
Credit markets (e.g., interest rates)	12.0	27.4	26.9	10.3	14.6	8.9
Tax	10.5	28.1	34.3	9.9	9.2	8.1
Rent contracts	4.9	15.2	35.1	22.7	12.8	9.3
Commercial	3.2	14.4	43.6	16.7	12.6	9.5
Intellectual property	1.9	10.5	35.1	20.1	22.7	9.7

Note: The question read, "In your opinion, in which types of cases is it more frequently the case that decisions reflect more the political beliefs of the judges than a rigorous interpretation of the law?"
Source: Pinheiro (2001).

Third, judicial performance could be greatly improved with educational, management, and organizational reforms.

Differential Impacts on Small Borrowers

Conditions faced by small borrowers, whether individuals or small businesses, in the retail market differ from those prevailing in the middle and corporate markets not only due to loan size but also by the different ways the judicial system affects borrower–creditor relationships. There are five main reasons for this differential impact of judicial enforcement on the access of small borrowers to credit. First, for creditors, the costs involved in judicial action, as a ratio of loan value, against small borrowers is high. Second, incentives to initiate judicial action against small borrowers are reduced by the tax allowances available for small loans (creditors may deduct even unsecured loans up to R$30,000 independent of judicial action). Third, small borrowers often lack sufficient executable assets to cover repayment. This is true not only for individuals but also for small businesses, in which case the firm's and its owner's assets are often mixed together. For this reason, in retail operations collateral plays a minor role. Fourth, because small loans are often extended to poor individuals or small enterprises, they are more likely to benefit from the sort of judicial activism described in the previous section, not the least because banks charge very high interest rates in retail market loans. And fifth, small loans are less likely to be self-executable, as they are usually extended using less formal 'contracts.' The problem is often compounded in the case of special checks or guaranteed accounts by the fact that banks take decisions not foreseen in the contract (for example, the client borrows beyond the credit ceiling established in the initial contract, a fact accepted by the bank, which charges fees and higher interest for this extra credit). All these features make these debts far from liquid and certain.

For these various reasons, in the retail market, banks do not count on the judicial system to enforce payment. First and foremost, banks rely on the law of large numbers, correcting the loan spread to cover the expected loss in each loan. Because retail loans are of short maturity and very numerous, this mechanism is effective. For similar reasons, some banks extend overdrafts to small-company loans as well, by buying the company's receivables at a discount. This is the case, for instance, of postdated checks. The absence of effective judicial remedies for cases of default or nonpayment increases the expected losses banks must face in these mass credit market segments and thus increases the spread charged. This contributes to more severe credit rationing than would occur in a market with a more effective judicial system.

Second, creditors are increasingly relying on credit-reporting services, such as SCPC , SERASA, and others to provide incentives for repayment. Given that the reputational collateral of small borrowers may be their only real collateral, these can be a key source of creditor pressure. Third, in the case of default, creditors transfer collection to specialized companies. All retail credit collection is outsourced soon after the debt is due.

Ongoing Government Measures and Suggestions for Further Reform

The government has attempted to pass legal reforms to increase creditor protection in retail markets. These include, first, the creation of the Cédula de Crédito Bancário (Bank Credit Bill; CCB), an executable security to be used in retail market operations, which allows banks to start judicial collection with an execution action, jumping therefore the cognizance action. Initially created as a provisional measure, it was formally enshrined in the legal system with Constitutional Amendment 32 (September 11, 2001). Its introduction was partly motivated by a decision of the Superior Tribunal of Justice ruling that a debt through overdraft (*cheque especial*) was not executable on the basis of bank statements showing how much was drawn and the interest due. This was deemed to lack certainty and liquidity. It was also perceived that the bank statement is a unilateral document and that in many instances contained other charges, not related to the debt, perceived as abusive by the judiciary.

In principle, the CCB can reduce costs (it does not need to be registered in a public registry), speed up credit recovery (it is an executable title), and even be sold and bought by third parties. In practice, however, it has been little used, as banks have been insecure about how the judiciary will treat it, but this may have been before the constitutional amendment of 2001. Some of the banks that did use it did not follow the norms established for the CCB, adopting contract forms typical of other credit securities, such as promissory notes.

Second, the Superior Tribunal of Justice has tried to clarify the conditions under which banks can capitalize interest rates, despite the still outstanding Usury Law of 1933. But these rules leave aside informal retail operations, as they require the use of instruments regulated by law in which the capitalization of interest is explicitly cited in the contract. To allow a more general use of compounded interest rates, the government legislated, through Provisional Measure 1963, of August 2000, that financial institutions were allowed to charge compounded interest rates. The possible revocation of this measure is now under consideration at the Supreme Court.

Third, because many of the issues that delay judicial decisions concern the discussion of the value of interest that has accrued on the loan, the Central Bank has suggested that the discussion of interest and principal repayment should be separated. If implemented, this would allow the creditor to ask the court to immediately tell the debtor to pay the principal while discussion continues on the value of interest payments. By reducing the benefit of postponing a decision, this would also tend to discourage ill-intentioned borrowers to use the judiciary only to postpone debt payment. However, although the spirit of the proposal is sound, some of the bank lawyers interviewed point out that this could increase costs, for it would require two processes instead of one. Moreover, as judges have a tendency to group actions pertaining to the same matter, they would almost certainly do this in this instance. An additional potential complication is that pledged assets would be the same for the principal and interest, and separation of these would require two execution actions and raise complicated issues concerning the sale of those assets.

Fourth, in house financing, one of the market segments most affected by the weakness of creditor protection in Brazil, the government approved new legislation in 1997 extending the use of chattel mortgage (fiduciary alienation) to the financing of real estate. This instrument, successfully used in car finance, keeps property of the financed asset with the creditor until the debt is fully paid. In this way, it tries to circumvent the restriction imposed by the judiciary on the repossession of the debtor's home when this is given as collateral in house-financing loans. In practice, however, this instrument has failed to boost house financing, especially by private banks, largely because of concerns of judicial interpretation. All Brazilians are entitled to housing as a constitutional principle, and this may block the repossession of the debtor's house. Therefore, until disputes involving this law reach the Supreme Court and jurisprudence is established, the use of fiduciary alienation will be slower than desired.

Finally, the government is working with Congress on the passage of a new bankruptcy law, which is a marked improvement over the existing legal framework for both the reorganization of companies in financial difficulties and for increased protection to creditors and better asset recovery in bankruptcy proceedings. Brazil's main efforts to update its corporate insolvency legislation started in 1993 and were finally approved by the lower house in Congress in October 2003.[13] Changes in Brazil's 1966 Tax Code (Código Tributário Nacional; CTN) were simultaneously voted on, which reinforced the strengthening of creditor rights by removing the prior claims of tax authorities on the proceedings from bankruptcy. These changes are very significant, and once finally approved, will bring the legal framework for bankruptcy in Brazil substantially in line with good international practice.[14]

As the preceding discussion shows, the issues are complex and solutions difficult to find. Nevertheless, it also reveals that there are potential areas for reform which, by strengthening creditor rights, could extend loan services and reduce the costs of such services. These suggestions are:

- A major effort must be made to work with the judges and society at large to show that decisions benefiting a specific borrower in a specific case have broad repercussions that harm borrowers as a whole, at a wider level. As a political process, judicial activism must be dealt with in the political arena by building the constituency in favor of the strict enforcement of credit contracts.
- Judicial education is additionally desirable to establish a better understanding of specific financial instruments, such as self-executable instruments and *cédulas*, and to establish more uniformity in jurisprudence.
- In addition, the self-execution of instruments used for small borrowers in the modern context can be reinforced, for example, the overdraft facilities offered over the ATM or the *duplicatas* of small firms. In keeping with new technology, legal recognition of these debts could be explored.

- The most promising area of reform in the short term is in changing the procedural codes to speed up judgments, an initiative that would likely be supported by the magistracy. Judges largely agree that judicial slowness could be substantially decreased with a reform of procedural codes to reduce the possibilities of postponing a decision or of appeal processes.
- To reduce costs and time for judicial execution of debt, the Special Courts could be opened to small credits. These courts judge exclusively low-value disputes, operate with much lighter procedures, and do not require the parties to be represented by a lawyer; also, their decisions cannot be appealed. For that, either the law that created the *Juizados Especiais* would have to be amended to allow banks and other financial institutions to act as plaintiffs, or a new law would be necessary to create special claims courts able to judge small-debt collections. The proposed new courts could be designed to combine pro-debtor services as well as the settlement of small loans, in order to make them socially and politically acceptable.
- Finally, current tax write-offs against profits on uncollected small claims can be evaluated in a wider context, as these may be sending perverse signals to both borrowers and financial institutions for debt repayment. International practice in the design of more incentive-compatible tax treatment for small claims can be investigated.

Security Interests

As the previous section discussed, debt recovery processes are complex, and there are advantages in this process for secured creditors, who enjoy priority over other creditors in the payment of debtor's liabilities.[15] The Brazilian legal system provides for various types of security interests, such as pledges, mortgages, and 'fiduciary sales.'[16] Other possible structures are based on conditional sales and leasing. The efficiency, reliability, and cost of the process of registration of security interests thus directly affects creditor risk and cost, and hence, the availability and cost of credit.

Institutions and Services Required for Securing Credit Interests

Security interests in real or personal property are perfected through registration, either at a Real Estate Registry or at a Registry of Deeds and Documents.[17] Notarial services, or cartório de notas, which include the preparation of deeds and certification of copies, may also be required as a part of the process of perfection of a security interest. Brazil has more than 21,000 registry offices.[18] An illustrative list of registry offices in state capitals and in two major cities in the state of São Paulo is given in table 6.3.

Table 6.3 Registry Offices in State Capitals and Two Major Cities in São Paulo, Brazil

Capital of state/city	*Real estate registry*	*Registries of deeds and documents*	*Notaries public*
São Paulo City (state capital)	18	10	30
Campinas, São Paulo	3	8	
Ribeirão Preto, São Paulo	2	5	
Pôrto Alegre, capital of Rio Grande do Sul	3	1	6
Florianópolis, capital of Santa Catarina	2	1	4
Curitiba, capital of Paraná	9	4	12 (capital) 19 other town districts
Rio de Janeiro City (state capital)	11	6	24
Vitória, capital of Espírito Santo	3	1	6
Belo Horizonte, capital of Minas Gerais	7	2	10
Salvador, capital of Bahia	7	2	14
Aracaju, capital of Sergipe	4	1	11
Maceió, capital of Alagoas	3	2	6
Recife, capital of Pernambuco	4	2	8
João Pessoa, capital of Paraíba	2	2	10
Natal, capital of Rio Grande do Norte	3	1	7
Fortaleza, capital of Ceará	6	1	3
Teresina, capital of Piauí	3	1	6
São Luís, capital of Maranhão	2	1	4
Palmas, capital of Tocantins	1	1	4
Goiânia, capital of Goiás	4	2	10
Brasília, Federal District Government	9	7	19
Campo Grande, capital of Mato Grosso do Sul	5	1	10
Cuiabá, capital of Mato Grosso	4	1	11
Porto Velho, capital of Rondônia	2	1	6
Rio Branco, capital of Acre	2	1	2
Manaus, capital of Amazonas	4	1	6
Boa Vista, capital of Roraima	1	1	2
Belém, capital of Pará	2	2	10
Macapá, capital of Amapá	1	1	2

Note: Offices in accordance with Law No. 8.935/94
Source: Felsberg and Associates (2003).

Notarial Services

Notarial services in Brazil are provided by individuals, under federal legal provisions, supplemented by state laws and regulations on judicial organization enacted by the Corregedorias Gerais de Justiça of each state.[19] Selection of notaries public is today undertaken by a competitive public service examination for individuals who also fulfill certain professional qualifications and meet standards of integrity. Appointments are specific to a given municipality. The notarial function enjoys judicial oversight and inspection, although each state determines the form and level of such oversight. Each state has an association with which all notaries public and protest notaries are affiliated, the Colégio Notarial, constituted as a private corporation and working in collaboration with the government as to improve notarial services. The Notary Association for each state is affiliated with a Federal Council, which in turn is affiliated to the International Union of the Latin Body of Notaries (União Internacional do Notariado Latino), headquartered in Buenos Aires with an administrative office in Rome. This international recognition of Brazil's notaries facilitates overseas business transactions.

The present integrity and oversight of the notarial office in Brazil represents huge progress compared to the system that prevailed 15 years ago. Before the enactment of the Federal Constitution of 1988, the power to provide public notary and registry service was delegated by the governor of each state, without any objective or fair criteria. Positions were held on a lifelong basis and, in some cases, were inherited, purchased, or sold. The award of a registry or notarial appointment was a valuable franchise, not to be easily given up. The notary function had evolved over time as a position to benefit those who enjoyed political favor, and its reform is relatively recent. Unfortunately, several notary and registry offices managed by individuals who were delegated such powers before these rules still function today, and they may not be removed except in rare circumstances.[20]

Security in Personal Property: The Registry of Deeds and Documents

The Registry of Deeds and Documents enables public access to contracts and records agreements that establish security interests. Such agreements include pledges (*penhor*) of movables (for example, equipment, machinery, inventory, vehicles), credit instruments, bonds or bearer securities, livestock, and any other recordings not expressly attributed to any other registry. To be valid and enforceable in Brazil, the written pledge agreement must be registered with a Registry of Deeds and Documents, by the borrower or the lender. There are also provisions under the law for pledges of receivables, rights, and corporate stock. Other security interests that may be recorded are fiduciary sales (under Articles 1361–1368 of the New Civil Code), which guarantee a debt using personal property as collateral. Other ways of securing transactions consist of structuring deals as conditional sales[21] or lease transactions.[22] Personal property may be used to secure different kinds of debts. Banks usually require most businesses to offer collateral for their loans, and even normal businesses require their clients to put up collateral for transactions.

If a search on a pledge deed or asset is needed, the party contacts the Deeds and Documents Registry where the pledgor and pledgee reside. If there is more than one registry office at the location, there is a Central Distribution Office for Registries of Deeds and Documents, at least in larger locations. However, even these offices are specific to a given region or area such as a large metropolitan region. If the company's office location changes, a search is needed in all districts where the company held an office.

SECURITY IN REAL PROPERTY: REAL ESTATE REGISTRIES

Security interests in real property in Brazil that are registered at the Real Estate Registry Office are mortgages (*hipoteca*),[23] fiduciary sales (*alienação fiduciária*),[24] and pledges of immovable assets that are registered in the real estate registry.[25] These must be filed with the Real Estate Registry Office where the concerned property or immovable is recorded, as larger judicial districts contain more than one Real Estate Registry Office and, unlike deeds and documents registries, no Central Real Estate Registry Office exists.

Each Real Estate Registry has various books, recording different types of security interests. For example, agreements that are not directly related to the real estate recorded, such as rural and industrial credit instruments, pledges of machines and instruments used for industrial purposes (industrial pledge), and rural pledge agreements, are filed in Book III of the Real Estate Registry Office. Mortgaged securities are recorded in Book II of each Real Estate Registry Office. If there is more than one mortgage security in a transaction, each at a different location, registration must be filed in each one of the districts. This could significantly affect the extent to which mortgages could be 'bundled,' as, for example, in a securitization process. In this case, each mortgage and credit instrument will be filed in Book III in each office that has recorded the documents creating the respective mortgages. When a pledge and a mortgage are simultaneously established, they may thus be filed with several registries.

Cost of Public Deeds and Registries

Costs and fees associated with public registries (*custas e emolumentos*) are provided for in state statutes with separate price lists, collection procedures, and rules for each kind of registry. Registration fees are often regarded as high, but as these fees are a good revenue source, proposals for changing state laws to reduce these fees find no support either before the Brazilian Congress or before state Legislative Assemblies.

Fees for Notary Publics

Costs for drafting documents and related notarial acts depend on the transaction fee and the underlying value of the assets involved. Although fees rise with transaction values, the incremental fees charged, as transaction value increases, decrease. The implication is that these fees are regressive in terms of economic incidence. Thus, individuals at the lower end of the income scale, with smaller transaction values or small enterprises, would proportionally pay more for notarial transactions than people or enterprises involved in larger-value transactions. As shown in table 6.4, notarial fees as a percentage of transaction value declined from 14 percent for a mortgage value of R$1,000 to around 1.7 percent for a mortgage of R$50,000 and to only 0.2 percent or less for mortgages in excess of R$3 million.

Fees at Real Estate Registries

Fees associated with Real Estate Registries function similarly, with a tiered structure based on the economic value of the legal transaction under registration, the fair market value of the property established by the municipality (for urban property), or by a federal agency (for rural property). Fees are capped at the upper end, and only large operations can benefit from this. Thus, again, costs are proportionally higher for smaller and simpler transactions (figure 6.2).

Fees at Registries of Deeds and Documents

Not surprisingly, fees at Registries of Deeds and Documents are structured similarly (table 6.5). Although fees rise in absolute terms with the value of the contract to be registered, fees decline in proportional terms as contract value increases. Fees are also disassociated with costs, as registration costs are regardless of the number of pages of the document to be registered. In cases in which documents have to be manually transcribed and can run into hundreds of pages, there would appear to be a prima facie case for taking this into consideration.

Search Processes at Registries

Current search systems in Brazil for secured credit interests, even once registered, are not easy. A personal visit to the relevant registry by the interested party or a representative is required. Search results are often

Table 6.4 Notarial Fees for Drafting a Public Deed of Mortgage in the State of São Paulo

Average mortgage value (R$'000)	*Fees payable (R$)*							*Costs/average mortgage value (%)*
	Notarial fees	*Federal government*	*IPESP*	*Civil registries*	*Justice*	*Charity*[a]	*Total cost*	
0.2	64	18	13	3	3	1	102	44.97
1	95	27	20	5	5	1	153	14.05
4	212	60	45	11	11	2	341	7.92
29	403	115	85	21	21	4	649	2.26
52	541	154	114	29	29	5	872	1.69
107	871	247	183	46	46	9	1,402	1.31
287	1,073	305	226	56	56	11	1,728	0.60
402	1,190	338	251	63	63	12	1,916	0.48
935	1,826	519	384	96	96	18	2,940	0.31
3,214	4,018	1,142	846	211	211	40	6,468	0.20
4,967	5,661	1,609	1,192	298	298	57	9,115	0.18
7,597	8,400	2,388	1,769	442	442	84	13,525	0.18
9,934	10,592	3,010	2,230	557	557	106	17,053	0.17

a. Santa Casa Hospital. For complete table go to http://www.anoregsp.org.br/leis/tabelaI_03.htm.
Source: ANOREG-SP (São Paulo data), http://www.anoregsp.org.br/.

Figure 6.2 Registration Costs of Mortgages in the State of São Paulo

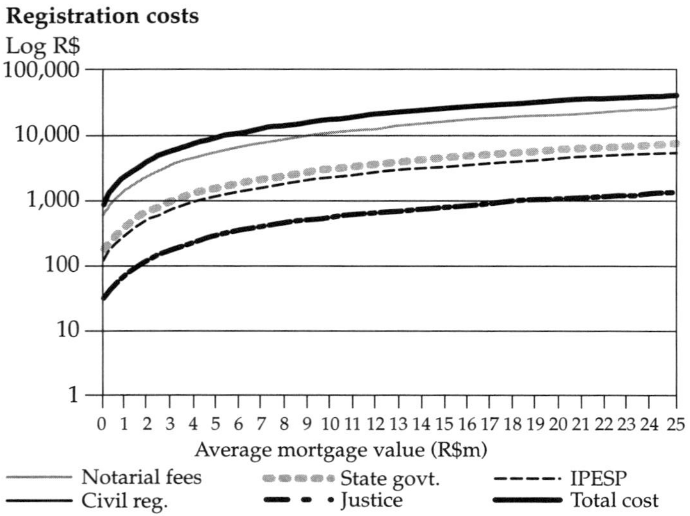

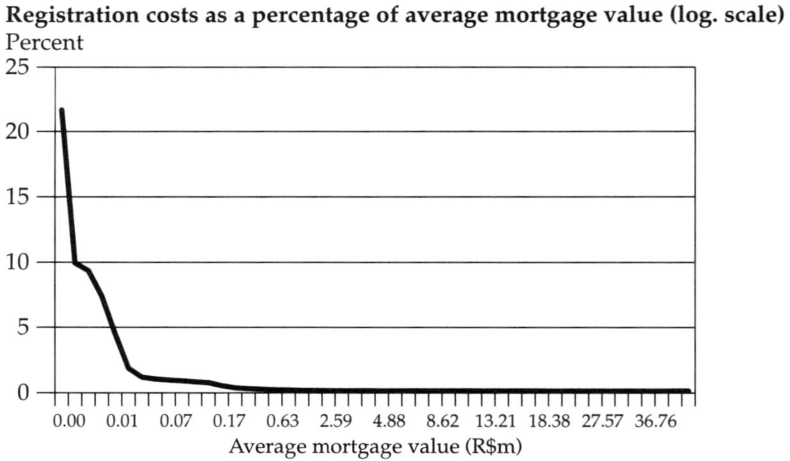

Average mortgage value (R$'000)	*Fees payable (R$)*						*Costs/average mortgage value (%)*
	Notarial fees	*State government*	*IPESP*	*Civil registries*	*Justice*	*Total cost*	
0.3	47	13	10	2	2	75	21.68
1	75	21	16	4	4	120	9.94
9	242	69	51	13	13	388	4.50

Source: ANOREG-SP (São Paulo data), http://www.anoregsp.org.br/leis/tabelaII_03.htm

Table 6.5 Registration Costs for Deeds and Documents in the State of São Paulo

Average mortgage value (R$'000)	*Fees payable (R$)*						*Costs/average mortgage value (%)*
	Notarial fees	*State government*	*IPESP*	*Civil registries*	*Justice*	*Total cost*	
0.3	22	6	5	1	1	34	10.01
1	32	9	7	2	2	52	4.29
4	70	20	15	4	4	112	2.60
9	108	31	23	6	6	172	2.67
46	266	76	56	14	14	425	0.93
93	395	112	83	21	21	632	0.68
350	396	113	83	21	21	634	0.18
1,023	588	167	124	31	31	941	0.09
4,383	977	278	206	51	51	1,563	0.04
10,227	1,754	499	369	92	92	2,807	0.03
20,453	2,976	846	626	157	157	4,761	0.02
29,219	3,753	1,067	790	198	198	6,005	0.02

Source: ANOREG-SP (São Paulo data).

given orally by the notary or an office clerk, although a written certificate may be requested. A search takes approximately five business days in the São Paulo area.

There is no particular relationship between the different registry systems in Brazil, except for large Judicial Districts, where a Central Distribution Office for Registries of Deeds and Documents exists. São Paulo city has such a Central Distribution Office. It also has an Association of Real Estate Registry Offices called Associação dos Registradores Imobiliários de São Paulo (ARISP), but this is unusual. Given the lack of linkages between registries of different types, and even of the same type in different locations, it is difficult to conduct a search on a security interest without some prior knowledge of the type of secured credit and location of asset, pledgor, or pledgee as applicable, depending on the type of asset.

For example to find out if a given piece of real estate is mortgaged, research should be done at the Real Estate Registry Office in that specific geographic area. If conducting research regarding pledge agreement involving movable assets of a company, the inquiry must be addressed to the Registry of Deeds and Documents in the area where the company is headquartered, or if there is more than one registry, to the Central Distribution Office for Registries of the region. Thus, unravelling a variety of security interests in the assets of, say, an enterprise could be a difficult undertaking. Ideally, a national system for all related types of registries would be required to ease this.

One partial alternative, which could be authorized by each state's Corregedoria Geral de Justiça, is to consolidate requests for consultation and certificates in one office per city, where all files of that city could be accessed. The ARISP office for the 18 Registries of Real Estate in the capital city of São Paulo provides one such example. A second example of better information management is given by the pilot system of the Caixa Econômica Federal (National Savings Banks; CEF).

New Search Systems: ARISP and CEF

In 1998, ARISP launched a certification service for integrating the 18 Real Estate Registry Offices in the capital city. Before 1998, to know, for instance, whether or not someone owned real properties in the city, it would have been necessary to visit each city registry. It would be virtually impossible to check on the situation for the entire state or in all 26 Brazilian states or the more than 5,500 municipalities. Since 1998, ARISP has introduced two new processes for search and certification requests. Under the first system, approved by the Corregedoria Geral da Justiça, a person may request a certificate from any participating Real Estate Registry at any office in town. Certificates can be collected at the office where the request was made or at any other participating office. The second alternative is to request a certificate directly at ARISP through their website (www.arisp.com.br).

A second innovation is being introduced by the CEF, which is responsible for almost 70 percent of housing financing in Brazil, together with the Brazilian Notary and Registry Association (Associação dos Notários e Registradores do Brasil; ANOREG). These entities entered into an agreement on June 9, 2002, to reduce costs and expedite the housing financing process in addition to facilitating securitization transactions. Under this agreement, people would be able to obtain certificates through electronic media at Internet Caixa (www.caixa.com.br). Available documents will initially include attestations of ownership and liens as well as certificates issued by land registries in the city of São Paulo. Documents will be issued in two versions: a certified electronic version and another version in hard copy, to be sent through the mail to the person who requested it.[26] The pilot project will be carried out at registry offices in São Paulo.

As discussed further below, documentary requirements for any housing finance transaction are complex and require a series of documents, normally issued by several offices, such as certificates relating to tax foreclosure and civil lawsuits (Certidão dos Distribuidores Cíveis), certificates issued by the offices for the protest of commercial paper (Certidão dos Cartórios de Protestos), and updated certificates relating to the whole history of a given real estate property (Certidão Atualizada de Inteiro Teor da Matrícula do Imóvel). Implementation of the agreement between CEF and ANOREG will end the need to visit all the individual offices concerned with this, as all information needed will be available at CEF on the Internet.

Electronic certification of documents will also enable securitization transactions and boost the creation of a secondary market for housing securities, where an investor may buy a 'bundle' of standardized contracts from an institution. Without electronic records, documentation requirements pertinent to each individual contract would be nearly impossible on any scale. Securitization is important for the increase of long-term investments in the real estate market.

Other Obstacles Faced in the Registration Process

Documentary Requirements

When there is a need to purchase or encumber a real estate property, multiple documents need to be requested to safeguard the safety of the transaction. It is not enough to verify the status of the real estate at the registry according to the real estate files. It is also necessary to see if there are any encumbrances on the property. The creditor or the purchaser must also check the debtor's or the seller's personal documents and other docu-

Documentation Requirements for Securing a Credit Interest in Real Estate

These include, first, documents pertaining to the property, including (1) a certificate issued by the Real Estate Registry Office, listing the individuals who had title to the property during the past 20 years and confirming that the property is unencumbered; (2) a clearance certificate regarding urban property tax issued by the municipality; (3) a statement issued by the condominium regarding the settlement of the respective condominium fees; and (4) a property value assessment, required in case of collateral for mortgage purposes and, inter alia, for the purposes of claiming eligibility for funding from the Housing Finance System, used for lower-income housing.

Next, there are documentary requirements pertaining to the owner, his or her spouse, and former owners for periods that can be up to the past 20 years, including (1) State Court statement regarding judicial actions, including reorganization and bankruptcy, interdiction and guardianship; (2) court records for protested commercial papers; (3) a Federal Court statement regarding any judicial actions; (4) a State Revenue Service statement related to any state tax foreclosures; (5) a Municipal Revenue Service statement related to any local tax foreclosures; (6) a clearance certificate related to labor claims; and (7) a list of outstanding federal debts.

There are additional documents required if the seller or former owners are a legal entity, including (1) State Court certificates pertaining to judicial actions, including reorganization and bankruptcy; (2) court records on protested commercial papers; (3) a Federal Court statement regarding any judicial actions; (4) a State Revenue Service statement related to any state tax foreclosures; (5) a Municipal Revenue Service statement related to any local tax foreclosure; (6) a clearance certificate related to labor claims; (7) a list of outstanding federal debts; (8) a clearance certificate issued by the Social Security Agency related to social security taxes; and (9) a clearance certificate issued by the Federal Revenue Service related to federal taxes.

ments related to the real estate. Bureaucratic documentation requirements for carrying out a secured credit transaction are extensive.

Time Taken for Registration: Equipment Limitations of Smaller Offices

While Deeds and Documents Registries equipped with microfilm equipment are able to register agreements submitted to their offices in a day (as is the case in most metropolitan cities), to register a pledge agreement on movable property in a small office without a microfilm system is time consuming and burdensome. The agreement must be manually transcribed, which may take a long time.[27] Again, this particularly adversely affects small-value transactions and the possibility of the use of collateral for individuals and microproducers. There are no provisions in public records law for deadlines that the Registries of Deeds and Documents should meet for undertaking registration. Small cities lack motivation as well as the means to move away from a manual recordation system.

Suggestions for Simplifying the Creation of Security Rights

As the preceding sections show, the process for securing creditor rights, in practice, is not always easy, and this impedes the development of secured transactions. Several measures have also emerged in this discussion, which if adopted could lead to an improvement in the process. These include

- Expedite the adoption of electronic filing, retrieval, and indexation systems at all registration offices in the country.
- Establish networks for the interlinkage of registries, initially if necessary on a pilot basis within cities, regions, or state, and eventually, across regions and across the different types of registries required for different types of security interests (for example, pledges versus mortgages, currently under different registries).
- Adopt deadlines for turnover time for registries of deeds and documents, which will shorten the time taken for these processes and may encourage the adoption of modern technologies. Investigate the five-day time and costs taken to conduct a search and certification, which could both be reduced by a self-guided web search.
- Examine any modifications that may be required in the legal framework, at both the federal or state levels, which could be necessary to accompany such a process of networking of registries.
- Investigate tariff structures of registries and notaries public, which at present are regressive in their incidence, with disproportionately high costs for smaller transactions. Remove the caps on the upper end of the scale and, if necessary, use the proceeds to lower transaction costs for small-scale transactions.
- Examine the documentation requirements for secured transactions in real estate to evaluate the scope for simplification or consolidation.
- Finally, examine through the offices of judicial oversight the extent to which notarial and registration services are still operating on a franchise basis and assess the extent to which this is likely to remain a longer-term problem. Investigate measures that could be adopted within the present legal framework to ameliorate its impact in the near term.

Credit Information and Credit Reporting

Credit information registries are especially important in countries such as Brazil, where debt recovery is difficult. By improving the lender's ability to evaluate credit risk, credit registries reduce the time and cost associated with loan processing and strengthen credit quality. In competitive credit markets, this means greater access to credit on more competitive terms. Credit registries provide rapid access to standardized information on past behavior of potential borrowers, recognized to be one of the best predictors of their future behavior. Such 'reputation collateral' provides borrowers with an incentive to meet their commitments in much the same way as does a pledge of physical collateral.

Credit reporting is a rapidly growing industry internationally, due both to improved conditions for finance in many developing countries and to technological advances in computing and software, which make it possible to collect and analyze large quantities of data at a low cost and in a timely fashion. Seven of the 15 member nations of the European Union have public credit registries, as do most nations in Latin America.[28] Together with credit decision tools like credit scoring, these promise increased access to credit to previously underserved segments of the population.

Low-income consumers and micro- and small businesses, which operate mainly on a cash-flow basis and lack physical collateral, can particularly benefit from credit reporting. However, it is important to ensure that particularly small-business reporting does not fall between the cracks of consumer and commercial credit bureaus. A viable credit information infrastructure of a country would typically consist of public and private credit registries, covering different kinds and sizes of borrowers, from consumers all the way up to large corporates (figure 6.3). Although public registries would serve supervisory functions and require lenders to report loans above a minimum amount, private credit registries enable lenders and investors to make better credit decisions. As the consumer credit history of the owner of a small business is one of the most predictable pieces of information in making a credit decision for a small business, it is important to link and integrate small-business reporting with consumer reporting. Even in the United States it took some time to close the missing gap of reporting on small businesses, and good examples of integrated systems are Italy and Australia, among others.

As shown in the following sections, relative to most other emerging markets, Brazil has a fairly developed credit-reporting environment. However, the market remains fragmented, and only a very limited amount of positive credit data is available in credit reports. Given both the size of the market and the sophistication of its financial industry,

Figure 6.3 Use of Credit Registries by Different Entities

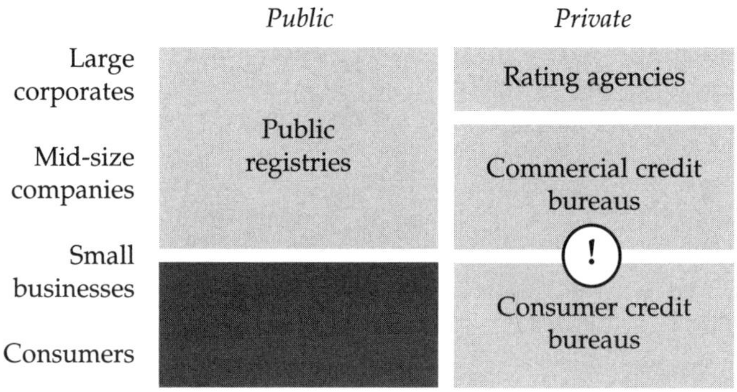

Note: The exclamation point = most widely used

Brazil would greatly benefit from further improvements to its credit information infrastructure. Priorities in this sector include reforms to the legal and regulatory framework to facilitate the reporting of positive credit information and steps to increase competition and overcome fragmentation in the private reporting industry making credit allocation decisions.

Sources of Credit Information in Brazil

Brazil enjoys several established sources of credit information, including two competing private credit bureaus, SERASA and Equifax do Brasil (formerly SCI; Segurança ao Crédito e Informações; Credit and Information Security), registries focused on retail credits administered by state and local Chambers of Commerce (of which the São Paulo registry is largest); a credit registry maintained by the Central Bank, known as the Central de Risco; and also a database for outstanding public-sector financial credit transactions such as fees and taxes, Cadasto Informativo de Crèditos não Quitados do Setor Público Federal (Registry of Citizens and Firms in Default with the Federal Government; CADIN) (table 6.6).

SERASA is the largest private credit-reporting firm in the developing world, with annual sales in excess of $100 million. It provides information for more than 300,000 direct and indirect customers and processes more than 2.5 million queries per day. Data available from SERASA include information on about 8.6 million companies legally established in Brazil, out of which 4.2 million are active, and 65 million individual consumers. Established in 1968 by Brazil's domestic banks to enable them to exchange information, it mainly focuses on negative information on borrowers.

Table 6.6 Major Credit Information Providers in Brazil, 2002

Name	*SERASA*	*São Paulo Chamber of Commerce*	*Equifax do Brasil*	*Central de Risco*
Date established	1968	1956	SCI 1974; Equifax purchased 80% in 1998	1997
No. of employees	1600	800	n.a.	6
No. of customers	44,000	100,000 (est.)	25,000	450
Sales (US$ millions)	112	25		
No. of individuals in database[a] (millions)	65	10.7	23	4.6
No. of firms in database (millions)	4.2	8.8	4	0.7
Main products	*SERASA*—Individuals *RELATO*—Businesses *ACHE*—*Recheque*— Bad-checks database, Cheque Scoring Credit Bureau Scoring	UseCheque— Bad-checks database SCPC—consumer loans database	Equifax Empresarial— Business behavior Equifax Pessoal—Credit report on individual Score Empresarial Cheque Pessoal (Empresarial) —Bad-check report on individuals (firms)	Bad-checks list; information on loans outstanding within financial system
Sources of information	Banks (200) Firms Public sources	Banks (64) Firms Public sources	Banks (very few) Firms Public sources	Banks (442)

Note: n.a. = not applicable.

a. Usually there is more than one entry for each individual or firm, for example, several lines of credit.

Source: World Bank staff interviews, field visits, and estimates.

Public banks, such as Banco do Brasil and Caixa Econômica Federal, also share information with SERASA.

Next in importance as a major provider of credit information are Chambers of Commerce led by the chamber in the city of São Paulo (Associação Comercial de São Paulo). Their credit registry, known as the SCPC, contains approximately 40 million records on about 10 million individuals and provides information to about 100,000 clients. Until recently, the data in these registries was almost exclusively from retail merchants in relation to store credits. This is changing, however, and banks now comprise a significant share of both the information provided to and demanded from SCPC. Similar databases are managed by the Chambers of Commerce in hundreds of other cities in the state of São Paulo, as well as in cities in the other Brazilian states. A recent important initiative is the creation of a computer network to link these registries across the states and country. As a nonprofit venture, SCPC has more restricted funding for investments in technology and infrastructure, as well as a less aggressive pricing policy. The cost of a consultation is affected by volume discounts and runs from R$0.46 to R$0.70.

Third in overall popularity and second among private credit-reporting firms in Brazil is Equifax do Brasil. This firm is majority owned by the U.S. credit-reporting agency Equifax, which purchased an 80 percent interest in the firm, previously known as SCI, in 1998. Since then, Equifax has invested heavily in technology, new product development, and a new office building in the financial district of São Paulo. The Equifax do Brasil database contains records on 13 million enterprises (out of which about 4 million are active), which consists primarily of header data (nonfinancial information such as name, address, and so forth) and 23 million consumers. The firm has a customer base of approximately 25,000 and focuses on providing reports to firms. The traditional focus of SCI was trade credit, where it maintains a dominant position in this market segment. The firm is also interested in challenging SERASA's dominance in the consumer credit-reporting market, but this is a difficult task.

New clients question whether it is worth providing data to Equifax, which has a smaller database than SERASA and which may not provide them additional useful information. Equifax do Brasil is focusing on value-added services and working intensively on the development of decision analysis tools, such as credit scoring. It has an exclusive relationship with Fair Isaac, the largest credit-scoring firm in the world, to develop these products. (Fair Isaac had been working with SERASA until summer 2001, when this relationship was terminated, and they began working with Equifax.)

The Central de Risco, run by the Brazilian Central Bank, began operation in 1998 and has steadily expanded since, progressively reducing the

Principal Credit-Reporting Products in Brazil, by Company

SERASA's reports aim to provide comprehensive information solutions tailored for specific customer groups integrating data from several sources. SERASA's principal products include

- *Credit Bureau SERASA*—Individual credit data bank, with data on market commitments; payment habits; negative information for each tax number, including protested notes, court proceedings, financial pending matters, and other information.
- *RELATO*—A business behavior data bank for all trade relationships, guaranteed up-to-date.
- *ACHEI-Recheque*—Checks with insufficient funds and those reported suspended, stolen, missing, or cancelled. Protested checks and opposition to payment.
- *Credit Bureau Scoring Models*—Estimates the likelihood of a credit applicant defaulting within a 12-month period.
- *Cheque Scoring Models*—Indicate the likelihood of postdated checks being returned, based on the issuer's reference file data.

The Chamber of Commerce of the City of São Paulo is the next major provider of credit information. Its two main products are

- *UseCheque*—Information on checks with insufficient funds for consumers and firms. To make a query, a client can put in the telephone number of the individual or firm, tax identification number, name of the bank that has issued the check, and bank account number or check number.
- *SCPC*—Database of consumer loans based mostly on reports of retailers. Queries by name and date of birth or tax identification number are possible, which yield data on unpaid debts, including, for enterprises, contract number, date of missed payment, and amount unpaid.

Equifax do Brasil focuses particularly on trade credit and enterprise credit. Its products include:

- *Equifax Empresarial*—A comprehensive report on businesses operating in Brazil, including identification information, judicial records, and payment behavior records.
- *Core Empresarial*—Statistical model evaluating the level of credit risk of a given enterprise.
- *Equifax Pessoal*—Comprehensive credit report on an individual.
- *Cheque Pessoal (Empresarial)*—Bad-check report on individuals (firms).

threshold of loan size recorded.[29] The initial minimum loan size of R$50,000 has now been reduced to R$5,000. The public credit registry collects data on defaults and delinquencies and information on the size of outstanding balances by borrower and risk classification, thus reflecting its primary purpose—banking supervision. Different credit lines are clustered in the same line of information, if the operations belong to the same borrower and have a common risk classification. Due to bank secrecy restrictions, data is aggregated before it is distributed, so banks requesting data obtain a borrower's total indebtedness in the system, broken down only by the risk classifications of debts. This consolidated overview of a client's position in the system is a key contribution of the public registry.

Formal authorization from the borrower is required for a bank to obtain a report from the Central de Risco. Information is available only for institutions supervised by the Central Bank, and credit-reporting firms do not have access to this database. The Central de Risco is now at a critical point, as they plan to expand information requested of banks, especially for firms. Data could include information on firms' owners, industrial activity, type of organization, and financial data. Fees to access the data are minimal and are debited to banks' reserve accounts at the Central Bank. The Central Bank also maintains a bad-check list—Cadastro de Cheques sem Fundo—which can be accessed by financial institutions as well as by credit bureaus.

Finally, CADIN is a public-sector database that catalogs debts with public authorities, including tax debts, social and labor fees owed by employers, late or delinquent payments to state-owned utilities, and similar transactions. CADIN is located in Brasilia and is not consumer friendly; once a name appears in CADIN, it is difficult to remove, even if the debt is paid. The data from CADIN is not considered to be of good quality.

Competition has increased in recent years in the market for credit information in Brazil, which is a welcome development. Data collected by Chambers of Commerce have been improved, including the creation of a network of these databases to provide statewide, and eventually national, access to the data they contain. The registry developed by the São Paulo Chamber of Commerce (SCPC) is of growing interest to banks who are trying to penetrate the consumer market. Although the SCPC began largely as a file of information on credit at retail establishments, banks are now major contributors and users of this data. Equifax do Brasil is also increasing its presence in both firm and consumer markets, moving from what had been a database focused on trade credits to a more full-service credit-reporting firm. Given their association with Fair Isaac, Equifax do Brasil may be successful in increasing their share of the commercial market for credit-reporting and related services; however, the consumer market is likely to be harder to enter. SERASA remains the market leader in the credit information market in Brazil—especially for consumer credit data—due to its unmatched access to credit data from banks who are its shareholders.

At this time, public-sector databases do not provide any data to the private credit-reporting industry. Data in the Central de Risco is available only to supervised financial institutions, and data in CADIN is available only within the public sector. It appears that banks use the data from the Central de Risco mainly as a check for their large customers and not as a primary source of information.

Many low-income consumers in Brazil obtain credit from banks and finance companies that focus on this market segment or from retailers of consumer durables who sell on installment plans. Often these loans have high interest rates and other fees and charges that consumers do not fully understand. When customers are late with a payment or default on one of these loans, they are often reported to SERASA, SCPC, or both. The Brazilian Consumer Protection Agency (A Fundação do Proteção e Defesa do Consumidor; PROCON) in São Paulo indicated that the majority of the complaints they receive and investigate on credit reporting are found in this segment of the credit market.

Low-income consumers have particularly benefited from the credit-reporting industry, as it has enabled them to access store credit in Brazil through those retailers of consumer durables such as the Casas Bahia, Ponto Frio, and Electro of the Pão de Açucar Group. Some of the main financial intermediaries serving the low-income consumer segment in Brazil are Cacique, Panamericano, Losango, and Fininvest (owned by Unibanco). Cacique offers a service in which they will bring loan funds to the door of the low-income consumer, in amounts of two to three times a person's monthly salary. Losango operates primarily as the financing arm of Casas Bahia, and Fininvest is working to expand its microcredit program. These financial institutions report some information to both SCPC and SERASA, but it appears they do not report to SCI Equifax. Interest rates charged are typically very high. One of the most common forms of credit for low-income consumers is installment payments for goods, typically distributed over 4 to 12 months. In many stores in Brazil, prices are displayed in terms of the monthly installment price, for example, 4 × R$10, to indicate four installments of R$10. Low-income consumers often are unaware of the very high rates of interest implicit in these installment plans, which can exceed 100 percent or even 200 percent per annum. Once a consumer falls behind in the payments, delinquent charges compound the difficulty of repayment. Low-income consumers may also have more difficulty navigating in the system and taking the steps required to clear their record.

Although a full-fledged credit bureau for low-income consumers already exists, the law restricts access. In addition to the data on low-income consumers found in the main archives of SCPC and SERASA, the latter established a service known as the 'Credit Bureau' several years ago that focuses on low-income consumers and that is estimated to contain approximately 25 million consumer records. A group of five lenders, mostly finance or consumer credit companies and banks active in the lower-income segment, are members of the credit bureau: Panamericano, Losango, Cacique, Fininvest, and ABN AMRO (the automobile loan department only). These five have provided full payment histories to SERASA on their client base, much as would exist in countries such as the United States. However, the five remain concerned about their liability due to the Bank Secrecy Law, and thus data is retrieved from the database only on consumers who authorize access to the data in writing and for the exclusive use of these five lenders. Currently, only 5 to 10 percent of the data in this bureau is being used. If legal issues on credit information are resolved, there would be more future interest in expanding membership and coverage.

Interestingly, SERASA tried to start a similar positive information credit bureau among major banks in Brazil but was unsuccessful. However, it has recently launched a recent initiative with consumer finance companies (October 2002). Mainstream banks may have been more zealous in guarding their client information or may have alternative sources of information available for middle-income consumers, such as payroll stubs from formal jobs, rent or mortgage histories, and so forth. Access to credit records may, therefore, be less valuable for higher-income clients than for the lower segment.

Brazil's Credit-Reporting Industry: International Comparisons

Brazil has one of the largest markets for credit reporting among all emerging markets. However, unlike mature markets in the United States, the United Kingdom, or South Africa, where credit bureaus have access to largely the same information and compete fiercely on value-added services, the credit bureaus in Brazil still compete and differentiate themselves primarily by having access to different information sources. Although this is changing, for example, as banks are signing on to SCPC or retailers are reporting to SERASA and Equifax, the market still remains largely fragmented. Further, there is still no positive credit reporting of any significance. As a result, the overall credit information infrastructure is suboptimal, resulting in more limited access and a higher cost of credit than would likely be the case in a nonfragmented, fully positive credit-

Figure 6.4 International Examples of Credit Registry Information

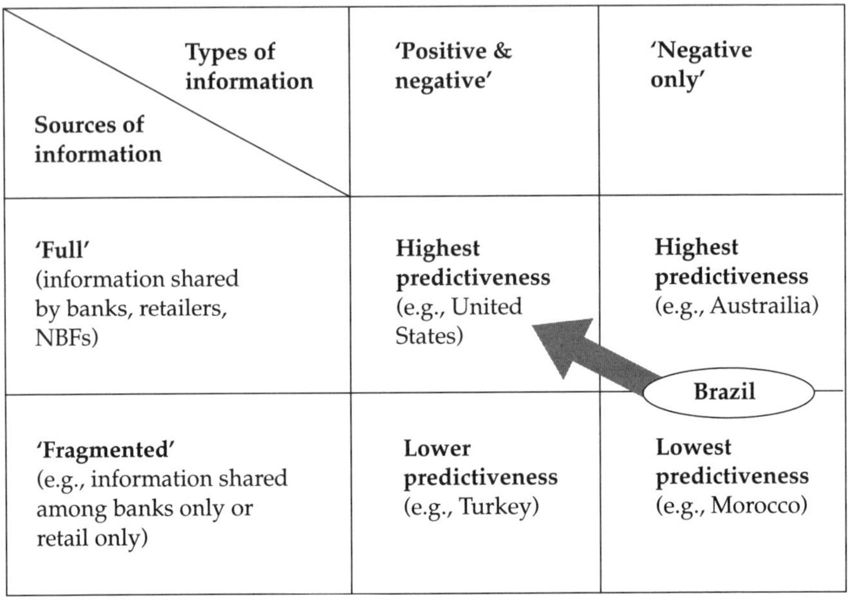

reporting environment.[30] As can be seen in figure 6.4, Brazil needs to move in the direction of full, nonfragmented credit reporting, which includes both positive and negative information, to maximize the predictive power of the data and its usefulness in the credit-granting process. Brazil's credit-reporting firms have been in business for decades and are capable of incorporating both positive data and more complete data (data from more sources) in credit reports almost immediately as such information becomes available.

A comparison of Brazil's credit-reporting system with neighboring countries in Latin America reveals that Brazil's largest system, SERASA, is unusually large, and its database coverage of 59 percent of the population in the age group 15–64 is the highest in the region, high even compared to some major credit bureaus in developed countries. Brazil is slightly behind regional averages in terms of the historical record contained in credit reports. Due to legal restrictions, credit data in Brazil can be maintained only 5 years, which is relatively shorter than other countries in the region, which have set the period from between 6 to 10 years (table 6.7).

The greatest weakness of Brazil's credit-reporting system is the virtual absence of positive payment history information, due both to the Bank Secrecy Law and to the reluctance of banks to share information on good borrowers. Moreover, due to restrictions on collection of positive infor-

Table 6.7 Key Characteristics of Cross-Country Comparisons of Private Credit Bureaus

	Argentina	*Brazil*	*Chile*	*Colombia*	*Mexico*	*Peru*	*United Kingdom*	*Italy*	*United States*
Established	1957	1968	1979	1970	1996	1995	1980	1989	1980
Employees	195	1,600	395	350	86	95		380	
Sales (1998, US$ millions)	28	147	36	1.5	5.5	4.8		15	
Ownership	Private, with bank ownership	Private, with bank ownership	Private, no bank ownership	Private, no bank ownership	Private, with bank ownership	Private, with bank ownership	Private	Private, with bank ownership	Private
Foreign participation	More than 50% (Equifax, 94)	Domestic	Foreign (Equifax, 97)	Domestic	Less than 50% (Trans Union)	More than 50% (Equifax, 95, 98)	Domestic	Domestic	
Institutions that provide data	6,000	1,500	580	180	150	400	350	70,000	
No. of banks that provide data	72	200		15	30	12	29	300	
Does your registry only include data from a limited group?	No	No	No	Yes (bank superintendency)	No	No	No	Yes (financial institutions)	No
No. of individuals with records in past 5 years (millions)	6.51	65	3	2.5	12	4.6	40	19	200

(table continued next page)

Table 6.7 *(continued)*

	Argentina	*Brazil*	*Chile*	*Colombia*	*Mexico*	*Peru*	*United Kingdom*	*Italy*	*United States*
% population with credit report	28.5[a]	59[a]	31[a]	9.7[a]	20[a]	30[a]	67[b]	48[a]	72[b]
No. of firms ('000)	622	4,500	500	200	100	285	4,000	1,100	15,500
Frequency of reporting	Monthly	Daily	Monthly	Monthly	Monthly	Monthly	Daily	Daily	Monthly
Positive or negative data	Both	Both (primarily negative)	Both	Negative	Both	Both	Both	Both	Both
Reciprocity	Yes	No	No	Yes	Yes	No	Yes	Yes	No
Maximum years' data	6–10	5	6–10	6–10	Over 10	6–10	6–10	4–5	Over 10
Loan presentation	Each credit, each institution	Consolidated by institution	Other	Each credit, each institution	Each credit, each institution	Consolidated debt in system	Each credit, each institution	Each credit, each institution	Each credit, each institution
Share of the market		80	70		90	70	73	70	30

Note: Coverage of population in 15–64 age group for the United Kingdom is 103% and for the United States, 112%.

a. Coverage of population as a percentage of total population ages 15–64 years.

b. Coverage of population as a percentage of total population.

Source: Survey data, World Bank.

mation, Brazil's credit bureaus remove data from their files on repayment of past-due credits once the matter has been resolved. Only two other registries in the region remove negative information from a record once the debt in question has been repaid. Second, Brazil has strict consumer attention guidelines and notification obligations (table 6.8). Among the countries surveyed, Brazil is the only country where credit bureaus are required by law to notify consumers if negative information is received. Third, procedures for removing incorrect information from the database are onerous. Brazil is the only sample country where contested data can only be removed after legal action by the individual or firm. The most common correction mechanism (cited by 12 firms) is to remove or change data on advice from the reporting institution; however, 7 other firms stated that they do not remove data under any circumstances but will make corrections. The complexities associated with notifying consumers of their inclusion in a credit registry and related to correcting disputed data increase the cost of preparation of credit reports, which is then passed on to the credit markets.

Cost Differentials in Credit Reporting

Entry costs in the credit-reporting industry do not appear to be prohibitive, as there are several operating credit bureaus. However, for low-income consumers, report costs could be a constraint, making their use less likely for small-value loans. Anecdotal information suggests reports in Brazil are relatively expensive, discouraging their use for small loan sizes. In table 6.9, prices of basic and detailed consumer credit reports are listed for specific firms in several Latin American countries. These prices are based on a one-off purchase of a report, which would not be the typical price paid by financial institutions, who are able to negotiate volume discounts. Banks and other institutions that purchase hundreds and even thousands of reports monthly would likely pay only a fraction of the prices listed. In addition, the type of data contained in a 'basic report' varies greatly from firm to firm and country to country, which further complicates price comparisons. Price comparisons are rendered difficult as different firms compute these on different bases. Indicative estimates are given in table 6.9. If reporting prices are high, these would particularly constrain the participation of microlenders in credit reporting, because they may choose not to provide data to a system if credit reports are too costly for them to purchase when reviewing small loans.

Legal and Regulatory Issues

As alluded to above, one key legal issue that considerably affects Brazil's credit-reporting industry is the Bank Secrecy Law, which is a major deter-

Table 6.8 Cross-Country Comparison of Customer Attention Issues in Private Credit Bureaus

	Argentina	*Brazil*	*Chile*	*Colombia*	*Mexico*	*Peru*	*United Kingdom*	*Italy*	*United States*
Legally required to respond to consumer complaints	Yes	Yes	Yes	Yes	Yes	No	Yes	Yes	Yes
Must creditors notify consumers that info is transferred when									
Relationship is established	No	Yes	No	Yes	No	No	Yes	Yes	No
New information is provided	No	Yes	No	No	No	No	Yes		No
The customer defaults	No	Yes	No	No	No	No	Yes		No
Must credit registry notify consumers if									
Negative information is received	No	Yes	No	No	No	No	No	No	No
Positive data is received	No	No	No	No	No	No	No	No	No
Credit report is emitted	No	No	No	No	No	No	No	No	No
How can data be removed if contested?	Cannot be removed, only corrected	After legal action by individual or firm	Only at the request of data provider	After grievance procedure	Only at the request of data provider	Only at the request of data provider	Only at the request of data provider	Only at the request of data provider	At request of provider

Can individual request that his or her entire record be removed?	No	Yes	No	No	No	No	No	Yes	No
How long do cancelled debts remain on file?	8–10 years	Data is removed when debt is repaid	3–4 years	Data is removed when debt is repaid	Negative data is never removed	5–7 years	5–7 years	5–7 years	More than 10 years
How long do unpaid debts remain on file?	8–10 years	5 years	5–7 years	8–10 years	Negative data is never removed	8–10 years	5–7 years	5–7 years	7 years

Table 6.9 Cost of a Credit Report in Brazil and Other Countries

	Cost of basic report	*Cost of detailed report*
Brazil (SERASA)	US$1.35[a]	US$1.50[a]
Brazil (SCPC)	US$0.5–1.00	Do not provide
Argentina (Veraz)	US$1.00–1.25 (before devaluation US$2.00–2.50)	US$5 (before devaluation $10)
Chile (Dicom)	Do not provide	US$5.20 (consumer report) US$0.50 (banks)
Peru (INFOCORP)	Do not provide	US$0.80–$5.00 US$8.00–$10.00 (individuals)
El Salvador (INFORED)	US$0.40	Do not provide
Uruguay (Clearing de Informes)	Do not provide	US$7.10

a. Price per individual report, contingent on monthly fee of US$35.00 by the subscribing institution, for between 1–25 reports.
Source: World Bank data.

rent to the sharing of positive information by financial intermediaries in Brazil. Although the law was amended in December 2000, the principal change from the credit-reporting perspective was to clarify the legal environment facing the Central de Risco in the Central Bank. Private banks do not believe the legal changes adequately protect even the Central de Risco against charges of noncompliance with the Bank Secrecy Law, if it were to substantially increase access to positive data. At this time, banks require customers to sign a waiver to permit the sharing of their payment history or positive data with other banks.

The consumer-credit-reporting industry is also affected by the law for consumer protection, which includes an article related to the sharing of consumer data (Section VI, Article 43, Law No. 8.078, September 11, 1990); however, this impact is uneven over the country. In São Paulo, the Consumer Protection Foundation (PROCON) is responsible for enforcing the consumer protection law and is involved in court proceedings with both SERASA and SCPC. PROCON is generally against the collection of positive information, such as payment history data, which they view as a violation of an individual's privacy. It has also brought a case against SCPC for giving lenders information on the number of times a person's credit report has been requested in the recent past. There is a strong correlation between the number of times a report has been requested and the likelihood of default, as individuals who seek many lines of credit in a short period of time may be having economic difficulties or become overextended. This data is a standard part of credit evaluation in the U.S. credit market.

The PROCON also requires consumers to be notified in writing every time negative information on them is sent to a credit-reporting firm. Either the lender or firm reporting the data can inform the consumer, or the credit-reporting firm can do so. The Ministry of Justice in Brasilia supports this requirement and believes it should be stronger (notification must be confirmed to have been received by the consumer) for negative Congress, which would greatly add to the cost of credit reporting in Brazil. For example, SCPC in São Paulo already sends approximately 400,000 letters each month to notify consumers they have been included in the database. Each letter costs almost US$1.00 to prepare and send. This cost could double or triple if individuals were required to sign for the letters and if the credit-reporting firms were required to maintain these records.

Despite the active interest of PROCON and the consumer protection offices of the Ministry of Justice in the credit-reporting industry, some consumer protections usual elsewhere are lacking in Brazil. These include a right to know when an adverse action was taken based on information contained in a credit report, who has accessed your credit report, the right to request that data in a credit report not be shared with marketing firms, and the right to request that recipients of credit reports change data in their records that was obtained from a credit report and then shown to be erroneous.

Another legal issue that can affect the credit-reporting industry concerns the notary publics in Brazil, which have concessions to run *cartórios*, where delinquent payments can be registered. Lenders can obtain 'protest letters' from the *cartórios* if they register a delinquent loan there. This letter has a certain legal status, even though it does not mean that any assessment has been made as to the justification of the complaint. Facing falling demand for their services, the *cartórios* have tried to make it a requirement that delinquent payments or loans first be registered with them and that protest letters be prepared before notification can be sent to a credit-reporting firm. In December 2001, a judge in the state of Alagoas ruled in favor of this approach for the first time, stating that only protest letters can be included in the local SCPC. Although this action has a valid basis for self-executable security interests, it is not clear whether this requirement also has been applied in the case of other credits.

The judge's ruling in the Alagoas case underlines other legal hurdles facing credit reporting in Brazil: nonuniformity in case law and poor understanding of this industry by the judiciary. Frequently, judges have ruled to remove *all* information on plaintiffs from credit information registries when there is a dispute on one piece of data, including the Central de Risco run by the Central Bank, as well as private registries. In cases of corporate restructuring and bankruptcy, judges may also rule that information on delinquent accounts cannot be communicated to credit-reporting firms, because it would cut off other sources of finance. Moreover, judges in some cases penalize firms for reporting negative information to credit bureaus and support compensation.

Laws related to the regulation of utilities also affect the type of information that can potentially be reported to credit registries. When the gas, telephone, and electricity companies in Brazil were privatized, the regulations governing these industries included a requirement of 'universal' service coverage. This means that firms in these industries cannot deny service to someone, even if they know the person is in bankruptcy or otherwise unlikely or unable to pay. In the case of telephone service, homes must be connected if there is a nearby trunk line, and service can be cut off only after 90 days of nonpayment. Similar regulations are in force for energy utilities. As a result, these firms do not conduct background checks on the credit history of new clients, as they cannot use this information to deny service. They do report negative payment histories to the main credit bureaus. In the case of the telephone industry, the 'telephone secrecy' law is unclear in regard to the sharing of data on payment history of a customer.

A unified common approach to the nature, scope, and regulation of this industry is lacking within the government. The Ministry of Justice is concerned with protecting individual privacy, while the Central Bank believes credit reporting supports financial soundness as well as access to credit. These divisions are evident in laws with conflicting objectives regarding this industry. Brazil also lacks a regulatory body responsible for the supervision of the credit-reporting industry, with the legal right to access information in the databases of credit-reporting firms to verify compliance with rules and the right to request audits for this purpose.

Curiously, there is no regulation regarding limitations on the type of information that can be put into scoring techniques. It is likely that credit-reporting firms use restricted data, such as positive information or information older than five years. Use of such scores for businesses does not seem to raise any problems, although scores for consumers could constitute a violation of privacy. This fact evidently slows the introduction of credit scoring for consumer lending in Brazil.

Suggestions for Policy: Strengthening the Credit-Reporting Industry

Based on the discussion above, a plan of action to strengthen credit reporting in Brazil could include the following elements:

- Generate dialogue to formulate a consistent and common vision of the role of credit reporting across different parts of the government, which takes cognizance of the importance of broad-spectrum and low-cost credit information in improving access to finance particularly for lower-income segments.

- Re-evaluate and reform the Bank Secrecy Law with regard to restrictions on the sharing of positive information, to ease sharing existing information databases. Evaluate the experience of Acrefi Positivo to explore the prospects for its extension to larger organizations.
- Permit the collection of information on positive payment histories. International data protection guidelines and the legal experiences of other nations should provide guidance in this reform process.
- Reconsider current time restrictions of five years of credit data.
- Clarify the legal basis for credit/consumer reporting with regard to the circumstances under which sharing data for credit and consumer reporting is permissible. Inter alia evaluate current guidelines on notification, as well as pending new proposals, against international norms. The Fair Credit Reporting Act of the United States is one example of this type of law.
- Examine the role that notarial services may have with regard to the filing of protests for credit claims other than those that are self-executable, and reconsider legislative proposals to first register debts with *cartórios*.
- Reformulate regulations related to the dissemination and collection of payment data from utilities to enable data from these sectors to enter credit reports. Permit utilities to allow service providers to take into account the credit standing and capacity to pay when providing services. Recognize the value of such positive information for low-income consumers, who may lack a formal credit history.
- Prepare consistent strategic direction for the Central de Risco, at Brazil's Central Bank, including its role for supervision and possible access to its data by the existing credit bureaus. Examine access also to databases such as CADIN, which are currently limited.
- Launch judicial education and outreach programs on the benefits of credit reports and prepare records of case law in this regard to promote the consistent application of current and new laws.
- Develop outreach programs for consumers, especially low-income ones, so that they are aware of their rights, understand more fully how credit works, and understand their obligations. Examine areas in which consumer protection may currently be less than international norms, for example, with regard to notification of access of a credit record and the taking of adverse actions based on such records, limits on the marketing of information, and changing erroneous data.

7
Enlisting the Government

Today, we have a government that spends a lot and spends badly. We spend a lot on our public employees as a whole, but there are several categories with outdated salaries. We spend a lot on the public administration, but our society receives back little of the many direct and indirect taxes that are levied upon it. In these times, our society requires a modern and efficient management of public funds so as to guarantee the fulfillment of our constitutional obligations with social policies, citizen's access to basic public goods, such as health and education, as well as public investment in infrastructure.

ANTONIO PALOCCI FILHO,
MINISTER OF FINANCE, BRAZIL (JANUARY 2003)

To what extent will markets eventually solve the problem of financial exclusion, without government intervention? As the preceding chapters have shown, the role and presence of the government is pervasive. The nature of its regulation of financial entities significantly affects the services they can offer and also the appropriateness of these services for those who are financially excluded. Many observers believe that the government's role needs to be more proactive, even if not with financial support, then with inducements to formal financial institutions to expand access.[1]

When bankers in the United Kingdom were asked whether the financial exclusion problem will be solved by banks without government help, they generally translated the question into a profit argument: If it is profitable, then it will happen; if it is not, then it will not (Donovan and Palmer 1999). Thus, there are two issues at hand. First is the possibility of market failures, due to perceptions of high risk, in turn based on limited information or due to externalities or issues of scale economies in the provision of such services. In such cases there is a clear reason for government intervention, whether through start-up or demonstration. However, exclusion also may result from risks and costs, which are genuinely high and are unlikely to decline with scale.

Some observers point out that governments have a particularly significant leverage on banks due the latter's particular status. Banks' strategic economic position, coupled with their state charters and guaranteed deposit insurance, renders them to be more socially responsible than ordinary undertakings (Giuseppi 2001). But social responsibilities may conflict with private profit. To what extent should the government exercise its influence or authority over the banking system to achieve social objectives? These issues are examined in the present chapter, based largely on the experience of major developed countries.

As pointed out at the outset of this study, issues of access to financial services cannot be analyzed only in terms of distribution; the overall depth of financial services is a first consideration. And the overall depth of financial services is influenced by a spectrum of government policies, which lie largely outside the financial sector. The first section of this chapter therefore examines the influence of such policies. These include, first and foremost, overall macroeconomic policy, which has a major influence on financial system deepening. Macroeconomic stability, with sound fiscal management, helps establish the environment for inflation-free growth and provides an appropriate environment for financial system deepening. The government's taxation and borrowing requirements are a central part of this environment that affects the financial system. Second, government policies in a range of regulatory areas also affect the financial system. For example, bank branch openings are affected not only by regulations pertaining to banks and other financial intermediaries but also by prevailing competitive forces and labor laws. These factors affect interest rates and spreads and, hence, the costs of financial intermediation.

However, given the increased recent recognition of many of these influences, a detailed analysis of these factors is not undertaken.[2] Instead, most of the attention of this concluding chapter of the study is devoted to the investigation of areas in which the government can take supportive steps toward resolving financial exclusion, based on the experience of other countries. For financial-sector authorities, macroeconomic forces or even regulatory changes in other areas of the economy are often largely outside their control, and as such it is difficult for agents of the financial system acting on their own to take remedial steps in these areas. But both the government and financial-sector authorities can relatively easily adopt some of the smaller proactive measures discussed in chapter 2 of this study, as undertaken already in other countries.

A first summary observation of this chapter is that access to financial services is shaped by government policies in several areas that lie beyond the financial sector. A significant expansion of financial access in the absence of attention to these factors would be difficult. In the context of Brazil today, these factors include, particularly,

- Macroeconomic policies with high borrowing requirements, financed though the issue of domestic debt, held largely by the financial system, which has 'crowded out' lending to the private sector.

- High taxation of the domestic financial system, both explicit and implicit (through high reserve requirements) and a consequent disincentive toward financial transactions.
- A high proportion of directed credit in total credit, which has tended to raise the cost of freely allocated credit.
- Uneven effects of regulatory policy across different parts of the financial system, with consequent 'regulatory arbitrage' throughout the system, which explains a substantial part of the relative 'success' of some segments of the system as compared to others.
- Regulatory policy in other areas that indirectly affect the financial system, notably, labor market policies that add a considerable burden to hiring costs in the formal sector, thus providing incentives for the development of financial-sector segments outside this system.
- Not detailed here is competition policy; increased attention to competition in some formal financial-sector segments may broaden the base of support for expanded access.

Given the macroeconomic and regulatory setting, the second part of this chapter suggests that, nevertheless, policies favorable toward the expansion of access to financial services can be, and have been, adopted in several countries. Based largely on the experience of developed countries, especially the United Kingdom, the United States, and Canada, a series of policies favoring access are investigated. Broad lessons to emerge from the cross-country examples are

- Government support, through legislation or enabling regulation that takes the form of consumer protection (for example, for the prevention of discrimination or predatory practices, for better disclosure of lending practices, for the collection of quality data on these practices), is critical to inform good policy and to alter the behavior of institutions. Disclosure, and the implied moral suasion, are powerful tools in shaping the behavior of financial institutions, especially if there is an alignment of financial and nonfinancial incentives to reinforce legislation.
- There may be a case for obligatory provision of some form of basic banking services; this is a widespread practice. It may be useful in such basic accounts to emphasize, first, access to money transmission mechanisms and the payments system, and second, deposit facilities. Services such as check writing and credit need not form a part of a basic account. To be useful, such a service would need to be very competitively priced. Electronic funds transfers for federal payments could accelerate the reduction of the 'unbanked,' but such requirements may leave many people outside its net today.

- Encouraging partnerships, first of all, of financial institutions with community-based credit providers to use alternative delivery channels and, second, between the public and private sectors, built around shared understandings of their different roles and what each brings to any transaction, can be very productive.
- In terms of financial support, most successful examples of credit support for products that serve disadvantaged populations entail indirect support by government, where private credit providers still share in the risk. These can be combined with policies to promote access by financial institutions to secondary credit markets, and also, such activities can be designed to complement rather than compete with activities of the private sector.
- A range of supporting institutions needs to be involved in the efforts of financial outreach. These include not only business administration and fund administration agencies but also nonprofit agencies and community investment agencies who work closely with target communities.
- The role of programs of financial education and literacy are also key; in this context, programs that offer incentives for family support to financial planning are also interesting.
- Finally, issues of competition may sometimes be present, even if this is not immediately apparent. Brazil's banking structure, dominated by a handful of institutions, bears some resemblance to that of the United Kingdom. Some of the issues encountered in this regard, for example, the payment of service charges for access to money transmission, have been encountered in other countries, too. A full evaluation of the status of competition in the provision of 'downscaling' in this context may be worth consideration.

Government Policy and Access: Macro- and Regulatory Environment

Government's Borrowing Requirement

As discussed in chapter 1, the overall depth of financial intermediation in Brazil ranks average on a cross-section basis today, compared to other emerging market economies. How has financial depth behaved over time? Following the Real plan, and the ensuing drop in inflation and improved overall economic stability, there was some expansion in bank credit to the economy. In absolute terms, credit grew at an estimated real rate of 2 percent per year between 1995 and 2002 (Canuto and Mattos 2003). However, despite this growth, credit as a percentage of gross domestic product (GDP) has declined over this period (figure 7.1).

One factor associated with the recent slowdown in the expansion of credit is the expansion of the government's borrowing needs over the same period. Despite careful controls on the primary fiscal surplus as well as on the expansion of public borrowing at the provincial and state level, public-borrowing requirements at the federal level continued to increase in recent years, as witnessed by the rising debt-to-GDP ratio (figure 7.1). Together with the increase in the domestically financed component of the government's borrowing requirements, this has meant an increase in the holding of government paper by domestic agents. The bulk of this increased holding of government paper has been shouldered by the financial system. It is reflected in the increased share of securities in banking assets and in the high proportion of fixed income (government) securities held by mutual funds and investment funds, as indicated in broad measures of money supply.

In figure 7.2, the share of securities in bank assets, which had shown some decline in the period of stability of March 2000 to March 2001, increased once again through most of 2001 and early 2002. The effect of these factors has been a continuous 'crowding out' of credit to the private sector and thus generally reduced access to financial services. At the margin, it is more profitable for a bank to hold government paper than to lend. This is clear from the segments of the banking industry that remain profitable: overdrafts, consumer loans at very high interest rates, and sight and special savings deposits for smaller-net-worth individuals.

Taxation

Another consequence of the high public-sector borrowing needs is the high level of financial-sector taxation. Certain financial-sector taxes have many advantages in terms of low administrative costs and relatively low possibilities of evasion. Explicit taxes, such as the Tax on Financial Operations (Imposto sobre Operações Financeiras; IOF) and Financial Transactions Tax (Contribuição Provisória sobre Movimentação; CPMF), have affected all financial transactions. In addition, high reserve requirements on sight and savings deposits constitute an additional, implicit tax on Brazil's financial system. Although reserve requirements decreased from 75 percent to 45 percent of demand deposits from early 1999 to 2001, marginal requirements have been raised periodically in times of macroeconomic turbulence (figure 7.3). Brazil's average reserve requirements on demand deposits, of 45 percent, are very high compared to its neighboring Chile (14 percent) or to developed countries such as those in Europe or the United States, which have rates of around 10 percent each. Reserve requirements were raised once again to 60 percent in February 2003.[3]

Figure 7.1 Ratios of Credit to GDP and Debt to GDP over Time in Brazil, January 1995 to March 2003

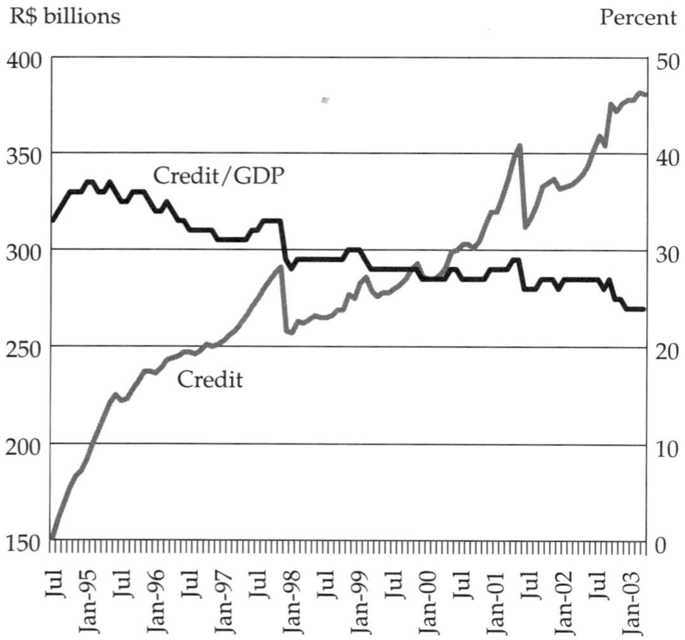

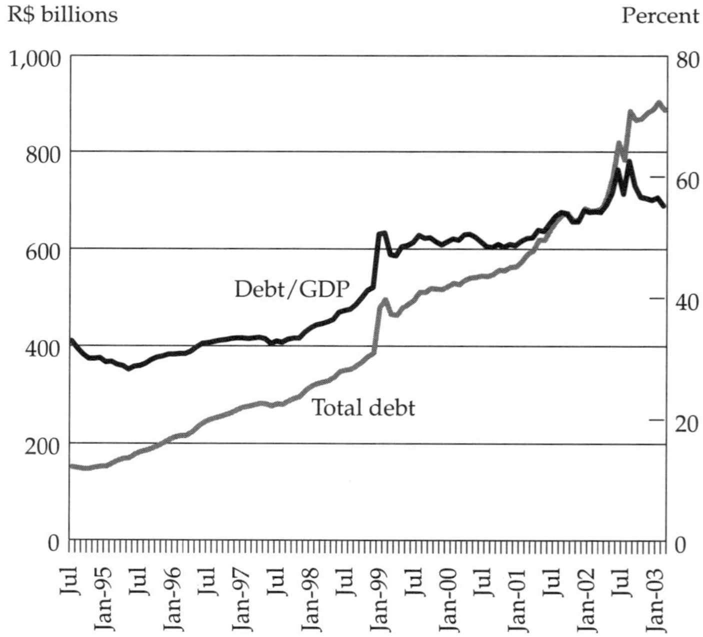

Source: Constructed from data from the Central Bank of Brazil.

Figure 7.2 Shares of Securities in Bank Assets (December 1999 to December 2002) and Money Supply in Brazil (July 1994 to June 2003)

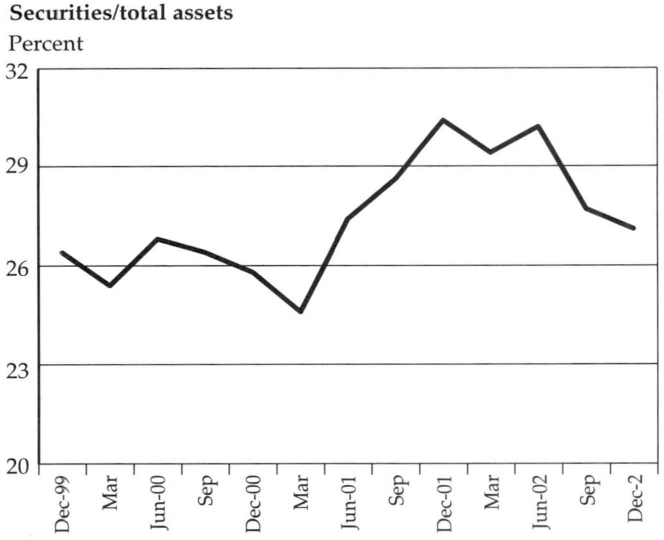

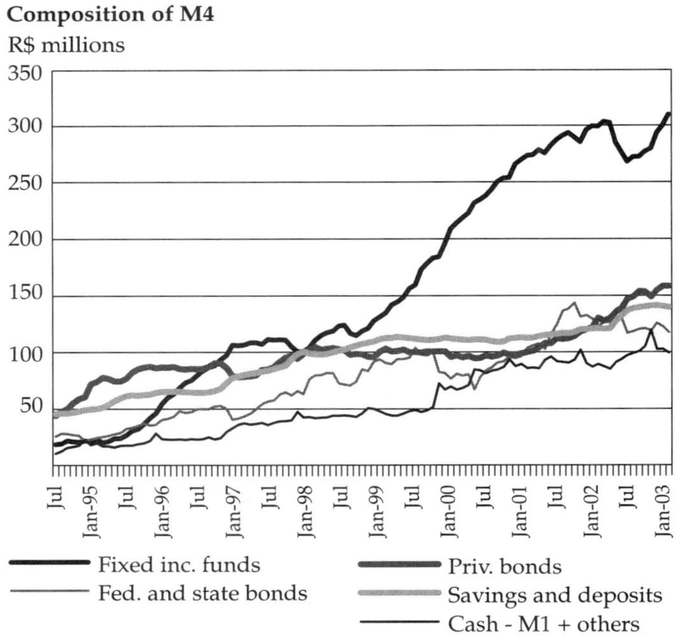

Note: M1 = government held cash + sight deposits; M4 = government held cash + sight deposits + remunerated special deposits + savings deposits + securities issued by deposit-taking institutions + fixed income fund quotas + promissory transactions registered with the Selic + high liquidity public securities.
Source: Constructed from data from the Central Bank of Brazil.

Figure 7.3 Trends in Spreads and Reserve Requirements in Brazil, January 1995 to March 2003

Bank spreads and reserve requirements
Percent

Credit/GDP ratio and reserve requirements
R$ millions

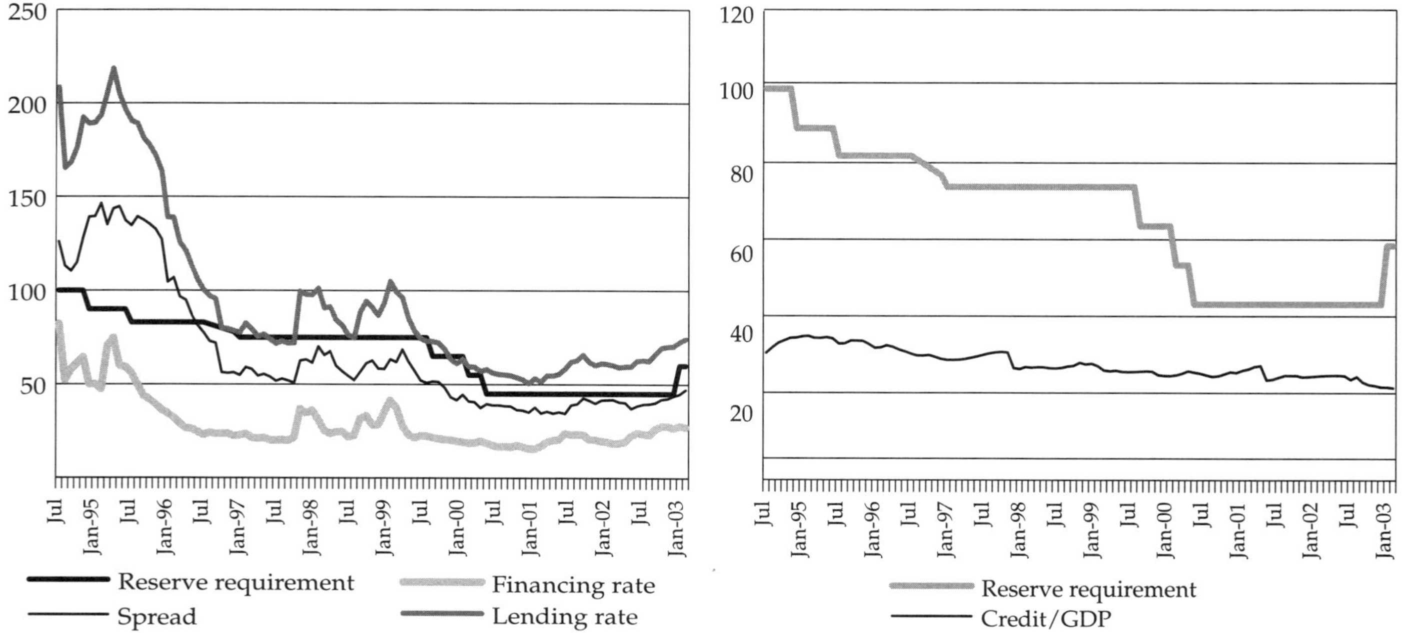

Source: Constructed from data from the Central Bank of Brazil.

Although high financial-sector taxation and high public-borrowing needs may not be the only factors behind the high interest rates in Brazil, as well as high spreads, these have certainly been contributing factors, as confirmed by recent work of the Central Bank of Brazil on spreads, although precise quantification is complex (see chapter 6; also see Afanasieff, Villa Lhacer, and Nakane 2001). The study itself subsumes many factors under the general category of 'overheads,' which could also include such factors as the impact of large and less-efficient public banks and the effects of cross-subsidization and directed credit programs, as in the case of the housing and rural-lending obligations of special savings deposits and sight deposits, respectively.

Directed Credit

More than one-third of total bank loans are directed to specific sectors, often at below-market rates of interest.[4] These requirements lower the potential return banks can make on their collected funds, and therefore increase the costs of capital. Under the rules for special deposits, 65 percent must be allocated to housing finance. Of that total, at least 80 percent must be allocated to loans under the government-mandated Sistema Financeiro de Habitação (Housing Financial System), with strictly regulated terms and conditions. The remaining 20 percent is allocated at market rates, but at least half should be directed to housing financing as opposed to mortgage loans. In addition, 15 percent of these savings deposits balance must be held as cash reserves, so that only 25 percent is available for free investment. And 25 percent of average-demand deposit balances must be allocated to rural credit. These directed lending obligations have been progressively relaxed during the past decade, but directed credit remains high in Brazil, even compared to its regional neighbors such as Mexico, which have largely dismantled such programs. These quantitative lending targets, often combined with social programs for lending at below-market interest rates, lead to financial market segmentation and price distortions and contribute toward the raising of the overall cost of capital.

Labor Market Policies

The high cost of labor and difficulties of contesting labor disputes affect the selection of financial instrument and service mechanisms. For example, high labor costs reduce incentives to open branches. As in the case of debtors, judges in Brazil tend to favor labor in disputes with employers, a factor that affects banks and all nonfinancial companies in their expansion decisions. Some legal encumbrances increase labor costs. For instance, labor in the banking sector is limited to six hours a day. Even if workers were kept for longer hours on an overtime basis, and if this overtime was paid, labor has contested this in court on numerous occasions. Recently, labor unions have been objecting to the use of banking correspondents, which they view as a way to overcome labor regulations for bank employees. Finally, labor costs (including social contributions) are affected by various earmarked taxes for funds to support employees, so that total social contribution (an implicit tax) paid by the employers above the salary amount to a steep 83 percent of the latter (of which 59 percent are taxes, 11 percent social security contributions, and 12 percent additional benefits). All this makes banks reluctant to expand their network because of the high labor costs and risks that entails. High labor costs also affect spreads.

Regulatory Segmentation

The impact of the factors discussed above is not uniform on different segments of the financial system, and the resulting distortions offer several opportunities for regulatory arbitrage across different segments of the financial system. Brazilian regulation includes significant differences in treatment to different types of financial institutions. There are large differences in explicit taxes, implicit taxes (required reserves and directed lending), and also documentation and reporting requirements between banks and other types of financial institutions. This creates incentives for banks to offer services to this clientele via separate vehicles, such as consumer finance companies (although finance companies, or *financeiras*, receive the same treatment as banks, in terms of minimum capital and reporting requirements, as they are not deposit-taking institutions, they are not subject to reserve requirements or deposit insurance). However, such choices create constraints on the range of products that can be offered to these clients (a consumer finance company, apart from not being able to collect deposits, cannot offer loans for productive purposes). In practice, financial conglomerates have developed, with separate subsidiaries for different product categories.

For example, choices between leasing and consumer finance companies have clearly varied with the differences in regulation toward them (discussed in chapter 4). Choices of organizational form for different legal entities in microfinance are also determined by regulatory tradeoffs. Choices between correspondents versus bank branches also reflect, in part, the regulatory considerations relevant to each segment. To expand the role of Brazilian banks with lower segments, differences in treatment relative to the multiple regulatory windows offered by nonbanks, specialized credit card companies, and other entities that offer similar activities could be reduced.

Proactive Government Policies: Supportive Microeconomic Measures

Although the indirect impact of macroeconomic and regulatory policy on overall levels of financial access may be difficult to control, Brazil's government has made major direct efforts to address issues of financial access. Historically, in Brazil, the principal vehicles for the expansion of access have been a series of specialized programs targeted at specific end users at preferential prices, in tandem with public banks, which have provided the channels for the implementation of these programs. As discussed in chapter 5 of this study, there is an emerging international consensus of the potential limitations of public banks and directed credit policies in this regard, due to their adverse effects on the financial institutions themselves as well as on credit markets in a wider sense due to their distortive effects on relative prices.[5] Government-supported downscaling through the state ownership of assets or control of pricing may instead contribute inadvertently to the displacement or crowding out of private credit to the desired sectors. In 2003, Brazil added new measures for emphasizing access, which include a range of financial institutions, although public banks expect to play a major role through individual specialized schemes.[6]

The following section looks at other paradigms for government support for financial access, in view of the experience of specific developed countries. These examples illustrate that support for the expansion of access is not easy. Governments have supported the expansion of access through direct or indirect legislation, the promotion of disclosure on financial practices and the implementation of monitoring systems to track financial practices, and support for financial-sector competition, as well as through direct support and institutional building. Beyond this, governments have in some cases provided financial guarantees or support for such initiatives, albeit on a small scale and using mechanisms that do not distort market prices. Governments have also supported institutions that contribute, primarily indirectly, toward aiding access. Such measures are discussed on the basis of international experience, with a particular emphasis on the experience of the United States, the United Kingdom, and Canada.

Looking at individual countries, the United States illustrates a case in which direct support for community outreach was combined with powerful provisions on disclosure, nondiscrimination, and fairness. However, financial support for expanded outreach has been sparing and, in general, incentive compatible in design. That is, there are built-in incentives to maintain or improve efficiency in these markets. Few other developed countries have followed the U.S. example in terms of adopting legislative provisions encouraging disclosure-backed outreach. In the United Kingdom, strong cooperation has been fostered among government, banks, the private sector, and other organizations, coupled with recently enhanced disclosure and restrictions against anticompetitive practices in lending to small entities.[7] At the same time, the principle of financial sustainability has been upheld in all measures against financial exclusion. It is acknowledged that, only if financial products and services are cost effective for all players will they be willing to participate on a long-term basis. The importance of providing targeted clients with needed financial education to understand their rights and responsibilities and learn to access appropriate financial products and services is also acknowledged.

In recent years, the United Kingdom has implemented several initiatives—similar to those in place in the United States—to expand the financial services provided to deprived communities and to better support small-business development. Differences between the United States and the United Kingdom, however, have resulted in different needs, priorities, and solutions. Key differences include the concentration of banking assets in four banks; the role played by Community Development Financial Institutions (CDFIs) as lenders of last resort for those rejected by mainstream banks, the predominance of social enterprises and nonprofits in community finance, the provision of extensive subsidized housing (but without encouragement of ownership for certain segments of the population), and the absence of a history of redlining in ethnic communities.

Canada's main preoccupation in terms of financial access has been support for specialized programs and entities that serve lower-income, geographically remote, native Canadians and also small-enterprise populations.[8] As in the United Kingdom, there was traditionally a reluctance to formalize policies for financial institutions to promote access; however, the recent Canadian Bank Act of 2001 formally supports enhanced access to basic financial services and the collection and disclosure of data on bank-lending patterns. But it does not address the provision or availability of credit, and its information disclosure requirements are not detailed or onerous. Instead of emphasizing downscaling, the government has created specialized institutions to serve those markets and promoted market competition among banks, credit unions, and specialized vehicles to increase services to consumers. In terms of direct financial support, loan guarantee programs exist, but there does not seem to be any systematic or sophisticated use of such programs by the larger banks in conjunction with the regional capital pools or other risk-mitigating resources. As in the United Kingdom, Canadian banks do not have separate or specialized divisions or subsidiaries to focus on community banking. Apart from their dedicated lending teams for Aboriginal banking, the banks integrate small-business and other community lending into their main operations, without specific incentives or performance targets.

Legislative Provisions to Expand Outreach

ANTIDISCRIMINATION AND OBLIGATIONS TOWARD OUTREACH: THE CRA AND ASSOCIATED LEGISLATION

The United States emphasizes targeted legislation relating especially to nondiscrimination, fairness, and disclosure, with more limited regulation requiring expanded outreach. Much of its proactive policy includes associated financial supports or enhancements. Its legacy of special programs and entities has its origins in Depression-era programs that were focused on reducing the threat of foreclosure on homes and making home ownership more affordable. Included among these were regulations creating the Federal Housing Administration (FHA), which made insured, self-amortizing, 30-year mortgage loans and enabled home buyers at all income levels to avoid the refinancing associated with short-term, nonamortizing loans; loan guarantees for veterans under the Veterans Administration from 1944; the Federal National Mortgage Association (Fannie Mae), which provided a secondary market for the 30-year FHA-insured mortgage loans; and the Home Owners Loan Act, which authorized the federal government to charter savings and loan associations.

It was realized that, even with such laws, discriminatory practices limited outreach to affordable housing. This led to the Fair Lending Act (1968) and the Equal Credit Opportunity Act (1976), which are the backbone of federal nondiscrimination law.[9] More recently, the Truth in Lending Act, the Truth in Savings Act, and the Home Ownership and Equity Protection Act attempt to enable less-well-informed consumers to make informed financial decisions. There remains concern about 'predatory-lending' practices against more vulnerable consumers, as recent studies illustrate (U.S. Department of the Treasury and U.S. Department of Housing and Urban Development 2000).

Shortly after the Equal Credit Opportunity Act, the Community Reinvestment Act (CRA) was enacted in 1977, which required the federal banking regulators to "assess [a bank's] record of meeting the credit needs of its entire community, including low- and moderate-income neighborhoods, consistent with the safe and sound operation of such institution." Congress adopted the CRA in response to evidence that banks drew deposits from their local communities but limited their lending back to those communities, sometimes through discriminatory practices against poor people or ethnic minorities. The CRA has no legal enforcement mechanism other than that bank regulators are to take an institution's record 'into accoun' when applications are made (for example, for branch openings or mergers). What made the CRA effective was its combination with disclosure requirements (Litan and others 2000). The Home Mortgage Disclosure Act (HMDA; 1975) required mortgage lenders to report the location (by census tract) of their mortgage loans, demonstrating that few mortgage loans were made in minority census tracts. Next, the HMDA was amended to require far more information, including the number and location of mortgage applications, the race and income of applicants, and approval status. Public disclosure of CRA examinations and ratings since 1990 also gives banks additional incentives to comply with the CRA. Indeed, the CRA requires banks to post in their offices a CRA notice and make available on request their CRA performance. The effect of these changes was huge.

CRA regulations were further revised in 1993 to require large depository institutions to provide reporting on small-business lending activities. This has significantly improved the amount of data available about small-business lending in the nation and has prompted research on its effectiveness. Early research highlighted the lack of a well-developed secondary market for small-business loans (Haag 2002). This ultimately led Congress to pass new laws removing regulatory obstacles to the securitization of small-business loans as part of the Riegle Act. Difficulties in implementation of the CRA led to further revisions in 1995, which provided for specific tests to evaluate CRA performance (www.ffiec.gov/cra/history/ htm). It also reduced considerably the amount of paperwork and record-keeping that all banks, but especially small ones, must produce for a CRA examination.

CRA examinations are conducted by the federal agencies that are responsible for supervising depository institutions: the Board of Governors of the Federal Reserve System, the Federal Deposit Insurance Corporation, the Office of the Comptroller of the Currency, and the Office of Thrift Supervision (www.ffiec.gov/cra/history/htm). These regulators are also required to include public comment on the institution's community lending record in banks' CRA performance (Agpar and Duda 2002).

Some commentators on the CRA point out that it has had an overall positive impact not only on low-income and minority communities but also on the banks that have invested in these communities. According to a CRA loan survey by the Federal Reserve, banks appear to have realized positive returns overall, in line with or superior to their other investment (Federal Reserve Board 2000). Communities have benefited from stronger community organizations and from increased social infrastructure, business investments, home ownership, and home improvements. However, the overall impact of the CRA on poverty reduction is not very clear, as the CRA has helped only a small portion of low-income people.

How Does the Community Reinvestment Act Work?

A major change in the CRA occurred in 1995 after widespread complaints by the banking industry and community advocates complained that CRA evaluations were not results based. New procedures examined actual performance in their assessment areas, defined as one or more metropolitan statistical areas in which the bank has its main office, branches, and deposit-taking ATMs and also the surrounding areas in which the bank has originated or purchased a substantial portion of its loans.

The 1995 revision establishes specific tests to be used by federal banking regulators when assessing CRA performance for different lender types, sizes, and businesses (large retail, small retail, and wholesale/limited-purpose institutions). These tests consist of three parts: lending, investment, and services.

The lending test evaluates a bank's lending activity in its assessment area. This includes home mortgage, small-business, credit card, automobile, and community development lending. Regulators look at the number and amount of loans; their geographic distribution among low-, moderate-, middle-, and upper-income areas; and borrower characteristics, including income and size. Lending is the most heavily weighted component in the overall rating equation and is most widely scrutinized by community advocates.

The investment test evaluates a bank's qualified investments that benefit its community or a broader geographic area that includes the bank's community. A qualified investment is any investment or grant that makes community development as its primary purpose.

The service test evaluates a depository institution's record of helping to meet the credit needs of its assessment area by analyzing the availability and effectiveness of its systems for delivering retail banking services and the extent and innovativeness of its community development services.

Despite the effort to focus on quantitative results, it is claimed that the CRA examination is subjective, as examiners apply the relevant tests taking into account the context of the particular institution and the market in which it operates. This 'performance context' is defined to include information about the economic and demographic characteristics of the institution's assessment area; lending, investment, and service opportunities in that area; the institution's product offerings and business strategy; its capacity and constraints; its past performance and the performance of similarly situated lenders; information and public commentary contained in the institution's public CRA file; and any other information the regulator deems relevant. The new rules also attempted to reduce both paperwork and subjectivity. For all types of institutions, public comment is encouraged by requiring that each banking regulator publish a list of banks that are scheduled for CRA examinations in the upcoming quarter.

Today, some commentators believe that the CRA is losing some of its relevance and no longer conforms to the realities of the current financial services industry. When Congress modernized financial services through the 1999 Gramm–Leach–Bliley Financial Modernization Act, which broke down residual barriers to multiple banking and banking across geographic boundaries, it did not scrutinize the impact of these changes on the CRA. Given that the CRA was founded on the assumptions of local deposit-taking and local community provision of banking services, its context is no longer clear. Moreover, new banking delivery channels such as phone or Internet banking also contribute to weaken the role of branch banking and the links between these bank branches and local communities.

Finally, with the changing structure of the mortgage industry, less than 30 percent of all home purchase loans are subject to intensive review under the CRA (Apgar and Duda 2003). In some metropolitan areas, this share is less than 10 percent. Mortgage lending is now dominated by large national firms. At the time when the CRA was enacted, banks and thrifts originated the vast majority of home purchase loans. The link between mortgage lending and the branch-based deposit-gathering on which the CRA was based is no longer strong.

Other countries have considered CRA-type legislation, and some have adopted it while others have considered it inappropriate in their circumstances. In South Africa, the postapartheid government has been very proactive in its effort to address the problem of financial exclusion. The Home Loan and Mortgage Disclosure Act, modeled after the HMDA in the United States, was passed by the South African Parliament in 2000. This legislation encourages banks to grant home loans and requires banks to disclose annual financial statements so that their lending practices can be monitored. The Community Reinvestment Bill, which will most likely become law in 2003, follows in the footsteps of the CRA. In its draft form, the bill compels financial institutions to set aside a portion of their home loan funding to low- and middle-income households and to disclose their reasons for rejecting mortgage loan applications.

There has been a popular movement to enact CRA-type legislation in Canada, although no formal legislative proposal has been presented. The Ottawa-based Canadian Community Reinvestment Coalition mobilizes a broad coalition of Canadians to support measures to make the banks serve individuals, small businesses, and local communities much better. However, despite heavy pressure from pro-CRA lobby groups, this venture has not gone very far, partly because of structural differences compared to the United States. The Canadian banking system is national in scope and dominated by six major banks. Hence, a case for reinvestment in the local community is limited. Besides, the CRA in the United States works largely through the process of applications for mergers, which suggests a banking system with a relatively large number of banks (www.parliament.nsw.gov.au).

The United Kingdom, which has a similarly concentrated banking system (four banks hold 90 percent of system assets), has also rejected the idea of CRA-style legislation (Donovan and Palmer 1999). However, the threat to pass a CRA-type bill has led the financial industry to release data showing how much money deposited in deprived areas is reinvested into the local economy, based on the recommendations of a Social Investment Task Force under the Treasury Department.[10]

'Lifeline Banking' and Basic Accounts

To promote universal access to financial services, many countries have enacted legislation requiring commercial banks to offer low-cost bank accounts, known as 'lifeline' accounts. Legislation introduced by the government in mid-2003 introduced a form of lifeline banking in Brazil, through a scheme for the free provision of basic accounts with no checking facilities and a cap on monthly transactions.[11] Conditions for opening such bank accounts have also been simplified. As discussed below, forms of such basic banking are provided in many countries. Monitoring of costs to try to ensure sustainability is desirable in tandem with lifeline banking.

In the United States, many states require banks to serve the population at large. "Lifeline banking laws were first proposed in several states in the early to mid-1980s. Thus far, seven states—Illinois, Massachusetts, Minnesota, New Jersey, New York, Rhode Island, and Vermont—have enacted legislation creating lifeline banking accounts. These laws range from authorizing the state banking department to monitor bank fees and, when appropriate, regulating them, to mandating that all state-chartered banks offer a low-cost checking account" (Doyle and Saidenberg 1998). New York State law is a good example of a comprehensive form of lifeline legislation. The Omnibus Consumer Protection and Banking Deregulation Act, enacted in January 1995, requires state-chartered banks in New York to offer low-cost checking accounts. Such accounts can be opened with as little as $25, have no minimum balance requirement, carry a maximum maintenance fee of $3 per month, and must allow at least eight monthly transactions. In France, if a French resident can prove that two banks have rejected him or her as clients, Banque de France will select a bank that is then directed to accept the new client. "In practice, those appealing receive a very simple account based at the post office, which allows deposits and withdrawals but little else. In Sweden, it is a condition of a bank's license that they are obliged to accept deposits" (Donovan and Palmer 1999).

The main banks in the United Kingdom have started providing basic bank accounts to meet the special needs of low-income people. Typically, these accounts do not include an overdraft option or checkbook; the Bank of Scotland has gone further, offering a bill payment account linked to the basic account. The 2001 Bank Act of Canada requires chartered banks to provide basic bank accounts for low-income people. Although these accounts do not include overdraft and checkbook options, they are available to clients who would normally be refused by banks based on their credit scoring. The act imposes penalties for noncompliance (essentially fines of up to C$100,000). While the bill mandates access to basic retail services to help low-income individuals build assets as part of the financial system, it does not address access to credit. The government wants to extend financial services to the low-income population and pays all government wages, salaries, and benefits into these basic accounts via automated credit transfer; checks and cash can also be deposited. In addition, clients with basic accounts have access to cash machines and bill payment through direct debit. Some banks also provide other services linked to basic accounts, such as debit cards.

It should be noted that analyses of the impact of lifeline banking are limited and mixed. Lifeline banking legislation would have a positive impact on the unbanked if it reduces the cost of basic financial services (especially for payments) and if consumers are sensitive to this price change. But evidence on cost reduction is mixed, and analysis suggests that many consumers may not be sensitive to these price changes. These analyses conclude that such initiatives must be accompanied by consumer education and more convenient banking services to be fully effective.

Electronic Transfer Accounts and First Accounts

The Debt Collection Improvement Act of 1996, intended primarily to reduce the cost to the U.S. federal government of making payments and collecting debts, had an unintended but major impact on the downscaling of financial services. The act required that electronic funds transfers be used to make federal payments, revealing the very large number of recipients who did not have a bank account at all (estimated by the Treasury Department at about 6 million people but recently re-estimated by the General Accounting Office at 11 million, or 18 percent of all benefit recipients). Treasury discovered that there were many barriers to providing such individuals with accounts, including cost, financial institutions' lack of interest, and popular mistrust.

In response, the Treasury developed the Electronic Transfer Account (ETA), a debit-based, low-cost account into which federal benefits can be directly deposited. The ETA is complemented by a low-cost, electronic banking account for the 'unbanked' who receive federal benefits, known as the First Accounts. First Accounts, a recent U.S. program to combat unbankedness (January 2, 2002), targets the working poor who are unbanked and do not receive government checks. Since the ETA was launched in July 1999, more than 400 financial institutions with more than 2,500 locations have committed to offer the ETA. The Treasury Department puts particular emphasis on trying to reach unbanked employees through their employers or through their employers' financial institutions (www.ustreas.gov/press/releases/).

The program still requires careful evaluation. According to some banks, it is not very successful due to limited use and high start-up costs despite subsidies for start-up. There are successful examples elsewhere. The Australian government makes 6 million welfare payments by electronic transfer each fortnight, and the transition to EFT should be effective in Britain by 2005 (Stegman 2003).

Monitoring and Information Tracking

Apart from the disclosure requirements discussed above, additional information is collected in some countries, which helps to raise consumer and public awareness on the distribution of financial services. In the United States, relatively more information is available on the distribution of housing finance, compared to other financial services.[12] Advocacy groups track the availability of financial services for low-income consumers and small businesses and by various geographic criteria (Bradford 2002; National Community Reinvestment Coalition 2003). There is also original survey and analytical work, frequently on a local basis. For example, the Woodstock Institute recently published a report on the effectiveness of CDFIs and has previously published a report on Chicago-area credit union services to low-income consumers (Jacob, Bush, and Immergluck 2002; Woodstock Institute 2003). As a result, the National Credit Union Association began to produce its own report on credit union services to this population in 2003.

In the United Kingdom, government actors who take an interest in the financing of underinvested communities and lower-income groups include the Treasury Department, the Competition Commission, and the Department of Trade and Industry. The Bank of England also publishes an annual report on small-enterprise financing (Bank of England 2002). The Treasury set up a Social Investment Task Force in 2001 to investigate enhanced private financing to disadvantaged communities. The Task Force recommended increased bank disclosure of lending to deprived communities. The main banks, responding to government pressure, are establishing strategies and departments to increase financing to CDFIs, social enterprises, and deprived communities. The British Bankers Association report, *Access to Finance and Business Support by Ethnic Minority Firms in the UK*, was published in September 2002 (Ram, Smallbone, and Deakins 2002). Also in 2002, the Department of Trade and Industry set up a Social Exclusion Unit to focus on the needs of underserved communities.

The U.K. experience is also useful in terms of thinking of locally targeted policies, based on definitions of location, which are much smaller than regions or states. For several years, the United Kingdom has compiled Indices of Local Conditions, more recently referred to as Indices of Multiple Deprivation, or Local Deprivation, where the unit for the targeting of policies has been as narrowly defined as the local ward or census numeration district (discussed further below), and this index is used for determining eligibility when targeting policies for financial support, such as those available through the Phoenix Fund. Also valuable is the incorporation in this exercise of highly skilled university-level expertise in the construction and interpretation of such indices.[13] These indices then have been used in the analytical work undertaken on small-business financing by entities such as the Bank of England in its annual report on this subject.

The 2001 Bank Act of Canada created a consumer agency that will be responsible for collecting and publishing small-business lending data by authorization level (loan approval amounts) from all financial institutions. The new agency will use Statistics Canada to produce annual data on the lending activity of all financial institutions by regional geography and loan approval size, greatly enhancing the information reporting and transparency of small-business financing.[14] In contrast to the United States, Canadian data collection and disclosure requirements focus on the number of loans that financial institutions (for example, banks, credit unions, *caisses populaires*) have approved by authorization level or by size of loan approved. The Financial Consumer Agency will not collect bank lending data by demographic characteristics of the borrower (such as race or ethnicity), by geographic location (other than by province), by size of business, or by type of business. According to the Canadian Bankers Association, this would be deemed to be a violation of privacy laws. This raises the important point that laws on information collection and monitoring of lending practices for any country will have to be tailored to the privacy provisions of each country's legal framework.

Financial Support

The experience of the past two decades has demonstrated that moral suasion and monitoring may go much further than imagined hitherto in promoting financial downscaling. Even in countries such as the United States, the United Kingdom, or Canada, experience with the extension of explicit financial support has been much older. Financial support programs in these countries have been mainly small and largely indirect. A review of their experience provides important insights into how targeting may be most effectively used.

The United States Part 1: SBA

In the United States, government support for downscaling financial services has been primarily indirect—typically providing partial guarantees or insurance for credit provided by private financial institutions to targeted groups. Although borrowers pay fees for the insurance and guarantees, the loan quality in these programs has led the Federal Office of Management and Budget to conclude that, at various times, they do represent a subsidy. Yet, many such programs with financial supports have proven to be effective devices for encouraging private capital toward entities that might not otherwise have received it. Such programs have been most effective where they have covered only a part of lenders' or investors' financial exposure, so that there are still incentives to underwrite the transactions prudently. Ease of processing and use is another key factor.

Among the oldest such programs are those run by the U.S. Small Business Administration (SBA), created in 1953, which offers several programs that provide partial guarantees and other support to participating banks. Its major programs are the Section 7(a) Loan Guaranty Program, which provides pro rata guarantees for up to 75 to 85 percent of private-sector loans to small businesses. Interest rates on SBA-guaranteed loans are negotiated between the borrower and the lender, subject to certain maxima, and range from around 2.25 to 4.75 percent above prime.

Although SBA loan guarantees carry some administrative burdens for lenders, those financial institutions that have invested in understanding and applying program rules have found them to be effective. More recently, SBA has introduced a low-documentation option for very small loans as well as a line-of-credit alternative. The program has also been successful in reaching difficult-to-serve populations. Roughly one-third of Section 7(a) loans go to minority- and women-owned businesses; a roughly comparable proportion serves new enterprises.

The SBA offers other programs. The Section 504 Certified Development Company Loan Program provides substantial guarantees for loans to small businesses made by nonprofit corporations created to contribute to the economic development of their communities in conjunction with private lenders. There are currently 270 certified development corporations for this program throughout the United States. Proceeds under Section 504 loans may be used to finance fixed assets such as land and improvements or for the purchase of long-term machinery and equipment.

Third, a venture-capital program, known as the Small Business Investment Company (SBIC) Program, was authorized in 1958, which provides capital to licensed venture funds that target small businesses. SBICs can be independently owned by small groups of investors, affiliated with banks, or publicly traded venture-capital companies. SBICs may issue SBA-guaranteed debentures for amounts equal to up to 300 percent of their private capital, to a maximum of about $100 million. This permits these specialized companies to access capital on terms that would not otherwise be available to them. The SBIC Program has contributed meaningfully to total venture-capital investing in the United States. In the past 40 years, licensed SBICs have provided more than $36 billion in financing to small businesses. Since 1997, financings reported by SBICs have amounted to between one-third and more than one-half of the total number of venture-capital financings made in the United States in any given year and from 5 percent to 15 percent of the annual dollar volume of venture-capital financings. Among the companies that received SBIC-financed capital when they were small business are Apple Computers, Intel Corporation, Sun Microsystems, and Federal Express.

The United States Part 2: Community Development Finance

During the 1990s, Congress enacted several new programs involving financial support focused on expanding banking services to low-income and minority people and to small businesses. These included the establishment of the CDFI Fund, and the Assets for Independence Act, which provides grants to establish and enroll low-income working families in Individual Development Account (IDA) programs.[15] These programs are relatively small, and their impact has been largely by example and through partnerships. The largest is the CDFI Fund, which has made $608 million in awards to community development organizations and financial institutions since it was established in 1994.

The American Community Development Banking and Financial Institutions Act (1994) created a fund to stimulate investment in alternative financial institutions through two main programs: the CDFI program and the Bank Enterprise Award (BEA) program. The CDFI program funds the operations of CDFIs through equity investments, capital grants, loans, and technical assistance. The CDFIs are federally certified financial institutions that provide financial services to low-income communities and other groups unable to get approved by traditional banks. CDFI services may span credit, deposits, investments, and developmental services. Some are chartered banks; others are credit unions; and many operate as self-regulating, nonprofit institutions (www.microenterpriseworks.org/links/glossary/organization.htm#B).

The act also authorizes the fund to provide incentives through the Bank Enterprises Award program to promote investment in CDFIs. The BEA program provides cash prizes to banks that lend and invest directly in low-income communities and that support CDFIs operating in these communities. In 1996 and 1997, 79 banks were awarded a total of $30 million. These banks provided $133 million of support to CDFIs and $143 million in direct lending and financial services (Donovan and Palmer 1999, p. 63).The CDFI Fund is now also administering the $15 billion New Markets Tax Credit program, which subsidizes eligible community development entities.[16]

THE UNITED STATES PART 3: CAPITAL ACCESS PROGRAMS

Since 1986, more than two-fifths of all states in the United States and two cities have established Capital Access Programs (CAPs) to encourage banks to lend to small businesses. Under CAPs, participating states match funds that lenders contribute to their loan-loss reserves for such loans—typically between 3 and 7 percent of loan value. A study published by the U.S. Treasury in 2001 concluded that CAPs have proven to be a cost-effective means to encourage lending to small enterprises (U.S. Department of the Treasury 2001). CAPs allow banks to apply their own underwriting guidelines without prior government approval. Because of their administrative simplicity, CAPs impose small additional costs on lenders; banks consistently report that they are able to staff these programs with between 1 and 1½ full-time equivalents. Nearly 400 banks were actively originating CAP loans in June 2000. Cumulative losses under CAP loan programs have amounted to $58 million, or about 3.7 percent of the volume of such loans originated. The Treasury concluded that CAPs benefit groups of borrowers that are not well served by other credit enhancement programs, including minority-owned businesses and firms that are located in low- and moderate-income communities. Factors that appeared to contribute to the success of these programs include active marketing by states to banks as well as state funding levels that banks view as sufficient to meet their likely demand.

Over the past several years, Congress has considered proposals to provide a tax credit to banks offering special savings accounts (Individual Development Accounts; IDAs) to cover the cost of their administration and matching funds. IDAs are special savings vehicles for low-income individuals in which savings are both directed toward a specific asset-building goal (such as buying a home, higher education, or starting a business) and matched, often on a greater than 1:1 basis, by an outside party. The Senate passed the proposal in early 2003; it awaits House action. Whether other types of incentives, either through direct awards or the tax system, are proposed or enacted will depend at least in part on the outcome of the First Accounts program.

Financial Support in the United Kingdom and Canada

There are many similarities today between models in the United States and United Kingdom, although the use of the programs differs, and they are of different vintages. The Phoenix Fund was established in 1999, based on the recommendations of the *Enterprise and Social Exclusion* report commissioned by HM Treasury. Modeled after the CDFI Fund run by the U.S. Treasury, the Phoenix Fund is designed to encourage entrepreneurship in disadvantaged areas. The Phoenix Fund includes (1) a Development Fund to promote innovative ways of supporting enterprises in deprived areas; (2) a pilot network of volunteer mentors to pre- and early start-up; (3) capital, revenue, and loan guarantee support for CDFIs; (4) Community Venture Capital Funds (see below); and (5) City Growth Strategies designed to encourage towns and cities to develop and implement strategies that put enterprise and business at the heart of regeneration, focusing on the competitive economic advantages of inner-city areas rather than their social disadvantages. Four pilot projects are operating in Nottingham, Plymouth, St. Helens, and parts of London. In its 2002 Spending Review, a further £50 million was authorized by the government to enable the Phoenix Fund to continue through 2006.

The United Kingdom also offers tax credits for investing in CDFIs. The Community Investment Tax Credit was approved in 2002. The first 11 CDFIs were approved for tax credits in March 2003. Tax relief (5 percent per annum of the amount invested for five years) is provided to an investor who invests in an accredited CDFI, which in turn lends to or invests in a qualifying profit-distributing enterprise or community project. One such CDFI, Bridges Community Ventures, was established and launched in 2002. It raised £20 million from the private sector, matched with £20 million from the government. The fund focuses on providing traditional venture capital to small businesses located in the most deprived 25 percent wards on the Index of Multiple Deprivation. These businesses provide employment in the deprived ward and serve disadvantaged communities.

Community Loan Funds provide more conventional loan finance to businesses, charities, and social enterprises. An example of a U.K. Community Loan Fund is Aston Reinvestment Trust (ART). Focused on access to finance and charging commercial rates, ART was set up in 1997 to promote economic and social regeneration in Birmingham by providing loans for small businesses and voluntary-sector organizations that could not access finance from conventional sources. Based on the U.S. community-banking model, ART's aim is to help regenerate urban areas abandoned by mainstream banks.

Like the United States, the United Kingdom also has a Small Loan Guarantee Fund program for loans to small firms. However, there does not seem to be any systematic or sophisticated use of the guarantees in the way that some U.S. banks have segmented the U.S. market using SBA and CAP support for different markets, loan sizes, and credit risks. In response to the British Bankers' Association's report on *Access to Financing for Ethnic Minorities,* the guarantee was expanded to additional sectors that were considered to be particularly important to ethnic minorities, and its maximum turnover limit for the service sector was raised to £3 million per annum.

The U.K. government provides tax relief as a way to encourage savings and promote individual provision for retirement. Because this provision offers no incentive if income is too low to be taxable, however, it is of no benefit to most low-income people. The policy instead targets the middle- and higher-income population. Recognizing this drawback, in 2001 the U.K. government introduced the Stakeholder Pensions, a new, low-cost pension for moderate-income people. Its goal is to encourage this population to provide for itself. Because this initiative is relatively new, empirical evidence of its effectiveness is not yet available. The U.K. government has also encouraged the accumulation of financial assets through tax incentives. The former government introduced two initiatives: Personal Equity Plans and Tax Exempt Special Savings Accounts. The new government introduced Individual Savings Accounts in 1997, superseding the two earlier initiatives.[17]

The United Kingdom also introduced IDAs and the Saving Gateway accounts that are matched by additional funds based on specific ratios. They are intended to encourage low-income people to establish banking relationships and to increase their savings. The U.K. used the U.S. model but also explored a geographically targeted policy—provided by the local community organization and funded by different sources—to support the regeneration of deprived communities. IDAs are to be used for targeted purposes such as home ownership, education, buying a business, and training.

The Saving Gateway allows more flexibility in the use of funds than the IDA (which restricts use to home ownership, enterprise, and education). This lack of restriction makes the Saving Gateway more like a pure financial product and less like an antipoverty tool. Although some argue that this lack of restriction will prevent the Saving Gateway from creating a lasting change in savings habits, U.K. policymakers do not wish to introduce restrictions that will increase the complexity of program administration. The Saving Gateway includes a financial education component. Focused on three stages (account opening, account lifetime, and account maturity), this component aims to promote wider financial literacy and financial inclusion goals. The policy is still at the launching phase. Pilot programs for this initiative started in August 2002 in five areas around England. These will last for 18 months, after which it is the stated aim of the government to roll the policy out nationally. The most innovative feature of the Saving Gateway is the concept of matched saving—an incentive first used in U.S. IDAs. Also as with IDAs, only certain groups will be eligible for the Saving Gateway, and they will last for a restricted length of time (www.ippr.org.uk/research/files.team27/).

Observers of the U.K. system point out that the geographically targeted policy approach has three primary advantages. First, it is trusted by potential clients, who are familiar with the local organizations involved. Second, it can be more flexible in responding to specific needs, adapting its design, and delivery to changing local conditions. And third, it is better able to pilot and test new approaches.

In April 2003, the U.K. government approved implementation of the Child Trust Fund. Its goal is to increase opportunities for young people, help them manage their transition to independent adulthood, and improve their financial literacy. The fund, which will provide savings accounts for all newborn babies (resulting in nest eggs for all young adults), is aimed at opening up opportunities for all. The fund operates as follows: The government provides an endowment, paid into an account at birth, for all newborn babies (with a higher amount provided for poorer families). At the ages of 5, 11, and 16 years, additional payments will be made; again, higher amounts are paid to those with lower income. Although the account is locked away until the child reaches the age of 18, parents, friends, relatives, and others are encouraged to add money to this account. At the age of 18, the child is given access to the account, with no restrictions on the use of the funds it contains.

As in the case of the United Kingdom and United States, the federal government of Canada provides support through partial guarantees through the Canada Small Business Financing Program, a loan guarantee program for loans smaller than C$250,000. The bank receives an 85 percent guarantee of the loan principal, pays a 2 percent transaction fee (usually passed on to the borrower), and charges a maximum of prime +1.25 percent. Like the SBA (Section 7a) loan guarantees in the United States, the program's guarantees enhance collateral value and reduce the risk of marginal loans, encouraging more transactions.

Since the program's restructuring in 1999, annual volume by banks has declined steadily; obviously, the program is not achieving its goals. This failure is due in part to the difficult economic climate and in part to the disincentives built into the guarantee program (such as paperwork requirements, a longer response time to the borrower, and less-flexible loan structuring).[18] The total number of loans has dropped from 16,635 in fiscal year 1999–2000 to 11,142 in 2001–2002 (http://strategis.ic.gc.ca/epic/internet/incsbfp=pfpec.nsf/vwapg/la01260e_A_tii.html/$FILE/la01260e_A_tii.html). Total dollars lent through the program fell from C$1.2 billion to C$915 million. Because the guarantees are only eligible for loans up to $250,000, bankers complain that the loan guarantee program offers too little upside for all the additional paperwork and transaction costs.

In addition to the federal government's Canada Small Business Finance Program, regional intermediaries of federal funds have created innovative and flexible programs to encourage banks and credit unions to make loans to smaller entrepreneurs. For example, Western Economic Diversification is a regional division of the federal government now in its seventh year. Known simply as WD, it promotes economic diversification and job creation in the western provinces of Canada. WD's tools include direct loans to small enterprises and loan-loss reserves for sector-specific loan pools created by individual banks. Just as with Capital Access Programs in the United States, any bank or credit union can apply for loan-loss reserve support for a portfolio of loans in a particular sector (such as technology, health, microloans up to C$35,000, and conservation business loans up to C$500,000). In this program, however, WD puts up the loan-loss reserve, and the originating bank receives an 80 percent guarantee on any individual loan without any paperwork.

This program works extremely well for smaller loans (under C$50,000) and loans with minimal collateral. The partnering bank projects its disbursements for the next quarter and then receives cash for the reserve equal to 80 percent of the total projected loan amount. The bank books only 20 percent of the loan value on its own books (because that is all that is at risk). For example, Vancouver City Savings Credit Union in British Columbia (the largest credit union in Canada, with C$6.3 billion in assets) has issued C$11 million in Self-Reliance Loans (loans less than $35,000). The maximum loss exposure is 20 percent of the total principal lent, and there is no cap on the interest rate that Vancouver City can charge (currently, prime +4 percent). WD worked with Vancouver City to review its alternative credit scoring for situations not qualifying for conventional loans, helping Vancouver City understand how the loan pool would allow the credit union to make loans that would otherwise not be feasible.[19]

The Business Development Bank of Canada (BDC) is a development financial institution wholly owned and capitalized by the government of Canada. BDC's mandate is to help create and develop Canadian small and medium-size businesses. The bank provides senior and subordinated loans, venture capital to finance business growth, and customized services through individual business consulting. In 1995, revisions were brought about to (1) significantly raise its C$3 million loan ceiling; (2)

change the capital structure so that the bank could access capital from both the government and the private capital markets; and (3) redefine its role, so that it complements other commercial financial institutions rather than serving as the 'lender of last resort.' This has enabled BDC to colend with banks more often, to compete with banks (on interest rates, terms, and acceptable loan-to-value ratios), and to meet its internal goal of financial self-sufficiency.

For fiscal year 1999–2000, BDC's loan group disbursed C$1352 million, with 56 percent of loans being smaller than C$100,000 and 88 percent being less than C$500,000 in size. The venture-capital group makes investments ranging from C$300,000 to C$3 million and made commitments of C$44 million in 36 small and microenterprises (SMEs; Industry Canada 2001). According to its website, BDC's venture-capital portfolio is currently C$400 million, and the bank is looking to grow it to C$1 billion over the next five years. BDC focuses on industry sectors with significant job creation and economic development potential. Although BDC does not target small entrepreneurs seeking modest amounts of debt financing, it does offer many resources and a nationwide delivery system through local branches.

Institutional Support

As a counterpoint to the consolidation that was occurring in the commercial banking sector in the 1980s and 1990s, community development banks and other nonprofit financial intermediaries emerged in both urban and rural markets across the United States to serve the financial needs of low-income and minority people and small businesses. The majority of these institutions are nonprofit corporations whose stated missions target certain segments of the underserved populations or geographic markets. In some respects, these community-focused institutions took on the role that credit unions and mutual savings banks traditionally played in providing financial services to populations not otherwise served by the mainstream banking sector. Although credit unions continue to play an important role as providers of financial services to these populations, community development loan funds have emerged as an important provider of credit to these individuals and businesses.[20]

The growth in the number of these alternative delivery vehicles was in part stimulated by the creation of the CDFI Fund in 1994 by the Riegle Community Development and Regulatory Improvement Act. In addition to providing capital to lend for qualified activities, the CDFI Fund offers technical assistance to nascent, qualified community development financial institutions. These technical assistance funds are leveraged with other funding sources, such as foundations or large U.S. financial institutions.

Indeed, direct financial support for this type of activity from the government is modest. Instead, much of the support for these smaller community-based organizations comes indirectly through partnerships. For example, all 12 U.S. Federal Reserve district banks have Community Affairs Offices that facilitate communication among banking institutions, community groups, and government agencies and provide research on the community development finance industry.

The Federal Home Loan Banks (FHLBs), although in existence since the 1930s, have become more significant players in the community development field since the passage of the Gramm–Leach–Bliley Act. A provision of the act expanded the types of collateral member banks could use when obtaining liquidity advances from the FHLB. Being able to pledge small-business loans as collateral has increased the small-business lending activity of these community financial institutions. In addition, the FHLB system, through its Community Investment Program, has provided more than $20 billion in below-market-rate loans to its member institutions since 1990, enabling them to extend long-term financing for housing and economic development. It also offers extensive services focused on operational efficiency and training to its more than 8,000 member institutions.

There is a precedent for large national banks and thrifts in the United States to support smaller community-based financial providers. Under the SBA's Microloan Program, the SBA makes funds available to community-based lenders (intermediaries) which, in turn, onlend to eligible small businesses and individuals. The average loan size according to the SBA is $10,500. The local provider handles all underwriting and decision-making. Loan applicants may also receive technical assistance and training by participating in the Microloan Program.

Another notable program to encourage business-to-business collaboration is BusinessLINC. It was initiated as a joint effort by the Treasury and the SBA in 1998 and encourages linkages between large, private-sector companies and small or minority-owned firms operating in the same industry. The LINC stands for *l*earning, *i*nformation, *n*etworking, and *c*ollaboration. It offers technical advice, market access, endorsement and credibility, financial access, and potential partnering to small and minority-owned businesses. Although originally started by a government entity, the program was intended to turn management over to the private sector. The Business Roundtable, a private-sector organization, now runs day-to-day management of the program.

These examples highlight efforts by large commercial banks and thrifts to partner with government to increase the institutional capacity of community-based financial service providers. These community organizations fill gaps in the market not otherwise served by the national firms, who find it more efficient to partner with and provide financial and technical assistance to community-based providers rather than offer the products and services directly. Often, the delivery of the financial and technical assistance is provided by third-party practitioners, such as ShoreBank, that work to strengthen the institutional capacity of these community-based organizations directly.

Support for downscaling has also come through support for financial literacy. In particular, the Federal Deposit Insurance Corporation developed and has been an active promoter of a comprehensive financial literacy curriculum called Money Smart. It has entered into partnerships with hundreds of government entities and private organizations to teach the curriculum to low-income individuals, including such hard-to-reach populations as ex-offenders and teenagers coming out of foster care.

INSTITUTIONAL SUPPORT IN THE UNITED KINGDOM AND CANADA

Established in 2000 as an agency of the Department of Trade and Industry, the main responsibility of the Small Business Service (SBS) is to ensure that the interests of small businesses receive a higher priority. In addition, the SBS aims "to promote enterprise across society, and particularly in under-represented and disadvantaged groups" (Small Business Service 2001). The SBS provides grants to small businesses for capacity building, especially in technology, and guarantees bank loans to riskier small-business projects under the Small Firms Loan Guarantee. The SBS also manages the accreditation process for the Community Investment Tax Credit. The Phoenix Fund is also under the SBS and focuses on disadvantaged areas in particular.

The U.K. government enacted the Regional Development Agency Act in 1998 and established nine Regional Development Agencies (RDAs) by mid-2000 under the oversight of the Department of Trade and Industry. RDAs are nondepartment public bodies with a primary role as strategic drivers of regional economic development. RDAs aim to coordinate regional economic development and regeneration, enable the English regions to improve their relative competitiveness, and reduce the imbalances that exist within and among regions. The government is increasingly focusing on reducing the 'equity gap' for small businesses and businesses in deprived areas. For small businesses, regional venture-capital funds are being established totaling £270 million, backed by £80 million of government funding. For deprived areas (those defined by the European Union as Objective 1 areas requiring regeneration), separate regional funds have been established. Each RDA also supports various business development services, mentoring, and other financial schemes for start-ups and small businesses that match the region's development strategies. This often includes deprived areas and low-income groups but is not exclusively focused on this area.

Advantage West Midlands, one of the regional development agencies, has made providing access to finance for all SMEs in its region a priority. It has created a Regional Finance Forum to bring together experts to focus on both demand and supply issues and is setting up a £30 million regional venture-capital fund providing equity funds of between £250,000 and £500,000 to fill the equity gap many SMEs face. Advantage West Midlands is also in the process of setting up a fund-of-funds to ensure that all types of funding are provided to all the different types of businesses requiring access to finance in the region.

CDFIs are financial services providers (including community development banks, community loan funds, and community development venture funds) whose mission specifically requires them to achieve social objectives. The CDFIs (or CFIs, as they are called in the United Kingdom) typically emphasize financial services for businesses and social economy organizations, although some do provide personal lending. They may provide equity, quasi-equity, or debt services. To some extent, CDFIs are considered lenders of last resort, although they do not officially require customers to have been formally rejected by banks or other sources of funding to qualify as clients. The products provided, however, typically would not be available to such clients from a bank. Although some U.K. CDFIs are regulated as banks or building societies, most do not have deposit-taking status. Most CDFIs are nonprofits, legally established as Industrial and Provident Societies; in association with their charitable status, the companies are limited by guarantee. CDFIs are self-regulated, and the Association of the CDFIs, launched in April 2002, is working on establishing benchmarks for the sector. Three banks—Triodos, Unity Trust, and Charity Bank—are considered to be part of the CDFI sector, although none specifically focus on low-income or deprived communities. The estimated size of the sector is £400 million.

The United Kingdom also recognizes Development Trusts and Social Enterprises, which take on some activities associated with economic regeneration. Social Enterprises have historically had strong access to grant funding. Their debt financing tends to be performed by CDFIs, bank community development finance departments, and special-purpose banks such as Triodos and Charity Bank. As is the case with microfinance institutions or nonprofit governmental organizations in developing countries, many traditional banks are unfamiliar with the organizational structure, the use of grants, and the lack of profit maximization involved. For these reasons, Social Enterprises may have difficulty obtaining traditional bank debt financing on reasonable terms. The Bank of England published a report on the financing of Social Enterprises in mid-2003 (Brown and Murphy 2003).

Finally, U.K. banks work with government and other partners to promote financial education and training for individuals and small businesses. Banks are now educating individuals on how to use and maintain basic accounts and provide free money management advice for people having financial difficulties. The British Bankers Association is also active in supporting government financial education programs in schools.

Other than the Business Development Bank of Canada, there are fewer privately capitalized and managed development finance vehicles in Canada than in the United States. Programs focused on microbusiness lending in Toronto and elsewhere in Canada, for example, have been privately financed and managed. These, however, became a model that several regional governments have sought to encourage through financial incentives to support such programs (such as the loan capital pools created by Western Economic Diversification, described above). Those nongovernmental development finance institutions that do exist typically receive a combination of private and regional government dollars. For example, Western Economic Diversification manages a program called Community Futures, which provides seed capital for local loan funds and operational support. These local organizations are rural community development corporations. Many of these programs appear to be regional or province based rather than federal.

Enhancing Competition in the Provision of Financial Services

A Treasury-sponsored independent review of U.K. banking published in March 2000, led by Don Cruickshank, head of the London Stock Exchange, accused banks of making excess profits at the expense of consumers. It maintained that there is even less competition in the small-business market, where just a few banks dominate (Cruickshank 2000). Cruickshank was particularly critical of the four major banks—Barclays, NatWest, HSBC, and Lloyds TSB—which control 80 percent of personal accounts. More specifically, it found the industry particularly uncompetitive in the following: payments systems, such as charges for cash machines and debit cards, and banking services for SMEs and the poor population. In the first market, the report found that banks' charges were excessively high. The Cruickshank report recommended new regulation for banks' cash and payments networks. It also acknowledged that technological progress and better information could help spur competition.

With regards to SME banking, the report called for a Competition Commission study to investigate small-business charges. The conclusions of the study were finally announced in March 2002, and all its recommendations were accepted. The Competition Commission found that the four major banks, which provide 90 percent of services to SMEs, formed—along with other banks—a complex monopoly (HM Treasury 2001). The commission found that 10 practices by eight banks restricted or distorted competition, causing SMEs to be overcharged and making it difficult for them to switch to other banks. Some of the specific charges included (1) restricting SMEs to business rather than personal bank accounts; (2) failing to inform SMEs about possible benefits from 'set-off-and-sweep' facilities (which allow for credit balances in one account to be set off against debit balances in another) and from the automatic transfer of funds between accounts to prevent overdrafts; (3) failing to compete on prices, by refusing to pay interest on current accounts, and paying low rates of interest on smaller, short-term deposit accounts; (4) maintaining a structure of charges not related to costs; and (5) overcharging their SME customers.

The commission proposed radical remedies, including price controls and bank split-offs to generate competition. The Cruickshank report called for more downscaling efforts from the U.K. banking system. It asked banks to cater to the needs of the low-income community by making their services more affordable and providing services for low-income households in poor neighborhoods. The Competition Commission and the government asked the Director General of Fair Trading to ensure that the banks implement several remedies over the next two to three years and to seek undertakings from the four largest banks to offer to any SME customer (1) an account that pays interest of at least the Bank of England's base rate minus 2.5 percent, (2) a current account free of money transmission charges, or (3) a choice between the two. Three of the big four banks chose the first option, except Barclays, which offered a choice between credit interest and reduced money transmission charges. Most of the changes were implemented at the beginning of 2003.

These investigations in the United Kingdom have led to the raising of similar questions with regard to competitive practices in other countries. Notably in South Africa, a recent study on small-business finance also raised the issue of a possible need for investigation into competitive practices, in terms of banks' access to the payments system.[21] Given the relatively concentrated structure of the banking system in Brazil and issues already alluded to above, for example, difficulties in the sharing of ATM networks, the above reports may provide interesting insights.

Conclusion

Many of the programs discussed above could be introduced in a Brazilian context. First of all, the power of disclosure of social banking practices is considerable, especially if based on the regular collection and monitoring of appropriate data and even more so if used in the context of regular banking supervision. However, the relevance of community development models in the context of Brazil's banking sector, with nationwide branching for major banks, has to be weighed carefully.

Brazil has already embarked on the obligatory provision of basic banking services; this is a widespread international practice. In accordance with recognized good practice, in Brazil such basic accounts emphasize first, access to money transmission mechanisms and the payments system, and second, deposit facilities. Services such as check writing and credit are not usually deemed to be a part of a basic account, and in this respect Brazil is unusual in permitting holders of such accounts access to low-cost credit. To be useful, basic services need to be very competitively priced. In Brazil they are offered free of charge, which increases the implicit tax on the banking system. Electronic funds transfers for federal payments can accelerate the reduction of the unbanked, but such requirements may leave a huge number of persons outside its net today.

If financial support is to be provided by the government, there are many devices that, for relatively small outlays, seek to leverage public funds and also make sure that donor and beneficiary incentives are compatible. Such programs include, for example, the partial guarantees and the matching grants for loan-loss reserves, together with more traditional start-up loans and venture-capital funds. Tax credits to the private sector for investment in venture-capital funds are another way to provide incentives for the formation of partnerships in downscaling.

A range of supporting institutions needs to be involved in the efforts of financial outreach. These include not only business administration and fund administration agencies but also nonprofit agencies and community investment agencies who work closely with target communities, such as the CDFIs of the United Kingdom and United States, which are distinct from commercial banks.

The role of programs of financial education and literacy is also key; in this context, programs that offer incentives for family support to financial planning are also interesting.

Finally, issues of financial-sector competition may sometimes be present, even if this is not immediately apparent. Brazil's banking structure, dominated by a handful of institutions, bears some resemblance to that of the United Kingdom. Some of the issues encountered in this regard, for example, the payment of service charges for access to money transmission, have been encountered in other countries, too. A full evaluation of the status of competition in the downscaling of financial services is clearly worth consideration.

Appendix
Statistical Tables

Appendix Table A1.1 Brazil: Number of Institutions in Operation and Assets, 1993–2002

1. Institutions (nos.)	*1993*	*1994*	*1995*	*1996*	*1997*
Multiple and commercial banks[b]	241	244	240	229	215
Development banks	7	6	6	6	6
Investment banks	17	17	17	23	22
Savings banks (incl. CEF)	2	2	2	2	2
Finance companies	41	41	42	47	48
Leasing companies	67	72	78	74	78
Real estate/savings and loan	27	27	23	22	22
Total these items	402	409	408	403	393
Credit cooperatives	877	946	980	956	1,015
Microcredit companies (SCMs)					
Construction consortia	485	490	462	446	433
Investment funds[c]	839	1,279	2,195	2,765	3,500
Others[d]	745	734	692	621	564
Total all items	3,348	3,858	4,737	5,191	5,905
2. Different types of institutions in total nos. of institutions (% shares)					
Multiple and commercial banks[b]	7.20	6.32	5.07	4.41	3.64
Development banks	0.21	0.16	0.13	0.12	0.10
Investment banks	0.51	0.44	0.36	0.44	0.37
Savings banks (incl. CEF)	0.06	0.05	0.04	0.04	0.03
Finance companies	1.22	1.06	0.89	0.91	0.81
Leasing companies	2.00	1.87	1.65	1.43	1.32
Real estate/savings and loan	0.81	0.70	0.49	0.42	0.37
Credit cooperatives	26.19	24.52	20.69	18.42	17.19
Microcredit companies (SCMs)	0.00	0.00	0.00	0.00	0.00
Construction consortia	14.49	12.70	9.75	8.59	7.33
Investment funds[c]	25.06	33.15	46.34	53.27	59.27
Others[d]	22.25	19.03	14.61	11.96	9.55
Total shares	100.0	100.0	100.0	100.0	100.0
3. Assets of institutions (% total financial system)					
Multiple and commercial banks[b]	68.84	67.45	68.58	67.86	68.37
Development banks	8.14	8.44	7.81	7.08	7.69
Investment banks	3.08	3.10	1.24	1.67	1.53
Savings banks (incl. CEF)	11.92	12.16	13.77	13.64	13.83
Finance companies	0.33	0.56	0.29	0.59	0.52
Leasing companies	2.43	2.90	3.33	3.36	4.17
Real estate/savings and loan	1.23	1.23	1.18	1.11	1.09
Credit cooperatives	0.10	0.15	0.20	0.25	0.31
Construction consortia	n.a.	n.a.	n.a.	n.a.	n.a.
Investment funds[c]	n.a.	n.a.	n.a.	n.a.	n.a.
Microcredit companies (SCMs)	—	—	—	—	—
Others[e]	3.93	4.01	3.60	4.44	2.49
Total	100.0	100.0	100.0	100.0	100.0

Note: — = not available; n.a. = not applicable.

a. Considers single institutions and portfolios of the same type.

b. Includes branches of foreign banks.

c. Includes investment funds authorized and in operation.

d. Mortgage, security brokerage, exchange brokerage, security distribution companies, and development agencies (including institutions authorized to operate by Central Bank of Brazil, including group buyer consortia).

e. Same as note *d*, less exchange brokerage companies.

Source: Central Bank of Brazil.

1998	*1998*[a]	*1999*	*1999*[a]	*2000*	*2000*[a]	*2001*	*2001*[a]	*2002*
201	185	193	175	191	173	181	160	166
6	21	5	18	5	17	4	15	4
22	128	21	126	19	123	20	121	23
2		1		1		1		1
42	187	41	182	42	176	39	169	46
80	100	79	103	77	109	71	105	65
21	86	19	77	18	73	18	74	18
374	707	359	681	353	671	334	644	323
1088		1,183		1,235		1,333		1,374
		3		6		14		26
422		406		404		397		375
3617		4,034		4,656		5,195		5,833
528		524		497		487		475
6,029		6,509		7,151		7,760		8,406

3.33	2.97	2.67	2.33	1.97
0.10	0.08	0.07	0.05	0.05
0.36	0.32	0.27	0.26	0.27
0.03	0.02	0.01	0.01	0.01
0.70	0.63	0.59	0.50	0.55
1.33	1.21	1.08	0.91	0.77
0.35	0.29	0.25	0.23	0.21
18.05	18.17	17.27	17.18	16.35
0.00	0.05	0.08	0.18	0.31
7.00	6.24	5.65	5.12	4.46
59.99	61.98	65.11	66.95	69.39
8.76	8.05	6.95	6.28	5.65
100.0	100.0	100.0	100.0	100.0

65.74	66.63	69.04	72.84	72.17
10.02	10.11	10.50	10.52	11.54
0.90	1.02	0.91	1.21	0.95
14.01	13.82	12.63	9.07	9.62
0.41	0.53	0.85	0.49	0.87
5.24	5.42	3.87	3.29	2.66
1.10	0.45	0.37	0.33	0.31
0.41	0.54	0.62	0.75	0.86
n.a.	n.a.	n.a.	n.a.	n.a.
n.a.	n.a.	n.a.	n.a.	n.a.
—	—	—	—	—
2.17	1.48	1.21	1.50	1.02
100.0	100.0	100.0	100.0	100.0

Appendix Table A1.2 Brazil Bank Services, Branches, and ATMs: Number of Facilities in Operation, 1994–2002

Type of service outlet	*1994*	*1995*	*1996*	*1997*	*1998*	*1999*	*2000*	*2001*	*2002*
Branches	17,400	17,181	16,583	16,255	16,002	16,189	16,396	16,841	17,049
Bank service outposts (a) internal (PABs)	10,125	9,075	8,268	7,787	7,211	6,614	6,562	7,318	7,108
in municipalities with bank branches	9,776	8,780	7,987	7,513	6,987	6,425	6,407	7,183	6,988
in municipalities with no bank branches	349	295	281	274	224	189	155	135	120
Bank service outposts (b) external (PAAs)				52	334	503	582	619	654
ATMs—individual network (PAE)	2,874	3,922	4,841	6,015	6,709	10,808	12,681	14,923	20,347
ATMs—associate network (PAE)	572	674	696	744	1,010	1,369	1,772	1,825	2,081
Cooperative services (PAC)	48	305	361	445	600	849	1,129	1,344	1,485
Rural credit outposts (PACRE)[a]	10	9	8	7	7	5	5	5	2
Payment posts (PAP)	1,786	1,643	1,340	1,164	942	719	697	402	325
Other (PCO[b] & UAD[c])	672	689	610	508	505	506	520	553	566
Total these items	33,487	33,498	32,707	32,977	33,320	37,562	40,344	43,830	49,617
Bank correspondents							10,589	12,311	16,453
o/w lottery shops							6,253	7,823	8,961
Others								4	2,083
Total all items	33,487	33,498	32,707	32,977	33,320	37,562	50,933	56,141	66,070
Municipality-level services	*1994*	*1995*	*1996*	*1997*	*1998*	*1999*	*2000*	*2001*	*2002*
Municipalities	5,011	5,076	5,300	5,546	5,597	5,626	5,636	5,654	5,658
Municipalities with no services[d]	1,137	1,223	1,474	1,749	1,739	1,679	1,659	1,681	1,665
Municipalities with one outpost	1,402	1,488	1,597	1,659	1,773	1,906	1,972	2,013	2,060
Municipalities with 1 branch	1,402	1,488	1,597	1,607	1,439	1,403	1,390	1,394	1,406
With PAA	..	..	..	52	334	503	582	619	654

Note: .. = negligible.
a. PACRE is Posto Avançado de Crédito Rural.
b. PCO is Posto de Compra de Ouro.
c. UAD is Unidade Administrativa Desmembrada.
d. Banking service outlets are not included in these numbers.
Source: Central Bank of Brazil.

Appendix Table A1.3 Brazil: Number of Branches across Different Ownership Groups and over Time, 1995–2001

(nos.)

Ownership group	*March 1995*	*1997*	*1998*	*1999*	*2000*	*2001*
Branches						
Federal banks	7,232	6,552	5,260	5,615	5,472	5,611
State banks	1,863	1,332	2,267	1,842	1,084	1,084
o/w CEF	—	—	—	—	1,693	1,689
Multiple and commercial banks	—	—	—	—	4,863	5,006
Private domestic banks	4,507	6,252	6,085	5,587	6,147	6,347
o/w banks with foreign participation	—	—	—		758	930
Foreign banks	915	2,254	2,390	3,145	3,693	3,799
Total branches	14,517	16,390	16,002	16,189	16,396	16,841
Other services						
Bank service outposts (a) internal (PABs)	—	—	—	—	6,636	7,323
ATMs (PAE)	—	—	—	—	12,675	14,986
Bank service outposts (b) external (PAAs)	—	—	—	—	582	619
Total all items	—	—	—	—	36,289	39,769

Note: — = not available.
Source: Central Bank of Brazil.

Appendix Table A1.4 Brazil: Percentage Participation of Banking Institutions, by Ownership and Institutional Type, 1996–2002

Net worth	*1996*	*1997*	*1998*	*1999*	*2000*	*2001*	*2002*
Banks under foreign control	10.29	14.29	21.86	25.46	28.31	30.72	32.89
Private banks	55.32	51.82	49.75	46.69	50.33	51.14	48.66
Public banks (including State Savings Bank)	12.40	11.49	11.35	11.10	5.66	3.46	4.60
CEF	8.85	9.09	5.42	5.22	3.82	3.90	3.91
Banco do Brasil	11.87	11.76	10.03	9.73	9.89	8.76	7.77
Credit cooperatives	1.27	1.55	1.59	1.80	1.99	2.02	2.17
Total	100.0	100.0	100.0	100.0	100.0	100.0	100.0
Assets							
Banks under foreign control	9.79	12.82	18.38	23.19	27.41	29.86	27.38
Private banks	39.00	36.76	35.29	33.11	35.23	37.21	36.93
Public banks (including State Savings Bank)	21.92	19.06	11.37	10.23	5.62	4.30	5.87
CEF	16.47	16.57	17.02	17.06	15.35	10.97	11.66
Banco do Brasil	12.52	14.42	17.44	15.75	15.63	16.76	17.12
Credit cooperatives	0.30	0.37	0.50	0.66	0.76	0.9	1.04
Total	100.0	100.0	100.0	100.0	100.0	100.0	100.0
Deposits							
Banks under foreign control	4.36	7.54	15.14	16.80	21.14	20.14	19.82
Private banks	34.06	32.85	33.08	31.82	33.93	35.33	36.60
Public banks (including State Savings Bank)	18.66	17.09	13.26	11.54	7.36	7.15	7.41

CEF	26.58	24.05	20.52	19.91	19.49	19.09	16.92
Banco do Brasil	16.00	18.00	17.41	19.14	17.05	16.98	17.73
Credit cooperatives	0.34	0.47	0.59	0.79	1.03	1.31	1.53
Total	100.0	100.0	100.0	100.0	100.0	100.0	100.0
Credit operations							
Banks under foreign control	8.64	11.71	14.88	19.75	25.16	31.51	29.94
Private banks	32.74	35.35	30.97	31.66	34.53	42.13	39.73
Public banks (including State Savings Bank)	23.47	10.30	8.86	8.13	5.12	3.09	4.78
CEF	24.00	30.93	32.31	28.74	23.00	7.13	7.61
Banco do Brasil	10.62	10.97	12.05	10.58	10.95	14.53	16.17
Credit cooperatives	0.53	0.74	0.93	1.14	1.24	1.61	1.77
Total	100.0	100.0	100.0	100.0	100.0	100.0	100.0

Source: Central Bank of Brazil.

Appendix Table A1.5 Brazil: Number of Financial Institutions in Operation, by Region and Type, 1999–2002

Region	*Multiple banks and commercial banks*	*Development banks*	*Investment banks*	*Savings banks*	*Financial companies*
2002					
Northeast	12	0	0	0	2
North	3	0	0	0	0
Central–West	4	0	2	1	1
Southeast	131	3	21	0	31
South	16	1	0	0	12
Total, 2002	166	4	23	1	46
2001					
Northeast	13	0	0	0	2
North	3	0	0	0	0
Central–West	4	0	2	1	1
Southeast	143	3	18	0	31
South	18	1	0	0	8
Total, 2001	181	4	20	1	42
2000					
Northeast	13	1	0	0	2
North	3	0	0	0	0
Central–West	4	0	2	1	2
Southeast	152	3	17	0	32
South	20	1	0	0	7
Total, 2000	192	5	19	1	43
Dec 1999					
Northeast	14	1	0	0	2
North	3	0	0	0	0
Central–West	4	0	2	1	2
Southeast	153	3	19	0	31
South	20	1	0	0	7
Total, Dec 1999	194	5	21	1	42
Jan 1999					
Northeast	15	1	0	0	2
North	5	0	0	0	0
Central–West	4	0	2	1	2
Southeast	160	3	19	0	34
South	20	2	1	0	6
Total, Jan 1999	204	6	22	1	44

Source: Central Bank of Brazil.

Leasing companies	*Real estate/ savings & loan*	*Micro-credit companies*	*Coopera-tives*	*Construc-tion consortiums*	*Others*	*Total*
2	6	3	154	26	36	241
0	1	1	82	4	8	99
1	2	1	129	37	3	181
56	5	25	760	186	284	1502
6	4	7	305	123	39	513
65	18	37	1,430	376	370	2,536
2	6	2	146	28	36	235
0	1	0	78	4	7	93
1	2	1	125	40	5	182
61	5	18	759	200	303	1541
8	4	2	271	127	44	483
72	18	23	1,379	399	395	2,534
2	6	0	124	27	35	210
0	1	0	72	3	7	86
1	2	1	112	39	5	169
67	5	9	753	209	324	1571
8	4	1	250	129	49	469
78	18	11	1,311	407	420	2,505
3	7	0	110	24	36	197
0	1	0	64	3	7	78
1	2	0	104	39	4	159
69	5	4	740	214	336	1574
8	4	0	235	126	50	451
81	19	4	1,253	406	433	2,459
2	7	0	105	25	36	193
0	1	0	58	3	4	71
1	2	0	96	42	3	153
73	6	0	721	220	346	1582
7	4	0	224	131	54	449
83	20	0	1,204	421	443	2,448

Appendix Table A1.6 Brazil: Bank Services by Region and Municipality, Branches, PABs, and PAAs, 1998–2002

(nos.)

Region	*No. of municipalities*	*Total of branches*	*Total of PAAs*	*Total of PABs*	*Municipalities w/1 branch*
2002					
Northeast	1,840	2,396	242	841	409
North	470	580	60	356	54
Central–West	482	1,262	72	509	122
Southeast	1,670	9,361	102	3,952	533
South	1,196	3,450	178	1,450	288
Total, 2002	5,658	17,049	654	7,108	1,406
2001					
Northeast	1,838	2,369	242	829	409
North	470	562	59	337	50
Central–West	480	1,233	48	532	118
Southeast	1,670	9,254	99	4,191	537
South	1,196	3,423	171	1,429	280
Total, 2001	5,654	16,841	619	7,318	1,394
2000					
Northeast	1,837	2,327	221	822	405
North	470	557	54	304	50
Central–West	464	1,194	47	454	116
Southeast	1,669	8,942	100	3,657	539
South	1,196	3,376	160	1,325	280
Total, 2000	5,636	16,396	582	6,562	1,390
1999					
Northeast	1,846	2,331	n.a.	853	413
North	471	552	n.a.	294	50
Central–West	464	1,185	n.a.	457	115
Southeast	1,669	8,763	n.a.	3,699	542
South	1,176	3,358	n.a.	1,311	283
Total, 1999	5,,626	16,189	n.a.	6,614	1,403
1998					
Northeast	1,826	2,360	n.a.	852	444
North	470	552	n.a.	285	53
Central–West	456	1,200	n.a.	545	114
Southeast	1,669	8,527	n.a.	4,072	542
South	1,176	3,363	n.a.	1,457	286
Total, 1998	5,597	16,002	n.a.	7,211	1,439

Note: n.a. = not applicable.

a. Does not include banking correspondents.

Source: Central Bank of Brazil.

Municipalities w/PAB and no branch	*Municipalities w/no services (a)*	*Nos. of branches/ municipality*	*Nos. of PAAs/ municipality*	*Nos. of PABs/ municipality*
57	818	1.30	0.13	0.46
6	260	1.23	0.13	0.76
2	119	2.62	0.15	1.06
38	261	5.61	0.06	2.37
17	207	2.88	0.15	1.21
120	1,665	3.01	0.12	1.26
54	817	1.29	0.13	0.45
7	265	1.20	0.13	0.72
24	121	2.57	0.10	1.11
40	263	5.54	0.06	2.51
10	215	2.86	0.14	1.19
135	1,681	2.98	0.11	1.29
69	822	1.27	0.12	0.45
7	269	1.19	0.11	0.65
25	107	2.57	0.10	0.98
37	259	5.36	0.06	2.19
17	202	2.82	0.13	1.11
155	1,659	2.91	0.10	1.16
83	841	1.26	n.a.	0.46
8	284	1.17	n.a.	0.62
25	105	2.55	n.a.	0.98
54	263	5.25	n.a.	2.22
19	186	2.86	n.a.	1.11
189	1,679	2.88	n.a.	1.18
86	860	1.29	n.a.	0.47
9	315	1.17	n.a.	0.61
44	93	2.63	n.a.	1.20
60	292	5.11	n.a.	2.44
25	179	2.86	n.a.	1.24
224	1,739	2.86	n.a.	1.29

Appendix Table A1.7 Brazil: Regional Indicators, 2000

(nos.)

Region/state	*GDP R$ millions*	*GDP per capita*	*Branches*	*Area ('000 km^2)*	*Branches/ '000 km^2*	*Population (millions)*	*Branches/ 100,000*	*Municipalities w/no services*
North	50,650	3,907	557	3,853.3	0.14	12.90	4.32	269
Rondônia	5,625	4,065	24	237.6	0.10	1.38	1.74	25
Acre	1,703	3,037	13	152.6	0.09	0.56	2.33	14
Amazonas	18,873	6,668	120	1,570.7	0.08	2.81	4.27	40
Roraima	1,117	3,417	247	224.3	1.10	0.32	76.14	11
Pará	18,914	3,041	74	1,247.7	0.06	6.19	1.20	63
Amapá	1,968	4,098	13	142.8	0.09	0.48	2.73	11
Tocantins	2,450	2,110	66	277.6	0.24	1.16	5.70	105
Northeast	144,135	3,014	2,327	1,554.3	1.50	47.74	4.87	822
Maranhão	9,207	1,627	106	332.0	0.32	5.65	1.88	91
Piauí	5,330	1,872	727	251.5	2.89	2.84	25.57	187
Ceará	20,800	2,794	322	148.8	2.16	7.43	4.33	60
Rio Grande do Norte	9,293	3,343	241	52.8	4.56	2.78	8.68	122
Paraíba	9,238	2,681	147	56.4	2.60	3.44	4.27	175
Pernambuco	29,127	3,673	415	98.3	4.22	7.92	5.24	42
Alagoas	7,023	2,485	101	27.8	3.64	2.82	3.58	44
Sergipe	5,921	3,310	124	21.9	5.66	1.78	6.95	18
Bahia	48,197	3,680	144	564.7	0.26	13.07	1.10	83
Southeast	636,394	8,774	8,942	924.5	9.67	72.41	12.35	261
Minas Gerais	106,169	5,925	283	586.5	0.48	17.89	1.58	225
Espírito Santo	21,530	6,931	1,774	46.1	38.50	3.10	57.28	2
Rio de Janeiro	137,877	9,571	1,565	43.7	35.82	14.39	10.87	2
São Paulo	370,819	9,995	5,320	248.2	21.43	37.03	14.37	32

South	193,534	7,692	3,376	576.4	5.86	25.11	13.45	202
Paraná	65,969	6,882	1,250	199.3	6.27	9.56	13.07	63
Santa Catarina	42,428	7,902	1,344	95.3	14.10	5.36	25.09	44
Rio Grande do Sul	85,138	8,341	782	281.7	2.78	10.19	7.68	95
Central–West	76,542	6,559	1,194	1,606.4	0.74	11.64	10.26	107
Mato Grosso do Sul	11,861	5,697	261	357.1	0.73	2.08	12.56	13
Mato Grosso	13,428	5,342	510	903.4	0.56	2.50	20.36	47
Goiás	21,665	4,316	208	340.1	0.61	5.00	4.16	39
Distrito Federal	29,587	14,405	215	5.8	37.06	2.05	10.48	8
Brazil	1,101,255	6,473	16,396	8,514.9	1.93	169.80	9.66	1,661

Source: Instituto Brasileira de Geografia e Estatistica (IBGE).

Appendix Table A1.8 Analysis of Demand, Urban Survey: Access and Geographic Location, by Region

Item	*Northeast*	*North*	*Central–West*	*Southeast*	*South*
Had a bank account	29	25	53	45	55
	0.00[a]	0.00[a]	0.00[a]	0.00[a]	0.00[a]
Used banks as their primary financial institution	38	30	48	50	42
Used correspondent banks as the primary financial institution	53	70	52	48	53
Used mainly nonbank institutions	9		1	2	5
	0.00[a]	0.00[a]	0.00[a]	0.00[a]	0.00[a]
Used mainly private banks	27	16	28	34	26
Used mainly public banks	73	84	72	66	74
	0.00[a]	0.00[a]	0.00[a]	0.00[a]	0.00[a]
Reached the financial Institution on foot	55	24	59	57	38
	0.00[a]	0.00[a]	0.00[a]	0.00[a]	0.00[a]
Had a saving or a current or a term deposit account	19	6	50	28	38
	0.00[a]	0.00[a]	0.00[a]	0.00[a]	0.00[a]
Had deposits in public sector	3	10	21	11	33
Had deposits in private sector	6	7	30	22	16
Had deposits in other sectors	n.a.	4	10	1	0
Didn't have deposits	90	79	39	66	50
	0.00[a]	0.00[a]	0.00[a]	0.00[a]	0.00[a]
Applied for loan and received it	9	3	4	12	10
Applied for loan and didn't receive it	4	0	8	5	3
Didn't apply for loan	88	97	88	83	87
	0.00[a]	0.00[a]	0.00[a]	0.00[a]	0.00[a]
Received credit from other sources	n.a.	47	40	46	43

Received credit from public banks	50	40	0	17	39
Received credit from private banks	50	13	60	37	17
	0.02[a]	0.02[a]	0.02[a]	0.02[a]	0.02[a]
Had a debit card	18	16	44	24	40
	0.00[a]	0.00[a]	0.00[a]	0.00[a]	0.00[a]
Had a credit card	19	10	16	22	16
	0.04[a]	0.04[a]	0.04[a]	0.04[a]	0.04[a]
Used cash for all payments	89	81	74	79	79
Used credit card or debit card for all payments	10	12	11	2	7
Used transfer or direct deposits	2	7	15	20	14
	0.00[a]	0.00[a]	0.00[a]	0.00[a]	0.00[a]
Made the major part of payments at other points services	68	57	34	58	71
Made the major part of payments at private banks	11	11	9	22	10
Made the major part of payments at public banks and lottery shops	21	32	58	20	19
	0.00[a]	0.00[a]	0.00[a]	0.00[a]	0.00[a]
Made the major part of payments at bank in person	23	50	61	23	53
Made the major part of payment by other methods	77	50	39	77	48
	0.00[a]	0.00[a]	0.00[a]	0.00[a]	0.00[a]

Note: n.a. = not applicable. Numbers indicate percentage frequencies in each category. Values of chi-square tests of independence are cited below the frequencies.

a. Significant statistic at 5 percent level.

Source: World Bank staff estimates; World Bank survey of access to financial services in urban areas of Brazil, 2002.

Appendix Table A1.9 Analysis of Demand, Urban Survey: Access and Location, by Area, Neighborhood, and Home

	1. Area		*2. House*		*3. Construction*		*4. Rooms*	
Item	*Illegal*	*Legal*	*Unique*	*Collective*	*Regular home/ apartment*	*Shack/ room*	*>2 rooms per person*	*<0.5 rooms per person*
Had a bank account	37	45	43	38	45	34	55	13
	0.01[a]	0.01[a]	0.81	0.81	0.00[a]	0.00[a]	0.00[a]	0.00[a]
Used banks as their primary financial institution	45	47	46	53	47	40	56	32
Used correspondent banks as the primary financial institution	53	50	50	44	49	59	40	64
Used mainly nonbank institutions	3	4	4	3	4	1	4	4
	0.51	0.51	0.5	0.51	0.01[a]	0.01[a]	0.00[a]	0.00[a]
Used mainly private banks	30	31	31	27	33	23	39	19
Used mainly public banks	70	69	69	73	67	77	61	81
	0.53	0.53	0.37	0.37	0.00[a]	0.00[a]	0.00[a]	0.00[a]
Reached the financial institution on foot	59	52	54	74	52	58	52	62
	0.02[a]	0.02[a]	0.01[a]	0.01[a]	0.17	0.17	0.06	0.06
Had a savings or a current or a term deposit account	23	30	29	19	30	20	41	7
	0.01[a]	0.01[a]	0.03[a]	0.03[a]	0.00[a]	0.00[a]	0.00[a]	0.00[a]
Had deposits in public sector	9	15	14	7	15	11	18	3

Had deposits in private sector	17	19	19	24	20	14	28	6
Had deposits in other sectors	1	2	2	3	2	–	3	1
Didn't have deposits	73	64	65	66	64	75	51	90
	0.00[a]	0.00[a]	0.28	0.28	0.00[a]	0.00[a]	0.00[a]	0.00[a]
Received credit from other sources	48	44	43	67	45	45	42	100
Received credit from public banks	10	25	23	17	26	6	30	
Received credit from private banks	41	30	34	17	29	48	28	
	0.18	0.18	0.17	0.17	0.02[a]	0.02[a]	0.25	0.25
Applied for a loan and received it	8	11	10	15	11	9	13	1
Applied for a loan and didn't receive it	6	5	5	20	4	6	4	5
Didn't apply for a loan	86	84	85	65	85	85	83	94
	0.16	0.16	0.00[a]	0.00[a]	0.19	0.19	0.02[a]	0.02[a]
Had a debit card	24	26	26	10	26	22	34	5
	0.59	0.59	0.37	0.37	0.17	0.17	0.00[a]	0.00[a]
Had a credit card	17	21	20	14	21	16	25	6
	0.16	0.16	0.47	0.47	0.00[a]	0.00[a]	0.00[a]	0.00[a]
Used cash for all payments	84	75	76	79	75	85	69	91
Used credit card or debit card for all payments	8	10	10	11	10	9	11	7
Used transfer or direct deposits	8	15	14	11	15	6	20	1
	0.00[a]	0.00[a]	0.28	0.28	0.00[a]	0.00[a]	0.02[a]	0.02[a]

(table continued next page)

Appendix Table A1.9 *(continued)*

	1. Area		*2. House*		*3. Construction*		*4. Rooms*	
Item	*Illegal*	*Legal*	*Unique*	*Collective*	*Regular home/ apartment*	*Shack/ room*	*>2 rooms per person*	*<0.5 rooms per person*
Made majority of payments at other service points	24	25	25	12	26		23	33
Made majority of payments at private banks	16	18	17	24	17	67	23	5
Made majority of payments at public banks and lottery shops	60	58	58	65	56	33	55	62
	0.01[a]	0.01[a]	0.21	0.21	0.00[a]	0.00[a]	0.01[a]	0.01[a]
Made majority of payments at bank in person	47	56	54	63	55	50	55	44
Made majority of payments by other methods	53	44	46	37	45	50	45	56
	0.00[a]	0.00[a]	0.06	0.06	0.33	0.33	0.29	0.29

Note: Numbers indicate percentage frequencies in each category. Values of chi-square tests of independence are cited below the frequencies.
a. Significant statistic at 5 percent level.
Source: World Bank staff estimates; World Bank survey of access to financial services in urban areas of Brazil, 2002.

Appendix Table A1.10 Analysis of Demand, Urban Survey: Public and Private Banks and Access to a Financial Institution

	Banks—narrow definition			*Banks—including correspondents*		
Item	*Private*[a]	*Public*[a]	*Test*	*Private*[b]	*Public*[b]	*Test*
Geographic region						
North	50	50	0.01[c]	16	84	0.00[c]
Northeast	48	52	0.01[c]	27	73	0.00[c]
Central–West	58	42	0.01[c]	28	72	0.00[c]
Southeast	62	38	0.01[c]	34	66	0.00[c]
South	48	52	0.01[c]	26	74	0.00[c]
Area						
Illegal areas	58	42	0.46	30	70	0.53
Legalized area	58	42	0.46	31	69	0.53
Type of dwelling						
Unique permanent house	59	41	0.61	31	69	0.37
Collective house	50	50	0.61	27	73	0.37
Type of building						
House or apartment	59	41	0.02[c]	33	67	0.00[c]
Cottage or rooms	52	48	0.02[c]	23	77	0.00[c]
Number of room per person						
More than 2 rooms for person	63	37	0.00[c]	39	61	0.00[c]
Less than 0.5 rooms for person	52	48	0.00[c]	19	81	0.00[c]
Gender						
Man	60	40	0.00[c]	34	66	0.00[c]
Woman	56	44	0.00[c]	28	72	0.00[c]

(table continued next page)

Appendix Table A1.10 *(continued)*

	Banks—narrow definition			*Banks—including correspondents*		
Item	*Private*[a]	*Public*[a]	*Test*	*Private*[b]	*Public*[b]	*Test*
Role in household						
Head of household	60	40	0.10	32	68	0.43
Dependent	56	44	0.10	30	70	0.43
Income						
Lowest quintile	51	49	0.00[c]	22	78	0.00[c]
Highest quintile	64	36	0.00[c]	49	51	0.00[c]
Wealth/collateral						
Possessing house or car	60	40	0.02[c]	36	67	0.00[c]
Without collateral	50	50	0.02[c]	25	75	0.00[c]
Education level						
Less than primary	57	43	0.00[c]	26	74	0.00[c]
More than secondary	69	31	0.00[c]	59	41	0.00[c]
Having a job						
Having a job in the last month	59	41	0.00[c]	33	67	0.04[c]
Not having a job in the last month	57	43	0.00[c]	29	71	0.04[c]
Role in workplace						
Employer	44	56	0.00[c]	22	78	0.04[c]
Self-employment	60	40	0.00[c]	35	65	0.04[c]
Employee with work certificate	59	41	0.00[c]	36	64	0.04[c]
Employee without work certificate	58	42	0.00[c]	28	72	0.04[c]

Full- or part-time						
Employed full-time	60	40	0.20	32	68	0.06
Part-time or irregular	58	42	0.20	35	65	0.06

Note: Numbers indicate percentage frequencies in each category. Values of chi-square tests of independence are cited to the right of the frequencies.

a. Private or public banks only.

b. Private includes post office with banking services. Public includes lottery shops with banking services.

c. Significant statistic at 5 percent level.

Source: World Bank staff estimates; World Bank survey of access to financial services in urban areas of Brazil, 2002.

Appendix Table A1.11 Analysis of Demand, Urban Survey: Public and Private Banks, Access to Deposit, Payment, and Credit Facilities

	Deposits				
Item	*Public*	*Private*	*Other*	*None*	*Test*
Geographic region					
North	3	6		90	0.00[a]
Northeast	10	7	4	79	0.00[a]
Central–West	21	30	10	39	0.00[a]
Southeast	11	22	1	66	0.00[a]
South	33	16	0	50	0.00[a]
Area					
Illegal areas	9	17	1	73	0.00[a]
Legalized area	15	19	2	64	0.00[a]
Type of dwelling					
Unique permanent house	14	19	2	65	0.28
Collective house	7	24	3	66	0.28
Type of building					
House or apartment	15	20	2	64	0.00[a]
Cottage or rooms	11	14		75	0.00[a]
Number of rooms per person					
More than 2 rooms for person	18	28	3	51	0.00[a]
Less than 0.5 rooms for person	3	6	1	90	0.00[a]
Gender					
Man	17	22	2	59	0.00[a]
Woman	11	15	2	72	0.00[a]
Role in household					
Head of household	15	22	1	62	0.02[a]
Dependent	14	16	2	68	0.02[a]
Income					
Lowest quintile	7	6	3	84	0.00[a]
Highest quintile	25	42	1	32	0.00[a]
Wealth/collateral					
Possessing house or car	14	20	2	64	0.01[a]
Without collateral	12	13	1	73	0.01[a]
Education level					
Less than primary	9	10	3	78	0.00[a]
More than secondary	29	45	2	25	0.00[a]

Payments				*Credit*			
Public banks or lottery shops	*Private banks*	*Other*	*Test*	*Informal source*	*Public banks*	*Private banks*	*Test*
68	11	21	0.00[a]		50	50	0.02[a]
57	11	32	0.00[a]	47	40	13	0.02[a]
34	9	58	0.00[a]	40		60	0.02[a]
58	22	20	0.00[a]	46	17	37	0.02[a]
71	10	19	0.00[a]	43	39	17	0.02[a]
60	16	24	0.81	48	10	41	0.18
58	18	25	0.81	44	25	30	0.18
58	17	25	0.21	43	23	34	0.17
65	24	12	0.21	67	17	17	0.17
56	17	26	0.00[a]	45	26	29	0.02[a]
67	17	17	0.00[a]	45	6	48	0.02[a]
55	23	23	0.01[a]	42	30	28	0.25
62	5	33	0.01[a]	100			0.25
59	19	22	0.00[a]	43	20	37	0.17
57	15	28	0.00[a]	47	27	26	0.17
59	19	22	0.08	41	22	37	0.36
57	16	27	0.08	48	24	28	0.36
59	10	30	0.00[a]	33	42	25	0.48
56	31	13	0.00[a]	42	24	34	0.48
58	18	24	0.08	41	26	33	0.02[a]
60	13	27	0.08	64	8	28	0.02[a]
58	11	31	0.00[a]	52	17	30	0.11
41	38	21	0.00[a]	52	10	38	0.11

(table continued next page)

Appendix Table A1.11 *(continued)*

	Deposits				
Item	*Public*	*Private*	*Other*	*None*	*Test*
Having a job					
Having a job in the last month	18	26	2	54	0.00[a]
Not having a job in the last month	9	11	2	78	0.00[a]
Role in workplace					
Employer	34	22	3	41	0.00[a]
Self-employment	14	29	3	54	0.00[a]
Employee with work certificate	23	31	1	45	0.00[a]
Employee without work certificate	14	15	3	68	0.00[a]
Full- or part-time					
Employed full-time	18	26	2	54	0.00[a]
Part-time or irregular	18	26	2	53	0.00[a]

Note: Numbers indicate percentage frequencies in each category. Values of chi-square tests of independence are cited to the right of the frequencies.

a. Significant statistic at 5 percent level.

Source: World Bank staff estimates; World Bank survey of access to financial services in urban areas of Brazil, 2002.

Payments				*Credit*			
Public banks or lottery shops	*Private banks*	*Other*	*Test*	*Informal source*	*Public banks*	*Private banks*	*Test*
58	20	22	0.00[a]	49	21	30	0.41
58	13	29	0.00[a]	39	26	35	0.41
53	21	26	0.00[a]	71	14	14	0.64
57	19	24	0.00[a]	54	17	29	0.64
58	25	18	0.00[a]	42	18	40	0.64
61	17	23	0.00[a]	52	24	24	0.64
58	21	21	0.00[a]	47	22	31	0.76
59	18	23	0.00[a]	51	19	30	0.76

Appendix Table A1.12 Analysis of Demand, Urban Survey: Public and Private Banks, Access to Pension Deposits and Housing Finance

	Pension contributions			
	Didn't contribute	*Public fund*	*Private fund*	*Test*
Geographic region				
North	89	11	n.a.	0.00[a]
Northeast	94	3	2	0.00[a]
Central–West	87	8	5	0.00[a]
Southeast	96	2	2	0.00[a]
South	76	21	3	0.00[a]
Area				
Legalized area	92	8	n.a.	0.00[a]
Illegal areas	93	5	3	0.00[a]
Type of dwelling				
Unique permanent house	93	6	2	0.82
Collective house	97	3	n.a.	0.82
Type of building				
House or apartment	93	5	2	0.00[a]
Cottage or rooms	92	7	1	0.00[a]
Number of rooms per person				
More than 2 rooms for person	90	6	5	0.01[a]
Less than 0.5 rooms for person	94	6	n.a.	0.01[a]
Gender				
Man	92	6	2	0.74
Woman	93	5	2	0.74
Role in household				
Head of household	91	6	3	0.07
Dependent	94	4	2	0.07
Income				
Lowest quintile	96	3	1	0.00[a]
Highest quintile	82	11	7	0.00[a]
Wealth/collateral				
Possessing house or car	92	6	2	0.01[a]
Without collateral	96	3	1	0.01[a]
Education level				
Less than primary	95	3	1	0.00[a]
More than secondary	79	11	10	0.00[a]

Home purchase					
Savings	*Credit (CEF)*	*Private bank*	*Constr. co., consortium, co-op*	*Family/ friends*	*Test*
70	10	10	n.a.	10	0.02[a]
53	6	n.a.	n.a.	22	0.02[a]
49	9	3	5	5	0.02[a]
56	22	11	n.a.	n.a.	0.02[a]
69	7	6	4	n.a.	0.02[a]
53	9	4	4	5	0.35
61	5	n.a.	2	11	0.35
57	8	4	3	5	0.01[a]
25	50	n.a.	n.a.	25	0.01[a]
55	9	3	4	6	0.01[a]
54	6	6	2	8	0.01[a]
58	13	n.a.	4	3	0.09
75	n.a.	n.a.	n.a.	25	0.09
56	9	2	3	6	0.65
53	8	5	5	7	0.65
47	8	n.a.	2	9	0.02[a]
57	9	5	5	5	0.02[a]
49	5	7	5	19	0.05[a]
39	18	n.a.	7	7	0.05[a]
54	9	4	4	6	0.15
62	4	n.a.	4	15	0.15
40	12	n.a.	4	4	0.02[a]
66	16	n.a.	13	n.a.	0.02[a]

(table continued next page)

Appendix Table A1.12 *(continued)*

	Pension contributions			
	Didn't contribute	*Public fund*	*Private fund*	*Test*
Having a job				
Having a job in the last month	90	8	3	0.00[a]
Not having a job in the last month	96	2	1	0.00[a]
Role in workplace				
Employer	68	22	11	0.00[a]
Self-employment	89	8	3	0.00[a]
Employee with work certificate	89	8	3	0.00[a]
Employee without work certificate	95	3	2	0.00[a]
Full- or part-time				
Employed full-time	90	8	2	0.00[a]
Part-time or irregular	88	8	4	0.00[a]

Note: n.a. = not applicable. Numbers indicate percentage frequencies in each category. Values of chi-square tests of independence are cited to the right of the frequencies.
a. Significant statistic at 5 percent level.
Source: World Bank staff estimates; World Bank, survey of access to financial services in urban areas of Brazil, 2002.

Home purchase					
Savings	*Credit (CEF)*	*Private bank*	*Constr. co., consortium, co-op*	*Family/ friends*	*Test*
57	10	3	1	7	0.14
50	7	5	8	7	0.14
29	n.a.	14	n.a.	29	0.05[a]
50	13	2	2	2	0.05[a]
51	11	2	6	9	0.05[a]
70	8	3	3	11	0.05[a]
61	8	3	7	4	0.23
44	16	2	4	7	0.23

Appendix Table A1.13 Analysis of Demand, Urban Survey: Respondent Characteristics and Access to Financial Services, Physical Access and Deposit Facilities

	Bank account		*Access to financial institution*				
Item	*Had a bank account*	*Test*	*Banks*	*Correspondent banks*	*Nonbank institutions*	*Test*	*Private banks*
Gender							
Male	50	0.00[a]	50	47	3	0.00[a]	34
Female	37	0.00[a]	42	54	4	0.00[a]	28
Role in household							
Head of household	50	0.00[a]	48	50	3	0.08	32
Dependent	37	0.00[a]	44	52	4	0.08	30
Income							
Lowest quintile	15	0.00[a]	34	61	5	0.00[a]	22
Highest quintile	64	0.00[a]	69	30	1	0.00[a]	49
Wealth/collateral							
Possessing house or car	45	0.00[a]	48	49	3	0.02[a]	33
Without collateral	35	0.00[a]	40	57	4	0.02[a]	25
Education							
Less than primary	28	0.00[a]	38	58	4	0.00[a]	26
More than secondary	84	0.00[a]	83	16	1	0.00[a]	59
Having a job							
Having a job in the last month	55	0.00[a]	50	47	2	0.00[a]	33
Not having a job in the last month	30	0.00[a]	42	53	5	0.00[a]	29
Role in workplace							
Employer	63	0.00[a]	47	50	3	0.00[a]	22
Self-employed	51	0.00[a]	47	49	4	0.00[a]	35
Employee with work certificate	68	0.00[a]	58	41	1	0.00[a]	36
Employee with no work certificate	44	0.00[a]	42	56	2	0.00[a]	28
Full- or part-time							
Employed full-time	56	0.00[a]	49	50	1	0.00[a]	32
Part-time or irregular	55	0.00[a]	53	42	4	0.00[a]	35

Note: Numbers indicate percentage frequencies in each category. Values of chi-square tests of independence are cited to the right of the frequencies.

a. Significant statistic at 5 percent level.

Source: World Bank staff estimates; World Bank survey of access to financial services in urban areas of Brazil, 2002.

		Physical access		*Accounts*		*Deposits*				
Public banks	*Test*	*Reached fin. institution on foot*	*Test*	*Savings, current or term deposit*	*Test*	*Public*	*Private*	*Other*	*No deposits*	*Test*
66	0.00[a]	52	0.22	34	0.00[a]	17	22	2	59	0.00[a]
72	0.00[a]	55	0.22	23	0.00[a]	11	15	2	72	0.00[a]
68	0.43	51	0.04[a]	32	0.01[a]	15	22	1	62	0.02[a]
70	0.43	55	0.04[a]	26	0.01[a]	14	16	2	68	0.02[a]
78	0.00[a]	54	0.22	9	0.00[a]	7	6	3	84	0.00[a]
51	0.00[a]	47	0.22	47	0.00[a]	25	42	1	32	0.00[a]
67	0.00[a]	52	0.01[a]	30	0.00[a]	14	20	2	64	0.01[a]
75	0.00[a]	59	0.01[a]	22	0.00[a]	12	13	1	73	0.01[a]
74	0.00[a]	55	0.09	19	0.00[a]	9	10	3	78	0.00[a]
41	0.00[a]	43	0.09	67	0.00[a]	29	45	2	25	0.00[a]
67	0.04[a]	51	0.06	38	0.00[a]	18	26	2	54	0.00[a]
71	0.04[a]	56	0.06	19	0.00[a]	9	11	2	78	0.00[a]
78	0.04[a]	45	0.1	51	0.00[a]	14	29	3	54	0.00[a]
65	0.04[a]	54	0.1	37	0.00[a]	34	22	3	41	0.00[a]
64	0.04[a]	47	0.1	47	0.00[a]	23	31	1	45	0.00[a]
72	0.04[a]	56	0.1	25	0.00[a]	14	15	3	68	0.00[a]
68	0.06	50	0.06	38	0.00[a]	18	26	2	54	0.00[a]
65	0.06	55	0.06	40	0.00[a]	18	26	2	53	0.00[a]

Appendix Table A1.14 Analysis of Demand, Urban Survey: Respondent Characteristics and Access to Financial Services, Loans, Credit, and Payment Services

	Loan application				*Receiving credit*				*Debit and*	
Item	*Received it*	*Didn't receive it*	*Didn't apply*	*Test*	*Other sources*	*Public banks*	*Private banks*	*Test*	*Had a debit card*	*Test*
Gender										
Male	11	5	84	0.52	43	20	37	0.17	30	0.00[a]
Female	10	5	85	0.52	47	27	26	0.17	21	0.00[a]
Role in household										
Head of household	13	5	83	0.01[a]	41	22	37	0.36	30	0.00[a]
Dependent	8	5	87	0.01[a]	48	24	28	0.36	21	0.00[a]
Income										
Lowest quintile	3	5	92	0.00[a]	33	42	25	0.48	5	0.00[a]
Highest quintile	24	2	74	0.00[a]	42	24	34	0.48	40	0.00[a]
Wealth/collateral										
Possessing house or car	11	4	85	0.02[a]	41	26	33	0.02[a]	27	0.00[a]
Without collateral	9	7	84	0.02[a]	64	8	28	0.02[a]	19	0.00[a]
Education										
Less than primary	10	5	85	0.00[a]	52	17	30	0.11	15	0.00[a]
More than secondary	23	1	76	0.00[a]	52	10	38	0.11	54	0.00[a]
Having a job										
Having a job in the last month	13	4	83	0.00[a]	49	21	30	0.41	34	0.00[a]
Not having a job in the last month	8	5	87	0.00[a]	39	26	35	0.41	17	0.00[a]
Role in workplace										
Employer	18	5	77	0.02[a]	71	14	14	0.64	39	0.00[a]
Self-employed	11	5	85	0.02[a]	54	17	29	0.64	27	0.00[a]
Employee with work certificate	15	3	82	0.02[a]	42	18	40	0.64	44	0.00[a]
Employee with no work certificate	10	5	85	0.02[a]	52	24	24	0.64	26	0.00[a]
Full- or part-time										
Employed full-time	12	4	84	0.01[a]	47	22	31	0.76	34	0.98
Part-time or irregular	14	4	82	0.01[a]	51	19	30	0.76	34	0.98

Note: Numbers indicate percentage frequencies in each category. Values of chi-square tests of independence are cited to the right of the frequencies.

a. Significant statistic at 5 percent level.

Source: World Bank staff estimates; World Bank survey of access to financial services in urban areas of Brazil, 2002.

credit cards		*Payment method*				*Payments—institution type*				*Payment location*		
Had a credit card	*Test*	*Cash*	*Credit card or debit card*	*Transfer or direct deposits*	*Test*	*Other service points*	*Private banks*	*Public banks and lottery shops*	*Test*	*At a bank in person*	*Other methods*	*Test*
23	0.00[a]	76	10	14	0.77	59	19	22	0.00[a]	56	44	0.15
17	0.00[a]	77	9	13	0.77	57	15	28	0.00[a]	52	48	0.15
23	0.07	76	9	15	0.37	59	19	22	0.08	56	44	0.05[a]
17	0.07	77	10	12	0.37	57	16	27	0.08	52	48	0.05[a]
7	0.00[a]	82	9	8	0.00[a]	59	10	30	0.00[a]	45	55	0.00[a]
34	0.00[a]	62	12	26	0.00[a]	56	31	13	0.00[a]	57	43	0.00[a]
22	0.00[a]	74	11	15	0.00[a]	58	18	24	0.08	55	45	0.01[a]
12	0.00[a]	87	5	8	0.00[a]	60	13	27	0.08	48	52	0.01[a]
9	0.00[a]	90	6	4	0.00[a]	58	11	31	0.00[a]	45	55	0.00[a]
48	0.00[a]	38	15	47	0.00[a]	41	38	21	0.00[a]	62	38	0.00[a]
26	0.00[a]	72	11	17	0.00[a]	58	20	22	0.00[a]	57	43	0.01[a]
14	0.00[a]	82	8	10	0.00[a]	58	13	29	0.00[a]	51	49	0.01[a]
45	0.00[a]	51	14	34	0.00[a]	53	21	26	0.00[a]	74	26	0.13
21	0.00[a]	77	11	13	0.00[a]	57	19	24	0.00[a]	76	24	0.13
32	0.00[a]	64	13	23	0.00[a]	58	25	18	0.00[a]	82	18	0.13
20	0.00[a]	83	8	9	0.00[a]	61	17	23	0.00[a]	77	23	0.13
26	0.93											
26	0.93											

Appendix Table A1.15 Analysis of Supply: Economic and Financial Indicators across Brazilian States

State	*Total population (millions)*	*Area ('000 km²)*	*Branches 1995*	*Branches 2000*	*Share of small firms*	*Share of work-force in agriculture*
Rondônia	1.23	237.6	94	73	80.1	0.59
Acre	0.48	152.5	37	24	80.7	1.95
Amazonas	2.39	1,571.0	131	120	76.5	0.21
Roraima	0.25	224.1	21	13	85.8	0.81
Pará	5.51	1,247.7	284	246	72.8	1.67
Amapá	0.38	142.8	16	13	79.2	1.54
Tocantins	1.05	277.3	103	66	84.9	5.30
Maranhão	5.22	331.9	280	151	81.5	2.36
Piauí	2.67	251.3	114	83	83.5	1.24
Ceará	6.81	145.7	374	291	82.9	1.47
Rio Grande do Norte	2.56	53.1	126	106	79.0	2.39
Paraíba	3.31	56.3	178	127	77.8	1.20
Pernambuco	7.40	98.5	486	390	73.7	1.58
Alagoas	2.63	27.8	152	97	78.5	0.76
Sergipe	1.62	22.0	167	128	73.5	0.82
Bahia	12.54	564.3	835	680	78.1	2.12
Minas Gerais	16.67	586.5	1,842	1,749	80.1	2.02
Espírito Santo	2.80	46.0	313	280	77.6	1.46
Rio de Janeiro	13.41	43.8	1,385	1,509	67.7	0.34
São Paulo	34.12	248.2	4,884	5,218	76.7	1.42
Paraná	9.00	199.3	1,351	1,243	79.8	1.34
Santa Catarina	4.88	95.3	814	776	79.9	1.55
Rio Grande do Sul	9.63	268.8	1,462	1,331	83.7	1.17
Mato Grosso do Sul	1.93	357.1	297	214	79.6	3.81
Mato Grosso	2.24	903.4	284	208	81.8	3.37
Goiás	4.51	340.1	589	504	80.5	1.70
Distrito Federal, Brasília	1.82	5.8	228	205	74.1	0.33

Note: Unless otherwise indicated, all numbers are for 1996. The residual branch intensity is the deviation of the actual from the predicted number of branches relative to the predicted number, from a regression of the number of branches on GDP, land area, and population for 28 countries. Positive numbers indicate that the actual number of branches is higher than the predicted number.

Source: World Bank staff estimates; data provided by Central Bank of Brazil, IPEA, and IBGE.

Share of rural population	*Population density*	*Income per capita*	*Credits/ GDP*	*Deposits/ GDP*	*Credits per capita*	*Deposits per capita*	*Residual branch intensity*
38.0	5.2	5,095	19.6	3.3	1,061	179	–0.30
34.8	3.2	4,168	7.0	5.3	292	222	–0.36
26.1	1.5	4,838	8.4	6.8	407	329	–0.22
29.5	1.1	4,581	20.8	4.6	1,126	248	–0.36
46.5	4.4	3,504	31.8	6.8	1,153	248	–0.34
12.9	2.7	3,900	4.9	4.8	194	189	–0.68
29.3	3.8	1,470	31.2	9.1	472	138	0.37
48.1	15.7	1,670	12.5	7.1	245	140	–0.21
41.8	10.6	1,662	18.0	8.7	334	162	–0.41
30.8	46.7	2,312	23.1	20.8	534	480	–0.26
28.0	48.2	2,787	11.5	7.8	327	222	–0.41
31.6	58.7	2,103	9.5	8.3	214	186	–0.30
26.0	75.1	2,860	23.0	19.5	667	564	–0.18
36.9	94.7	2,738	51.3	9.1	1,408	249	–0.31
29.8	73.9	3,038	12.7	12.4	386	378	0.06
37.6	22.2	2,978	16.5	44.5	492	1,326	–0.02
21.6	28.4	5,355	12.4	12.3	684	678	0.12
22.4	60.9	5,057	14.3	16.1	742	837	0.04
4.5	306.1	7,471	15.1	21.2	1,143	1,608	–0.16
6.9	137.5	10,076	41.3	27.0	4,168	2,722	–0.01
22.1	45.2	5,934	27.4	16.9	1,658	1,024	0.33
26.9	51.2	5,764	16.8	12.6	986	739	0.54
21.3	35.8	6,608	23.5	17.1	1,574	1,148	0.30
16.8	5.4	6,516	24.2	4.5	1,574	295	0.29
24.2	2.5	4,398	36.3	5.6	1,643	254	0.42
14.2	13.3	4,082	38.8	7.6	1,665	327	0.42
7.1	314.0	12,854	122.3	87.9	15,716	11,295	–0.32

Appendix Table A1.16 Analysis of Supply: Branch Intensity across Different Ownership Groups and over Time

Year/item	*Federal banks*	*State banks*	*Private banks*	*Foreign banks*
1995				
Assets per branch	32,730	17,108	26,920	27,661
Loans per branch	17,907	6,900	11,929	15,761
Deposits per branch	13,984	7,494	11,544	10,007
Employees per branch	43.5	36.4	37.5	48.4
1997				
Assets per branch	43,442	31,094	27,613	36,416
Loans per branch	21,340	8,583	11,031	14,489
Deposits per branch	16,674	14,869	9,722	10,350
Employees per branch	38.1	27.3	29.3	28.2
2000				
Assets per branch	45,156	19,115	29,852	54,129
Loans per branch	23,040	4,937	13,451	23,149
Deposits per branch	15,542	12,212	10,312	12,812
Employees per branch	39.4	27.8	26.6	24.0

Note: The financial data are in R$, deflated by the CPI (base year = 1995). All ratios are calculated for the aggregates and are for March 1995, December 1997, and September 2000. One bank is excluded because of data problems.
Source: World Bank staff estimates; data provided by Central Bank of Brazil.

Appendix Table A1.17 Analysis of Supply: Branch Intensity across Private Banks of Different Size and over Time

Year/item	*Large banks*	*Medium banks*	*Small banks*
1995			
Assets per branch	22,333	38,384	38,527
Loans per branch	9,652	19,325	20,582
Deposits per branch	10,385	13,549	13,315
Employees per branch	37.6	44.1	32.3
1997			
Assets per branch	23,830	81,307	46,759
Loans per branch	9,397	32,803	22,801
Deposits per branch	8,227	24,114	13,672
Employees per branch	28.1	37.1	28.1
2000			
Assets per branch	27.959	118,557	82,167
Loans per branch	12,553	49,823	37,134
Deposits per branch	8,949	31,794	19,643
Employees per branch	25.6	29.5	28

Note: These ratios are for private domestic and foreign banks only. The financial data are in R$, deflated with the CPI (base year = 1995). All ratios are calculated for the aggregates and are for March 1995, December 1997, and September 2000. One bank is excluded because of data problems.
Source: World Bank staff estimates; data provided by Central Bank of Brazil.

Appendix Table A1.18 Analysis of Supply: Structure of the Loan Portfolio across Brazilian Banks over Time

Year/item	*Federal banks*	*State banks*	*Private banks*	*Foreign banks*
1995				
Private borrowers	72.8	69.1	97.2	98.0
Agriculture	16.8	4.8	3.1	1.9
Residential mortgage	34.6	30.1	15.8	5.1
Individuals	3.1	10.3	12.6	12.8
Federal government	7.3	0.3	0.2	0.2
State government	19.0	27.4	2.1	0.7
1997				
Private borrowers	78.4	94.0	98.0	99.2
Agriculture	16.3	7.4	5.9	6.7
Residential mortgage	44.4	32.8	9.7	4.8
Individuals	4.0	16.5	15.5	20.8
Federal government	5.1	0.1	0.3	0.0
State government	14.9	2.0	1.1	0.2
2000				
Private borrowers	76.6	98.9	98.9	99.4
Agriculture	13.6	9.8	5.0	4.0
Residential mortgage	42.2	26.0	6.5	4.8
Individuals	7.6	24.5	17.8	23.1
Federal government	19.3	0.0	1.0	0.4
State government	3.0	0.3	0.1	0.1

Note: Ratios are for aggregates and are for March 1995, December 1997, and September 2000.
Source: World Bank staff estimates; data provided by Central Bank of Brazil.

Appendix Table A1.19 Analysis of Supply: Structure of the Loan Portfolio across Private Banks over Time

Year/item	*Large banks*	*Medium banks*	*Small banks*
1995			
Private borrowers	98.7	93.7	98.3
Agriculture	3.8	1.5	0.2
Residential mortgage	18.9	4.0	12.8
Individual	12.4	10.0	29.5
Federal government	0.1	0.4	0.0
State government	1.2	3.6	1.0
1997			
Private borrowers	99.0	96.7	99.0
Agriculture	8.1	1.9	1.6
Residential mortgage	11.0	2.1	5.4
Individual	15.1	20.9	23.7
Federal government	0.4	0.1	0.0
State government	0.3	1.9	0.3
2000			
Private borrowers	99.2	99.3	100.0
Agriculture	5.3	1.8	6.9
Residential mortgage	7.1	1.3	2.5
Individual	15.8	28.9	29.6
Federal government	0.8	0.4	0.0
State government	0.0	0.3	0.0

Note: Numbers are for March 1995, December 1997, and September 2000 and are for private domestic and foreign banks only.
Source: World Bank staff estimates; data provided by Central Bank of Brazil.

Appendix Table A2.1a BNDES PCPP Microfinance Portfolio
(June 2001)

MFIs with BNDES contracts	*Initiation of activities* (*mm/yy*)	*Date of first contract*	*Total value of BNDES contracts*	*Total value of BNDES disbursements (R$'000)* *Jun–01*
Portosol	Jan–96	Jan–97	4,800	4,867
VivaCred	Apr–97	Sep–97	1,600	1,610
CEAPE–Bahia	Mar–94	Dec–97	1,825	228
CEAPE–Goiás	Jun–94	Dec–97	300	304
CEAPE–Paraíba	Apr–94	Dec–97	4,800	4,867
CEAPE–Pernambuco	Oct–92	Dec–97	1,600	1,610
CEAPE–Rio Grande do Norte	Apr–90	Dec–97	1,825	228
Banco da Mulher/Bahia	Jun–88	Apr–98	300	304
Banco da Mulher/Paraná	Apr–86	Apr–98	1,840	396
FAEP	Aug–97	Apr–98	4,280	1,705
Blusol	Aug–97	Jul–98	2,805	2,924
CEAPE–Espírito Santo	Jul–97	Jul–98	300	301
CEAPE–Sergipe	Oct–91	Aug–98	966	908
Casa do Empreendedor	Nov–97	Aug–98	2,000	1,101
CEAPE– Rio Grande do Sul	Feb–87	Sep–98	2,000	2,051
CEAPE–Pará	Dec–94	Oct–98	200	201
FAEJ	May–98	Feb–99	3,390	994
Vitória Credisol	Jun–98	Mar–99	1,000	1,056
Banco da Mulher/ Santa Catarina	Oct–98	May–99	2,780	989
Banco do Povo de S. André	May–98	May–99	210	211
ORGAPE/Ceará	Mar–97	Feb–00	1,000	534
Banco do Povo/Minas Gerais	May–99	Jul–00	1,000	503
Visão Mundial/Minas Gerais	Sep–97	Jul–00	500	508
Visão Mundial/Pernambuco	Oct–96	Jul–00	2,000	1,017
Visão Mundial/Bahia	Sep–97	Jul–00	1,000	477
Visão Mundial/FUNDAF/ Rio Grande do Norte	Oct–00	Jul–00	600	311
Visão Mundial/Ceará	Aug–00	Jul–00	600	464
Credimais/Goiás	Jun–98	Oct–00	950	0
Conquista Solidária/Bahia	May–99	Nov–00	600	103
Microcred	Nov–99	Feb–01	600	647
Rótula	Nov–99	Feb–01	500	411
Total			48,171	31,830

Source: BNDES, Social Programs Department, and World Bank staff estimates.

Active portfolio	Loans in arrears >30 days (%)	Credits granted (nos.)		Avg. loan value (R$)		Total loan value (R$'000)		Active clients (nos.)
	Jun–01	2000	Jun–01	1998	Jun–01	2000	Jun–01	Jun–01
3,881	4.23	4,030	6,302	2,953	1,093	6,221	6,890	2,135
2,043	4.50	2,569	1,331	1,799	1,603	4,147	2,133	1,905
1,102	5.90	4,391	2,067	783	941	3,766	1,944	1,457
777	4.20	2,176	1,261	927	971	2,495	1,224	944
910	6.90	5,034	2,413	668	754	3,596	1,819	1,596
3,377	23.00	12,371	4,793	1,015	1,173	13,373	5,621	4,527
3,829	3.19	11,786	7,433	681	887	11,339	6,590	5,145
433	4.50	1,485	787	1,085	859	1,256	676	726
1,091	4.35	995	931	2,013	1,568	1,666	1,459	958
1,274	1.47	1,060	544	1,963	2,036	2,417	1,108	853
2,467	1.50	986	661	2,967	4,023	4,002	2,659	950
624	6.80	1,714	260	1,123	1,765	2,076	459	736
1,747	7.50	7,567	3,003	736	1,098	7,631	3,299	2,755
1,435	5.70	836	454	2,764	2,718	2,132	1,234	722
1,029	5.50	9,782	2,146	1,139	734	6,771	1,576	1,479
823	14.77	2,691	778	1,026	1,914	4,074	1,489	557
412	0.50	306	141	2,244	2,905	847	410	204
978	5.80	861	452	1,827	2,302	1,847	1,041	693
848	0.50	591	210	1,208	4,144	1,091	870	650
463	1.59	395	224	2,287	2,453	976	550	264
684	3.70	746	608		437	1,027	266	882
391	0.50	177	232		1,332	225	309	442
597	3.91	621	356		1,883	651	670	916
421	3.36	587	577		939	524	542	672
233	3.98	371	787		391	320	308	392
190	0.74	197	709		681	342	483	341
151	2.14	40	277		803	30	222	262
400	3.10	300	67		2,563	804	172	208
306	3.90	75	501		845	66	423	537
154	7.25		59		1,927	0	114	61
823	2.22		233		1,405	0	327	387
33,893		74,740	40,597	1,091	1,155	85,714	46,888	34,356

Appendix Table A2.1b BNDES PCPP Microfinance Portfolio

(December 2002)

MFIs with BNDES contracts	*Initiation of activities* (*mm/yy*)	*Date of first contract*	*Total value of BNDES contracts*	*Total value of BNDES disbursements (R$'000)* 2002
Portosol	Jan–96	Jan–97	7,800	7,948
VivaCred	Apr–97	Sep–97	4,580	4,711
CEAPE–Bahia	Mar–94	Dec–97	225	228
CEAPE–Goiás	Jun–94	Dec–97	300	304
CEAPE–Paraíba[a]	Apr–94	Dec–97	390	396
CEAPE–Pernambuco	Oct–92	Dec–97	1,680	1,705
CEAPE–Rio Grande do Norte	Apr–90	Dec–97	2,805	2,861
Banco da Mulher/Bahia	Jun–88	Apr–98	300	301
Banco da Mulher/Paraná	Apr–86	Apr–98	950	95
FAEP	Aug–97	Apr–98	1,500	1,542
BluSol	Aug–97	Jul–98	3,500	3,532
CEAPE–Espírito Santo	Jul–97	Jul–98	200	201
CEAPE– Sergipe	Oct–91	Aug–98	3,390	994
Casa do Empreendedor	Nov–97	Aug–98	1,000	1,037
CEAPE–Rio Grande do Sul	Feb–87	Sep–98	2,780	989
CEAPE–Pará	Dec–94	Oct–98	210	211
FAEJ	May–98	Feb–99	1,000	500
Vitória Credisol	Jun–98	Mar–99	1,000	503
Banco da Mulher/Santa Catarina	Oct–98	May–99	500	508
Banco do Povo de S. André	May–98	May–99	2,000	1,667
ORGAPE/Ceará[a]	Mar–97	Feb–00	1,000	817
Banco do Povo/Minas Gerais	May–99	Jul–00	600	434
Visão Mundial/Minas Gerais	Sep–97	Jul–00	525	502
Visão Mundial/Pernambuco	Oct–96	Jul–00	850	300
Visão Mundial/Bahia	Sep–97	Jul–00	500	300
Visão Mundial/FUNDAF/ Rio Grande do Norte	Oct–00	Jul–00	625	637
Visão Mundial/Ceará	Aug–00	Jul–00	500	400
Credimais/Goiás	Jun–98	Oct–00	1,000	880
Conquista Solidária/Bahia	May–99	Nov–00	1,000	500
Microcred	Nov–99	Feb–01	1,000	372
Rótula	Nov–99	Feb–01	1,000	1,004
Banco da Mulher/Rio de Janeiro	Jun–98	Nov–03	1,000	400
Ipatinga	Jun–98	—	1,000	700
Maringá Crédito Solidário[a]	May–03	—	1,000	379
Socialcred	Apr–03	Dec–03	2,000	2,051
Total			49,710	40,772

a. These companies did not provide all the necessary data to BNDES.

Source: BNDES, Social Programs Department, and World Bank staff estimates.

Active portfolio	*Loans in arrears >30 days (%)*	*Credits granted (nos.)*		*Avg. loan value (R$)*		*Total loan value (R$'000)*		*Active clients (nos.)*
	2002	*2001*	*2002*	*2001*	*2002*	*2001*	*2002*	*2002*
3,708	3.85	14,123	14,256	1,036	998	14,626	14,221	1,916
2,157		2,394	2,474	1,590	1,621	3,806	4,010	2,225
1,158	3.55	4,430	4,512	868	1,014	3,843	4,577	1,711
1,087	3.70	3,838	5,974	899	902	3,449	5,390	876
		4,621	4,007	790	803	3,648	3,219	
3,371	4.00	8,894	8,892	1,198	1,251	10,656	11,120	3,704
3,369	0.88	14,752	15,556	936	873	13,805	13,575	5,623
441	2.90	1,619	1,458	873	903	1,414	1,316	734
844	6.83	1,700	1,300	1,573	1,624	2,673	2,111	830
2,397	2.14	1,338	2,003	1,856	1,920	2,483	3,845	1,797
3,991	0.70	1,320	2,229	4,103	3,517	5,415	7,838	1,349
398	5.40	426	314	2,011	2,430	857	763	429
2,270	2.75	6,396	7,472	1,029	1,011	6,582	7,555	2,916
1,708	4.90	984	1,127	2,718	2,687	2,674	3,028	887
485	5.00	4,001	2,212	744	882	2,978	1,952	598
323	16.77	1,388	738	1,804	1,917	2,504	1,415	288
335	6.10	295	235	2,782	2,602	821	612	209
1,074	4.70	865	1,093	2,171	2,080	1,878	2,274	828
2,074	0.40	1,400	2,349	1,866	1,404	2,612	3,297	2,031
995	4.98	486	1,098	2,747	1,884	1,335	2,068	677
		546	546	1,208	962	660	525	
1,258	0.74	554	1,316	1,250	1,387	693	1,825	1,192
839	1.42	1,360	1,766	1,123	1,154	1,527	2,037	1,165
586	2.90	1,248	1,633	874	869	1,091	1,420	958
443	4.80	837	1,157	801	840	670	972	758
403	3.55	1,279	1,162	1,165	983	1,490	1,143	352
381	2.67	1,084	1,747	712	711	772	1,242	745
777	3.44	133	382	2,621	3,539	349	1,352	356
363	4.90	1,123	1,182	866	1,100	972	1,300	656
226	1.85	313	418	1,781	1,941	557	812	104
1,865	4.78	2,342	3,159	1,388	1,562	3,251	4,935	679
81	7.70	83	185	1,092	1,114	91	206	116
1,142	2.90		1,254		1,618		2,029	1,047
			1,101		1,078		1,187	
974	4.77	459	2,140	2,295	1,665	1,054	3,564	271
41,516		86,631	98,447	1,169	1,206	101,237	118,734	38,027

Appendix Table A2.2 Products Offered by Main Microfinance Providers in Brazil

Name of institution	*Type of loans offered*	*Loans extended to*
CrediAmigo	Working capital (WC) fixed assets	Solidarity groups (3 to 5 people)
CEAPE	90% working capital 10% fixed assets	Solidarity groups (3 to 6 people) or individuals
Banco do Povo de São Paulo	21% working capital 68% fixed assets 11% mixed loans	Individuals or associations of business partners
PortoSol	Working capital fixed assets mixed loans	Solidarity groups, individuals, or production associations
BluSol	33% working capital 67% fixed assets	Solidarity groups or individuals
Banco da Mulher	Working capital	Individuals
VivaCred	70% working capital 30% fixed assets	Individuals
Banco do Povo de Juiz de Fora	74% working capital 26% fixed assets	Solidarity groups (3 to 7 members) or individuals
RioCred	66% working capital 18% fixed assets 16% business remodeling	Individuals
SindCred	Fixed assets	Individuals

Note: n.a. = not applicable. In June 2001, the loan portfolio of the institutions included in this sample represented 92 percent of the total loan portfolio of the sample of 46 institutions included in table 2.3, chapter 2. Data are for June 2001.
Source: BNDES, individual institutions.

Maximum maturity	*Loan size*	*Use of collateral*
6 months	First loan: R$300 to R$700; Repeat loan: up to R$4,000	None
6 months for WC, 12 for fixed assets	Up to R$15,000	Cosigner for loans to individuals
18 months	R$200 to R$5,000 for individuals Up to R$25,000 for associations	Cosigner or collateral
9 months for WC, 15 for fixed assets	R$200 to R$15,000	Cosigner or collateral for loans to individuals
n.a.	R$250 to R$12,800	Cosigner or collateral for loans to individuals
n.a.	n.a.	n.a.
12 months	R$100 to R$5,000	Cosigner
6 months for WC, 12 for fixed assets	R$200 to R$5,000 for WC Up to R$10,000 for fixed assets	Cosigner or collateral
12 months for WC, 18 for fixed assets	R$400 to R$5,000	Cosigner
12 months	R$100 to R$5,000	Cosigner

Appendix Table A2.3 Distribution of Credit Cooperatives and Other Financial Institutions in Brazil, by State

(April 2002)

State	*Multiple and commercial banks*	*Investment banks*	*Housing and development banks*	*Development agencies*
Acre				
Alagoas				
Amapá				1
Amazonas	1			1
Bahia	4			1
Ceará	2			
Distrito Federal	3	2	1	
Espírito Santo	1		1	
Goiás	1			1
Maranhão	1			
Mato Grosso				
Mato Grosso do Sul				
Minas Gerais	8	1	1	
Pará	2			
Paraíba	1			
Paraná	6	1		1
Pernambuco	3			
Piauí	1			
Rio de Janeiro	22	5	1	
Rio Grande do Norte			1	1
Rio Grande do Sul	10		1	1
Rondônia				
Roraima				1
Santa Catarina	1			1
São Paulo	104	12	5	
Sergipe	1			
Tocantins				
Total	172	21	11	9

Source: Central Bank of Brazil: www.bcb.gov.br.

a. Included in this category are security brokerage companies, security distribution companies, exchange brokerage companies, and leasing companies.

Holding companies	*Finance companies*[a]	*Savings and loans*	*Microcredit companies*	*Credit cooperatives*	*Total*
				4	4
2		1		8	11
					1
1	3	1		4	11
5	6	1		64	81
5	16	2	2	16	43
16	5	1		28	56
6	7			49	64
17	1			32	52
2	2			2	7
2			1	48	51
4		1		18	23
38	25	2	6	296	377
2	1			40	45
2				22	25
46	22		2	87	165
2	12	1	1	17	36
1		1		2	5
26	88	2	8	107	259
3	1			13	19
48	27	3		112	202
1				24	25
				1	2
32	7	1		81	123
124	256	1	5	310	817
6				2	9
				8	8
391	479	18	25	1,395	2,521

Appendix Table A2.4 Regional Distribution of Loans to Microcredit Institutions Supported by BNDES

	1998		1999		2000		2001 (Jan–Sep)	
Institutions	*Clients (nos.)*	*Value (R$'000)*	*Clients (nos.)*	*Value (R$'000)*	*Clients (nos.)*	*Value (R$'000)*	*Clients (nos.)*	*Value (R$'000)*
South (6: Banco da Mulher SC and PR, Casa do Empreendedor, CEAPE RS, PortoSol, BluSol)								
Paraná (PR)	625	1,466	1,166	2,785	1,831	3,798	243	446
Rio Grande do Sul (RS)	5,399	7,707	11,571	13,075	13,812	12,982	1,541	1,387
Santa Catarina (SC)	621	1,842	921	2,814	1,577	5,092	250	677
Average loan size		1,658		1,367		1,270		1,234
Subtotal	6,645	11,015	13,658	18,675	17,220	21,873	2,034	2,510
% share	15.7	24.1	20.9	25.5	23.2	25.9	28.2	30.7
Southeast (10: CEAPE ES, Vitória Credisol, Banco do Povo ACP, FAEP, Rotula, Visão Mundial MG, VivaCred, Banco do Povo de Santo André, FAEJ, Microcred)								
Espírito Santo (ES)	2,529	2,925	2,758	4,126	2,575	3,923	98	195
Minas Gerais (MG)	499	1,096	666	1,715	1,858	3,294	607	914
Rio de Janeiro (RJ)	1,236	2,224	1,446	2,550	2,569	4,147	180	287
São Paulo (SP)			859	2,071	701	1,824	111	254
Average loan size		1,464		1,826		1,712		1,656
Subtotal	4,264	6,245	5,729	10,462	7,703	13,188	996	1,649
% share	10.1	13.6	8.8	14.3	10.4	15.6	13.8	20.2
South plus Southeast (%)	25.8	37.7	29.7	39.8	33.6	41.5	42.0	50.9
Northeast (13: Visão Mundial AL, BA, CE, PE, RN; Banco da Mulher BA; CEAPE BA, PE, PB, RN, SE; Conquista Solidária; ORGAPE)								
Alagoas (AL)							12	10
Bahia (BA)	3,474	2,917	4,739	3,852	6,322	5,408	731	629

Ceará (CE)					786	1,057	184	125
Paraíba (PB)	3,384	2,648	5,166	3,534	5,034	3,596	434	367
Pernambuco (PE)	12,354	11,303	18,025	18,568	12,958	13,897	750	817
Rio Grande do Norte (RN)	5,707	4,867	8,939	7,597	11,786	11,339	1,162	1,156
Sergipe (SE)	3,725	3,925	5,767	6,023	7,567	7,631	393	369
Average loan size		896		928		966		948
Subtotal	28,644	25,661	42,636	39,574	44,453	42,927	3,666	3,474
% share	67.7	56.0	65.3	54.1	59.9	50.8	50.9	42.5
Central–West (2: CEAPE GO, Rio Verde Inst. de Crédito Popular)								
Average loan size		1,044		1,123		1,147		890
Goiás (GO)	1,690	1,765	1,829	2,055	2,176	2,495	425	378
Subtotal	1,690	1,765	1,829	2,055	2,176	2,495	425	378
% share	4.0	3.9	2.8	2.8	2.9	3.0	5.9	4.6
North (CEAPE PA)								
Average loan size		1,026		1,608		1,514		1,867
Pará (PA)	1,071	1,099	1,486	2,389	2,691	4,074	86	161
Subtotal	1,071	1,099	1,486	2,389	2,691	4,074	86	161
% share	2.5	2.4	2.3	3.3	3.6	4.8	1.2	2.0
North, Northeast, and Central-West (%)	74.2	62.3	70.3	60.2	66.4	58.5	58.0	49.1
Total	42,314	45,784	65,338	73,154	74,243	84,557	7,207	8,172

Note: ACP = Popular Credit Association (Associação de Crédito Popular). The table does not include data on the one MFI in the Federal District of Brasília, CEAPE Nacional.

Source: BNDES Social Programs Department.

Appendix Table A2.5 Clientele of the Main Microfinance Institutions Active in Brazil

Name of institution	*Target clientele*	*Breakdown by sector*	*% informal sector*	*% women*	*Average loan size (R$)*
CrediAmigo	Established microentrepreneurs	81% commerce 15% industry 4% services	n.a.	48	729
CEAPE	Microentrepreneurs above 21 years of age, with a business in existence for at least six months	76% commerce 13% industry 11% services[a]	89[a]	56[a]	918
Banco do Povo de São Paulo	Microentrepreneurs, with a business in existence for at least six months, with annual earnings < $45,000 and who have been living in São Paulo for at least two years	48% commerce 8% industry 44% services	68	52	2,237
PortoSol	Microentrepreneurs, with a business in existence for at least six months	46% commerce 20% industry 34% services	38	39	1,093
BluSol	Established microentrepreneurs	41% commerce 22% industry 37% services	38	44	4,023
Banco da Mulher[b]	Low-income women entrepreneurs	54% commerce 18% industry 28% services	70	69	1,559

VivaCred	Microentrepreneurs, with a business in existence for at least 12 months	68% commerce 8% industry 24% services	92	45	1,603
Banco do Povo de Juiz de Fora	Microentrepreneurs, with a business in existence for at least six months and who reside or have their business in the municipality	47% commerce 21% industry 32% services	52	46	2,036
RioCred	Microentrepreneurs, with a business in existence for at least 12 months	68% commerce 8%s industry 24% services	Accepts informal clients	n.a.	1,205
SindCred/Credito Cidadão	Microentrepreneurs, with a business in existence for at least nine months	n.a.	Accepts informal clients	n.a.	1,049
Weighted average of total sample[c]		70% commerce 14% industry 16% services	77[d]	51	1,087

Note: n.a. = not applicable. Data are for June 2001.
a. Estimates based on data provided to BNDES by nine CEAPE entities.
b. Three entities affiliated to WWB only.
c. Sample includes all the 46 institutions listed in table 2.3.
d. Excludes CrediAmigo, RioCred, and SindCred.
Source: BNDES, individual institutions.

Appendix Table A2.6 Disbursements of BNDES to Micro, Small, and Medium-Size Companies by Loan Product and Ranking of Active Agents

(R$ millions)

	1998		1999	
Item	*Clients*	*Value*	*Clients*	*Value*
Automatic BNDES loan	12,245	908	27,192	894
Investment support	5,094	605	4,047	682
Agricultural programs[a]	7,151	303	23,145	212
FINAME	8,203	796	7,087	704
FINAME leasing	870	89	570	55
FINAME agriculture	9,632	372	19,503	732
FINEM	63	84	110	222
BNDES–Exim	38	16	42	36
Capital markets	6	6	10	65
Risk capital	6	6	9	11
Other			1	54
Nonreimbursable funds	29	24	75	45
Total	31,092	2,301	54,599	2,818

Agents (rank) Jan–Sep 2001	*Only MPME (a)*	*Total (b)*	*(%) MPME participation (a)/(b)*	*Number of operations*
1 Banco do Brasil	613	932	65.8	52,641
2 Bradesco	354	920	38.5	5,898
3 CNH Capital	314	314	100.0	5,078
4 BCN BM	192	247	77.7	1,202
5 Rabobank	183	183	100.0	3,859
6 Banco do Nordeste	162	196	82.7	8,575
7 Banespa	150	186	80.6	4,076
8 John Deere	140	140	100.0	1,629
9 DaimlerChrysler	130	236	55.1	877
10 Banrisul	97	186	52.2	10,367
11 Royal	93	96	96.9	322
12 BRDE	84	156	53.8	2,472
13 Unibanco	67	985	6.8	210
14 Volvo	64	87	73.6	347
15 Badesc	57	72	79.2	375
16 Volkswagen	55	64	85.9	619
17 BVA	55	74	74.3	86
18 ABN AMRO	50	169	29.6	465
19 Safra	49	219	22.4	151
20 Itaú	49	768	6.4	284
21 Boston BC	45	203	22.2	466
22 CEF	40	58	69.0	305

2000		2001		2002	
Clients	Value	Clients	Value	Clients	Value
47,624	1,081	77,384	1,570	42,790	1,638
4,068	791	4,099	1,036	3,365	989
43,556	290	73,285	534	39,425	649
1,225	1,376	13,966	1,750	18,125	2,363
506	70	1,260	139	1,753	224
37,422	1,347	43,936	1,841	54,486	3,006
127	322	93	202	110	739
89	125	97	199	231	313
15	39	9	50	9	12
15	39	9	50	9	12
		0		0	
83	46	80	34	67	42
87,106	4,445	214,218	7,405	160,370	9,987

Agents (rank) Jan–Mar 2003	Only MPME (a)	Total (b)	(%) MPME participation (a)/(b)	Number of operations
1 Banco do Brasil	180	259	69.7	2,549
2 Bradesco BM	156	291	53.6	1,478
3 Volkswagen	130	148	87.9	1,517
4 CNH Capital	94	94	99.9	1,072
5 BCN BM	85	98	86.1	675
6 Dibens	75	76	98.9	800
7 DaimlerChrysler	60	79	75.6	528
8 Volvo	58	68	86.5	223
9 BRDE	45	75	59.4	993
10 Unibanco	41	121	33.5	204
11 Itaú	40	133	30.1	99
12 BVA	37	56	66.1	70
13 DLL Brasil	36	36	100.0	485
14 Banco Santos	33	161	20.3	35
15 Safra	31	172	17.8	91
16 John Deere	27	27	100.0	137
17 ABN AMRO	27	49	55.9	154
18 Badesc	24	40	59.6	168
19 Rural	21	21	99.6	102
20 Safra AM	20	30	69.0	117
21 Banespa	20	23	87.3	365
22 BCN	20	24	83.0	152

(table continued next page)

Appendix Table A2.6 *(continued)*

Agents (rank) *Jan–Sep 2001*	*Only MPME (a)*	*Total (b)*	*(%) MPME participation (a)/(b)*	*Number of operations*
23 Caterpillar	37	55	67.3	192
24 Santos	37	233	15.9	24
25 Bansicredi	36	36	100.0	3,644
Top 25 agents (c)	3,153	6,815	46.3	104,164
All 119 agents (d)	3,786	9,623	39.3	112,578
(c)/(d)	83.3	70.8	n.a.	92.5

Note: n.a. = not applicable.
a. Created by Central Bank Resolutions: Procaju, Propasto, Prodamel, Prodecap, Prodevinho, Profruta, Pronaf, Prosolo, Provarzeasul, Aqüicultura, and Floricultura e Armazenagem.
Source: Boletim MPME, March 2003 and September 2001.

Agents (rank) Jan–Mar 2003	*Only MPME (a)*	*Total (b)*	*(%) MPME participation (a)/(b)*	*Number of operations*
23 Banrisul	19	40	48.8	219
24 Royal BI	18	18	100.0	38
25 Dibens AM	17	18	95.8	208
Top 25 agents (c)	1,314	2,156	60.9	12,479
All 119 agents (d)	1,603	3,007	53.3	15,664
(c)/(d)	81.9	71.7	n.a.	79.7

Appendix Table A2.7 Disbursements of BNDES to MPMEs, by Region and by Sector

(nos., R$ millions)

	1998		1999		2000		2001[a]		2002	
Region/sector	*Clients*	*Value*	*Clients*	*Value*	*Clients*	*Value*	*Clients*	*Value*	*Clients*	*Value*
By region										
North	442	47.8	672	94.8	1,379	137.1	2,727	101.2	1,838	312.6
Northeast	5,175	531.4	6,786	457.2	14,947	623.1	10,670	506.4	6,101	978.2
Southeast	9,416	842.9	12,425	1,070.5	25,166	1,792.0	20,798	1,576.3	30,574	2,878.8
South	13,035	641.7	29,597	780.6	47,830	1,266.5	72,004	1,317.4	64,949	2,812.8
Central–West	3,018	230.8	5,109	349.8	8,794	586.9	6,520	447.2	14,109	1,354.9
Total	31,086	2,294.6	54,589	2,752.9	98,116	4,405.6	112,719	3,948.5	117,571	8,337.3
By sector										
Agriculture	19,203	928	44,234	1,098	82,468	1,820	118,601	2,551	94,794	3,885
Industry	4,155	425	3,680	485	5,292	918	6,512	1,207	6,783	1,309
Infrastructure	4,568	568	3,608	690	5,834	856	6,813	1,239	9,152	2,113
Commerce and services	2,833	263	2,679	299	3,928	486	4,339	595	6,306	792
Education and health	327	111	388	181	594	326	560	193	536	237
Total	31,086	2,295	54,589	2,753	98,116	4,406	136,825	5,785	117,571	8,337

a. Regional data for 2001 cover January to September only.
Source: Boletim MPME, September 2001 and March 2003.

Appendix Table A2.8 Total BNDES Disbursements for Programa Brasil Empreendedor (PBE), by Institution and by Region

(nos., R$ millions)

	PBE I (Oct-99 to Sep-02)		*PBE I (Oct-02 to Mar-03)*		*PBE total*	
Institution/region	*Value*	*Clients*	*Value*	*Clients*	*Value*	*Clients*
BNDES	9,043	50,015	2,826	14,429	11,869	64,444
BNDES–microcredit	293	248,115	70	56,761	363	304,876
Banco da Amazônia	51	146	13	15	64	161
Banco do Nordeste	323	1,827	14	63	337	1,890
Banco do Brasil	562	3,478	134	749	696	4,227
Caixa Econômica Federal	227	1,283	27	262	254	1,545
Total, institutions[a]	10,498	304,864	3,084	72,279	13,582	377,143
North	435	6,765	89	716	524	7,481
Northeast	1,290	141,970	269	27,805	1,559	169,775
Southeast	4,520	54,189	1,412	16,742	5,932	70,931
South	2,392	80,384	955	21,751	3,347	102,135
Central–West	698	14,822	172	4,176	869	18,998
Total, region[b]	9,335	298,130	2,896	71,190	12,231	369,320

a. Includes all credits of BNDES with MPMEs.
b. Excludes credits through other federal financial institutions.
Source: Boletim MPME, March 2003.

Appendix Table A2.9 Loan Approvals from the Fundo de Garantia para a Promoção da Competitividade
(R$ millions)

	1998		*1999*		*2000*		*2001 (up to Sep)*	
Item	*Clients*	*Value*	*Clients*	*Value*	*Clients*	*Value*	*Clients*	*Value*
Automatic BNDES loan	256	27	745	109	1,590	343	1,181	324
FINAME	13	2	321	35	1,758	161	1,990	188
FINEM					1	3		
BNDES–Exim	31	4	26	26	59	59	24	30
Total	300	33	1,092	170	3,408	566	3,195	542

Source: Boletim MPME, September 2001.

Appendix Table 2.10 Comparison of Select Microfinance Institutions between Brazil and other Latin American Countries
(December 31, 2001)

Company	*Country*	*Portfolio (US$ millions)*	*Clients ('000)*
Banco Sol	Bolivia	81.0	61.4
Caja los Andes	Bolivia	52.6	43.5
CMAC Arequipa	Peru	50.0	50.2
Calpia	El Salvador	31.9	36.3
FIE	Bolivia	27.4	22.6
CMAC Trujillo	Peru	27.4	47.0
Compartamos	Mexico	24.8	92.8
CrediAmigo	Brazil	20.7	85.3
Edyficar	Peru	20.0	20.5
CMAC Sullana[a]	Peru	19.9	45.3
Visión	Paraguay	19.3	35.1
FinAmérica	Colombia	18.9	16.5
WWB Cali	Colombia	17.7	38.1
CMAC Cusco[a]	Peru	17.3	22.0
Confia	Nicaragua	13.5	13.5
CMAC Ica	Peru	12.3	12.1
CMAC Tacna	Peru	10.1	13.5
ADOPEM	Dom. Republic	9.9	28.1
WWB Popayán	Colombia	9.6	36.0
CEAPE[b]	Brazil	7.3	26.4
Finde	Nicaragua	7.3	5.3
Fondesa	Dom. Republic	5.4	3.4
Proempresa	Peru	5.0	5.5
WWB Bucaramanga	Colombia	4.9	19.6
WWB Medellín	Colombia	3.9	10.9
Crear Tacna	Peru	3.5	2.9
WWB Bogotá	Colombia	3.3	10.1
F.J. Nieberowski[a]	Nicaragua	2.9	4.2
Crear Arequipa	Peru	3.0	3.1
Confianza	Peru	3.7	3.6
Enlace	El Salvador	1.5	9.5

a. Clients = number of loans.
b. June 2001 data.
Source: Abrams, von Stauffenberg, and Farrington 2002.

Appendix Table A2.11 Credit Cooperatives in Brazil, by Type and by State, 2001

	Mutual	*Luzzatti*	*Rural*
Acre	1		
Alagoas	2		1
Amapá			
Amazonas	3		
Bahia	9	1	12
Ceará	9	3	
Distrito Federal	17		
Espíritu Santo	32		9
Goiás	8		14
Maranhão	1		
Mato Grosso	10		19
Mato Grosso do Sul	8		7
Minas Gerais	182		114
Pará	34		
Paraíba	10		1
Paraná	7		29
Pernambuco	10		1
Piauí			
Rio de Janeiro	77	1	5
Rio Grande do Norte	4		7
Rio Grande do Sul	39	1	61
Rondônia	3		5
Roraima			
Santa Catarina	27	1	33
São Paulo	177	3	36
Sergipe			
Tocantins			1
Brazil, total	670	10	355

Source: Organização das Cooperativas Brasileiras: www.ocb.org.br.

Appendix Table A2.12 Regulatory Framework for Credit Cooperatives in Brazil

CMN Resolution No.	*Date*	*Comments*
2.025	Nov 24, 1993	Alters and consolidates the norms concerning the opening, maintenance, and transfers of deposit accounts.
2.099	Aug 17, 1994	Approves regulation about access to the financial system, minimum net worth, and branches of financial institutions and other institutions authorized to function by the Central Bank of Brazil.
2.193	Aug 31, 1995	Regulates the creation and functioning of commercial banks with the exclusive participation of credit cooperatives.
2.267	Mar 29, 1996	Deals with the appointment of the person responsible for the accounting and auditing.
2.554	Sep 24, 1998	Regulates the implementation of internal control systems and auditing.
2.645	Sep 22, 1999	Establishes conditions for statutory positions in financial institutions and other institutions authorized to function by the Central Bank of Brazil.
2.692	Feb 24, 2000	Establishes criteria for calculating the net worth for institutions referred to in Annex IV of Resolution No. 2.099/94.
2.788	Nov 30, 2000	Permits the creation of multiple cooperative banks.
3.106	Jun 25, 2003	Approves bylaw that regulates the creation and functioning of credit cooperatives and eases membership criteria for credit cooperatives.
CMN Circular No.	*Date*	*Comments*
1.958	May 10, 1991	Introduces the simplified client information form.
2.452	Jul 21, 1994	Establishes additional standards concerning the opening, maintenance, and transfers of deposit accounts.

(table continued next page)

Appendix Table A2.12 *(continued)*

CMN Circular No.	*Date*	*Comments*
2.932	Sep 30, 1999	Establishes procedures concerning the employment in statutory positions of financial institutions and other institutions authorized to function by the Central Bank of Brazil.
3.201	Aug 20, 2003	Establishes complementary procedures to be observed by credit cooperatives regarding process instructions.
CMN Circular Letter No.	*Date*	*Comments*
2.613	Sep 02, 1996	Establishes procedures about sending and updating information forms of statutory positions of financial institutions and other institutions authorized to function by the Central Bank of Brazil.

Note: This table lists key recent National Monetary Council Resolutions and Circulars that have had a direct impact on cooperative credit.
Source: Bittencourt 2001.

Appendix Table A2.13 Balance Sheet for BANSICREDI and BANCOOB

(R$'000)

	BANSICREDI		*BANCOOB*	
Balance sheet	*Dec 2001*	*Dec 2000*	*Jun 2001*	*Dec 2000*
Current assets	1,000,336	590,781	461,722	308,393
Cash and banks	2,816	949	629	5,362
Interbank funds applied	621,822	376,294	29,758	90,090
Securities	18,553	17,148	204,445	128,858
Interbank accounts	82,854	61,673	104,749	431
Net loans	265,787	131,783	211,898	145,408
Other receivables	8,368	2,914	10,043	8,183
Fixed and other assets	11,859	3,408	8,559	7,320
Total assets	1,012,059	594,169	570,081	385,652
Current liabilities	944,263	542,107	468,680	291,962
Deposits	179,184	95,873	246,484	141,361
Demand deposits	6,262	4,378	1,782	969
Interbank deposits	22,616	11,003	81,502	56,052
Time deposits	150,306	80,492	163,200	84,340
Money market repos	551,112	330,733	122,637	145,435
Interbank accounts	69,417	45,791	81,915	
Borrowings	4,646	2,049		
Rediscounts: public and foreign	117,485	55,422	8,522	
Other liabilities	22,419	12,239	9,122	5,166
Long-term liabilities	26,818	23,214	67,065	60,203
Shareholders' equity	40,978	28,848	34,336	33,487
Capital	38,190	26,690	31,000	31,000
Reserves	1,191	1,056	333	291
Retained earnings	1,597	1,102	3,003	2,196
Total liabilities and capital	1,012,059	594,169	570,081	385,652

Source: Atlantic Rating: BANCOOB—Banco Cooperativo do Brasil S.A., June 2001; BANSICREDI: SICREDI communications to authors of this paper, March 4, 2002.

Appendix Table A2.14 Income Statement for BANSICREDI and BANCOOB

(R$'000)

Income statement	*BANSICREDI Jun 2001*	*BANCOOB Jun 2001*
Interest income	48,754	29,057
Loan and leasing income	17,042	10,255
Securities trading and compulsory placements	30,758	18,802
Foreign exchange income	954	
Interest expense	(42,480)	(24,341)
Deposits, money market and interbank funds	(37,816)	(22,864)
Borrowings and onlendings, leasing expenses	(3,977)	(1,155)
Provisions	(687)	(322)
Gross interest income	6,274	4,716
Operating revenues and expenses	(4,344)	(3,138)
Fees from services	2,067	8,507
Personnel and other administrative expenses	(5,992)	(10,511)
Tax expenses	(490)	(1,208)
Earnings from affiliates	(143)	(345)
Other operating revenues and expenses	214	419
Operating profit	1,930	1,578
Nonoperating income/(expenses)	(4)	38
Income before taxes	1,926	1,616
Income tax and social contribution	(901)	(777)
Net income	1,025	839

Source: Atlantic Rating: BANCOOB—Banco Cooperativo do Brasil S.A., June 2001; BANSICREDI: SICREDI communications to authors of this paper, March 4, 2002.

Appendix Table A2.15 WOCCU: Advocated Prudential Standards for Credit Unions

WOCCU International Credit Union Prudential Standards of Excellence		
	P–E–A–R–L–S ratios[a]	*Goals*
P	*Protection*	
	1. Allowance for loan losses/delinq. >12 mo.	100%
	2. Net allowance for loan losses/delinq. 1–12 mo.	35%
	3. Complete loan charge-off of delinquency > 12 mo.	Yes or no
	4. Annual loan charge-offs/average loan portfolio	0%
	5. Accum. charge-offs recovered/accum. charge-offs	100%
	6. Solvency	100%
	7. Allowance for investments at risk/investments at risk	100%
E	*Effective financial structure*	
	1. Net loans/total assets	Between 70 and 80%
	2. Liquid assets/total assets	Max 20%
	3. Financial investments/total assets	Max 10%
	4. Nonfinancial investments/total assets	0%
	5. Savings deposits/total assets	Between 70 and 80%
	6. External credit/total assets	0 to 5%
	7. Member share capital/total assets	Max 20%
	8. Institutional capital/total assets	Min 10%
	9. Net capital/total assets	Min 10%
A	*Asset quality*	
	1. Total delinquency/total loan portfolio	Less than 5%
	2. Nonearning assets/total assets	Less than 7%
	3. Zero cost funds/nonearning assets	Greater than or equal to 100%
R	*Rates of return and costs*	
	1. Net loan income/average net loan portfolio	Entrepreneurial rate
	2. Liquid assets income/avg. liquid assets	Market rates
	3. Fin. investment income/avg. fin. investments	Market rates
	4. Nonfin. inv. income/avg. nonfin. investments	Greater than or equal to R1
	5. Fin. costs: savings deposits/avg. savings deposits	Market rates
	6. Fin. costs: external credit/avg. external credit	Less than or equal to R5
	7. Fin. costs: member shares/avg. member shares	Greater than or equal to R5
	8. Gross margin/average assets	Cover R9, R10 increase capital
	9. Operating expenses/average assets	Between 3 and 10%
	10. Provisions for risk assets/average assets	Sufficient for estimated losses

(table continued next page)

Appendix Table A2.15 *(continued)*

WOCCU International Credit Union Prudential Standards of Excellence	
P–E–A–R–L–S ratios[a]	*Goals*
R *Rates of return and costs (continued)*	
11. Other income or expense/average assets	Minimum
12. Net income/average assets	Enough to reach the goal for E8
L *Liquidity*	
1. Liquid assets—ST payables/total deposits	Minimum 15%
2. Liquidity reserves/total savings deposits	10%
3. Nonearning liquid assets/total assets	Less than 1%
S *Signs of growth (annual growth rates)*	
1. Loans	Sufficient to achieve goal in E1
2. Liquid assets	Sufficient to achieve goal in E2
3. Financial investments	Sufficient to achieve goal in E3
4. Nonfinancial investments	Sufficient to achieve goal in E4
5. Savings deposits	Sufficient to achieve goal in E5
6. External credit	Sufficient to achieve goal in E5
7. Share capital	Sufficient to achieve goal in E7
8. Institutional capital	Sufficient to achieve goal on E8
9. Net capital	Sufficient to achieve goal on E9
10. Membership	Minimum 5%
11. Total assets	More than inflation

a. The table records prudential operating standards for credit cooperatives in protection, effective financial structure, asset quality, rates of return and costs, liquidity, and signs of growth, or P–E–A–R–L–S.

Source: World Council of Credit Unions: www.woccu.org.

Appendix Table A3.1 Brazil: Structure of Aggregate Deposits, by Type and Institution
(December 2001)

	All deposits		*Term deposits*		*Sight deposits*		*Special savings deposits*	
Value and no. of clients	*Value (R$ billions)*	*Clients (millions)*	*Value (R$ billions)*	*Clients (millions)*	*Value (R$ billions)*	*Clients (millions)*	*Value (R$ billions)*	*Clients (millions)*
All institutions	312.5	94.0	128.9	3.3	50.6	43.3	119.5	51.2
All public	134.7	48.3	32.7	2.5	23.1	17.5	68.6	28.3
o/w Banco do Brasil	48.0	20.1	12.9	1.3	13.9	10.9	21.2	7.9
CEF	56.0	17.5	6.0	neg.	4.6	2.7	35.3	14.8
All private	177.9	45.6	96.1	0.8	27.6	25.8	51.0	22.9
o/w National								
Bradesco	42.1	17.0	15.5	0.2	7.9	7.0	18.0	9.8
Itaú	24.9	9.9	2.1	0.4	6.6	7.1	15.7	5.2
Foreign participation								
Unibanco	24.6	7.5	19.4	neg.	1.9	6.6	2.9	0.9
Foreign controlled								
Santander	14.6	2.9	8.2	neg.	2.9	2.4	3.4	1.0
HSBC	8.9	2.3	5.0	neg.	2.3	1.1	1.5	1.1
ABN AMRO	8.9	3.2	2.2	neg.	2.1	0.8	4.5	2.4
Sudameris	4.6	0.4	3.0	neg.	0.6	0.2	1.0	0.9
BBV Banco	4.2	0.6	3.4	neg.	0.2	0.2	0.6	0.4
Foreign								
Citibank	1.6	0.1	0.8	neg.	0.7	0.1	0.1	neg.
ING	0.2	neg.	0.2	neg.	neg.	neg.	0.0	0.0

(table continued next page)

Appendix Table A3.1 *(continued)*

	All deposits		*Term deposits*		*Sight deposits*		*Special savings deposits*	
% composition	*% of total deposits*	*% of total clients*	*% of total term deposits*	*% of total term deposit clients*	*% of total sight deposits*	*% of total sight deposit clients*	*% of total special savings deposits*	*% of total special savings clients*
All institutions	100.0	100.0	100.0	100.0	100.0	100.0	100.0	100.0
All public	43.1	51.4	25.4	75.3	45.6	40.3	57.4	55.3
o/w Banco do Brasil	15.4	21.4	10.0	39.2	27.5	25.3	17.7	15.4
CEF	17.9	18.6	4.6	0.2	9.2	6.2	29.5	28.9
All private	56.9	48.6	74.6	24.5	54.5	59.5	42.6	44.7
o/w National								
Bradesco	13.5	18.0	12.0	6.0	15.6	16.1	15.0	19.1
Itaú	8.0	10.5	1.6	12.0	12.9	16.3	13.1	10.2
Foreign participation								
Unibanco	7.9	8.0	15.1	0.9	3.8	15.2	2.4	1.7
Foreign controlled								
Santander	4.7	3.1	6.3	0.9	5.6	5.5	2.8	1.9
HSBC	2.9	2.4	3.9	0.3	4.6	2.5	1.3	2.1
ABN AMRO	2.9	3.4	1.7	0.9	4.2	1.7	3.8	4.6
Sudameris	1.5	0.5	2.3	0.4	1.2	0.4	0.9	1.8
BBV Banco	1.3	0.7	2.6	0.1	0.4	0.5	0.5	0.9
Foreign								
Citibank	0.5	0.1	0.6	neg.	1.5	0.2	0.1	neg.
ING	0.1	neg.	0.2	neg.	neg.	neg.	0.0	0.0

Note: Neg. = negligible.
Source: World Bank calculations based on data from the Central Bank of Brazil.

Appendix Table A3.2 Brazil: Structure of Deposits below R$5,000, by Deposit Type and Institution
(December 2001)

	Value				Clients			
Deposits	*Total value, all deposits (R$b)*	*Total value below R$5,000 (R$b)*	*Institutional % of total deposits*	*Institutional % of total deposits below R$5,000*	*Total clients, all deposits (millions)*	*Total clients below R$5,000 (millions)*	*Institutional % of total clients*	*Institutional % of total clients below R$5,000*
1. Total—all deposits								
All institutions	312.5	37.5	100.0	100.0	94.0	87.4	100.0	100.0
All public	134.7	17.5	43.1	46.6	48.3	44.7	51.4	51.1
o/w Banco do Brasil	48.0	7.6	15.4	20.4	20.1	18.7	21.4	21.4
CEF	56.0	7.8	17.9	20.7	17.5	16.1	18.6	18.4
All private	177.9	20.0	56.9	53.4	45.6	42.7	48.6	48.9
o/w Bradesco	42.1	6.4	13.5	16.9	17.0	16.0	18.1	18.3
Itaú	24.9	4.5	8.0	12.0	9.9	9.1	10.6	10.4
Unibanco	24.6	1.4	7.9	3.6	7.5	7.3	8.0	8.3
2. Term deposits								
All institutions	128.9	1.6	100.0	100.0	3.3	2.6	100.0	100.0
All public	32.7	1.2	25.4	79.9	2.5	2.1	75.5	79.1
o/w Banco do Brasil	12.9	0.6	10.0	40.5	1.3	1.1	39.5	41.1
CEF	6.0	neg.	4.6	neg.	neg.	neg.	0.2	neg.
All private	96.1	0.3	74.6	20.1	0.8	0.5	24.5	20.9
o/w Bradesco	15.5	0.1	12.0	8.5	0.2	0.1	6.8	4.1
Itaú	2.1	0.1	1.6	7.4	0.4	0.4	12.5	14.8
Unibanco	19.4	neg.	15.1	0.6	neg.	neg.	0.9	0.1

(table continued next page)

Appendix Table A3.2 *(continued)*

	Value				*Clients*			
Deposits	*Total value, all deposits (R$b)*	*Total value below R$5,000 (R$b)*	*Institutional % of total deposits*	*Institutional % of total deposits below R$5,000*	*Total clients, all deposits (millions)*	*Total clients below R$5,000 (millions)*	*Institutional % of total clients*	*Institutional % of total clients below R$5,000*
3. Sight deposits								
All institutions	50.6	12.5	100.0	100.0	43.3	42.0	100.0	100.0
All public	23.1	5.9	45.5	47.1	17.5	16.9	40.4	40.2
o/w Banco do Brasil	13.9	3.7	27.5	29.8	10.9	10.5	25.3	25.1
CEF	4.6	1.2	9.1	9.4	2.7	2.5	6.2	6.1
All private	27.6	6.6	54.5	52.9	25.8	25.1	59.6	59.9
o/w Bradesco	7.9	1.6	15.6	12.9	7.0	6.8	16.1	16.2
Itaú	6.6	1.7	12.9	13.5	7.1	6.9	16.3	16.5
Unibanco	1.9	0.6	3.7	4.9	6.6	6.3	15.3	14.9
4. Special savings deposits								
All institutions	119.5	24.2	100.0	100.0	51.2	46.6	100.0	100.0
All public	68.6	12.9	57.4	53.4	28.3	25.7	55.3	55.2
o/w Banco do Brasil	21.2	3.3	17.7	13.5	7.9	7.1	15.4	15.2
CEF	35.3	6.6	29.5	27.3	14.8	13.5	28.9	29.0
All private	51.0	11.3	42.6	46.7	22.9	20.9	44.7	44.8
o/w Bradesco	18.0	4.6	15.0	19.1	9.8	9.1	19.1	19.4
Itaú	15.7	3.1	13.1	12.6	5.2	4.6	10.2	9.8
Unibanco	2.9	neg.	2.4	neg.	0.8	0.3	1.7	0.7

Note: Neg. = negligible.
Source: World Bank calculations based on data from the Central Bank of Brazil.

Appendix Table A3.3 Brazil: Structure of Sight and Special Savings Deposits below R$5,000, by Deposit Size and Institution

(December 2001)

		Value					
Deposits	*Deposits, all deposits (R$b)*	*Total value, % of total deposits*	*Institutional % of total deposits below R$100*	*Institutional % of total deposits from R$101 to R$500*	*Institutional % of total deposits from R$501 to R$1,000*	*Institutional % of total deposits from R$1,001 to R$5,000*	*Institutional % of total deposits below R$5,000*
1. Sight deposits							
All institutions—value (R$ billions)	Value	50.6	0.9	1.5	1.9	8.3	12.5
All institutions	50.6	100.0	100.0	100.0	100.0	100.0	100.0
All public	23.1	45.5	13.6	47.1	47.3	50.6	47.1
o/w Banco do Brasil	13.9	27.5	7.8	29.5	29.5	32.3	29.8
CEF	4.6	9.1	2.3	9.3	9.5	10.1	9.4
All private	27.6	54.5	86.7	53.0	52.6	49.4	52.9
o/w Bradesco	7.9	15.6	5.3	15.8	14.2	12.8	12.9
Itaú	6.6	12.9	5.9	16.6	15.5	13.3	13.5
Unibanco	2.9	5.7	70.0	0.7	3.3	2.5	7.1
2. Special savings deposits							
All institutions—value (R$ billions)	Value	119.5	0.5	2.4	3.0	18.2	24.2
All institutions	119.5	100.0	100.0	100.0	100.0	100.0	100.0
All public	68.6	57.4	53.8	52.8	52.7	53.6	53.4
o/w Banco do Brasil	21.2	17.7	13.0	11.6	12.1	14.1	13.5
CEF	35.3	29.5	30.4	29.4	27.9	26.8	27.3

(table continued next page)

Appendix Table A3.3 *(continued)*

Deposits	*Deposits, all deposits (R$b)*	*Total value, % of total deposits*	*Value* *Institutional % of total deposits below R$100*	*Institutional % of total deposits from R$101 to R$500*	*Institutional % of total deposits from R$501 to R$1,000*	*Institutional % of total deposits from R$1,001 to R$5,000*	*Institutional % of total deposits below R$5,000*
2. Special savings deposits (continued)							
All private	51.0	42.6	46.0	47.4	47.6	46.4	46.7
o/w Bradesco	18.0	15.0	20.6	22.4	21.2	18.2	19.1
Itaú	15.7	13.1	9.4	10.5	12.0	13.1	12.6
Unibanco	2.9	2.4	1.7	1.8	1.7	2.0	1.9

Deposits	*Total clients, all deposits*	*Institutional % of total clients*	*Clients* *Institutional % of total clients below R$100*	*Institutional % of total clients from R$101 to R$500*	*Institutional % of total clients from R$501 to R$1,000*	*Institutional % of total clients from R$1,001 to R$5,000*	*Institutional % of total clients below R$5,000*
1. Sight deposits							
All institutions—clients (millions)	nos.	43.3	29.7	5.8	2.7	3.8	42.0
All institutions	43.3	100.0	100.0	100.0	100.0	100.0	100.0
All public	17.5	40.4	37.0	46.7	46.7	50.1	40.2
o/w Banco do Brasil	10.9	25.3	23.1	29.3	29.1	31.8	25.1
CEF	2.7	6.2	4.7	9.2	9.4	10.0	6.1
All private	25.8	59.6	63.0	53.4	53.5	49.9	59.9

o/w Bradesco	7.0	16.1	16.8	16.0	14.1	13.0	16.2
Itaú	7.1	16.3	16.8	16.9	15.4	13.8	16.5
Unibanco	6.6	15.3	21.1	0.9	4.3	2.7	15.6
2. Special savings deposits							
All institutions—clients (millions)	nos.	51.2	24.6	9.8	4.3	7.9	46.6
All institutions	51.2	100.0	100.0	100.0	100.0	100.0	100.0
All public	28.3	55.3	57.2	53.0	52.6	53.4	55.2
o/w Banco do Brasil	7.9	15.4	17.6	11.6	12.1	13.7	15.2
CEF	14.8	28.9	29.5	29.9	27.9	26.9	29.0
All private	22.9	44.7	42.9	47.0	47.4	46.6	44.8
o/w Bradesco	9.8	19.1	18.3	22.2	21.2	18.6	19.4
Itaú	5.2	10.2	8.2	10.2	11.9	12.9	9.8
Unibanco	0.8	1.6	1.3	1.9	1.7	1.9	1.6

Source: World Bank calculations based on data from the Central Bank of Brazil.

Appendix Table A3.4 Brazil: Sight Deposit Accounts; Fees and Services for Standard Packages of Services at Major Banks

Service	*Public*			
	Banco do Brasil		*CEF*	
Service package	*Basic*	*Special*	*Basic*	*Special*
Monthly fee (R$)	3.50	8.50	3.50	12.00
Services included				
Account service fee	incl.	incl.	incl.	incl.
Account balance—ATM	unltd.	unltd.	unltd.	unltd.
Account balance—at agency	incl.	incl.	incl.	incl.
Withdrawals—ATMs	incl.	incl.	incl.	incl.
Withdrawals—at agency	incl.	incl.	incl.	incl.
Monthly statement	incl.	incl.	incl.	incl.
Written statement—ATM	2	4	1 p/week	incl.
Internet banking	unltd.	unltd.	unltd.	unltd.
Telephone service—electronic	unltd.	unltd.	incl.[a]	incl.[a]
Telephone service—personal attendance	unltd.	unltd.		
Debit card service fee	1st card	1st card	1st card	1st card
Transfer—between accounts	incl.	incl.		incl.[b]
Checkbook issue	n.a.	2	n.a.	2
Overdraft/special credit limit[c]		incl.		incl.
Automatic debit	incl.	incl.	incl.	incl.
Bill payments	incl.	incl.	incl.	incl.
Additional services				
Cash deposits	unltd.	unltd.	unltd.	unltd.
Checks deposited	incl.	incl.		
Direct debit/electronic check			incl.	incl.
Checks debited into current acc.				
Check stopping				
E-mail/WAP/fax banking		fax		fax
Special savings account transactions				
Minimum initial deposit (R$)	0	0	variable	variable

Note: n.a. = not available.

a. Includes written statements and account balance.

b. Includes one DOC-type (Credit Order Document or Interbank transfer) transfer per month.

c. Subject to interest charges.

Source: World Bank staff estimates based on data from individual bank websites.

Private							
Bradesco		*Itaú*			*ABN AMRO–Banco Real*		
1	*2*	*Electronic*	*Basic*	*Total*	*1*	*2*	*3*
3.50	12.50	6.00	8.00	15.00	4.00	8.00	14.00
incl.	incl.	incl.	incl.	incl.	incl.	incl.	incl.
unltd.	unltd.	unltd.	unltd.	unltd.	unltd.	unltd.	unltd.
incl.	incl.					1	2
incl.	incl.	5	6	20	8	10	20
incl.	incl.	2	2	4	2	4	4
incl.	incl.	incl.	incl.	incl.	incl.	incl.	incl.
incl.	incl.	4	4	8	4	4	8
unltd.	unltd.	unltd.	unltd.	unltd.	50 times	50 times	unltd.
unltd.	unltd.	unltd.	unltd.	unltd.	unltd.	unltd.	unltd.
unltd.	unltd.		2	20	20	20	20
1st card	1st card	1st card	1st card	1st card	1st card	1st card	1st card
incl.	incl.	10	10	30	15	25	30
n.a.	incl.	n.a.	incl.	incl.	n.a.	incl.	incl.
	incl.	incl.	incl.	incl.	incl.	incl.	incl.
incl.	incl.	incl.	incl.	incl.	incl.	incl.	incl.
incl.	incl.	10	10	30	25	30	30
unltd.	unltd.	10 (cash + checks)	10 (cash + checks)	unltd.	unltd.	unltd.	unltd.
incl.	incl.			40	20	40	50
					incl.	incl.	incl.
			4	20		10	20
		n.a.		1			2
fax, email	fax, email	incl.	incl.	incl.			
incl.	incl.	incl.	incl.	incl.			
0	0	0	0	0	variable	variable	variable

Appendix Table A4.1 Brazil: Sources of Enterprise Credit, by Type of Instrument, June 2000–December 2002

(R$ millions or percentage)

Date	New loans	Delinquency rates (%) 15 to 90 days	Delinquency rates (%) More than 90 days	Delinquency 15 to 90 days	Delinquency More than 90 days	Outstanding loans[a]	Interest rate (% p.a.)[b]	Average maturity (days)
Overdrafts—Conta Garantida								
Jun-00	11,583	2.67	1.94	329	239	12,326	59.68	24
Dec-00	12,185	1.19	1.15	178	173	15,008	54.34	23
Jun-01	12,644	1.30	1.80	229	318	17,620	55.64	23
Dec-01	13,664	1.10	1.20	218	238	19,860	63.74	23
Jun-02	13,988	1.00	1.50	209	313	20,880	63.23	24
Dec-02	16,595	1.40	1.60	283	324	20,247	66.30	22
Feb-03	14,671	1.50	1.70	312	354	20,797	68.27	22
Discount of duplicatas[c]								
Jun-00	3,049	2.69	2.53	106	100	3,932	46.60	37
Dec-00	3,305	6.15	2.05	324	108	5,270	44.66	38
Jun-01	3,412	2.73	3.13	141	162	5,175	45.89	33
Dec-01	3,750	2.20	3.00	132	181	6,022	50.14	40
Jun-02	3,660	3.00	3.80	177	224	5,895	50.12	37
Dec-02	4,458	1.50	4.40	91	266	6,045	50.48	32
Feb-03	4,089	1.50	4.20	89	249	5,920	51.58	32
Working capital								
Jun-00	3,881	3.28	5.39	427	702	13,030	34.34	121
Dec-00	5,565	2.10	3.31	347	547	16,542	32.53	138
Jun-01	4,987	2.37	4.36	409	750	17,211	33.97	150

Dec-01	6,891	3.10	3.20	685	708	22,110	37.70	162
Jun-02	5,178	3.30	4.30	741	965	22,441	37.83	263
Dec-02	9,035	2.40	3.40	709	1,005	29,562	37.99	238
Feb-03	5,847	3.00	3.60	875	1,050	29,176	39.11	231
Fixed assets								
Jun-00	392	2.07	2.65	26	33	1,264	31.18	256
Dec-00	816	3.26	2.87	72	63	2,201	30.72	362
Jun-01	752	3.82	1.49	118	46	3,094	30.40	314
Dec-01	731	4.30	2.00	155	72	3,593	34.43	320
Jun-02	785	4.10	2.00	165	81	4,030	33.80	286
Dec-02	991	3.60	1.80	154	77	4,278	35.64	258
Feb-03	919	3.70	1.90	155	79	4,177	37.19	251
Vendor credit								
Jun-00	1,450	4.76	0.79	219	36	4,594	23.75	63
Dec-00	2,663	0.73	0.54	47	35	6,470	20.76	79
Jun-01	2,513	2.05	0.61	120	35	5,828	22.71	64
Dec-01	2,877	0.70	0.30	48	20	6,802	25.10	82
Jun-02	2,245	1.70	0.40	102	24	5,992	25.09	73
Dec-02	3,573	0.60	0.40	47	31	7,852	26.00	70
Feb-03	2,877	0.80	0.40	59	29	7,374	27.41	67
"Hot money"—commercial bills (less than 30 days)								
Jun-00	820	2.39	5.97	11	28	466	44.93	24
Dec-00	1,052	0.85	5.44	5	32	583	39.38	13
Jun-01	999	0.65	5.04	3	25	502	45.16	11
Dec-01	990	1.40	3.70	6	17	462	46.11	15
Jun-02	931	3.40	5.90	16	27	461	48.21	12
Dec-02	1,340	7.50	4.70	46	29	619	49.09	10
Feb-03	961	0.80	12.70	4	70	551	50.53	11

(table continued next page)

Appendix Table A4.1 *(continued)*

Date	New loans	*Delinquency rates (%)*		*Delinquency*		Outstanding loans[a]	Interest rate (% p.a.)[b]	Average maturity (days)
		15 to 90 days	*More than 90 days*	*15 to 90 days*	*More than 90 days*			
Promissory note								
Jun-00	660	2.75	0.87	22	7	811	55.15	31
Dec-00	673	1.61	1.18	14	10	868	50.20	37
Jun-01	526	1.49	3.13	12	25	799	50.24	29
Dec-01	444	1.00	2.00	6	13	637	56.13	34
Jun-02	362	1.30	2.00	6	10	482	55.55	29
Dec-02	424	0.90	2.20	5	11	520	51.88	34
Feb-03	288	1.60	2.80	6	11	405	52.08	32

a. End of period.
b. Average interest rates weighted by outstanding loans until May 2000 and by daily or monthly average of new loans since May 2000.
c. Commercial invoices.
Source: Central Bank of Brazil.

Appendix Table A4.2 Brazil: Sources of Credit for Individuals by Type of Instrument, June 2000–December 2002

(R$ millions or percentage)

Date	New loans	*Delinquency rates (%)* 15 to 90 days	*Delinquency rates (%)* More than 90 days	*Delinquency* 15 to 90 days	*Delinquency* More than 90 days	Outstanding loans[a]	Interest rate (% p.a.)[b]	Average maturity (days)
Overdrafts—cheque especial								
Jun-00	10,087	2.60	2.75	167	176	6,409	163.28	21
Dec-00	10,132	2.79	4.26	181	278	6,517	152.71	20
Jun-01	12,278	2.76	6.19	239	535	8,651	147.07	19
Dec-01	12,287	3.30	8.30	269	676	8,141	160.18	20
Jun-02	12,409	2.70	9.40	246	856	9,105	158.89	20
Dec-02	13,555	2.40	8.40	205	718	8,545	159.63	21
Feb-03	12,905	2.50	7.70	228	702	9,115	161.63	21
Personal loans								
Jun-00	2,202	4.69	3.48	627	465	13,368	70.05	175
Dec-00	2,622	5.04	4.73	825	775	16,381	67.72	182
Jun-01	2,839	5.85	5.44	1,243	1,157	21,248	74.40	198
Dec-01	2,662	6.20	8.20	1,440	1,905	23,233	84.25	197
Jun-02	2,797	6.40	9.30	1,628	2,365	25,432	83.88	208
Dec-02	2,480	5.60	8.60	1,378	2,116	24,601	85.31	220
Feb-03	3,004	5.80	8.30	1,469	2,102	25,330	87.46	209
Vehicles acquisition								
Jun-00	1,273	4.79	2.42	399	202	8,332	35.54	458
Dec-00	1,973	5.64	1.78	880	277	15,616	35.05	512
Jun-01	1,707	6.82	2.28	1,478	494	21,664	38.61	533

(table continued next page)

Appendix Table A4.2 *(continued)*

Date	New loans	*Delinquency rates (%)* 15 to 90 days	More than 90 days	*Delinquency* 15 to 90 days	More than 90 days	Outstanding loans[a]	Interest rate (% p.a.)[b]	Average maturity (days)
Vehicles acquisition (continued)								
Dec-01	1,825	7.90	3.10	1,950	765	24,685	38.24	516
Jun-02	1,513	7.90	3.10	2,150	844	27,214	41.51	515
Dec-02	1,708	7.60	2.90	2,047	781	26,933	46.21	517
Feb-03	1,693	7.60	3.80	2,059	1,030	27,093	48.15	514
Other assets acquisition								
Jun-00	512	11.27	8.55	242	184	2,148	84.30	116
Dec-00	756	8.90	6.58	294	217	3,303	66.54	147
Jun-01	578	6.75	5.04	242	181	3,588	64.54	158
Dec-01	720	9.30	12.00	354	457	3,810	69.59	174
Jun-02	575	9.00	13.80	345	528	3,828	66.38	174
Dec-02	858	7.70	11.40	353	522	4,579	69.08	165
Feb-03	661	8.60	11.60	405	547	4,714	70.66	160

a. End of period.
b. Average interest rates weighted by outstanding loans until May 2000 and by daily or monthly average of new loans since May 2000.
Source: Central Bank of Brazil.

Appendix Table A4.3 Brazil: Number of Finance and Leasing Companies, by State, December 2001

State	*Number of finance companies*	*Number of leasing companies*
Acre	0	0
Alagoas	0	0
Amapá	0	0
Amazonas	0	0
Bahia	1	0
Ceará	1	2
Distrito Federal	1	1
Espírito Santo	3	1
Goiás	0	0
Maranhão	0	0
Mato Grosso	0	0
Mato Grosso do Sul	0	0
Minas Gerais	2	4
Pará	0	0
Paraíba	0	0
Paraná	3	3
Pernambuco	0	0
Piauí	0	0
Rio de Janeiro	3	8
Rio Grande do Norte	0	0
Rio Grande do Sul	3	4
Rondônia	0	0
Roraima	0	0
Santa Catarina	2	1
São Paulo	20	47
Sergipe	0	0
Tocantins	0	0
Total	39	71

Source: Central Bank of Brazil.

Appendix Table A4.4a Brazil: Evolution of Leasing Industry Receivables Portfolio, by Sector, 1996–February 2003

	1996		*1997*		*1998*		*1999*
Sector	*US$ millions*	*%*	*US$ millions*	*%*	*US$ millions*	*%*	*US$ millions*
Services	4,751	47	5,289	33	3,545	25	2,208
Commerce	2,400	24	2,166	13	1,273	9	979
Industry	1,887	19	1,781	11	1,199	8	854
State-owned	25	0	182	1	101	1	60
Individuals			4,683	29	6,577	46	4,358
Other	966	10	2,013	13	1,770	12	1,168
Total	10,029	100	16,114	100	14,465	100	9,626

Source: ABEL (Brazilian Leasing Companies Association).

	2000		2001		2002		Feb 2003	
%	*US$ millions*	*%*	*US$ millions*	*%*	*US$ millions*	*%*	*US$ millions*	*%*
23	2,086	32	2,086	39	1,219	41	1,266	47
10	717	11	753	14	444	15	397	15
9	720	11	777	15	520	18	469	17
1	55	1	52	1	32	1	31	1
45	1,891	29	1,011	19	300	10	268	10
12	1,086	17	668	12	445	15	286	11
100	6,556	100	5,347	100	2,959	100	2,717	100

Appendix Table A4.4b Brazil: Evolution of Leasing Industry Outstanding Portfolio, by Type of Asset, 1996–February 2003

(US$ millions)

	1996		*1997*		*1998*		*1999*
Sector	*US$ millions*	*%*	*US$ millions*	*%*	*US$ millions*	*%*	*US$ millions*
Vehicles	5,995	69	11,295	82	13,859	84	9,405
Machines	1,366	16	1,255	9	928	6	571
Computers	726	8	756	6	1,260	8	366
Other	42	1	112	1	188	1	164
Real estate	415	5	318	2	178	1	79
Machines—operational leasing		0		0		0	
Aircraft	42	1	32	0	29	0	23
Buildings	38	0	39	0	27	0	15
Computers—operational leasing		0		0		0	
Furniture	45	1	38	0	22	0	16
Ships	3	0	4	0	3	0	2
Total	8,672	100	13,849	100	16,494	100	10,641

Source: ABEL (Brazilian Leasing Companies Association).

Appendix Table A4.4c Brazil: Evolution of Factoring Companies Portfolio, by Sector, 1993–1999

(percent)

Sector	*1993*	*1994*	*1995*	*1996*	*1997*	*1998*	*1999*
Other industries	14	15	15	21	25	30	32
Metallurgic industries	25	28	20	15	18	18	22
Commerce	11	12	10	25	21	20	18
Services	10	3	20	22	20	18	13
Chemical industries	18	20	15	8	10	7	8
Printing industry	12	10	8	5	3	4	4
Textile industry	8	10	10	3	2	2	2
Sugar–alcohol industries	0.5	1	1	0.5	0.5	0.5	0.5
Transportation	1.5	1	1	0.5	0.5	0.5	0.5
Total	100	100	100	100	100	100	100

Source: ANFAC (Brazilian Factoring Association).

	2000		2001		2002		Feb 2003	
%	*US$ millions*	*%*	*US$ millions*	*%*	*US$ millions*	*%*	*US$ millions*	*%*
88	5,751	79	3,885	70	1,661	59	1,548	57
5	726	10	919	17	682	24	688	26
3	423	6	410	7	342	12	332	12
2	266	4	186	3	50	2	42	1.6
1	66	1	56	1	10	0	24	0.9
0		0	33	1	29	1	15	0.6
0	23	0	22	0	19	1	18	0.7
0	12	0	16	0	19	1	9	0.3
0		0		0	9	0	5	0.2
0	12	0	15	0	3	0	10	0.4
0	1	0	4	0	1	0	1	0
100	7,280	100	5,543	100	2,825	100	2,692	100

Appendix Table A4.5 Brazil: Evolution of Factoring Companies, by State, 1999–2001

	Members			*Net worth (R$ millions)*			*Banking credit limit*			*Mutual members/ associates (R$ millions)*		
States	*'99*	*'00*	*'01*	*'99*	*'00*	*'01*	*'99*	*'00*	*'01*	*'99*	*'00*	*'01*
São Paulo	279	256	255	700.0	903.0	908.0	10.0	23.5	23.7	345.0	462.0	465.0
Rio Grande do Sul	79	70	74	185.0	200.0	203.0	6.0	7.0	7.8	17.5	18.0	19.0
Rio de Janeiro	66	68	79	48.0	54.0	56.0	7.0	4.0	4.9	13.0	12.0	12.5
Paraná	36	34	40	31.0	35.0	36.0	1.2	1.8	1.9	5.0	7.0	7.0
Pernambuco	36	39	40	17.0	30.0	32.5	1.8	8.0	9.0	4.5	12.0	13.0
Santa Catarina	33	38	43	30.0	38.0	39.5	1.0	9.0	9.7	3.5	4.5	4.9
Ceará/Piauí/ Maranhão	32	40	38	10.0	22.0	23.0	3.5	6.0	7.0	3.0	6.0	7.0
Bahia/Sergipe	31	26	27	2.0	1.5	1.9	0.1	0.5	0.9	0.2	0.2	0.3
Distrito Federal	27	23	23	8.0	7.0	8.2	1.0	0.8	0.9	2.0	0.3	0.3
Minas Gerais	25	22	19	17.0	23.0	26.0	3.6	20.0	21.0	5.0	12.0	13.0
Amazonas/Pará/ Rondônia	21	21	24	0.7	0.9	1.0	0.2	0.2	0.3	0.8	1.0	1.4
Mato Grosso/Mato Grosso do Sul	18	17	17	41.0	42.5	43.1	5.0	3.5	3.8	5.0	4.0	5.0
Goiás/Tocantins	17	17	16	16.0	21.5	22.6	4.0	5.0	5.7	4.0	6.0	6.5
Espírito Santo	15	18	9	0.4	2.0	2.8	0.1	0.3	0.5	2.0	3.0	3.8
Rio Grande do Norte/Paraíba	7	8	8	0.2	1.5	1.7	0.1	0.2	0.4	0.2	0.2	0.2
Alagoas	6	6	5	0.8	1.0	1.3	0.5	0.2	0.2	0.6	0.1	0.2
Total	728	703	717	1,107.1	1,382.9	1,406.4	45.0	89.9	97.5	411.3	548.2	559.1

Source: ANFAC (Brazilian Factoring Association).

Portfolio (R$ millions)			Default (%)			Employees			Client companies		
'99	'00	'01	'99	'00	'01	'99	'00	'01	'99	'00	'01
13,000	16,762	18,597	2.4	2.5	3.0	2,200	2,150	2,190	17,000	17,900	18,050
1,600	2,160	2,598	3.2	3.1	3.2	620	650	670	6,300	7,800	8,100
900	1,240	1,472	3.8	3.8	3.7	580	600	605	4,300	4,800	4,850
425	526	569	3.8	3.7	3.5	370	385	390	3,100	3,900	3,950
550	600	812	4.0	4.0	3.9	180	250	255	3,500	3,950	4,000
500	590	625	3.0	2.9	3.2	300	380	387	3,600	4,300	4,400
260	550	577	4.4	4.2	4.1	260	300	310	5,500	4,700	4,750
17	26	29	4.0	4.5	4.4	75	85	90	1,350	1,400	1,450
50	96	99	3.2	3.5	3.6	65	67	75	1,300	1,500	1,570
500	660	795	3.6	3.7	3.7	280	270	278	2,800	2,850	2,900
18	24	37	4.6	4.2	4.3	65	75	76	1,400	1,600	1,650
560	600	648	4.2	4.3	4.1	360	350	358	3,800	3,750	3,800
350	395	425	3.4	3.7	3.8	260	270	285	2,800	2,950	2,980
3	63	72	4.0	4.0	3.9	65	85	90	1,100	1,385	1,560
8	16	23	4.3	4.1	3.8	55	60	65	1,100	985	1,030
18	16	19	4.5	4.0	4.2	55	58	62	1,400	980	1,030
18,759	24,324	27,397	3.8	3.8	3.8	5,790	6,035	6,186	60,350	64,750	66,070

Appendix Table A4.6 Brazil: Ranking of Leasing Companies, February 2003

(present value of portfolio and number of contracts)

Ranking		*R$ (millions) company*	*US$ (millions)*	*Number of contracts (thousands)*	*Percent*
1	Bradesco BCN	1,379	387	32	15.4
2	Safra	1,036	291	44	11.6
3	IBM Leasing	1,018	286	1	11.4
4	Itaúleasing	733	206	126	8.2
5	BankBoston	410	115	2	4.6
6	Volkswagen	385	108	25	4.3
7	Sudameris	369	104	15	4.1
8	Hewlett-Packard	360	101	2	4.0
9	Unibanco	332	93	14	3.7
10	BB Leasing	299	84	21	3.3
11	DaimlerChrysler	254	71	5	2.8
12	Citibank	251	70	2	2.8
13	Santander	197	55	18	2.2
14	Alfa	183	51	2	2.0
15	BBV Leasing	159	45	2	1.8
16	Dibens	157	44	9	1.8
17	Panamericano	136	38	31	1.5
18	HSBC	129	36	4	1.4
19	Banrisul	119	33	7	1.3
20	Santander Banespa	116	33	9	1.3
21	Lloyds	111	31	4	1.2
22	Finasa	106	30	5	1.2
23	Compaq Financial	104	29	0	1.2
24	Cit Brasil	87	25	0	1.0
25	Finaustria	87	24	4	1.0
26	Sistema	66	18	2	0.7
27	Inter American Express	59	17	0	0.7
28	BV Leasing	58	16	6	0.7
29	Banco Finasa	40	11	8	0.4
30	Mercantil do Brasil	26	7	1	0.3
31	BMW	24	7	1	0.3
32	BMC	23	6	0	0.3
33	Banestes	22	6	2	0.2
34	GM Leasing	17	5	3	0.2
35	BIC	16	4	0	0.2
36	Banco Guanabara	16	4	0	0.2
37	Toyota	14	4	1	0.2
38	Industrial do Brasil	12	3	0	0.1
39	Banestado	11	3	0	0.1
40	Lease Plan	10	3	1	0.1

Ranking		*R$ (millions) company*	*US$ (millions)*	*Number of contracts (thousands)*	*Percent*
41	BMG	8	2	5	0.1
42	Societe	7	2	0	0.1
43	Fibra	5	1	2	0.1
44	Zogbi	3	1	0	0.0
45	Honda	1	0	0	0.0
46	BESC	1	0	0	0.0
47	BGN	0	0	0	0.0
48	NorChem	0	0	0	0.0
49	BancoCidade	0	0	0	0.0
50	BFB	0	0	0	0.0
	Total, all	8,956	2,513	416	100

Source: ABEL (Brazilian Leasing Companies Association).

Appendix Table A4.7 Brazil and Other Countries: Factoring Turnover

(US$ millions, 2000)

	Number of companies	*Domestic*	*International*	*Total*
Europe				
Austria	3	1,585	690	2,275
Belgium	7	5,500	2,500	8,000
Cyprus	3	1,300	110	1,410
Czech Republic	5	760	245	1,005
Denmark	8	2,700	1,350	4,050
Finland	4	6,915	215	7,130
France	39	48,250	4,200	52,450
Germany	15	18,660	4,823	23,483
Greece	8	1,300	200	1,500
Hungary	13	258	86	344
Ireland	6	6,000	500	6,500
Italy	45	105,000	5,000	110,000
Netherlands	7	11,500	4,400	15,900
Norway	7	4,650	310	4,960
Poland	6	2,055	30	2,085
Portugal	8	8,500	495	8,995
Spain	19	18,870	630	19,500
Sweden	15	10,160	2,150	12,310
Switzerland	2	1,000	300	1,300
Turkey	113	5,400	990	6,390
United Kingdom	70	117,700	6,070	123,770
Subtotal	435	378,705	35,678	414,383
Americas				
Argentina	5	1,700	15	1,715
Brazil	703	12,000	12	12,012
Canada	31	1,921	335	2,256
Chile	25	2,525	125	2,650
Cuba	1	105	3	108
Mexico	13	4,970	60	5,030
United States	293	116,000	4,000	120,000
Subtotal	1,114	139,671	4,578	144,249
Africa				
Morocco	2	15	30	45
South Africa	10	5,500	50	5,550
Tunisia	2	45	15	60
Subtotal	14	5,560	95	5,655
Asia				
China	3	180	32	212
Hong Kong, China	8	1,600	800	2,400

	Number of companies	*Domestic*	*International*	*Total*
Asia (continued)				
India	5	450	20	470
Israel	3	50	410	460
Japan	20	57,358	1,115	58,473
Malaysia	12	570	15	585
Singapore	15	1,800	300	2,100
Korea, Rep. of	1	0	115	115
Taiwan, China	5	2,100	1,550	3,650
Thailand	16	1,260	8	1,268
Subtotal	98	65,493	4,372	69,865
Australasia				
Australia	20	7,200	120	7,320
New Zealand	8	100	0	100
Subtotal	28	7,300	120	7,420
Total, world	1,689	596,729	44,843	641,572

Source: Factors Chain International 2001.

Appendix Table A4.8 Leasing Legal Framework in Brazil: Basic Legislation

Federal laws (Leis Federais)	
Law No. 6,099, of December 12, 1974	On the tax treatment of commercial lease operations and other measures.
Law No.7,132, of October 26, 1983	Amends Law No. 6,099, of December 12, 1974, "on the tax treatment of commercial lease operations and other measures," and Decree–Law No. 1,811, of October 27, 1980
Ordinances	
Ordinance No. 2,309, of August 28, 1996	Disciplines and consolidates norms relative to commercial lease operations.
Ordinance No. 2,465, of February 19, 1998	Amends the Regulation attached to Ordinance No. 2,309, dated August 28, 1996.
Ordinance No. 2,493/98 of May 7, 1998	Sets conditions for the transfer of credits to special purpose corporations.
Central Bank—Circulating Letters (Cartas Circulares)	
Circulating Letter No. 2,436 of June 30, 1994	Reasonability of considerations—on assets and liabilities operations subject to minimum terms performed in the financial marketplace, their respective compensations and consolidating norms in this respect.
Ministry of Finance Ordinances (Ministerio da Fazenda)	
Ordinance MF No. 564 of November 3, 1978	Income tax—on the verification of results, for tax purposes, of commercial lease operations.
Ordinance MF No. 140, of July 27, 1984	Income tax—establishes norms relative to commercial lease considerations as regards the inclusion into the net profit on the taxable period in which they were due.
Ordinance MF No. 113, of February 26, 1988	On the depreciation of goods object of commercial lease.
Normative Instructions (Secretaria da Receita Federal)	
Normative Instruction by the Secretariat of Federal Revenues No. 103, of October 17, 1984	Income tax—depreciation of used goods acquired; admitted life span.

Source: ABEL (Brazilian Leasing Companies Association).

Appendix Table A5.1 Sources of Finance for Rural Credit, 1998–2002

(R$ millions and percentage)

	1998		1999		2000		2001		2002	
Sources	*Total*	*%*	*Total*	*%*	*Total*	*%*	*Total*	*%*	*Total*	*%*
National Treasury	185.0	1.7	13.1	0.1	2.6	0.0	289.1	1.6	376.6	1.7
Obligatory resources	4,534.5	40.7	4,747.7	40.3	7,137.6	51.8	10,577.9	59.0	11,832.6	52.7
BNDES/FINAME	452.3	4.1	593.0	5.0	779.6	5.7	1,082.2	6.0	1,623.5	7.2
INCRA	127.4	1.1	34.5	0.3	4.3	0.0	273.0	1.5	214.8	1.0
Rural savings	1,449.5	13.0	2,216.8	18.8	1,976.2	14.3	1,851.9	10.3	2,827.7	12.6
Special remunerated deposits	0.0	0.0	0.0	0.0	1.4	0.0	—	—	—	—
FAT (Workers' Fund)	1,765.4	15.9	1,914.5	16.2	1,751.2	12.7	1,789.4	10.0	2,283.5	10.2
Commodity funds	5.8	0.1	6.6	0.1	7.7	0.1	15.3	0.1	13.0	0.1
Freely allocated resources	520.2	4.7	578.0	4.9	651.8	4.7	722.4	4.0	1,159.4	5.2
State governments	19.9	0.2	14.9	0.1	15.3	0.1	13.3	0.1	26.5	0.1
Extramarket Fund	124.1	1.1	0.3	0.0	0.0	0.0	—	—	—	—
External resources	318.7	2.9	168.0	1.4	150.2	1.1	31.9	0.2	22.4	0.1
FUNCAFÉ	617.3	5.5	571.4	4.8	296.4	2.2	194.7	1.1	501.8	2.2
FNE[a]	342.7	3.1	435.4	3.7	190.3	1.4	130.3	0.7	170.9	0.8
FNO[b]	138.1	1.2	323.9	2.7	409.3	3.0	323.5	1.8	313.2	1.4
FCO[c]	302.8	2.7	115.8	1.0	206.8	1.5	630.6	3.5	1,060.5	4.7
Other sources	230.1	2.1	52.3	0.4	198.8	1.4	16.5	0.1	17.0	0.1
Total	11,133.8	100.0	11,786.2	100.0	13,779.5	100.0	17,942.1	100.0	22,443.3	100.0

a. Constitutional Fund for the Northeast.
b. Constitutional Fund for the North.
c. Constitutional Fund for the Central–West.
Source: Central Bank of Brazil, 1998–2002, *Annual Report on Rural Credit.*

Appendix Table A5.1a Sources of Finance for Rural Credit, 2002

(R$ millions and percentage)

			Credit operations not linked to			
Sources	*Total*	*%*	*Financing*	*%*	*Invest-ment*	*%*
National Treasury	376.6	1.7	2.8	0.0	78.1	2.0
Obligatory resources	11,832.6	52.7	7,730.9	67.7	685.6	17.7
BNDES/FINAME	1,623.5	7.2			1,611.9	41.6
INCRA	214.8	1.0				
Rural savings	2,827.7	12.6	2,399.3	21.0	4.1	0.1
Special remunerated deposits						
FAT (Workers' Fund)	2,283.5	10.2	35.1	0.3	105.4	2.7
Commodity funds	13.0	0.1	12.7	0.1	0.2	0.0
Freely allocated resources	1,159.4	5.2	617.8	5.4	90.0	2.3
State governments	26.5	0.1	0.7	0.0	25.7	0.7
Extramarket Fund						
External resources	22.4	0.1	14.7	0.1	6.0	0.2
FUNCAFE	501.8	2.2	471.7	4.1		
FNE	170.9	0.8	15.8	0.1	67.6	1.7
FNO	313.2	1.4	55.9	0.5	257.3	6.6
FCO	1,060.5	4.7	40.5	0.4	947.0	24.4
Other sources	17.0	0.1	17.0	0.1		
Total	22,443.3	100.0	11,414.8	100.0	3,879.0	100.0

Note: See abbreviations list for spelling of agricultural support programs and organizations in note *a* and source for appendix tables 5.1a–e.

a. Includes resources allocated to PRODECER (I and II), to PROEST, to PROINAP, and to Cacauicultura or cocoa bean production.

Source: Central Bank of Brazil, Defin/Diate/Susep.

special programs		*Credit operations linked to special programs*							
Commercial-ization	%	*PRONAF*	%	*PROCERA*	%	*PROGER*	%	*Others*[a]	%
0.1	0.0	294.6	12.2					1.0	7.6
3,269.9	81.4	146.3	6.1					0.0	0.0
								11.6	92.3
				214.8	100.0				
424.3	10.6								
		1,654.4	68.5	488.6	100.0				
0.1	0.0								
292.3	7.3	159.2	6.6						
1.7	0.0								
30.2	0.8								
0.1	0.0	87.3	3.6						
		73.0	3.0						
4,018.6	100.0	2,414.9	100.0	214.8	100.0	488.6	100.0	12.6	100.0

Appendix Table A5.1b Sources of Finance for Rural Credit, 2001

(R$ millions and percentage)

			Credit operations not linked to			
Sources	*Total*	*%*	*Financing*	*%*	*Invest-ment*	*%*
National Treasury	289.1	1.6	3.0	0.0	32.2	1.1
Obligatory resources	10,577.9	59.0	6,263.2	71.3	710.9	25.3
BNDES/FINAME	1,082.2	6.0	0.1	0.0	989.3	35.2
INCRA	273.0	1.5				
Rural savings	1,851.9	10.3	1,802.1	20.5	0.6	0.0
Special remunerated deposits						
FAT (Workers' Fund)	1,789.4	10.0	27.3	0.3	29.6	1.1
Commodity funds	15.3	0.1	14.5	0.2	0.7	0.0
Freely allocated resources	722.4	4.0	396.7	4.5	90.6	3.2
State governments	13.3	0.1	0.1	0.0	13.2	0.5
Extramarket Fund						
External resources	31.9	0.2	11.7	0.1	20.3	0.7
FUNCAFE	194.7	1.1	189.2	2.2	5.5	0.2
FNE	130.3	0.7	8.5	0.1	62.2	2.2
FNO	323.5	1.8	43.1	0.5	280.4	10.0
FCO	630.6	3.5	4.8	0.1	573.6	20.4
Other sources	16.5	0.1	16.5	0.2		
Total	17,942.1	100.0	8,780.8	100.0	2,809.2	100.0

a. Includes resources allocated to PRODECER (I and II), to PROEST, to PROINAP, and to Cacauicultura.

Source: Central Bank of Brazil, Defin/Diate/Susep.

special programs		*Credit operations linked to special programs*							
Commercial-ization	*%*	*PRONAF*	*%*	*PROCERA*	*%*	*PROGER*	*%*	*Others*[a]	*%*
0.0	0.0	253.8	11.5						
3,412.9	93.9	190.9	8.6						
								92.7	98.9
				273.0	99.9				
49.1	1.4								
		1,593.9	72.1			138.6	100.0	0.0	0.0
0.1	0.0								
173.5	4.8	61.6	2.8						
		59.3	2.7	0.3	0.1			0.0	0.0
		51.1	2.3					1.1	1.1
3,635.6	100.0	2,210.7	100.0	273.4	100.0	138.6	100.0	93.8	100.0

Appendix Table A5.1c Sources of Finance for Rural Credit, 2000

(R$ millions and percentage)

			Credit operations not linked to			
Sources	*Total*	*%*	*Financing*	*%*	*Investment*	*%*
National Treasury	2.6	0.0	2.1	0.0	0.5	0.0
Obligatory resources	7,137.6	51.8	4,400.3	61.6	368.9	17.1
BNDES/FINAME	779.6	5.7			745.0	34.6
INCRA	4.3	0.0				
Rural savings	1,976.2	14.3	1,893.7	26.5	0.3	0.0
Special remunerated deposits	1.4	0.0				
FAT (Workers' Fund)	1,751.2	12.7			186.4	8.6
Commodity funds	7.7	0.1	7.5	0.1	0.2	0.0
Freely allocated resources	0.0	0.0	0.0	0.0		
State governments	651.8	4.7	250.0	3.5	97.0	4.5
Extramarket Fund	15.3	0.1	3.6	0.1	11.7	0.5
External resources	150.2	1.1	120.0	1.7	30.2	1.4
FUNCAFE	296.4	2.2	296.4	4.1		
FNE	190.3	1.4	14.7	0.2	142.1	6.6
FNO	409.3	3.0	48.3	0.7	327.5	15.2
FCO	206.8	1.5	1.4	0.0	158.3	7.3
Other sources	198.8	1.4	104.9	1.5	88.2	4.1
Total	13,779.5	100.0	7,142.9	100.0	2,156.2	100.0

a. Includes resources allocated to PRODECER (I and II), to PROEST, to PROINAP, and to Cacauicultura.

Source: Central Bank of Brazil, Defin/Diate/Susep.

special programs		*Credit operations linked to special programs*							
Commercial-ization	%	*PRONAF*	%	*PROCERA*	%	*PROGER*	%	*Others*[a]	%
2,193.6	86.8	174.7	9.4						
								34.6	99.8
				4.3	70.7				
82.2	3.3								
1.4	0.1								
0.0	0.0	1,515.8	81.3			48.9	100.0	0.1	0.2
242.9	9.6	61.9	3.3						
		31.8	1.7	1.8	29.3				
		33.6	1.8						
		47.1	2.5						
5.7	0.2								
2,525.8	100.0	1,864.9	100.0	6.1	100.0	48.9	100.0	34.7	100.0

Appendix Table A5.1d Sources of Finance for Rural Credit, 1999

(R$ millions and percentage)

			Credit operations not linked to			
Sources	*Total*	*%*	*Financing*	*%*	*Invest-ment*	*%*
National Treasury	13.1	0.1	2.8	0.0	10.4	0.8
Obligatory resources	4,747.7	40.3	3,126.4	50.4	230.3	18.1
BNDES/FINAME	593.0	5.0			211.3	16.6
INCRA	34.5	0.3	11.3	0.2	23.2	1.8
Rural savings	2,216.8	18.8	1,964.5	31.7	0.0	0.0
Special remunerated deposits						
FAT (Workers' Fund)	1,914.5	16.2	88.4	1.4	87.9	6.9
Commodity funds	0.3	0.0	0.3	0.0		
Freely allocated resources	6.6	0.1	6.4	0.1	0.2	0.0
State governments	578.0	4.9	225.8	3.6	66.7	5.2
Extramarket Fund	14.9	0.1	1.3	0.0	13.6	1.1
External resources	168.0	1.4	124.1	2.0	34.9	2.7
FUNCAFE	571.4	4.8	571.4	9.2	0.0	0.0
FNE	435.4	3.7	8.6	0.1	207.7	16.3
FNO	323.9	2.7	31.5	0.5	292.4	22.9
FCO	115.8	1.0	1.3	0.0	87.7	6.9
Other sources	52.3	0.4	36.5	0.6	9.1	0.7
Total	11,786.2	100.0	6,200.6	100.0	1,275.2	100.0

a. Includes resources allocated to PRODECER (I and II), to PROEST, to PROINAP, and to Cacauicultura.

Source: Central Bank of Brazil, Defin/Diate/Susep.

special programs		*Credit operations linked to special programs*							
Commercial-ization	*%*	*PRONAF*	*%*	*PROCERA*	*%*	*PROGER*	*%*	*Others*[a]	*%*
1,216.5	68.7	174.6	9.8						
								381.7	94.5
252.3	14.3								
0.4	0.0	1,447.9	81.5			289.9	100.0	0.0	0.0
285.6	16.1								
8.9	0.5								
0.0	0.0	149.9	8.4	69.2	100.0			0.0	0.0
		4.5	0.3					22.2	5.5
6.8	0.4								
1,770.4	100.0	1,777.0	100.0	69.2	100.0	289.9	100.0	404.0	100.0

Appendix Table A5.1e Sources of Finance for Rural Credit, 1998

(R$ millions and percentage)

Sources	Total	%	Credit operations not linked to			
			Financing	%	Investment	%
National Treasury	185.0	1.7	1.6	0.0	0.3	0.0
Obligatory resources	4,534.5	40.7	2,948.6	51.2	310.5	20.5
BNDES/FINAME	452.3	4.1	0.0	0.0	416.2	27.5
INCRA	127.4	1.1				
Rural savings	1,449.5	13.0	1,447.5	25.1	2.0	0.1
Special remunerated deposits						
FAT (Workers' Fund)	1,765.4	15.9	35.8	0.6	94.6	6.3
Commodity funds	124.1	1.1	124.1	2.2		
Freely allocated resources	5.8	0.1	4.8	0.1	0.6	0.0
State governments	520.2	4.7	266.1	4.6	61.5	4.1
Extramarket Fund	19.9	0.2	7.3	0.1	12.6	0.8
External resources	318.7	2.9	236.0	4.1	58.8	3.9
FUNCAFE	617.3	5.5	617.3	10.7	0.0	0.0
FNE	342.7	3.1	7.7	0.1		
FNO	138.1	1.2	16.3	0.3	121.8	8.1
FCO	302.8	2.7	0.1	0.0	253.0	16.7
Other sources	230.1	2.1	44.1	0.8	180.9	12.0
Total	11,133.8	100.0	5,757.3	100.0	1,512.8	100.0

a. Includes resources allocated to PRODECER (I and II), to PROEST, to PROINAP, and to Cacauicultura.

Source: Central Bank of Brazil, Defin/Diate/Susep.

special programs		*Credit operations linked to special programs*							
Commercial-ization	%	*PRONAF*	%	*PROCERA*	%	*PROGER*	%	*Others*[a]	%
178.5	11.8			0.0	0.0			4.6	1.3
1,117.5	73.6	157.8	11.7						
								36.1	10.0
				127.4	59.7				
0.1	0.0	1,104.8	82.2	0.0	0.0	427.3	100.0	102.8	28.6
0.5	0.0								
192.6	12.7								
23.9	1.6								
0.6	0.0	81.5	6.1	36.6	17.2			216.3	60.1
		0.5	0.0	49.2	23.1				
5.1	0.3								
1,518.8	100.0	1,344.6	100.0	213.3	100.0	427.3	100.0	359.8	100.0

Appendix Table A5.2 The Brazilian Rural Credit System: Specific Lines of Credit for Agricultural Investment

Program	*Coverage*	*Purpose*
PROSOLO	National	Agricultural productivity
PROLEITE	National	Modernize milk production
PROPASTO	National	Recover pastures
FRUTICULTURA	National	Upgrade quality/ competitiveness
CAJUCULTURA	National	Cashew agribusiness
OVINOCAPRINOCULTURA	National	Livestock production
VITIVINICULTURA	South	Wine/grape juice production
APICULTURA	National	Honey production
AQÜICULTURA	National	Aquaculture production
Sistematização de Várzeas	Rio Grande do Sul	Systemizing cultivated plains
FLORICULTURA[b]	National	Horticulture production/ quality
Armazens na Propriedades Rurais[b]	National	Storage facilities
Subtotal		
MODERFROTA	National	Modernize tractor fleet
Total		

Note: n.a. = not applicable.
a. Upper limits for 2002 crop year.
b. New programs for 2002.
Source: Ministry of Agriculture.

Budget (R$m)	*Actual (R$m)*	*Usage (%)*	*Max. per client*[a]	*Interest rate*	*Max. term*	*Grace period*
300.0	65.1	21.7	80,000	8.75	5	2
200.0	27.1	13.6	60,000	8.75	5	2
400.0	96.4	24.1	150,000	8.75	5	2
100.0	5.9	5.9	100,000	8.75	8	3
50.0	2.3	4.6	40,000	8.75	8	3
70.0	4.9	7.0	40,000	8.75	8	3
20.0	3.9	19.5	40,000	8.75	8	3
20.0	1.2	6.0	20,000	8.75	5	2
50.0	2.2	4.3	80,000	8.75	5	2
50.0	0.4	0.7	40,000	8.75	5	2
			50,000	8.75	5	2
			100,000	8.75	8	3
1,260.0	209.3	16.6				
1,627.0	1,484.0	91.2	n.a.	8.75–10.75	6–8	n.a.
2,887.0	1,693.3	58.7				

Appendix Table A5.3 Rural Financing, by Source of Resources, 1985–2002

(percent)

Source of resources[a]	*'85*	*'86*	*'87*	*'88*	*'89*	*'90*	*'91*
National Treasury	64.0	64.9	37.3	24.5	24.0	26.7	24.2
Obligatory resources	32.4	24.6	34.3	35.8	14.5	27.4	22.4
Rural savings			22.6	36.2	51.6	20.0	32.3
Free resources					7.8	19.9	10.3
Constitutional funds					0.8	4.5	3.2
State government resources					0.3	0.1	0.1
FAT (Workers' Fund)							
FAE (Extramarket Fund)							
FUNCAFE							
Commodities Fund							
BNDES/FINAME							
INCRA/PROCERA							
External resources—rural							
Other sources	3.7	10.6	5.8	3.4	1.1	1.4	7.5
Total	100	100	100	100	100	100	100

a. Resources = financing + investment + commercialization.

Source: Central Bank of Brazil.

'92	'93	'94	'95	'96	'97	'98	'99	'00	'01	'02
23.0	26.7	27.1	19.7	3.5	1.5	1.7	0.1			1.7
18.7	11.0	11.6	13.1	16.9	44.9	40.7	41.7	54.6	59.1	52.7
45.5	43.2	34.9	36.1	9.1	8.4	13.0	19.5	15.4	10.5	12.6
6.8	11.7	15.9	16.3	8.1	6.0	4.7	5.1	4.8	3.0	5.2
3.2	5.5	5.0	9.0	14.9	5.6	7.0	5.8	5.4	5.9	6.9
0.1	0.1	0.3	0.4	0.3	0.2	0.2	0.1	0.1		0.1
				22.0	18.4	15.9	15.9	8.7	9.8	10.2
				13.9	6.7	1.1				
					3.6	5.5	5.0	2.3	1.1	2.2
					0.1	0.1	0.1	0.1		0.1
					3.4	4.1	4.7	6.0	5.6	7.2
					0.5	1.1	0.3			1.0
						2.9	1.5	1.2		0.1
2.8	1.7	5.2	5.4	11.4	0.7	2.1	0.4	1.3	5.0	0.1
100	100	100	100	100	100	100	100	100	100	100

Appendix Table A5.4 Behavior of Rural Credit Interest Rates: Controlled Resources, Working Capital

Period	*Interest rate (% p.a.)*	*IGP*[a] *(% p.a.)*	*Real interest rate*[b] *(% p.a.)*
1995/96	16.00	14.58	1.24
1996/97	12.00	7.68	4.01
1997/98	9.50	3.67	5.62
1997/98–PRONAF	6.50		2.73
1998/99	8.75	10.41	–1.50
1998/99–PRONAF	5.75		–4.22
1999/2000	8.75	16.68	–6.80
1999/2000–PRONAF	5.75		–9.37
2000/2001	8.75	13.28	–4.00
2000/2001–PRONAF	4.00	—	–8.19

Note: — = not available. The following rural credit resources are considered 'controlled': (a) Obligatory, based on the sight deposits of financial institutions; (b) Official Credit Operations (OOC) under the supervision of the Ministry of Finance; (c) Rural savings (*caderneta de poupança*); (d) Resources from the Worker's Fund (FAT) and the Investment Fund 'Extra–Mercado,' when invested in designated operations for tax equalization; and (e) Others specified by the National Monetary Council.

a. Obtained by using July's IGP–DI (General Price Index–Internal Availability) from each year in relation to June from the previous year.

b. Real interest rate is equal to $[(1 + i)/(1 + p)] - 1$, where i is the nominal interest rate and p is the variation in the price index in the year.

Source: Central Bank of Brazil.

Appendix Table A5.5 Brazil: Direction of Rural Credit Flows, 1998–2002

(R$ billions and percentage)

			Credit operations not linked to special programs						Credit operations linked to special programs							
Year	Total	%	Financing	%	Investment	%	Commercialization	%	PRONAF	%	PROCERA	%	PROGER	%	Others[a]	%
2002	22.4	100	11.4	50.9	3.9	17.3	4.0	17.9	2.4	10.8	0.2	1.0	0.5	2.2	0.0	0.1
2001	17.9	100	8.8	48.9	2.8	15.7	3.6	20.3	2.2	12.3	0.3	1.5	0.1	0.8	0.1	0.5
2000	13.8	100	7.1	51.8	2.2	15.6	2.5	18.3	1.9	13.5	0.0	0.0	0.0	0.4	0.0	0.3
1999	11.8	100	6.2	52.6	1.3	10.8	1.8	15.0	1.8	15.1	0.1	0.6	0.3	2.5	0.4	3.4
1998	11.1	100	5.8	51.7	1.5	13.6	1.5	13.6	1.3	12.1	0.2	1.9	0.4	3.8	0.4	3.2

a. Includes resources allocated to PRODECER (I and II), to PROEST, to PROINAP, and to Cacauicultura.

Source: Central Bank of Brazil.

Appendix Table A5.6 Distribution of Rural Credit, by Purpose and Lending Institution, 2000

Lending bank/capital	*Credit (R$m)*	*Share (%)*	*Contracts ('000s)*	*Share (%)*
Federal banks	6,896.3	50.05	1,021.1	75.68
Working capital	5,094.5	36.97	792.3	58.72
Investment capital	1,482.3	10.76	226.6	16.80
Marketing credit	319.5	2.32	2.2	0.16
State banks	316.8	2.30	28.7	2.13
Working capital	224.0	1.63	22.7	1.68
Investment capital	55.2	0.40	5.2	0.39
Marketing credit	37.6	0.27	0.8	0.06
Private banks	5,856.5	42.50	204.6	15.16
Working capital	3,107.0	22.55	163.6	12.13
Investment capital	727.9	5.28	26.6	1.97
Marketing credit	2,021.6	14.67	14.4	1.07
Rural credit co-ops	709.9	5.15	94.8	7.03
Working capital	493.3	3.58	72.1	5.34
Investment capital	69.5	0.50	11.5	0.85
Marketing credit	147.1	1.07	11.1	0.82
Total	13,779.5	100.00	1,349.2	100.00
Working capital	8,918.8	64.73	1,050.7	77.88
Investment capital	2,334.9	16.94	269.9	20.00
Marketing credit	2,525.8	18.33	28.5	2.11

Source: Central Bank of Brazil 2000a.

Appendix Table A5.7 Brazil: Interest Rates for Different Programs of Rural Finance, 2001

Description		Financial charges
Programs/special lines of credit	*Index*	*Effective interest rate*
Rural credit—controlled resources—MCR 2–4–3–a.		8.75% p.a.
Rural credit—noncontrolled resources—MCR 2–4–3–b.		Agreed independently
Rural credit—rural savings—MCR 2–4.	TR[a]	Agreed independently
Rural credit—official credit operations—investment—MCR 2–4–3–c.		To be established with the disclosure of lines of credit
Prodecer III—Res. 2,816, from Feb. 22, 2001.		10.75% p.a.
Banco da Terra—financing up to R$15,000.00—Res. 2,728, from June 14, 2000.		6% p.a., with early payback bonus of 50%
Banco da Terra—financing above R$15,000.00 and up to R$30,000.00—Res. 2,728, from June 14, 2000.		8% p.a., with early payback bonus of 50%
Banco da Terra—financing above R$30,000.00 and up to R$40,000.00—Res. 2,728, from June 14, 2000.		10% p.a., with early payback bonus of 50%
FUNCAFÉ (financing, harvest, precommercialization and CPR)—Res. 2,865, from July 3, 2001, 2,831 from April 25, 2001, 2,868, from July 4, 2001 and 2,871 from July 3, 2001.		9.5% p.a.
Daily adjustments and premiums financing program in the futures and options market, supporting resources from FUNCAFÉ—Res. 2,898, from October 31, 2001.	TJLP[b]	3% p.a.
Recuperation program for Bahian cacao farming—Res. 2,887, from August 31, 2001.		8.75% small and medium producers, with early payback bonus of 15%; 0.75% large producers, with early payback bonus of 15%

(table continued next page)

Appendix Table A5.7 *(continued)*

Description		*Financial charges*
Programs/special lines of credit	*Index*	*Effective interest rate*
Debt renegotiation—securitization—Res. 2,919, from Dec. 26, 2001.		3% p.a. + *equivalência em produto*
Debt renegotiation—PESA—up to R$500,000.00—Res. 2,471, from Feb. 26, 1998, and Art. 3 of Res. 2,579, from Dec. 23, 1998 and Res. 2,904, from Nov. 21, 2001.	IGP–M;[c] limited to 9.5% p.a.	3% p.a.
Debt renegotiation—PESA—larger than R$500.000,00 and up to R$1,000,000.00—Res. 2,471, from Feb. 26, 1998, and Art. 3 of Res. 2,579, from Dec. 23, 1998 and Res. 2,904, from Nov. 21, 2001.	IGP–M;[c] limited to 9.5% p.a.	4% p.a.
Debt renegotiation—PESA—larger than R$1,000,000.00—Res. 2,471, from Feb. 26, 1998, and Art. 3 of Res. 2,579, from Dec. 23, 1998; Res. 2,904, from Nov. 21, 2001; and Res. 2,919, from Dec. 26, 2001.		5% p.a.
Debt renegotiation—mini and small producers—financing operations and investment contracted in the period of June 20, 1995 to Dec. 31, 1997—Res. 2,765, from Aug. 10, 2000.		Fees originally agreed (up to 09.11.99)
Debt renegotiation—mini and small producers—financing operations and investment contracted in the period of June 20, 1995 to Dec. 31, 1997—Res. 2,765, from Aug. 10, 2000.		3% p.a. (after 10.11.99)
RECOOP—investment, debts with financial institutions, suppliers, and collaborators, receivables from collaborators, taxes and workers fees—Res. 2,681, from Dec. 21, 1999 to Res. 2,903, from Nov. 21, 2001.	IGP–DI (previous month),[d] limited to 9.5% p.a.	4% p.a.
RECOOP—working capital—Res. 2,681, from Dec. 21, 1999.		8.75% p.a.
PRONAF—financing—MCR 10–4–1.		4% p.a.

PRONAF—investment—Group A—MCR 10–5–3–c.		1.15% p.a.
PRONAF—investment—Group B—MCR 10–5–5–b.		1% p.a.
PRONAF—investment—Group C—MCR 10–5–6–b.		4% p.a. with early payback bonus of 25% for each payment made before the due date
PRONAF—investment—Group D—MCR 10–5–7–b.		4% p.a. with early payback bonus of 25% % for each payment made before the due date
PROGER Rural—investment—Res. 2,953, from July 3, 2001.		8.75 % p.a.
Programs supported with resources administered by BNDES	*Index*	*Effective interest rate*
Special Agricultural FINAME—acquisition or maintenance/ recuperation of machines, tractors, harvesters, equipment and agricultural implements—Res. 2,854, from July 3, 2001.		11.95% p.a.
MODERFROTA— income less than R$250.000,00—Res. 2,877, from July 26, 2001.		8.75% p.a.
MODERFROTA—income equal to or greater than R$250.000,00—Res. 2,877, from July 26, 2001.		10.75% p.a.
National Recuperation Program for Degraded Pastures—PROPASTO—Res. 2,856, from July 3, 2001.		8.75% p.a.
Support Program for the Development of Tilapia, Shrimp, and Shellfish Production—Res. 2,859, from July 3, 2001.		8.75% p.a.
Support Program for Horticulture—PROFRUTA—Res. 2,860, from July 3, 2001.		8.75% p.a.

(table continued next page)

Appendix Table A5.7 *(continued)*

Description		*Financial charges*
Programs supported with resources administered by BNDES	*Index*	*Effective interest rate*
Support Program for the Development of Viticulture—PRODEVINHO—Res. 2,865, from July 3, 2001.		8.75% p.a.
Development Program for Ovine/Caprine Raising—PRODECAP—Res. 2,861, from July 3, 2001.		8.75% p.a.
Development Program for Cashew farming—PROCAJU—Res. 2,862, from July 3, 2001.		8.75% p.a.
Development Program for Apiculture—PRODAMEL—Res. 2,858, from July 3, 2001.		8.75% p.a.
Sustained Development Program for Horticulture—PRODEFLOR—Res. 2,866, from July 3, 2001.		8.75% p.a.
Incentive Program for the Construction and Modernization of Storage Units on Rural Properties—PROAZEM—RES. 2,867, from July 3, 2001.		8.75 % p.a.
PROLEITE—Res. 2,857, from July 3, 2001.		8.75 % p.a.
PROSOLO—Res. 2,855, from July 3, 2001.		8.75% p.a.
Constitutional funds for the financing of the North, Northeast, and Central–West	These are not fixed by the National Monetary Council (CMN)	

a. TR = referential interest rate.
b. TJLP = long-term interest rate.
c. IGP–DI = general price index–internal availability.
d. IGP–M = general price index–average.
Source: Central Bank of Brazil, 2001, *Annual Report on Rural Credit*.

Endnotes

Chapter 1

1. World Bank 2002f. The Millennium Development Goals outlined in this document have been embraced by the World Bank, the community of the United Nations, and the government of Brazil.

2. The most recent census numbers (end-2000) do not show a significant change in the Gini coefficient. This is consistent with cross-country studies showing the persistence of Gini coefficients over time.

3. Extreme poverty is defined to include persons living in households with per capita income of less than R$65 per month. At this extreme, Brazil had a poverty headcount in 1999 of 22.6 percent (see World Bank [2001a]).

4. Discussions of the association between growth and poverty reduction may be found in Dollar and Kraay (2001). See World Bank (2001d) for a discussion of this issue. The discussion of the association between growth and the financial system can be traced through King and Levine (1993); Rajan and Zingales (1998); and Levine, Loayza, and Beck (1999). See also the IMF working paper by Holden and Prokopenko (2001) for a well-documented survey of the literature.

5. The fiscal costs of banking crises have been as much as 50 percent of GDP in the 1999 Indonesia crisis (World Bank 2001h). See also Honohan and Klingebiel (2000) and Caprio and Klingebiel (1996).

6. Using a measure of financial assets as constructed in table 1.2 for 1999/2000.

7. In December 2002, there were 58.3 million savings accounts and 45.6 million current accounts in Brazil's banks, according to data maintained by the deposit insurance fund, Fundo Garantidor de Créditos (FGC). FEBRABAN (Federação Brasileira dos Bancos), the association of Brazil's banks, pointed out that estimates for current account numbers could be higher, because FGC excludes accounts in deficit. Assuming that some persons have only a current account while others have only a savings account, the figure of 58.3 is thus a lower bound on the total number of bank account holders.

8. Financial exclusion is not a problem of emerging economies alone. Even today (2003), the Federal Reserve estimates that almost 13 percent of families in the United States do not have a checking account, and that almost 60 percent of that group are low income, nonwhite or Hispanic, or both. According to one source, an estimated 8 percent of the population is 'unbanked' in England and Wales and 15 percent for Scotland as a whole. In another investigation, HM Treasury of the United Kingdom reported in 1999 that approximately 1.5 million U.K. households use no financial services. An estimated one in every six adults in Britain, representing up to 15 percent of households, have no current account and

hence no access to money transmission services. Formal saving is largely nonexistent among low-income people. Between 32 percent and 37 percent of people over the age of 16 have no savings (How People on Low Incomes Manage Their Finances, Economic and Social Research Council seminar, Westminster, December 2002). Financial exclusion is also a problem across transitional countries. A third of all Hungarian households do not have a banking relationship, including a quarter of all households in Budapest and 45 percent in outlying villages (Stegman 2003). By these standards, Brazil's achievement of bank accounts for at least a third of its population, which implies a much higher proportion of families with bank accounts, is far from insignificant, especially in view of its income distribution, albeit low compared with developed countries.

9. The microeconomic underpinnings of the welfare implications of improved access to financial intermediation are discussed in annex 1.1, which points out that intermediation enables intertemporal choices in consumption and investment for the individual; allows the determination of the cost of capital, thus helping guide investment to its most productive use; and permits the social reallocation of savings from low- to high-productivity uses, thus raising social welfare.

10. The role of savings and borrowing in protecting consumption against unexpected shocks, first discussed by Milton Friedman (1957a) in the 'permanent income hypothesis,' has since been extensively tested empirically, as discussed in Bond and Townsend (1996).

11. The 'life cycle' hypothesis as an explanation for savings and borrowing behavior was discussed in Ando, Modigliani, and Brumberg in a series of articles in the 1950s and 1960s. See Mayer (1972) and Romer (1996) for overviews.

12. These difficulties, referred to as problems of 'moral hazard' and 'asymmetric information,' have been extensively discussed by economists. Besley (1994) provided a survey.

13. Such theories of 'credit rationing' have been discussed, for example, by Stiglitz and Weiss (1981) and Williamson (1986). Besley (1994) and Morduch (1999) discussed this specifically in the case of communities such as small farmers and microfinance providers, and Bond and Townsend (1996) raised the possibility of such rationing with regard to minority communities in the inner city of Chicago.

14. For example, a discussion of these issues in the context of South Africa may be found at the South African Banker's Institute's website. See "Extending Appropriate Financial Services to Low-Income Communities" at http://www.ahi.co.za/current/.

15. Morduch (1999) described the increasing interest in microfinance as a vehicle for addressing the needs of the underserved.

16. Housing finance issues, also investigated during the study, have been omitted from this report because of their detailed treatment in a parallel World Bank study (2002d).

17. Some evidence in this regard is presented in Padilla and Requejo (2000) and Galindo and Micco (2001).

18. This issue was studied extensively in three consecutive Central Bank reports on interest rate spreads, *Juros e Spreads Bancário no Brasil,* 1999–2001. A partial analysis of some specific factors affecting spreads is undertaken in chapter 6 of this study.

19. In the United Kingdom, for example, bank credit to regions broadly indicated as 'deprived,' based on a standardized index of deprivation, must now be documented (see chapter 7 of this study).

20. This section is based largely on Beck (2002).

21. Bank mergers or purchases, especially with regard to the privatization of state banks under the Programa de Incentivo à Redução do Setor Público Estadual na Atividade Bancária (Reduction of State Level Participation in Banking Activities; PROES) scheme, were frequently conditional on the maintenance of branch service provision.

22. Statistics for microfinance entities do not include those outside the formal financial system (chapter 2).

23. Meanwhile, there was an increase in the numbers of municipalities, from 5,011 in 1994 to 5,597 by 1998 and 5,658 by 2002.

24. These changes in composition are also associated with changes in the delivery of different types of financial services. Although public banks had a low share (one-third) in banking system net worth in 1996, they accounted for almost 60 percent of credit operations and more than 60 percent of deposits in that year. By December 2001, the public bank share of system net worth had declined to 16 percent and their share in credits to 25 percent, but they still accounted for 43 percent of all deposits (appendix table A1.4). Foreign bank shares in credit and net worth grew from around 10 percent to some 31 percent over the same period.

25. It is possible that there have been policy-driven pressures to maintain at least one service outpost in each municipality, and these pressures dominate other considerations. Also on economic grounds, the presence or absence of a branch is linked to overall GDP. However, that branch density is linked to per capita income may not be surprising. An area may need to have a certain minimum critical economic mass (as represented by GDP) in client potential to make it worth installing a bank branch there, but decisions to further increase bank presence may depend more on average incomes and also, as discussed below, on the entire pattern of income distribution.

26. Access measured by branch density is an exception, but here the overall association is weak.

27. As we shall see in chapter 3, this is not a surprising finding; private banks have a large involvement in the small loan market that could be associated with densely populated and poorer urban areas.

28. At the 1 percent level, using chi-squared tests of differences.

29. This part of the study was undertaken in partnership with a team from the Instituto de Pesquisa Econômica Aplicada (IPEA), the University of Niteroi in Brazil, and a group of Brazilian advisors. Data were collected and tabulated by the firm Sensus of Belo Horizonte.

30. The individual rather than the household was chosen for a combination of reasons: financial characteristics are not common to all household members, and there are variations across the age spectrum in terms of financial access as well as financial needs. Some questions, especially those relating to credit, depend on individual characteristics. See Kinnon Scott in Grosh and Glewwe (2000), chapter 21, on the reasons for selecting the individual as the point of data collection.

31. The cities in the survey are Belém, Belo Horizonte, Brasília, Curitiba, Fortaleza, Goiânia, Pôrto Alegre, Recife, Rio de Janeiro, Salvador, and São Paulo. The sample of cities, which includes locations in each region and cities of a range of sizes, follows the selection used for the periodic consumer expenditure surveys (Pesquisa de Orçamentos Familiares; POF) of the Instituto Brasileira de Geografia e Estatistica (IBGE), Brazil's statistical institute, and is based on the IBGE Census 2000 results for the distribution of population by city. The advantage of this procedure was that a ready-made, existing sampling frame was available and known to be representative. The sample was constructed on a probabilistic basis for census sectors and for domiciles within the sector, with a requirement of a minimum of 10 interviews per city and quotas for sex and age. In designing the questionnaire, efforts were made to build on financial data collected in previous surveys in Brazil (in particular the PPV, Pesquisa Sobre Padrões de Vida, or household survey), and also to draw on ongoing parallel efforts under way in the World Bank for Mexico and Colombia. Additional details of sample construction, frequencies, or other sample results are available from the task team at the World Bank.

32. Other forms of 'unbundling' could be used. For example, the typology used in a recent study, conducted by the National Community Investment Fund (NCIF) in the United States, distinguishes between 'first-order' or prior needs to help financial access (adequate income and minimal financial literacy); immediate financial needs, including liquidity, money orders, bill payments, and remittances (wire transfers); short-term credit during emergencies; and long-term financial needs, including savings, access to borrowing, home ownership, insurance, and investment.

33. Unibanco 2003. However, the parameters of the surveyed population in the Unibanco sample are not known. The figure is also highly plausible in view of aggregate statistics on bank accounts in Brazil, which amount to at least a third of the population. The present sample, moreover, only covers adults in major cities; thus, a higher mean ratio would be expected.

34. A second question was included as a cross-check. It is, however, also possible that some persons who are intensive users of banks use the accounts of family members without setting up their own account.

35. Discussed in greater detail in chapter 3 of this study. Around 40 percent of respondents cited 'other' reasons for not having accounts.

36. Personal guarantees were the most common (six cases), followed by business inventory/bank accounts and institutional guarantees (three cases each).

37. At a different point in the questionnaire, it was asked how real estate had been financed. The response was that only 37 percent of respondents used a financial institution to obtain a loan for real estate purchase and renovation.

38. Information on loan maturity suggests that 78 percent of loans were for a period of 12 months or less and 20 percent were for less than one month. Interest rates on a monthly basis averaged 85 percent.

39. Differences in the distributions of variables among the parameters examined (different regions, different institutions, different socioeconomic categories, and so forth) are tested for significance using chi-squared tests of independence. Significant statistics reported here, unless noted, are significant at a 1 percent level. Detailed results are available in background papers. Results presented here are summaries only; more detailed background papers are available.

40. Differences cited in this section are all based on the results of chi-squared tests of independence of distributions (see annex 1.2, Technical Note on Estimation) and are significant at the 1 percent or 5 percent level. Results with the corresponding test statistics are detailed in appendix tables A1.8–A1.14.

41. For credit cards, there are also differences in proportions, which are significant but weaker.

42. Deposit balances were defined in this case as money in a special savings account, a current account, or a term deposit account. A generic definition of deposits yielded similar results: 52 percent of persons living in a house with more than 2 rooms per person had no deposits; in contrast, 90 percent of people in homes with less than 0.5 rooms per person had no deposits.

43. To analyze overall access to formal financial institutions, two separate measures of public versus private banks were adopted. In the first, wide definition, correspondent banking outlets (lottery shops with banking services for public banks and post offices with banking services for private banks) were included. In the alternative, narrow definition, correspondent outlets were not included. Results turned out to be very sensitive to these alternative definitions.

44. A resolution of the National Monetary Council (Resolution 3110 of July 31, 2003) has expanded the scope of services offered by correspondents.

45. This is corroborated by data discussed in chapter 3 of this study.

46. See appendix tables for a summary of the results. The estimation methods used are detailed in annex 1.2, Technical Note on Estimation. Explanatory variables selected are those demonstrated to have significant differences across groups in the analysis of the preceding section (chi-squared tests of independence). Probit models were used for binary independent variables, while multinomial logit models were used for multivariate independent variables. The usual care has to be applied in interpreting the results, bearing in mind that although significant findings can help to predict some type of access, these results do not imply causality.

47. A detailed analysis of parameters explaining access was also undertaken separately using data from a household survey undertaken in Brazil in 1997. This

analysis, which defined a series of levels of access, depending on the range of services included, also had very similar overall results: World Bank, Access to Financial Services in Brazil—an empirical evaluation based on the Pesquisa Sobre Padrões de Vida (PPV 1996/97), mimeo, Rio de Janeiro, June 2002. Coordinated by Rosane Mendonça with a technical note by Daniel Santos.

48. Annex 1.1 is based on Cobbaut (1997).

Chapter 2

1. Global recognition was given to the potential role of microfinance in addressing poverty alleviation at the Microcredit Summit in Washington, D.C., in 1997, when summit campaign members representing some 1,500 institution members prepared a declaration undertaking to extend credit to 100 million of the poorest by 2005. As of December 2001, some 2,200 institutions had accessed 55 million clients, of whom 27 million were among the poorest. See www.microcreditsummit.org for details.

2. *Microbanking Bulletin,* November 2002, based on its 147 participating institutions, available through www.cgap.org. Several agencies and websites now provide rich information on microfinance, as do the publications of the Consultative Group to Assist the Poorest, including the above, the *Focus Notes,* and the *Microfinance Gateway. Finance for the Poor* is a quarterly periodical of the Asian Development Bank, and the *Microenterprise Americas* magazine is a publication of the Inter-American Development Bank. PlanetFinance, Women's World Banking, and other agencies such as Accion International are rich private sources. The literature on the experience of microfinance is huge; surveys are available in Morduch (1999), Robinson (2001), and others.

3. SEBRAE (www.sebrae.com.br), based on Brazilian Institute of Geography and Statistics (Instituto Brasileira de Geografia e Estatistica; IBGE) data from 1994. These definitions are based on the number of employees. The IBGE defines *microenterprises* as those with up to 19 employees in industry and up to 9 employees in services and commerce and defines *small enterprises* as those with up to 99 employees in industry and 49 employees in services and commerce. Alternative definitions based on sales turnover are also used.

4. DIEESE 2002. These numbers do not include an estimated 4 million small rural enterprises. In all it is estimated that the majority of Brazil's 70 million economically active people work in or are linked to small enterprises.

5. National Credit Union Administration (United States) at www.ncua.org and the World Council of Credit Unions, www.woccu.org, provide detailed historic as well as comparative experience.

6. The 753 members of the SICOOB network, which accounted for more than half Brazil's cooperatives in 2002, had 972,000 members. According to the Central Bank of Brazil, there were 1.5 million co-op members at end-2001.

7. World Bank estimates and Goldmark, Nichter, and Fiori (2002).

8. The team contributing to this chapter includes Mcdonald Benjamin, Susana Sanchez, and Sophie Sirtaine (World Bank staff) and Alfredo Ebentrich, Lydie Ehouman, Ricardo Gonçalves, Adam Parsons, and Robert Vogel (consultants).

9. Article 8 of Law 5764 of December 16, 1971 (Cooperatism Law). However, the first central cooperative to commence its operations was not established until October 1980.

10. Considerable recent literature on Brazil's microfinance sector is now available, beginning from Schonberger (2001); Goldmark and Vechina (2000); Goldmark, Pockross, and Vechina (2000); Goldmark, Nichter, and Fiori (2002); Central Bank of Brazil (2002a, 2002b); Mezzera (2002); and UNDP (2001)

11. A more extensive discussion of the regulatory framework is available later in this chapter.

12. *Medida Provisória* 1914-4 of June 28, 1999, excluded both OSCIPs and SCMs from the Usury Law.

13. Law 9790 of March 23, 1999, which came to be known popularly as the New Law of the Tertiary Sector, established the OSCIP; Decree No. 3100 of June 30, 1999, provided details on its authorization, functioning, and supervision. Reporting requirements are minimal, but for lines of credit through public entities, external audits are required. For details see especially Communidade Solidária (2001), which discusses the implications of the OSCIPs.

14. Central Bank Resolution 2627 of August 2, 1999, established the SCM. Guidelines for its authorization and functioning were issued rapidly after (Central Bank Circular No. 2915 of August 5, 1999), and further circulars established reporting requirements to the Central Bank as well as public disclosure requirements for financial statements (Circular No. 2964 of February 3, 2000) and a standardized chart of accounts in COSIF (Carta-Circular No. 2898 of the Central Bank of February 29, 2000).

15. Law No. 10194 of February 2001 extended funding sources to include the SEBRAE and also companies registered with the CVM and investment funds. OSCIPs were permitted to own SCMs.

16. As discussed later in this chapter, MFIs under separate and formal regulatory windows would have reporting requirements that are harder to elaborate and require better information systems. There is a tradeoff between the supervisory value of such reporting requirements and the point at which they become excessive and a burden rather than a tool to improve the managing of their operations.

17. However, the retention rate has dropped to 47 percent, partly due to the economic slowdowns and perhaps also less understood demand factors.

18. Banco Nacional de Desenvolvimento Econômico e Social (BNDES) and the Serviço Brasileiro de Apoio às Micro e Pequenas Empresas (SEBRAE). SEBRAE, established in 1990, focuses largely on technical assistance for micro- and small enterprises in Brazil, as well as on the maintenance of information, advice on credit, and support to business incubators.

19. PortoSol, VivaCred, and BluSol, all of which have pioneer status, and large clusters of MFIs belonging to groups, including nine in the CEAPE network, three in the network of Banco da Mulher, and five belonging to Visão Mundial.

20. Supported by a technical assistance loan from IADB. It launched the development of rating systems for MFIs (in collaboration with Planet Finance) and auditing systems (based on CGAP audit principles) (www.portaldomicrocredito.org.br). Tools were provided on the website for performance evaluation, including a set of performance indicators and methodology for self-assessment.

21. Note that all rates would have changed with the new measures introduced in 2003.

22. These 'good principles' of microfinance have now been accepted by several authors; see below for a fuller discussion. The erratic adhesion of BNDES-supported entities to these principles has also been pointed out elsewhere, notably Goldmark, Nichter, and Fiori (2002).

23. The federal government, BNDES, and SEBRAE each offer different definitions of micro-, small, and medium enterprises. BNDES defines *microenterprises* as businesses with gross annual revenues of up to R$900,000, while *small businesses* are classified by revenues between R$900,000 and R$7,875,000, and *medium businesses* are classified by revenues between R$7,875,000 and R$45,000,000. This includes businesses from industry, commerce, and services.

24. Regional development policy and export promotion are also goals that are explicitly supported and given additional weight, together with energy conservation, environmental safeguards, and so forth.

25. Created by Law No. 9531 of December 12, 1997 (Insurance Fund for Promoting Competitiveness [Fundo de Garantia do Tempo de Serviço; FGPC]) and Decree 3113 of July 6, 1999 (regulates Law No. 9531).

26. Working capital loans are accepted if they complement a long-term financing loan and represent less than 50 percent of the total.

27. There is now a sizable literature on microfinance in Brazil, which began with Schonberger (2001) and has been added to notably by the DAI/BNDES group publications: Goldmark, Pockross, and Vechina (2000); Goldmark and Vechina (2000); Goldmark, Nichter, and Fiori (2002); Brusky and Fortuna (2002); Martins, Winograd, and Salles (2002); and Mezzera (2002).

28. A multinational bank, ABN AMRO, is developing a pilot project, in the context of a USAID credit line, to start providing loans to microentrepreneurs. The project, located in Northeast Brazil and São Paulo, would use distinct facilities and specially trained credit officers, but ABN AMRO's branch network would be used to channel funds. However, this activity is not intended to become a real business line of the bank.

29. Estimates based on DAI (Goldmark, Nichter, and Fiori 2002), based on an aggregation of data on banks, SCMs, credit OSCIPs, NGOs, and government initiatives.

30. RioCred, a joint venture of Fininvest and the International Finance Corporation, has since undergone a transformation of its regulatory status as well as its name and is now operating as MicroInvest.

31. Some sources detect a recent slowdown, as witnessed by the slow loan renewal rate even in CrediAmigo (Goldmark, Nichter, and Fiori 2002). However, against this, the number of SCMs has clearly increased rapidly.

32. Development Alternatives, Inc., estimated the average percentage of gross loans overdue by more than 30 days for a representative sample of 12 Brazilian MFIs at 7.5 percent (with a range from 2.3 to 12.0 percent) in 1999 and found that this compared poorly with a reference rate of 4.6 percent (with a range from 0.6 to 13.0 percent) for a sample of 17 MFIs in Latin America in 1998. Differences in results are likely attributable to fluctuations over time and sample selection, both of which have high variation, as discussed above.

33. It must be remembered that guidelines adopted by BNDES require that, if bad loans exceed 8 percent in two consecutive quarters, loans must be returned.

34. MicroRate is a private rating agency dedicated to the evaluation of MFIs in Latin America. It has been operating since 1997 and has analyzed a total of about 70 institutions. The extent to which loan classification and recognition of bad loans differs materially across countries is not taken into account.

35. Ten percent on loans overdue by 1 to 30 days, 50 percent on loans overdue by 31 to 60 days, 75 percent on loans overdue by 61 to 90 days, and 100 percent on loans overdue by more than 90 days.

36. *Operational self-sufficiency* is defined as the ratio of total loan income/total operational expenses. *Financial self-sufficiency* is defined as the ratio of (total loan income + total income from financial investments)/(total operational expenses + total financial expenses).

37. These comparisons are only approximate, however, given differences between base rates and other market conditions across countries.

38. Yaron 1994; Morduch 1999. The subsidy dependence index measures the percentage of increase in the average lending rate required to compensate for eliminating subsidies, including the subsidy an MFI receives by paying a below-market interest rate on its borrowed funds and imputing a market-level cost of equity.

39. The SELIC rate was at 19 percent in November 2001; 26.5 percent in March 2003. BNDES long-term financing is officially provided at the long-term interest rate (Taxa de Juros de Longo Prazo; TJLP), but in practice, institutions only pay 6 percent p.a., and the difference between the TJLP and 6 percent is amortized over the same period as the principal of the loan. The TJLP has varied between 11 percent and 14 percent over the years. SEBRAE's funding is also based on the TJLP or on the reference rate (Taxa Referencial) plus a margin.

40. For instance, MicroRate estimated that demand for BNDES funds would go beyond US$200 million by 2003.

41. See also chapter 3 of this study.

42. Caixa Econômica Federal commissioned an analysis of 13 MFIs to identify those suitable for onlending but concluded that none was adequately equipped.

43. *Microbanking Bulletin* (November 2002) notes in its highlights that MFIs that target the low-end clients cover almost all of their costs and have an average financial self-sufficiency ratio of 92 percent, compared to 42 percent for all its 147 participating institutions. There is other evidence to support this: Wenner (1995) finds in a survey of village banks in Costa Rica supported by the Foundation for International Community Assistance (FINCA) that delinquency rates are higher in better-off towns; Sharma and Zeller (1996) also found this to be the case in village programs in Bangladesh. However, other studies are less conclusive, and more empirical investigation of this issue is needed.

44. Interviews of microentrepreneurs in São Paulo and Recife confirmed that most of them had never heard of MFIs (Brusky and Fortuna2002).

45. The growing literature in this area includes, in particular, Christen and Rosenberg (2000); van Greuning, Gallardo, and Randhawa (1999); Staschen (1999); and CGAP (2002). See also a discussion of issues in the *Sa-Dhan Newsletter* of October 2002 (www.sa-dhan.org), an association of MFIs in India.

46. Christen and Rosenberg (2000) mentioned the following cases: BASIC (India), K-REP (Kenya), BancoSol (Bolivia), Kafo Jiginew (Mali), BRAC Bank (Bangladesh), FinAmerica (Colombia), Compartamos (Mexico), FINSOL (Honduras), CARD Bank (Philippines), Financiera Calpia (El Salvador), ACEP (Senegal), Genesis (Guatemala), Banco ADEMI and Banco de la Pequeña Empresa (Dominican Republic), CERUBEB (Uganda), Banco Solidario (Ecuador), and MIBANCO (Peru).

47. Entry capital for different types of banks is given in a Central Bank notification of August 29, 2001 (Acesso ao Sistema Financeiro Nacional); for SCMs, the most recent requirements are in a circular of March 27, 2003. Limits are currently R$100,000 for SCMs and R$17.5 million for commercial banks and R$12.5 million for multiple banks (higher if foreign exchange operations are sought).

48. These types of indirect supervision are commonly used in the supervision of closed credit cooperatives, because the risks faced by the credit cooperative are self-contained in it and would affect only its shareholder (discussed further below).

49. In the case of Peru, it was estimated that, if all the costs of supervising MFIs were charged to these institutions, interest rates would increase by an estimated 3 percent to meet these additional costs.

50. Resolution No. 3106 of June 25, 2003 (Requirements and Procedures for Credit Cooperatives). The resolution allows new 'open-admission' credit cooperatives (in municipalities with up to 100,000 inhabitants), subject to the approval of the Central Bank, thus allowing them to be created by location, as well as by activity or profession. Existing credit cooperatives, operating for more than three years, can transform into open-admission credit cooperatives, in municipalities (or contiguous municipalities) with up to 750,000 inhabitants. Minimum capital require-

ments for the transformation are R$6 million for entities located in municipalities in metropolitan regions with more than 100,000 inhabitants and R$3 million for the rest. In the North and Northeast, this requirement is reduced by 50 percent.

51. As these two cover at least three-quarters of all credit cooperatives and have reliable member information, data here are based principally on their information.

52. Eligible services were specified under Resolution 2771 of the National Monetary Council and later by Resolution No. 3106 of June 2003.

53. See chapter 5.

54. Based on data from the WOCCU, which reports more than 100 million members in almost 37,000 credit unions in 91 countries. However, WOCCU does not report members in such important countries for credit unions as Italy and Germany, and in other countries, only some of the national credit union networks are members of WOCCU. For example, in Brazil, WOCCU lists 423 credit unions, or less than half of all credit unions in the country. Nonetheless, even allowing for understatement, the conclusions would remain correct.

55. See the related paper on rural finance by Yaron and Benjamin (2002).

56. Atlantic Rating, a local rating company in Brazil.

57. Bittencourt (2001) on the CRESOL cooperative network. Central Bank norms require provisioning of 0.5 percent for loans that are 15 days overdue, 3 percent after 30 days, and 100 percent after 6 months. In the case of CRESOL, about 20 percent to 25 percent of the provisioning for loan losses is eventually reversed into revenues due to loan recoveries.

58. This appears to be a frequently encountered difficulty for credit unions. Recently, ABCUL, the Association of British Credit Unions, has recommended that a central services organization be established in the United Kingdom to provide credit unions with central treasury and liquidity management functions, in the hope that this will assist credit unions to grow (ABCUL 2001).

59. The 1988 Constitution, in Article 192, provides for distinct treatment for cooperatives relative to other financial institutions.

60. Resolution No. 3106 of June 25, 2003, which superseded the rules of August 2000. These were followed by Circular No. 3.196/03 of July 17, 2003, of the Central Bank, which specified new capital adequacy rules for credit cooperatives—11 percent for affiliated co-ops (as in banks) and 15 percent for cooperatives not affiliated with a central cooperative.

61. See the National Credit Union Administration, www.ncua.org, for the United States case. In the case of Brazil, credit cooperatives are exempted from the 1.5 percent IOF tax on financial transactions, the income tax on profits, and reserve requirements, although the cooperative banks that they own need to meet these requirements in the same way as regular commercial banks.

62. There are clearly no exposure limits upward regarding the placement of deposits by member cooperatives in their central cooperative or cooperative bank.

63. Resolution 3106 of June 25, 2003, of the National Monetary Council, which requires a minimum of 50 percent of the mean value of daily balances of monthly deposits to be used for credit.

64. Resolution 2798 of November 30, 2000 (see chapter 6 for a further discussion).

65. In Latin America, Peru, Ecuador, and Argentina have formal deposit insurance for credit cooperatives, but in reality they do not work. In the case of more developed countries like Germany and the United States, credit cooperatives have their own deposit insurance fund. Brazil and Colombia are moving toward establishing their own deposit insurance fund. See Arzbach and Duran (2002a) for a discussion.

66. In the United States, the revised Federal Credit Union Act of 1998 includes in the Title III the National Credit Union Central Liquidity Facility to improve general financial stability by meeting the liquidity needs of credit unions.

67. The idea is that cooperatives can hardly expand their services to a large geographic area, as their qualifying members are usually concentrated in one area. But limiting geographic spread may increase risk concentration.

68. Regulation on this matter has already been implemented in Bolivia, Peru, and Germany.

69. The National Credit Union Administration is the independent federal agency that supervises and insures the federal credit unions and state-chartered credit unions.

70. See especially Campion and Halpern (2001) and Marker, McNamara, and Wallace (2002) for recent surveys.

71. For more information on ATMs, see chapter 3 on the downscaling of private banks.

72. For more information, see Smart Money Goes Multilingual, June 13, 2001, available at http://news.bbc.co.uk/2/low/business/1386310.stm.

73. See also chapter 6 on financial infrastructure.

74. AIS has developed tools that can measure and manage credit, liquidity, and market risks (www.ais-int.net).

75. See especially chapter 3.

76. In terms of the active portfolio levels.

Chapter 3

1. Note that banks are obliged to direct 25 percent of the total of their unremunerated sight deposits to the rural sector (in addition to reserve requirements, applicable also to other deposits). Rules regarding special savings deposits are complex. Remunerations are indexed to the TR (Taxa Referencial) plus 6 percent, and are tax exempt. However, at least 65 percent of these deposits must be directed to housing finance, four-fifths of which must be loaned at controlled terms of credit (TR + 12 percent to individuals and TR + 13 percent to builders). In practice, such deposits can still be very profitable.

2. Banks in Brazil divide their clients into five notional income groups: classes A (the wealthiest) to E (the least-well-off). Limits for each class at the beginning of 2002 were approximately: A (above R$3,000), B (above R$1,000), C (above R$500), D (above R$250), and E (below).

3. Note that this does not establish effective demand at prevailing prices. Table 3.8 suggests that a large number of persons believe that their lack of 'money' (which could be either income or wealth) is an obstacle to access to bank services and, also, that prices of services are 'high.'

4. The Brazilian Treasury (Tesouro Nacional), http://www.tesouro.fazenda.gov.br/tesouro_nacional, issued Ordinance No. 554 on December 12, 2001, which approved the regulation of the public offering of bonds to individuals via the Internet and offers that began on January 7, 2002.

5. Note that Unibanco appears to have a smaller share in the small-loan market than its natural market share would suggest, but this is in part because it concentrates small loans in its subsidiary, Fininvest.

6. In mid-2003, new regulations were introduced (CMN Resolution 3104 of June 25, 2003, and CMN Resolution 3113 of July 31, 2003), which permit the opening of basic bank accounts for low-income clients, with eased requirements. Such accounts, which offer limited services, are now available free of charge. Further details are in Expanding Access to Banks in Brazil: New Measures Introduced in 2003 (on page 170 of this book).

7. In the World Bank survey, of the some 1,150 persons who did not have bank accounts, only 700 persons or 64 percent wanted a bank account. In a parallel survey by Unibanco of Brazil, a very similar 60 percent of the 'unbanked' wanted an account. The Unibanco survey also ranked the reasons why persons did not have accounts, and financial reasons (insufficient income, insufficient proof of income, or insufficient money for opening or maintaining balances), together with costs, were the first four reasons cited, accounting for 80 percent of responses. Next came bureaucracy and documentation and, finally, adverse credit reports.

8. Official regulations on minimum information and other data required to open any type of deposit account can be found in Resolution 2025 (article 1) of the National Monetary Council, as amended, especially by Resolution 2747 (article 1) and also by Resolutions 2078, 2303, 2817, as well as Circulars 2452, 2520, 2556, 2677, and 3006. Requirements are basically the same for demand deposits and savings deposits, with some additional regulations for term deposits. An individual must furnish name, parents' names, nationality, date and place of birth, gender, civil status, name of wife or husband, profession, and an official document of identification. Legal entities must present documents in relation to the entity (statutes, principal activity, form and date of constitution), as well as to the individuals authorized to operate the accounts, including their residential and commercial addresses, phone numbers, references, and signatures. Financial institutions must maintain copies of these documents. Banks are also obligated to provide some information to their clients. For demand deposits, information on

minimum balances to maintain the account current, conditions for furnishing a checkbook, fees charged for inactive accounts, and so forth must be included in the contract. Checkbooks may not be furnished until client data have been verified.

9. The CPF (Cadastro de Pessoa Física) is the tax registration number for Brazilian individuals at the Secretaria da Receita Federal (the Brazilian Internal Revenue Services). Although all citizens are supposed to have a CPF, only 11 million of the estimated 170 million Brazilians paid income taxes in 1999.

10. New regulations were introduced in 2003 that offered subsidized low-interest loans to small entrepreneurs. Again, look for details in Expanding Access to Banks in Brazil: New Measures Introduced in 2003 (on page 170 of this book).

11. Official recognition was first given by Resolution No. 2707 of March 30, 2000, and extended by Circular No. 2978 of April 19, 2000, Circular No. 2983 of June 7, 2000, and Resolution No. 2953 of April 25, 2002. Most recently the scope of activities was extended by Resolution of the National Monetary Council, No. 3110 of July 31, 2003, which expanded the outreach of correspondent banks, authorizing them to offer many banking services such as opening accounts (sight deposits, savings deposits, term deposits, and investment funds) and payment and credit facilities.

12. An estimated 25 percent of the total population do not or are not able to use bank services. Of these, about 4 million live in municipalities without a bank, but with a post office.

13. These figures include the number of Electronic Service Points of each bank (Postos de Atendimento Bancário Eletrônico as defined by the Central Bank of Brazil), plus the Banco24Horas ATM network shared by 61 financial institutions in Brazil.

14. Brazil's two largest public banks, Banco do Brasil and Caixa Econômica Federal, have indicated a willingness to begin sharing their ATM networks, and there are plans to launch a pilot program in major cities after early-2004, with a subsequent countrywide rollout later in the year. Banco do Brasil and Caixa Econômica Federal alone make up 40 percent of all ATM transactions in Brazil.

15. See chapter 6 of this study for details. Credit scoring is an automated statistical method used to assess the risk of default of a credit applicant. This substantially reduces costs of underwriting a credit because it reduces the role of human evaluation, thus allowing financial institutions to profitably underwrite credits of smaller sizes.

16. For example, Bradesco financed about 20,000 computers, but these were directed first to its employees, many of whom were well-to-do.

17. Estimates all confirm huge cost differentials. Based on U.S. data for 1996, Booz Allen Hamilton estimated that the average transaction cost through the Internet is less than 1 percent of that of a transaction at a branch and about 4 percent of ATM transactions. *Institutional Investor Magazine* (www.institutionalinvestor.com) estimated that transactions at a teller cost US$1.53 in the United States, versus US$0.60 at an ATM and US$0.10 via the Internet.

18. Bradesco revealed, for instance, that 83 percent of their Internet clients have an income above R$15,000 (US$6,700) and 65 percent have a university degree. Unibanco estimated that more than 75 percent of their Internet clients are in the richest income class and less than 5 percent in the two lowest groups. Internet clients are most numerous in a few of Brazil's largest cities, Brasília coming first, followed by São Paulo and Rio de Janeiro.

19. Brazil is not alone in its limited success in using the Internet for outreach of financial services. Citibank in India initiated a small-savings-based Internet scheme, Citibank Suvidha, which accepted initial deposits of as little as R$500 (US$10). But low-income depositors have been few, and the initial deposit doubled within a short while of the opening of the scheme. See www.citibank.com/india/suvidha/.

20. Comitê Gestor da Internet–Brazil. In 2000 alone, there were 5,997 reported successful system intrusions. A recent report by the Gartner group indicated that while the largest 500 companies in Brazil spent an average of 16 percent of their budgets on information technology in 2001, very little of this was spent on security. Gartner's survey stated that Brazilian security investments were just under 2 percent of their technology budget against a worldwide trend of around 4 to 6 percent. Only 13 percent of the largest 500 Brazilian firms are prepared for large losses; 28 percent have some kind of crisis management and business continuity plans; and an estimated 36 percent have insurance plans against sizable losses.

21. Some of these initiatives admittedly had disappointing results, though these could have been the result of unsound banking practices. According to the Economist Intelligence Unit, Unifer, now a subsidiary of Absa, admitted that it had overstated profits by some 10 percent, and that poor lending had resulted in a shortfall in provisions. Saambou, one of the smaller institutions active in microlending, issued a profit warning and said that it was likely to record a half-year loss of R$5 million (US$436,510). Unifer and Saambou financed personal capital purchases with aggressive sales targets.

22. Banco de Credito del Peru is the largest bank in Peru, measured by the size of its assets as of June 2002. It is followed by Banco Wiese Sudameris and Banco Continental BBV.

23. Consumer loans are a close cousin of microfinance and are quickly moving closer. According to Christen and Drake (2001), small commercial banks and finance companies are more flexible and adaptable than the large banks, although the latter have a large network of branches and information systems that are very important for the provision of microfinance services.

24. One of the four leading U.K. banks recently set up a separate community banking unit focusing on providing savings and loan services for housing-association tenants, banking social enterprises, childcare organizations, and community development trusts. This bank has also created an innovative financial inclusion product. It announced a partnership with Prospect Community Housing Associa-

tion whereby Prospect's tenants would be able to open savings accounts (paying interest of 2.75 percent) and apply for loans of up to £2,000 (up to four times savings). Bank personnel would be trained to accept rent books and power bills as forms of identification. Prospect staff would assist tenants to take advantage of these products, reducing their reliance on subprime lenders.

25. Main banks in the United Kingdom have also started providing basic bank accounts to meet the special needs of low-income people. Typically, these accounts do not include an overdraft option or checkbook; the Bank of Scotland has gone further, offering a bill-payment account linked to the basic account.

26. Caskey 2001. The term 'unbanked' here refers to individuals who do not have deposit accounts of any type.

27. Law No. 10735 of September 11, 2003 (formerly Provisional Measure No. 122 of June 25, 2003), CMN Resolution 3109 of July 24, 2003, and CMN Resolution 3128 of October 30, 2003, created additional measures that include microfinance operations destined for low-income earners and small businesses.

28. This annex is based on a background paper prepared by ShoreBank Advisory Services for the World Bank.

29. ShoreBank points out that there are significant differences in cross-border concepts of low financial access. For example, in the United States, ShoreBank's target markets in the South Side of Chicago suffered exclusion 30 or 40 years ago largely because of minority status and location in less-desirable neighborhoods. As commercial banks have discovered the business opportunities offered in these communities, access to financial services has become more a function of income level, business size, credit history, and immigrant status. In the transitional economies of Eastern Europe, access is low because of political instability (or continued military conflict), nascent financial systems, and short operational histories of small businesses or microenterprises. In Latin America, income level, geography, race, and business size all limit access to financial services, as do popular distrust of financial institutions following currency crises and other shocks to the financial system.

30. Ed Jacob, Manager, North Side Community Federal Credit Union, Periodic Report, March 31, 2003.

31. CLHS is a nonprofit agency that seeks to increase the resources of low-income households through improved access to public entitlement programs.

32. At Ceska Sporitelna, to qualify for a credit line, the customer needs to have been a bank customer for a minimum of two years (either through an account or a lending relationship with the bank) and have documented annual sales of at least $30,000 for the last two years. ShoreBank usually includes a credit line as part of a larger financing package, and traditional cash-flow analysis is performed on the entire package.

Chapter 4

1. For example, multiple banks had 34 leasing portfolios at the end of 2001. However, according to the Central Bank, if these activities are undertaken through separate subsidiaries, such assets would not be included in these data.

2. See chapter 3, table 3.10.

3. Overdrafts for individuals are referred to as *cheque especial* lending; overdrafts for enterprises are included in the category referred to as the *conta garantida*. Export notes, letters of credit, lines of credit, and import finance are important, accounting for a significant 42 percent of outstanding enterprise financing (December 2002).

4. The yearly factor has been calculated by annualizing the monthly factor for December 2001 provided by ANFAC of 3.9 percent, i.e., (1.039)^12 = 1.582, or 58.2 percent.

5. Credit card receivables are issued by special credit card companies, which are nonbanking commercial activities that finance themselves either through the securitization of their receivables or through conventional bank loans, for which receivables provide the collateral. Credit card receivables are due at the end of 30 days and, if not paid off by the expiration date, loans are originated by the sponsoring financial institutions.

6. December 2001. Figures for February 2003 are R$79 billion for total consumer credit.

7. The corresponding figures are 0.7 percent and R$8.9 billion for February 2003.

8. The principal author of this chapter is Mario Guadamillas, World Bank, with input also provided by Professor Ricardo Leal and a team from Coppead Business School, Rio de Janeiro.

9. Factoring as defined in Brazil conforms to international practice. Brazil, together with 53 other countries, accepted the definition adopted at the Ottawa Diplomatic Convention on International Factoring in May 1988, organized by the Institut International pour l'Unification du Droit Privé (International Institute for the Standardization of Private Laws). The definition was formally adopted in Brazil in Article 28 of Law No. 8981/95, ratified by Resolution 2144/95 of the National Monetary Council and by Article 58 of Law No. 9532/97.

10. Articles 191–220 of Brazil's Commercial Code and Articles 1,065–1,078 until January 11, 2003, and since then by Brazil's new Civil Code, which unified civil and commercial obligations (Articles 286–298, Law No. 10406, of January 10, 2002). The provision of services attached to a factoring contract is regulated by Articles 594–609 of the new Civil Code.

11. These are the factoring companies affiliated with ANFAC. Because factoring is deemed to be a nonfinancial activity, data on factoring companies are not readily available through institutions such as the Central Bank, which maintains data on all financial institutions. ANFAC provides a valuable service in terms of providing a focal point for the industry and its causes.

12. ANFAC distinguishes three groups of members of factoring companies according to size of turnover: (1) below R$1 million (30 percent), (2) between R$1 million and R$5 million (60 percent), and (3) above R$5 million (10 percent of all members).

13. The CDB is a fixed-income security with an average term of 30 days.

14. Discussed in chapter 6.

15. When the buyer does not pay, the factor may file a delinquency declaration with a notary public, called a *protesto,* which serves as a proof of the existence of the debt. Thus, a cognizance action is not necessary, and the debt is self-executable (see chapter 6).

16. Law Nos. 4595/64, the basic financial institutions law in Brazil (Articles 17 and 18), and 7492/86 (Articles 1 and 16) define operations of financial intermediaries that cannot be carried out by factoring companies, including bank discounts or payment or receipt of interest.

17. These rules provide legal support, standardize and consolidate the terminology used by the sector, and oblige affiliates and their counterparties to adhere to the principles stated in the *Code of Ethics.*

18. A previous regulation, under Circular 703/82, had created some confusion, stating that factoring activity had similar characteristics to financial intermediaries subject to Central Bank authorization. This was, however, clarified in 1988. Subsequent laws and regulations (8981/95, ratified by Law Nos. 9249/95, 9430/96, 9532/97; CMN Resolution 2144/95; and Declaratory Act [Ato Declaratório] 51/94 of the Secretária de Receita Federal [Internal Revenue Service]) endorse the position that factoring activities are regulated by commercial law.

19. Presented by Senator José Fogaça in July 1996, it was approved by the Comissão de Assuntos Econômicos do Senado (Economic Affairs Commission of the Senate) and passed to the Comissão de Constitução e Justiça (CCJ; Commission for Justice and the Constitution) of the Senate, where it remains. In parallel, the Congress has discussed eight draft laws directly or indirectly dealing with factoring. In November 2001, the Comissão de Economia da Câmara dos Deputados (Economic Commission of the Chamber of Deputies [Lower House]) approved another draft law pertaining to factoring, presented by Deputy Emerson Kapaz. This is currently seeking approval at the CCJ da Câmara. Both projects, in Senate and Congress, are very similar, although the project presented to Congress has been more recently updated.

20. When the operation is with recourse from the merchant, it is said to be undertaken on a pro soluto basis.

21. Some countries, such as Italy and Spain, have introduced the concept of passive solidarity, which allows for recourse financing, thus diminishing the risks faced by factoring companies.

22. A discussion of the various taxes on financial intermediation is available in the documentation for Brazil's Second Financial Sector Programmatic Loan.

23. However, most local entities accept the principle that tax must be charged only on services provision revenues and not on revenues from the purchase of receivables.

24. From December 1, 2002, PIS ceased to be calculated on a cascading basis. COFINS ceased to be calculated on a cascading basis with the passing of the new Tax Reform, Provisional Measure No. 135 of October 30, 2003 (later converted into Law No. 10833 of December 29, 2003).

25. Leasing is relatively new even in the United States. It followed President Franklin D. Roosevelt's wartime Lend and Lease Act. In the 1950s, this activity expanded to the business sector, initially largely for equipment leasing. Brazil's legal framework for leasing was introduced with Law No. 6099/74 and modified by Law No. 7132/83. However, these define only the fiscal treatment of leasing and its oversight by the Monetary Council, respectively. Thus, leasing activities are governed by the Civil Code for issues concerning property, rent, penalty, or repossession. A comprehensive law on leasing is under preparation and is to be submitted to Congress.

26. ABEL, at http://www.leasingabel.com.br/, the leasing association of Brazil, is very active in advancing the interests of its associates and the industry.

27. Leasing payment flows in Brazil are defined to be of not less than 30 days and not more than 180 days, except in the case of leasing activity for the rural sector, for which payment flows up to one year are permitted (Central Bank Resolution 2309/96, Article 7 IV).

28. Defined, respectively, in Resolutions 2309/96 and 2465/98 of the National Monetary Council.

29. In terms of contract type and pricing, leasing contracts may have fixed interest rates (*pré-fixados*), U.S. dollar–indexed rates, or rates indexed to a reference or benchmark domestic rate (for example, the Taxa Referencial or Taxa Básica Financeira). The law does not include indexation to the consumer price index (Índice de Preços ao Consumidor), although this, too, has been used in some contracts.

30. This indexation to the long-term interest rate (Taxa de Juros a Longo Prazo) is normally used when the leasing operation is financed with BNDES resources (FINAME leasing). The FINAME leasing credit line is devoted to legal entities (if national shareholders do have the control of the firm) and individuals (transport and rural-sector professionals) for the leasing of machines, vehicles, and new equipment registered at FINAME and financed by BNDES resources.

31. International leasing is regulated by Resolutions 1969/92 and 2302/96 of the Monetary Council; Circulars 2249/92, 2397/93, and 2731/96; and Law No. 9959/00.

32. In 1997, the Central Bank implemented an electronic system for approval, called Siscomex, which reduced the average term for approval from 120 days to 15–20 days.

33. The contract is signed by a Brazilian lessor and a foreign lessee, just the opposite of international leasing, in which the lessor is from abroad and the lessee Brazilian.

34. Under Resolutions 2921 and 2923 of 2002 of the Monetary Council, which permitted 'derivative' credit operations and related operations (*operações vinculados*), more flexible limits many be established within diversification limits permitted for each client.

35. International Accounting Standard 17 issued by the International Standards Accounting Committee and Financial Accounting Standards Board Statement 13 in the United States.

36. In operational leases the present value of payments must not be greater than 90 percent of the cost of the asset.

37. Even some companies from the real sector entered in the competition for providing leasing from a financial perspective. For example, IBM's strategy in the early 1990s was to provide finance through leasing not only for IBM products but in general for information technology solutions. This strategy changed in the late 1990s, and their leasing operations were only concentrated on facilitating the acquisition of IBM products.

38. In those cases the higher risk is worthwhile as operational leasing helps to strengthen sales, keeps clients captive, facilitates access to secondary markets, and normally comes with services provision increasing the value added of the lessor.

39. There are some examples at the international level of how important secondary market considerations are for operational leasing. In one case, one important car manufacturer launched a new model before selling in the secondary market an important stock of the old model car, creating huge losses. On other occasions, some car manufactures had a very aggressive leasing policy, concentrating the maturity of the lease contracts in such a way that a huge car supply went at the same time to the secondary market, creating an important price drop. So, even experts in the markets have experienced important losses when, for several reasons, they have been unable to adequately price used assets coming from operational leases.

40. The real went from R$1.12 for US$1.00 to more than R$2 after the depreciation of 1999, stabilizing afterward in a R$1.70–R$1.80 range. It depreciated again to R$2.55 in September 2001.

41. In the cases of normal financial operations subject to *alienação fiduciaria*, the repossession of the collateral is done by means of a process—*busca e apreensão*—that takes longer than the *reintegração de posse* used in the case of leasing.

42. The concept of direct consumer credit was originally introduced in Decree Law Nos. 7583/45 and 9603/46. A later regulation, Portaria 309/59, defined finance companies' activities to include the financing of purchases and sales; issue of *duplicatas*, promissory notes, and bills of exchange; working capital finance; and export and import finance. But later Central Bank Resolution 45/66 banned their issue of *duplicatas* and promissory notes. With subsequent Resolutions (103/68), working capital finance was capped at 60 percent of a finance company's operations. Export and import finance was also forbidden (by Circular 29/66).

43. For more information on ACREFI, visit http://www.acrefi.com.br/.

44. See chapter 6. A self-executable contract cannot be structured unless both parties sign.

Chapter 5

1. Although this study was intended to include housing finance issues in its study of specialized financial segments, this was omitted because of the ongoing parallel advisory work in this area, initially launched jointly with the present study. See World Bank (2002b) and World Bank (2002d).

2. Is there a case for intervention in rural finance markets because of the existence of real market failures in such markets? This is a widely debated issue and is briefly discussed in Two Perspectives on Market Failure: The Argument for and against Intervention (on page 312 of this book). Besley (1994) has pointed to imperfect information, high transaction costs, contract enforcement problems, and the need to safeguard against the monopoly powers of some lenders as factors that reinforce the case for intervention in such credit markets. Even if market interventions are considered necessary, there is a case for increasing their efficiency and effectiveness according to clearly defined criteria. This issue is discussed further in the fourth section of this chapter, Designing Rural Financial Systems: Principles and Experience.

3. In Mexico and India, for example, nationalized financial institutions bore a large part of the responsibility for rural lending. In the Philippines, as well as in India, rural lending was also an obligation for private banks.

4. Similarly, in the case of directed credit for housing, it can be shown that the principal beneficiaries are middle-class homebuyers. These findings of the 'capture' of selective credit by the better-off is common and have been pointed out by other authors (see, for example, Adams and Vogel [1996]).

5. Specifically, we assume that rural credit, R$35 billion, is at an average rate of TJLP – 3 percent, because many rural credit programs are at rates below TJLP; housing credit, R$22 billion, is at TR + 5 percent, because rates vary from TR + 3 to TR + 6 percent, depending on income; and BNDES credit, R$85 billion, is at TJLP + 2 percent, because BNDES charges a spread on most of its lending. Under this scenario, and assuming that the opportunity cost remains the SELIC rate, total government financial outlay declines little, from R$18.6 billion to R$18.1 billion.

6. At a minimum, a fifth of such resources are to be used for livestock and up to R$60,000 per borrower. The government pointed out, however, that limits per borrower are lower for crops generally cultivated by large producers.

7. These funds mentioned here, including the FAT and FCO, are not used exclusively for rural credit; they are used for a range of purposes, such as rural infrastructure.

8. In recent years private bank participation has been conceded for some earmarked funds, for example the Fundo de Defesa da Economia Cafeeira or FUNCAFÉ (National Monetary Council Resolution 2779 of October 18, 2000).

9. Note that the substituting payment option allows the producer to benefit from a potential gain if prices rise above the projected price that was assumed when the transaction was agreed upon initially.

10. Note that the *cédula* for rural producers parallels a series of other *cédulas,* notably the bank bill of exchange (*cédula de crédito bancário*) and more recently also for real estate (the *cédula de crédito immobiliário*). The self-executable nature of this security and its legal advantages are also discussed in chapter 6 of this study.

11. Information on premiums in the Brazilian insurance industry and benchmarking with other countries can be obtained from FENASEG at the following web address: http://www.fenaseg.org.br/.

12. The spikes in land prices in 1986 and 1994 were in part driven by speculative buying on the assumption that the Plan Cruzado (1986) and the Real Plan (1994) would trigger large increases in land prices.

13. This contrasts sharply with countries such as Thailand, where about 85 percent of farming households have a bank account with the state-owned agricultural bank, which receives only a relatively modest subsidy but provides clients with a range of efficient financial services.

14. Implicitly, nonpriority sectors are taxed through lower deposit rates and higher lending rates in light of the cost of directing 25 percent of reserve requirements to agriculture.

15. This estimate applies the concept of the Subsidy Dependence Index (SDI) methodology, a tool that can be used to assess the extent to which the interest rate must be raised to eliminate lending subsidies. A detailed discussion of its rationale, benefits, and estimation technique is presented in annex 5.1.

16. The most outstanding success story in the past two decades has been the Unit Desa or village bank system of Bank Rakyat Indonesia (BRI), an Indonesian agricultural development bank (annex 5.3).

17. Schiff and Valdés (1992) discussed the 'eight pillars' of urban-biased policies. Yaron, Benjamin, and Piprek (1997) argued that the consequences are broader than that: countries with the highest degree of discrimination against agriculture have had the lowest rates of economic growth.

18. Broader issues relating to judicial issues, collateral, registries, and credit information systems are discussed in chapter 6 of this study.

19. Law No. 9848 of October 26, 1999, extended these privileges to include Banco do Brasil, Banco da Amazônia, Banco do Nordeste, and cooperative banks.

20. This annex was adapted from Yaron (1992b).

Chapter 6

1. La Porta and others 1998. Empirical evidence supporting this view is presented in Beck (2000) and Galindo and Micco (2001).

2. Cardoso and Koyama (1999) further discuss the different components of banks' lending rates, highlighting the importance of taxes, the high cost of fund-

ing, and large default rates. A cross-country comparison by Demirgüç-Kunt and Huizinga (1999), with averages for 1988–95, shows that the large net interest margin of Brazilian banks (5th largest among the 76 countries considered in the study) reflects the high ratios of overhead (the highest among the 76 countries), taxes (5th largest), loan loss provisions (13th largest), and net profits (24th highest) to total assets.

3. For a discussion of arguments and empirical evidence in favor of strong protection to creditor rights, see, for instance, Shleifer and Vishny (1996), La Porta and others (1998), and Demirgüç-Kunt and Huizinga (1999).

4. However, strong creditor protection, some authors point out, can be costly to the economy, by discouraging banks from properly screening projects to be financed or reducing the incentives of entrepreneurs to enter into risky but worthwhile projects. See Padilla and Requejo (2000) for a discussion.

5. The benefits of credit reporting are discussed in Petersen and Rajan (1994), Berger and Udell (1995), and Cate and Staten (2003).

6. This section is drawn largely from a background working paper prepared for this study by Armando Castelar Pinheiro and from Pinheiro and Cabral (2001). Further legal details are available in the background paper.

7. Creditors are usually unwilling to rely on laws or legal instruments until a body of judicial rulings has been established for them. Judicial interpretations about capitalized interest rates (*anatocismo*), the liquidity and certainty of some loan instruments, and the possibility of executing certain kinds of guarantees are examples. This also explains why chattel mortgage (fiduciary alienation) is well accepted for car financing, but the same instrument for housing finance has not had the expected impact.

8. Each is ruled by specific legislation: Law No. 5475 of July 18, 1968 (*duplicatas*); Decree 2044 of December 31, 1908 (bills of exchange and promissory notes); Decree Law 413 of January 9, 1969, and Law No. 6840 of March 11, 1980 (industrial and commercial credit *cédulas*), and Law No. 7357 of September 2, 1985 (checks).

9. The priority ascribed to workers and the tax authority under bankruptcy law is frequently pointed to. A detailed investigation of Brazil's bankruptcy law and proposals for modification was undertaken by a World Bank team as part of a Report on the Observance of Standards and Codes and through technical assistance to the Central Bank.

10. The survey was conducted by IDESP with 602 businesspeople from different states, and it asked them to rate the judiciary with respect to agility, fairness, and costs. It included state enterprises, private national firms, and foreign companies of medium to large size. See Pinheiro (2001) for details.

11. Pinheiro (2001) used a stratified sample of 741 judges (about 6 percent of the total population), covering the federal, labor, and state justices in the Federal District and 11 states: Rio Grande do Sul, Santa Catarina, São Paulo, Rio de Janeiro, Minas Gerais, Bahia, Pernambuco, Mato Grosso, Pará, Roraima, and Goiás. The sample included judges in first degree, second degree, and higher courts.

12. See Pinheiro and Moura (2001) for a description of the main credit registries list used by creditors in Brazil.

13. Amendments added to the plenary amendments made to the substitutive document adopted by the Special Commission for Draft Law No. 4376-B/1993 (Draft Law No. 205 of 1995, appended).

14. Bill of Law No. 72/03 (Emenda Aglutinadora Substitutiva Global ao Projeto de Lei Complementar No. 72/03), which amends certain provisions of Law No. 5172 of October 25, 1966 (the National Tax Code).

15. Although under currently prevailing bankruptcy law, secured creditors' rights follow after the rights of labor, accidents, labor claims, tax claims, and expenses of the bankrupt estate.

16. *Alienação fiduciária*, or fiduciary sale, is a transfer of the title of a given property to a creditor to secure a debt. In Brazil, this type of security is currently applied to real estate properties, too.

17. The perfection of guarantees involving ships, aircraft, and cars requires additional registration, respectively, at the Maritime Tribunal, the Brazilian Aeronautical Registry, and the State Traffic Authority.

18. Statistics provided by the Ministry of Justice.

19. Article 236 of the 1988 Constitution, Law No. 9835 of November 18 1994, and the Public Records Law No. 6015 of December 31, 1973, govern notarial services at the federal level. The Corregedoria Geral da Justiça is a division of the judiciary that oversees and regulates the services it provides.

20. Voluntary retirement or resignation, physical or mental impairment, death, or loss of commission for reasons specified by law.

21. Governed by Articles 125 and 521–528 of the new Civil Code.

22. Governed by Law No. 6099/74 and Law No. 8880/94 and the National Monetary Council Resolution 2309/96.

23. Mortgages are governed by Articles 1473–1488 of the new Civil Code, and full registration is subject to the requirements of Law No. 6015/73.

24. Fiduciary sale for goods and chattel is governed by Articles 1361–1368 of the new Civil Code, while fiduciary sale for real property is governed by Law No. 9514/97.

25. Governed by Articles 1438–1450 of the new Civil Code.

26. The electronic version would conform to the rules of ICP/Brasil—Brazilian Public Key Infrastructure.

27. Two months on average in the experience of one law firm, as each security agreement contains, on average, 300 pages, and the registrar had to transcribe the entire agreement manually, which caused much discomfort.

28. Miller 2003. The surveys of credit registries worldwide conducted in this study show that half of the private credit-reporting firms that have participated in the survey were created after 1989. Margaret Miller and Nataliya Mylenko are the principal contributors to this section.

29. Resolution 2.390 of May 22, 1997, of the National Monetary Council, Central Bank of Brazil establishes the legal foundation for Central de Risco, while Central Bank Circulars 2.768 of July 16, 1997, Circular 2.977 of April 6, 2000, and Circular 2.999 of Autust 24, 2000, specify details of its operations.

30. Research commissioned by the World Bank and conducted by Barron and Staten have specified these costs to financial institutions and the economy in terms of higher loss rates and, also, lower acceptance rates of credit applications (Staten 2001).

Chapter 7

1. For example, see Tomlinson (2002): "The lesson drawn from extending financial services to low-income people have clearly shown that it will not happen if the market is left to its own devices. The government does not possess sufficient resources to make things happen but is key to induce downscaling."

2. See in particular in-depth analyses by Canuto and Mattos (2003) on credit for the enterprise sector and a presentation by the Ministry of Finance (2003a, 2003b) on Brazil's international capital markets.

3. As the economy stabilized, basic reserve requirements were reduced once more to 45 percent in August 2003. However, new mandatory reserves of 2 percent were imposed on banks for microlending, lending to low-income groups, and related schemes.

4. As discussed in chapter 5 of this study.

5. Direct control of interest rates, to make credit available at a reasonable cost for specific sectors of the economy, was very common in the 1960s and 1970s. Brazil's Usury Law predates this by some decades. The South African Usury Act was another example. But such absolute quantitative limits on prices can have undesirable effects, for example, on microfinance. This has now been eliminated in South Africa.

6. Chapter 2 and chapter 3 of this report provide more details on these measures.

7. Competition is a greater preoccupation in the United Kingdom than in the United States, due to the dominance of its financial system by four big banks, which control an estimated 90 percent of banking assets.

8. As in the United Kingdom, the Canadian financial system is dominated by a handful of banks (the 'Big Five'), with national branch networks.

9. Emulated in South Africa's Promotion of Equality and Prevention of Unfair Discrimination Act (2000), which prevents unfair discrimination.

10. October 2000. The report described disadvantaged communities as underinvested and made several recommendations: a Community Investment Tax Credit, Community Development Venture Capital Funds, bank disclosures on lending to underinvested areas, ease in investments in community development initiatives, and support for community development financial institutions. Regarding disclosure, banks agreed, through the British Bankers Association, to

disclose their lending to significantly deprived communities. Barclays will become the first bank to publish these lending figures. Barclays also has started to compare credit factors (such as bad debts or nonperforming loans) in deprived areas versus all areas.

11. CMN Resolution 3104 of June 25, 2003, and CMN Resolution 3113 of July 31, 2003, establish new 'special deposit accounts' for sight deposits, which will offer a basic package of bank services. Chapter 3 provides more details on these measures.

12. The Federal Reserve Board does a triennial interview, Survey of Consumer Finance, which includes a good deal of information about how households of various ages, income groups, and ethnicities use the financial services system. Data are published at the national and regional (but not local) level. The Department of Housing and Urban Development regularly publishes information about the homeownership rate, by age, income group, geography, and ethnicity, and has also published a survey on housing discrimination with relatively local data. The Joint Center for Housing Studies at Harvard University publishes an annual report on the state of the nation's housing that includes information about affordability, with a specific emphasis on lower-income families. Fannie Mae and Freddie Mac publish information about how they are meeting their housing goals (discussed above) and also more general information about the mortgage system. Fannie Mae publishes an annual National Housing Survey, which covers attitudes of Americans about housing, housing finance, and affordability; in 2001, for example, it focused on credit-impaired borrowers. The National Association of Realtors publishes quarterly housing affordability and first-time homebuyer affordability indices, which use a combination of mortgage interest rates, home prices, and incomes to assess whether housing is becoming more or less affordable to buy.

13. Full information on the U.K. Index of Deprivation may be found at the website of the Office of the Deputy Prime Minister, at http://www.urban.odpm.gov.uk/research/. In December 1998, a review of the index was commissioned at the University of Oxford, and a series of background papers has been prepared on issues of measurement and construction.

14. Statistics Canada has provided an annual survey of the suppliers of small-business financing since 2000. This study breaks out suppliers of credit by category (such as banks and credit unions) and then by loan approval amounts (less than C$25,000, between C$25,000 and C$50,000, and so on).

15. And the First Accounts program (discussed above).

16. The New Markets Tax Credit, a new program, and the Low Income Housing Tax Credit, enacted in 1986, use tax credits to lower the cost of production of, in the one case, rental housing for low- and moderate-income families and, in the other, business lending (including commercial real estate lending) in underserved communities.

17. Individual Savings Accounts are tax-free savings account schemes designed by the U.K. government to help low-income people save. Their main

benefits are flexible access to savings and low account-associated charges. However, these accounts have attracted primarily middle- and high-income savers. Low-income people simply do not have the spare income to save. In addition, as they pay at the lowest tax rates, low-income people benefit less from the tax incentives.

18. Interview with Marion Roble, Canadian Bankers Association.

19. Interview with Vicky Scully, Director of Community Lending, Vancouver City, May 1, 2003.

20. The Coalition of Community Development Financial Institutions reports there are between 800 and 1,000 CDFIs currently operating in the United States. In a recent survey of 512 of these groups, the coalition found that the 512 CDFIs had $5.7 billion of financing outstanding at the end of fiscal year 2001. Of the groups surveyed, 46 percent were community development loan funds, 45 percent were credit unions, 5 percent were venture-capital funds, and the remaining 4 percent were community development banks (see www.cdfi.org/cdfiproj.asp).

21. See Task Group of the Policy Board for Financial Services and Regulation (2001). Financial-sector competition issues for microfinance have also been examined in South Africa (Meagher and Wilkinson 2001).

Bibliography

ABCUL (Association of British Credit Unions). 2001. *Financial Exclusion and Credit Unions.* Manchester, United Kingdom.

ABECIP (Associação Brasileira das Entidades de Crédito Imobiliário e Poupança). 1998. *30 Anos, História e Futuro do Crédito Imobiliário.* São Paulo, Brazil.

ABECIP and Luiz Henrique Rocha. 2000. *Mortgage Lending in Brazil.* São Paulo, Brazil: ABECIP.

Abrams, Julie, Damian von Stauffenberg, and Todd Farrington. 2002. *The Finance of Microfinance.* Arlington, Va.: Microrate.

Adams, Dale W. 1995. Using Credit Unions as Conduits for Micro-enterprise Lending—Latin-American Insights. Poverty-Oriented Banking Working Paper No. 12. International Labour Office, Geneva.

Adams, Dale W., and Robert Vogel. 1996. *Old and New Paradigms in Development Finance: Should Directed Credit Be Resurrected?* Arlington, Va.: International Management and Communications Corporation.

Adams, Dale W., and Robert C. Vogel. 1997. "Costs and Benefits of Loan Guarantee Programs." *The Financier* 4(1 & 2).

Adrien, Peter. 1997. "The Financial Services Industry: Emerging Trends in the OEC's Credit Union Sector." *Savings and Development* 11(3).

Afanasieff, Tarsila Segalla, Priscilla Maria Villa Lhacer, and Márcio I. Nakane. 2001. The Determinants of Bank Interest Spread in Brazil. Working Paper No. 46. Central Bank of Brazil, São Paulo.

Aith, Marcio. 2000. "O Impacto do Judiciário nas Atividades das Instituições Financeiras," in A. C. Pinheiro, ed., *O Judiciário e a Economia no Brasi* [*The Impact of the Judiciary in the Activities of Financial Institutions*]. Rio de Janeiro: IDESP.

Alberdi, Baralides, Achim Duebel, and M. Vitor Serra. 2000. *Housing Markets in Brazil: Policy Issues in Finished and Progressive Housing.* Washington, D.C.: Infrastructure, Finance, and Private Sector Department, Brazil Country Management Unit, Latin America and the Caribbean Regional Office, World Bank.

Albuquerque, Pedro H. June 2001. *Impactos Econômicos da CPMF: Teoria e Evidência* [*The Economic Impact of the CPMF: Theory and Evidence*]. Central Bank of Brazil: São Paulo.

Almeyda, Gloria. 1997. Microfinance Services in Colombia: Case Study of Solidarios Financial Cooperative. Sustainable Banking with the Poor Program. World Bank, Washington, D.C.

Almeyda, Gloria, and Brian Branch. 1997. Microfinance in Guatemala: UPA and Union Popular Credit Unions. Sustainable Banking with the Poor Program. World Bank, Washington, D.C.

Amaral, Carlos, Caio Márcio Silveira, and Ricardo Mello. 1994. *Crédito popular—Iniciativas em damento no Brasil* [*Popular Credit: Initiatives Under Way in Brazil*]. Rio de Janeiro: Núcleo de Assessoria Planejamento e Pesquisa and Federação de Órgãos para Assistência Social e Educacional.

Andrietta, António J. 2000. *Microcrédito: Banco do Povo em Santo André.* São Paulo.

Annamalai, Naga, Stijn Claessens, Karen Furst, Tom Glaessner, Leora Klapper, and Daniela Klingebiel. 2004. Excerpts from South Africa—Electronic Finance and the Delivery of Financial Services to Lower Income Groups. Mimeo. World Bank, Washington, D.C.

Annan, Kofi. 2000. "We the Peoples: The Role of the United Nations in the 21st Century." Available from http://www.un.org/millenium/sg/report/summ.htm.

Apgar, William C., and Mark Duda. June 2003. "The Twenty-Fifth Anniversary of the Community Reinvestment Act: Past Accomplishments and Future Regulatory Challenges." *FRBNY Economic Policy Review* 9(2).

Araujo, Paulo F. C., Ricardo Shirota, and Richard L. Meyer. 1990. "Brazilian Agricultural Credit Policy Revisited in the 1980s." *Savings and Development* 14(1): 101–16.

Arzbach, Matthias, and Alvaro Duran. 2002a. *Protección de Depósitos para Bancos y Cooperativas de Ahorro y Crédito en América Latina* [*Deposit Protection for Banks and Savings and Credit Cooperatives in Latin America*]. San Jose, Costa Rica: DGRV.

————. 2002b. *Regulación y Supervisión de Cooperativas de Ahorro y Crédito en América Latina* [*Regulation and Supervision of Savings and Credit Cooperatives in Latin America*]. San Jose, Costa Rica: DGRV.

Aspen Global Forum. April 1999. Brazil–US Global Forum—Expanding Primary and Secondary Mortgage Markets and Housing Opportunity in Brazil. London.

Atlantic Rating, BANCOOB (Banco Cooperativo do Brasil S.A.). June 2001. BANSICREDI: SICREDI personal communications, March 4, 2002.

Attuch, Roberto, and Marcelo Telles. 1999. *Internet Banking, Equity Research—Latin America.* New York: Credit Suisse First Boston Garantia.

Azevedo, João Pedro Wagner de. February 2002. *Credit and Entrepreneurship in the Slums of Rio de Janeiro.* Newcastle Upon Tyne, U.K.: University of Newcastle Upon Tyne, Department of Economics.

Balkenhol, Bernd. 1999. *Credit Unions and the Poverty Challenge—Extending Outreach, Enhancing Sustainability.* Geneva: International Labour Organisation.

Bank Indonesia and GTZ (German Technical Co-operation Agency). 2000. *Legislation, Regulation, and Supervision of Microfinance Institutions in Indonesia.* Jakarta: Project ProFi.

Bank of England, Domestic Finance Division. April 2002. *Finance for Small Firms—A Ninth Report.* London.

Barham, Bradford, and Stephen Boucher. 1994. Credit Unions in Guatemala 1987–1992: The Role and Impact of Credit Unions in Guatemalan Financial Markets: Helping to Meet the Needs of Small-Scale Producers. Monograph Series No. 6. Madison, Wisc.: WOCCU.

Barham, Bradford L., Stephen Boucher, and Michael R. Carter. 1996. "Credit Constraints, Credit Unions, and Small-Scale Producers in Guatemala." *World Development Oxford* 24(5): 793–806.

Barres, Calmeadow I. 2000. *Benchmarking for Microfinance Institutions—The Micro Banking Standards Project—Performance of Four Brazilian Institutions.* Rio de Janeiro: BNDES.

Barton, Clifton, and Marshall Bear. March 1999. *Information and Communications Technologies: Are They the Key to Viable Business Development Services for Micro and Small Enterprises?* Bethesda, Md.: Development Alternatives.

Batra, Geetra, Daniel Kaufman, and Andrew H. W. Stone. 2003. Investment Climate Around the World: Voices of the Firms from the World Business Environment Survey. World Bank, Washington, D.C.

Bass, Jacqueline, and Katrena Henderson. October 2000. Warehouse Receipts: Financing Agricultural Production, Innovations in Microfinance. Technical Note No. 5. USAID Microenterprise Best Practice Project. USAID, Washington, D.C.

Baydas, Mayda, Douglas Graham, and Liza Valenzuela. 1997. Commercial Banks in Microfinance: New Actors in the Microfinance World. Microenterprise Best Practices, available at http://www.mip.org/pdfs/mbp/commer.PDF.

Beck, Thorsten. 2000. Impediments to the Development and Efficiency of Financial Intermediation in Brazil. Policy Research Working Paper 2382. World Bank, Washington, D.C.

———. 2002. Access to Financial Services in Brazil: An Overview. Mimeo. World Bank, Washington, D.C.

Beck, Thorsten, Asli Demirgüc-Kunt, and Vojislav Maksimovic. 2002a. Bank Competition, Financing Constraints, and Access to Credit. Mimeo. World Bank, Washington, D.C.

———. 2002b. Financing Constraints and Firm Growth: Does Size Matter? Policy Research Working Paper 2382. World Bank, Washington, D.C.

Beck, Thorsten, Ross Levine, and Norman Loayza. 1999. Finance and the Sources of Growth. Policy Research Working Paper No. 2057. World Bank, Washington, D.C.

———. 2000. "Finance and the Sources of Growth." *Journal of Financial Economics* 58: 261–300.

Beebe, Christianna. 2000. Palm Pilots: Lending Efficiency to Microcredit. Interaction—Monday Developments. Washington, D.C. Available at http://www.accion.org/PDF/ventures_fall99.

Benartzi, Shlomo, and Richard Thaler. 1995. "Myopic Loss Aversion and the Equity Premium Puzzle." *Quarterly Journal of Economics* 110: 73–92.

Benjamin, McDonald, Alfredo Ebentreich, Anjali Kumar, and Ricardo Pires Gonçalves. 2002. Credit Cooperatives in Brazil. Mimeo. World Bank, Washington, D.C.

Benjamin, McDonald, and Joanna Ledgerwood. 1999. The Dominican Republic—ADEMI. Sustainable Banking with the Poor Project. World Bank, Washington, D.C.

Berger, Allen N., and Gregory F. Udell. 1995. "Relationship Lending and Lines of Credit in Small Firm Finance." *Journal of Business* 68(3): 351–81.

Bernstein, Steven A. August 1999. *Real Estate Finance in Brazil: The State of the Market, 1999*. Washington, D.C.: Mortgage Bankers Association of America.

Bertaud, Alain. 1989. The Regulatory Environment of Urban Land in Indonesia: Constraints Imposed on the Poor. Unpublished memorandum. World Bank, Washington, D.C.

Bertaud, Alain, Marie-Agnes Bertaud, and James O. Wright, Jr. 1988. Efficiency in Land Use and Infrastructure Design: An Application of the Bertaud Model. Policy Planning and Research Staff Discussion Paper, Report INU 17. World Bank, Washington, D.C.

Besley, Timothy. 1994. "How do Market Failures Justify Interventions in Rural Credit Markets?" *The World Bank Research Observer* 9:27–48.

Besley, Timothy, and Stephen Coate. 1991. Group Lending, Repayment Incentives, and Social Collateral. Princeton, N.J.: Princeton University, Woodrow Wilson School of Development Studies.

Biety, Monnie. 1998. *Operational Guidelines for the Development of and Early Stages of Credit Union Operations*. Madison, Wisc.: WOCCU.

Binswanger, Hans, Klaus Deininger, and Gershon Feder. 1993. Power, Distortions, Revolt, and Reform in Agricultural Land Relations. Policy Research Working Paper WPS 1164. World Bank, Washington, D.C.

Bittencourt, Gilson. 1999. Cooperativas da Crédito. CONTAG/CUT, Série Experiências 09. CONTAG/CUT, São Paulo.

————. 2001. Cooperativismo de Crédito Solidário: Constituição e Funcionamento. ADS/CNDRS/NEAD/MDA. Estudos NEAD 4. São Paulo.

Bittencourt, Gilson, and Ricardo Abramovay. 2001. Inovações Institucionais no Financiamento à Agricultura Familiar: O Sistema CRESOL. Mimeo. UNICAMP, São Paulo.

BNDES. 2000a. Conferência Internacional sobre Microfinanças [Internacional Microfinance Conference], Brazil.

————. 2000b. Ensaios e Experiências. Seminario BNDES Microfinanças. Brazil.

————. 2000c. Plano Estratégico—BNDES—2000–2005 [Strategic Plan]. Brazil.

————. 2001a. Criaçao e Fechamento das Firmas Brasileiras: Uma Análise por porte. Informe-se #33. Brazil.

————. 2001b. *Nova Sistemática de Parceria com os Agentes Financieros do BNDES*. Brazil.

————. September 2001, August 2002. *BNDES Boletim MPME—Micro, Pequenas e Medias Empresas [BNDES Bulletin—Micro, Small and Medium Businesses]*. Rio de Janeiro.

Bond, Philip, and Robert Townsend. 1996. "Formal and Informal Financing in a Chicago Ethnic Neighborhood." *Economic Perspectives* 20(4): 3–27.

Booz Allen Hamilton. 2000a. Instituições Financeiras Públicas Federais: Alternativas para a Reorientação Estrategica [Public Federal Financial Institutions: Alternatives for Strategic Reorientation]. Mimeo. São Paulo.

————. 2000b. *Modelagem das Instituições Financeiras Públicas Federais [Modeling of Public Federal Financial Institutions]*. São Paulo.

Borges, L., and S. Bergamini. 2001. "O Risco Legal na Análise de Crédito." *Revista do BNDES* 8(16).

Boucher, Stephen, Bradford Barham, and Brian Branch. 1992. *Credit Unions in Guatemala 1987–1992, Report 2. Financial Market Niche: Member Behavior Profile.* Madison, Wisc.: WOCCU.

Bowman, David, Deborah Minehart, and Matthew Rabin. 1997. *Loss Aversion in a Consumption-Savings Model.* New York: Elsevier.

Bradford, Calvin. 2002. *Risk or Race? Disparities in Sub-Prime Lending.* Washington, D.C.: Center for Community Change.

Branch, Brian. 1999. *A Conceptual Framework for Legislative and Regulatory Systems for Credit Union Supervision.* Madison, Wisc.: WOCCU.

————. March 12, 2003. Credit Union Rural Finance—SICREDI Brazil. Powerpoint presentation. WOCCU, Madison, Wisc.

Branch, Brian, and Gloria Almeyda. 1997. Microfinance in Ecuador: Progreso and Oscus Credit Unions. Sustainable Banking with the Poor Program. World Bank, Washington, D.C.

Branch, Brian, and Anna Cora Evans. 2002. *A Technical Guide to PEARLS—A Performance Monitoring System*. Madison, Wisc.: WOCCU.

Branch, Brian, Nathalie Gons, and Mark Cifuentes. 2001. *The Road to Jinotega*. Madison, Wisc.: WOCCU.

Branch, Brian, and Dave Grace. 2000. *Model Law for Credit Unions*. Madison, Wisc.: WOCCU.

Branch, Brian, and Janette Klaehn. 2002. *Striking the Balance in Microfinance—A Practical Guide to Mobilizing Savings*. Madison, Wisc.: WOCCU.

Branch, Brian, Janette Klaehn, and Anna Cora Evans. 2002. *A Technical Guide to Savings Mobilization—Lessons from the Credit Union Experience*. Madison, Wisc.: WOCCU.

Briceno, Marc. 1998. GSM Cloning. Available at http://www.isaac.cs.berkley.edu/isaac/gsm-faq.html.

Brown, Hilary, and Emma Murphy. 2003. *The Financing of Social Enterprises: A Special Report by the Bank of England*. London: Bank of England.

Brusky Bonnie, and João Paulo Fortuna. 2002. Entendendo a Demanda para as Microfinancas no Brasil: Um Estudo Qualitativo de Duas Cidades [Understanding the Demand for Microfinance in Brazil: A Qualitative Study of Two Cities]. BNDES/PDI, Rio de Janeio.

Burgess, Robin, and Rohini Pande. 2002. Do Rural Banks Matter? Evidence from the Indian Social Banking Experiment. CEPR Discussion Paper No. 4211. Centre for Economic Policy Research, London.

Caixa Econômica Federal. 2002. Projeto Estruturar Proposta de Nova Política Habitacional, Sumarío dos Temas Principais e Dinâmica das Atividades [Project to Structuralize the Proposal of New Housing Policies]. Brasília.

———. 2000. *Annual Report*. Brasília.

———. June 2001. Trazendo o Futuro a Valor Presente [Bringing the Future of the Present Value]. Re-capitalization Plan. Brasília.

———. September 24, 2001. *Diretoria de Desenvolvimento Urbano* [*Urban Development Directory*]. Brasília.

Campion, Anita, and Sahra S. Halpern. 2001. Automating Microfinance—Experience in Latin America, Asia, and Africa. Occasional Paper No. 5. The Microfinance Network, Washington, D.C.

Canadian Cooperative Association. June 2001. *Promise the Future—A Collection of Essays on Cooperatives and Poverty*. Ottawa.

Canadian Government. 2003. *CSBFA Annual Report 2001–2002*. http://strategis.ic.gc.ca/epic/internet/incsbfp-pfpec.nsf/vwapj/la01260e_A_tii.html.

Canuto, Otaviano, and César Mattos. January 2003. *Credit for Small and Medium Companies in Brazil: Problems and Agenda*. Brazil.

Caprio, Gerard, and Patrick Honohan. April 2001. Finance for Growth. Report No. 22239. World Bank, Washington, D.C.
Caprio, Gerard, and Daniela Klingebiel. July 1996. Bank Insolvencies: Cross Country Experience. Policy Research Working Paper No. WPS1620. World Bank, Washington, D.C.
Card Industry Directory. 2002. *Card Industry Directory, 2002 Edition*. New York: Thomson Media.
Cardoso, Renato Fragelli, and Sergio Mikio Koyama. 1999. *A Cunha Fiscal sobre a Intermediação Financeira, in Juros e Spread Bancário no Brasil* [*The Fiscal Cost of Financial Intermediation in the Central Bank's Interest Rates and Bank Spreads in Brazil*]. Brasília: Banco Central.
Cardoso, Ruth, Augusto de Franco, and Miguel Darcy de Oliveira. 1997. *Um Novo Referencial para a Ação Social do Estado e da Sociedade, Comunidade Solidaria e PNUD* [*A New Frame of Reference for Social Actions of State and Society: The Solidarity Community and the UNDP*]. Brasília: Comanidade Solidaria e PNUD.
Carroll, Chris. 1994. "How Does Future Income Affect Current Consumption?" *Quarterly Journal of Economics* 109:111–47.
Carroll, Christopher. 1997. "Buffer-Stock Saving and the Life Cycle/ Permanent Income Hypothesis." *Quarterly Journal of Economics* 112:1–55.
Carvalho, Carlos Eduardo, Rogerio Studart, and Antonio Jose Alves, Jr. 2002. Desnacionalizacao do Setor Bancario e Financiamento das Empresas: A Experiencia Brasileira Recente [Privatization of the Banking Sector and Company Financing: The Recent Brazilian Experience]. CEPAL/IPEA, Textos para Discussao. IPEA, Brasilia.
Carvalho, Fernando J. Cardim de. 2001. The Recent Expansion of Foreign Banks in Brazil: First Results. Working Paper Cbs-181-01. Oxford Centre for Brazilian Studies, Oxford, U.K.
Caskey, John P. 1989. "The IMF and Concerted Lending in Latin American Debt Restructurings: A Formal Analysis." *Journal of International Money and Finance* 8:105–20.
———.1992. Bank Representation in Low-Income and Minority Urban Communities. Research Working Paper. Research Division, Federal Reserve Bank of Kansas City, Kansas City, Mo.
———. 1993. Who Has a Bank Account and Who Doesn't: 1977 and 1989. Research Working Paper. Research Division, Federal Reserve Bank of Kansas City, Kansas City, Mo.
———. 1995. *Fringe Banking, Check-Cashing Outlets, Pawnshops, and the Poor.* New York: Russell Sage Foundation.
———. 1997a. *Beyond Cash and Carry: Financial Savings, Financial Services, and Low-Income Households in Two Communities.* Report for the Consumer Federation of America. Washington, D.C.

———. 1997b. *Lower Income American, Higher Cost Financial Services.* Madison, Wisc.: Filene Research Institute.

———. 2001. Reaching Out to the Unbanked. Available at http://www.chicagofed.org/cedric/2001/session1paper3.pdf.

Cate, Fred H., and Michael E. Staten. 2003. The Impact of National Credit Reporting under the Fair Credit Reporting Act: The Risk of New Restrictions and State Regulation. Working Paper 67. Georgetown University–McDonough School of Business, Washington, D.C.

CEAPE (Centro de Apoio aso Pequenos Empreendimentos). 1998. *Relatório Anual* [*Annual Report*]. Brazil.

———. 2001. *Desempenho do Sistema CEAPE no Período de Janeiro a Junho de 2001* [*Development of the CEAPE System in the Period from January to June 2001*]. Brazil.

Center for Community Change. 2002. *Risk or Race? Disparities in Sub-Prime Lending*. Washington, D.C.

Central Bank of Brazil. 1997–2003. *Boletim do Banco Central do Brasil* (various issues).

———. 1999. *Juros e Spreads Bancário no Brasil* [*Interest Rates and Bank Spreads in Brazil*]. Brasília: Departamento de Estudos e Pesquisa.

———. 1999–2003. *Focus Reports.* Various issues. Brasília.

———. 2000a. *Anuário Estatístico do Crédito Rural* [*Annual Statistics on Rural Credit*]. Brasília.

———. December 2000b. *Evolution of the National Financial System, Annual Report*. www.bcb.org.br.

———. 2000c. *Juros e Spreads Bancário no Brasil: Avaliação de 1 Ano do Projeto.* Brasília: Departamento de Estudos e Pesquisa. Available at www.bcb.org.br.

———. 2001a. *Annual Statistical Report on Rural Credit.* Brasília.

———. 2001b. *Evolution of the National Finance System, Annual Report 2000.* Brasília.

———. December 11, 2001c. Interest Rates and Banking Spreads. Focus Report.

———. 2001d. Juros e Spreads Bancário no Brasil: Avaliação de 2 Anos do Projeto. Available at www.bcb.org.br.

———. 2001e. *Nota Para a Imprensa—Política Monetaria e Operaçoes de Crédito do Sistema Financeiro.* Brasília.

———. 2001f. Recent Developments in the Brazilian Supervisory Framework—Consolidated Supervision in Brazil. Available at www.bcb.gov.br/ingles/public/recdevsupfram.pdf.

———. 2001g. *Sistema Financeiro da Habitação (SFH), Estatísticas Básicas.* Brasília.

———. 2001h. Useful Information, 3rd Quarter, 2001. Brasília.

———. 2002a. As Cooperativas De Crédito e o Banco Central do Brasil. Nota Técnica. Brazil.

———. 2002b. Democratização do Crédito no Brasil—Principais Desafios—Atuação do Banco Central [Popularization of Credit in Brazil—Principal Challenges—An Update by the Central Bank]. Nota Técnica. Brasília.

———. 2002c. Economica Bancária e Crédito—Avaliação de 3 Anos do Projeto Juros e Spreads [An Evaluation of Three Years of the Project on Interest Rates and Spreads]. Bancário, Brazil. Available at www.bcb.org.br.

———. 2002d. *Evolution of the National Financial System, Annual Report of December 2000*. Available at www.bcb.org.br.

———. 2002e. *Nota Para a Imprensa*. Brasília.

CGAP (Consultative Group to Assist the Poorest). 1995. Maximizing the Outreach of Microenterprise Finance: The Emerging Lessons of Successful Programs. Focus Note No. 2. World Bank, Washington, D.C.

———. 1997a. Commercial Banks in Microfinance: New Actors in the Microfinance World. Focus Note No. 12. World Bank, Washington, D.C.

———. 1997b. Effective Governance for Micro-Finance Institutions. Focus Note No. 7. World Bank, Washington, D.C.

———. 1997c. Introducing Savings in Microcredit Institutions: When and How? Focus Note No. 8. World Bank, Washington, D.C.

———. 1997d. State-Owned Development Banks in Micro-Finance. Focus Note No. 10. World Bank, Washington, D.C.

———. 1998. Savings Mobilization Strategies: Lessons from Four Experiences. Focus Note No. 13. World Bank, Washington, D.C.

———. 2001a. Commercialization and Mission Drift, The Transformation of Microfinance in Latin America. Occasional Paper No. 5. World Bank, Washington, D.C.

———. 2001b. Linking Microfinance and Safety Net Programs to Include the Poorest: The Case of IGVGD in Bangladesh. Focus Note No. 21. World Bank, Washington, D.C.

———. 2002. Consensus Microfinance Policy Guidance: Regulation and Supervision. World Bank, Washington, D.C.

Chaves, Rodrigo, and Claudio Gonzalez-Vega. 1992. Principles of Regulation and Prudential Supervision: Should They Be Different for Microenterprise Finance Organizations? Occasional Paper No. 1979. Rural Finance Program. Ohio State University, Columbus.

Chaves, Rodrigo A., and Saul Schor. 2001. Ukraine Financial Markets in Rural Areas. Policy Note. Department for Environmentally and Socially Sustainable Rural Development of the Europe and Central Asia Region, World Bank, Washington, D.C.

Chen, Martha Alter, and Donald Snodgrass. 1999. An Assessment of the Impact of SEWA Bank in India: Baseline Findings. U.S. Agency for International Development, Office of Microenterprise Development, Assessment of the Impact of Microenterprise Services, Washington, D.C.

Chiquier, Loic. December 14, 2001. Access to Financial Services in Brazil—Housing Finance Section. Draft. World Bank, Washington, D.C.

Christen, Robert. 1999. Trip Report: Visit to Banco do Nordeste do Brazil, April 14–25, 1999. Unpublished manuscript.

Christen, Robert Peck, and Deborah Drake. 2001. Commercialization of Microfinance. Working Draft. Microenterprise Best Practices Project, USAID, Washington, D.C.

Christen, Robert Peck, and Richard Rosenberg. 2000. The Rush to Regulate: Legal Frameworks for Microfinance. Occasional Paper No. 4. CGAP, Washington, D.C.

Christen, Robert Peck, Elisabeth Rhyne, Robert C. Vogel, and Cressida McKean. 1995. *Maximizing the Outreach of Microenterprise Finance: The Emerging Lessons of Successful Programs.* Arlington, Va.: International Management and Communications Corporation.

Claessens, Stijn, and Thomas Glaessner. 1997. *Are Financial Sector Weaknesses Undermining the East Asian Miracle?* Washington, D.C.: World Bank.

————. 1998. The Internationalization of Financial Services in Asia. Policy Research Working Paper 1911. World Bank, Washington, D.C.

Claessens, Stijn, Thomas Glaessner, and Daniela Klingebiel. 2000. Electronic Finance: Reshaping the Financial Landscape around the World. Financial Sector Discussion Paper No. 4. World Bank, Washington, D.C.

————. June 2001. E-Finance in Emerging Markets: Is Leapfrogging Possible? Financial Sector Discussion Paper No. 7. World Bank, Washington, D.C.

Clarke, George, Robert Cull, and Maria Soledad Martinez Peria. 2001. Does Foreign Bank Penetration Reduce Access to Credit in Developing Countries? Evidence from Asking Borrowers. World Bank Policy Research Working Paper No. 2. World Bank, Washington, D.C.

Cobbaut, Robert. 1997. *Théorie Financière.* Collection Gestion, Série: Politique Générale, Finance et Marketing. Paris: Economica.

Cocco, João, Francisco Gomes, and Pascal Maenhout. 1998. Consumption and Portfolio Choice over the Life Cycle. Mimeo. Harvard University, Department of Economics, Cambridge, Mass.

Cochrane, John. 1997. Where Is the Market Going? Uncertain Facts and Novel Theories. NBER Working Paper No. 6207. National Bureau of Economic Research, Cambridge, Mass.

Coelho, Isaias, Liam P. Ebril, and Victoria P. Summers. 2001. Bank Debit Taxes in Latin America: An Analysis of Recent Trends. Working Paper 6207. IMF, Washington, D.C.

Community-Driven Mortgage Lending. March 27, 2002. A Proposal to the Ministry of Lands and the Ministry of Agriculture of Malawi. Powerpoint presentation.

Computer Security Institute and the San Francisco Federal Bureau of Investigation's Computer Intrusion Squad. 2001–02. Computer Crime and Security Survey. San Francisco.

Comunidade Solidária. 2000. Organização da Sociedade Civil de Interesse Público, A Lei 9.790/99 como Alternativa para o Terceiro Setor [Organization of Civil Societies and Public Interest OSCLIPs, Law No. 9790/00, as an Alternative for the Tertiary Sector]. Brazil.

————. 2001. A Expansão do Microcrédito no Brasil, Continuação da Quinta Rodada de Interlocução Política do Conselho da Comunidade Solidaria [The Expansion of Microcredit in Brazil: Continuation of the Fifth Round of Policy Discussions of the Council of Community Solidarity]. Brazil.

Comunidade Solidária, IPEA. 1997. *Interlocução Política*. Brazil.

CrediAmigo. 1999a. *Gestão Do Risco e Controle de Qualidade da Carteira [Management of Risk and Portfolio Quality]*. Brazil.

————. 1999b. *Manual Básico CrediAmigo*. Brazil.

————. 1999c. *Plano de Negócios*. Fortaleza, Brazil.

Credit Union National Association. 2003. *Serving Members of Modest Means Survey Report*. Alexandria, Va.

Cruickshank, Don. March 2000. Competition in UK Banking: A Report to the Chancellor of the Exchequer, HM Treasury UK. Press Release 128/00.

CSI/FBI. 2001–02. Computer Crime and Security Survey. Computer Security Institute. San Francisco.

Dantas, Valdi de Araújo. 1998. *A Tecnologia do Microcrédito*. Brazil: Federação de Apoio aos Pequenos Empreendimentos.

————. 2000. Experiência de um Participante do DelNet, Sistema CEAPE (Brasil). DelNet numero 4. Organização Internacional do Trábalo (OIT), Especial Microcrédito, Italy.

Deaton, Angus. 1991. "Saving and Liquidity Constraints." *Econometrica* 59:1221–48.

de Basto, Maria Emília Xavier. 1998. *Menos de 500 Milhões de Pobres até 2005? O Microcrédito como Solução*. Lisbon: Instituto de Cooperação Portuguesa.

de Ferranti, David, and Guillermo Perry. 2000. Securing Our Future in a Global Economy. Report No. 20655. World Bank, Washington, D.C.

Deininger, Klaus, and Lyn Squire. 1996. "Measuring Income Inequality: A New Database." *The World Bank Economic Review* 10:565–91.

De Oliveira, Vergolino, José Raimundo, Gustavo Maria Gomes, and Arístides Monteiro Neto. 2000. Produtos Internos Brutos dos Municipios Brasileiros: 1970, 1975, 1980, 1985, 1990 e 1996. Instituto de Pesquisa Econômica Aplicada, Rio de Janeiro.

Demirgüç-Kunt, Asli, and Harry Huizinga. 1999. "Determinants of Commercial Bank Interest Margins and Profitability: Some International Evidence." *The World Bank Economic Review* 13(2).

Development Bank of Canada. 2001. *Supporting Small Business Innovation: A Review of the Business Development Bank of Canada*. Ottawa: Industry Canada.

DGRV (German Confederation of Credit Cooperatives). October 2002. Auditing of German Co-operative Banks. Bonn.

DIEESE (Departamento Intersindical de Estatísticas e Estudos Socioeconómicos). 2002. São Paulo. www.dieese.org.br.

Dollar, David, and Aart Kraay. 2001. Growth Is Good for the Poor. Policy Research Working Paper No. WPS2587. World Bank, Washingtion, D.C.

Donovan, Nick, and Guy Palmer. July 1999. Meaningful Choices: The Policy Options for Financial Exclusion. New Policy Institute. Available at http://www.npi.org.uk/reports.

Dowall, David E. November 1991. "The Karachi Development Authority: Failing to Get the Prices Right." *Land Economics* 67(4).

————. 1992. A Second Look at the Bangkok Land and Housing Market." *Urban Studies* 29(1).

————. 1995. The Land Market Assessment: A New Tool for Urban Management. Urban Management Program UMP 4. World Bank, Washington, D.C.

————. 1997. A Retrospective Look at the Land Market Assessment. Working Paper 697. University of California, Institute of Urban and Regional Development, Berkeley.

Dowall, David E., and P. Alan Treffeisen. 1991. "Spatial Transformation in Cities of the Developing World: Multinucleation and Land-Capital Substitution in Bogota, Colombia." *Regional Science and Urban Economics* 21.

Doyle, Joseph, Jose Lopez, and Marc Saidenberg. 1998. "How Effective Is Lifeline Banking in Assisting the 'Unbanked'?" *Current Issues in Economics and Finance* 4(6).

Düebel, Achim. 2000. Housing Finance Reforms Policy Note. Internal document. World Bank, Washington, D.C.

Dunham, Constance R. 2001. *The Role of Banks and Nonbanks in Serving Low- and Moderate-Income Communities*. Washington, D.C.: OCC.

Ebentreich, Alfredo. 2002. *Regulation and Supervision of Microfinance—Why, What, Who, and How? Lessons from International Experiences.* Washington, D.C.: World Bank.

Eisenhauer, Janet Marie. 1995. Malawi Union of Savings and Credit Cooperatives: Member Impact Survey. WOCCU, Madison, Wisc.

Escritório Técnico de Estudos Econômicos do Nordeste. 1999. Trabalho Avaliação CrediAmigo [An Evaluation of the Work of CrediAmigo]. Brazil.

Factors Chain International. 2001. *Annual Report 2001.* Amsterdam.

Falkena, Hans, and Reserve Bank of South Africa. 2002. SMEs' Access to Finance in South Africa—A Supply-Side Regulatory Review. Available at http://www.finance.gov.za/documents/sme/.

Farah, Douglas. July 14, 1996. "Satellites Solve Salvadoran Farm Disputes." *The Washington Post,* p. A26.

Farrington, Todd. 2000. "Efficiency in Microfinance Institutions." *The MicroBanking Bulletin* 4.

FASE (Federação de órgãos para Assistência Social e Educacional). *Proposta Magazine* 75.

Federal Reserve Board. July 2000. The Performance and Profitability of CRA-Related Lending. Executive Summary. Washington, D.C.

Felszberg, Thomas. 2001. Country Report—Brazil, Bankruptcy, and Insolvency. Draft. World Bank, Washington, D.C.

Felsberg and Associates. 2003. Background paper for World Bank study on access to financial services. Draft. São Paulo.

Ferguson, Charles, and Donal McKillop. 1997. *The Strategic Development of Credit Unions.* New York: John Wiley & Sons.

Fleisig, Heywood, and Nuria de la Peña. 1996. *Creating a Legal and Regulatory Framework to Promote Access to Rural Credit.* Washington, D.C.: Center for the Economic Analysis of Law.

———. 1999. *Romania: How Problems in the Framework for Secured Transactions Limit Access to Credit.* Washington, D.C.: Center for the Economic Analysis of Law.

Fountain, Wendell V. 1994. *The Credit Union Director—Roles, Duties, and Responsibilities.* Jacksonville, Fla.: FAI Publishing.

Friedman, Milton. 1953. *Essay in Positive Economics.* Chicago: University Press of Chicago.

———. 1957a. "The Permanent Income Hypothesis: Comment." *American Economic Review* 48:990–91.

———. 1957b. *A Theory of Consumption Function.* Princeton, N.J.: Princeton University Press.

———. 1960. "Comments." In Irwin Friend and Robert Jones, eds., *Proceedings of the Conference on Consumption and Saving,* Vol. 11, 191–205. Philadelphia: University of Pennsylvania, Wharton School of Finance and Commerce.

———. 1963. "Windfall, the 'Horizon,' and Related Concepts in the Permanent Income Hypothesis." In Carl F. Christ, ed., *Measurement in Economics*, pp. 3–28. Stanford, Calif.: Stanford University Press.

Galindo, Arturo. 2001. Creditor Rights and the Credit Market: Where Do We Stand? Working Paper No. 448. Inter-American Development Bank, Washington, D.C.

Galindo, Arturo, and Alejandro Micco. 2001. Creditor Protection and Financial Cycles. Working Paper No. 443. Inter-American Development Bank, Washington, D.C.

Gallagher Terence, Fernanda Castanheira, Daniele Vechina, and Elizabeth Toder. 2001. *A Indústria Brasileira de Microcrédito* [*The Microcredit Industry in Brazil*]. Rio de Janerio: Development Alternatives, Inc.

Gallardo, Joselito. 2001. *A Framework for Regulating Microfinance Institutions: The Experience in Ghana and Philippines.* Washington, D.C.: Financial Sector Development Department, World Bank.

Gibbons, David S., and Jennifer W. Meehan. 2000. The Microcredit Summit's Challenge: Working towards Institutional Financial Self-Suficiency While Maintaining a Commitment to Serving the Poorest Families. Microcredit Summit, Washington, D.C.

Giuseppi, James. 2001. European Banks' Environmental and Social Policies and Business Practices Survey. The Giuseppi Report. London: Jon Carpenter.

Glaessner, Thomas, Thomas Kellermann, and Valerie McNevin. May 2002. E-security: Risk Mitigation in Financial Transactions. Mimeo. World Bank, Washington, D.C.

Glaessner, Thomas, Sophie Sirtaine, and Daniela Klingebiele. 2002. The Privately Owned Banks Serving Low-Income Segments in Brazil: Constraints and Possibilities. Access Study. World Bank, Washington, D.C.

Goldmark, Lara, Simeon Nichter, and Anita Fiori. July 2002. *Understanding Microfinance in the Brazilian Context.* Rio de Janeiro: BNDES Microfinance.

Goldmark, Lara, Steve Pockross, and Daniele Vechina. May 2–3, 2000. The Status of Microfinance in Brazil. Briefing paper for speakers at the BNDES seminar. BNDES-BID de Microfinanças. Rio de Janeiro.

Goldmark, Lara, and Daniele Vechina. 2000. A Situação no Brasil. BNDES/OIT, Especial Microcrédito, DelNet numero 4. Organização Internacional do Trábalo, Italy.

Gomez, Arelis, Thomas Fitzgerald, and Robert Vogel. 2000. *Regulation and Supervision of Microfinance Activities: The Philippine Case Study.* Washington, D.C.: International Management and Communications Corporation.

Gomez, Arelis, Germán Tabares, and Robert Vogel. 2000. *Microfinance, Bank Regulation, and Supervision: The Bolivian Case Study*. Washington, D.C.: International Management and Communications Corporation.

Goncalves, José Pereira. March 1997. *Acesso ao Financiamento para Moradia pelos Extratos de Media e Baixa Renda [Access to Housing Finance for Medium and Low-Income Earners]*. Brasília: CEPAL.

Goncalves, Ricardo Pires, and Anjali Kumar. December 3, 2001. Access to Financial Services in Brazil: Background Note on the BNDES Bank and Microcredit. Draft. World Bank, Washington, D.C.

Goodwin, Ruth. 1997. Key Issues for Profitable Commercial Bank Engagement in Microfinance. Draft for Discussion at Asia Regional Conference on Sustainable Banking with the Poor.

Goodwin-Groen, Ruth. 2000. Do Asian MFIs Access Funds from Commercial Banks? Independent consultancy, New York.

Government of Brazil. June 6, 1999. Housing Reforms. Preliminary Report of the Working Group Established by Interministerial Rule Number. Translated in October 1999.

Government of Brazil, Secretaria de Política Econômica. December 2000. *Orçamento de Renúncias Fiscais e Subsídios da União*. Brazil.

Gropp, Reint, John Karl Scholz, and Michelle White. 1997. "Personal Bankruptcy and Credit Supply and Demand." *Quarterly Journal of Economics* 112(1).

Grosh, Margaret, and Paul Williams Glewwe. 2000. *Designing Household Survey Questionnaires for Developing Countries: Lessons from 15 Years of the Living Standards Measurement Study*. Volumes 1, 2, and 3. Washington, D.C.: World Bank.

Gudger, Michael. 1997. "Sustainability of Credit Guarantee Systems." *The Financier* 4(1/2).

Guerrero, Javier Alvaro. 2000. *As Microfinanças e o Crédito Rural—América Latina*. Peru: Centro de Estudios Peruanos.

Haag, Susan White. 2002. "Community Reinvestment: A Review of Urban Outcomes and Challenges." *International Regional Science Review* 25(3).

Hall, Robert. 1978. "Stochastic Implications of the Life-Cycle Permanent Income Hypothesis: Theory and Evidence." *Journal of Political Economy* 86:971–87.

Hallberg, Kristin. 2001. A Market-Oriented Strategy for Small and Medium-Scale Enterprises. IFC Discussion Paper No. 40. International Finance Corporation, Washington, D.C.

Hannig, Alfred, and Edward Katinbo-Mugwanya, eds. 2000. *How to Regulate and Supervise Microfinance—Key Issues in an International Perspective*. Washington, D.C.: World Bank.

Hawkins, John, and Dubravko Mihaljek. 2001. "The Banking Industry in the Emerging Market Economies: Competition, Consolidation, and Systemic Stability—An Overview." In The Banking Industry in the Emerging Market Economies: Competition, Consolidation, and Systemic Stability. BIS Paper No. 4. Bank for International Settlements, Basel, Switzerland.

Hazell, Peter. March 27–28, 1995. Managing Default Risks in Rural Finance: The Experience with Credit Insurance Programs. Paper presented at the Workshop on Finance against Poverty. Reading University.

Helmuth, Pabst. 2001. *Mejores Practicas en la Supervisión y Regulación de las Cooperativas de Ahorro y Crédito.* Santiago: DGRV.

HM Treasury. March 6, 2001. *Supply of Banking Services by Clearing Banks to SMEs: The Commission's Provisional Conclusions on Complex Monopoly.* London.

————. 2002a. *Enterprise Britain: A Modern Approach to Meeting the Enterprise Challenge, UK Pre-Budget.* London.

————. 2002b. Small Business Service: Pre-Budget Report 2002—Key Issues for Small Business. Available at http://www.businesslink.org/cgi-bin/bv1/detail.jsp?PCOID=-9038&POID=1073783364&furl param = pbr.

Hoek-Smit, Marja. May 2002. *Towards a National Housing Policy for Brazil.* Washington, D.C.

Holden, Paul, and Vassili Prokopenko. 2001. Financial Development and Poverty Alleviation: Issues and Policy Implications for Developing and Transition Countries.Working Paper WP/01/160. IMF, Washington, D.C.

Holtmann, Martin, Ilonka Rühle, and Adalbert Winkler. 2000. "SME Financing: Lessons from Microfinance." *SME Issues—New Ideas from the World of Small and Medium Enterprises* 1(1).

Honohan, Patrick, and Daniela Klingebiel. September 2000. Controlling the Fiscal Costs of Banking Crises. Policy Research Working Paper No. WPS2441. World Bank, Washington, D.C.

Hubbard, Glenn, Jonathan Skinner, and Stephen Zeldes. 1995. "Precautionary Saving and Social Insurance." *Journal of Political Economy* 103: 360–99.

IBGE (Instituto Brasileira de Geografia e Estatística). 2000. National Household Survey. Rio de Janeiro.

Industry Canada. 2001. *Supporting Small Business Innovation: A Review of the Business Development Bank of Canada.* Ottawa.

————. 2003. Canada Small Business Financing Program, Canada Bank's Data, Appendix A. Ottawa.

Ingram, Gregory K. 1982. "Land in Perspective: Its Role in the Structure of Cities." In Matthew Cullen and Sharon Woolery, eds., *World Congress on Land Policy, 1980*. Lexington, Mass.: Lexington Books.

Instituto de Pesquisa Economica Aplicada (IPEA)/Diretoria de Estudos Regionais e Urbanos. 2001. Study. World Bank, Washington, D.C.

IPM. 2000. Pre-Feasibility Study: Brazilian Micro-Finance Institution. Prepared for Opportunity International. Illinois.

Jacob, Katy, Malcolm Bush, and Dan Immergluck. 2002. *Rhetoric and Reality: An Analysis of Mainstream Credit Unions' Serving Low-Income People*. Chicago: Woodstock Institute.

Jansson, Tor. 2000. *Issues in Regulating and Supervising Microfinance—Latin America*. Washington, D.C.: Inter-American Development Bank.

———. 2001. *The Building Blocks of Microfinance Regulation*. Washington, D.C.: Sustainable Development Department, Inter-American Development Bank.

Jansson, Tor, and Mark Wenner. 1997. *Financial Regulation and Its Significance for Microfinance in Latin America and the Caribbean*. Washington, D.C.: Inter-American Development Bank.

Jiménez, Soto, Max Alberto, and Alan Thompson Chacon. 1999. Recomendaciones para la Adecuación de los Marcos Regulatorios y de Supervisión Financiera en Centroamérica al Financiamiento no Convencional [Recommendations for the Adjustment of Regulatory Marks and Financial Supervision in Central America for Nonconventional Financing]. Project PAR-FOLADE-DID-BCIE. Canadian International Development Agency, Quebec.

Kessel, Moysés. 2001. O Crédito Rural no Brasil [Rural Credit in Brazil]. Nota Técnica. Central Bank of Brazil–DEPEC, Brasília.

King, Robert G., and Ross Levine. 1993. Finance and Growth: Schumpeter Might Be Right. Policy Research Working Paper No. 1083. World Bank, Washington, D.C.

Kirkpatrick, Colin, and Samuel Munzele Maimbo. 2002. "The Implications of the Evolving Microfinance Agenda for Regulatory and Supervisory Policy." *Development Policy Review* 20(3): 293–304.

Klapper, Leora. May 23, 2001. Access to Electronic Services. World Bank, Washington, D.C.

Kochar, Anjini. 1997. "An Empirical Investigation of Rationing Constraints in Rural Credit Markets in India." *Journal of Development Economics* 53:339–71.

Koyama, Sergio Mikio, and Marcio I. Nakane. July 2001. Os Efeitos da CPMF sobre a Intermediação Financeira. Trabalhos para Discussão 23. Banco Central do Brasil. Brazil.

Krebsbach, Karen. September 2, 2002. "Following the Money." *U.S. Banker*.

Lacoursiere, Robert, Juan Partida, and Paulo Roberto Ribeiro. January 18, 2001. "Brazilian Banks, Coming to Term with the Risk of Growth." In *Global Equity Research Latin America*. New York: Lehman Brothers.

Laibson, David. 1997. "Golden Eggs and Hyperbolic Discounting." *Quarterly Journal of Economics* 112:443–77.

La Porta, Rafael, Florencio Lopez-de-Silanes, Andrei Shleifer, and Robert W. Vishny. 1998. "Law and Finance." *Journal of Political Economy* 106(6).

Latin America Newsletters. 2001. Banking in Latin America. Mimeo. London.

Leal, Ricardo P. C. 2001a. *Access to Credit in Brazil, An Exploratory Study*. Washington, D.C.: World Bank.

————. 2001b. *A Descriptive Analysis of the Capital Structure of a Broad Sample of Brazilian Firms*. Washington, D.C.: World Bank.

————. 2001c. *Characteristics and Instruments of the Brazilian Credit Market*. Washington, D.C.: World Bank.

————. 2001d. A Review of the Empirical Evidence and of the Factors That Influence Brazilian Business Financing. Mimeo.

Leite, Luiz Lemos. 2001. *Factoring no Brasil*. São Paulo: Editora Atlas.

Levine, Ross, Norman Loayza, and Thorsten Beck. 1999. Financial Intermediation and Growth: Causality and Causes. Policy Research Working Paper 2059. World Bank, Washington, D.C.

Linares, Carlos. 1989. *Revised Planning and Design Standards for BTN Financed Housing*. Jakarta: Lembaga Management and Flagler Management Group.

Litan, Robert, Nicholas P. Retsinas, Eric S. Belsky, and Susan White-Haag. April 2000. *The Community Reinvestment Act after Financial Modernization: A Baseline Report*. Washington, D.C.: U.S. Department of the Treasury.

Lora, Eduardo. 2001. Structural Reforms in Latin America: What Has Been Reformed and How to Measure It? Working Paper 466. Inter-American Development Bank, Washington, D.C.

Lora, Eduardo, Patricia Cortés, and Ana Maria Herrera. 2001. *Los obstáculos al Desarrollo Empresarial y el Tamaño de las Firmas en América Latina* [*Obstacles to Enterprise Development and Firm Size in Latin America*]. Washington, D.C.: Inter-American Development Bank.

Lundberg, Mattias, and Lyn Squire. 2001. Growth and Inequality: Extracting the Lessons for Policymakers. Mimeo. World Bank, Washington D.C.

MacPherson, Ian. 1999. *Hands Around the Globe—A History of the International Credit Union Movement and the Role and Development of World Council of Credit Unions, Inc.* Victoria, British Columbia: WOCCU and Horsdal & Schubart Publishers Ltd.

Mahajan, Vijay, and Bharah Ramola Gupta. 1996. "Financial Services for the Rural Poor and Women in India: Access and Sustainability." *Journal of International Development* 8(2): 211–24.

Mankiw, Gregory N. 1982. "Hall's Consumption Hypothesis and Durable Goods." *Journal of Monetary Economics* 10: 417–25.

Marker, Phil, Kerry McNamara, and Lindsay Wallace. 2002. *The Significance of Information and Communication Technologies for Reducing Poverty*. London: Department for International Development.

Martins, Paulo, H., Andrei Winograd, and Renata de Carvalho Salles. 2002. *Regulamentação das Microfinanças* [*Microfinance Regulation*]. Rio de Janeiro: BNDES.

Maurer, Klaus. 1999. Bank Rakyat Indonesia (BRI): Indonesia (Case Study). Consultative Group to Assist the Poorest, Washington, D.C.

Mayer, Thomas. 1972. *Permanent Income, Wealth, and Consumption: A Critique of the Permanent Income Theory, Life-Cycle Hypothesis, and Related Theories*. Berkeley: University of California Press.

McKinsey and Co. 2001. "Brazil's Head Start in Online Banking." *The McKinsey Quarterly* 2.

McKinsey Global Institute. 1998. *MGI Report: Productivity—The Key to an Accelerated Development Path for Brazil*. New York.

McLean, Douglas, and Matthew Gamser. October 11, 1995. Hi-Tech at the Frontier: Reducing the Transaction Cost of Lending in Swaziland with the SmartCard. Presentation at the Sustainable Banking with the Poor Seminar Series. World Bank, Washington, D.C.

Meagher, Patrick, Doris Muyinga, and Betty Wilkinson. 1999. *Zambian Laws Affecting Microfinance: Review and Recommendations for Reform*. College Park: University of Maryland, Center for Institutional Reform and the Informal Sector.

Meagher, Patrick, and Betty Wilkinson. September 26, 2001. *Filling the Gap in South Africa's Small and Micro Credit Market: An Analysis of Major Policy, Legal, and Regulatory Issues*. College Park: University of Maryland, Center for Institutional Reform and the Informal Sector.

Mesbah, Dina. 1998a. *The Role of Credit Unions in Nicaraguan Financial Markets: Improving the Financial Access of Small Savers and Borrowers*. Madison, Wisc.: WOCCU.

————. 1998b. *The Role of Credit Unions in Salvadoran Financial Markets: Expanding and Improving the Delivery of Financial Services to the Rural Poor*. Madison, Wisc.: WOCCU.

Mesbah, Dina, Connie Dey-Marcos, and World Council of Credit Unions. 1997. The Role of Credit Unions in Ecuadoran Financial Markets: A Case Study of 11 Credit Unions. Research Monograph Series. Madison, Wisc.: WOCCU.

Meyer, Richard L. 2000. Iniciativas Asiáticas para Desenvolver Mercados Financeiros Rurais: Algumas Idéias para o Brasil [Asian Initiatives for Developing Rural Financial Markets—Some Ideas for Brazil]. Seminario Internacional de Microfinanças. BNDES, Rio de Janeiro.

Mezzera, Jaime. 2000a. *A Expansão do Microcrédito no Brasil, Dados Brasileiros, e Reflexões de 20 anos de Experiencia.* Brasília: Organização Internacional do Trabalho.

———. 2000b. A Situação das Microfinanças na América Latina [The Condition of Microfinance in Latin America]. Especial Microcrédito, DelNet 4. Organização Internacional do Trabalho, Brasília.

———. November 2002. "Microcredit in Brazil: The Gap between Supply and Demand." *MicroBanking Bulletin* 8.

MicroBanking Standards Project. 1999. *MicroBanking Bulletin* 3.

———. November 2001. "Focus on Transparency." *MicroBanking Bulletin* 7.

———. 2002. "Focus on Standardization." *MicroBanking Bulletin* 8.

Microcredit Summit. 1997–2003. State of the Microcredit Summit Campaign Report. Washington, D.C.

Micro-Finance Regulatory Council. 2001. *The Second Annual Report of the Micro-Finance Regulatory Council Covering the Period July 2000 to August 2001.* Parktown, Johannesburg.

Miller, Margaret. 2003. *Credit Reporting Systems around the Globe: The State of the Art in Public and Private Credit Registries.* Washington, D.C.: World Bank.

Miller, Margaret, and Nataliya Mylenko. 2002. Credit Reporting around the World. Executive Summary. World Bank, Washington, D.C.

Ministry of Agricultural Development. 2000. *Novo Retrato da Agricultura Familiar—O Brasil Redescoberto* [*A New Portrait of Family Agriculture—Brazil Rediscovered*]. Brasília: Ministry ofAgricultural Development/ Instituto Nacional de Colonização e Reforma Agrária.

———. 2001. Pecuária e Abastecimento. Plano Agrícola e Pecuário 2001–2002 [Agriculture and Cattle Plan 2001–2002]. http://200.252.165.21/spa/spa_09.htm.

Ministry of Finance, Secretariat of International Affairs. January 14, 2003a. Brazil and the International Financial Architecture. Mimeo. Brazil.

———. January 14, 2003b. Credit Flows to the Private Sector. Mimeo. Brazil.

Miranda, Jose Carlos. 2001. Liberalizacao Financeira, Estrategias Bancarias e Desempenho do Mercado Financeiro no Brazil nos Anos 1990 [Financial Liberalization, Bank Strategies, and Financial Market Performance in Brazil in the 1990s]. Mimeo.

Mollin, Jason. March 2001. *Brazilian Banks, Initiation of Coverage, Equity Research, Emerging Markets.* New York: Bear Stearns.

Moody's. December 2001. *South Africa Banking Sector Outlook.*

Morduch, Jonathan. 1999. "The Microfinance Promise." *Journal of Economic Literature* 37:1569–14.

———. 2000. "The Microfinance Schism." *World Development* 28(4): 617–29.

Morris, Kelly J. 1995. The Effects of Using Credit Unions as Onlending Agents for External Lines of Credit: The Experience of the International Credit Union Movement. Poverty-Oriented Banking Working Paper No. 14. International Labour Office, Geneva.

National Community Reinvestment Coalition. 2003. *America's Best and Worst Lenders: A Consumer's Guide to Lending in Metropolitan Areas.* Washington, D.C.

Nelson, Eric R. July 1999. Financial Intermediation for the Poor—Survey of the State of the Art. African Economic Policy Discussion Paper No. 10. World Bank, Washington, D.C.

Netcash. 2000. Apresentação da Companhia [Company Presentation]. São Paulo.

Nobrega, Mailsonda, Gustavo Loyola, Ernesto Moreira Guedes Filho, and Denise Pasqual. 2001. O Mercado de Capitais: Sua Importancia para o Desenvolvimento e os Entraves com que Se Defronta no Brasil [The Complete Market: Its Importance for Development and Constraints Faced in Brazil]. Mimeo. Estudos para o Desenvolvimento do Mercado de Capitais, Bovespa.

Ohls, James, Richard Weisberg, and Michelle White. 1974. "The Effects of Zoning on Land Value." *Journal of Urban Economics* 1:428–44.

Orbeta Jr., Aniceto C., Cristina G. Lopez, and Dale W. Adams. September 1998. *An Assessment of Loan Guarantee Programs for Small-Scale Borrowers in the Philippines.* Manila: Credit Policy Improvement Program, Secretary of Finance.

Ouattara, Korotoumou, Mayada Baydas, and Douglas Graham. 1995. *Credit Unions in the Financial Markets in Niger.* Columbus: Ohio State University, Department of Agricultural Economics.

Padilla, Atilano Jorge, and Alejandro Requejo. 2000. The Costs and Benefits of the Strict Protection of Creditor Rights: Theory and Evidence. Working Paper 384. Inter-American Development Bank, Washington, D.C.

Parente, Silvana. 2000. Microcredit Policy as a Financial Market Mechanism to Reduce Poverty—The Experience of the Banco do Nordeste do Brazil. Mimeo. Cambridge, Mass.: MIT.

Paulson, Jo Ann, and James McAndrews. 1999. *Financial Services for the Urban Poor, South Africa's E-Plan.* Washington, D.C.: World Bank.

Paxton, Julia. 2002. "Depth of Outreach and Its Relation to the Sustainability of Microfinance Institutions." *Savings and Development* 26(1): 69–86.

Paxton, Julia, and Carlos Cuevas. 1998. *Outreach and Sustainability of Member-Based Rural Financial Intermediaries in Latin America—A Comparative Analysis*. Washington, D.C.: Sustainable Banking with the Poor Program, World Bank.

Petersen, Mitchell, and Raghuram Rajan. 1994. "The Benefits of Lending Relationships: Evidence from Small Business Data." *Journal of Finance* 49:3–37.

Petrie, Ragan. 2002. *Report on Member and Non-Member Survey Rwanda Credit Unions*. Madison, Wisc.: WOCCU.

Pinheiro, Armando Castelar. April 27, 2001. Judges' View on the Judiciary and Economics. Paper presented at the seminar Reforma do Judiciário: Problemas, Desafios e Perspectivas, IDESP, São Paulo, Brazil.

Pinheiro, Armando Castelar, and Celia Cabral. 1998. "Credit Markets in Brazil: The Role of Judicial Enforcement and Other Institutions." *Ensaios BNDES* 9.

————. 2001. "Credit Markets in Brazil: The Role of the Judiciary and Other Institutions," In M. Pagano, ed., *Defusing Default: Incentives and Institutions*. Washington, D.C.: Inter-American Development Bank.

Pinheiro, Armando Castelar, and Alkimar Moura. 2001. Segmentation and the Use of Information in Brazilian Credit Markets. BNDES Textos para Discussão No. 88. Rio de Janeiro.

Planet Finance. July 2000. Country Study India. Paris.

Poyo, Jeffrey. 1995. Expansion of Rural Financial Services: The Development of a Community-Based Rural Credit Union Network in the Dominican Republic (1984–1993). Poverty-Oriented Banking Working Paper No. 10. Inter-American Development Bank and International Labour Office, Geneva.

Puga, Fernando Pimentel. 1999. Sistema Financeiro Brasileiro: Reestruturação Recente, Comparações Internacionais e Vulnerabilidade à Crise Cambial [Brazilian Financial System: Recent Restructuring, International Comparisons, and Vulnerability to Exchange Crisis]. Texto para Discussão No. 68. BNDES, Rio de Janeiro.

————. 2000. Experiências de Apoio às Micro, Pequenas e Médias Empresas nos Estados Unidos, na Itália e em Taiwan. Textos para Discussão No. 75. BNDES, Rio de Janeiro.

Rajan, Raghuram, and Luigi Zingales. 1998. "Financial Dependence and Growth." *American Economic Review* 71(3): 559–86.

Ram, Monder, David Smallbone, and David Deakins. 2002. *Ethnic Minority Businesses in the UK: Access to Finance and Business Support*. London: British Bankers' Association.

Ramola, Bharti, and Vijay Majahan. 1996. Financial Services for the Rural Poor and Women in India: Policy Issues on Access and Sustainability. Sustainable Banking with the Poor Occasional Paper No. 6. World Bank, Washington, D.C.

Reed, Larry, and David Befus. 1993. Transformation Lending: Helping Microenterprises Become Small Businesses. GEMINI Working Paper No. 37. USAID, Washington, D.C.

Renaud, Bertand. 1989. "Compounding Financial Repression with Rigid Urban Regulations: Lessons of the Korean Housing Market." *Review of Urban and Regional Development Studies* 1:3–22.

Republic of South Africa. 2002. Promotion of Equality and Prevention of Unfair Discrimination Act. Pretoria.

Richardson, David C. 2000. "Unorthodox Microfinance: The Seven Doctrines of Success." *Microbanking Bulletin* 4.

Richardson, David C., and Barry Lennon. October 2001. *Teaching Old Dogs New Tricks—The Commercialization of Credit Unions, Microenterprise Best Practices*. Bethesda, Md.: Development Alternatives Inc.

Richardson, David, Barry Lennon, and Brian Branch. March 1993. *Credit Unions Retooled—A Road Map for Financial Stabilization*. Madison, Wisc.: WOCCU.

Richter, Lisa, and Christopher Tan. 2002. *Innovative Products and Services for Low-Income and Unbanked Customers*. Chicago: National Consumer Investment Fund.

RioCred—Diretoria de Risco. 2001. *Indicadores de Risco*. Brazil.

Roberts, Bradford. 2001. State Economic Memorandum: Micro, Small, and Medium Enterprises in Northeast Brazil. International Finance Corporation, Washington, D.C.

Robinson, Marguerite S. 2001. *The Microfinance Revolution: Sustainable Finance for the Poor*. Washington, D.C.: World Bank.

Roemer, Michael, and Mary Kay Gugerty. March 1997. *Does Economic Growth Reduce Poverty?* Cambridge, Mass.: Harvard Institute for International Development.

Romer, David. 1996. *Advanced Macroeconomics*. New York: McGraw-Hill.

Rosales, Ramon. 2000. *Marco Jurídico para as Instituições de Microcrédito—América Latina* [*Judicial Mark for Microcredit Institutions—Latin America*]. International Consulting Corporation.

———. 2002. *Tendencias Recientes en la Regulación del Financiamiento a la Microempresa* [*Recent Trends in the Regulation of Microenterprise Financing*]. Washington, D.C.: Inter-American Forum on Microenterprise.

Rosenberg, Richard. 1994. Beyond Self-Sufficiency: Licensed Leverage and Microfinance Strategy. Unpublished draft.

Salomon Smith Barney. November 2001. Foreign Financial Institutions in Latin America. Mimeo. New York.

Sánchez, Susana. 2002. *Bringing Microfinance Services to the Poor: The Successful Story of CrediAmigo in Brazil, In Brief*. Washington, D.C.: World Bank.

Sánchez, Susana, and Steven Schonberger. 1999. *CrediAmigo: Financial Evaluation*. Washington, D.C.: World Bank.

———. 2000. *Central de Microcrédito do Nordeste—A Case Study, Credi-Amigo.* Washington, D.C.: World Bank.

Sánchez, Susana, Steven Schonberger, and Jacob Yaron. 2000. The New Approach to Rural Finance: Its Application in Brazil. Mimeo. World Bank, Washington, D.C.

Sánchez, Susana, and Walter Zunic. February 2002. Brazil Access Study—Background Note on Banco do Nordeste (BNB) and Banco da Amazonia (BASA). Mimeo. World Bank, Washington, D.C.

Santo, Benedito Rosa do Espirito. 2001. *Eos Caminhos da Agricultura Brasileira* [*The Paths of Brazilian Agriculture*]. São Paulo: BM&F and Editora Evoluir.

Schiff, Maurice, and Alberto Valdés. 1992. *The Plundering of Agriculture in Developing Countries.* Washington, D.C.: World Bank.

Schmidt, Reinhard H., and Claus-Peter Zeitinger. 1994. Critical Issues in Small and Microbusiness Finance. Working Paper No. 1. IPC, Frankfurt, Germany.

Schonberger, Steven. 1999. Microfinance Prospects in Brazil. Mimeo. World Bank, Washington, D.C.

———. 2000a. Microfinance Prospects in Brazil. Forthcoming Economic and Sector Work, LCSES, Latin America and the Caribbean Region, World Bank, Washington, D.C.

———. 2000b. Microfinance Prospects in Brazil. Mimeo. World Bank, Washington, D.C.

———. 2001. Microfinance Prospects in Brazil. Latin America and Caribbean Region Sustainable Development Working Paper No. 12. World Bank, Washington, D.C.

Schonberger, Steven N., and Robert Peck Christen. 2001. *A Multilateral Donor Triumphs over Disbursement Pressure.* Washington, D.C.: CGAP, World Bank.

Schor, Gabriel. 1997. Commercial Financial Institutions as Micro-Lending Partners, Some Lessons of the Micro Global Program in Paraguay. Working Paper No. 15. IPC, Frankfort.

Schreiner, Mark, 2000. *Credit Scoring for Microfinance: Can It Work?* St. Louis, Mo.: Washington University, Center for Social Development.

SEBRAE. 1999. *SEBRAE Orienta Pequenas Empresas em Relação a Crédito Bancário—Brasil* [*SEBRAE Orients Small Enterprises to Bank Credit*]. Brasília.

SEBRAE website: www.sebrae.com.br. Accessed in 2004.

Secretaria do Emprego e Relações do Trábalo de São Paulo. 2001. *Banco do Povo, Acreditando em Quem Produz, Bases para Parceria Estados e Municípios* [*The People's Bank: Believing in Those That Produce, a Basis for State and Municipal Partnership*]. São Paulo: Government of the State of São Paulo.

SEDU. October 2001. Principais Legislações da Area de Habitaçã [Principal Laws in the Area of Housing]. Compiled for the World Bank Mission. Mimeo. Brasília.

Sharma, Manohar, and Manfred Zeller. 1996. Repayment Performance in Group-Based Credit Programs in Bangladesh: An Empirical Analysis. Discussion Paper. International Food Policy Research Institute, Washington, D.C.

Shleifer, Andrei, and Robert W. Vishny. 1996. "A Survey of Corporate Governance." *Journal of Finance* 52:737–83.

ShoreBank, and the Center for Law and Human Services. 2001. *Money in the Bank: The Extra Credit Savings Program.* Chicago.

Sinclair, Stephen P. 2001. Financial Exclusion: An Introductory Survey. CRSIS Briefing. Edinburgh College of Art, Heriot Watt University, Edinburgh.

Sirtaine, Sophie. 2001. On the Services Offered by Post Offices—A Cross-Country Study. Mimeo. World Bank, Washington, D.C.

Soares, Marden. 2001. *Microcrédito.* Brasília: Banco Central do Brasil, DINOR,

Small Business Service. 2001. Entrepreneurs in Deprived Areas and Disadvantaged Groups to Benefit from Further Phoenix Fund Supports. SBS-related press release. http://www.sbs.gov.uk/default.php?page=/press/news50.php.

Squire, Lyn. December 8, 1995. What We Expect from a Bank Project—The Rural Finance Context. Seminar presentation at the World Bank, Washington, D.C.

Stallings, Barbara, and Rojerio Studart. 2001. Financial Regulation and Supervision in Emerging Markets: The Experience of Latin America since the Tequila Crisis. Mimeo. ECLAC, Economic Development Division, Santiago, Chile.

Staschen, Stefan. 1999. *Regulation and Supervision of Microfinance Institutions: State of Knowledge.* Eschborn, Germany: Deutsche Gesellshaft für Technische Zusammenarbelt.

Staten, Michael. 2001. "The Value of Comprehensive Credit Reports: Lessons from the U.S. Experience." In *Making Small Business Lending Profitable—Proceedings from the Global Conference on Credit Scoring.* Washington, D.C.: IFC.

State of California. September 2001. Payday Lending Fact Sheet. Available at http://www.corp.ca.gov/pub/payday.htm.

Stegman, Michael. 2003. "Banking the Un-banked: Connecting Residents of Social Housing to the Financial Mainstream." In *Housing and Social Change: An International Perspective.* London: Routledge.

Stiglitz, Joseph E. 1994. "The Role of the State in Financial Markets." *Proceedings of the World Bank Annual Conference on Development Economics.* Washington, D.C.: World Bank.

Stiglitz, Joseph E., and Andrew Weiss. 1981. "Credit Rationing in Markets with Imperfect Information." *American Economic Review* 71(3).

Studart, Rojerio. 2000. "Pension Funds and the Financing of Productive Investment: An Analysis Based on Brazil's Recent Experience." *Série Financiamiento del Desarollo* 102, LC/L.1409-P.

Studart, Rojerio, and Jennifer Hermann. 2001. Sistemas Financeiros no Mercosul: Perspectivas a Partir das Reformas dos Anos 1990 [Financial Systems in the Mercosul: Perspectives on Reforms in the 1990s]. Texto para Discussão 799. IPEA, Rio de Janeiro.

Sukarno, Imam. 1999. *How to Regulate and Supervise Microfinance: Key Issues in an International Perspective—The Case of Indonesia.* Proceedings of the High-Level Policy Workshop. FSD Series No. 1. Kampala: Bank of Uganda/FSD.

Sullivan, Richard. 2000. *How Has the Adoption of Internet Banking Affected Performance and Risk in Banks?* Kansas City, Mo.: Federal Reserve Bank of Kansas City.

Sutoro, Ann Dunham, and Roes Haryanto. 1990. KUPEDES Development Impact Survey. BRI Briefing Booklet. Jakarta.

Task Group of the Policy Board for Financial Services and Regulation. 2001. SMEs' Access to Finance in South Africa—A Supply Side Regulatory Review. Internal Report. South African Government, Treasury Department, Pretoria.

The Financier. February/May 1997. "Analyses of Capital and Money Market Transactions." Philadelphia.

Theodore, Leslie, and Jacques Trigo. 2001. The Experience of Microfinance Institutions with Regulation and Supervision: Perspectives from Practitioners and a Supervisor. Working Draft. Microenterprise Best Practices, USAID.

The Secretary, Joint Audit Committee. January 5, 1994. Management Response to OED: A Review of Bank Lending for Agricultural Credit and Rural Finance. World Bank, Washington, D.C.

Tomlinson, Mary. 2002. Extending Appropriate Financial Services to Low-Income Communities. Internal Discussion Paper Draft 3. AHI. Pretoria, South Africa.

Townsend, Robert, with Anna Paulson, Sombat Sakuntasathien, Tae Joeng Lee, and Michael Binford. 1997. *Risk, Insurance, and the Family.* Rockville, Md.: National Institute of Child Health and Human Development and National Science Foundation.

Townsend, Robert, and Jacob Yaron. 2001. The Credit Risk Contingency System of an Asian Development Bank. 3Q/2001 Economic Perspectives. Federal Reserve Bank of Chicago, Chicago.

Tully, Shawn. April 14, 2003. "Bank of the Americas; BofA Is Betting Its Future on the Hispanic Market." *Fortune.* gihttp://www/fortune.com/fortune/fortune500/articles/0,15114,438340,00.html.

Udry, Christopher. 1990. "Credit Markets in Northern Nigeria: Credit as Insurance in a Rural Economy." *World Bank Economic Review* 4(3): 251–69.

———. 1995. "Risk and Saving in Northern Nigeria." *American Economic Review* 85(5):1287–1300.

Udry, Christopher, and Ernest Aryeetey. 1995. "The Characteristics of Informal Financial Markets in Africa." *Journal of African Economies* 6(1).

U.K. Government. February 2001. Opportunity for All in a World of Change. White Paper. DTI Publications, London.

UNDP. 2001. Status of Microfinance in Brazil. Mimeo. Brazil.

Unibanco. February 2003. Presentation of Unibanco at the World Bank seminar on Access to Financial Services. Washington, D.C.

Uppal, Mahesh. 2003. When Can ICTs Benefit Microfinance? Mimeo. World Bank, Washington, D.C.

U.S. Department of the Treasury. January 2001. *Capital Access Programs: A Summary of Nationwide Performance.* Washington, D.C.

U.S. Department of the Treasury and U.S. Department of Housing and Urban Development. June 2000. *Curbing Predatory Home Mortgage Lending: A Joint Report.* Washington, D.C.

Valenzuela, Liza. 2001. Getting the Recipe Right: The Experiences and Challenges of Commercial Bank Downscalers. Working Draft. Microenterprise Best Practice Project. USAID, Washington, D.C.

van Greuning, Hennie, Joselito Gallardo, and Bikki Randhawa. 1999. A Framework for Regulating Microfinance Institutions. Policy Research Working Paper No. 2061. Financial Sector Development Department, World Bank, Washington, D.C.

Vittas, Dimitri. 1998. Institutional Investors and Securities Markets: Which Comes First? Paper presented at the ABCD LAC Conference, June 28–30, 1998, San Salvador, El Salvador.

Vogel, Robert C. 1999. *Other People's Money: Regulatory Issues Facing Microenterprise Finance.* Washington, D.C.: International Management and Communications Corporation.

———. 2002. Brazil's Micro Finance Institutions: Regulatory Environment and Institutional Performance. Mimeo. World Bank, Washington, D.C.

Von Amsberg, Joachim. 2001. *Attacking Brazil's Poverty.* Washington, D.C.: World Bank.

Von Pischke, J. D. 1991. *Finance at the Frontier.* Washington, D.C.: Economic Development Institute, World Bank.

Watts, Harold W. 1960. An Objective Permanent Income Concept for the Household. Cowles Foundation Discussion Paper No. 99. Yale University, Cowles Foundation for Research in Economics, New Haven, Conn.

Weil, Phillipe. 1989. "The Equity Premium Puzzle and the Risk-Free Rate Puzzle." *Journal of Monetary Economics* 24:401–21.

———. 1990. "Non-expected Utility in Macroeconomics." *Quarterly Journal of Economics* 105:29–42.

Wenner, Mark D. 1995. "Group Credit: A Means to Improve Information Transfer and Loan Repayment Performance." *Journal of Development Studies* 32:263–81.

Westercamp, Christine. 1999. Federation of the Agricultural Savings and Credit Unions, Benin (Case Study). Consultative Group to Assist the Poorest, Working Group on Savings Mobilization, Washington, D.C.

Westley, Glenn D. 2001. Can Financial Market Policies Reduce Income Inequality? Sustainable Development Department Technical Papers. Inter-American Development Bank, Washington, D.C.

Westley, Glenn D., and Brian Branch. 2000. *Safe Money—Building Effective Credit Unions in Latin America.* Washington, D.C.: IADB and WOCCU.

Wilcox, David. 1989. "Social Security Benefits, Consumption Expenditure, and the Life Cycle Hypothesis." *Journal of Political Economy* 97: 288–303.

Williams, Marva, and Kimbra Nieman. January 2003. The Foundation of Asset Building, Financial Services for Lower Income Consumers. Woodstock Institute, Chicago.

Williamson, Stephen D. 1986. "Costly Monitoring, Financial Intermediation, and Equilibrium Credit Rationing." *Journal of Monetary Economics* 18.

Witzeling, Ruth. 1994. *Credit Union Handbook.* Madison, Wisc.: WOCCU.

WOCCU (World Council of Credit Unions). Statistical Reports. Madison, Wisc.

———. July 2001. *Credit Unions—Vehicles for Providing Sustainable Microfinance.* Madison, Wisc.

———. 2002a. *Ecuador, Spotlights on Development.* Madison, Wisc.

———. 2002b. *Guatemala, Spotlights on Development.* Madison, Wisc.

———. 2002c. *Nicaragua, Spotlights on Development.* Madison, Wisc.

———. October 26, 2002. *Examination Process—Investment and Cash Analysis, Development Best Practices in Credit Union Supervision.* Madison, Wisc.

———. October 28, 2002. *Examination Process—Final Examination Report, Development Best Practices in Credit Union Supervision.* Madison, Wisc.

———. October 29, 2002. *Examination Definition, Objectives, Scope, and Process, Development Best Practices in Credit Union Supervision.* Madison, Wisc.

———. October 29, 2002. *Examination Process—General Ledger Review, Development Best Practices in Credit Union Supervision.* Madison, Wisc.

———. November 4, 2002. *Examination Process—Management Review, Development Best Practices in Credit Union Supervision*. Madison, Wisc.
———. December 2002. *Strengthening Credit Unions, WOCCU Technical Services*. Madison, Wisc.
———. December 4, 2002a. *Board of Directors Duties and Responsibilities, Development Best Practices in Credit Union Supervision*. Madison, Wisc.
———. December 4, 2002b. *Operational Management Duties and Responsibilities, Development Best Practices in Credit Union Supervision*. Madison, Wisc.
———. December 5, 2002a. *Credit Committee/Loan Officer Duties and Responsibilities, Development Best Practices in Credit Union Supervision*. Madison, Wisc.
———. December 5, 2002b. *Supervisory Committee Duties and Responsibilities, Development Best Practices in Credit Union Supervision*. Madison, Wisc.
———. December 6, 2002. *Code of Conduct/Conflict of Interest, Development Best Practices in Credit Union Supervision*. Madison, Wisc.
———. December 9, 2002a. *Credit Union Legislation, Development Best Practices in Credit Union Supervision*. Madison, Wisc.
———. December 9, 2002b. *Model Credit Union Bylaws, Development Best Practices in Credit Union Supervision*. Madison, Wisc.
———. December 10, 2002. *Regulatory Standards, Development Best Practices in Credit Union Supervision*. Madison, Wisc.
———. December 11, 2002. *Internal Control Requirements, Development Best Practices in Credit Union Supervision*. Madison, Wisc.
———. December 12, 2002. *Administrative Actions, Development Best Practices in Credit Union Supervision*. Madison, Wisc.
———. December 27, 2002. *Chartering New Credit Unions, Development Best Practices in Credit Union Supervision*. Madison, Wisc.
———. December 30, 2002. *Registration of Existing Credit Unions with a Regulatory Authority, Development Best Practices in Credit Union Supervision*. Madison, Wisc.
———. December 31, 2002. *Supervision of Problem Credit Unions, Development Best Practices in Credit Union Supervision*. Madison, Wisc.
———. January 7, 2003. *Accounting Norms and Principles, Development Best Practices in Credit Union Supervision*. Madison, Wisc.
———. January 9, 2003. *Problem Resolution by Credit Union Management, Development Best Practices in Credit Union Supervision*. Madison, Wisc.
———. *International Remittance Network, Spotlights on Development*. Madison, Wisc.
Woodstock Institute. 2003. Community Development Banks Substantially Outscore Other Banks in Serving Low-Income and Minority Communities: Federal Policies Threaten Community Development Banks' Success. Chicago.

World Bank. 1984. India Urban Land Management Study. Internal memorandum. World Bank, Washington, D.C.

———. 1989. *Malaysia: The Housing Sector, Getting the Incentives Right.* Washington, D.C.: Infrastructure Division Country Department II, Asia Regional Office.

———. April 1993. *Housing: Enabling Markets to Work.* Washington, D.C.

———. 1995. Brazil: A Poverty Assessment. Report No. 14323-BR. Washington, D.C.

———. October 1997. Brazil—Central Bank Modernization Technical Assistance Project. Project Appraisal Document No. 16867. Washington D.C.

———. 1999. The World Bank and Microenterprise Finance: From Concept to Practice. Report No. 19895. Operations Evaluation Department, Washington, D.C.

———. 2000a. Brazil—Selected Issues in Social Protection, Vols. 1 and 2. Report 20054. Washington, D.C.

———. September 2000b. Housing Finance in Brazil: The Legacy of the SFH and the Road Ahead. Draft Internal Technical Note. Washington, D.C.

———. 2000c. Project Appraisal Document on a Proposed Loan in the Amount of US$50.0 Million to the Bank of Northeast for a Northeast Microfinance Development Project. Report No. 20330-BR. Washington, D.C.

———. 2000d. "SME Financing: Lessons from Microfinance." *SME Issues* 1(1).

———. 2000e. *Telecommunications Regulation Handbook.* Washington, D.C.

———. 2000f. World Business Environment Survey. Washington, D.C.

———. 2001a. Brazil: Attacking Brazil's Poverty: A Poverty Report with a Focus on Urban Poverty Reduction Policies, Vols. 1 and 2. Sector Report No. 20475-BR. Washington, D.C.

———. August 2001b. Brazil—Financial Sector Technical Assistance Loan Project. Project Appraisal Document No. 22603. Washington, D.C.

———. April 2001c. Brazil—Financing Municipal Investment: Issues and Options. Economic Report No. 20313. Washington, D.C.

———. April 26, 2001d. Brazil: First Programmatic Financial Sector Adjustment Loan (PFSECAL MOP). Report No. P7448-BR. Washington, D.C.

———. August 7, 2001e. *Brazil: Progressive and Low Income Housing.* Washington, D.C.

———. November 21, 2001f. Brazil: The New Growth Agenda, Vols. 1 and 2. Report No. 22950-BR. Washington, D.C.

———. November 21, 2001g. Broadening Access to Financial Services in Mexico and Colombia—How Can the Banking Sector Reach the Urban "Unbanked"? Concept Paper. LAC FPSI. Washington, D. C.
———. 2001h. Finance for Growth: Policy Choices in a Volatile World. Policy Research Report No. 22239. Washington, D.C.
———. August 2001i. Information and Communication Technologies. Sector Strategy Paper. Washington, D.C.
———. 2001j. Microfinance in India: Issues, Constraints, and Potential for Sustainable Growth. Report No. 22531-IN. Finance and Private Sector Development Unit, South Asia Region, Washington, D.C.
———. April 20, 2001k. Rural Poverty Reduction in Brazil: Towards an Integrated Strategy, Vols. 1 and 2. Report No. 21790-BR. Washington, D.C.
———. 2001l. State Economic Memorandum—Micro, Small, and Medium Enterprises in Northeast Brazil. Washington, D.C.
———. 2001m. World Business Environment Survey. Washington, D.C.
———. 2002. Brazil: Report on the Observance of Standards and Codes (ROSC)—Insolvency and Creditor Rights Systems. Unpublished. Washington, D.C.
———. May 2002a. Brazil—Jobs Report, Vols. 1 and 2. Report No. 24408. Washington, D.C.
———. 2002b. Brazil Progressive Low-Income Housing: Alternatives for the Poor. Report No. 22032-BR. Washington, D.C.
———. May 2002c. Brazil—Second Programmatic Financial Sector Adjustment Loan Project. Program Document No. 24067. Washington, D.C.
———. 2002d. Housing Policy in Brazil: Maintaining Momentum for Reform. Report 24335–BR. Draft. Washington, D.C.
———. April 2002e. *Information and Communication Technologies*. Washington, D.C.
———. 2002f. *The Millennium Development Goals*. Washington, D.C.
———. August 18–23, 2002g. Policy Dialogue. Aide Memoire Mission. Washington, D.C.
———. June 2002h. Policy Notes on Housing Finance, Assistance Policies, and Land Issues. Draft. Washington, D.C.
———. June 2002i. Using Information and Communications Technology to Reduce Poverty in India. PREM Notes 70. Washington, D.C.
———. 2002j. Survey of Access to Financial Services in Urban Areas of Brazil. Washington, D.C.
———. January 2003. Viewpoint: Sustainable Telecenters. Washington, D.C.
Yaron, Jacob. 1992a. Assessing Development Finance Institutions: A Public Interest Analysis. Discussion Paper 174. Washington, D.C.

———. 1992b. Successful Rural Finance Institutions. World Bank Discussion Paper No. 150. Washington, D.C.

———. 1994. "What Makes Rural Finance Institutions Successful?" *The World Bank Research Observer* 9(1): 49–70.

———. 2000a. Brazil: Agricultural Credit and Rural Finance—Initial Diagnosis. Washington, D.C.

———. May 8, 2000b. Financial Sector Economic and Sector Work—Focus Note. Washington, D.C.

———. 2002. Brazil: Rural Finance Agricultural Insurance and Related Issues. Draft. Washington, D.C.

Yaron, Jacob, and McDonald Benjamin. January 1998. *Challenges and Best Practices in Rural Finance, Finance and Development*, Vol. X. Washington, D.C.

———. 2002. *Brazil: Access to Financial Services in Rural Areas.* Washington, D.C.

Yaron, Jacob, McDonald Benjamin, and Gerda Piprek. 1997. Rural Finance: Issues, Design, and Best Practices. Environmentally and Socially Sustainable Development Studies and Monographs Series No. 14. Washington, D.C.

Zeldes, Stephen. 1989a. "Consumption and Liquidity Constraints: An Empirical Investigation." *Journal of Political Economy* 97:305–46.

———. 1989b. "Optimal Consumption with Stochastic Income: Deviations from Certainty Equivalence." *Quarterly Journal of Economics* 104: 275–98.

List of Institutions and Web Addresses

ABA (Associação Brasileira de Anunciantes): www.aba.com.br
ABEL (Associação Brasileira das Empresas de Leasing): www.leasing abel.com.br/
ABRACOOP (Associação Brasileira para o Desenvolvimento do Cooperativismo): www.abracoop.com.br
ACCION: www.accion.org
ACREFI (Associação Nacional das Instituições de Crédito, Financiamento e Investimento): www.acrefi.com.br/
Alternative Finance: www.alternative-finance.org.uk
ANDIMA (Associação Nacional das Instituições do Mercado Aberto): www.andima.com.br/
ANFAC (Associação Nacional das Sociedades de Fomento Mercantil): http://www.anfac.com.br/home/index.jsp
BCB (Central Bank of Brazil): www.bcb.gov.br
BNDES (Banco Nacional de Desenvolvimento Econômico e Social): www.bndes.gov.br
BIS (Bank for International Settlements): www.bis.org
Basix: www.basixindia.com
COFIDE (Corporación Financiera de Desarrollo): www.cofide.com.pe
Conselho da Comunidade Solidária, Brasília
CrediAmigo: www.banconordeste.gov.br/CrediAmigo/
CVM (Comissão de Valores Mobiliários): www.cvm.com.br
Comite Gestor da Internet–Brazil: www.cg.org.br/
DIEESE (Departamento Intersindical de Estatísticas e Estudos Socioeconômicos): www.dieese.org.br
Digital Dividend: www.digitaldividend.org
Digital Partners: www.digitalpartners.org
SUSEP, DETEC (Departamento Técnico Atuarial): www.susep.gov.br
ECT (Empresa Brasileira de Correios e Telégrafos): www.correios.com.br
FEBRABAN (Federação Brasileira dos Bancos): www.febraban.org.br
FENASEG (Federação Nacional das Empresas de Seguros Privados e de Capitalização): www.fenaseg.org.br
FIESP (Federação das Indústrias do Estado de São Paulo): www.fiesp.org.br

FINCA (The Foundation for International Community Assistance): http://villagebanking.org
FONDESIF (Fondo de Desarrollo del Sistema Financiero y de Apoyo al Sector Productivo): www.fondesif.gov.bo
FGV (Fundação Getúlio Vargas): www.fgv.br
Grameen Bank: www.grameen-info.org/index.html
Grameen Foundation USA: www.gfusa.org
IBGE (Instituto Brasileiro de Geografia e Estatística): www.ibge.gov.br
ILO (International Labour Organisation): www.ilo.org
IMF (International Monetary Fund), International Financial Statistics database: www.imf.org
Instituto Cidadania: www.icidadania.org.br
International Finance Corporation, Emerging Markets Database, Washington, D.C.
International Telecommunication Union Database: www.itu.int/ITU-D/ict/Statistics/
IPEA (Instituto de Pesquisa Econômica Aplicada): www.ipea.gov.br
Kroll Risk Consulting Group: www.krollworldwide.com/
MDIC (Ministerio do Desenvolvimiento, Industria e Comercio Exterior), Brazil, www.desenvolvimento.gov.br/sitio/inicial/index.php
MFRC (Microfinance Regulatory Council): www.mfrc.co.za/services/circulars.asp
Ministério do Desenvolvimento Agrário: www.pronaf.gov.br
NAFIBO (Nacional Financiera Boliviana): www.nafibo.com.bo
OCB (Organização das Cooperativas Brasileiras): www.ocb.org.br
Planet Finance: www.planetfinance.org
Profund: www.profundinternational.com
SBEF (Superintendency of Banks and Financial Entities), Bolivia: www.sbef.gov.bo
SBS (Superintendency of Banking and Insurance Companies), Peru: www.sbs.gob.pe
SERT (Secretaria de Emprego e Relações de Trabalho), São Paulo, www.emprego.sp.gov.br/
Share Microfin: www.sharemicrofin.com/home.htm
SICOOB (Sistema de Cooperativas de Crédito do Brasil): www.sicoob.com.br
SICREDI (Sistema de Crédito Cooperativo): www.sicredi.com.br
The Microfinance Gateway: www.microfinancegateway.org/
The Phoenix Fund, Small Business Service, Department of Trade and Industry, U.K. Government: www.sbs.gov.uk/default.php?page=/phoenix/default.php
TowerGroup Research: www.marketresearch.com/vendors/viewvendor.asp?SID=86543348-300061617-348788805&VendorID=2491

UNIDROIT (Institut International pour l'Unification du Droit Privé): www.unidroit.org/
United Nations Development Programme (UNDP), Brasília
Universidade Federal de Rio de Janeiro (UFRJ), Rio de Janeiro
VivaCred, Rio de Janeiro
WOCCU (World Council of Credit Unions): www.woccu.org
WorldScope database: www.rimes.com/wscp.xmp

Index

Figures and tables are indicated by f and t, respectively.